Library of
Davidson College

An Introduction to Cognitive Psychology

An Introduction to Cognitive Psychology

Danny R. Moates

Gary M. Schumacher

Ohio University

WADSWORTH PUBLISHING COMPANY, INC.
BELMONT, CALIFORNIA
A Division of Wadsworth, Inc.

Psychology editor: Kenneth King

Editing, design, production supervision: Brian K. Williams

Design: Rick Chafian

Cover painting: Mark Rothko, *Number 18, 1948,* 1949

Copyediting: Sylvia Williams

Technical illustrations: John Foster and Mary Burkhardt

Composition: Graphic Typesetting Service

153
M687i

© 1980 by Wadsworth, Inc. All rights reserved. No part of this book may be reproduced, stored in a retrieval system, or transcribed, in any form or by any means, electronic, mechanical, photocopying, recording, or otherwise, without the prior written permission of the publisher, Wadsworth Publishing Company, Belmont, California 94002, a division of Wadsworth, Inc.

Printed in the United States of America

1 2 3 4 5 6 7 8 9 10—83 82 81 80

Library of Congress Cataloging in Publication Data

Moates, Danny R
  An introduction to cognitive psychology.

Bibliography: p.
Includes index.
  1. Cognition. I. Schumacher, Gary M., joint author. II. Title.
BF311.M56   153   79-9188
ISBN 0-534-00724-4

80-6694

Acknowledgments and Copyrights

Cover painting. Reproduced by permission of Vassar College Art Gallery, gift of Mrs. John D. Rockefeller 3rd (Blanchette Hooker '31).

Figure 2.3, p. 12. From Sperling, 1960, p. 11. Copyright 1960 by the American Psychological Association. Reprinted by permission.

Figure 2.4, p. 13. From Sperling, 1963, p. 21. Reprinted by permission of the Johns Hopkins University Press. © The Human Factors Society.

Figure 2.5, p. 14. From Darwin, Turvey, & Crowder, 1972, p. 259. Copyright 1972 by Academic Press, Inc. Reprinted by permission.

Figure 2.6, p. 15. From Conrad & Hull, 1968, p. 136. Copyright 1968 by the Psychonomic Society, Inc. Reprinted by permission.

Figure 2.13, p. 21. From Posner, Goldsmith, & Welton, 1967, p. 30. Copyright 1967 by the American Psychological Association. Reprinted by permission.

Figure 2.14, p. 24. From Lindsay & Norman, 1977, p. 231. Copyright 1977 by Academic Press, Inc. Reprinted by permission.

Figure 2.15, p. 25. From Lindsay & Norman, 1977, p. 233. Copyright 1977 by Academic Press, Inc. Reprinted by permission.

Figure 2.16, p. 26. From Lindsay & Norman, 1977, p. 233. Copyright 1977 by Academic Press, Inc. Reprinted by permission.

(Continued on page 348)

To my parents, Chester and Hazel Moates,
without whom I would never have begun
thinking about thinking.
DANNY R. MOATES

To my wife, Kathy, and my daughters, Kelly and Kristin.
Without their love and support this writing
about thinking could not have been done.
GARY M. SCHUMACHER

Contents

Preface ix

1. **Issues in Cognitive Psychology** 1

   Cognitive Psychology as a Science 2
   Antecedents of Cognitive Psychology 2
   Topics and Themes 4

2. **Perception and Attention** 7

   Sensory Registers 10
   Perception 16
   Attention 39
   Automatic Processes 46
   Consciousness 47
   Conclusion 49

3. **The Temporary Retention of Information** 51

   Models of Memory 53
   Characteristics of Temporary Retention 55
   Structures in Temporary Retention 70
   Conclusion 77

4. **The Structure of Permanent Memory** 81

   The Meaning of Permanent Memory 82
   Episodic versus Semantic Memory 82
   Models of Permanent Memory 83
   Conclusion 104

5. **The Permanent Retention of New Information** 105

   Storage Processes in Permanent Memory 107
   Retrieval of Information from Permanent Memory 126
   Conclusion 131

6. **Language** 135

   Properties of Language 137
   The Structure of Language 138
   Functions of Language 147
   Competence and Performance 149
   Language Production 149
   Language Comprehension 159
   A Computer Model of Language Processing 178
   Conclusion 181

7. Comprehension and Retention of Prose Materials   183

Context and Language Comprehension   184
Schemata   190
The Role of Schemata in Processing Prose Materials   193
Inference Processes in Comprehension and Retention   199
Schemata and Semantic Memory   204
Conclusion   206

8. Concepts   207

Concept Structure   209
Learning Concepts   209
Concepts, Memory, and Language   224
Conclusion   229

9. Problem Solving   231

Gestalt Theory   234
Information-Processing Theory   247
Conclusion   276

10. Deductive Reasoning   277

Linear Series Problems   279
Propositional Reasoning   286
Reasoning with Syllogisms   293
Conclusion   301

11. Motor Skills   303

Properties of Motor Skills   306
Learning a Motor Skill   307
Feedback   309
Processing Information   312
Practice   317
Central Processes   322
Conclusion   330

References   331

Name index   353

Subject index   358

Preface

The purpose of this book is to convey to advanced undergraduate students a picture of what is now known about the cognitive processes. Three principles have guided us in our writing. First, we have sought to be comprehensive. We have been struck with the diversity of topics and issues that come under the rubric of cognitive functioning. Cognition is not a narrow field; rather it encompasses topics as various as perceiving, reasoning, motor skills, remembering, and the production and comprehension of language. We have tried to capture this diversity by making our treatment of topics related to cognition comprehensive. We hope that students will thereby appreciate the scope of human cognition.

Comprehensiveness, however, can be overwhelming. Our second guiding principle, integration, is designed to offset this problem. We have sought to show how the concepts and processes involved in one aspect of cognitive functioning relate to those of another. Some ideas flow throughout the text. A good example is the cyclic nature of cognition, in which the environment affects cognitive processing but is also being interpreted by the processes it affects. This notion of cyclic interaction is fundamental to many types of cognitive functioning and is the primary reason why the concept of schema, discussed frequently in this book, has had such a resurgence in recent years.

Our final guiding concern has been for readability. All our other efforts will be blunted if the reader must struggle to understand the material. To that end we have aimed for clarity and evenness of style. To heighten interest we have used numerous examples, story lead-ins for some of the chapters, and discussions of everyday applications. We have used boxed inserts to discuss certain experiments in some detail as well as to present particularly relevant examples. All these devices are designed to capture the attention of readers and help them relate what they are reading to what they already know. Both of us have taught our cognitive processes course many times, and we have accumulated a considerable repertoire of such experiences, which we have integrated into this text.

We believe this text is appropriate for most one-term courses in cognitive psychology. We are aware that instructors differ in the topics they emphasize, but we think the comprehensiveness of the material will provide a solid framework for most courses.

The work of many people besides the authors is involved in any text. While we cannot individually mention all those who have aided us in our writing, a few people do deserve special acknowledgment. We wish to thank George Miller, Alan Lesgold, Richard C. Anderson, Hal Arkes, Richard Mayer, and Lawrence Meyers for their useful and insightful comments at various stages in the manuscript. Their comments were invaluable. In addition, we wish to thank the anonymous reviewers who gave us valuable suggestions for improving the manuscript, and Ken King and the entire editorial and production staff from Wadsworth for their help, their support, and their patient prodding. Finally, we wish to thank our many colleagues, students, and friends and our families for the encouragement and support they so willingly gave us during our most frustrating hours. Had it not been for them, this book would not be before you now.

An Introduction to
Cognitive Psychology

1 Issues in Cognitive Psychology

Cognitive Psychology as a Science
Antecedents of Cognitive Psychology
Topics and Themes

This book is about the **cognitive processes,** those mental activities familiar to us in such forms as seeing, attending, remembering, talking, and solving problems. They are those processes that receive, transmit, and operate upon information. We use cognitive processes in every waking moment. Indeed, we would be robbed of our human identity if we were to be divorced from our ability to see and hear, to remember the past, or to use language. The rich development of these processes is one of the characteristics that gives human beings their special niche in the phylogenetic scale; a better scientific understanding of these processes thus should give us a fuller appreciation of what it means to be human.

COGNITIVE PSYCHOLOGY AS A SCIENCE

You may question whether the cognitive processes can be studied scientifically, and you would not be alone in doing so. There are several good reasons for raising the question. First, you may wonder whether science can add anything to what you already know about how these processes operate. These activities seem so intimately familiar, so fundamental, that it seems unnecessary to examine them at all. Our personal means of knowing about these activities, however, is somewhat special: It is the method of introspection, which is our consciousness of what we are doing as we talk, see, remember, and so on.

Introspection gives us a special avenue to the cognitive processes, but it does not tell all. Talking, for example, is a natural act—one we all carry out with ease. Yet few of us are aware of what we are going to say until it issues from our mouths. We are aware of the product of talking but not of the process. Similarly in perceiving; whether it be through seeing, hearing, touching, or whatever means, we are subjectively aware of what we perceive yet unaware of the processes that led to that end state. Cognitive psychologists seek an understanding of how these processes work, sometimes with the aid of introspection but more often through other methods.

A second problem lies in the almost paradoxical character of studying the cognitive processes. Such study is a reflexive act; that is, the processes we are studying are the very ones we are using to carry out the study. Can the eye behold itself? Perhaps not; this seems to be one of the shortcomings of the introspective method. However, we can study one another and thereby separate the object from the observer.

Finally, we must acknowledge that the cognitive processes are largely private processes. However real our perceptions or memories may seem to us, they can be known to others only in a secondhand way by our talking about them or expressing them in some other way. Doesn't this make them unavailable to scientific study? Cognitive psychologists think not. Physicists study subatomic particles that are far too small for direct visual inspection, and astronomers hypothesize such mind-stretching objects as black holes on the basis of quite indirect evidence such as star formations. In cognitive psychology as well, the scientist works within the constraints of incomplete information.

The method is the same for each discipline; it is the scientific method. From the observations at hand we generate hypotheses that may explain these observations. Through a cycle of observation and the generation of hypotheses, we arrive at a theory to explain our observations.

ANTECEDENTS OF COGNITIVE PSYCHOLOGY

Scientific interest in the cognitive processes has developed at an almost explosive rate since the 1960s. For half a century prior to that, American psychology was dominated by **behaviorism,** a movement that was guided by a firm methodological commitment—namely, that scientific psychology be based on fully objective observations. The privateness of mental events led behaviorists to conclude that these experiences are not a legitimate topic for scientific study. They argued that objective data are limited to observable behavior in humans and other animals and to the environmental conditions in which such behavior appears. Behavior, they said, is to be analyzed into a set of responses that are assumed to be governed by stimulus conditions in the environment.

This methodological orientation led behaviorists to play down the significance of internal processes and to concentrate instead on environmental and behavioral events that were available for direct inspection. A small number of behaviorists denied the very existence of conscious experiences. Others, more cautious perhaps, concluded that little that was scientifically useful could come from the study of mental events.

The major theoretical orientation within behaviorism was learning theory. Psychologists, impressed with the theory of evolution, asked themselves how human beings adapted to their environment in order to survive as a species. James B. Watson, a pioneer behaviorist, championed classical conditioning as nature's means of molding people to adaptive behavior. Edward L. Thorndike offered the law of effect as an explanation of adaptive behavior; and this law is the historical forerunner of present-day theories of reinforcement, such as Skinner's operant conditioning.

Both classical and operant conditioning depicted the human being as a relatively plastic, passive organism, an "empty organism," whose behavior is shaped by environmental events. Many behaviorists assumed that the laws of learning, once they were fully developed, would account for all forms of human behavior and would do so without recourse to explanations based on internal processes.

The 1960s saw a surge of interest in the cognitive processes. New theories appeared in the areas of perception, memory, language, and problem solving that made strong assumptions about the way internal activities influence overt behavior. These new theories depicted the human being as a processor of information, an active organism having a rich set of resources that it uses in its interactions with the environment.

The environment, though still important, was no longer the preeminent source of explanations for behavior. Instead, the environment provided the information that was to be coded, stored, and operated upon by the multiplicity of cognitive processes that underlie overt behavior. The empty organism characterized under behaviorism had become a full organism indeed with the advent of cognitive psychology.

The interest in cognitive processes arose from several sources. First, there was increasing dissatisfaction with the progress of psychology under behaviorism. Learning theory, the major theoretical orientation within behaviorism, had come under critical attack and was found to contain substantial flaws that dethroned it as a general theory of human behavior. For example, there was the very real problem of generalizing to human behavior from the animal data that served as the primary evidence for theories of behavior.

Second, other disciplines were experiencing dramatic advances that held strong implications for psychology. Linguistics, for instance, was undergoing a revolution from its behavioristic orientation to a new rationalism. The new interpretation presented language not just as another form of behavior but as a uniquely organized skill, highly abstract in structure and calling for a complex set of psychological processes for its use. Similarly, applied mathematics was making great strides, which led to the appearance of information theory as well as the rapid development of the digital computer.

The digital computer had a special impact on the growth of cognitive psychology. It provided a model of information processing in a highly objective form. Psychologists began to borrow the programmer's concepts of coding and transforming information and to incorporate them into models of the cognitive processes. Moreover, some of these models could be translated into computer programs, which then served as working models of the cognitive processes for comparison with human beings carrying out the same tasks. Thus computer technology provided a source of ideas about how the cognitive processes might function and offered as well a means of objectively representing the cognitive processes. The latter offered genuine promise of easing the subjectivity problem that had so hampered the study of cognitive processes in earlier decades.

In the brief span of 25 years cognitive psychology has evolved into a very active branch of psychology, full of the ferment of new ideas and the excitement of the promise inherent in its conceptualization of human functioning. This conceptualization projects the human being as a dynamic organism in continual, cyclic interaction with its environment. It assumes that we humans constantly search our environment for new information, a search guided by our expectations of what we will find. The new information in turn modifies our expectations, altering the direction of future searches for information. Through these cyclic interactions we code information into the vast reservoir of permanent memory. Permanent memory then serves as a resource for the use of that information in speaking, writing, motor skills, problem solving, and the many other ends we set for ourselves.

Overt behavior is thus only the tip of the iceberg of cognitive activity. From that overt expression psychologists draw clues about the nature of the internal functions. They design experiments that seek to isolate these processes in order to clarify our understanding of them and predict the kind of behavior they lead to. This work is far from done, but therein lies much of the excitement.

TOPICS AND THEMES

In the chapters that follow we have tried to capture the major concepts of contemporary cognitive psychology. Each chapter develops a particular aspect of cognitive functioning, identifying both the structures and the processes involved in that function and describing the research upon which the characterization is based.

The cognitive processes, of course, are not a set of isolated engines, humming away at independent tasks. Rather they are an organic whole, each serving the other in a highly interrelated fashion. We have tried to delineate some of these interrelationships in each chapter by drawing upon ideas developed in preceding chapters. Books, however, are intractably two-dimensional and thus you may find yourself flipping back from time to time in pursuit of an earlier topic. But this is an effort we think will pay off in a fuller appreciation of the way the cognitive processes interact.

In Chapter 2 we introduce the processes of perception and attention, concentrating on the way patterns are recognized in the early stages of perception and the selective manner in which attention and our expectations influence the flow of incoming information. At the outset of the chapter we describe an everyday situation, which we then use to illustrate the transformations that information undergoes in the early stages of processing. In succeeding chapters we elaborate upon the conceptual processes in that situation and show how they interact.

In Chapter 3 we take up temporary memory for information and describe the way in which it is encoded as well as forgotten. In Chapters 4 and 5 we discuss permanent memory—its organization and the ways in which information is added, retrieved, and forgotten. The ideas in these two chapters are fundamental to understanding the topics that follow.

In Chapter 6 we treat language, especially the processes of producing speech and understanding the speech of others. In Chapter 7 we expand these ideas in a discussion of how human beings process the contextual relations in prose materials. In Chapter 8 we introduce the learning of concepts, which returns us to some of the themes in permanent memory.

In Chapter 9 we undertake an analysis of problem solving, one of the clearest forms of goal-oriented activity in the cognitive processes. Here we introduce some of the extensive work in the computer simulation of cognitive processes. In Chapter 10 we describe some of the cognitive processes underlying a special form of problem solving: deductive reasoning.

In Chapter 11 we close with a description of motor skills and the cognitive processes that underlie the body movements with which we humans express ourselves in work, sports, and artistic activity.

As you read this book, you will notice several recurring themes. Prominent among these is the active nature of the cognitive processes. Human beings do not wait passively for information; rather we actively seek information that is relevant to our purposes. A psychological concept that captures such activity especially well is the concept of **schema.** A schema is a mental structure that accepts information from the environment. It also directs the search for such information and can be modified by the information it receives. The concept of schema plays a prominent role in recent theories of perception and the processing of prose materials.

A second theme is that of novelty, the problem of dealing with the ever-present uniqueness of information. Thus we are capable of recognizing a face from an angle that we have never seen it from before, or of understanding a sentence we have never heard before, or of returning a tennis ball from a stance we have never experienced before. The problem of handling novel information pervades all of the cognitive processes, and thus several chapters take up the mechanisms by which we selectively code that information in ways that are relevant to the task at hand.

A third theme is the goal-oriented character of many of the cognitive functions and the closely related notion of controlling the processes involved in achieving these goals. Goals tell us when to terminate cognitive processes. The goal of problem solving is the solution; in memory it is the retrieval of an item, and in motor skills it is the successful completion of an intended act. The problem of control lies in selecting a mechanism for attaining these goals.

In closing, one of our purposes in this book is to present a broad and synthetic description of the cognitive processes. Nonetheless, there are relevant topics we have not discussed. We say nothing of the neurophysiological bases of the cognitive processes and little about the development of these processes in the early stages of life. Similarly, we have chosen not to discuss the expression of cognitive functioning in personality and social interaction. What we have chosen to do with the present work is to give you a unified set of ideas about the cognitive processes which we believe will go with you and enrich your future encounters in this field of study.

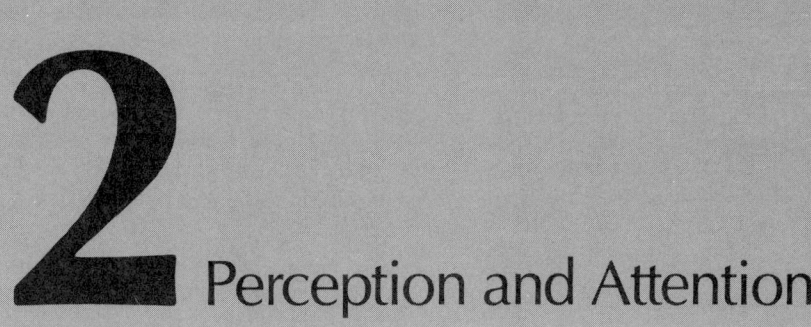

2 Perception and Attention

Sensory Registers
    Visual Register
    Auditory Register
Perception
    Pattern Recognition
        Templates
        Prototypes
        Feature Analysis
            Physiological mechanisms
            Pandemonium
            Distinctive features
    Expectations and Perception
        Expectations and Schemata
        Context
Attention
    Early Selection Model
    Attenuation Model
    Full-Processing Model
    Data and Resource Limitations
Automatic Processes
Consciousness
Conclusion

In the next four chapters we will explore **perception, attention,** and **memory.** Since these processes and their interactions are sometimes complex, it may help first to set them in perspective.

In Figure 2.1 we have diagrammed a simplified model of the major components involved in perception, attention, and memory. This model also shows how these components interact with one another, allowing the individual to process information from the world around him.

We begin our description by asking you to focus on the left side of this figure at the place marked environmental input. A great deal of our interest in cognitive functioning is concerned with how individuals take in, understand, put into memory, and retrieve from memory new information from the environment. We thus begin by describing the environmental situation in

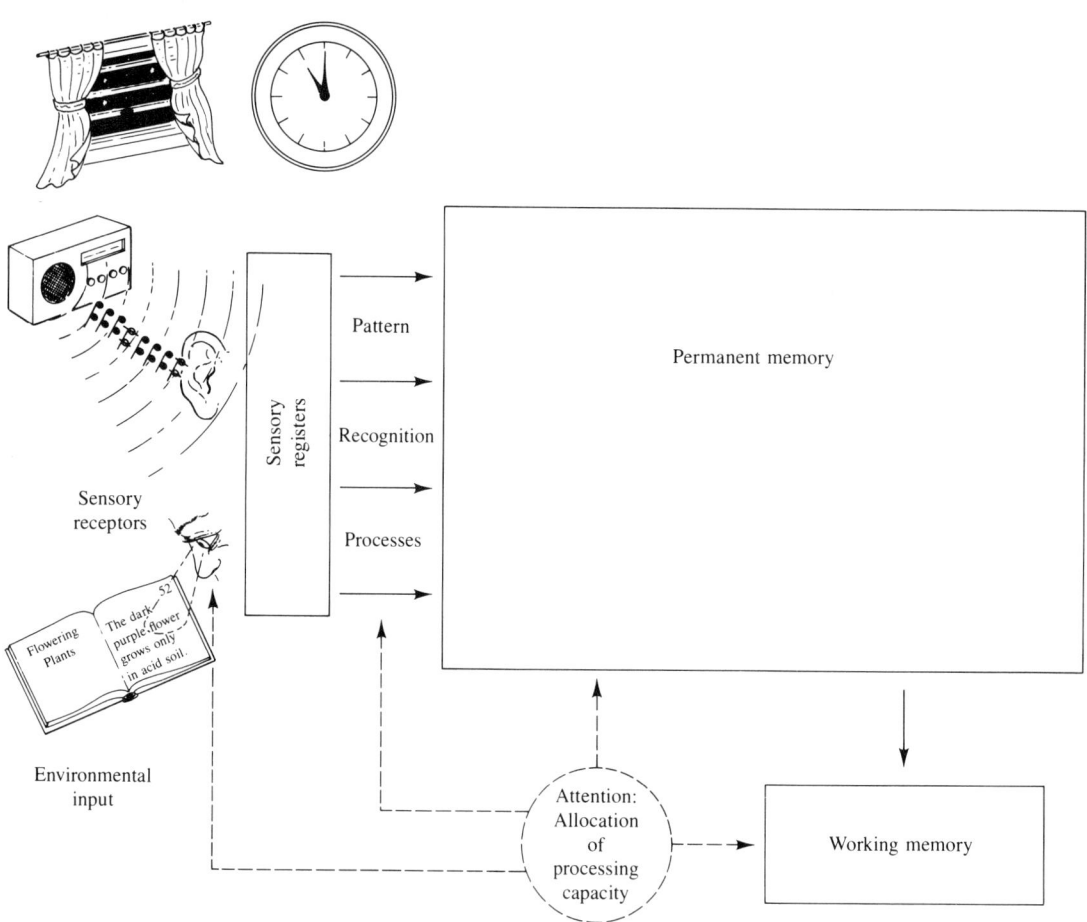

Figure 2.1 Schematic model of the components of the information-processing system.

which the individual typified by this setting (we call him Peter) is located. We see that Peter is reading a book about flowering plants and his eyes are currently focused on the word *flower* in the middle of page 52. It appears in the sentence "The dark purple flower grows only in acid soil." The book Peter is reading is a textbook for a difficult botany course he is taking. Peter is studying for an exam to be given the next day. It is currently 11 P.M. on a warm, balmy night. He has the radio tuned to a local radio station that primarily plays music. It is currently playing Beethoven's Fifth Symphony.

Six major information-processing components are involved as Peter continues to read and study his book. These are the *sensory receptors, sensory registers, permanent memory, pattern recognition processes, attention,* and *working memory.* The first of these—the sensory receptors such as the eyes and ears—are composed of millions of specialized cells that first respond to the environmental input. While these represent the first step in processing any environmental information, we will not deal with them in this book. Our focus lies in more central processing, a set of changes information undergoes as it leaves the receptors and moves into the central nervous system.

Perception is the process of determining the meaning of the stimuli that impinge upon us. A statement such as this one could lead to deep philosophical debates about what meaning is (for example, see Kintsch, 1977). We do not wish to enter such a debate but wish merely to suggest that perception involves more than a simple determination that something exists in the environment; we would call that detection. Perception, on the other hand, involves the determination of the sense of the stimuli. This process usually, but not always, means the determination of a concept to which the stimuli are related. For example, the object you are reading is a book or the music you are hearing is Beethoven's Fifth Symphony. Several of our six information-processing components are directly involved in perception. Let us consider the one we have called the **sensory registers.**

In order for meaning to be derived, a number of processes must be carried out on environmental stimuli. Each of these processes takes time; that is, they do not occur instantaneously. This leaves us with an interesting problem. Since the environment may change quickly and since a stimulus may terminate before the perceptual processes are complete, we might expect that the analysis of many stimuli must be terminated midstream before their meaning has been determined. In fact, this occurs infrequently because we are equipped with holding systems for briefly maintaining a rather complete representation of stimuli so that perceptual analyses can be completed. It is these holding systems that are the sensory registers depicted in Figure 2.1; they compose the second major component in the information-processing system.

To say that perception involves the determination of the meaning of stimuli implies that individuals have a permanent repository of knowledge about their world. This repository must be consulted so that the meaning of a given event can be determined. Thus if Peter had no knowledge of the alphabet, spelling rules, or what flowering plants are, he would not be able to perceive the meaning of *flower.* In our model we have labeled this component **permanent memory.** It is the third component of our information-processing system.

It is unlikely that the stimuli existing in our environment are in exactly the same form as the knowledge of our world that we store in permanent memory. If they were, we would have to have a very large head indeed to store our knowledge of elephants, whales, and sailing ships. Thus in order for Peter to be able to determine the meaning of stimuli from his environment, he must transform and analyze them so that they can be compared to what is in permanent memory. This involves a number of processes, which we have labeled **pattern recognition processes.** In Figure 2.1 these are shown as occurring between the sensory registers and permanent memory. They are the fourth component of our information-processing system.

There is an unlimited amount of environmental stimulation that Peter could pay attention to. There are millions of color shades, cloud formations, and facial expressions he could analyze and perceive. Since it takes time to perceive each of these, Peter is soon faced with a difficult problem. He must select which part of the environment he chooses to analyze and process. In other words, he must decide how to allocate his limited processing capability to the many tasks he could do. For example, he may try to read, listen to the radio, and watch TV simultaneously—or he may do one at a time. This is the process of **attention.** We have included this component of our information-processing model in the dashed circle at the bottom of Figure 2.1.

One key part of Peter's information-processing capability lies in his ability to bring certain aspects of his cognitive functioning into a working memory. We shall see later that working memory is related to what is commonly called conscious awareness. Peter thus becomes able to monitor or modify some processing that he is doing. This is a key aspect of cognitive functioning, since it allows Peter to plan ahead or to generate unique combinations of information he has never seen before. For example, Peter may plan how to drive to his friend's house a new way or he may ruminate about what is involved in building a better mousetrap. This sixth key component of our information-processing system, called **working memory,** is indicated in the box below permanent memory.

These six components provide the underlying foundation for explaining how Peter gets meaning from, pays attention to, and becomes able to remember information about his environment. In the remainder of this chapter and the next four chapters we will elaborate this model as we look in greater depth at each of these components. We begin with the sensory registers.

SENSORY REGISTERS

Probably the most common phenomenon we experience as we interact with our environment is the derivation of meaning from what happens to us. As we walk down a street and see an object in the distance, we extract information from this object until we are able to conclude that it is a friend, a car, a beer can, or whatever. This process of deriving the meaning of what we see involves a multitude of different processes, which we will be discussing in the pages that follow.

In one important respect each of these processes is like any other behavior humans carry out. It takes time. That is, in the same manner that it takes us 10 minutes to get to work or 50 minutes to eat dinner, it takes us a finite amount of time to carry out each of the processes involved in determining meaning from the world around us. The time durations for these perceptual analyses are on a much smaller scale, often milliseconds (msec, a thousandth of a second) in length, but they nevertheless do take a specifiable amount of time.

This fact presents the psychologist studying how people extract meaning from the environment with an intriguing dilemma. The world around us is not always going to wait until our perceptual analyses are complete. Many environmental events occur and disappear before our processes are complete. Thus one of two things must occur: Either many processes are cut off before they reach completion, leaving us with numerous fragments of processing, or there is some means of temporarily retaining environmental information after it has terminated. This temporary retention procedure would allow us to complete analyses so that meaning can be determined for an event.

Visual Registers

The most compelling evidence that such temporary retention exists was provided by the innovative work of George Sperling (Sperling, 1960). He had noticed that when subjects were presented a matrix of letters (see Figure 2.2) for a brief duration of say 50 msec, they could recall about 4 to 5 letters. This number did not change if the number of letters was varied from 4 to 12 or if the time duration was changed from 15 msec to 500 msec. As Crowder (1976) noted, it is possible that the remaining items were never registered, were registered but were subsequently lost before they could be reported, or were available in memory but were somehow not accessible at the time of recall.

In order to test these hypotheses, Sperling reasoned that if more information is available than subjects can report, it may be possible to sample their knowledge rather than request all of what they saw. This led to what is sometimes called the partial report procedure (in contrast to the usual whole report procedure), in which subjects are asked to recall only some part of what they saw. This method is similar to the teacher generating a test that samples a student's knowledge so that the teacher can infer how much the individual knows about the given topic.

Using this procedure, Sperling presented subjects with an array such as the one in Figure 2.2. In addition, he told them they would hear a tone after the matrix had disappeared. If the tone was of a high pitch, they were to recall the top row; if a middle-range pitch, the middle row; and if a low pitch, the bottom row. Since the subject was not given the tone until after the array terminated, improved recall performance would indicate that the person still had information available even though the array was no longer physically present. In addition, by varying the delay period between the time the array was terminated and the onset of the tone, Sperling was able to get an indication of the duration of the temporary retention of information.

As indicated in Figure 2.3, Sperling's data using the partial report procedure did show that subjects had more information available than they were able to report. If the tone occurred immediately after the offset of an array of 12 letters, the subject was able to report about 75 percent of any row requested. This indicates that about 75 percent of the array was available immediately after termination, or about 9 or 10 letters. If the tone were delayed even ½ sec (500 msec), performance was no better than if no tone at all were given. Apparently the subject was able to retain information about the environment for a period approaching ½ sec. Since the time it takes to read out 4 to 5 letters is longer than ½ sec, it is not surprising that by the time a person has indicated 4 letters, the remainder of the array has disappeared.

Sperling's work supports the contention that the human has a very brief holding mechanism that allows additional processing to continue for a brief period after the environmental stimulation has changed or terminated. A later study by Averbach and Coriell (1961) indicated that a better estimate of the time duration of this temporary holding system was about 250 msec, or ¼ sec. This temporary holding mechanism has become known as the visual sensory register, or the **Icon.**

Since these early studies on the Icon, our understanding has broadened extensively. It was unclear from the early studies whether the information held by the Icon had already been extensively processed or whether it was in a raw and relatively unprocessed state. Several pieces of evidence suggest that the latter is a more accurate description of what actually occurs.

```
        J    D    P    B

        F    R    K    Z

        G    M    S    H
```

Figure 2.2 A typical array of letters used in studies of sensory memory.

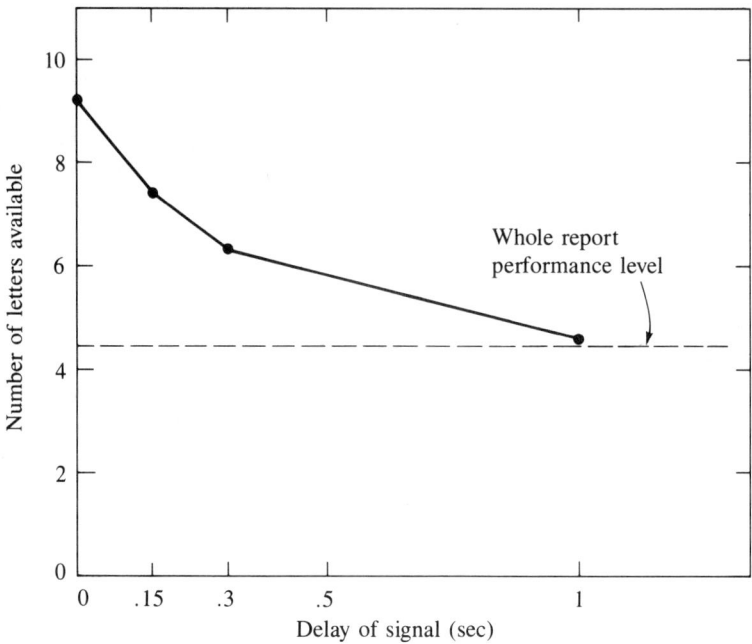

Figure 2.3 The number of letters available in the partial report situation after varying delay intervals. (From Sperling, 1960.)

Sperling (1960), for example, manipulated the lightness of the prestimulus and poststimulus field in some of his studies to see what impact this had on the Icon. That is, in some conditions the subjects were shown a stimulus matrix such as the one in Figure 2.2. The matrix was preceded and followed by a dark visual field. In other conditions, the subjects were shown the array, but the field was left illuminated, so that the eye was exposed to new visual stimulation.

As seen in Figure 2.4, a subject's ability to remember the array dropped off much sooner if the subject was exposed to an illuminated stimulus field than if the visual field was dark. Apparently the new visual stimulation erased much of the information being held in the Icon. This finding suggests that the Icon holds the information in a raw visual form that is easily interfered with by new visual stimulation.

A number of other so-called selection studies also support the notion that the Icon holds material in a relatively unprocessed state. In these studies subjects are shown arrays of letters and are given cues about which items in the array are to be recalled. The cues vary in the way they indicate which items are to be recalled. In some studies the cues indicate that a certain physical location (e.g., the top row) in the array is to be recalled (Sperling, 1960), as we saw above. In other cases the cues indicate that certain types of material are to be recalled. For example, Sperling (1960) and von Wright (1972) presented arrays that included both digits and letters. Subjects were then given a cue indicating whether they were to recall the digits or the letters.

Such cues are found to be ineffective. That is, subjects are unable to recall more of the array with these cues, unlike the studies that use cues for physical location. These results suggest that

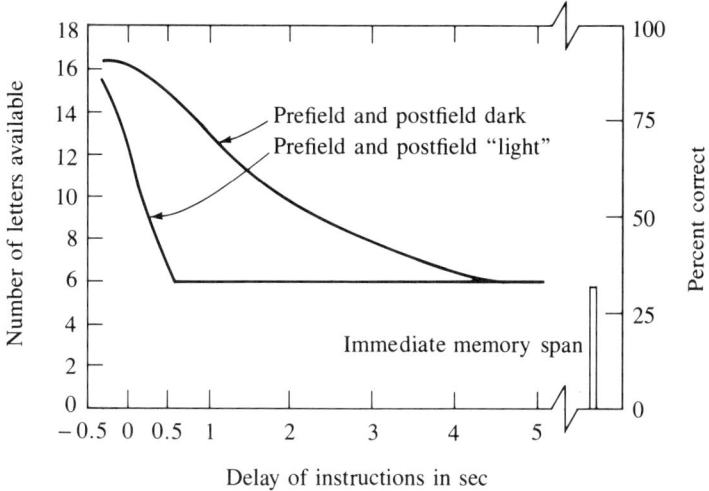

Figure 2.4 Comparison of information available to one observer after varying intervals of dark and light visual fields. (From Sperling, 1963.)

the arrays are held in a state of little processing, and hence cues that require the subject to have distinctions made between item classes (e.g., numbers and letters) are ineffective for recall.

Sakitt (1976) provides evidence that the locus of the Icon is in the photoreceptors of the eyes—primarily the rods but possibly also the cones. In a series of intricate studies using subjects who were rod monochromats (that is, they have no cone vision), she demonstrated that the locus of the Icon has to be very early in the processing system (but see Turvey, 1973, for an alternate point of view). She does not claim that the rods are the only place at which visual information is stored. Instead, she argues that rod storage is sufficient to explain most of the results attributed to the Icon.

Banks and Barber (1977) disagree with Sakitt's conclusions, claiming that the cones play a significant role in iconic memory. They found that subjects showed typical partial report performance under conditions in which the rods were inoperative. They consequently concluded that both the rods and cones are important in memory and thus suggested that iconic memory may not just be a peripheral retinal phenomenon.

Auditory Registers

We have concentrated our arguments on the human visual system. Logically, we may postulate that similar brief retention systems are necessary for the other sensory systems. While there has been little work on the systems of taste, touch, and smell which indicates the existence of sensory registers, such is not the case in audition. Darwin, Turvey, and Crowder (1972), for example, replicated the original Sperling work on vision using auditory presentation.

They presented their subjects with three short lists of letters and digits simultaneously so that each list appeared to come from a different part of the room. They then cued their subjects about which list to report at time intervals varying from 0 to 4 sec after the lists were presented. As can be seen in Figure 2.5, the more delayed the cue the poorer the recall. After about 3 to 4 sec, the subjects' performance was no better than

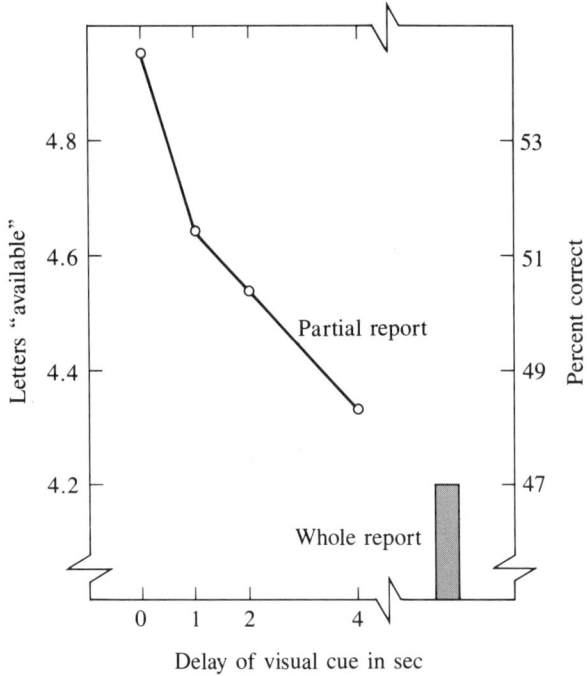

Figure 2.5 Comparison of whole and partial report performance with auditorially presented materials. (From Darwin, Turvey, & Crowder, 1972.)

that of subjects asked to remember all the items in the three lists. These data suggest the existence of an auditory sensory register much like the visual Icon except that its duration is on the order of 3 to 4 sec rather than ¼ sec. This sensory register has, not surprisingly, come to be called the **Echo**, or echoic memory.

In order to claim that the Echo is truly a sensory register and not a more central memory store, we need to consider how information is stored in the Echo. That is, does the Echo, like the Icon, store raw sensory information or has extensive processing occurred on information in the Echo? To answer this question we again turn to selection studies. Darwin et al. presented subjects with the same auditory arrays that we described above. However, in order to determine the extent of processing of the letters, these researchers told their subjects that the visual cues indicated that either the letters or the digits were to be recalled. These cues were much less effective in improving recall than were the cues indicating physical location. These findings suggest that the Echo, like the Icon, holds information in a relatively unprocessed state.

A number of recent studies suggest that the Echo plays a key role in the processing of language. Consider an interesting memory phenomenon called the *modality effect:* When people are given lists of seven or eight items to be remembered, they remember them better if the items are presented auditorially than if they are presented visually.

In Figure 2.6 we see that the modality effect can be traced primarily to the fewer errors subjects made in the last few serial positions for the

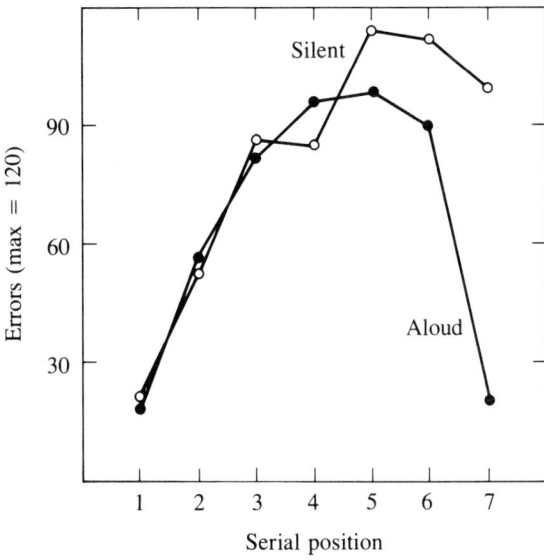

Figure 2.6 A demonstration of the modality effect. Subjects in both groups were shown the stimuli visually. However, subjects in the "Aloud" group spoke each letter orally, thus generating an auditory input. (From Conrad & Hull, 1968.)

auditorially presented list. (Serial position refers to the position of a word within a list; for example, a word in Serial Position 3 was the third item presented in a list.) Crowder (1976) claimed that the modality effect is due to the fact that the Echo is larger than the Icon. Otherwise, the contribution from the Icon at the end of the visually presented list should have offset the contribution from the Echo.

Interestingly, however, the modality effect does not occur equally for consonant and vowel information. When the consonants in the syllables *bah, dah, gah, pah, tah, kah* (called stop consonants) are presented, no modality effect appears. On the other hand, if vowels are changed instead of consonants, such as in *bah, bih,* and *beh,* the modality effect appears (Crowder, 1971; Darwin & Baddeley, 1974).

What might account for this unusual finding? As Crowder (1976) noted, we could argue that "Short-term memory has a larger capacity for auditory information than for visual information except when stop consonants are concerned, in which case the two capacities are equal" (p. 64). Such an argument would make little sense from the point of view of any memory theory. However, extensive research on speech perception shows that vowels and consonants are processed differently (Crowder, 1975) in a number of different experimental settings.

Is it possible that the Echo serves some very functional purpose as far as the processing of language? In particular, is it possible that the Echo is set up to handle speech information specifically related to the processing of vowel sounds—information that is important in understanding spoken human language? Crowder (1976) suggests this may be the case. He notes that features such as pitch, stress, and intonation contours, which are encoded only on vowels, are important in speech perception.

In order to know, for example, that the pitch of a word has changed from one part of a word to another, we must be able to remember both the beginning and end sounds of the word. Since this pitch information is unlikely to be coded in a symbolic fashion, it would seem a likely feature to be coded in a memory that has carried out relatively little processing on the incoming speech signal. Such a description fits well our characterization of the Echo.

We see then that the sensory registers play an important early role in our story of information processing. They play that first crucial function of maintaining a representation of the environmental stimulation long enough so that more elaborate processing can be completed. This is apparently important not only for relatively simple stimuli such as letters, words, or visual objects but even for complex information such as language. If we are to be able to understand speech, we must be able to hold certain types of information long enough so that additional analyses can be completed.

What is involved in these additional analyses? As we consider the processes of perception, we will discover answers to this question.

PERCEPTION

Consider the following situation: You are casually walking down a sidewalk when you suddenly note a glinting object several feet to one side. What follows is a likely series of events. You turn your head toward the glinting object and focus your eyes on it. You note that the object is small, round, and reflects light. Since the sidewalk borders an old deserted house with several trash cans, you surmise that the object is an old tin can. You maintain this view until you get within two or three feet of the object, when you note that there appears to be a face on the can surface. Suddenly you realize that what you are seeing is not a can but a silver dollar leaning up against a rock.

While this example might result in a good deal of elation for you, it serves a different function for us because it exhibits some key aspects of the process of perception.

Before we consider what these aspects are, let us first recall what we mean by perception. As we noted, perception is the process of determining the meaning of the stimuli that impinge upon us. Consequently, when we say that a person has perceived an object or event, we are saying that individual has determined some meaning for it. The meaning may vary from individual to individual, but nevertheless it is a meaning. Perception then involves more than just detecting stimulation in the environment, for we can detect an object and know that something occurred but yet have no specific meaning for that environmental stimulation.

What aspects of this process of perception are apparent in our example? First, our example indicates that perception depends on two different types of information—information from the environment and information from the perceiver. Obviously you would not have perceived anything if there had been no object beside the sidewalk to give off the glint of light. Not so obvious perhaps is the fact that there would have been no perception if you had had no information available in memory. That is, to determine the meaning of an event implies that we link up environmental stimulation with knowledge we already have. Thus we know that small glinting objects around trash cans are likely to be tin cans and that round shiny surfaces with profiles of faces on them are likely to be coins.

A second aspect of perception apparent in our example is that perception involves a number of subprocesses: first, orienting the sensory receptors (in this case the eyes) toward the source of stimulation and second, extracting numerous features from the environmental stimulation. Here, for example, features such as roundness and shininess were extracted from the stimulation. Third, we can note that the context, or setting, in which an event occurs can influence what we perceive. If the glinting object had occurred in a jewelry store rather than a vacant lot, your initial perceptions might have been quite different.

Finally, it is apparent that perception is a cyclic process of orientation, feature extraction, comparison to memory, and then additional orientation, feature extraction, and comparison. It involves a continuing cycle of such processes until a satisfactory perception is attained. In our example above, the first run through the cycle did not result in an accurate perception, but it narrowed the range of objects and guided further feature extraction so that the perceptual cycle could result in an accurate perception. In the following two sections on pattern recognition and the role of schemata in perception, we will provide greater detail about these aspects of perception.

Pattern Recognition

A large part of the current study of perception comes under the title of **pattern recognition.** In studies of pattern recognition we investigate how it is that an individual can determine that a particular set of lines and angles is the letter *A,* a particular set of sounds is the word *paper,* or a particular set of curved lines such as shown in Figure 2.7 is a human face. In essence then, pattern recognition is concerned with how an environmental stimulus comes to be identified as something that a given individual has stored in memory. Although there are a number of ways of conceptualizing the process of pattern recognition, each view hypothesizes that the stimulus is detected by the sensory receptors and maintained briefly in sensory memory while a number of analyses of the stimulus are carried out. These analyses involve a comparison to stored knowledge so that a pattern recognition decision can be reached.

The best way to conceptualize these analyses, however, has led to some dispute, and to understand this dispute we need to consider briefly how it is that information about our world is stored in permanent memory. Although we will leave an in-depth discussion of this topic to Chapter 4, we need to understand now the notion of the unit of permanent memory introduced in Chapter 1—a unit variously called the **concept** or the **schema** (plural, **schemata**). These terms refer to mental structures—units of organized knowledge that individuals have about their world. Thus a person's cat schema may include such information as the acoustic sounds of the word *cat,* the fact that cats have four legs, that cats are furry, and so on.

In a similar manner a person's automobile schema probably contains information about a body, wheels, and type of engine. It also contains certain information about the relationships among these various parts. This is clear by looking at Figure 2.8. Most of us would not recognize the top drawing in this figure as an automobile even though it contains the three sets of parts identified. Our schema apparently contains certain structural information as well—information such as that conveyed in the bottom part of Figure 2.8.

Figure 2.7 Schematic drawing of the human face.

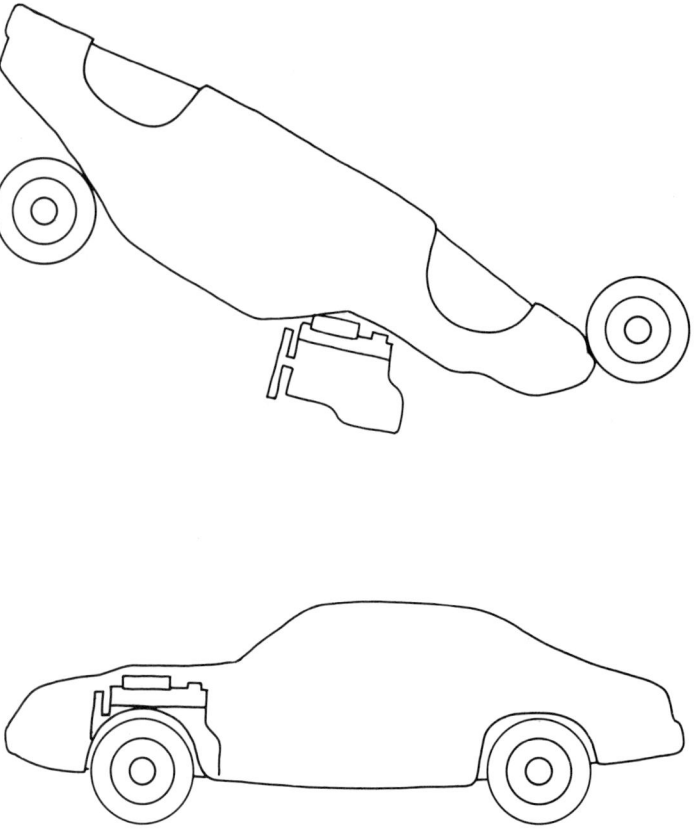

Figure 2.8 Two different representations of the relationships among the various parts of an automobile. The top is inconsistent with our schema of automobile. The bottom is highly consistent with our schema.

As the following chapters will illustrate, we have a vast number of such schemata, for we know about books, about flowers, and about how to hit a tennis backhand or make a line drawing of an object. These schemata vary in generality and may be linked to other schemata. Thus a cat schema may have some pieces of knowledge related to the lion schema but have little overlap with the book schema. All of a person's knowledge of his world is held in these various schemata.

What we have not specified here is what form this knowledge is maintained in. How, for example, is the letter A retained in memory? Do we have the equivalent of a photograph of the letter in memory (called a *template*)? Or do we have a list of features (called *distinctive features*) that would specify the letter A? Such a list might include one of each of the following:

$$/ \, , \, \backslash \, , \, - \, .$$

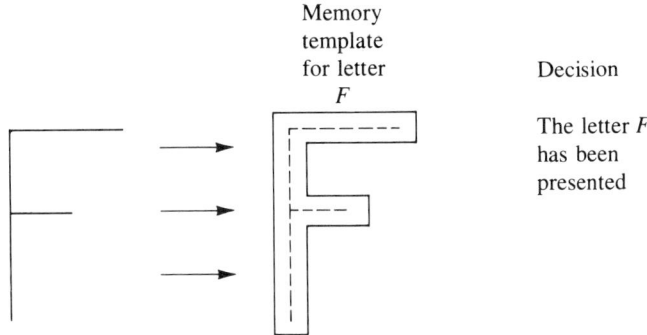

Figure 2.9 Template matching process for the letter *F*.

There are of course numerous views of the manner in which information is maintained in permanent memory. Although these will be discussed in detail later in the book, we wish to note here that the manner in which psychologists contend that human knowledge is stored in permanent memory plays a large role in how they view pattern recognition. Three principal views of how knowledge is stored have been hypothesized by those interested in pattern recognition: (1) storage by templates, (2) storage by prototypes (a variation of templates), and (3) storage by distinctive features. We need to consider each of these views and determine what they mean for the process of pattern recognition.

Templates. Probably the simplest view of pattern recognition hypothesizes that there are **templates,** or mental copies of environmental objects, stored in permanent memory. We might argue that a mental copy of the letter *F* is stored in memory in such a way that when *F* is presented to the individual, a match is made between the incoming stimulation and the stored copy. We have schematized such a possibility in Figure 2.9.

While at first glance this may seem a reasonable hypothesis, further analysis suggests a major logical problem. There would have to be a different template for every possible size and orientation of any given stimulus object. Thus if the letter *F* were presented as ⌒ or ⊢ or ℱ, we would probably not recognize it as the letter *F*, as is seen in Figure 2.10. To have that many different templates makes such an approach untenable.

Of course, it may be possible to do some manipulations of the incoming patterns to make them conform to some basic pattern. For example, we might argue that all letters are rotated such that their longest axis is vertical, that all objects are scaled to a standard size, and that all imperfections are removed. Thus the three letters shown above may be altered as seen in Figure 2.11.

This approach would certainly help the template model although it raises some additional difficulties. Such manipulations assume that the pattern recognition device has some idea of what the pattern is so that it can carry out the correct set of manipulations. For example, should ℱ be straightened to ⊢ or changed to make P?

These difficulties arise when our pattern recognition device is only expecting to recognize individual letters. What if we complicate the situation and present it with numbers, line drawings, and geometric forms? What if we go a step further and present it with real-life scenes having

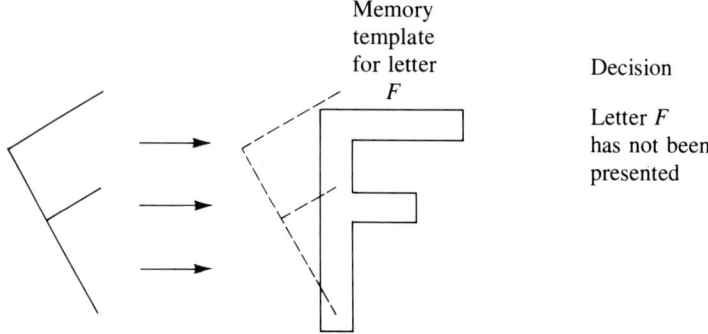

Figure 2.10 Orientation difficulty for template model of pattern recognition.

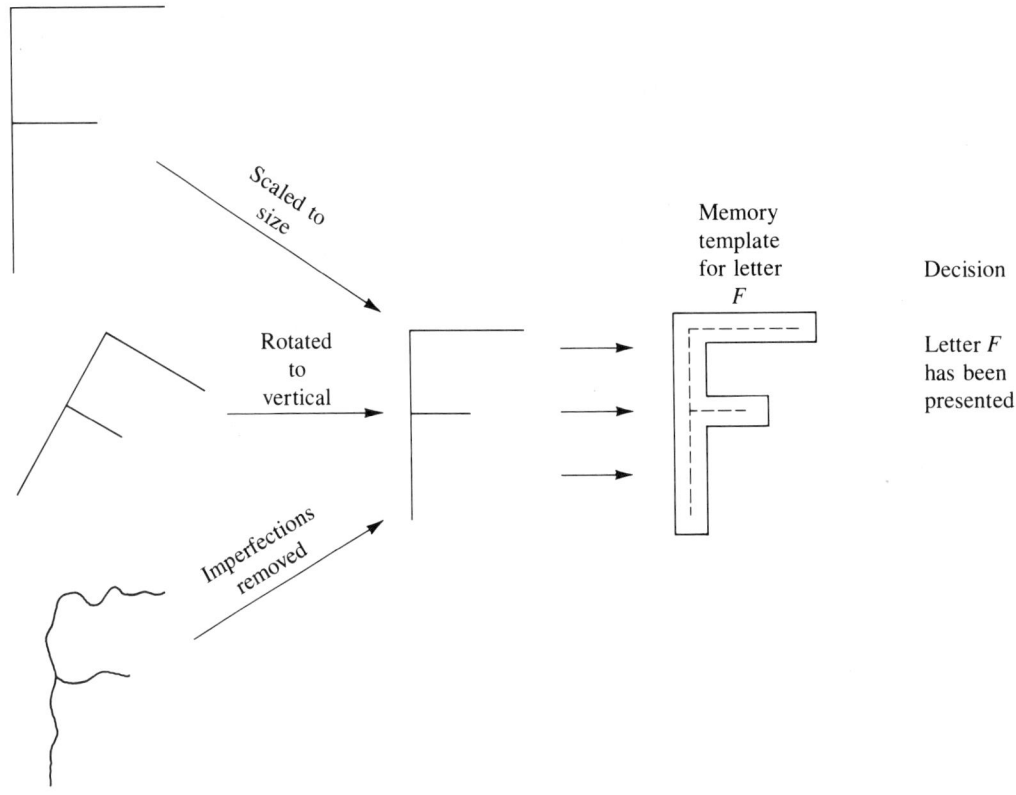

Figure 2.11 Transformation procedures used in cleaning up raw environment stimulation.

shadows and unusual orientations of objects? In such settings a template system seems unable to function efficiently.

It is possible to modify the template system even more radically and thus keep it as a viable candidate for pattern recognition. The needed modification would allow the template to be more general and less specific to individual patterns —or as Klatzky (1975) said, to allow some "slop" in the patterns coming to it. This modified form of template has come to be called a *prototype*.

Prototypes. Trees take many shapes. But if we were to ask you to draw a picture of a tree, you would probably sketch something like we have in Figure 2.12. This drawing is not of any particular tree but just of an average tree. It has the basic features of a tree in that it has a trunk and a type of foliage on top. Such a drawing characterizes what we mean by a **prototype**—a form that represents the key features of a set of objects. It does not represent any specific object and in that sense is not a template.

Some psychologists have argued that information is stored in memory in the form of such prototypes. Any particular object or event is stored by its prototype plus a list of variations. Pattern recognition then consists of determining whether an object matches the basic form found in the prototype. If it does, the item is recognized.

Do humans use prototypes in storing information? The answer appears to be yes. This is seen most clearly in work by Posner and Keele (1968, 1970). These authors presented subjects with patterns of nine dots such as those in Figure 2.13. These patterns were formed by taking a single pattern (the prototype) and generating variations by moving some of the dots. In essence, each of these new patterns was a variation on the original prototype. Subjects were asked to learn a single response for the several distortions of any given prototype. The subjects were required to

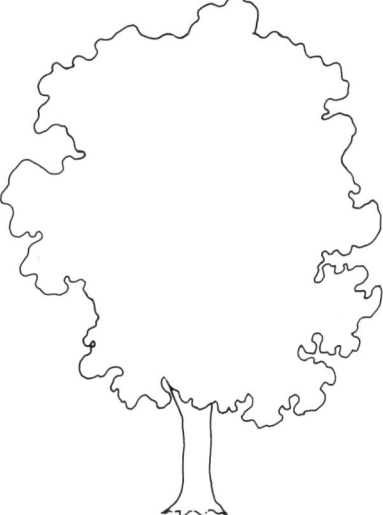

Figure 2.12 Prototype of a tree.

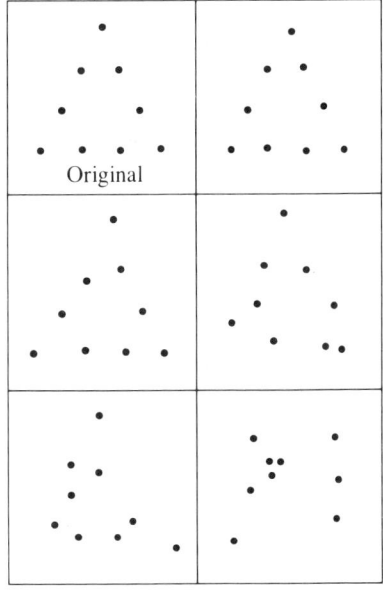

Figure 2.13 The top left box shows an original prototype. The remaining boxes show variations on this prototype. (From Posner, Goldsmith, & Welton, 1967.)

learn a new response for the set of distortions for each of three different prototypes.

After this learning experience, they were given another set of dot patterns and asked to classify them as to which set of patterns they belonged to. Included in the set to be classified were the actual prototypes (which the subjects had never seen before), new variations of the

---

Box 2.1   ARE PERSONALITY TRAITS PROTOTYPES?

A book on human cognitive processes may seem an unlikely place to discuss personality traits. However, a study by Cantor and Mischel (1977) suggests that personality traits such as introversion and extraversion may play the same role in processing personality-related information as prototypes do in processing geometric forms or dot patterns. If this is true, we may have gained an insight into some important personality phenomena.

Cantor and Mischel presented subjects with ten sentences describing the personality characteristics of different people. For example, one individual was described as being energetic, entertaining, impulsive, dominating, friendly, ambitious, honorable, logical, punctual, and neat. This was a description of an extraverted individual. This description was composed of six terms that are moderately related to extraversion and four that are unrelated to extraversion. Cantor and Mischel also generated descriptions of individuals who had characteristics unrelated to extraversion.

After hearing these descriptions, subjects were given a recognition memory test to see if they could recognize the terms that described the individuals. Included in the recognition test were a number of items the subjects had not seen before. These included items that were highly, moderately, or not-at-all related to extraversion.

Cantor and Mischel found that subjects were far more likely to claim that they had seen a term highly or moderately related to extraversion if they had been given the extraversion description than if they had been given a description composed only of terms unrelated to extraversion. Apparently subjects had built up a prototype of the individual from the description presented. This prototype biased the subjects toward information consistent with the prototype they had established.

The study by Cantor and Mischel is significant for two reasons: First, it suggests an important unity of processes across very diverse areas of psychology. The phenomena and processes observed in the studies of human cognition seem related to those in social and personality areas. Second, and more specific to our social functioning as human beings, we may be subject to some degree of bias in how we process information about the personality characteristics of individuals. That is, once we have characterized an individual as having certain personality characteristics, we may be more likely to pay attention only to those aspects that fit our view of the individual.

same three prototypes, and old variations of the three prototypes. Only the last set of patterns had ever been seen before by the subject.

Posner and Keele (1968) found that subjects classified the actual prototypes and the old variations as being members of the same class equally well. That is, they placed the prototype they had not seen before in the appropriate class as well as they did variations they had seen before. The new variations were classified less accurately. Thus it seems that a prototype, or average figure, had been entered into memory along with the specific instances. This is consistent with the view that subjects store prototypes of experiences from their world.

Recent work suggests that people not only form prototypes of visual objects but also of human faces (Reed, 1972), event sequences (Lindsay & Norman, 1977), personality patterns (Cantor & Mischel, 1977; see Box 2.1), and mental illness (Rosenhan, 1973). In many cases, such prototypes—or *stereotypes* as they are more usually called—play an important role in social interactions. Thus if we have a stereotype of a miser, a football player, or a mentally ill person, our behavior toward a given individual who falls in any one of those classes is going to be affected.

Prototypes are advantageous in that they are a more efficient means of storing information, but they have a drawback in that they lead us to treat all members of the same class in the same way. It is not surprising then that the intellectual football player or the handsome young miser may be difficult for us to respond to.

Feature Analysis. There is a third way to view the process of pattern recognition—**feature analysis.** It is not unrelated to the notions of template matching and prototype use, but it adds some properties that allow us to explain a broader array of perceptual phenomena. In addition, this model fits well with what is currently known about the physiological mechanisms underlying perception.

PHYSIOLOGICAL MECHANISMS. To help you understand feature analysis better, we need to summarize some fascinating and important findings about physiological mechanisms that detect features. In the 1960s, Hubel and Wiesel (1962, 1963, 1965, 1968) published a number of studies examining the firings of specific brain cells (neurons) following various types of visual stimulation. They implanted microelectrodes in the brains of cats and monkeys to monitor the neural activity of individual brain cells as the animals were shown different patterns of visual information. Over the years, they and other researchers have established a picture of brain activity related to the process of visual perception.

In general, they have shown that the brain carries out extensive analyses on specific properties (features) of incoming stimuli. These analyses are carried out through a very large number of brain cells, each responding to particular aspects of the stimulus. These cells may be roughly classified as follows (our description is based on that of Lindsay & Norman, 1977):

Simple cells. These are cells in the cortex of the brain which respond maximally to certain simple patterns of light falling on the retina of the eye. Three types of these cells are *edge detectors, slit detectors,* and *line detectors.*

Edge detectors respond most strongly when an edge of light falls across a particular location on the retina of the eye as shown in Figure 2.14. On the left side of this figure we have diagrammed a rough circle that symbolizes the retina of the eye. Lying across the retina is a dashed vertical line that demonstrates the receptive field of one particular neural cell—in this case an edge detector. The receptive field of a cell is the region on the retina which a neural cell is sensitive to. In Figure 2.14 we show a region of high intensity light which exactly lines up with the receptive field of the edge detector. This results in maximum firing of the cell as indicated by the high density of vertical strokes when the light is turned on. When the light is off, this cell

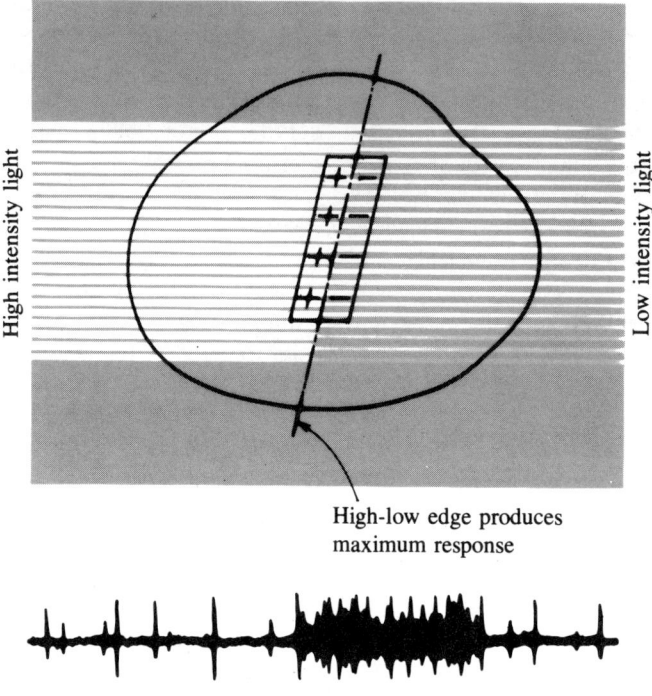

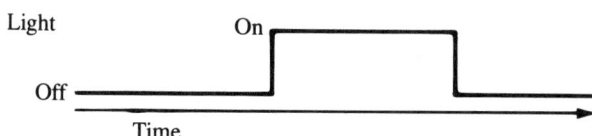

Figure 2.14 Example of receptive field and firing pattern for an edge detector cell. (From Lindsay & Norman, 1977.)

resumes a much lower firing rate. The edge detector cell shown here will fire maximally only if the light source aligns exactly with the receptive field of the cell.

In contrast to edge detectors, slit detectors respond most strongly to a bright line of stimulation surrounded by two dark areas as in Figure 2.15. Again the orientation and location of the light source are important.

Line detectors are complementary to slit detectors and respond maximally to two light areas of stimulation surrounding a dark line as shown in Figure 2.16.

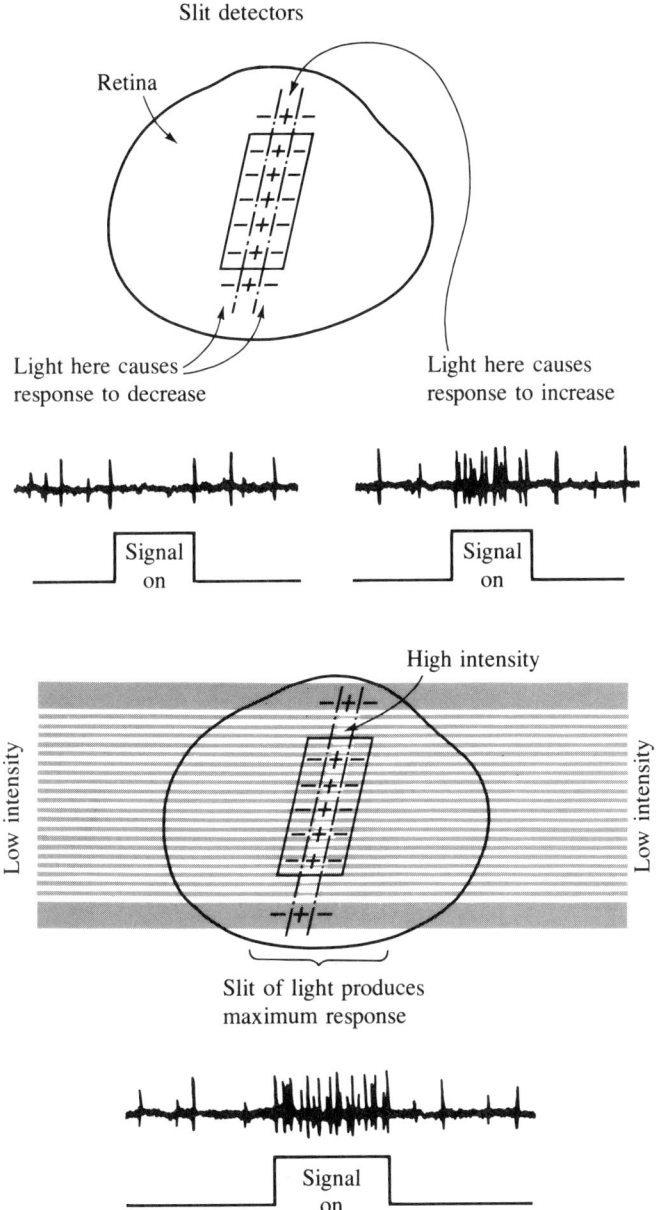

Figure 2.15 Example of receptive field and firing pattern for a slit detector cell. (From Lindsay & Norman, 1977.)

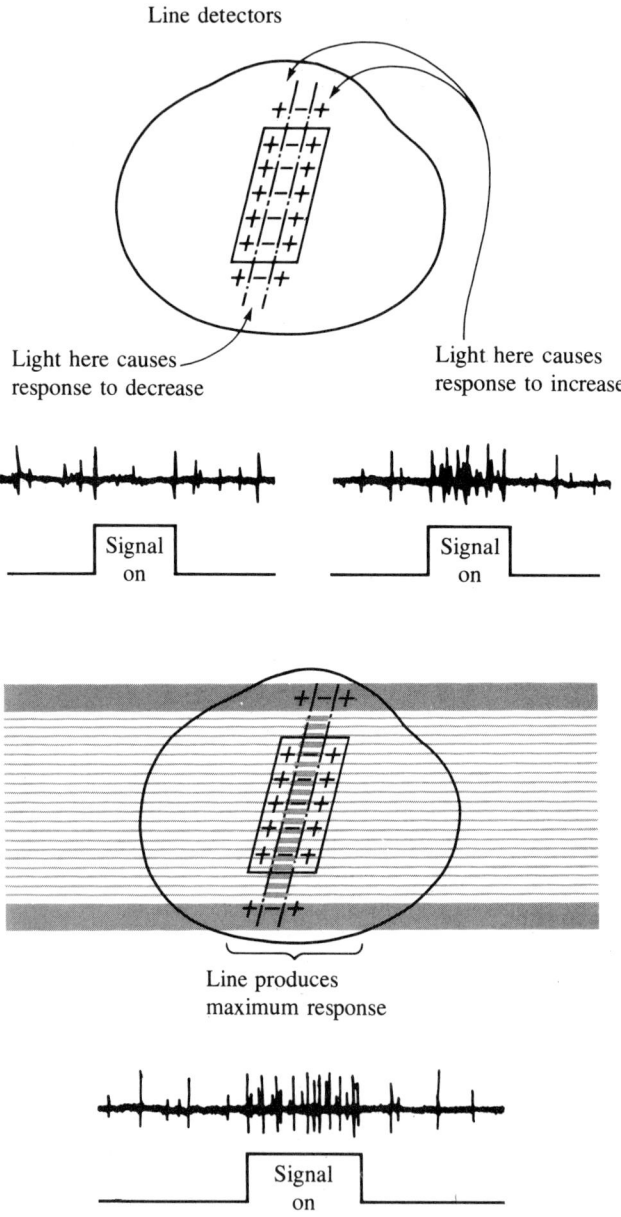

Figure 2.16 Example of receptive field and firing pattern for a line detector cell. (From Lindsay & Norman, 1977.)

Complex cells. These cells respond to the same general types of stimulation as simple cells, but they are not so influenced by location on the retina. That is, for a particular complex line detector cell to respond maximally, it must be given a line of a particular orientation and width, but the location of the line on the retina is not of as much importance. These cells are thus more complex in that they respond to a more general type of stimulation than do simple cells.

Hypercomplex cells. These cells react to properties of the stimulus which simple and complex cells do not. For example, one such cell may respond maximally only if the lines and slits have a particular length and move in a particular direction. This allows the cell to determine the size and movement of specific types of stimulation.

Thus we see in Figure 2.17 a hypercomplex cell responding maximally to a line of one length moving in one direction (line A), but not to a line of a different length moving in the same direction (line C), or to a line of any length moving in the opposite direction (lines B and D). Some hypercomplex cells also respond differentially to certain angles of light stimulation, thus providing for a means of detecting angular information from stimulus arrays.

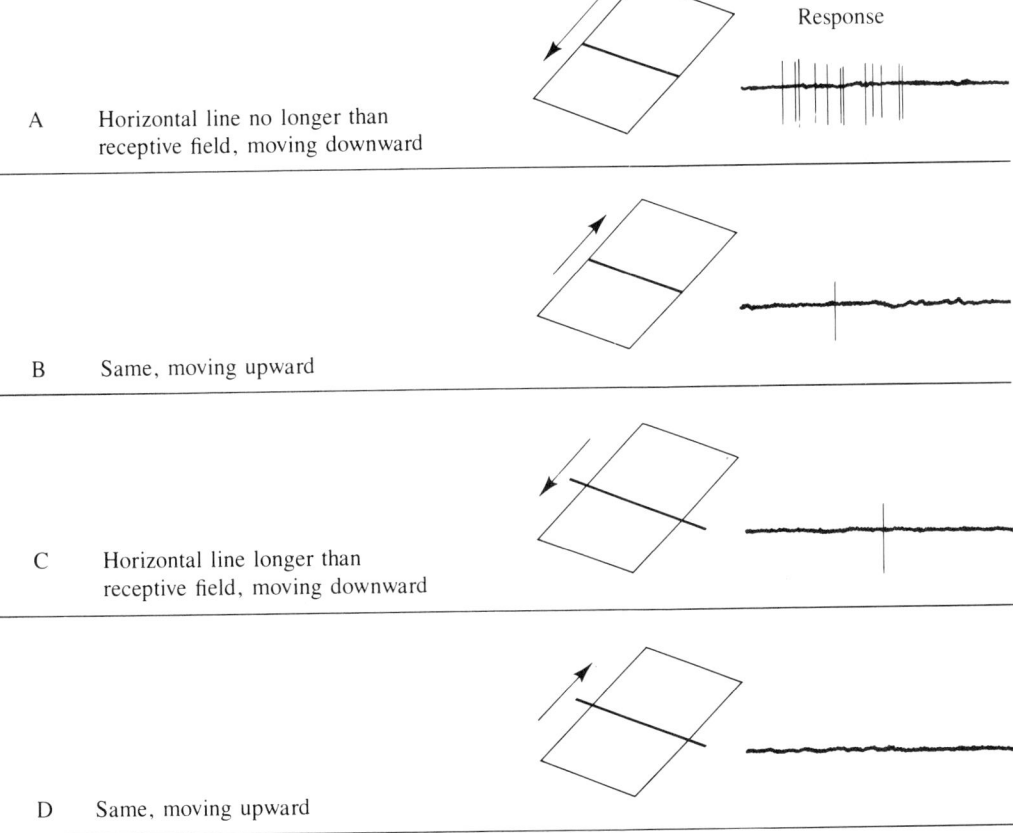

A Horizontal line no longer than receptive field, moving downward

B Same, moving upward

C Horizontal line longer than receptive field, moving downward

D Same, moving upward

Figure 2.17 Example of a hypercomplex cell firing pattern. Note that the firing pattern is influenced by both the direction of movement and length of the line. (From Hubel & Wiesel, 1965.)

W, X, Y cells. Recently another classification of neural cells has been added: W, X, and Y cells. These labels indicate roughly the speed of transmission of certain cells, with Y being very fast, X intermediate, and W slow. Y cells are most sensitive to movement and are good for detecting change. X cells are more sensitive to continual stimulation and indicate what the steady state properties of the stimulation are.

These sets of specialized cells appear to be the foundation of an elaborate feature analysis system involved in recognizing patterns of visual stimulation in the world around us.

PANDEMONIUM: A MODEL OF FEATURE DETECTION. One way to characterize the feature analysis system is called **Pandemonium** (Selfridge, 1959). Pandemonium is a computer model of a process that Selfridge claimed can recognize common patterns such as letters or numbers. This system is characterized in Figure 2.18, again using the letter *F,* and it involves a number of processes, called *demons,* which work on the input stimuli, each doing different things. We have already discussed the duties of some of these demons as will be evident, although we did not call them by that name.

The first level of demon in Pandemonium is called the *image demon.* These demons simply hold a record of the external signal briefly. Hence they play the same role that sensory registers did in our discussion earlier in this chapter. At the next level in Pandemonium is a set of *feature demons.* These demons analyze the image held by the image demon, looking for certain properties. As we see in Figure 2.18, each such demon looks for a different type of information. One may search for vertical lines, another for horizontal lines, another for diagonal lines, and so on. When a given demon sees the particular stimulation it is looking for, it starts shouting or signaling that its type of stimulation is available.

Feature demons in Pandemonium may be related to some of the specialized brain cells we have described; in particular, the capabilities of the complex and hypercomplex cells seem analogous. You will recall that these cells respond to lines of particular orientation, width, and length but that location of the lines on the retina is of little importance.

At the next level in Pandemonium are *cognitive demons*. These demons look at the signals from the feature demons; each looks for a particular pattern of features. Thus there would be cognitive demons for each letter of the alphabet and for other patterns of stimulation. When a cognitive demon finds evidence for its pattern, it starts shouting. The more features it finds for its pattern, the louder it yells.

Finally, Pandemonium calls for a *decision demon,* who listens to all the cognitive demons and decides which is signaling the loudest, thus indicating which pattern is occurring in the environment.

Describing Pandemonium in this way with all its demons and shouting makes it sound quite unscientific. Obviously we do not have demons shouting in our heads; but as we have tried to indicate, there are physiological mechanisms within the brain which can effectively do what these demons are thought to do. When a complex cell is firing rapidly, indicating its feature is available, it is signaling other cells just as surely as humans signal each other by shouting or yelling. Similarly, when even more complex cells fire only when they see certain patterns of features, they too are sending signals to other brain cells. Thus Pandemonium becomes a real possibility for a model of how humans recognize patterns of stimulation in the environment around them.

DISTINCTIVE FEATURES. Before leaving our discussion of feature analysis, we need to discuss a major question facing feature analysis models of pattern recognition. What *is* a feature? There are

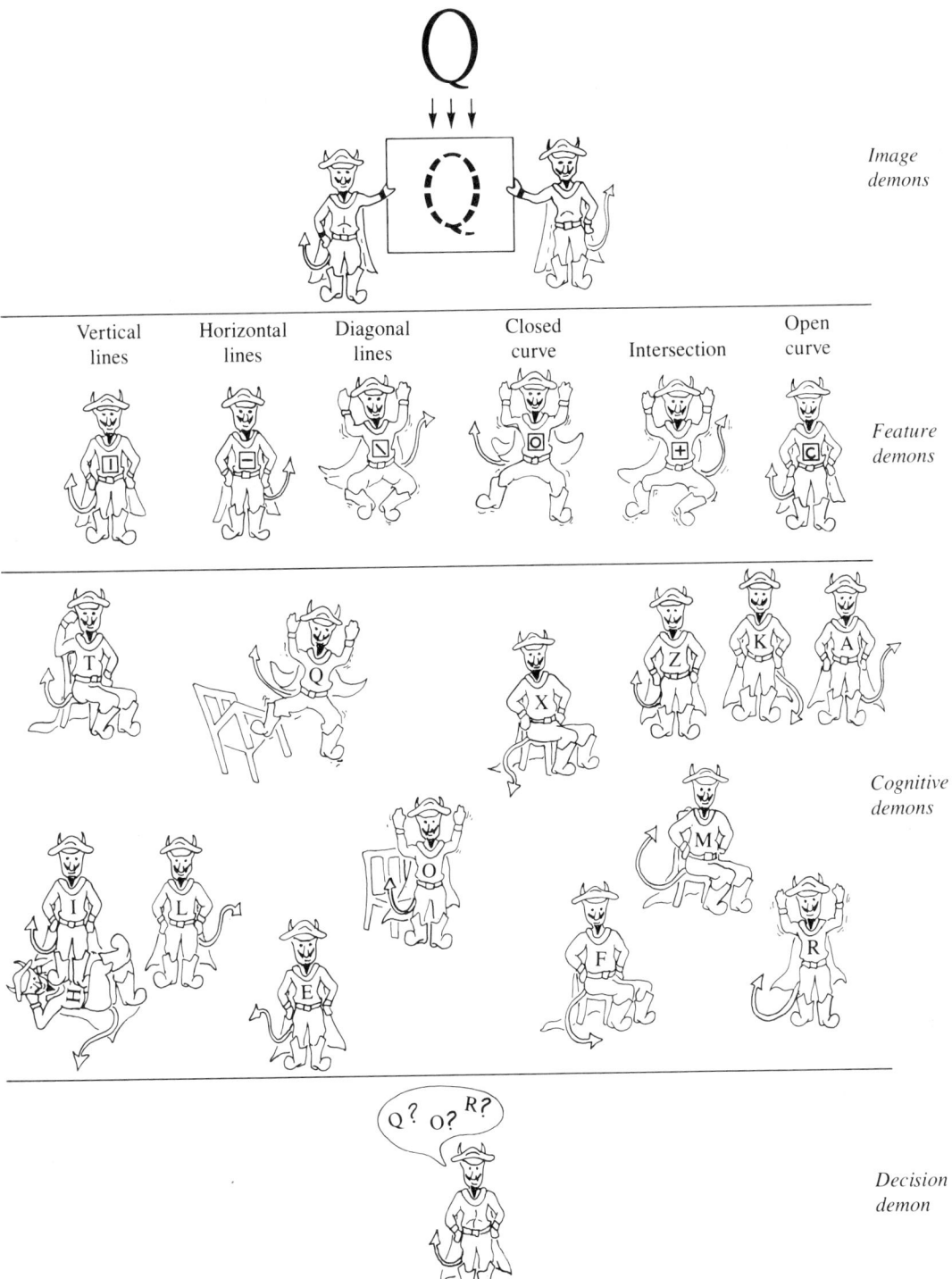

Figure 2.18 Characterization of Selfridge's Pandemonium system.

obviously a large number of different characteristics that could be singled out for any given object. This seems especially the case when we consider the complex visual and acoustical stimuli that frequently occur in everyday settings. Which of these characteristics, or features, become important in the recognition of environmental patterns?

It is difficult to answer this question definitively at the present time. The bulk of work by psychologists on pattern recognition has dealt with rather simple patterns such as letters. With these types of stimuli we can generate a list of so-called *distinctive features*. These refer to a set of features that can distinguish among all members of the set of objects being considered.

For example, the list of features indicated in Table 2.1 is a distinctive feature set for the printed letters of the alphabet. Thus combinations of horizontal, vertical, or diagonal lines, of closed or open curves, of intersections, and so on, uniquely indicate every printed letter of the alphabet. The letter *A,* for instance, can be indicated by the features of diagonal lines, horizontal lines, intersections, symmetry, and vertical discontinuity. The letter *H,* in contrast, is represented by the features of vertical lines, horizontal lines, intersections, symmetry, and vertical discontinuity. In a similar manner every printed letter can be represented by a unique combination of these simple distinctive features. (It is of interest to note, of course, that the set of features indicated here is not unrelated to the feature demons in the Pandemonium model of pattern recognition.)

The number of studies hypothesizing that humans use distinctive feature sets such as these in recognizing letters of the alphabet is quite compelling. For example, we might expect that the hardest letters to distinguish would be those that have very similar patterns of distinctive features. The printed letters *R* and *P* are quite similar, for instance, as are *C* and *G*. Studies have in fact shown that distinguishing letter pairs such as these is difficult (Kinney, Marsetta, & Showman, 1966), as the confusion matrix in Table 2.2 illustrates.

The leftmost column of this table shows the characters presented to the subjects in a brief flash on a screen. The horizontal row at the top of the table indicates the characters the subjects thought they saw. By reading across any row we can determine which characters—letters or figures—were most frequently confused with which other characters. For example, if we look at the errors made when the letter *R* was flashed on the screen, we note that most frequently (4 out of 6 times) it was confused with the letter *P*. This is not so surprising when we note in Table 2.1 that the letter *R* differs from *P* only by one distinctive feature, the addition of a diagonal line.

Additional support for the belief that we use distinctive features arises from the work on visual scanning behavior by Neisser and his colleagues (for a review, see Neisser, 1967). An excellent example of their evidence can be seen in a study in which Neisser asked subjects to scan a series of lists of letters such as those in Figure 2.19 for a particular target letter (Neisser, 1964).

These target lists varied in how similar the letters in the lists were to the target letter. For example, if the target letter in the two lists in Figure 2.19 were *Z*, List *b* would be more similar to the target than List *a*. List *b* is composed only of items made up of straight lines, as is *Z*. List *a*, however, is composed only of letters having some curved features, which *Z* of course does not have.

If subjects were matching each letter against the *Z* template, they should have been able to scan these two lists equally rapidly. If subjects were using a distinctive feature approach, however, they should have been able to scan List *a* more quickly since they needed only determine if a given letter had any curved feature to know that it could not be *Z*. This is, in fact, what Neisser found. Subjects were able to scan lists that were dissimilar to the target letter faster than they could lists that were similar.

Studies such as these, of course, do not prove that human pattern recognition is carried out by a feature recognition procedure, nor do they show that sets of distinctive features can be used to recognize very complex patterns of environmental stimulation. Nevertheless, they do indicate a plausible mechanism that could underlie complex pattern recognition processes.

A few years ago our consideration of pattern recognition and perception might have ended with this discussion of features and feature analyses. Some compelling investigations and theorizing in the past few years, however, suggest that to end here would be to present a distorted picture of human perception. The principal difficulty is that the models discussed so far do not take into account the importance of the context in which a pattern is presented in the recognition of

Table 2.1 Distinctive Feature Set for Written Letters of the English Alphabet

Feature		A	E	F	H	I	L	T	K	M	N	V	W	X	Y	Z	B	C	D	G	J	O	P	R	Q	S	U
Straight																											
Horizontal		+	+	+	+		+	+								+			+								
Vertical			+	+	+	+	+	+	+	+	+						+		+				+	+			
Diagonal	/	+							+		+	+	+	+	+	+											
Diagonal	\	+							+	+	+	+	+	+		+								+	+		
Curve																											
Closed																	+		+			+	+	+	+			+
Open V																					+							+
Open H																		+		+	+					+		
Intersection		+	+	+	+			+	+					+			+							+	+	+		
Redundancy																											
Cyclic change			+							+		+				+									+			
Symmetry		+	+		+	+		+	+	+		+	+	+	+		+	+	+		+						+
Discontinuity																											
Vertical		+			+	+	+		+	+	+	+				+								+	+			
Horizontal			+	+			+	+											+									

Source: From Gibson (1969).

Note: A "+" sign indicates that the letter has the indicated feature.

Table 2.2 Confusion Matrix for Visually Presented Characters

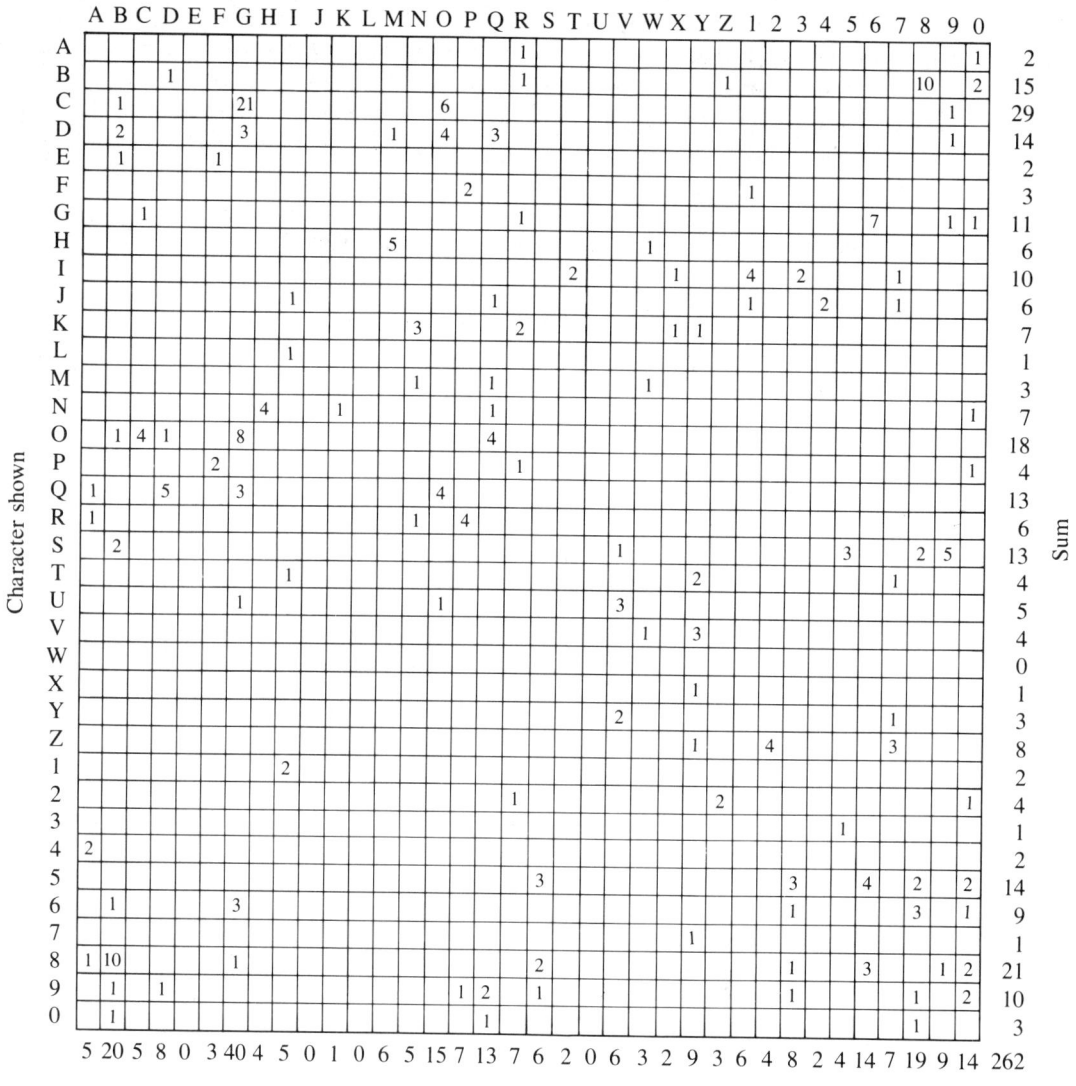

Source: From Kinney, Marsetta, and Showman, (1966). *Reprinted by permission.*

that pattern. Similarly, our discussion has not adequately indicated the importance of what the individual who is perceiving a situation brings to that perceptual setting. In fact, much of what human beings perceive depends on what they expect to perceive.

a	b
ODUGQR	IVMXEW
QCDUGO	EWVMIX
CQOGRD	EXWMVI
QUGCDR	IXEMWV
URDGQO	VXWEMI
GRUQDO	MXVEWI
DUZGRO	XVWMEI
UCGROD	MWXVIE
DQRCGU	VIMEXW
QDOCGU	EXVWIM
CGUROQ	VWMIEX
OCDURQ	VMWIEX
UOCGQD	XVWMEI
RGQCOU	WXVEMI
GRUDQO	XMEWIV
GODUCQ	MXIVEW
QCURDO	VEWMIX
DUCOQG	EMVXWI
CGRDQU	IVWMEX
UDRCOQ	IEVMWX
GQCORU	WVZMXE
GOQUCD	XEMIWV
GDQUOC	WXIMEV
URDCGO	EMWIVX
GODROC	IVEMXW

Figure 2.19 Examples of lists used in the visual scanning tasks of Neisser. (From Neisser, 1964.)

Expectations and Perception: There Is More to Seeing Than Meets the Eye

Our discussion to this point has portrayed the process of perception as a one-way street. This street begins with an event or object in the environment that is picked up by the sensory mechanisms, maintained in the sensory registers, and analyzed by pattern recognition processes until a match is achieved. We are becoming increasingly aware, however, that this is only half the story—an important half, of course, but it misleads us into viewing perception as a simple flow of information through ever more elaborate analyses until perception occurs.

Neisser (1976) argues with some forcefulness that it is more accurate to describe perception as involving a cycle of processing. A part of this cycle involves sampling information from the environment and analyzing it as we have described. Neisser, however, views this sampling as being guided by internal expectations. These expectations direct the sensory mechanisms to search for particular types of information. As this search for information gathers additional information, the expectations are modified. These newly modified expectations again guide further search, leading to yet additional modifications.

A review of our example beginning the section on perception portrays this cyclic nature of perception. You remember that the individual in that example notes a glint of light in the context of trash cans and activates an expectation of tin cans; this expectation guides further search, and the information derived from this search leads to a modification of the expectation in favor of a silver dollar. Here we see a constant interaction between environment and memory until satisfactory perception is achieved.

What are these expectations that play such an important role in the perceptual cycle? How can we best characterize them and how do they guide perception? What role does context play in our ability to perceive?

Expectations and Schemata. In order to understand expectations we must return to the notion of schema and elaborate our earlier discussion. The concept of schema has been a difficult one for psychologists. It has been used in a number of different ways by a number of prominent psychologists (Bartlett, 1932/1967; Neisser, 1976; Piaget, 1970). Generally the term is used to refer to a unit of organized knowledge about events, situations, or objects. A given individual has a schema for how to do long division, how to hit a tennis backhand, what a silver dollar looks like, or what to expect to see while riding to work on the bus. Thus schemata are mental structures, the units for representing our internalized knowledge of the world.

While this description gives us a general view of the character of schemata, we must be more specific in our description if we are to understand how schemata are related to perception. In particular, schemata have two important functions that lead them to play fundamental roles in perception.

First, schemata function as *information-accepting systems*. By this we mean that environmental information is meaningful only insofar as it fits into or relates to schemata that the individual has. In this sense schemata are like formats in computer-programming language. Such formats specify that information must be of a particular type before it can be interpreted (Neisser, 1976).

To help us make our point, we want you to turn the page and look at the picture of the man's face in Figure 2.20. In other words, we want you to have your man schema in mind as you look at this picture. A careful analysis indicates that some lines or marks in the picture are of less importance than others, and you would probably leave them out if we asked you to draw it from memory. In particular, the short line on the nose right under the glasses and the horizontal curved line between the mouth and the ear seem of little importance to the figure and are likely to be ignored in processing.

However, if we were to tell you to look at this figure again and note that it can also be perceived as a picture of a rat with a long curling tail, your acceptance of information in the picture is likely to change. The short line under the "glasses" (that is, the ears) now becomes important as the eye of the animal, and the line from the "mouth" to the "ear" now becomes important as the underbelly of the animal. Thus we see that information that fits the schema through which we are viewing a picture is likely to be processed. Information that does not is likely to be ignored.

A second major function of schemata is that they serve as *plans* for picking up information from the environment. Thus when we said that Figure 2.20 contained a man's face, we provided you with a plan to search the figure. Your plan may have gone something like this: "If this is a face, then there must be a nose, mouth, and eyes. Since the nose is below the eyes, those two big circles must be eyeglasses and this bump must be the nose."

This function of schemata is important to perception because it severely restricts where we must look for information and tells us what form the information we may find is likely to be in. Thus our schemata help dramatically to reduce the complexity of our world by providing us with hints about where we are likely to find certain types of environmental information. The perceptual expectations of which Neisser spoke are a natural offshoot of the functioning of our schemata. When any given schema receives environmental input that is appropriate to it—that is, when a schema is activated—it results in a set of perceptual expectations about what is likely to occur next.

The functions of schemata we have described here are important whether we are discussing how we perceive words in reading (Rumelhart, 1977b), how we see a room after opening a door (Minsky, 1975), or how we see pictures. Rumelhart (1977b), for example, describes a detailed step-by-step analysis of the interaction between environmental input and stored knowledge that occurs in the reading process. In the same manner that our face schema prepares us to see eyes, nose, and ears, our schematic knowledge of spelling patterns, syntactical patterns, and possible meanings prepares us for certain words in particular reading settings. For example, our knowledge of spelling prepares us for an *e* to follow the letters *th*, or the word *the* prepares us to see a noun instead of a verb. Thus we are ready for certain types of stimulation.

You should be aware that expectations based on activated schemata do not always lead to faster or more veridical perception. Schemata prepare us for particular types of stimulation, and if that stimulation occurs, we can process it quickly and well. However, if an unexpected type of stimulation occurs, we may have trouble identifying it. For example, if we are waiting for our short-haired bespectacled friend Hal at the airport and a long-haired nonbespectacled Hal walks toward us, we may not recognize him for some time. We are searching for the wrong type of stimulation.

Bruner and Potter (1964) found some evidence for this phenomenon in a study in which subjects were shown a series of pictures out of focus. The authors varied the level of initial blur of the pictures but brought the pictures to a common point of focus at which time the subjects had to guess what the picture was. Bruner and Potter found that the greater the initial blur the less likely the subjects were to recognize the picture. The authors argued that the subjects made incorrect guesses about the pictures while they were still out of focus. These guesses served to activate schemata about the content of the pictures. When these pictures were further out of focus, the guesses were more likely to be wrong and hence the wrong schema was activated. Once a schema for a particular picture had been activated, the subject found it difficult to pick up information inconsistent with the schema. Hence the subjects stayed with their initial schema and incorrectly identified the picture.

Thus we see that schemata play a crucial role in our perception of the world around us. They prepare us to see certain characteristics of stimuli, and consequently they normally allow us to operate more efficiently in our environment. In general, this concept has led psychologists to some significant breakthroughs in understanding processes such as perception and comprehension. Chapter 7, for example, will show how this concept has helped us to understand the way people process prose passages. But here let us consider a fundamental question about perception: How do the various schemata we have become activated? To answer this question we need to consider the role of context in perception.

Context. By **context** we mean the overall setting in which an item to be perceived is embedded. We begin our description of the role of context by considering two different modes of activating schemata—*data-driven,* or bottom-up, activation and *conceptually driven,* or top-down, activation. To say that a schema is data driven means that the schema in memory becomes activated because of pattern recognition analyses carried out on events from the environment. For example, if you are sitting quietly in your room and without any prior warning a voice suddenly cries "Help!", a schema for reacting to that situation is activated from the bottom up. Its activation comes entirely from analyzing an environmental event. Thus we might have labeled our initial discussion of pattern recognition as the data-driven phase of perception.

Recently Norman and his colleagues (Norman, 1976; Norman & Bobrow, 1976) have emphasized that a schema can also be activated through other schemata, or from the top down. That is, a given schema may be activated by an instruction (e.g., to listen for the bad tone from the piano), or by other related schemata (e.g., the flower schema might be activated after discussing plants, roses, or rain showers). In none of these cases is a schema being directly activated from an item being perceived; rather we can say it is activated by the context of the item being presented.

It is easy to demonstrate that contextual activation can dramatically influence perception. As early as 1962, Miller demonstrated that words are more easily perceived in the presence of masking noise when they are set in a sentence context than when they are embedded in a list of random words. He presented subjects lists of five words such as *brought, wet, who, socks, some* either in this random order or in a correct grammatical order such as *who brought some wet socks.* Miller found that subjects could identify the words in the sentence form more easily than in the list form. Apparently subjects were able to make use of grammatical constraints to aid them in perceiving the individual words.

Another interesting demonstration of the importance of context in perception comes from the work of Meyer, Schvaneveldt, and Ruddy (1975). They had subjects carry out a task in which the subjects had to determine as quickly as possible whether a given string of letters was a word or a nonword. The subjects were given two fixation points on a screen. After ½ sec the first fixation point was replaced by a string of letters. The subjects then had to indicate as quickly as possible whether the string of letters was a word or not. After another brief delay a second string of letters was flashed. Again the subjects had to respond as quickly as possible. Meyer et al. measured the amount of time it took for the subjects to respond *Yes* or *No*—that is, their reaction time.

Of special interest was the condition in which both letter strings were words. On some occasions the first word was unrelated to the second word *(bread, doctor)*; on others it was related *(bread, butter)*. Meyer et al. found that reaction time to the second word was shorter if the word was related to the first word than if it was not related. This finding indicates that presentation of the first word provides an appropriate context for related words, which increases expectations for related words and makes them more easily seen.

Data-driven and conceptually driven processes complement each other in the process of perception. As more contextual information is made available to perceivers, they need less information directly from the object in order to achieve veridical perception. Palmer (1975) has discussed this point in an interesting paper. He noted that if we are to recognize the parts of a human face such as those shown in Figure 2.21, we must have quite complete drawings if we are asked to perceive them independently of the factual information. However, if we are given the contextual information about the face (see Figure 2.22), we can attain veridical perception of the features with far less information.

Figure 2.20 Figure used by Bugelski and Alampay (1961, p. 206) in their study of perceptual set.

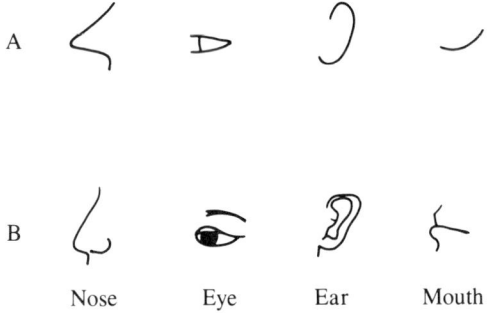

Nose   Eye   Ear   Mouth

Figure 2.21 Two collections of line drawings of facial features (after Palmer, 1975). Individuals have greater difficulty recognizing those items in row A when not in the context of the face than they do those in row B.

It seems that the key to human perception is to obtain as much information as possible about the object to be perceived. We can obtain this information directly from the object or indirectly from context. The more information we have from one procedure, the less we need from the other. In most everyday settings contextual information abounds. Thus we are often able to perceive a given object or event quickly because we know from context exactly what type of stimulation should be occurring and we can more readily find the information to confirm our expectation.

We must be aware, as noted earlier, that contextual information can also lead us to misperceive. Contextual information is based on our past experience of what has usually occurred in a given setting. If we have usually seen our friend Muriel driving a red Volkswagen station wagon, we expect her to be the driver on all occasions. Thus if we see this particular red Volkswagen drive by us on the street, we may report that Muriel just drove by. However, if Muriel has just traded cars and the new owner is driving the red car, our expectations have misled us to make an inaccurate perception.

Contextual information thus allows us to perceive our environment with less direct information. To the extent that this contextual information is accurate, our perception will be aided. To the extent that context misrepresents the present situation, we will misperceive our environment.

Let us summarize what we know about the process of perception. Perception involves deriving the meaning of events and objects in the environment. This process involves the activation and modification of schemata that individuals have about their environment. Activation can occur by operating directly on the to-be-perceived event or by contextual information surrounding the event. In most everyday circumstances both of these procedures are involved in the perceptual process. The more contextual information we have about an event, the less direct information we have to have. If we lack contextual information, we have to draw more heavily on the object to be seen in order to reach a satisfactory perception.

With our added knowledge of the process of perception, it is now useful to reconsider the model of information processing presented at the

Face

Figure 2.22 The same sparse figures shown in Figure 2.21 become easily recognizable when placed by Palmer (1975) in the context of the full face.

beginning of this chapter (see Figure 2.1). In that figure we sketched a skeleton of the model; we are now able to flesh out this model in part. We have schematized the expanded model in Figure 2.23.

You recall that Peter, our information processor, was reading a book on flowering plants in preparation for a test the next day. He was also listening to a radio playing music (Beethoven's Fifth Symphony) and the time was 11:00 P.M.

Peter was focusing on the word *flower* having just read *the dark purple*. Let us now describe how the various components of the information-processing system we have discussed play a role in Peter's perceptions.

The eye focuses on the word *flower* and the Icon retains the raw representation of the word. In a similar manner the Echo retains auditory information from the radio. While this raw information is being held in these sensory registers,

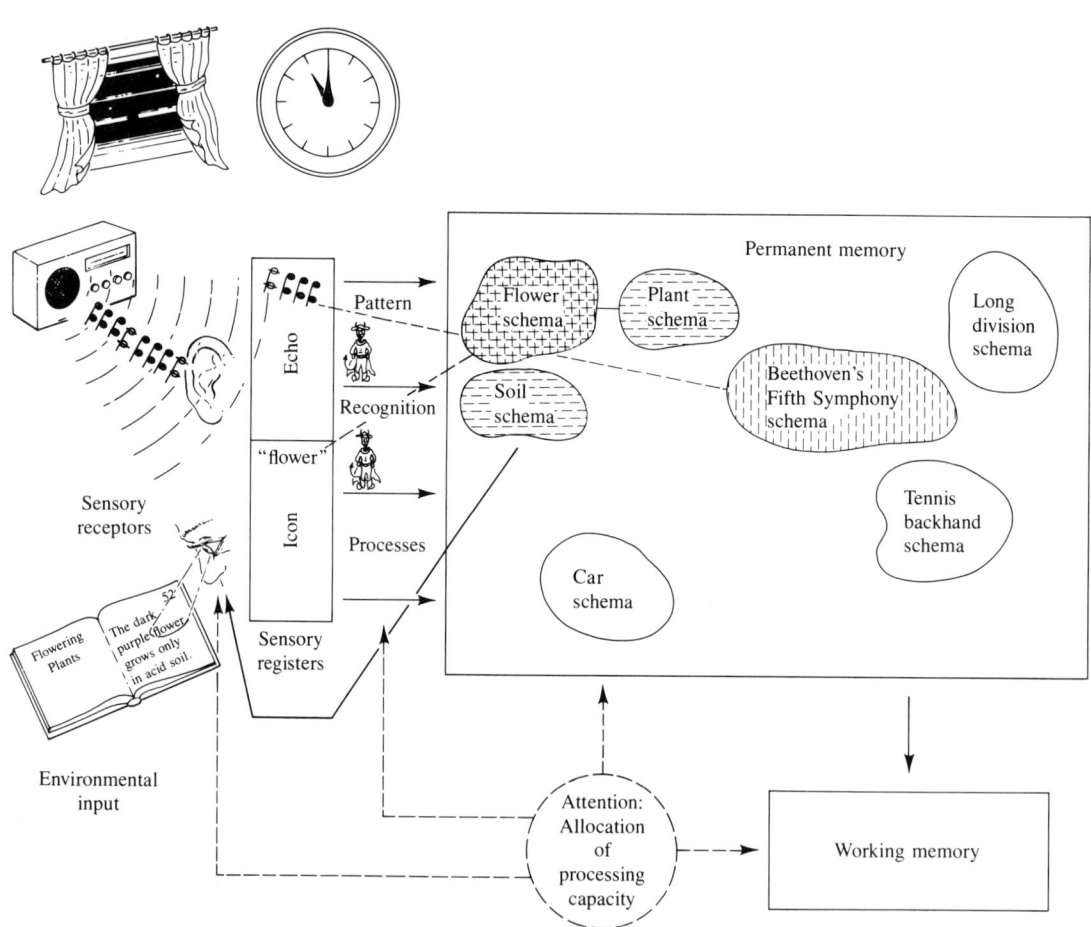

Figure 2.23 Expanded model of the components of the information-processing system.

the various pattern recognition demons are analyzing the input and beginning to shout according to what they see. As this information begins to accumulate, the flower schema in memory becomes more heavily activated. This activation, arising because of direct input on the word *flower,* is data-driven activation (bottom up) and is indicated in the figure by the vertical lines in the flower schema.

Note also that Peter knows he is reading a book about plants. Thus Peter has a strong context available to him from his earlier reading. We have indicated this by showing the plant schema being activated. Since the flower and plant schemata are highly related, the flower schema is also conceptually activated (top down) by the plant schema; this is indicated in the figure by the horizontal lines in the flower schema. This top-down activation makes it easier for Peter to perceive the word *flower.*

We have also indicated that the flower schema and soil schema are related and thus the soil schema is being conceptually activated by the flower schema. This activation will influence the sensory receptors and pattern recognition processes. In particular, an expectation for soil information has been created that will alert the sensory receptors and pattern recognition processes for information relevant to soil. This will make it easier for Peter to perceive the word *soil,* which he will soon be reading.

It is thus clear how the perceptual process is a cyclic one as indicated by Neisser; in addition, we can see the important role contextual information plays in the perception of our environment. At this point, however, we have not elaborated the bottom part of our model. We begin this by discussing the process of attention.

ATTENTION

Each of us has one fascinating yet frustrating characteristic that is crucial to investigate if we are to understand how we function cognitively: We are limited in the number of things we can do at any one time. This limitation may differ from one individual to another, or from one time to another within the same individual. Nevertheless, we have all experienced it. Some have experienced it when two or three people suddenly started talking to them all at once and they found themselves saying, "Hold it, one at a time please." Others have experienced it when they started into an unfamiliar section of curving, treacherous highway and suddenly found themselves leaning forward to turn off the radio or asking their riding companion to remain quiet for a moment.

This limitation is intimately related to what has come to be called **attention.** By attention we mean the general distribution of mental activity to the tasks being performed by the individual. Since we are limited in the number of things we can focus on, one key aspect of attention is concerned with the selection of tasks upon which the individual will concentrate. The famous psychologist William James was referring to this aspect of attention when he claimed that attention "implies withdrawal from some things in order to deal effectively with others" (James, 1890/1904, p. 404).

Thus if we walk down a busy street such as the one shown in Figure 2.24, only a very few items will be selected for concentrated analysis. We might, for example, note that the street was busy, that a bus drove by, and that a policeman was directing traffic. Much other information is not selected. The number of cars in the street, the name of the building in the background, the number of flags on the building, and the number of the trolley car may go unnoticed.

When do these selections occur? Do they occur very early in the processing cycle before much processing has taken place, or do they occur very late after extensive information about the environment has already been extracted? These questions have been of great interest to psychologists investigating attention and have led to much debate and theorizing.

Figure 2.24 Street scene. (Photo by Edgar and Patricia Cheatham.)

Early Selection Model

The first comprehensive views of attention argued that selection occurs very early. Broadbent (1958), for example, contended that there is only a limited processing capacity available to process the information held in the sensory registers. Selective attention then is the result of this limited capacity being focused on some small amount of environmental input. Any information that is not focused on goes unprocessed and is completely lost.

Broadbent argued that the selection of which information is to be processed is based on predetermined physical characteristics of the stimulation. Thus we might process the voice of a particular individual, or sounds of particular frequencies. In Figure 2.25 we have schematized a model of how attention was thought to occur by Broadbent.

Although this view seems too limited and simplistic now, early research found support for it. The bulk of this research involved dichotic listening tasks. These are tasks in which two different messages are presented simultaneously to a subject, one message to each ear. The subjects are asked to shadow (repeat) the message in one of the ears as the message arrives. Dichotic listening studies have consistently found that subjects can recall very little of the information from the unshadowed message except perhaps some simple physical properties such as whether the voice speaking was male or female.

On the basis of this evidence, Broadbent concluded that when too much information is presented to subjects for them to process with their limited capacity, their processing is directed, on the basis of physical properties, to a part of the message. Information that is not processed is lost.

It is important to note that Broadbent also claimed that to a small degree subjects may be able to switch back and forth from one type of information to another, thus appearing to be processing two types of information simultaneously. Switching capability was thought to be limited, however, and to become more difficult as the material in any given channel increases in complexity.

In recent years the view that selection occurs very early and that unselected information is completely lost has come under repeated attack.

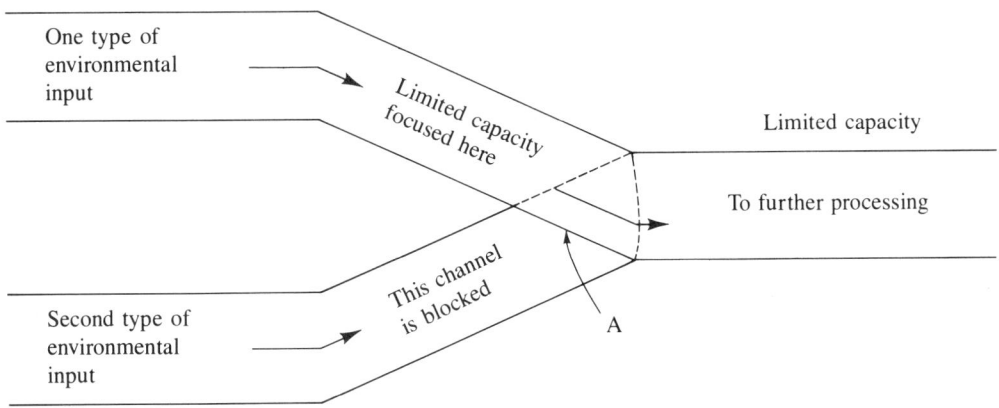

Figure 2.25 Model of attention according to Broadbent (1958). The blockage of the processing of material at point A is probably based on physical cues alone. The material in the blocked channel will be completely lost.

Both everyday observations and experimental evidence suggest that some processing is being carried out on unattended information and consequently that selection is occurring later.

An example will make this point apparent. When riding a bus and engaging in a conversation, you may suddenly hear your name or a friend's name being mentioned even though you were concentrating on your own conversation. This suggests that certain highly familiar information may be processed easily without our concentrating upon it. Several different investigations have confirmed this fact.

Treisman (1960), for instance, presented subjects with two different messages simultaneously, one to each ear. The subjects were requested to shadow the message coming to one ear. After a few words this passage was switched to the other ear and vice versa. For example, in one case the message to the shadowed ear was part of a prose passage. After the switch, the prose material was presented to the subject in the unshadowed ear. Thus if a subject were presented the messages indicated in Figure 2.26, that subject's shadowing near the transition point should have flowed as follows: "leaving on her passage an impression of grace is idiotic idea of almost there is a cabbage a horse . . ."

Treisman found, however, that occasionally subjects would briefly follow the passage meaning in their shadowing and read out, "leaving on her passage an impression of grace, charm and a . . ." This finding implies that some processing of the unshadowed ear must have been occurring. If the subjects had not processed beyond simple physical cues as Broadbent suggested, they should not have switched from ear to ear.

Employing slightly different logic, Moray (1970) also found evidence that subjects processed unshadowed information to some degree. He made use of the well-established fact that subjects show a galvanic skin response (GSR) when they are presented with emotionally charged words. A GSR is a form of electrical conductance by the skin. By presenting such emotionally charged words to the unshadowed ear, Moray could determine if subjects processed the unshadowed information sufficiently to result in a change in the GSR. His results supported his contention that more than physical properties of unshadowed information are processed.

Shadowed ear

While we were talking she would come and go with rapid glances at us leaving on her passage an impression of grace/ is idiotic idea of almost there is a cabbage a horse which was not always . . .

Unshadowed ear

The camera shop and boyhood friend from fish and screamed loudly singing men and then it was jumping in the tree/ charm and a distinct suggestion of watchfulness. Her manner presented a curious combination of shyness and audacity . . .

Figure 2.26 Examples of messages presented to subjects in Treisman's (1960) shadowing task. The slant line indicates where the messages were broken and shifted to the other ear.

The evidence seems clear then that some degree of processing of unattended information occurs. The question remains open, however, as to how much processing of this information occurs. Two principal views are possible. One says that only limited processing is accomplished before selection occurs; the other claims that a full and complete analysis of the information is carried out before selection of some part of it is made.

Attenuation Model

The principal advocate of incomplete processing of unattended information is probably Treisman, who supports a model such as the one shown in Figure 2.27. This model, like Broadbent's, contends that a limited processing capacity exists, but it also claims that varying channels of information can use this capacity simultaneously. Since the capacity is limited, however, the processing on some of the channels must be attenuated or reduced. This reduced processing is frequently sufficient nevertheless to pick up certain important pieces of information that can then be brought to full attention.

Treisman and Geffen (1967) provided compelling evidence for this view of processing capabilities in a study presenting prose passages dichotically to subjects. Subjects were requested to shadow the passage in one ear. At the same time subjects had to listen for a particular target word that might occur in either ear. As soon as they heard the target word, they were to tap.

If full processing occurs on the material in both the shadowed and unshadowed ears, there should be no difference in the subjects' ability to detect the target words in either ear. If, however, the subjects are able to carry out reduced processing only in the unshadowed ear, we might expect that detection of the target words would suffer in that ear.

The latter result is in fact the one that Treisman and Geffen found. Subjects were able to detect 87 percent of the target words in the

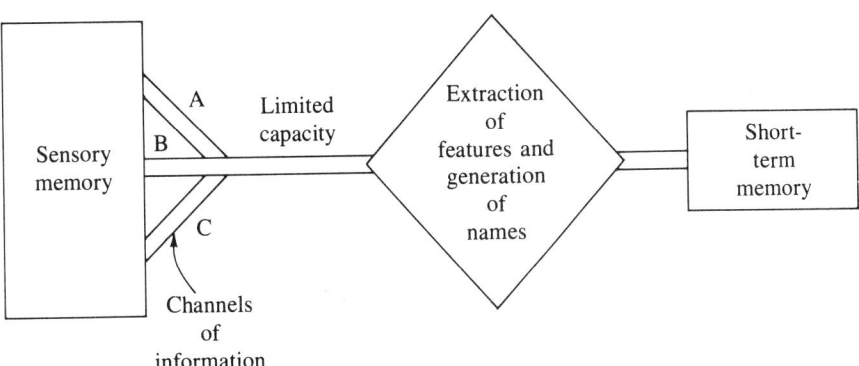

Figure 2.27 Schematized drawing of the attenuation model of attention. One of the channels of information (A, B, or C) will be the most heavily processed, while the other two channels will receive only a limited amount of processing. However, this limited amount of processing may be sufficient to have the information in that channel selected for further processing. In this further processing, additional features will be extracted from the stimulus, and the object's name may be determined. (From Kintsch, 1977.)

shadowed ear. When the target words appeared in the unshadowed ear, however, detection dropped to about 8 percent. This is strong support for limited or partial processing of unattended channels. In this model of attention then, selection of information to focus on occurs after some incomplete processing is carried out on environmental stimulation.

Full-processing Model

In contrast to the attenuation model of attention, the full-processing model suggests that the selection of information does not occur until pattern recognition processes are complete. It assumes that pattern recognition processes go on without conscious awareness (that is, automatically) as soon as they are given environmental stimulation to work on. These processes are thought to go to completion, at which time they present to working memory a relatively complete analysis of the input. On the basis of this information a selection is made of which type of information to concentrate on.

This view suggests that a large number of analyses can be carried out simultaneously with little or no limitation. Where then does the bottleneck in human information processing lie? According to this model, it is in the inability to retain or remember the results of all these analyses. That is, the results of these analyses are quickly lost if they are not picked up for further analysis. In effect then, the bottleneck is a memory bottleneck and not a processing one.

There is one real advantage to a model such as this one: The decision about what to select for additional processing is made with extensive information available. The person thus has a wide variety of information about the environment instead of having only physical information as Broadbent argued or limited information as Treisman argued. This model suggests then that the brain is an immensely capable processing machine that carries out extensive analyses of the environment automatically. The results of the completed analyses are presented to working memory, which allows for a more informed decision about what to treat to additional analysis.

As with the attenuation model of attention, some compelling evidence for the full-processing model is available. Shiffrin, Pisoni, and Casteneda-Mendez (1974) presented subjects with consonants against a background of white noise (random background noise). The subjects' task was to indicate whether or not a particular consonant had been heard. The key manipulation in the study involved the presentation of the consonants so that the subjects either (1) knew the consonants were coming to one particular ear or (2) did not know which ear the consonants would come to. This manipulation was important; if the subjects were unaware which ear the consonants were to be presented to, they had to process the information in both ears. In the single ear condition, they had half as much information to process.

The attenuation model of attention predicts that the single ear condition should result in better performance than the double ear condition. The full-processing model predicts equal performance, since the analysis in both ears should be completed automatically. The results of Shiffrin et al. support the full-processing model. They found that their subjects' ability to detect the consonants was independent of the amount of information they were monitoring.

Other investigations by Shiffrin and Gardner (1972), Posner and Boies (1971) and Sorkin and Pohlmann (1973) lead to essentially the same conclusions. Individuals carry out extensive analysis of incoming stimulation automatically. Only after these analyses are completed does the limited capacity of the organism come into play.

With these studies we seem to find ourselves in an uncomfortable position. Compelling evidence has been presented for both the attenuation and full-processing models of attention. As a matter of fact, the studies by Treisman and Geffen (1967) and Shiffrin et al. (1974) seem to be directly contradictory. How can this situation be resolved? The answer appears to lie in recent work regarding data-limited and resource-limited processes.

Data and Resource Limitations

A distinction can be made among two types of tasks individuals are asked to carry out: those which are resource limited and those which are data limited (Norman & Bobrow, 1975). To clarify the distinction between these tasks, we need to understand what is meant by the concept of **resources.** Resources refer to such things as psychological effort, memory capacity, and communication channels; these are things that may be assigned to a given task so that the task can be carried out. It is crucial to understand that these resources are limited; once they are all being used, there are no more resources available to assign to other tasks.

To say then that a given task is a **resource-limited** task means that performance on the task will improve if a greater amount of resources is assigned to it. In a task such as multiplying two-digit numbers, for example, performance will be poor if we have few resources to assign to it because we are also being asked to watch a television program closely to see a particular actor. However, if we are able to assign more resources to it (the television is turned off), performance will improve.

In contrast to resource-limited tasks, **data-limited** tasks are those upon which performance is limited not by the resources assigned but by the quality of data available. In a data-limited task, if the input data are poor, no amount of additional resources assigned to the task will improve performance. A good example of a data-limited task is one in which an individual is asked to detect a tone in a noisy room. Once some minimal level of resources has been assigned, the detection level for the tone becomes a function of the quality of the data. If the tone is too indistinct from the background noise, no amount of additional resources will allow it to be detected.

The distinction between resource-limited and data-limited tasks helps us to explain the contradictory data from the studies supporting the attenuation model and full-processing model of attention.

In the Treisman and Geffen (1967) study, shadowing the prose passage in one of the ears is a task that is assumed to use a large amount of resources. This leaves relatively few resources to carry out additional tasks. The second task that Treisman and Geffen had their subjects do (listen for the target word in the unattended ear) also requires extensive resources. Since this task does not have enough resources remaining for optimal performance (that is, it is resource limited), performance on this task is quite poor compared to performance in the attended ear.

When we consider the study by Shiffrin et al. (1974), we see a different situation. Their subjects had merely to detect a consonant over white noise. Since subjects only had to process to a depth of some acoustic information (instead of to semantic meaning as in the Treisman and Geffen study), this task demanded far less resources to be performed well. That is, such a task becomes data limited with far less resources being allocated to it than would have to be allocated in searching for a target word.

Therefore once the small amount of resources necessary to perform well on this task has been allocated to it, there still remains a considerable reservoir of resources that can be used in performing other tasks. Since the second task in the Shiffrin et al. study also used a small amount of resources (detecting a consonant in the second ear), sufficient resources were still available to perform this task at a high performance level. Thus Shiffrin et al. found that the subjects could detect the consonants as well in both ears as in one.

To summarize this view of attention, individuals have a limited amount of resources they can employ in carrying out tasks. As long as they have resources remaining, additional processing can be carried out either to do more tasks or to improve performance on the ones they are already doing (if the tasks are resource limited). Thus if we assign tasks that do not use all their resources, it will appear that they can fully process all of the available information before selection decisions are necessary. On the other hand, if the tasks we assign demand more resources than are available, the individuals will show decreased performance on some tasks in order to stay within the limit of their processing resources.

In sum, we cannot unequivocally say that selection occurs early or late in the processing cycle. It depends on the type of tasks a subject is asked to perform. This fact will become more clear as we consider the distinction between automatic and nonautomatic processes.

AUTOMATIC PROCESSES

Our discussion of resource-limited and data-limited processes leads naturally to consideration of a topic that is of increasing importance in models of human information processing and attention: **automatic processes.** Automatic processing refers to the activation of a learned sequence of elements or behaviors in permanent memory. This sequence is initiated by appropriate inputs and then automatically proceeds without any subject control (Schneider & Shiffrin, 1977). We all use such automatic processes as we go through each day. Consider the following examples:

You are driving down a city street and the brake lights of the car immediately in front of you suddenly go on. It is likely that an automatic process is set off. Your foot will leave the accelerator and move quickly to the brake pedal. You may also spin the steering wheel in order to avoid the car in front of you.

You are a well-trained basketball player and you have just decided to take a jump shot. As you bend your knees to jump, an entire sequence of behaviors will smoothly follow. The arms will move to a specified position, the fingers will impart a particular spin on the ball, and a smooth follow-through motion will occur after the shot.

You are an intermediate-level typist typing the word *plantation*. As you reach the last four letters of the word, your rate speeds up as the overlearned sequence of letters *tion* is activated.

Automatic processes such as these have a number of characteristic properties. First, they require few resources and hence may often be done in parallel with (at the same time as) other tasks. Second, they require extensive training to develop and once learned may be difficult to modify. Third, people are rarely conscious of the elements of such processes. Fourth, the performance level on such processes may increase across thousands of trials.

The types of automatic processes that we have discussed here appear to be fundamental to high levels of expertise that people show in certain areas. That is, great expertise in a particular area seems to depend upon having a large repertoire of highly differentiated and practiced automatic processes. For example, Simon and Chase (1973) have shown that chess masters appear to have a large number of highly automatic processes they employ in studying a chess board. These processes allow them to determine very quickly what situation a given chess game is in, which indicates why they are able to play a large number of games at once with players of somewhat lesser skill. We will consider this work in greater detail in Chapter 3 under the topic we call chunking.

Automatic processes are important in everyday functioning because they allow us to do quickly behaviors we are frequently asked to do. Since these behaviors are done more quickly, we have additional time and resources to carry out other processes. Such automatic processes play an especially important role in attention. As we noted in our discussion of resource-limited and data-limited processes, the type of task a subject is asked to do determines whether sufficient resources are available to carry out other tasks. The work on automatic processes suggests that not only is the task important but also the level of training on the task. We describe this point more fully in Box 2.2. The higher the level of training

> **Box 2.2 AROUSAL AND AUTOMATICITY: AN IMPORTANT INTERACTION**
>
> A young woman is diving for golf balls in a 12-foot pool of water. She surfaces in panic and then drowns. When her body is found, she still has on her weight belt and is clutching a heavy bag of golf balls. This is a true story reported by Bachrach (1970). It illustrates the close tie between the level of emotional arousal we are under and our performance in various types of tasks.
>
> Psychologists have known for years that as arousal level goes up, performance first improves. But as the arousal level goes still higher, performance begins to deteriorate. This is known as the Yerkes-Dodson law (Yerkes & Dodson, 1908). Norman (1976) argues that this phenomenon is related to the narrowing of attention to a central task. At first, narrowing aids by focusing attention on the relevant task only. But if attention narrows excessively, the person may focus on only a single detail of the task, perhaps an irrelevant one at that. Thus the diver above may have been excessively focusing on trying to swim harder for the surface, ignoring the other matters such as the weight belt and golf bag that impeded her progress.
>
> In order to eliminate stress-induced problems such as this one, diving instructors have their pupils overtrain extensively. The intent of this overtraining is for a single purpose—to make certain behaviors become as automatic as possible so that they can be carried out with no conscious attention. Such automatic processes are far less likely to be disrupted by high levels of arousal. Similar arguments hold for parachute jumpers, fliers, and even automobile drivers. It is interesting to note that while younger drivers may have a faster reaction time to stimulation, older experienced drivers may avoid accident situations more successfully because they have a wider repertoire of automatic responses to situations that arise on the road. Experience and practice are extremely important allies to have.

on a task, the fewer the resources needed to carry it out and consequently the more resources that are available for reassignment to other tasks.

We have all seen this principle operate in our own lives. When we first learn to drive a car, all our resources are needed to keep the car between the fenceposts (as an old farmer would say). However, as we become more proficient and practiced at driving, we are able to listen to the radio, carry on a conversation, and determine the quality of this year's corn crop. Athletic coaches and music teachers have known this for years as they have demanded their protegés to practice, practice. The basketball player who must concentrate on dribbling the ball will probably not see his teammate standing open under the basket. The piano student concentrating on finger movements will not be able to play an original interpretation of a piece of music.

CONSCIOUSNESS

One final topic needs to be considered before we complete our chapter on perception and attention: **consciousness.** Probably no concept in psychology causes as much debate as consciousness. It played an important role in major theories (such as Freud's psychoanalytic theory); and although it was, in effect, banned as a legitimate object of study by psychologists for many years, it now appears to have been resurrected, although cautiously, to play a role in theorizing about cognitive functioning. In this section we describe some recent views of consciousness as related to rational and verbal processes.

One of the major difficulties in working with the concept of consciousness is getting agreement on what is meant by it. Rather than attempt to define it formally here, we will try to convey what it is by describing the roles it plays in cognitive functioning.

Consciousness is closely intertwined with attention as we have described it in this chapter. It is not synonymous with attention, if by attention we mean the general distribution of mental resources and effort to the tasks being performed. It seems better equated with a particular type of resource, which is labeled differently by different theorists. Some refer to this resource as working memory or focal attention (Mandler, 1975), others as the central processor (Bjork, 1975), and still others as primary memory (James, 1890/1904; Waugh & Norman, 1965).

Identifying the characteristics and functions of this resource will help us to understand better what it is. It is a limited resource that is involved in

1. choices, selections, and decisions by the individual. It allows for the consideration of possible actions that have never before been performed.
2. the modification and questioning of long-range plans rather than immediate behaviors. For example, it is involved in decisions about whether you should go to college or attend a trade school. It allows for novel or unusual grouping of ideas as seen in creative behavior.
3. the retrieval of information from permanent memory, especially when an unusual route to information in memory is employed. For example, you try to remember what you were to do in town today by thinking about who told you to go to town. It is probably not involved in the automatic retrieval of well-learned information such as your name.
4. the storage of new combinations of ideas and thoughts in memory using mnemonic devices or categorization procedures. It may even serve a temporary memory function of holding information before us for a few seconds. We will discuss this property further in Chapter 3.
5. a troubleshooting function for mental structures that are carried out automatically. For example, the golfer who analyzes her stroke, movement by movement, in trying to find out why she is slicing every ball into the rough is making use of this function of consciousness (Mandler, 1975).

The role of consciousness in cognitive functioning then is the opposite of the role of automatic processes. It is the resource involved when new, unusual, or unique combinations of events are to be worked on in contrast to the automatic processes involved when highly learned and expected events are processed. Consciousness results in slow, serial processing, while automatic processing results in fast, parallel processing. Consciousness is involved when control of functioning is called for in new settings, automatic processes when control is called for in highly familiar situations. Yet both consciousness and automatic processes are key components of the overall attention system of the organism. They complement each other to lead to smooth functioning that is effective in the turmoil of the unexpected or the humdrum of the familiar.

While we are able to describe the functions of consciousness, we know unfortunately little of the mechanisms involved in carrying out these functions. Now that it is again legitimate to hypothesize and theorize about consciousness, we can hope the coming years will bring investigations that will allow us to understand better the mechanisms involved. Some recent speculations about the origins of consciousness by Jaynes (1976) may spur further work on this fascinating topic.

CONCLUSION

To help you summarize and integrate all that we have talked of in this multifaceted chapter, we present once again our model of cognitive functioning (Figure 2.28). We have elaborated it even further to include the new material we have presented. We ask you to follow through this figure as we summarize the processes involved in attention and perception.

As environmental inputs first reach Peter, they are very briefly held in the various sensory registers. These registers hold the information in a relatively unprocessed form and in a manner consistent with the receptor to which they are linked. As the material is held in these regis-

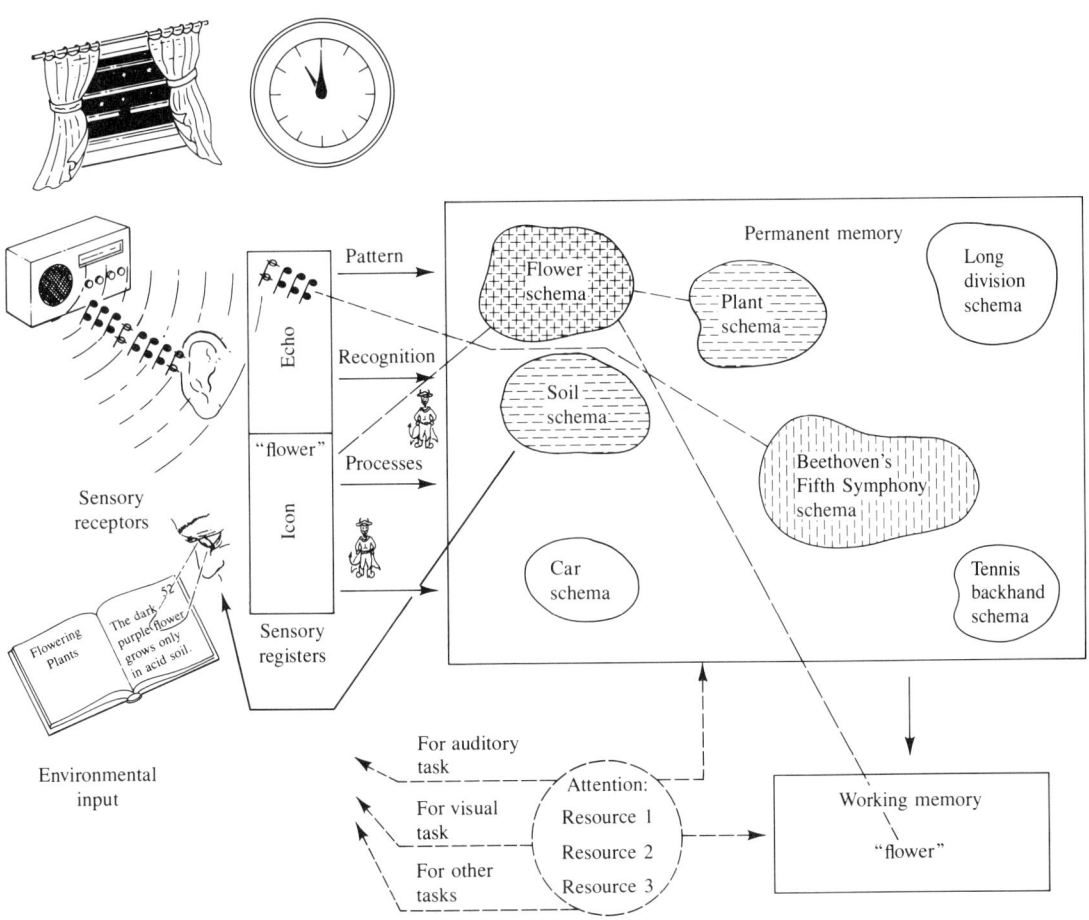

Figure 2.28 Expanded model of the components of the information-processing system.

ters, a number of pattern recognition processes are carried out which relate the information to structures stored in permanent memory.

Contextual information provided by earlier environmental inputs or by inputs occurring simultaneously dramatically influences the functioning of these perceptual processes (see the line from the soil schema to the sensory receptors). The more contextual information Peter has, the less he needs to glean from the environment (and vice versa) to reach a satisfactory perception of his world.

All the processes that Peter conducts in interacting with his world use resources to carry them out. Since there is a limited amount of resources available to conduct these processes, Peter has to allocate resources to the various processes going on. This is the problem of attention, and the dashed arrows from the attention circle show the directions that Peter's choices may take.

In order to determine if the various tasks being conducted will influence each other, we must take into account whether a given task is resource-limited or data-limited and what Peter's level of training on that task is. As Peter's tasks become more highly practiced, they demand less resources and allow Peter to carry out other activities.

Finally, to the extent that Peter's functioning necessitates working with new combinations of ideas, planning for future events, or evaluating what he is doing, a deliberate limited mechanism is necessary. This limited resource is what psychologists call working memory. In our figure the word *flower* is currently in Peter's working memory. The concept of working memory is closely related to what we commonly refer to as consciousness.

3 The Temporary Retention of Information

Models of Memory
    Interference Theory
    Two-Store Theory
    Levels of Processing
    Activation Models
Characteristics of Temporary Retention
    Capacity and Chunking in Temporary Memory
        Number of Chunks
        The Formation of Chunks
        Chunking Processes
    Rehearsal
    Encoding in Temporary Retention
        Acoustic Encoding
        Nonacoustic Encoding
    Forgetting from Temporary Memory
Structures in Temporary Retention
    Working Memory
    Temporary Memory Traces
        Trace Storage Structures
        Trace Retrieval Processes
Conclusion

Imagine, if you will, a man who wakes one morning to find that his memory has failed. As he looks around the room he cannot remember where he is. He cannot remember where he works, what his name is, or the fact that his alarm clock just woke him. When he goes into the bathroom and picks up his razor, he cannot remember the movements needed to adjust the blade or how to turn on the water faucet. As he tries to understand what has happened to him, he constantly loses his train of thought and forgets what he was just previously considering. He tries to tell his wife what has happened but no words can be recalled, and thus he is unable to construct sentences. As his wife moves toward him, she becomes a different object after each movement since he is no longer capable of remembering her from one location to another.

This description sounds like a story written by a science fiction author. But in actuality it describes what we might reasonably expect to happen to us if we were to lose our ability to remember. We would not only lose our ability to recall people's names or events that occur, but we could no longer solve problems, form concepts, speak, understand a language, or even perceive the events around us. The ability to remember is at the heart of all that we do and are.

What is this thing we call memory? Is it a unitary or multifaceted phenomenon? How does memory for a telephone number looked up but once, then dialed and forgotten, relate to the memory for childhood experiences? How does our memory of how to drive a car relate to our memory for the facts and theories in a textbook? How important for memory is our desire or intention to remember? Can we improve memory by practicing memorizing? What happens when we forget something? Each of these questions raises issues that need to be considered if we are to understand fully the processes involved in human memory.

But another question raises an issue that is basic and fundamental to the understanding of memory: Is the procedure for remembering an event that recently occurred—say within the last 20 to 30 seconds—the same as for remembering an event that occurred some time ago—10 minutes ago, or 36 hours, or 2 years? That is, is the process of remembering the same whether an event occurred recently or remotely, whether an event is to be retained temporarily or permanently?

At one level it is obvious that there are differences between memory for recent and remote events. For example, if you tell a friend the telephone number 592-8725 and immediately ask her to tell you the number, she can recall it easily. On the other hand, if you ask her whether the doorknob on the front door of the house she lived in during 1966 was on the left or right, she will take considerably longer to answer and will seem to go through a much different process than in remembering the telephone number.

Similarly, if after giving your friend the telephone number, you immediately ask her a whole series of questions necessitating quick replies and then ask her for the number, she will probably not remember it nor will she ever be able to recall it at a later time. But you could ask for the location of the doorknob at many different times and each time she would be able to recall it. The information about the doorknob is permanently remembered; the number is not.

In the past two decades there has been extensive documentation of the different characteristics of memory for recent and remote events, and we will be discussing these characteristics in the next five chapters. While most of these chapters will emphasize the properties of permanent memory, this chapter will emphasize the characteristics of the temporary retention of information, including how items temporarily held are encoded, forgotten, and structured. Our primary emphasis will be on the temporary retention of verbal rather than visual or motoric information simply because the bulk of the work on temporary retention has used verbal information.

There is little controversy over the fact that the characteristics of memory are different over different time spans, as our example of the doorknob and the telephone number has just illustrated. However, there is extensive controversy over whether the different characteristics of temporary and permanent retention are due to different memory systems or to one system working differently at various times. We need to consider the full implication of this point since it has had a large impact on the theories of human memory.

MODELS OF MEMORY

In the 1960s psychologists waged extensive debate between two major theoretical positions regarding the fundamental character of the human memory system. These positions were termed **interference theory** and **two-store theory.**

Interference Theory

Interference theorists such as Melton (1963) contended that a single set of variables could be used to explain retention, regardless of the duration of the memory. Thus they argued that the reason people lose information from memory (that is, forget) is that information learned prior to or subsequent to the learning in question interferes with the retention of the desired information.

This interference was thought to occur regardless of whether the information was just learned or had been learned long ago. These theorists argued that although memory for recent events may look different, this is simply due to the fact that the same variables are acting over different lengths of time and under different conditions. To interference theorists, therefore, any claim that fundamentally different mechanisms, processes, or variables are involved in the retention of information for short and long intervals was unjustified.

Two-Store Theory

Two-store theorists such as Atkinson and Shiffrin (1968) and Waugh and Norman (1965) contended that the retention of information for short intervals is accomplished in a remarkably different way than is retention over long time periods. They argued that memory involves two fundamentally different types of memory storage mechanisms called **stores.** A *short-term* or *primary memory* store was believed to hold information for up to 30 sec. The primary memory store was considered to be the place where incoming information is first held. It was assumed to have only a small capacity and to hold information for only a brief period.

For information held longer than approximately 30 sec, two-store theorists contended that information has to be moved to a *long-term,* permanent memory store called *secondary memory.* This store was thought to have a much larger capacity and to hold information relatively permanently. In the secondary memory store reside our accumulated experiences and knowledge. Thus according to two-store theorists, qualitatively different mechanisms are responsible for the retention of information for short and long intervals.

Levels of Processing

In the 1970s a third view of the temporary retention of information, called **levels of processing,** was formulated (Craik & Lockhart, 1972). This view, like interference theory, contended that it is unnecessary to postulate the existence of separate memory stores. It differed extensively, however, from the earlier interference theory. Instead of arguing in terms of interference and other variables drawn from behavioral theories, Craik and Lockhart contended that our ability to remember is a by-product of the various perceptual processes and analyses described in the last chapter.

In particular, Craik and Lockhart argued that we carry out a number of perceptual analyses such as pattern recognition in order to perceive our environment. As a result of carrying out these analyses, we are left with a **trace**—that is, with a record of the results of these analyses. This trace provides us with a means to remember the past. In essence then, our ability to remember is a by-product of the activities we carry out in order to give meaning to our environment.

The levels-of-processing theorists also noted that memory for recent events generally shows different characteristics from memory for remote events. However, rather than claiming this to be due to the holding of information in different stores, they saw it as a function of the fact that different perceptual analyses are carried out as the material is held longer.

Later versions of two-store theory (Shiffrin, 1975) and levels-of-processing theory (Craik & Jacoby, 1975; Craik & Tulving, 1975) have fuzzed the distinction between these views somewhat. However, the basic distinction between levels-of-processing and two-store theories still exists, and the ferment created by the levels-of-processing conception has generated extensive debate among theorists of temporary memory. Baddeley (1978) has summarized the arguments against the levels-of-processing viewpoint in some detail. Craik (1979) has reported, in return, that counterarguments exist to a number of the issues raised by Baddeley. While we will not detail this debate, we consider that its development has been a fruitful one for raising issues relevant to the temporary retention of information.

Activation Models

Since the mid-1970s still another model of memory has come forth, sometimes referred to as the **activation model.** This view is typified by the model of human cognitive functioning called *ACT* (Anderson, 1976; Anderson, Kline, & Lewis, 1977), which postulates that as human beings we have a large collection of knowledge about our environment. This knowledge is stored in a vast network of associations called the *data base*. Included in this data base are facts such as when Columbus discovered America, values such as the type of ice cream we like, and goals such as what we plan to do with our lives.

According to this model, we have access to only a small part of the data base at any one time. That information which we have access to is said to be *active*. This corresponds roughly to that information which is in working memory, or consciousness.

This model also postulates that information does not stay active for long time periods but rather becomes periodically deactivated. This process of deactivation occurs for any information that is in the active state except for the small amount of information necessary for ongoing functioning. This latter information is placed in a structure called the *ALIST*. This is a structure that can hold a small amount of information in an active state even when other information is being deactivated.

Thus the ACT model explains many of the temporary memory phenomena as being due to information in the person's data base that is in an active state. Such activation models have become increasingly popular in recent years. Since this model postulates a complete view of permanent memory as well, we will consider it in greater depth in Chapter 4.

Our interest in discussing these various viewpoints has not been to describe definitively any one of them or to prove that one presents a more accurate or fruitful view of temporary memory, for these considerations are beyond the scope of this book. Rather our intent was to provide different eyes through which you can view the many differences observed in memory performance when individuals are asked to retain information over long and short time periods. Any one of the last three theoretical viewpoints (the first one, interference theory, is infrequently discussed today) can explain most of the temporary memory phenomena. If you are interested in specific theoretical comparisons, we suggest Anderson (1976), Baddeley (1978), Craik and Jacoby (1975), Craik (1979), Kintsch (1977), and Shiffrin (1975).

Our approach in the remainder of this chapter will be to describe first the numerous phenomena that have been documented for the temporary retention of information. We will then attempt to glean the various structures or features of the human memory system that lead to these properties, returning to the theoretical positions described above to make use of the various constructs they offer as being responsible for the phenomena of temporary retention.

CHARACTERISTICS OF TEMPORARY RETENTION

There are several characteristics of the temporary retention of information that are important for us to consider if we are to understand how we remember information over short time periods. These characteristics are best described by the following four questions, each of which will be considered in detail:

1. What factors influence our capacity to retain information for brief periods?
2. How does recycling or repeating to-be-remembered information influence our ability to retain briefly that information?
3. How is briefly held information stored in memory?
4. What leads us to forget temporarily held information?

Capacity and Chunking in Temporary Memory

All of us have experienced what is sometimes called a cognitive overload. This is a situation in which we have too much information impinging on us at one time so that we cannot operate effectively. It may have come when several people were speaking simultaneously and we were trying to listen to each one. Or it may have occurred when someone was giving us a series of telephone numbers to remember or a set of grocery items to pick up. Psychologists suggest that our difficulties are due to the amount of information exceeding the capacity of working memory. While this phenomenon can be observed in any domain of cognitive functioning—problem solving, perception, concept identification, or memory—it is in the last area that it has been most frequently studied.

In the memory area, the question of capacity has revolved around the issue of the number of items that can be retained perfectly after a single presentation. This capacity is sometimes called *memory span*. As psychologists began to consider this issue, they found they needed to answer a prior question: What composes an item for memory?

This question may seem to be a strange one, but consider the work of Murdock (1961). He found that individuals could remember words as well as they could single consonants. He gave subjects either one word, three words, or three consonants and then gave them a three-digit number (for example, 785). The subjects were asked to count backwards by three from this number as rapidly as they could for varying time intervals in order to keep them from mentally practicing the memory items. The subjects were then asked to recall the items. Murdock found that the subjects were able to retain the three words as well as they could the three consonants although neither was recalled as well as the single word (see Figure 3.1). These results imply that although there is a restriction in capacity in temporary retention, several letters, if they form a word, use up no more of the capacity than does a single consonant.

Miller (1956) coined the word **chunk** to refer to the unit of temporary retention. He contended that the amount of information within a chunk may vary widely, but the number of chunks of information an individual can retain is seven plus or minus two items (7 ± 2). Several questions have been raised regarding the properties and characteristics of chunks. Two of these are of special importance: How many chunks can be retained, and how are chunks formed?

Number of Chunks. The notion that the memory span is limited to 7 ± 2 chunks has been one of the more widely accepted and cited characteristics of temporary retention. However, there

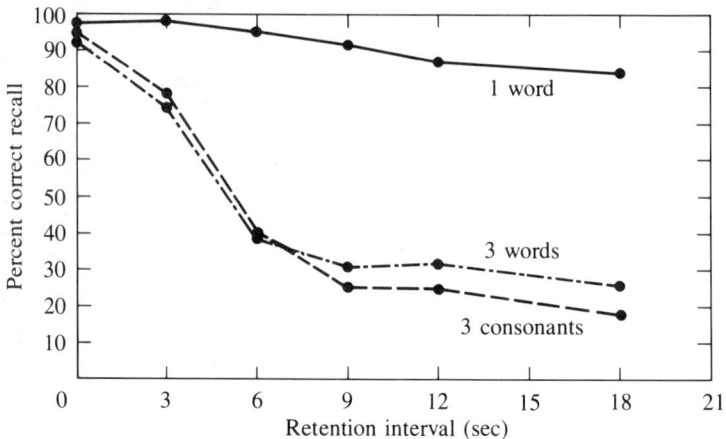

Figure 3.1 Recall performance after varying time intervals for stimulus patterns of one word, three consonants, or three words. (From Murdock, 1961.)

has been extensive debate as to the meaning of this particular result.

There seems little doubt that the number 7 ± 2 is a good estimate of memory span size, if we define memory span as the number of words or numbers that we can remember without error from a single presentation. There has been a tendency, however, to argue that this memory span outcome is the consequence of a single underlying cognitive process called short-term memory. As a consequence, it was sometimes argued not that the memory span was 7 ± 2 items but rather that short-term memory could hold 7 ± 2 items. This latter way of stating the matter has led to extensive debate and empirical research. In Box 3.1 we discuss the character of this debate. In the last paragraph of this box, we note that there is currently somewhat less attention directed to the topic of short-term memory capacity, partly because it is now believed that several processes may underlie temporary memory phenomena.

There is another reason, however, why determining an accurate number of chunks is of less concern now. As we noted in Chapter 2, carrying out various cognitive activities demands the use of a number of different resources such as focal attention. We noted that different tasks necessitate different amounts of these resources. If we extend this logic to memory tasks, the capacity of short-term memory will probably depend on the nature of the memory task given to the individual. If we give him an easy task, he may show a larger memory capacity and be able to remember a larger number of items over temporary time periods. On the other hand, if we give him a difficult task that puts a heavy load on his resources, we should expect that the number of items he will be able to retain (that is, his memory capacity) will probably be reduced.

The Formation of Chunks. The limitation on temporary memory has sometimes been referred to as a bottleneck in the information-processing system. If no effective way existed for reducing or offsetting this limitation, the human organism would be severely hampered in its interaction with the environment. One procedure used to offset this limitation is called **chunking.** Chunking refers to a process of combining several input elements into one group so that the combination

Box 3.1 THE CAPACITY OF SHORT-TERM MEMORY

Over the past two decades probably no topic related to temporary memory has received more attention than that of the size or capacity of short-term memory. George Miller's famous article on short-term memory (Miller, 1956) soundly established the first estimate of short-term memory capacity at 7 ± 2 chunks.

Several researchers, however, began to challenge this figure as an accurate estimate of short-term memory size (Broadbent, 1975; Glanzer & Razel, 1974). These challenges were raised for different reasons. Glanzer and Razel, for example, studied the size of short-term memory by looking at the recency effect in free recall studies. This effect refers to the very high level of recall of the last items on a free recall list. It is frequently argued that these items are better recalled because they are held in short-term memory. Glanzer and Razel claimed that this procedure overestimates the number of items in short-term memory since some of these items are held in long-term memory.

In order to test their contention, these authors used a formula developed by Waugh and Norman (1965) to generate a procedure to estimate the number of items in short-term memory. In this procedure the amount of information in long-term memory is estimated from the middle items in a free recall list. This estimate is then used to correct the recency effect for recall from long-term memory. By using this procedure, Glanzer and Razel came up with estimates that short-term memory could hold about two chunks, a markedly lower number than earlier estimates.

Broadbent, after reviewing several different kinds of evidence, also speculated that a capacity of seven was too large for short-term memory. For example, he noted that if people are given a continuous series of items, they are unable to respond at all reliably to items that occurred six or seven items earlier. Similarly, he noted that when subjects divide long strings of items into groups to aid their recall, they choose groups of three or four in length.

In the memory span studies, Broadbent noted that the usual span reported is the number of items that can be recalled perfectly on 50 percent of occasions. If, however, one looks at the number of items recalled with very high accuracy, the estimate is reduced. On these bases, Broadbent claimed that a more accurate estimate of capacity is three items, and that the higher estimates of five, six, or seven were due to particular task factors that aid in offsetting the limitation.

The fact that several different estimates of short-term memory capacity exist is somewhat disconcerting. However, criticisms by Postman (1975) and Simon (1974) have challenged the view that short-term memory is limited to two or three items. Postman, in particular, argued that unwarranted assumptions are made in arriving at these estimates. While this issue has never really been resolved, it is attracting less attention now since more complex views of

> the processes underlying temporary retention phenomena have been put forth. This issue arose primarily from early two-store theories that postulated only a single mechanism as being responsible for temporary memory phenomena. As we will see in the last section of this chapter, several processes seem implicated in these phenomena.

of elements takes up less space in working memory.

The process of chunking is closely related to the development of automatic processes discussed in the latter part of Chapter 2. In that discussion we noted that as a task becomes more and more automatic, it demands fewer and fewer resources for its execution. By combining memory items in certain ways, we in effect reduce the amount of resources we must use in order to remember these items.

The empirical work on chunking suggests that two major procedures are employed by subjects in combining to-be-remembered information in easier-to-remember chunks. First, the subjects make use of highly overlearned patterns of information which have frequently experienced. In fact, these patterns are so common that they are a part of each individual's permanent knowledge of the environment. Second, if such overlearned patterns of information are unavailable, the subjects may switch to more superficial aspects of the to-be-remembered information to help them form temporary chunks of information.

Chunking Processes. As we noted in our discussion of the study by Murdock (1961), three unrelated consonants influence memory capacity to the same extent that three separate words do. Similarly, digits use up as much capacity as do consonants or words. One explanation for these findings is that frequently used combinations of letters, words, or numbers come to form an entity in permanent memory, an entity that can be responded to as a unit rather than as a set of separate items. Thus the letters *b o o k* come to be responded to as the word *book* rather than four separate letters. Evidence to support this explanation comes from numerous sources.

Bower (1972b; Bower & Springston, 1970) looked at the ability of subjects to remember acronyms such as TV, FBI, and YMCA. He found that when the items were presented in a fashion in which the subjects could identify the acronyms, recall for the letter strings was quite good. For example, if the string was read as

FBI . . . . . . YMCA . . . . . . TV . . .

it was recalled better than if it was read

FB . . . . . . IYMC . . . . . . ATV . . .

Thus if subjects were able to identify an incoming set of information as something with which they were familiar, their recall was enhanced.

A fascinating look at the influence of highly practiced patterns on chunking has been provided by recent studies on the ability of chess players to remember chess positions. In a typical study, players are shown chess positions arranged either randomly or in situations that arose from games (but are unknown to the subjects). The players are then asked to reconstruct the board from memory. Players who were masters or grand masters in chess were able to replace most of the 20 to 25 pieces with few errors if the pieces were in a game arrangement. Subjects who were ordinary players could replace only a half dozen or so. However, if the pieces on the board were arranged randomly, the masters and grand masters performed no better than ordinary players (deGroot, 1965).

Simon and his colleagues (Simon, 1974; Simon & Chase, 1973) speculated that the improved performance of the masters and grand masters was due to their ability to chunk the 20-odd pieces into a half dozen or so chunks to get them within the limits of temporary retention capacity. In order to test these ideas, Simon measured the pauses between the replacement of each piece on the board. He argued that there should be relatively short pauses between pieces if they were held in one chunk but long pauses between pieces if the person was moving to a new chunk.

Such procedures for measuring chunking have been successfully used by other researchers. Using this measure, Simon found that the recall for game positions of one master player could be divided into about 7.7 chunks.

Thus the masters and grand masters of chess can apparently make use of their vast knowledge of possible chess orderings effectively to chunk the incoming information from the chess board into a reduced number of items to be remembered. In fact, Simon and his colleagues also estimated the number of chunks needed by master

---

Box 3.2   MEMORY FOR CHESS: STORAGE IN PERMANENT MEMORY?

Some question has arisen as to whether the more effective performance of chess masters in remembering chess-related information is due to more effective use of temporary storage procedures or to differences in permanent memory procedures. Charness (1976) employed an interesting experimental procedure to test this question. Subjects who were class A and C chess players were shown chess patterns for 5 sec. They were then subjected for 30 sec to a variety of interfering tasks such as summing digits, copying symbols, and shadowing digits. At the conclusion of these tasks, the subjects were required to reconstruct the chess patterns on an empty chess board.

If the chess information were being held in a temporary fashion, Charness expected that the interfering task would cause a significant drop in the subjects' ability to reconstruct the boards. In fact performance dropped by about 6 percent, which, although significant, was quite small compared to the subjects' ability to remember sets of letter trigrams after interpolated activity (a drop of 25 percent).

While there was little drop in the subjects' ability to remember the chess patterns, it took the subjects much longer to reconstruct the board at the time of retrieval. Charness interpreted these results as suggesting that virtually all the information obtained by the chess experts during the 5-sec exposure had been stored in permanent memory rather than obtained from permanent memory and stored in some temporary fashion. Apparently chess players are capable of quickly storing specific game information in some rather permanent form—a form not subject to interfering tasks that disrupt much temporarily held information.

players to carry out this process. The numbers fell in the range of 25,000 to 100,000 chunks, or a chess vocabulary of this size. This number is similar to the size of the word vocabulary of an educated adult.

It follows, of course, that using other types of information in permanent memory to organize incoming information into larger units should increase the amount of information that can be temporarily recalled. For example, syntactic rules in language or categories of words such as animals, fish, or furniture can also be used to organize input. Because these structures seem to be used more for the permanent retention of information, we will hold our discussion of them until we consider permanent memory. We wish only to note here that the processes of organization which we will discuss in permanent memory are not fundamentally different from the process of chunking.

It is worthwhile to note also one important implication of the role of well-practiced units in chunking: Since the ability to chunk depends on the total accumulated knowledge of the individual, there is little substitute for building a complete knowledge base. Such a knowledge base is built on extensive experience in an area. Simon and Chase (1973) noted, for example, that there is no person on record (including Bobby Fischer) who has reached a master or grand master level in chess without almost a decade of intense effort with the game. It takes thousands of hours of practice to attain a chess vocabulary of 25,000 to 100,000 chunks. Similarly, much of our schooling involves extensive amounts of experience aimed at building an accumulated knowledge that allows expertise in an area, as illustrated by the fact that training to become a medical specialist, lawyer, chemist, or psychologist takes years.

Obviously, we do not always have well-formed chunks existing in permanent memory which match information that we need to retain briefly. In such instances, the manner in which information is presented may markedly influence the chunks used by the subjects. For example, McLean and Gregg (1967) found in the recall of digits that the manner in which the items were divided up at presentation influenced the way in which the digits were recalled. Thus if the experimenter divided a string of numbers into groups of three, such as

271. . . . 594. . . .638. . . .293

the subjects were likely to recall them in these same groups. If no chunking pattern is highly practiced, the subject will apparently use whatever chunking pattern may be suggested by the manner of presentation.

It is apparent from our discussion of chunks and the chunking process that the formation of chunks plays a key role in the temporary retention of information by reducing the number of items to be recalled to a more manageable level. Another factor that plays an important role in temporary retention is the phenomenon of rehearsal.

Rehearsal

Kelly, a two-year-old girl, is going trick-or-treating for the first time. She has asked her parents repeatedly what she is to say when people open their doors for her. As she walks down the street, she is heard quietly repeating to herself, "Tick or treat, tick or treat, tick or treat." Kelly, a daughter of one of the authors, is making use of the well-known process of **rehearsal** to help her temporarily remember something.

Generally the term rehearsal refers to the temporary cycling of information through memory (Klatzky, 1975). It is frequently used in everyday settings calling for memory over a brief time period—for example, remembering a telephone number until it can be dialed or an address until it can be written down. Memory researchers and theorists have been quite interested in its role in the overall memory process.

Rehearsal was thought initially to be a unitary process that serves two different functions. The rehearsing, or recycling, keeps an item active in temporary memory and thus serves a *holding* or *maintenance* function. However, as an item is more and more frequently rehearsed, its trace in permanent memory is strengthened and hence rehearsal also serves a *transfer* function. In effect, each rehearsal accomplishes two tasks: keeping the item in temporary memory and simultaneously moving it into permanent memory.

Some studies have called this view into question. For example, Jacoby (1973) gave his subjects a series of five-word lists. Some subjects were asked to recall each list immediately, others were asked to recall following a 15-sec period of rehearsal. Finally, after many of the lists had been presented, the subjects were unexpectedly asked to recall all the words they had heard. Jacoby found no difference in recall for those who had rehearsed and those who had not. Apparently the rehearsal had not served to move the items into permanent memory. Craik and Watkins (1973) and Woodward, Bjork, and Jongeward (1973) reported similar findings with different types of experimental procedures.

These studies, in conjunction with earlier work showing that under certain conditions rehearsal *does* lead to better long-term retention (e.g., Howe, 1967), suggested that there may be two different types of rehearsal. If rehearsal is carried out in a manner in which an item is not related to any new information, then the item is simply maintained and no permanent change in memory occurs. This type of rehearsal has been variously called *maintenance* or *primary rehearsal*. If, however, an item being rehearsed is elaborated by being related to other incoming information, then it will be retained better over long time periods. This latter type of rehearsal has been variously labeled *elaborative, secondary,* or *constructive rehearsal*. (See Figure 3.2.)

In an attempt to better understand the characteristics of these two types of rehearsal, Bjork and his colleagues carried out a number of studies (Bjork & Jongeward, cited in Bjork, 1975; Elmes & Bjork, 1975). Generally their approach was to present subjects with five or six words and then instruct them to carry out either maintenance rehearsal or elaborative rehearsal for a period of time. The effects of these different instructions were quite dramatic. Subjects asked to do maintenance rehearsal remembered the words better than those doing elaborative rehearsal if recall was asked for within a short time period (20 sec). However, on an unexpected final recall at the end of the experiment, the subjects who were asked to do elaborative rehearsal both recalled and recognized better than those instructed to do maintenance rehearsal (Bjork & Jongeward, cited in Bjork, 1975).

Apparently different types of rehearsal are effective for different types of situations. If we just want to hold some item briefly, it is better not to try to rehearse it elaboratively because this takes up space in working memory and less information will be maintained. However, if we need to remember over long time periods, we should try to rehearse elaboratively in order to establish a more permanent trace even though we will be able to do this with a relatively small number of items. These findings point up the flexibility we have in making use of our memory processes.

The work on elaborative and maintenance rehearsal has been an important step forward in our understanding of rehearsal procedures for temporary retention. As a consequence, research on this topic has been of much interest during the mid-1970s (Craik, 1979). Some difficulties in finding pure examples of the two types of rehearsal, however, have led Craik to point out that a more viable description of rehearsal might "suggest a *continuum* of rehearsal operations running from the minimal processing necessary to repeat a word continuously to various types of elaborative processing involving either further enrichment of one item or associative linkage of several items" (p. 84). Research in the coming years should indicate whether this is a more useful view.

Figure 3.2 A well-known Austrian governess might not have been as famous had she required her children to use a maintenance rehearsal procedure (top) rather than an elaborative one (bottom) for learning the notes on the musical scale (do, re, mi, fa, so, la, ti, do).

Two other findings by Bjork and his colleagues are important in understanding the role of rehearsal in memory. In a study in which they induced their subjects to carry out different amounts of maintenance rehearsal, Woodward, Bjork, and Jongeward (1973) found that increased rehearsal did not improve long-term recall of the presented words. Surprisingly, however, these researchers did find that increased rehearsal improved final recognition of the words. That is, when the subjects were asked to pick out which words they had seen before from a long list of words including both new and old words, the subjects' accuracy improved with greater amounts of maintenance rehearsal.

This finding suggests a slight modification of the notion that maintenance rehearsal results in no permanent improvement of memory. Apparently some type of permanent change is being made via maintenance rehearsal, but this change is insufficient to result in better performance if the subjects have relatively little help during retrieval as is the case when they are attempting to recall the words. The rather surprising results of the Woodward et al. study have been supported by Glenberg, Smith, and Green (1977).

The second finding reported by Bjork and his colleagues provides a natural tie to our next topic—the nature of the way information is encoded for temporary retention. Elmes and Bjork (1975) looked at two types of errors subjects made during recall when they had been instructed to carry out maintenance versus elaborative rehearsal. In the first type of error, acoustic intrusions, they found that the subject replaces the correct word with one that is acoustically similar (*ban* for *van*). The second type of error, semantic intrusions, is of the same kind, except that the subject replaces the word with one similar in meaning (*bus* for *van*). Those subjects instructed to do maintenance rehearsal showed a higher proportion of acoustic than semantic intrusions: .34 and .03, respectively. However, for the subjects instructed to do elaborative rehearsal, the proportions were dramatically different: .19 and .16, respectively.

These results then show that those subjects who did maintenance rehearsal produced about twice as many acoustic errors (.34 to .19) but only one fifth as many semantic errors (.03 to .16) as did those who did elaborative rehearsal. Apparently these rehearsal differences result not only in differential recall and recognition patterns but lead also to different ways of encoding the information into memory.

Encoding in Temporary Retention

Coming out of the movie, Phil runs into a friend, Barb, who introduces Phil to her date.
"Phil, this is Cary Billings. He's in art."
"How're you doin'?" Phil asks, and without waiting for an answer launches into an analysis of the movie.
At the corner they part.
"See ya, Barb," says Phil. "Glad to meet ya, Gary."
Cary grins and says nothing.

Acoustic Encoding. Phil has just made an acoustic error while temporarily retaining a brief message. Such errors are not uncommon during temporary retention and are thought to be due to the way people encode information in short-term memory. By **encoding** we mean the way in which people place information in memory. Thus we speak of acoustic, visual, or semantic encoding when we mean that material is placed in memory according to its sound, its visual characteristics, or its meaning, respectively.

Soon after the advent of two-store models of memory, considerable effort was spent in determining the type of encoding predominant in short-term memory. Conrad (1964), for example, presented compelling evidence that encoding in short-term memory is based upon acoustic properties. He first constructed a matrix of confusions that subjects made in listening to letters presented over noise. (See Table 3.1.) This matrix showed which letters were confused with which others when subjects were listening to them in a hard-

Table 3.1 Listening Confusions

		STIMULUS LETTER							
RESPONSE LETTER		B	C	P	T	V	F	M	N	S	X
B	.	171	75	84	168	2	11	10	2	2
C	32	.	35	42	20	4	4	5	2	5
P	162	350	.	505	91	11	31	23	5	5
T	143	232	281	.	50	14	12	11	8	5
V	122	61	34	22	.	1	8	11	1	0
F	6	4	2	4	3	.	13	8	336	238
M	10	14	2	3	4	22	.	334	21	9
N	13	21	6	9	20	32	512	.	38	14
S	2	18	2	7	3	488	23	11	.	391
X	1	6	2	2	1	245	2	1	184	.

Source: From Conrad (1964).

to-hear context. For example, the letter *S*, if incorrectly heard, was frequently called *F,* but rarely *B* or *P*. The letter *P*, however, was frequently confused with *T* but rarely with *F* or *S*.

Conrad then conducted a temporary memory task in which the subjects were shown a string of six letters and asked to recall them. Conrad carefully analyzed the recall confusions and found that they followed a pattern remarkably similar to the listening confusions. For example, if a subject had been shown the letter *S* in a list of letters to remember and made a mistake, the most likely mistake was in calling it *F*. (See Table 3.2.) Letters likely to be confused in the perceptual task were also likely to be confused in the memory task.

Conrad thus argued that material in short-term memory is stored in terms of its acoustic properties. These results are even more important when it is noted that Conrad presented his letters for recall in a visual fashion. Apparently the subjects were translating the visually presented letters into an acoustic code for their representation in short-term memory.

Table 3.2 Recall Confusions

		STIMULUS LETTER							
RESPONSE LETTER		B	C	P	T	V	F	M	N	S	X
B	.	18	62	5	83	12	9	3	2	0
C	13	.	27	18	55	15	3	12	35	7
P	102	18	.	24	40	15	8	8	7	7
T	30	46	79	.	38	18	14	14	8	10
V	56	32	30	14	.	21	15	11	11	5
F	6	8	14	5	31	.	12	13	131	16
M	12	6	8	5	20	16	.	146	15	5
N	11	7	5	1	19	28	167	.	24	5
S	7	21	11	2	9	37	4	12	.	16
X	3	7	2	2	11	30	10	11	59	.

Source: From Conrad (1964).

Other studies using different paradigms have seemed to substantiate the conclusion that acoustic encoding is predominant in temporary memory. Some studies noted that word lists composed of similar sounding words are more difficult to recall than ones not so constructed (Conrad & Hull, 1964; Kintsch & Buschke, 1969). Others showed that memory is hindered if subjects have to carry out a distractor task (a task carried out during the retention period) that involves making verbal responses acoustically similar to the items to be recalled (Wickelgren, 1965). Based on these results, theorists speculated that people recode incoming information into an acoustic code so that they can easily rehearse the items to be remembered.

This initial view of encoding for temporary retention has changed rather dramatically since 1970. The change is based on both new empirical evidence and a more refined view of the structures involved in the temporary retention of information.

Nonacoustic Encoding. The initial studies of encoding left little doubt that acoustic features play a key role in encoding in temporary memory. Unfortunately, as Postman (1975) noted, there was a tendency to overinterpret these studies and claim that *only* acoustic encoding occurs in temporary memory. However, at least two other major encoding forms have been shown to play an important role in studies of temporary memory—visual and semantic. Although there is not complete agreement that these characteristics may be encoded in temporary memory (see Shallice, 1975), the evidence for them is mounting.

Posner and his colleagues (Posner, 1969; Posner, Boies, Eichelman, & Taylor, 1969; Posner & Mitchell, 1967), for example, have provided convincing evidence that in certain temporary memory situations people are able to maintain a visual code for a few seconds. The basic procedure employed in these studies involved a letter-matching task and a measurement of reaction time. Posner presented a letter (e.g., *D*) on a screen for a brief period. Then there was a period of time (called the *interstimulus interval,* or ISI) in which the subject saw only a blank field. Following the ISI, another letter appeared that was either identical in form *(D),* or in name *(d),* or different *(A).*

A subject's task was to report as quickly as possible whether the second letter was the same as or different from the first. The time between the onset of the second letter and the subject's report was that individual's reaction time. By manipulating various conditions and measuring the reaction time, the experimenters were able to deduce some characteristics of the individual's memory.

The important evidence for our question of whether visual information can be used in temporary memory arises from a comparison of the speed of identity matches versus name matches. An identity match (see Figure 3.3) occurs in the following manner: A letter (e.g., *B*) is presented followed by the ISI and an identical letter *(B).* A name match, on the other hand, involves the presentation of a letter (e.g., *A*) followed by the ISI and then a letter that differs in form but has the same name *(a).* To respond in the name match condition, the subject must perceive each letter, generate its name, compare these names, and then respond.

One might suppose that the identity match would require the same set of steps. If, however, a subject is able to hold a visual representation of the first letter in temporary memory, then the matching should go faster. The two letters could then be compared in their visual forms, without the necessity of generating and comparing names. Posner's data indicated this is indeed the case. When the ISI is less than about 2 sec, responses to identity matches are faster than responses to name matches.

If the ISI lasts longer than 2 sec, however, the name match is made as quickly as the identity match. These results thus suggest that visual information can be briefly held in temporary memory.

The visual information is apparently not being held in the Icon. If the ISI is filled with a

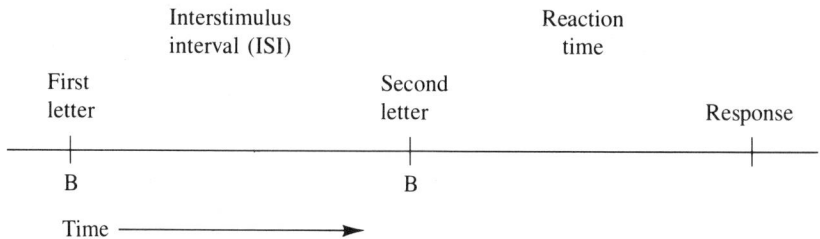

Figure 3.3 A sketch of the experimental paradigm for the identity match task in Posner's work. For a name match, the second letter would be replaced by *b*.

visual masking pattern, the difference between the identity and name matches is not obliterated (Posner et al., 1969). If the first letter were being held in the Icon, such a masking pattern should wipe it out, and hence the difference between the name matches and identity matches should likewise disappear.

Probably the most convincing evidence for a temporary visual code comes from the work of Kroll and his associates (Kroll, 1975; Parks, Kroll, Salzberg, & Parkinson, 1972). They combined the methodology used by Posner in his letter-matching tasks with a shadowing procedure. The shadowing procedure necessitated that a subject listen to and orally repeat a series of letters heard over a set of earphones. This procedure was added for two reasons. First, the Posner studies showed that the visual code could be held for up to 2 sec. However, it is of interest to know whether the visual code could be held for longer than this, say up to 1 min. The shadowing procedure can be used to force the subject to hold the visual code longer than was required in Posner's studies. Second, the shadowing procedure makes it difficult for the subject to recode the visual image into an auditory code, thus assuring that the subject uses only a visual code.

Kroll presented his subjects with a letter, followed by a period filled with shadowing, and then a second letter. The key comparison again involved a comparison between the name matches and identity matches. Once again, faster responding to the identity match provides evidence for the temporary retention of visual information. Using intervals of up to 8 sec, Kroll and his associates found that this was the case.

The evidence thus compiled using several different methodologies suggests that we are capable of briefly retaining information in a visual code as well as an acoustic code if the situation demands and allows it. Is there evidence that semantic codes can also be used? Apparently the answer is yes.

The most convincing evidence that semantic codes are maintained in temporary memory studies comes from work by Shulman (1970, 1972). Shulman used a probe recognition procedure to test for semantic effects. This procedure involved the presentation of a list of words (in this case ten words), followed immediately by a test item (the probe). Subjects were asked to judge whether the probe word matched a word in the list identically or was a synonym of the word. The subjects were unaware which type of judgment they were to make until just before the probe word was presented.

The key conditions were when the probe word was either synonymous with a word in the list or unrelated to any word in the list, and the subjects were asked to say whether the probe word was identical to some word in the list. For example, the probe word *male* might have the synonym *man* in the list, or it might have only unrelated words in the list.

The extent to which the subjects made more errors in the condition when the probe had a synonym in the list indicates how much they were holding semantic information. Shulman found that subjects did make more of these errors and they occurred even in the last words in the list, words that were truly being held temporarily. Thus subjects can hold semantic information in temporary memory if the conditions are conducive to it.

The evidence seems clear then that information stored for brief periods may involve many different memory codes, be they acoustic, visual, or semantic. The fact that they seem more frequently to involve acoustic properties may be partially a function of the tasks people are asked to do. We are probably most highly practiced at rehearsing acoustic codes, and we may naturally code information in this fashion unless task demands require otherwise.

In summary, acoustic codes appear to play an important role in temporary memory situations. However, it is possible to set up situations where it is more advantageous to code visual or semantic properties early. The beauty of such a processing system as ours is that it has a typical manner of processing that allows it to react quickly to common situations, but it also has extensive flexibility to handle the unusual processing situations that occasionally face any human being.

Forgetting from Temporary Memory

We have all experienced the frustration and occasional embarrassment of losing temporarily held information. Most of us can recall the time we went charging down the hallway only to stop halfway with a sheepish grin on our face because we could not remember what we were going to do, or the time we forgot the point we were going to make while talking to a group of people. Just as frustrating are the times we have been introduced to someone and started a conversation only to find that we could not recall the person's name.

Memory researchers have been much interested in this process of forgetting and have offered several hypotheses about it. The explanations for forgetting have centered around two main principles: that loss of temporary memory is due (1) to decay, or (2) to interference.

To say that information is forgotten because of decay from memory implies that the information becomes less and less available the longer the time has been since it was encoded. This does not mean, of course, that the passage of time has caused the memory loss, for time does not *cause* anything to occur. Rather, it implies that some unknown factor or factors that operate as time passes result in the eventual inability of the individual to remember a particular event.

Interference explanations of forgetting, in contrast, contend that material is lost because other information already in memory or new information coming into memory competes or interferes with retention of the material. This interference may take different forms. For example, if there is a limited capacity to temporary memory and this capacity is all taken up, incoming new information may displace some item that is already in memory. Alternatively, items that are highly similar may be more difficult to discriminate from one another or may take more space in working memory to discriminate, thus leading to memory loss.

It has proved difficult to disentangle which of these explanations, decay or interference, more correctly describes the loss of briefly stored information. It seems impossible to carry out an experiment that definitively separates the two explanations as can be seen if we consider how investigations of these two theories proceed.

In order to study forgetting, researchers make use of *interfering tasks*. These are tasks imposed upon subjects during the retention period, the time between when they are given something to be remembered and when they are asked to recall it. One type of interfering task involves placing a variety of tasks—counting backwards or listening for tones over noise—in the retention period. This type of interference task is called a *distractor* task. In a second type of interfering task, the *probe* task, subjects are given in the retention period additional items similar to the one to be remembered. For example, if a subject is going to be tested for recall of the digit 5 in the string 6 2 5 7 4 1 9 3 8, the last six numbers serve as interfering material.

The difficulty in carrying out a definitive comparison of decay and interference explanations lies in the fact that the decay hypothesis would necessitate a retention period during which the subjects carry out no interfering tasks. That is, they are not trying to remember additional information, nor are they carrying out any other mental activities. Since this condition is unobtainable, a definitive test does not seem possible. Nevertheless, approximations to this condition have allowed researchers to make useful statements.

Peterson and Peterson (1959), for instance, conducted one of the earliest studies of forgetting in temporary memory. These authors gave their subjects a series of trials set up as follows: The subjects were auditorially presented a trigram composed of three consonants, for example, *JTK*. This was immediately followed by a three-digit number from which the subjects were to count backwards by three at a rapid rate (the distrctor task). After various durations of counting backwards, the subjects were asked to recall the trigram.

It was argued that the counting task did not involve giving the subject any new memory material and so would be a noninterfering task. Hence a drop in the subject's ability to recall after the longer intervals of counting should be evidence for a decay theory of forgetting. The counting task was thought simply to prevent rehearsal but *not* interfere with the trigrams. Since no interference occurred, any memory loss was thought to be due to decay.

Peterson and Peterson did find rather dramatic forgetting as is seen in Figure 3.4. The longer the retention period filled with the counting task went on, the poorer recall became. At about 20 sec, recall was very poor. From these results it was concluded that the loss of temporarily held information was due to decay.

A number of other studies, however, found that the more similar a distractor task is to the material to be temporarily retained, the more dramatic is the memory loss. Wickelgren (1965),

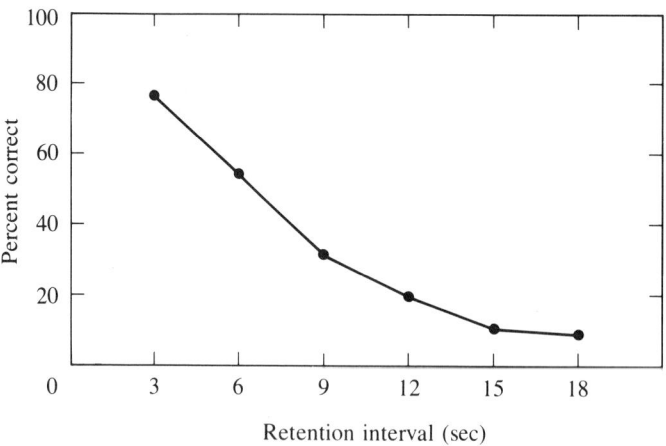

Figure 3.4 Recall as a function of the length of the retention interval. (From Peterson & Peterson, 1959.)

for example, found that when the distractor material sounded like the material to be remembered, there was more extensive forgetting than if it did not. These results suggest that the memory loss is due to interference.

These early studies then left the explanation of the forgetting of temporary information uncertain. Both decay and interference seemed to be involved, but there was concern that the distractor tasks used in the studies arguing for decay involved some degree of interference. This concern led to the use of a new type of distractor task, the signal-detection task, which presents a somewhat clearer view of the forgetting of temporary information.

This task involves filling the retention interval with a difficult tone-detection task. A tone is presented for detection over a background of noise that can be manipulated in loudness to make the task more or less difficult. This task has the benefit of keeping subjects from rehearsing and not giving them any new input to memory. Consequently, there should be no opportunity for either rehearsal or interference to occur.

Reitman (1971) was one of the first experimenters to employ this approach. She gave her subjects three words to remember and then had them listen for the tone for 15 sec. The tone-detection task was a difficult one, and the subjects were encouraged to attend to it carefully. In addition, their tone-detection performance was monitored to be sure they were paying attention to the task, and the subjects were asked if they had rehearsed. If either of these procedures suggested rehearsal, the subjects' data were not used. With these criteria, Reitman found that the subjects showed *no* loss over the 15-sec period, thus demonstrating that when no interfering material was presented and no rehearsal occurred, there was no loss of information. These results seemed to show that decay is not a factor in the loss of temporary information.

A second part of her experiment provided additional evidence that interference is involved in memory loss. Instead of having subjects listen for tones, she had them do a syllable-detection task that required them to listen for a syllable like *toh* among a series of *doh*s. This type of task led to a marked loss of information, suggesting that tasks that involve content similar to what is being stored in temporary memory cause a loss of information. Thus if we think back to the original Peterson and Peterson study, the counting-backwards task may have resulted in loss due to some interference rather than to decay. From these results it seems that decay plays little, if any, role in the loss of temporary information from memory.

Even this conclusion, however, has been called into question. Watkins, Watkins, Craik, and Mazuryk (1973) and even Reitman (1974) herself have questioned whether Reitman's original tone-detection task was demanding enough to completely prevent rehearsal on the subject's part. Of course, if the subjects were in fact rehearsing, this rehearsal might have accounted for their good retention over the 15-sec interval, and thus the test of decay still might not have been complete. Reitman (1974) therefore made an even more careful determination of whether the subjects were rehearsing. In this study the retention of those subjects who did not rehearse at all *dropped*. Thus some information had apparently decayed.

Watkins et al. (1973) supported this finding by giving their subjects a more demanding nonverbal interfering task. They had subjects shadow a series of piano tones and push different buttons corresponding to each. These researchers found that recall of five-word sequences dropped over a 20-sec retention period, evidence that some type of decay operates if rehearsal is prevented.

This complex set of research findings (see a graphic outline in Table 3.3) has thus led researchers back to arguing that the loss of temporarily stored information can evidently be traced to both the phenomena we have discussed—interference and decay. First, the more similar the new incoming information is to the temporarily stored information, the greater will be the memory loss. Very similar materials make it difficult for the structures involved in temporary memory to re-

Table 3.3 A Graphic Outline of Findings on Temporary Memory Loss

AUTHORS	ITEM TO BE REMEMBERED	DISTRACTOR TASK	RESULTS	CONCLUSION
Early Studies				
Peterson & Peterson (1959)	JTK	Count backwards by 3	Performance drops with time	Decay important
Wickelgren (1965)	GPTV	Write letters BCZDCBZD	Performance drops with similarity of distractor letters	Interference important
Initial Signal Detection Work				
Reitman (1971)	3 words	Listen for tone or Listen for syllable	No loss of information / Loss of information	Decay of little importance
Recent Study of Rehearsal				
Reitman (1974)	5 words	Employed an even more stringent test of rehearsal	Recall drops when subjects do not rehearse	Decay is important

Current conclusion: Both decay and interference play a role in temporary memory loss.

tain information. Thus interference is caused by the similarity of the material to be retained.

Second, if the individual is prevented from rehearsing the temporarily held information by a demanding interfering task (regardless of the similarity of the material being worked on), memory loss will also occur. This loss is, in effect, due to a decay process.

STRUCTURES IN TEMPORARY RETENTION

Now that we have characterized the temporary retention of information, we turn to a consideration of the structures underlying this process. Three principal structures are implicated: a sensory-memory holding mechanism, working memory, and temporary memory traces. The first structure, sensory memories, or registers, we have already discussed in Chapter 2, but we mention them briefly here to emphasize that they do serve an important temporary memory function.

We noted that when information first impinges on an individual, it is stored briefly in a sensory memory. Visual information is held briefly in iconic memory, and auditory information in echoic memory. These memories were found to differ in duration as well as in the form in which they held information. For example, iconic memory lasts for about ¼ sec and stores information in a visual fashion; echoic memory lasts for 2 to 4 sec and stores information in an acoustic fashion. In each case relatively little processing of the information takes place during the time the information is held in sensory memory. In effect, these memories serve as brief holding mechanisms that allow for more extensive processing of the information.

There is some debate over whether these registers are best thought of as separate from other temporary memory mechanisms. Shiffrin (1975), for example, contended that the characteristics of temporary memory thought to be due to these memory registers can be explained in terms of the short-term memory portion of his two-store memory model. He argued, for instance, that the loss of information from the sensory registers can be explained in the same manner as the loss of information from short-term memory.

In addition, and of more importance, he noted that the notion of a separate sensory memory system can be defended only if it involves a unitary store with a single processing procedure. However, investigations have shown that different levels of processing have been found within both the Echo and the Icon (Crowder & Morton, 1969; Massaro, 1972; Shiffrin & Geisler, 1973; Turvey, 1973). According to Shiffrin, thus, it is more parsimonious to treat the sensory memory phenomena as the product of a general short-term memory mechanism.

Regardless of the view one holds on this debate, it is apparent that the processing operations carried out during the initial stages of input into the organism result in a type of very brief retention of information which is crucial in the overall cognitive functioning of that organism. This temporary retention has properties markedly different from those that typify longer storage periods—namely, it is of short duration, nonsemantically coded, and easily interfered with.

Working Memory

In our discussion of attention in Chapter 2, we introduced the notion of a working memory capable of operating on only a limited number of inputs at one time, and we have noted that some refer to this as consciousness. It is the limitation of working memory that results in your limited extension of focal attention to a lecture, to the hardness of the seat in which you are sitting, or to your hunger pangs—but not to all three at once.

The concept of working memory has come to play an increasingly important role in explanations of the temporary retention of information (Craik, 1979) as well as permanent memory. In temporary retention, it must be remembered that what is in working memory is what is in the individual's consciousness. It is thus possible for the individual to simply "read out" that which is currently engaging working memory. If, for example, a person is consciously thinking of the telephone number *282-2571,* he can simply read out this information. Similarly, if a person is solving a problem or thinking about last night's dinner, these pieces of information can be communicated.

Since the information currently engaging working memory may have been recently presented to the individual, when he reads out the contents of working memory, it will appear that he has temporarily remembered this information. Mandler (1975), however, argues that we need to be careful in labeling such a readout as memory. When we call something a memory system, we imply that it involves retrieval; that is, we imply that items in memory must be recalled. Mandler, on the other hand, claims that what is in the momentary field of consciousness does not have to be retrieved or recalled; it is already available.

Such thinking has led Mandler to make an important distinction between the notion of consciousness and the notion of short-term memory as postulated by Shiffrin and other two-store theorists. Some of the recall in studies of temporary memory is due to the readout of information from consciousness; some is also due to other structures involved in retaining information for brief periods, such as memory traces of differing durations (see the next section). The concept of short-term memory frequently clouds the distinction among these different processes.

Regardless of one's view on Mandler's distinction, the process of reading out of consciousness, or working memory, is important in understanding the temporary retention of information.

One important characteristic of working memory is its flexibility. There are apparently some properties of stimuli which are difficult, if not impossible, to bring to conscious awareness. For example, one of the reasons it is difficult to tell a child how to ride a bicycle is that the motor skill information we use is difficult to bring to our consciousness and thus be available for transmission. However, much other information can easily be brought into consciousness. We can, for example, choose to attend to the background sounds of the room we are in or to carefully analyze the numerous colors that make up an oil painting.

The fact that working memory is flexible is important in our retention of information. In particular, as working memory is brought to bear on different characteristics of stimuli, different types of memory codes or traces are activated in memory. Many theorists (Craik & Jacoby, 1975; Shiffrin, 1975) argue that the type of trace formed by working memory makes a significant difference in the memory for information. For example, extensive research has shown that items coded in terms of their physical attributes (e.g., number of syllables in a word or number of e's) are remembered less well than items coded in terms of their semantic attributes (Arkes, Schumacher, & Gardner, 1976; Hyde & Jenkins, 1969; Till & Jenkins, 1973).

Temporary Memory Traces

In discussing any type of memory system, whether it be for the temporary or the permanent retention of information, two different properties of the system must be considered: the storage of information in the system and the retrieval of information from the system. That is, all memory systems first necessitate some processes for the registering and holding of information over some period of time. These processes are variously termed storage processes, encoding processes, and registration.

The outcome of carrying out these processes is some type of memory structure that serves to hold the information so that it can be used at some later time, and as we have noted these structures are called *memory traces*. Thus when we learn the name of a new acquaintance, Jane, we form a memory trace that can be used to recall her name the next time we see her.

We are all painfully aware, however, that the existence of a memory trace for an event does not guarantee that we will be able to recall that event later. The wife of one of the authors has frequently mentioned the occasion when her then fiancé could not remember her name while introducing her to one of his old buddies. Most of us have experienced similar circumstances when even well-known memory traces could not be retrieved.

Since all memory necessitates storage and retrieval, it is logical to consider whether the differences between the temporary and permanent retention of information arise from differences in how we store information in temporary and permanent memory or in how we retrieve information from temporary and permanent memory. Let us first consider memory storage.

Trace Storage Structures. As we noted earlier in this chapter, two important views of memory in the 1970s were the two-store conception of memory and the levels-of-processing conception. In the two-store view of memory it has been argued that in addition to the information that currently engages working memory, there is another type of temporary storage structure. It has been given different names and different properties by various theorists.

Broadbent (1958) called it the S system (in contrast to the P system, which was working memory) and characterized it as a temporary buffer memory store from which information was quickly lost with the passage of time. That is, information was thought to decay quickly from the *S* system unless it was brought into the *P* system and reactivated. For information to be held permanently it had to be moved into a third or long-term memory store, which was infinite in capacity and from which information was lost only by interference from other memories. Such interference made it difficult to retrieve an item, but the item was not lost as it was from the *S* system.

Thus for Broadbent some of the temporary memory phenomena were due to the different manner in which recent traces were held in a short-term buffer storage system. In effect, some information was held in a relatively unstable temporary state from which it could be quickly lost.

Waugh and Norman (1965) ascribed some temporary retention phenomena to a storage structure they called *primary memory*. Primary memory involved a very limited capacity system from which information was lost by being replaced by new information once the system had reached capacity. Thus if primary memory could hold six words presented one after the other, the presentation of a seventh word replaced one of the first six items. In effect then, earlier items were not lost by decay but by interference from incoming new items.

Probably the most famous view of memory which proposed a separate short-term storage structure was that of Atkinson and Shiffrin (1968). This model postulated the existence of a sensory register, a short-term store, and a long-term store (see Figure 3.5). The sensory register is similar to the sensory memory discussed above. The long-term store is a relatively permanent store from which information is lost primarily by interference. The short-term store involves both a buffer store (temporary storage structure) and a processor for placing information into the long-term store. According to Atkinson and Shiffrin, items can be lost from the buffer store by decay in about 15 to 20 sec if they are not rehearsed.

These three views of two-store theory thus postulate the existence of some type of separate short-term memory storage system. Several of the characteristics of the temporary retention of information are traced to these short-term memory stores. For example, it is argued that these stores primarily hold acoustic information, which would explain why many errors in studies of temporary memory are acoustic confusions (recalling b for p, f for s). Similarly, the reason the most recent words on a memory list can be recalled so easily is because they are being retrieved from these short-term memory stores.

Although recent evidence raises doubts about the usefulness of such short-term memory buffer systems to explain temporary retention phenomena, a large number of researchers and theorists of memory still argue for their existence.

A different view of the role of storage processes in the phenomena of temporary retention is described by the levels-of-processing model of Craik and Lockhart (1972). These authors changed the emphasis in the study of memory from temporary memory stores to the type of processing carried out on information as it is encoded and stored. They contended that the memory trace laid down during storage is best viewed as a by-product of the carrying out of certain perceptual processes on incoming information.

That is, as we described in Chapter 2, once information strikes the sensory surfaces, various analyses are carried out. Angles are considered, the length and orientation of lines are analyzed, sounds and syllables are processed, and the sets of operations involved in pattern recognition are carried out. The result of doing these analyses is a memory trace that can be used in subsequent attempts to recall the particular event.

According to Craik and Lockhart, perceptual analyses produce memory traces that vary in

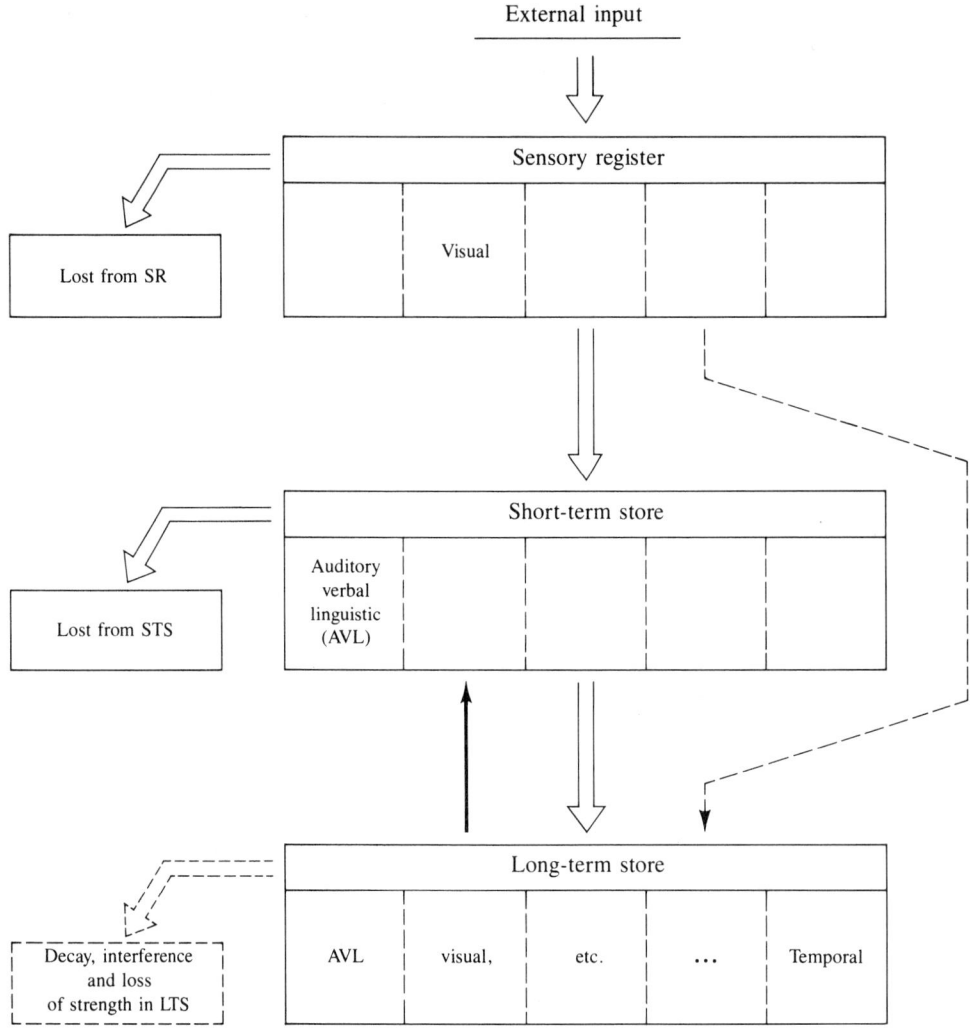

Figure 3.5 A schematic of the memory system proposed by Atkinson and Shiffrin (1968). The figure shows the three major components of the system and the type of material held in each component.

their elaborateness. In particular, they argued that the durability of the traces differs with the level of processing the inputs receive. If a stimulus is only processed to a shallow, sensory level, its trace is transient and easily lost. If, on the other hand, the trace is deeply processed to include semantic properties, its trace is persistent and durable.

Thus a person who considered the number of *e*'s and *t*'s in the words *bottle* and *president* would have a shallow trace that would disappear quickly. Considering the meaning of the words and how they related to other words, however, would create a durable trace for which recall would be good. We will present considerable empirical evidence speaking to these phenomena in our section dealing with encoding processes in permanent memory in Chapter 5.

Craik and Lockhart contended that some of the differences between temporary and permanent retention are due to the nature of the trace laid down during the perceptual analysis. They argued that it is not necessary to postulate the existence of a separate temporary memory store for recent information; rather they claimed that very recent information is more likely to have a trace based on shallow perceptual analyses which disappears quickly.

In a revision of his two-store theory, Shiffrin (1975) also argued for a series of stages of processing of incoming information. The initial stages are concerned with physical attributes such as contrasts, line segments, and open spaces. Later stages involve codes such as letters or word names, followed finally by semantic correlates of the word such as synonyms or previous uses of the word.

In accord with Craik and Lockhart, Shiffrin argued that the results of the earliest stages of processing are most quickly lost. The principal difference between Craik and Lockhart's view and Shiffrin's view is that Shiffrin still claims the existence of a separate short-term memory, which consists of all the features that have been activated in memory by the various analyses. That is, Shiffrin claims that the various features of words or stimuli are all stored in long-term memory, but in an inactive state. When these features are activated by various processing procedures, they are then in short-term memory.

In essence then, short-term memory to Shiffrin is that part of long-term memory which has been activated by various analyses. This view is summarized in Figure 3.6. This later position by Shiffrin seems to be a blend of the views that temporary memory is due to a short-term store and to the different types of traces resulting from different perceptual analyses. In addition, this view seems quite consistent with at least part of Anderson's ACT model (Anderson, 1976).

In summary, there are two principal views of trace storage that have been postulated to underlie the phenomena of the temporary retention of information. First, there is the view that a separate temporary storage system exists that holds information for brief durations. This store is thought to have markedly different properties from the more permanent long-term memory store.

Second, there is the view that there is only one type of memory store, but that different types of traces of incoming information are laid down by varying perceptual analyses. These traces have different durabilities and hence account for the different characteristics of temporary memory. Both of these views treat the differences in temporary memory as memory-trace *storage* differences. Some memory differences, however, may be due to different retrieval procedures between information stored temporarily and permanently.

Trace Retrieval Processes. Most concern with retrieval processes has been directed at studies of permanent memory, primarily because retrieval from temporary memory occurs with such ease that it seems almost automatic. In recent modifications of the levels-of-processing theory (Craik & Jacoby, 1975; Lockhart, Craik, & Jacoby, 1976), however, greater attention has been paid to the role of retrieval processes in temporary retention. Craik and his colleagues claim that some of the differences seen between temporary and permanent retention of information can be traced to the effectiveness of two different memory retrieval processes at varying times.

In particular, they claim that once information is no longer in working memory, it is in a form of long-term memory called *episodic memory*. Episodic memory refers to a system of permanent retention that maintains the order in which a series of events has occurred. For exam-

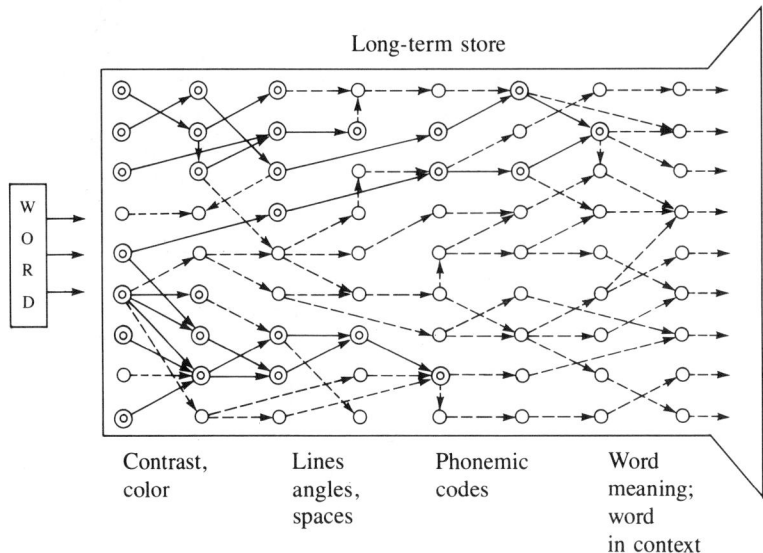

Figure 3.6 A conception of short-term store as involving particular activated pathways through long-term store. In the drawing, solid lines indicate information from long-term store currently in short-term store. This typifies what the memory system would be like shortly after a word was presented to a person. The early stages of processing (on the left) involve simple physical attributes, while later stages involve more semantic attributes. (From Shiffrin, 1975.)

ple, episodic memory includes the memory of such events as the time you fell and broke a collarbone, the food you ate at dinner last night, or the fact that you just read about breaking a collarbone. Retrieval from episodic memory means bringing back these particular events into working memory.

Craik and Jacoby claim that episodic memory is ordered from the most recent events to the most remote. A person who needs to retrieve from episodic memory can carry out one of two procedures. First, the person can *scan* recent items in episodic memory looking for some particular trace. The key factor in the success of this scanning process is the *distinctiveness* of the items being scanned. If the traces being scanned are all very recent, then extensive information about all the features that have been analyzed should be available and the traces should be easily distinguished. If the items are not as recent, much information about the item may have been lost and hence the scan is less effective.

In essence then, some of the phenomena of temporary retention may be due to the effectiveness of the scanning retrieval procedure at short intervals and the ineffectiveness of such a procedure at long intervals. For example, a trace of a word presented within the last 10 sec is likely to include acoustic, visual, and semantic information, any type of which would permit an accurate retrieval of the material. The more of these features that have decayed or been lost, the less effective will be the scan and retrieval.

If, on the other hand, it has been some time since a memory trace has entered episodic memory, a second retrieval process may be used—namely, *reconstruction*. In this retrieval process the instruction to recall an item initiates an attempt on the person's part to re-create or reconstruct the initial trace. In effect he goes through the same (or similar) analyzing processes at recall as he did when he initially stored the item. As he goes about constructing a new trace, he compares it to stored traces and is guided in his reconstruction by these traces.

Thus if a person is told the name of a new acquaintance one day, he may carry out certain perceptual and cognitive analyses on the person's name in an attempt to form a permanent trace. He may, for example, note the features of the woman's face and link her name to one of these features. Upon meeting the woman a week later, he may then reconstruct his trace of her name until he reaches a match with the now old name trace.

Craik and Jacoby thought that this reconstruction procedure would more probably be used when information is being retrieved over long retention periods. They did note, however, that reconstruction may be accomplished more effectively if an item has been coded into memory recently. Thus it is possible that some of the differences between temporary and permanent retention may be due to a more accurate reconstruction of a trace if the event to be remembered has only recently occurred.

The work on retrieval processes and their influence on the temporary retention of information is still in a very early state with considerable debate occurring as to the types of retrieval procedures and their characteristics. Further work should help to clarify these matters.

It is apparent nonetheless that several different structural features of the human memory system are involved in the temporary retention of information. These include some type of sensory retention mechanism, a working memory, and various encoding and retrieval procedures. Whether these are put together in a single box and called short-term memory or kept separate as part of the mechanisms involved in cognitive functioning is still a matter of debate among theoreticians.

Several implications for everyday functioning arise from the research on temporary retention. These implications, discussed in Box 3.3, may aid you in integrating and understanding some of the complex ideas we have presented in this chapter.

CONCLUSION

The principal thrust of this chapter has been to consider the major characteristics of temporary memory and the structures and processes thought to underlie these characteristics. We considered four major characteristics that are crucial in understanding the temporary retention of information: capacity and chunking, rehearsal, encoding, and forgetting. To help you understand these phenomena, we return to the model of information processing that we presented in Chapter 2, further modified in Figure 3.7.

We had shown before that Peter was reading a textbook while listening to music on the radio. We now see that the radio broadcast has just been interrupted to present the winning lottery number for a contest in which Peter was entered. The number is long and is read off in a monotone fashion by the announcer, "2-7-8-5-0-6-9-8-7." Peter is without a pencil. He is now faced with a dilemma because this number is beyond temporary memory *capacity;* it is composed of too many chunks of information. However, Peter attempts to aid his temporary retention by *chunking* the number into 278—506—987. This gives him fewer chunks to remember. Peter also makes use of *rehearsal* by mentally recycling the number to himself.

Because Peter is only interested in retaining the number until he can look up his lottery ticket, he will probably encode it in an acoustic manner since this is necessary for rehearsal. If the circumstances called for it, however, he could temporarily hold visual or semantic information also. Finally, Peter may lose this temporarily held information if he is unable to rehearse it (it will *decay*) or if he is given new similar informa-

> **Box 3.3 PRACTICAL IMPLICATIONS OF TEMPORARY MEMORY PHENOMENA**
>
> It is quite easy to derive important practical implications from our current understanding of temporary memory. Let us consider three key ones. First, it is apparent that the limitations imposed by working memory can markedly affect our everyday functioning. When we overload working memory, information will be lost and efficiency impaired. When a student is attempting to study in a noisy unpredictable environment (street noise, for instance, or a radio going with an unpredictable event such as a ballgame), information is frequently going to be lost before it can be moved to permanent memory. This is a function of the way the organism is structured.
>
> Second, chunking is a good way to increase our efficiency in using working memory. The individual who has built up an excellent permanent organization of some aspect of his or her experience will be able to process more information more quickly than someone who does not have such organization. Thus the advanced student or experienced individual will glean more from each new setting than the novice. For an individual without such an organization, efficiency in handling information can be improved if his environment shows him how to chunk and structure it. When we tell someone our telephone number, we do not read it in a monotone such as "5-7-2-6-4-3-9," but rather say, "572-6439."
>
> Third, we can be better served in temporarily retaining information if we are aware of the flexibility we have in how we process information. If an individual knows that the string of names and addresses she is being given over the phone can be found in the phone book, she can rehearse only the names and look up the addresses later. If the names are not in the phone book, she may be better served to get one or two names and addresses right and let the others go so that she has some useful information rather than a collection of useless information. Thus by making intelligent use of elaborative versus maintenance rehearsal, her performance can be improved. Similarly, a person who is being shown some paintings in an art class and knows that he will be tested for visual recognition will perform better at test than his classmates who were expecting a verbal recall. By concentrating in class on visual rather than semantic encoding, his performance will be aided.

tion such as a telephone number to call *(interference)*.

In the latter part of this chapter we discussed some of the structures involved in temporary retention. These include working memory, shown at the bottom of Figure 3.7, and the trace storage structures shown in episodic memory. These structures were derived from one or more of the four major theoretical positions we described in the opening pages of the chapter: interference theory, two-store theory, levels-of-processing theory, and activation theory.

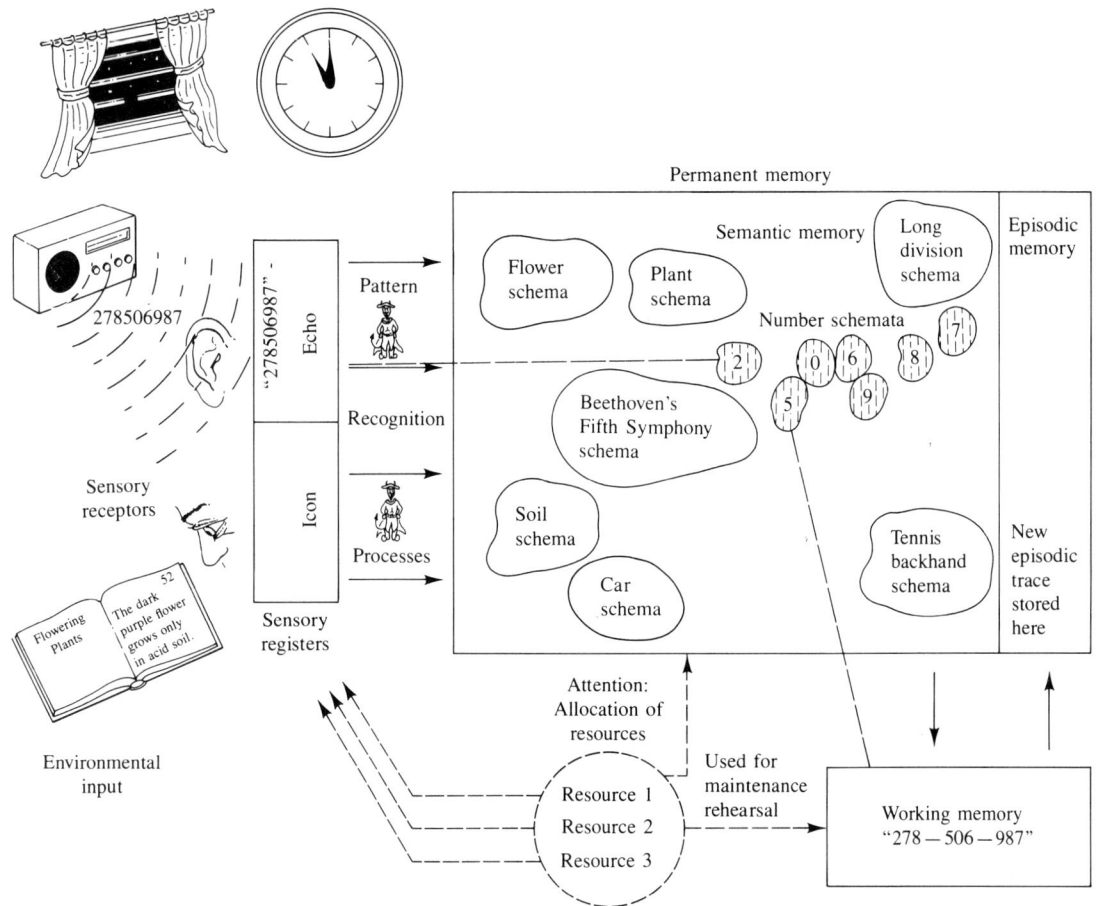

Figure 3.7 Expanded model of the components of the information-processing system.

4 The Structure of Permanent Memory

The Meaning of Permanent Memory
Episodic versus Semantic Memory
Models of Permanent Memory
    Analogical versus Propositional Representation
    Network Models of Semantic Memory
        The Collins and Loftus Network Model
        Investigations of Semantic Memory
            Reaction Time Methodology
            The Category Size Effect
            The Typicality Effect
            Priming Experiments
        ACT: A Network Model of Human Cognition
    Set Theory Model of Semantic Memory
    The Feature Comparison Model
    Images and Semantic Memory
Conclusion

"Hello, honey. How's the writing going?"

"Very slowly. I've been sitting here for almost two hours trying to think how to start the chapter on the structure of permanent memory. I just can't find the example I'm looking for."

"What kind of example do you want?"

"Well, I want to show that memory for events or lists of new information depends on making use of what we already know. That is the crux of permanent memory. I've thought of examples on remembering all the steps in developing film, remembering how to carry out an integration problem in calculus, or recalling the steps in landing an airplane. But I can't think of a way to develop these in order to make my point."

"I'm sure you'll come up with a good one. By the way would you bring some creamed corn, hamburger, tomatoes, bread, and ice cream when you come home?"

"Let's see. Hamburger, creamed corn, tomatoes, bread—those are easy. All I've got to do is remember the only casserole I know how to make—beef and corn casserole. What was the last item?"

"Ice cream."

"Beef and corn casserole a la mode. Who could forget that!"

Indeed, we are unlikely to forget such a concoction quickly. When we integrate new information into that which we already know, we form a permanent memory for this new information. The purpose of the next two chapters is to describe two key facets of the permanent retention of information: First, we describe how our permanent memories are structured and organized; second, we describe the processes involved in generating new permanent memories of the events we experience. We begin with a clarification of what we mean by permanent memory.

THE MEANING OF PERMANENT MEMORY

We have used the term *permanent* to describe the type of memory we are discussing in this chapter and the next. It is perhaps a misleading term in that it implies that a given fact or event is always available to the individual and can be brought to conscious awareness. Such is obviously not the case. Some information cannot be brought to awareness, or remembered, during some periods of time, a fact that all of us have experienced at one time or another. But is there some information, once known, which can never again be brought to awareness? That is, are some events completely and irrevocably forgotten, never to be remembered again? It is impossible to test this idea since we cannot test for some fact or event at all possible times and places. Thus the answer must remain unknown.

Nevertheless, there is suggestive evidence from physiological psychologists that the brain permanently stores an immense amount of information that can be brought into awareness under special conditions. For example, Penfield (1959) noted that when certain brain cells were electrically stimulated, the subjects reported recalling extensive details that were unavailable under normal circumstances. This, of course, does not prove that all information once in awareness is permanently stored, but it does suggest that a large amount may be.

The type of memory we are interested in throughout these two chapters then is dramatically different from that discussed in Chapter 3. There we were concerned with retention for periods up to 30 seconds; here we are concerned with retention over time periods lasting from minutes or hours to months and years. We will not use the term long-term memory in describing this memory, since that term is frequently used to refer to a stage of memory in two-store theory. Instead, we will use the term **permanent memory** as we explain the structures and processes involved in the retaining of information over relatively long time periods.

EPISODIC VERSUS SEMANTIC MEMORY

During the telephone conversation described in the opening of this chapter, we noted that memory for events depends on relating them to what we already know. As this fact has become clearer to psychologists, a distinction has been drawn between two types of permanent memory, **episodic memory** and **semantic memory** (Tulving, 1972).

Episodic memory refers to the memory a person has for temporally dated events and for relations between these events. For example, if you are asked to recall what clothes you wore yesterday, you are recalling information from episodic memory. Similarly, if you try to remember whether the Watergate break-in occurred before or after U.S. withdrawal from Vietnam, you are searching episodic memory.

Semantic memory, on the other hand, refers to the organized knowledge a person has about words, symbols, formulas, concepts, and rules. It includes the knowledge base necessary for the production and comprehension of language. It is the vast compendium of information that an individual knows about his or her world which is not tagged for a particular time. Included in semantic memory then are the various meanings of the term *hit,* the rules for carrying out long division, the order of letters in the spelling of *geography,* and the ingredients of the beef and corn casserole.

The distinction between episodic and semantic memory is a useful one and has helped clarify two important functions of memory: keeping an accurate record of particular experiences for an individual and making available a general knowledge base for carrying out the many cognitive functions of the individual. Until the early 1970s the bulk of work on memory was concerned with episodic memory. For example, the numerous studies on the variables influencing the recall of word lists were primarily studies of episodic memory.

With the publishing of Tulving's (1972) article, the popularity of studying the other function of memory increased dramatically, and the journals have been filled with studies on semantic memory. It should be noted, of course, that semantic memory is closely related to what was earlier called *concept structure* and the processes of concept identification.

There has been one basic difference in emphasis, however, between these earlier and later approaches to the study of semantic memory. The recent studies of semantic memory have been primarily concerned with structure—that is, with how the information stored in semantic memory is organized. As we discuss aspects of semantic memory in the remainder of this chapter, our interest will be primarily in this area. The earlier views of concepts and concept identification (see Chapter 8), were concerned with how we recognize and use concepts in new settings. Both approaches offer important insights into the study of the knowledge base of the individual.

Our discussion of episodic and semantic memory has implied that they are disjoint entities clearly distinguishable from one another. This is only partially true. Many memory aspects can be clearly placed under either one label or the other. Others, however, are not so easily classified. For example, is your memory for the gist of a prose passage you read two days ago an example of episodic or semantic memory? Is your reconstruction of a play you saw based on a particular episode or on your knowledge of how all plays unfold?

Perhaps we are unwise to characterize episodic and semantic memory as being two separate entities. Are they rather points on a continuum, with episodic memories having more clearly recognizable time tags whereas such tags have been lost from semantic memory?

At the present time we are unable to resolve this question of the separability of these two memories. Nevertheless, we are confident that the retention of new information is made easier by the employment of that knowledge which we already have. Of crucial concern then is how the knowledge that individuals have of their environment is organized. Depending on how this knowledge is structured it may be easy or difficult to relate new information to it.

MODELS OF PERMANENT MEMORY

Until the early 1970s psychologists were relatively uninterested in the organization of permanent memory. This neglect, if it can be labeled as such, was not intentional. Rather, psychologists were interested in the effects of factors such as instructions, word meaningfulness, and retrieval conditions on the ability of people to remember information they were given. As psychologists realized that the ability to remember was heavily influenced by the knowledge the person already had stored, interest increased in studying the organization and structure of this knowledge.

Since the investigation of this area is new and our knowledge is incomplete, it is not yet possible to choose among the various viewpoints of the structure of permanent memory which have emerged. Our intent is to sketch how each of the major viewpoints of the structure of permanent memory describes how that memory is organized and where necessary to note the problems that arise from taking one of these views.

Interestingly, as our knowledge of the structure of permanent memory has grown, the manner in which our everyday cognitive functioning is influenced by memory structure has become evident. Each of the views of permanent memory structure suggests some ways in which our everyday functioning is influenced. We will discuss these too as we move through the chapter.

A key issue that faces any viewpoint of the structure of permanent memory is whether the representation in memory is analogical or propositional.

Analogical versus Propositional Representation

Does the memory structure you have for representing your automobile reflect any of the properties of the automobile? Does it, for example, take you longer to mentally scan the car from front to back than from top to bottom? To the extent that our representations do mirror the world, they are called *analogical*. If the representation of our car were a complete visual image (as complete, say, as a photograph), we would have an example of an analogical representation.

We have characterized such a representational approach in the left half of Figure 4.1. This representation is like the real world in many ways. For example, it maintains the distance relationship between the car's length and height and maintains the relative size relationship among the windows. In addition, of course, information regarding shape and number of doors is also represented.

All representations, however, do not maintain information about the real world in such a literal form. Instead, representations can be composed of abstract statements that categorize the properties of the real-world situation. Thus the car may be stored as "red, two-door, sedan, Volkswagen . . ." as depicted in the right side of Figure 4.1. Such representations are called *propositional*.

There are advantages and disadvantages to both types of representational formats. Although

Figure 4.1 Examples of an analogical representation (left) and a propositional representation (right).

analogical representations seem more complete, they are in a form that makes them more difficult to communicate to others. Also, they seem wasteful of storage space, since they maintain information in so much detail. Propositional representations are in a form better organized for communication and less wasteful of storage space, but they are ill-suited to retain information of great variability—the myriad colors an auto may have, for example, or any other properties of a car which are easily misrepresented by categorical terms (e.g., long, dented, dirty).

The various views of the structure of permanent memory have handled this distinction between analogical and propositional representation in various ways. Some have argued for dual storage systems. Paivio (1975), for example, contended that any complete view of permanent memory must provide a system for representing both analogical and propositional information. His dual storage system calls for both an imagery-based system (analogical) and a language-based system (propositional).

Most other views have either ignored the issue or contended that a propositional representational system is a more general system and by appropriate extension can represent any type of information important to the organism.

Network Models of Semantic Memory

Most of us would agree that biologists, auto mechanics, and chess grand masters have different collections of knowledge about the world. One of the principal ways in which the knowledge of these specialists varies is in the concepts they have developed. The biologist is at ease in discussing mitosis and chlorophyll, the auto mechanic in discussing carburetors and transmissions, and the grand master in discussing opening moves and middle-game strategies. Such concepts are the basic building blocks of a person's knowledge of his or her world. In Chapters 7 and 8 we will discuss how such concepts are formed and used; here we will consider how they are interrelated and structured.

Several major classes or clusters of models of conceptual structure have been developed. The first major class has become known as **network models.** These models depict semantic memory as a vast collection, or network, of associated concepts. In some ways these network models of permanent memory are closely tied to a behavioral view of the human organism. As we stated in Chapter 1, behaviorists argue that basic associations or bonds are established between stimuli and responses through the process of learning. Thus in a behavioral view, the individual's knowledge of his or her world is also composed of a set of associations. However, the similarity between these views goes little further than this because the network models have been greatly elaborated from the early behavioral views as will become clear when we consider two major network models, the Collins and Loftus model and Anderson's ACT model.

A caution must be extended, however, before we continue our discussion of these models. Most current network models place prime importance on how the individual represents knowledge that can be transmitted via natural language. Thus the examples given to illustrate these models almost invariably involve concepts that are easily labeled, such as colors, animals, or furniture; or they involve relations, such as subject-predicate or relation-argument. But the reader should note that there exists much knowledge that is difficult if not impossible to convey linguistically, such as how to tie a shoelace or ride a bicycle. One test that must be used for any model of permanent memory is how well it represents the manner in which all types of human conceptual knowledge are organized, and it is this caution we must keep in mind as we turn to a consideration of the first major semantic network model.

The Collins and Loftus Network Model. The first and still influential view of the structure of permanent memory was proposed by Quillian in the late 1960s (Collins & Quillian, 1969; Quillian, 1968). It has recently been elaborated to handle some initial criticisms and some new empirical findings on semantic memory (Collins & Loftus, 1975). We will consider primarily this more recent view.

According to this view, semantic memory is best represented as a vast network of concepts interrelated to one another through a set of links or associations. A particular concept then refers to a node within this network. The various properties or characteristics of this concept are indicated by the types of links that relate this node to other nodes within the network. The links vary in kind; some links attach the concept to superordinate or subordinate concepts, while other links modify the concept or provide additional information about it. In addition, these links may be of different importance or criticality in determining the meaning of a concept. In other words, some properties of a concept are more important than others.

Because this description is so abstract, let us look at a particular example to make it clear. In Figure 4.2 we have diagrammed what a very small portion of semantic memory may look like. Think of this as a small subassembly of a much larger, more complex structure, much as the ignition system in an automobile is a subassembly of the entire automobile.

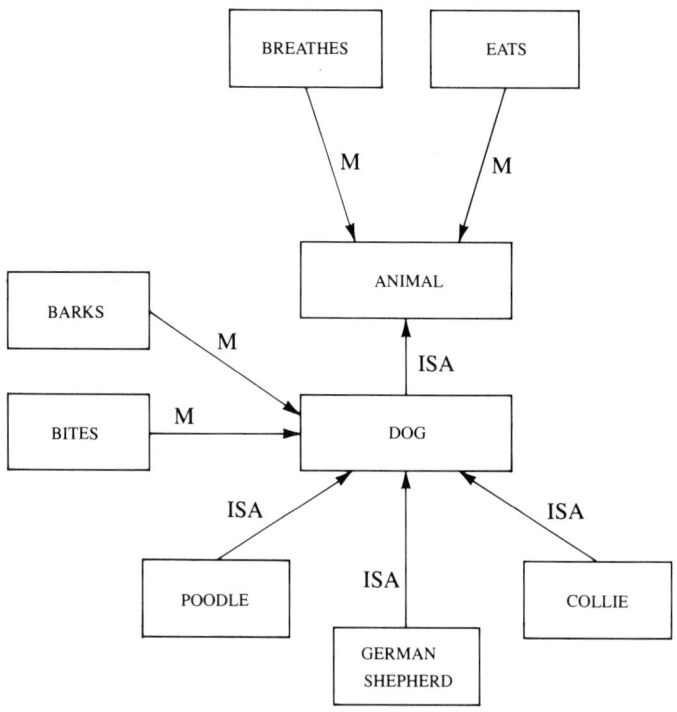

Figure 4.2 A schematic representation of the concept DOG in semantic memory. The labels *M* and *ISA* denote two different kinds of links: modifier links (M), which give properties of a concept, and superordinate links (ISA), which connect a concept to its superordinate. The length of lines indicates the degree of relatedness among concepts, a shorter line indicating a closer relationship.

The particular concept here is the node labeled DOG. We note that one link leading from this node is attached to the superordinate category of which dog is a member, ANIMAL. This type of superordinate link plays a large role in almost all concepts, according to Quillian. In Figure 4.2 superordinate links are marked by the label *ISA*. (Collie *is a* dog.) Other links may be referred to as *modifier* links or *properties*. For example, the links to the nodes of BARKS and BITES indicate characteristics of the concept DOG. These links are labeled by the letter *M* in the figure. All the various nodes linked to DOG provide the meaning of the concept DOG for the individual.

Some of these links, of course, are more essential to the meaning of DOG than are others; that is, they have high criteriality. The link to ANIMAL, for example, is an important one for the concept, whereas the links to POODLE, COLLIE, and BITES may be less essential to the meaning of DOG. Links of more importance or criteriality in this figure are shown by short lines. Remember that the set of nodes related to DOG is but a small subset of the entire semantic memory of the individual. Each node existing in this figure has similar sets of links that relate it to yet other nodes.

We have been discussing that part of the Collins and Loftus model which deals with what these theorists call the **semantic network.** This refers to the vast network of concepts interrelated to one another through various links. These links indicate how the various concepts are *semantically* related to one another. Although we have been labeling these nodes by particular words such as DOG and ANIMAL, they are in fact more abstract than words; for while many nodes correspond to a single word, others do not. For example, HAS FOUR LEGS, WHAT TO DO IF YOU SEE A GREEN LIGHT, and THE PARTICULAR HOUSE I OWN are also concepts that exist in the semantic network but are not labeled with a single word. The semantic network thus links abstract representations of our knowledge, some of which have simple labels and some of which do not.

In the Collins and Loftus model, the names of concepts are stored in a separate network called the **lexical network** or **dictionary.** This is a network organized principally by the phonemic properties of words, although it may also include orthographic (spelling) properties. This network also has links among the various nodes, although these links are related to sound and possibly spelling patterns. Of course, the lexical network is linked to the semantic network with links attaching each name node to one or more concept nodes. For example, the name node RIGHT is linked to at least two concept nodes—one dealing with directions (left, up, down) and the other with accuracy (wrong, correct).

Our description of the Collins and Loftus model thus far has emphasized its structural aspects. To complete our description we need to indicate what processes are involved in encoding, retrieving, and manipulating information in this model. Such processes play a crucial role in how the person adds information to that which is already in semantic memory and makes use of that which is already there to understand sentences and answer questions.

The major process used in carrying out these various tasks is what is called the *intersection search.* In this process when a question is asked of an individual—*Is a collie a bird?*—the individual enters the semantic network at the point of each concept named. Activation of nodes occurs outward from each concept node, first to all the nodes directly linked to that node and then to the nodes linked to these nodes and so on. This is referred to as the *spread of activation* (Collins & Loftus, 1975). An important assumption of the theory is that there is only a finite amount of activation that can occur within a limited time period.

Each time a node is activated in this process, a marker, or tag, is left indicating how it was activated—that is, from what node the activation started. At some point in this process the same node in the network will be activated from two different concepts. This is an intersection. The nature of this intersection is determined by checking the paths leading to it. Each path is then evaluated to determine if it is compatible with the original question, and a decision is reached. In the case of *Is a collie a bird?* the intersection will occur at the node of ANIMAL and not the node of BIRD. Since this is not consistent with what is stated in the question, the individual will answer *No*.

Investigations of Semantic Memory. In order to evaluate the Collins and Loftus model and also to set the stage for considering other models of semantic memory, we will look at some major empirical findings that need to be explained by any model of semantic memory. Most of these findings are from **reaction time studies,** a type of study which has produced extensive evidence about the structure of semantic memory.

REACTION TIME METHODOLOGY. Much of the research on memory is devoted to investigating people's ability to recall or recognize information that they have been given earlier. Good performance indicates a good memory under these conditions. In the process of studying the structure of permanent memory, however, this procedure is of little use, since we are not so much interested in what is recalled as in how it is recalled. Knowing how something is recalled gives us insight into the structure of permanent memory.

In the reaction time study, subjects are given a number of questions or statements to respond to as quickly as possible. For example, the following sentences have been given subjects in semantic memory studies: *Is a canary yellow? Do canaries fly? Do canaries eat? Is a banana a robin?* By carefully noting the time subjects take to respond to these sentences, we can determine whether some comparisons are made more quickly than others. Quick responses suggest that information is stored in a way that facilitates responding to the questions. For example, in the three sentences above dealing with canaries, Collins and Quillian (1969) found that the first sentence was responded to most quickly and the last, least quickly.

From these findings it was inferred that information about concepts such as CANARY is stored in a highly efficient hierarchical fashion. Information about canaries that is particular to canaries is stored most closely to CANARY, while information that is not unique is stored in concepts further up the memory hierarchy. This has been referred to as *cognitive economy,* since such a linking process economizes on storage space by requiring fewer links to represent the same information.

Such economy of storage can be seen most clearly by looking at the tree structure shown in Figure 4.3. In this representation, information about flying is not stored directly with CANARY but rather with the superordinate concept BIRD. Similarly, eating is stored with ANIMAL. The longer reaction time to respond to these latter questions arises then because the individual must go further in the memory hierarchy to verify the response to the question asked.

Although the particular interpretation of the data reported by Collins and Quillian has been disputed (see Box 4.1), their use of reaction time studies to investigate the structure of permanent memory exemplifies the techniques used in studying the structure of permanent memory. Reaction time studies have revealed several phenomena about semantic memory, the first known as the category size effect.

THE CATEGORY SIZE EFFECT. This effect refers to the consistent increase in reaction time in responding to questions of the type *Is X a Y?* as the size of category *Y* increases. For example, it is reliably found that subjects take more time in responding *True* to the question *Is a canary an animal?* than they do to the question *Is a canary a bird?* (Collins & Quillian, 1969; Meyer, 1970). The term **category size** arises from the fact that ANIMAL encompasses a larger number of items than does BIRD since birds are a subset of the ANIMAL category.

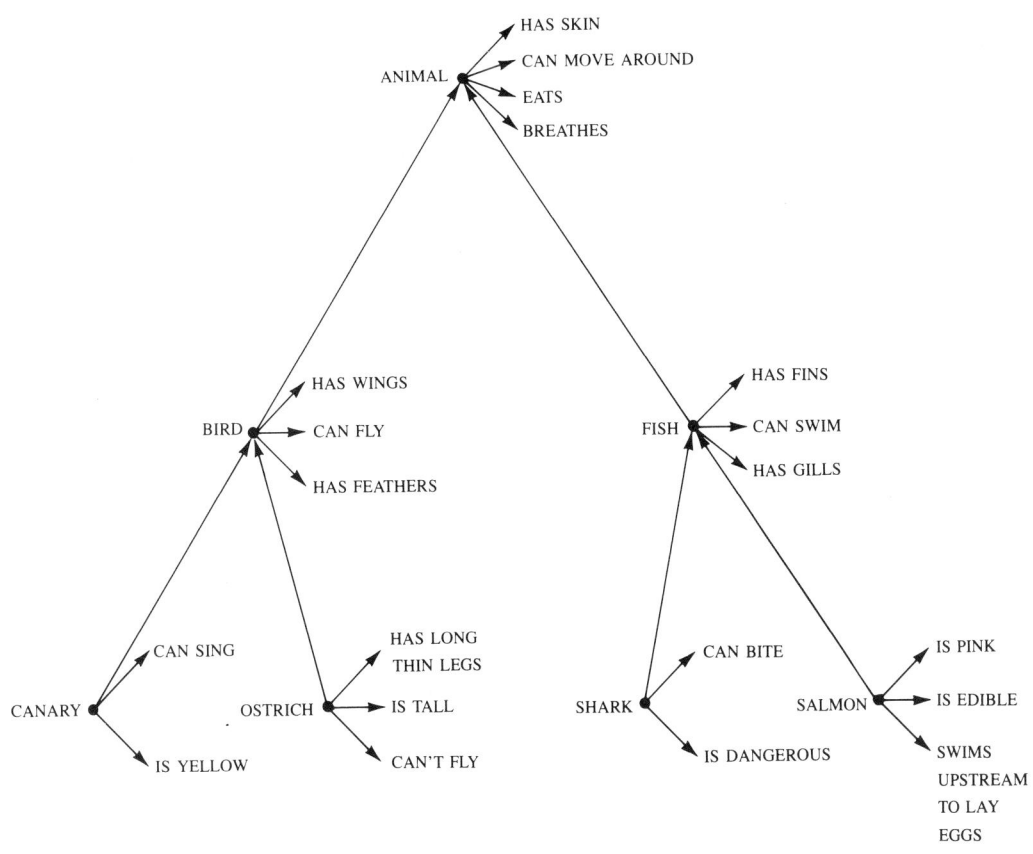

Figure 4.3 Hierarchical model of semantic memory. (From Collins & Quillian, 1969.)

Why does the category size effect occur? The explanation arising from the Collins and Loftus model is quite simple. Remember that in this model one of the links from each conceptual node is the superordinate link. Thus CANARY is linked to BIRD via its superordinate link. In addition, however, BIRD is linked to ANIMAL via a superordinate link. Thus for the individual to respond to the query *Is a canary a bird?*, only one link must be traversed. To respond to the query *Is a canary an animal?*, however, two links must be traversed. This can be seen graphically in Figure 4.3. Since we assume that traversing a link takes a set amount of time, it follows that the latter of these two questions is responded to more slowly than the first. There are, of course, other explanations of this effect, as we will see shortly.

THE TYPICALITY EFFECT. *Goose–bird, sparrow–bird*. Which pair of words is more closely related? Most people agree that the latter is. Would you expect that someone could more quickly respond to the question *Is a sparrow a bird?* than to the question *Is a goose a bird?* If

> **Box 4.1 COGNITIVE ECONOMY: PRO AND CON**
>
> Since the initial work on semantic memory by Collins and Quillian (1969), the concept of cognitive economy has intrigued researchers. It offers a partial solution to the tremendous information storage problem that would exist if each item in a category were linked to every property related to the category. For example, if we are to store with every type of bird every property related to birds, we would have to use immense amounts of storage space to store repetitious information. Thus if we have a storage system that stores the property of HAS FEATHERS only once, much storage space is saved.
>
> Two studies on the concept of cognitive economy are of special interest. Conrad (1972) challenged the notion of cognitive economy by providing evidence that the initial findings of Collins and Quillian are more parsimoniously explained by frequency of use rather than cognitive economy. She argued that subjects may have responded more slowly to sentences such as *Do canaries eat?* than to *Are canaries yellow?* because YELLOW is a higher frequency associate of CANARY than is EATS.
>
> Thus a true test of cognitive economy must use properties of concepts which are of the same frequency of association to both the subordinate and superordinate levels of the concept. When Conrad made such a test she found no significant differences in reaction time to properties referring to different superordinate levels. She concluded that the notion of cognitive economy is not necessary and that the effects Collins and Quillian found were probably due to frequency of association. End of scene one.
>
> Collins and Loftus (1975) carefully analyzed Conrad's procedures and concluded that a minor methodological change introduced in the Collins and Quillian procedure by Conrad may have accounted for her results. Unlike Collins and Quillian, Conrad gave the object concept to the subject 1 sec before she displayed the property concept. Thus she would show the subject the word *salmon* 1 sec before displaying the predicate of the sentence *has a mouth*. This time may have allowed the subject to bring the superordinates of SALMON (FISH and ANIMAL) to mind. Hence their properties of HAVING A MOUTH would have been activated, and any reaction time differences between superordinate levels would have been wiped out.
>
> Thus we see that the concept of cognitive economy cannot be ruled out. This series of studies indicates the extreme importance of careful methodological procedures if we are to make significant statements about semantic memory.

you answer *Yes*, you're correct. Researchers have come to call this phenomenon the **typicality effect.** Why does the typicality effect occur? What aspect of semantic memory structure makes it easier to respond to the one question than to the other?

Two reasons are put forth for this phenomenon by Collins and Loftus (1975). First, these authors claim that all the types of information that is relevant to two concepts and is gained in the process of an intersection search are combined in reaching a decision. If some information that is generated is consistent with a relationship and other information is not, a decision will be slowed. In our example of the *goose–bird* categorization, the fact that BIRD is superordinate to GOOSE provides evidence for the relationship. However, at the same time evidence is generated which indicates that geese are larger than most other birds, that geese are raised on farms whereas most other birds are not, and that geese are eaten by people. This information distinguishes geese from most other birds. Such conflicting information results in a slowing of response time.

Second, Collins and Loftus (1975) claimed that superordinate links differ in criteriality. Links that are commonly used *(sparrow–bird)* are of higher criteriality and hence are more accessible and easily generated than links that are rarely used. In Figure 4.4 we have sketched what the semantic network linking GOOSE, SPARROW, and BIRD may look like. This figure shows how the reaction time differences that have been reported may arise. Again, we caution that other interpretations of the typicality effect exist, some of which we will discuss below.

PRIMING EXPERIMENTS. What is the first word you can think of that is a fruit and begins with *P*? In tasks of this kind a subject must think of a word that has two properties: being in some category and having some characteristic. The subject's response is timed from the point at which the second property is mentioned. Does it make a difference whether the category is mentioned first or second? The answer appears to be yes. Freedman and Loftus (1971) found that subjects who were told the category first responded more quickly than those who were given the characteristic first.

Collins and Loftus (1975) explained this finding by noting that when a category (for example, FRUIT) is activated, the activation spreads to members of the category (APPLE, ORANGE, PEAR). However, since there is only a finite amount of activation that can occur within a given time period and since these concepts are closely related, this activation is spread over a small number of concepts, each of which is thus more ready to be reported. These concepts are said to be **primed.** However, if the characteristic (BEGINS WITH P) is presented first, the activation is spread over a much larger number of concepts, and hence it is less likely that the appropriate concept will be in a primed state ready to be output.

This differential priming effect is shown graphically in Figure 4.5. In each section of this figure the finite amount of activation is indicated by a total of 20 *X*s. Note that in 4.5b this activation is spread over many more links, resulting in less activation for any one of these links than for the concept in 4.5a. Thus the subject will be able to respond faster if the category FRUIT is activated first than if the letter P is activated first.

These investigations of category size, typicality, and priming are indicative of the types of studies carried out on semantic memory and suggest some phenomena that must be handled by any model of the structure of semantic memory. The Collins and Loftus model, of course, is not the only semantic network model. We turn now to another type of network model, which suggests a different picture of memory structure.

ACT: A Network Model of Human Cognition. One major approach to the study of human cognitive functioning is to simulate cognition with a computer. Such simulation usually begins with postulating some basic structures and processes for human cognitive functioning. By writing computer programs that have analogous structures and processes and testing them on the computer, a scientist can determine if the model of cognition he has proposed is a reasonable one.

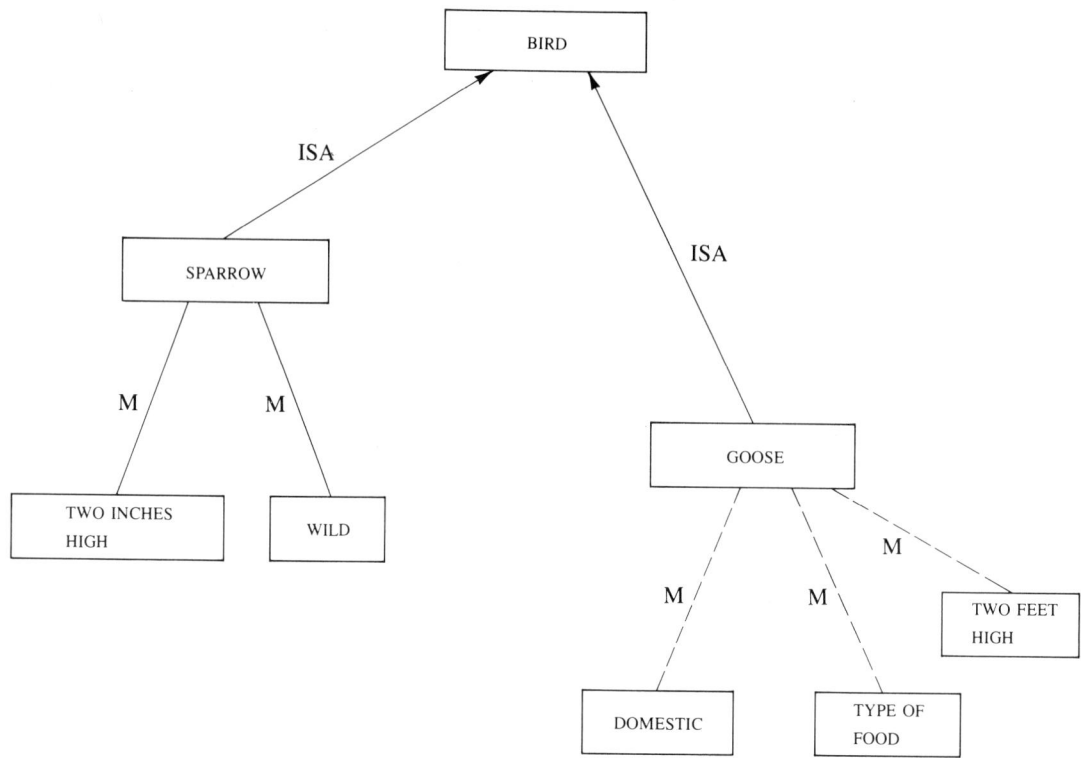

Figure 4.4 A portion of the semantic network linking GOOSE, SPARROW, and BIRD. The links drawn in solid lines indicate relationships that are consistent with most birds. Links drawn in dashed lines indicate relationships that are generally inconsistent with most birds. Such inconsistencies will result in slowed reaction times. Also, note the line connecting GOOSE with BIRD is longer than the one connecting SPARROW with BIRD, indicating a lower accessibility of that link and consequently slower reaction times.

We wish at this time to consider one such computer simulation model, because a prime component of this model is a network memory of the type we have been discussing.

This model, called *ACT,* was created by Anderson (Anderson, 1976; Anderson, Kline & Lewis, 1977) and is an elaboration of an earlier version of a simulation model called *HAM.* Anderson's ACT model is an extremely ambitious undertaking, because it attempts to create a single uniform theoretical framework to represent such diverse cognitive functions as language processing, memory, reasoning, and problem solving. While this model is far too complex for us to describe in this book, we do wish to present an overview of it in order to show how a network conception of semantic memory linked with some additional processes can present a comprehensive view of human cognitive functioning.

The **ACT model** proposes a basic distinction between two kinds of knowledge which humans have. One kind, called *declarative knowledge,*

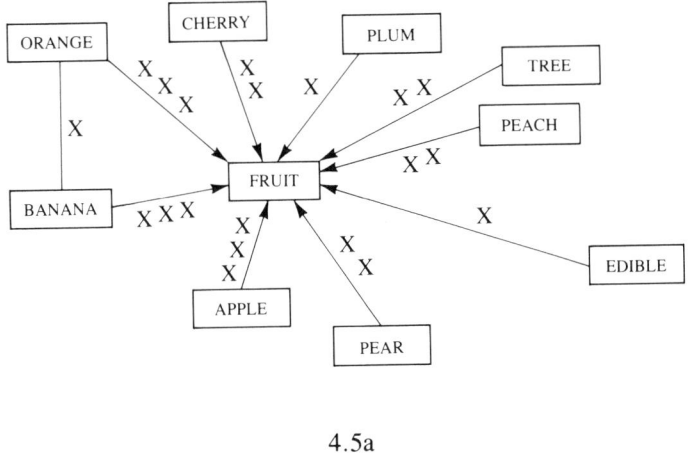

4.5a

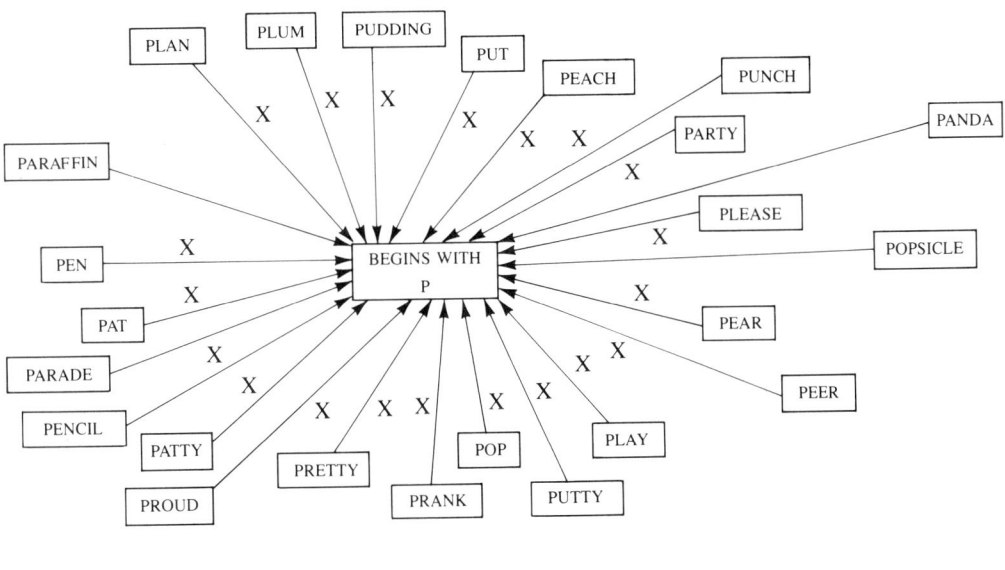

4.5b

Figure 4.5 A graphic representation of the priming effect. In each section of this figure there is the same amount of activation (indicated by the 20 *X*s), but in 4.5b in which the concept BEGINS WITH P is given first there are many more links that could be activated than in 4.5a in which the concept FRUIT is given first. Thus the links in 4.5b will be less accessible.

refers to the facts, concepts, and beliefs we have about our environment. For example, we know that George Washington was the first president, that solar energy refers to energy generated by the sun, and that ice cream is good. The second kind of knowledge, called *procedural knowledge*, refers to that which we know how to do. For example, we know how to tie a knot, how to ride a bicycle, or how to carry out long division. This basic distinction in knowledge types is reflected in the very structural foundation of the ACT model.

In ACT, all declarative knowledge is represented in a vast semantic network of labeled associations not unlike the one in the Collins and Loftus model. The basic unit of the network for ACT is the **proposition.** This is composed of two types of associations called *subject-predicate* and *relation-argument*. Examples of these two types of associations appear in Figure 4.6. In 4.6a the node in the network indicated by *X* stands for a proposition that uses a subject link *S* and a predicate link *P* to tie together the nodes for JOHN and GONE. Thus this proposition represents the meaning of the sentence *John is gone.*

In 4.6b we show a relation-argument association. The node in this figure, represented by *Y,* is linked to the node for LOVE by the relation link and to the node for KRISTIN by the argument link.

This association thus represents the concept of ALL LOVERS OF KRISTIN. These two basic types of associations are used in formulating complex propositions in the ACT system. An example of such a proposition is shown in 4.6c, which shows the proposition *Hannibal crossed the Alps.* Such propositions compose the basic semantic network of the ACT model.

As in the Collins and Loftus model, the various nodes and links in ACT are either in an active or inactive state, and activation can spread along the various links. In addition, the links within the propositional network have different strengths. The ACT model makes two additional assumptions that allow it to handle many of the temporary memory phenomena we discussed in Chapter 3. First, a maximum of ten nodes can be designated as being on an *active list (ALIST).* This list serves the functions of a working memory. Second, ACT postulates a *dampening* process, in which all activated links and nodes not on the ALIST are deactivated after a specified period of time. This is necessary to keep activation from continuously growing.

The aspect of the ACT model which makes it distinct from other network models is the postulation of a separate knowledge system to handle procedural knowledge. Anderson and his colleagues argue that such a separate system is

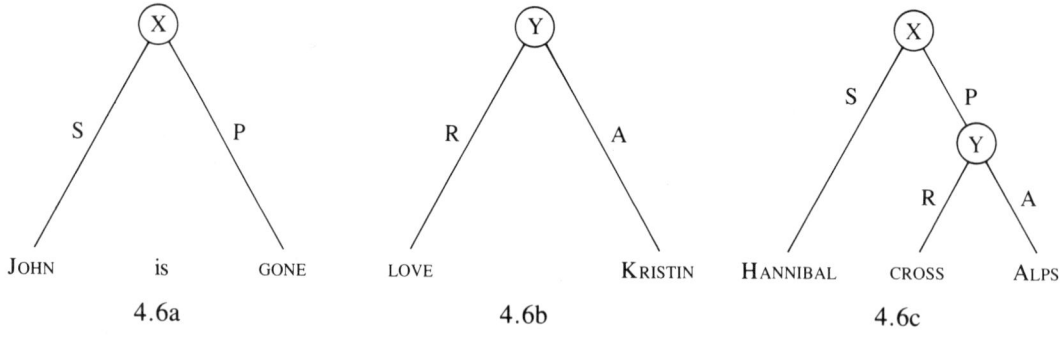

Figure 4.6 Examples of a subject-predicate association (4.6a) and a relation-argument association (4.6b). In 4.6c these two basic association types combine to form a complex proposition.

necessary because declarative and procedural knowledge are quite different in kind and function. For example, you may acquire declarative knowledge suddenly (Jane just got divorced), whereas you gain procedural knowledge gradually (your tennis backhand or chess game improves slowly). Declarative knowledge can be communicated to others, but procedural knowledge cannot. Procedural knowledge is used over and over again in much the same way, such as for generating sentences. Declarative knowledge, on the other hand, may be subject to many different uses. The fact that the United States is a democracy may be involved in discussions of politics, election procedures, the history of a nation, or discussions of true and false ideas.

The key component of the procedural knowledge system is the *production*. A production is composed of a *condition-action* pair. The condition specifies a set of features that must exist in the activated portion of memory. If these features exist, a particular action is carried out which results in a change in memory. Each production has a particular strength associated with it, and this strength is increased each time the production is carried out.

ACT postulates a two-stage process in determining which productions are chosen. During the first stage, all productions are partially tested against memory. All productions that make it through this screening process are placed on an APPLY LIST. During the second stage, the productions on this APPLY LIST are tested completely to see if their conditions are met. The one that best fits the memory conditions is executed, and through the ensuing action new memory structures are built. In this manner, changes in the knowledge base are brought about.

From our description it can be seen that ACT is a detailed and complex model of human cognitive functioning. However, it has also been a fruitful model. By postulating both an underlying network of concepts to represent declarative knowledge and a production system to represent procedural knowledge, the model is capable of handling a wide array of cognitive functions. It has been applied to various aspects of language, memory, inferential reasoning, and induction. Although it is not without its difficulties, the model shows that a network conception of memory can be the foundation of complex human cognitive functioning.

Set Theory Model of Semantic Memory

Not all views of the structure of semantic memory contend that memory is a vast network of interconnected associations. One alternative view, the **set theory model** put forth by Meyer (Meyer, 1970; Meyer & Schvaneveldt, 1976), contends that semantic memory is best conceptualized as sets of attributes, such as the set of all attributes of a poodle or of a cat.

This model has not been as extensively elaborated as some of the network models, but it has been used to explain some interesting types of data. Probably most well known are studies by Meyer and his colleagues which tested the ability of subjects to assess the truth value of various logical assertions—that is, to determine their truth or falsity. The assertions were of the form *All S are P* or *Some S are P,* where *S* and *P* refer to various categories. A specific example will illustrate these and test your predictive powers. Which of the following sentences can be evaluated for truth value more quickly: *All females are writers* or *Some females are writers*? If you chose the second sentence, you are correct. But why? What aspects of semantic memory structure allow someone to respond more quickly to that type of assertion?

Using a set-theoretical model of semantic memory, Meyer (1970) contended that such results occur because the subject must go through a two-stage verification process. In the first stage the subject determines what sets overlap with the *P* category. If any of the sets generated in this manner overlap with the *S* category, there is a match. In the example above (females and writers), such a determination would result in some overlap of the sets. Such a determination provides sufficient evidence to make a decision in the case of *Some females are writers,* and the verification process for this assertion can be terminated at this point.

However, if the assertion is of the type *All S are P,* the second stage of the process must be executed. This stage necessitates a determination that every attribute of the *P* category is an attribute of the *S* category—for example, every attribute of writers is an attribute of females. If the determination is *Yes,* the subject can respond positively to the assertion; if the determination is *No,* the subject can respond negatively to the assertion. In any event, the carrying out of the second stage of the process takes additional processing time, which makes the overall response to assertions of the type *All S are P* slower.

A set theory model of the type described here is capable of explaining the category size effect described earlier. Remember that the larger the category *Y* is in statements of the type *All X are Y,* the slower is the reaction time. In the set theory explanation, the larger that category *Y* becomes, the less overlap it has with category *X* and the longer it is likely to take to determine if any members of *X* are also members of *Y*. Thus one may have to search longer to find common members between CANARY and ANIMAL than between CANARY and BIRD.

Meyer and Schvaneveldt (1976) have discussed some interesting data in support of the set theory model which provide additional insights into our understanding of semantic memory. In general, these data may be summarized in this manner: If two categories have extensive overlap (that is, they have many common instances and attributes), both positive and negative benefits may accrue to the individual, depending on the tasks demanded of that person. If, for example, subjects are shown the word *bread* and then shortly thereafter shown the word *butter,* they can more quickly recognize the second item than if the second item is unrelated *(tree).*

If the task situation is changed, however, performance may be hindered by having closely related items. For example, subjects find it more difficult to evaluate the false assertion *All stones are rubies* than they do *All clouds are wrists.* The extensive overlap among the sets in the first assertion makes it more difficult to evaluate the assertion.

From these data it is apparent that the structure of semantic memory interacts with the types of tasks we are asked to carry out. The very aspect of memory structure which allows us to respond effectively in the first task described above impedes our responding in the second.

The Feature Comparison Model

A variation of the set theory model which has commanded considerable attention is the **feature comparison model** created by Smith, Shoben, and Rips (1974). As in other set theory models, the feature comparison model postulates that concepts are stored in semantic memory in the form of lists or sets of features relevant to the concept at hand. The principal characteristic that this model adds is to distinguish between features that are important and crucial to the meaning of the concept—the *defining features*—and those that are appropriate but less important—the *characteristic features.* For example, with the concept BIRD, the features of HAS WINGS, BREATHES, and HAS FEATHERS are defining features since all birds show these. Features such as FLIES, BUILDS NESTS IN TREES, and EATS WORMS are often but not always related to BIRD and are thus less important to the meaning of the concept; they are thus characteristic features.

The distinction between defining features and characteristic features has allowed Smith et al. to explain many of the semantic memory phenomena we have discussed above. For example, both the category size effect and typicality effect are handled easily by this model. To see that such is the case, let us consider the processes involved in making the categorization decisions involved in a task such as answering the question *Is a robin a bird?*

According to Smith et al., two stages are involved in such decisions. These two stages are shown graphically in Figure 4.7. In the first stage, comparisons are made among both defining and characteristic features of both categories. If there is extensive overlap of these features, the individual responds *Yes* to the question. If there is minimal overlap, the individual responds *No* to the question. In either case the task is completed. However, if there is a moderate amount of overlap, the individual must proceed to a second stage in order to make a decision. During this stage the comparisons are made only among the defining features of the categories. The outcome of these comparisons determines the *Yes/No* decision. Any task that demands involvement of the second stage of this process will require longer reaction times.

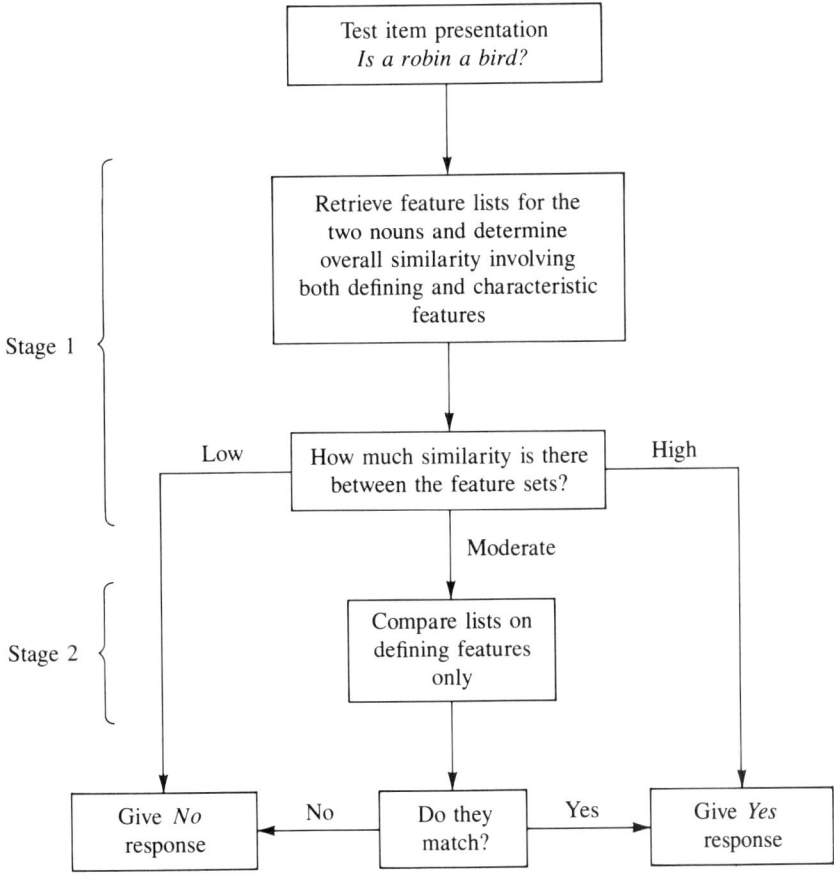

Figure 4.7 A graphic representation of the two processing stages involved in the feature comparison model for answering questions such as *Is a robin a bird?* (From Smith, Shoben, & Rips, 1974.)

Now consider the category size effect. The data show that it takes longer for individuals to decide that a robin is an animal than to decide that a robin is a bird. Why should this be the case? Smith et al. assume that features of ROBIN are more likely to be similar to its immediate superordinate, BIRD, than to the more remote category of ANIMAL. Hence Stage 2 processes are less likely to be needed in the first case than in the second, and reaction time will be faster.

A similar argument holds for the typicality effect. In this case people decide more quickly that a robin is a bird than they do that a chicken is a bird. This is explained by the fact that both ROBIN and CHICKEN will show the defining characteristics of BIRD, but ROBIN will show a greater number of characteristic features of BIRD than will CHICKEN. Therefore it is more likely in the chicken and bird task that the individual will have to move to a Stage 2 comparison on defining features in order to make a decision. Again, this would result in slower reaction times.

Thus it may be seen that the feature comparison model nicely accounts for these effects. It can also account for other types of semantic memory data (Loftus & Loftus, 1976). The model is not without its difficulties, however. The principal one stems from the fact that the distinction between defining and characteristic features is a troublesome one. Are people truly aware of the defining features of categories? Could you, for example, list the defining features of mammals, furniture, or boxes? People generally have a difficult time identifying such features.

In addition, critics have asked if defining features really exist for concepts. Collins and Loftus (1975) point out that a bird does not stop being a bird if it loses its feathers or its wings. Does a table have to have four legs, three legs, or for that matter, any legs? Such concerns raise questions about the desirability of basing a memory model on such a distinction.

To this point in our discussion of the structure of semantic memory, we have concerned ourselves with models that emphasize the storage of linguistic information. Most of us have had occasions when it seems as if we have information stored in quite complete visual detail, in what is frequently called images. Is there evidence that images are stored in a manner that is different from what we have already discussed? That is the subject of our next section. As you read this section, keep in mind our earlier distinction between analogical and propositional information storage.

Images and Semantic Memory

Imagine for a moment the scene that you see from the back window of your house or apartment. Can you "see" the garden, the dog house, your neighbors' back door? Most people find this task easy to do. Describing how we do it, however, has proved to be a very difficult task for students of human memory. In particular, theorists have puzzled over what type and structure of information we have stored which allows us to do this type of task.

In our discussion of the structure of memory, we have described theories that are verbally based. That is, memory structure theories such as network theories, set theories, and feature comparison theories are grounded in an abstract, verbally oriented base. Can such theories account for our ability to remember information such as the scene described above? Some researchers feel they cannot.

Perhaps the most vocal critic is Paivio (1971, 1974, 1975), a Canadian psychologist, who has done extensive work on imagery and its impact on memory. There have been two major thrusts from the work on imagery. One has been to study the manner in which instructions to generate and relate images of words can improve our memory for the words. The second has been to determine if a different set of memory structures are involved in the representation of images than are involved in the representation of other types of information. We will consider the first of these topics in the next chapter and take up the second one here.

Paivio (1974) argued that it is necessary to postulate two separate memory structures to represent figural information (images) and verbal information. In his **dual-coding model** of the structure of permanent memory, he labels the representational system that handles verbal information the *verbal system* and the one that handles figural information the *imagery system*. These systems are thought to be independent of one another, yet partially interconnected so that activity in one system may generate activity in the other.

Both systems are thought to be highly organized, although in different ways. The imagery system organizes elementary images into more complex structures so that output from the system has a spatial character. The verbal system organizes linguistic and verbal units into structures that are sequentially ordered. Paivio also contends that both systems are not static systems but rather are capable of transforming and manipulating information to meet various task demands. This will become more apparent when we consider some studies testing the dual-coding model.

Three important psychological implications arise from this conceptualization of the structure of permanent memory (Paivio, 1974). First, it is not necessary for the functioning of either of these systems to enter consciousness, although either may. Thus the experience we have of an image is simply the conscious expression of the activity of the image system, but it is not necessary for the system to operate.

Second, the independence of the two systems implies that there are types of information represented in one system that are not found in the other. For example, the appearance of the building in which you are now sitting has probably never been coded in the verbal system.

Finally, activity in one of the two systems may go on and interfere relatively little with activity going on simultaneously in the other system. On the other hand, carrying out different activities involving the same representational system is likely to be very difficult and lead to problems for the individual. Some recent experiments by Brooks, which we will discuss shortly, speak directly to these activity notions.

The fact that Paivio envisions the systems as interconnected is important in that it allows for some interchange between the systems. For instance, images can be connected with words and words with images, although these interconnections are limited in number.

Before we consider empirical evidence speaking to the validity of the dual-coding system, we need to discuss an issue related to imagery-based systems. The terms *image* and *imagery* are frequently interpreted in a very literal fashion. Such an interpretation suggests that images are almost complete photographs of the environment, stored in a rather raw, unprocessed state. This view is sometimes called the *literal copy* view of imagery. Such a view has come under extensive attack (and rightly so) and has been rejected by most researchers and theoreticians (for example, see Pylyshyn, 1973). Two studies will serve to illustrate this criticism.

If imagery is similar to a mental photograph, then images of hidden objects should be less effective in aiding memory than images of nonhidden objects. Neisser and Kerr (1973) tested this notion in a study with three different imagery conditions. In one condition, the subjects were asked to mentally picture two objects interacting with one another—for example, a harp sitting on the torch of the Statue of Liberty. This was called the pictorial condition.

In a second condition, the concealed condition, the subjects were to imagine a scene in which one object was hidden by the other—for example, a harp hidden inside the torch of the Statue of Liberty. Finally, in a third condition, the separate condition, the subjects were to imagine a scene in which the objects were not spatially close—for example, looking from one window to see a harp and from another window to see the Statue of Liberty.

Neisser and Kerr found that the separate condition, in which the objects were not interacting, led to the poorest performance. The crucial comparison, however, was between the concealed and pictorial conditions. If images are mental photographs, then the concealed condition should be worse than the pictorial one since the two objects cannot be represented by one photograph. Neisser and Kerr found that there was no difference between the concealed and pictorial conditions; they were both equally better than the separate condition. This finding provides support for the contention that images are not mental photographs but involve some type of different representational system.

A more recent study by Jonides, Kahn, and Rozin (1975) also indicates that the mental photograph model is inaccurate. These researchers compared congenitally blind college subjects with normal college students in a study involving mental images. They found that the blind subjects' performance was also improved by imagery instructions, suggesting that imagery instructions improve performance even for subjects who have never been able to see. It is apparent then that however the imagery system works, it is not simply a mental camera.

Nevertheless, there is significant evidence that suggests that the verbal and proposition-based memory systems discussed above have considerable difficulty accounting for some imagery system findings. Several studies converge on this point.

In an insightful study, Brooks (1968) asked his subjects to do an interesting combination of tasks. Subjects were given either sentences or line diagrams to remember and were then asked to perform different mental tasks on the remembered material. Brooks then measured the amount of time it took his subjects to respond. The tasks occurred under four different conditions. First, they were given a sentence to remember—for example, *A bird in the hand is not in the bush*—and then were told to go through the sentence mentally word by word saying *Yes* if a word was a noun and *No* if it was not. Second, they were given the sentence and a sheet of paper with several rows each showing the letters *Y* and *N* (yes and no). In this case the subject was to point to the correct letter indicating whether the word in the sentence was a noun *(Y)* or not *(N)* (see Figure 4.8).

In the other two conditions, Brooks had his subjects remember a diagram and respond about

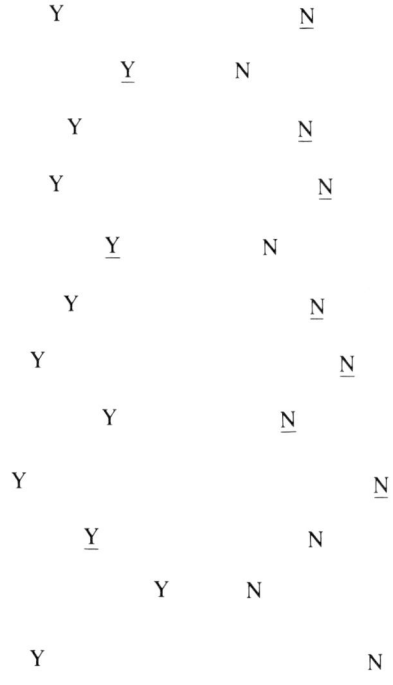

Figure 4.8 An example of an output sheet for the pointing condition in the Brooks (1968) experiment. The letters that have been underlined indicate the ones that would have been pointed to for the sentence *A bird in the hand is not in the bush*.

its characteristics either orally or by pointing to a set of letters. Brooks found that subjects took more time to respond whenever they were required to respond in a mode similar to the one in which they were remembering the material. For example, if a subject was remembering a sentence and had to respond orally whether each word was a noun, his performance was much slower than it was if he simply pointed to a letter (Y or N) indicating that the word was a noun or not a noun. Similarly, if a subject was remembering a diagram, she could respond more quickly orally than she could by pointing to letters indicating the characteristics.

Apparently subjects were using different memory modes to represent the verbal and spatial information. Performance was hindered when the same systems were activated to respond to the questions as were used to store the information. These results provide support for Paivio's contention that there are two separate representational systems and that these systems are able to operate relatively independently of one another.

There is an important practical implication in findings such as these. If we carry out tasks that demand multiple use of one type of representational system, we may create great difficulties for ourselves. For example, if we are making heavy use of our spatial capabilities in guiding a car down a winding road, it is possible that visualizing the plays from a football game on the radio may result in a catastrophic outcome (Baddeley, Grant, Wight, & Thomson, 1975).

Kosslyn, Ball, and Reiser (1978) also provide interesting evidence that appears to necessitate a type of analogical representational system such as the one described by Paivio. This evidence, which is difficult for a propositional system to explain, is described in Box 4.2.

Box 4.2 SCANNING VISUAL IMAGES

When we visualize an object, do we use processes similar to those we use in seeing a real-world object? Is an image-based representation of an object different from a propositional representation of that same object? By using reaction time methodology, Kosslyn, Ball, and Reiser (1978) suggested some answers to these questions.

Kosslyn and his colleagues presented subjects the map shown in Figure 4.9. After having their subjects memorize the map, they told them to image the map and to focus their attention on one of the objects on the map (e.g., the lake or the hut). Then these subjects were told to look for a particular object and indicate whether or not that object was also on the map. The properties varied in distance from the point of focus. Thus if the subject was focusing on the hut, the grass was a greater distance away than was the tree. Some properties mentioned by the experimenter were not part of the map (e.g., a bench) although they sensibly could have been included. If the subject decided the property was on the map, he or she was asked to scan to the property (in a straight line) as quickly as possible and was to push a button upon arrival there. The reaction time from the moment at which the object was mentioned until the subject pushed the response button was recorded.

The results of the study are seen in Figure 4.10 which plots the distance between the two mentioned objects against the reaction time to reach the

Figure 4.9 The fictional map used by Kosslyn, Ball, and Reiser (1978).

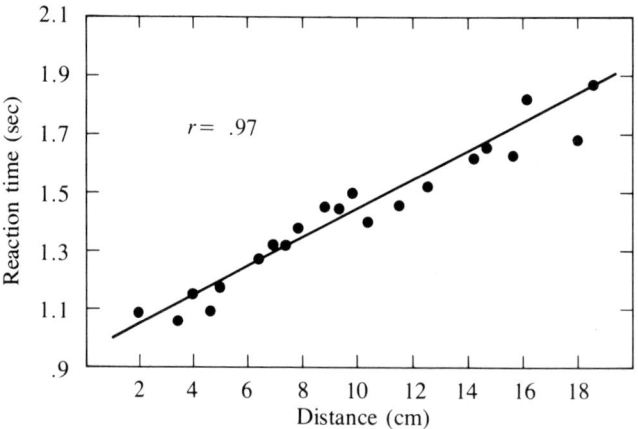

Figure 4.10 Reaction times to scan between all pairs of locations on the fictional map used by Kosslyn, Ball, and Reiser (1978).

second object. As can be seen, the greater the distance the object to be verified was from the focus object, the longer it took for subjects to reach the second object. This suggests that subjects were scanning their representation much as they would scan a real-world object. It appears that the subjects' representation of the map embodied distance relationships in much the same way these relationships are embodied in the visual perception of a picture.

In a follow-up experiment, Kosslyn and his colleagues attempted to rule out a nonimagery interpretation of the previous results. In this experiment they again asked their subjects to focus on a given location on the map and then judge whether a second named object was on the map. However, the subjects in this experiment were not required to make use of their images in making their judgments. They were simply to reach their decisions as quickly as possible. If the decisions in the prior study were made by scanning through an abstract propositional list, the same pattern of results should have occurred in this study. In fact, the pattern was different. Subjects' decisions in this second study were not influenced by the distance between the objects. Apparently distance only influences performance when subjects scan their images. If they use another representation system, the distance effects may not be found.

These data thus suggest that imaginal and proposition-based representation systems may indeed be different from one another and may be used in different ways in different tasks.

A number of other studies suggest that people can store figural information for either brief or long time periods. For example, Shepard and Metzler (1971) found that people can hold figural information for brief periods and can manipulate it mentally to respond to queries about the information.

Frost (1972) provided evidence that people can store visual representations in permanent memory. Frost gave her subjects simple line drawings of a number of common objects. It was possible to classify the objects either in terms of semantic categories (e.g., there were four animals, four vehicles) or in visual forms (the pictures occurred in various orientations). Frost told some of her subjects to expect a recognition test and others to expect a recall test. All of the subjects were actually asked to recall. Those subjects who expected to recall grouped their recall according to semantic categories. Those who expected recognition grouped their recall both in semantic and shape (orientation) clusters. Apparently these subjects had stored the visual information and were using it in their recall of the objects.

There is thus extensive evidence that figural and verbal information are handled differently. This is seen by the differential interference effects of figural and verbal materials shown by Brooks, the differential reaction time effects reported by Kosslyn et al., and the different recall patterns exhibited by Frost's subjects.

Even with this evidence, however, it is not yet clear whether the *manner* in which we represent visual information is fundamentally different from how we represent verbal information. It is possible that the underlying representational system is a single system but that *different cognitive processes* are applied to this base under different task circumstances. It will probably be some time before such questions can be answered. J.R. Anderson

(1978) has argued that it is not possible to determine from behavioral data whether we represent our environment on an imaginal or propositional basis. He suggests that the best we may be able to do is to determine that there is more than one code, but that we will probably not be able to determine the nature of the codes. Whether this contention is accurate remains to be seen.

CONCLUSION

With this we close our discussion of the structure of semantic memory—at least temporarily. It is apparent that several different views exist about how best to conceptualize the structure of semantic memory. Some believe semantic networks are most powerful; others claim set-theoretical or feature comparison models are better; still others suggest a need for differential representational procedures for verbal and nonverbal information. The empirical evidence as yet cannot provide us with a definitive choice among the available alternatives.

These are not the only alternatives, however. Within the past few years another major view of the structure of semantic memory has arisen based on the concept of schema—a view we will need to discuss in order to complete our own view of the structure of semantic memory. But first we will need to develop two other aspects of human cognitive functioning: how we use the structures discussed in this chapter to store and retrieve information (Chapter 5) and how humans understand and produce sentences, the area of language (Chapter 6). These two chapters will provide the context for a consideration of how people process complex materials such as prose passages. It is in this setting that we will return to our consideration of the structure of semantic memory and elaborate a schema-based model of this structure.

5 The Permanent Retention of New Information

Storage Processes in Permanent Memory
    Encoding Processes in Permanent Memory
    The Role of Organization in Permanent Memory
        Mediation
        Imagery
        Organization in Free Recall
            Material-induced Organization
            Subject-imposed Organization
        Mnemonics
            "One Is a Bun, Two Is a Shoe . . ."
            Method of Loci
            Substitution
            Stories
        Intentionality and Memory
    Retrieval of Information from Permanent Memory
        Encoding Specificity
        Processes of Memory Retrieval
            Recall and Recognition
            Reconstruction
Conclusion

James crouched behind the large pillar as the two guards strolled by. The hallway was bleakly lighted by bare lightbulbs spaced every 40 feet. The large metal doors on each cell had two small openings, one at the bottom for food, the other at the top for the guards to check the prisoners. Low murmurs could be heard from some of the cells with an occasional scream disturbing the relative quiet. The long hot spell had raised the temperature of the prison into the 90s, and even the relatively cool night had not lowered the temperature more than a few degrees. A stench of urine and diarrheic bowel movements pervaded the air.

As James waited for the guards' footsteps to fade away, a rush of memories came back to him. It had been three years ago that he had escaped from this hell hole. Even so, the memories were vivid. He remembered his cell mate Mark, six feet two inches tall but weighing only 110 pounds when he died from his last beating. Tim also came to mind; Tim had lost an arm to gangrene when the guards had slammed one of the steel doors on his hand, severing two fingers. They had refused to call in a doctor. He remembered Jacob, who would whimper like a dog when the guards would come to get him.

But he could also remember the number of steps from his cell to the interrogation room and the specific layout of the cells and how they were arranged in relation to the few exits from the prison. He remembered spending hours piecing together a large number of tidbits of information into a coherent map of the prison. Every time he was allowed to go a different route to his cell, he would take this new information and add to his mental map—gradually extending it to cover the whole prison wing. Unfortunately, some parts of his mental map of the prison were no longer so clear. Certain details stuck out but others had faded. He hoped he would be able to reconstruct the details when he needed them.

Suddenly James's attention snapped back to the present. The hallway was quiet. It was time to move. If he were to be successful in freeing John, the next few minutes would be crucial.

This rather brief episode depicting a rescue attempt displays several facets of permanent memory which we will introduce in this chapter. Let us detail a few of these. On a superficial level, of course, our story suggests that we can remember in some detail particular episodes we have experienced in the past. However, it is clear that some of the details of our memories may disappear with time and will have to be filled in or reconstructed by inference at a later time. Our story also suggests that our memories of the past may be triggered by the reinstatement of the conditions in which we first experienced those events. Thus James experienced a flood of memories in returning to the prison. Finally, our story makes it clear that permanent memory involves a lot of effort and processing on our part if we are to remember. We must organize and structure new information and compare it to that which we already know if we are to remember at some later time.

Generally the issues we have mentioned here can be divided into two major categories: the processes involved in the *storage* of new information in memory and the processes involved in the *retrieval* of information from memory. In the remainder of this chapter we will develop these two aspects of permanent memory in some detail.

Before we begin considering these two issues, we should comment on the type of studies we will be discussing in this chapter. For the most part we will be dealing with studies that have focused on memory for words and word lists. The voluminous research on these materials has been extremely fruitful in helping us develop a detailed and useful conception of permanent memory. This research has also revealed some fundamental characteristics and phenomena of permanent memory.

More recently, however, psychologists have begun working in earnest on memory for more complex types of stimulus materials—namely, sentences and prose passages. These materials have allowed us to explore how the context in which words and sentences are set influences how we process verbal information. This work has helped us refine our view of the storage and retrieval of new information in permanent memory. We will take up a detailed consideration of the memory for prose materials in Chapter 7 after we have discussed language and language processing.

STORAGE PROCESSES IN PERMANENT MEMORY

At the beginning of Chapter 4 we mentioned that a key aspect involved in permanently remembering new information is in relating that new information to knowledge the individual already has. This is not a new idea.

In the nineteenth century a renowned educator, Frances Herbart, argued that new ideas are retained by relating them to one's *apperceptive mass* (Murphy & Kovach, 1972). Although the concept of apperceptive mass was not clearly delineated, it appears to refer to the individual's accumulated knowledge of his or her environment. In recent years this view has become increasingly popular among psychologists interested in human memory. In fact, it has become the very heart of theories of human memory, whether these theories are based on studies of memory for words (Craik & Tulving, 1975) or for prose materials (Anderson, 1977).

While broad general statements of this kind are useful in establishing a framework in which to approach permanent memory, they do little to help us understand specifically how memory works. To do this we must become far more specific about what it means to relate new information to old knowledge. Current theory and research differentiate two major ways of conceptualizing how the new is related to the old. First, new information may be *directly related to that which is stored, with the current context in which the information is set being of little importance.* For example, a person may be asked to indicate whether each word in a list is a noun or a verb or has the letters *e* or *k* in it. In such tasks the individual is relating each word to what he knows, but the nature of the other words in the list is of little importance. Such noncontextual relating of new information to old we call **encoding** (Tulving, 1972).

The second major way in which new and old information are related *makes extensive use of the context in which the new information is presented.* For example, if the word *robin* is on a list composed of fish, furniture, domestic animals, and other birds, it will probably be more easily remembered than if it appears on a list of unrelated words. When the context plays a key role in memory we are studying **organization.**

You should be aware, of course, that the distinction between these two ways of relating information is not always sharp and clear; some studies seem to fit as well under one label as the other. This should not be cause for worry, however, since it is likely that the two lie on a continuum.

Encoding Processes in Permanent Memory

In our daily lives we are constantly bombarded by an immense amount of environmental stimulation. The words on a movie marquee, snatches of conversation from passersby, and a to-be-remembered grocery list provide grist for our sensory and perceptual mechanisms. As we saw in Chapter 2, a number of operations are carried out on this information as we attend to and perceive it. These operations include analysis of structural, acoustic, and semantic features of the stimuli. The outcome of these operations includes not only our attention to or perception of these events, however; it also includes an ability to retain or remember these events. In effect, it seems that each of these processes leaves a residue, called a *trace,* which enables us to remember the event (Craik & Lockhart, 1972).

A variety of studies suggest that the types of traces remaining after these encoding operations differ systematically in their ability to support memory. Perhaps the most compelling of these studies are those that make use of *orienting tasks.* These are tasks in which subjects are asked to carry out certain activities as they are presented lists of words or sections of prose materials. For example, a subject may be asked to indicate whether a given word has any *e*'s in it, whether it rhymes with *door,* or whether it is a pleasant or unpleasant word. Such studies allow us to view the impact of processing certain features of a word on the ability to remember that word at a later time.

Hyde and Jenkins (1973), for example, presented lists of words to their subjects and asked them to perform one of five orienting tasks on the words. These tasks were (1) to rate each word for its pleasantness or unpleasantness, (2) to estimate the frequency of use of each word, (3) to determine whether each word had the letters *e* and *g* in its spelling, (4) to determine the word's part of speech (e.g., noun, verb, adjective), and (5) to determine whether a given word did or did not fit in a sentence frame such as *It is _____* .

The first two orienting tasks require that subjects pay attention to the meaning of the word. To determine whether a word is pleasant or not, the subjects must consider its meaning. To determine whether a word is frequently used, they must determine its meaning and ask how often they have seen or heard that particular word.

The third task is a graphic one, which does not necessitate that the subjects consider the meaning of the word. They need only look at the form of the word to determine if it contains the letters *e* and *g*.

The last two tasks are most appropriately called syntactic tasks, for they ask the subjects to respond to the word in terms of different syntactic constraints. In neither of these tasks is it necessary for the subjects to consider the meaning of the term.

Hyde and Jenkins found that the subjects' ability to recall the words was a direct function of the type of orienting task. If they performed either of the semantic tasks, recall was as good as a control group told to remember the words and better than the recall from those subjects carrying out any of the nonsemantic orienting tasks. It is apparent that the type of encoding process used to relate the words to semantic memory dramatically altered the ability of the subjects to recall the words.

In other words, the memory traces left after carrying out semantic encoding operations better supported recall efforts than the traces left from the graphic and syntactic encoding operations. A number of other studies on word lists using a variety of orienting tasks have reported similar results (Craik & Tulving, 1975; Hyde & Jenkins, 1969; Till & Jenkins, 1973; Walsh & Jenkins, 1973).

An interesting variation of the orienting task paradigm gives further insight into how memory encoding operations may work. Rogers, Kuiper, and Kirker (1977) asked subjects to carry out both semantic and nonsemantic orienting tasks on a list of adjectives and found results similar to those described above. However, they also had subjects rate whether each of the presented adjectives described themselves. This last task resulted in by far the best performance of all the orienting tasks, suggesting that self-reference can function as an extremely effective way of relating incoming information to stored knowledge. Rogers et al. argued that the *self* is a very well organized concept or schema, which provides a rich place for us to relate new information to old.

Arkes, Schumacher, and Gardner (1976) extended the orienting task paradigm to prose materials and found results similar to those for word lists. Subjects who were asked to do graphic tasks, such as finding letters in words, remembered a prose passage more poorly than subjects asked to outline the material or sort the various sentences into related groups, tasks that demand greater semantic interaction with the passage.

Indeed, a large group of studies carried out by researchers interested in the factors that lead to better retention of prose materials seems to support the word list findings mentioned above. For example, Rothkopf (1972) and his colleagues have carried out numerous investigations into the effect of inserting questions into prose passages on the subject's ability to recall the passage. The general procedure in these studies is to insert one or more questions into a passage either before or after the information for answering the questions has been presented. The general finding has been that the insertion of postquestions leads to better overall recall of the passage than when no questions are inserted. The insertion of prequestions does not enhance total recall but only selects which particular part of the passage is recalled.

The above investigations suggest then that a number of operations are carried out on incoming information. The effect of these operations is to relate the information to semantic memory. This relationship may be on several levels, from formal or structural properties such as the letters composing words to semantic properties dependent on the meaning of the words. These operations and their resulting relationships leave a record or trace of the information for later use. The permanence of this record varies with the type of operation performed. Those operations resulting in semantic analyses leave relatively permanent records; those involving nonsemantic analyses leave less permanent records. These traces differentially support an individual's attempt to remember that which he or she has experienced.

From our discussion thus far it seems that these encoding operations are automatically carried out on any incoming information. They thus do not involve a conscious, organized attempt to aid recall. In great measure we think this is an accurate interpretation. Generally these encoding operations are a systematic routine that human beings must go through in order to perceive and attend to their environment—the operations involved in pattern recognition and perception discussed in Chapter 2. The fact that these processes also result in varying degrees of permanent memory for the events of the day is a beneficial offshoot of these operations, an offshoot that accounts for people's ability to generally reconstruct the events of the day (or of days long since passed).

Such a general-functioning, permanent memory system is necessary to the everyday functioning of human beings. But is such a system sufficient to explain all the aspects of permanent memory? We think not, for the various encoding operations do not make efficient and organized use of the context in which information occurs. In particular, there is no attempt to systematically organize and structure incoming information so it can more easily be remembered. This fact is seen most clearly when we consider the extensive work carried out on organization.

The Role of Organization in Permanent Memory

What do the following protocols have in common?

1. "Let's see, I must learn the pair of nonsense syllables *WIS–SEB*. *WIS* could be the abbreviation for Wisconsin. *SEB*. Hmm! *Seven*. Ah, yes, the 'Wisconsin Seven.' What a nasty bunch they were!"

2. "A 20-item grocery list to remember. That's going to be difficult. I need a plan. If I were to just put each item mentally in a different place.... We'll put the first item, potato chips, in the kitchen sink. They'll get good and soggy there. Napkins? Oh yes, there's the oven door wiping his big mouth with the napkin. A brussel sprout handle on the refrigerator—that would be a big selling item...."

3. "These chapters on permanent memory are difficult ones. I have to find out what the underlying structure is. According to the main captions, the authors are first talking about our accumulated knowledge or semantic memory and views on how that knowledge is organized. Then they consider how we learn new pieces of information by relating it to the accumulated knowledge. Right. Now I'm beginning to see."

In examining these protocols we can see that in each the individual is consciously attempting to relate the various parts of what he has to remember. The individual is making use of knowledge in semantic memory to develop a structure that binds the incoming information together in a coherent manner. This structure will provide an effective means of retrieving the new information at some later time.

Some psychologists maintain that the process of generating an organization relating the incoming information is necessary if we are to remember events effectively (Bellezza, Cheesman, & Reddy, 1977; Mandler, 1967). Bellezza et al., for example, maintain that the encoding processes discussed in the previous section are necessary for us to be able to recall information. However, they claim that such processes are not sufficient for good recall. Instead, they argue that relating items to one another is a crucial aspect of ensuring excellent retention. This process can take many forms, as we will see in the next several sections.

Mediation. One of the simplest forms of organization involves **mediation.** Certain processes are postulated to occur between a stimulus and response which explain why that response occurs. For example, in the first protocol described above, the individual added a suffix to the end of *WIS* to make the nonsense syllable more meaningful and allow it to be more easily related to semantic memory. She also substituted the letter *V* for *B* in *SEB*, and then added a suffix to make it *seven*. Finally by putting *Wisconsin* and *seven* together she formed a meaningful combination that was more likely to be recalled.

Mediation uses a variety of transformations to convert hard-to-remember items into something more meaningful and hence more easily remembered. We described two that may be used on nonsense syllables—substitution and suffixing. Others include the internal addition of letters (*wok* → *work*) and the deletion of letters (*dop* → *do*). Of course, mediators are not only useful in working with nonsense syllables. People frequently find that generating a sentence to link two words together will aid them in recalling the words. For example, if we want to remember *sky* when given the word *tree* as a stimulus, we may put them in the sentence, *The tree is in the sky.* Such sentences are effective mediators in aiding our recall.

Montague, Adams, and Kiess (1966) provide evidence for the effectiveness of mediators. They had their subjects write down the mediators they used (if any) while attempting to learn lists of paired-associate nonsense syllables. For example, if a subject was to learn the pair *jat–pon*, he might write down *jet plane*. When the subjects were being tested on their ability to recall the response words, they were also asked to remember their mediator if they had used one. Montague et al. found that a subject who had not used a mediator could recall only about 6 percent of the response terms. Subjects who used a mediator but were unable to recall it at the time of test could recall only 2 percent of the response terms. However, those who used a mediator and were able to recall it were able to recall 73 percent of the response terms. This provides strong evidence that mediators can improve our ability to remember information.

Imagery. A process very similar to mediation involves **imagery.** In this procedure people represent information in a visual image rather than a verbal form (see dual-coding theory in Chapter 4) to help them remember new episodic material.

The power of this technique has been demonstrated numerous times. Bower (1972a), for example, found that subjects given imagery instructions for learning noun pairs did much better than subjects merely told to remember the pairs. Bower's subjects were simply told to imagine the two nouns in an interacting manner. If the two nouns were *shower* and *brussel sprouts,* for instance, the subject might imagine a man standing in a shower being pelted by brussel sprouts (which might be even more invigorating than a shower massage). Such instructions resulted in about one third better recall than the nonimagery instructions.

A number of variables have been found to influence the ease of using imagery to aid episodic memory. Perhaps the most potent variable is the concreteness or *imagery value* (I) of words, which can be defined as the average rating subjects have given the words when asked to rate how easy it is to image them. Words such as *honesty* and *integrity* are low in imagery value, while words such as *cup* and *car* are high in imagery value. Words high in imagery value are more easily remembered than words low in imagery value.

Another variable found to influence the use of imagery in memory is whether subjects are asked to image words in an interactive manner. Subjects merely told to image items as resting side by side, for example, will remember those items more poorly than if they image them in an interactive manner (Bower, 1972a). In Figure 5.1 the word pair *piano–cigar* will be better remembered if imaged as in 5.1a than if imaged as in 5.1b. Apparently the combined image provides a more direct and powerful retrieval link between the items.

Finally, many professional memory experts (mnemonists) argue that when using imagery to aid memory, it is best to conjure up bizarre images such as those shown in Figure 5.2. Their rationale is that such images are more striking and captivating and thus support recall better than nonbizarre images. Although several studies have not found experimental support for this contention (Collyer, Jonides, & Bevan, 1972; Wollen, Weber, & Lowry, 1972), Neisser (1976) claims that this may be simply because these studies use naive subjects and immediate recall procedures. Further work seems necessary to clarify the impact of this variable.

Image techniques such as the ones described here play important roles not only in paired-associate tasks but also in serial learning tasks and in many mnemonic techniques, and we will take up this latter topic in greater detail later. Before leaving our discussion of imagery, however, we wish to point out that the use of imagery can aid an important part of second language learning—namely, the acquisition of vocabulary. Atkinson (1975) devised a mnemonic procedure called the *keyword method* to help learn foreign words. This procedure involves first finding some word that sounds like some part of the foreign word. For example, as shown in Figure 5.3, the Spanish word *pato* sounds like the English word *pot*. The second step is to form an image relating this English word to the translated meaning of the Spanish word; in this case an image is to be formed between *pot* and *duck* (see Figure 5.3 on page 114).

In an experiment comparing this technique to a standard vocabulary-learning procedure, subjects employing the keyword procedure translated 72 percent of the test items correctly compared to only 46 percent for subjects using the normal procedure. In a test 6 weeks later, the keyword subjects were correct on 43 percent of the items compared to only 28 percent for the normal procedure. Apparently imagery procedures can be a powerful aid in learning the English translation of foreign words.

It is apparent that mediators and imagery play a key organizational role in memory. However, because the bulk of the work on these topics has been carried out in paired-associate tasks, we are limited in our ability to determine the general importance of organization in memory. We get a broader view of organization in our next two sections: organization in free recall and mnemonics.

Organization in Free Recall. The most extensive investigations of the role of organization in memory have been carried out in studies involving free recall. In the free recall paradigm subjects are given a list of words and then at some later time are asked to recall these words in any order they wish. Since the subjects are allowed to output the words as they wish, we have a special

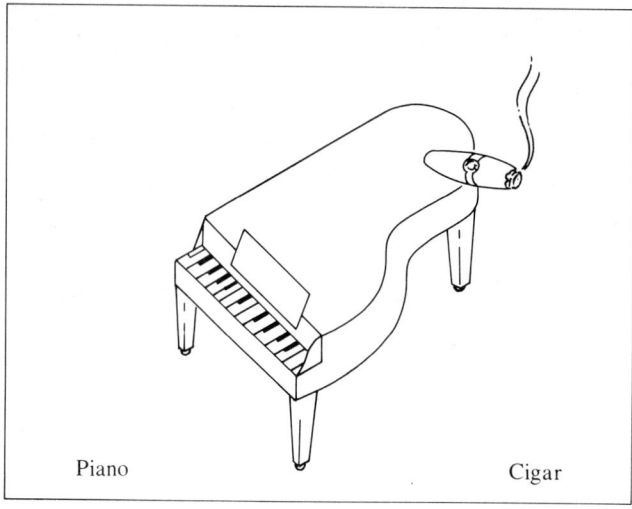

5.1a

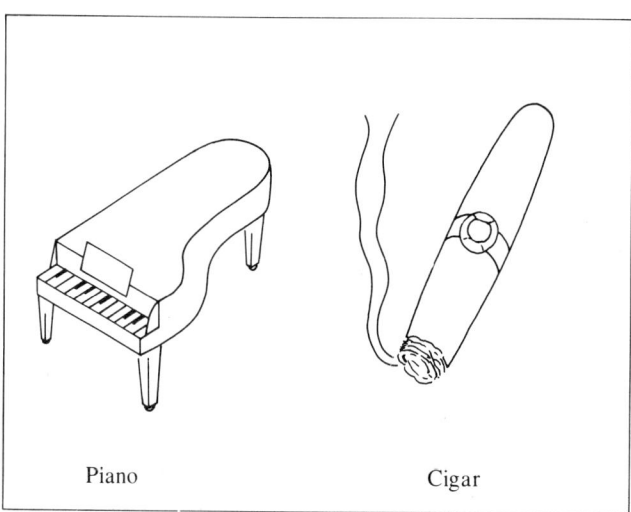

5.1b

Figure 5.1 Interacting and noninteracting images involving a piano and cigar. (From Wollen, Weber, & Lowry, 1972.)

opportunity to observe the manner in which they recall. By carefully studying the order of recall, we can infer how the subjects are organizing the words presented to them.

Two principal approaches have been employed in studying organization in free recall. In the first approach, subjects are given word lists in which some organization is apparent in the

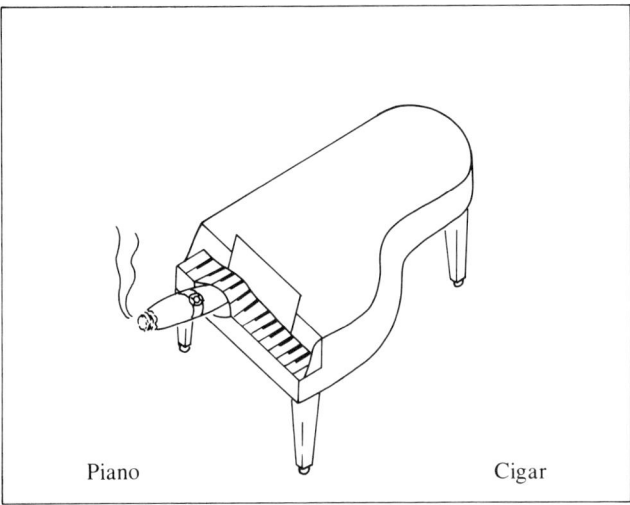

5.2a

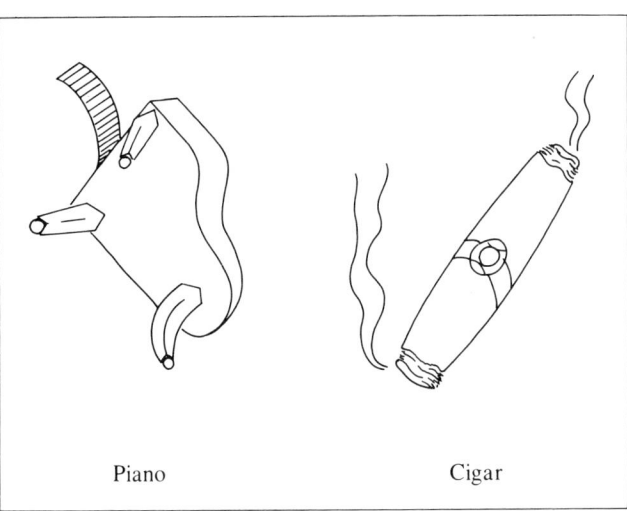

5.2b

Figure 5.2 Examples of interacting and noninteracting bizarre images involving a piano and cigar. (From Wollen, Weber, & Lowry, 1972.)

material. For example, subjects may be given a list in which there are four different word categories represented: fish, furniture, animals, and birds. In these studies researchers determine whether subjects are able to make use of the given structure to aid recall. In the second approach, subjects are given word lists in which there is no inherent structure. In this condition it

PATO — POT — DUCK

Figure 5.3 Example of keyword method for remembering foreign language vocabulary. (From Atkinson, 1975.)

is possible to determine if subjects impose organization even in situations where such structure is not immediately obvious.

MATERIAL-INDUCED ORGANIZATION. In the early 1950s two important studies were reported which were to have significant impact on the study of memory. In 1952, Jenkins and Russell reported a study in which they gave subjects a 48-word free recall word list composed of 24 pairs of words which were high associates of one another—for example, *man–woman, black–white*. These 48 words were presented in randomized order. When the subjects were asked to recall the words, however, they did so in a highly systematic fashion. Words that were high associates of one another tended to be associatively clustered (recalled together) regardless of the order in which they had been presented. Apparently the subjects' associations among the words were influencing recall. Their recall pattern did not mirror how the words were presented but rather seemed to be based on some internal structuring of the words.

The second influential study carried out in the 1950s was conducted by Bousfield (1953). Using a related procedure, he presented subjects with a 60-word free recall list composed of four categories of 15 words each—for example, animals: *giraffe, baboon, zebra;* occupations: *milkman, typist, florist*. As in the study by Jenkins and Russell these words were presented in a random order and the subject could recall them in any order he wished.

Bousfield too found that the order in which the words were recalled was unlike the input order, since the words within a category were recalled together more frequently than one would expect by chance. This was called *category clustering* and was measured by the ratio of repetitions. This ratio is a number reflecting the proportion of words recalled that were recalled in clusters from any of the four categories.

These two studies initiated a whole area of research concerned with the manner in which subjects make use of the associations and categories available in semantic memory to aid their memory. It was argued that by making use of associations or categories already known, the subject is able to provide a more coherent meaning or structure to a list of words and thus is better able to remember it.

However, the evidence from studies of material-induced organization that support this conclusion has not been overwhelming. Several early studies (Bousfield, Cohen, & Whitmarsh, 1958; Jenkins, Mink, & Russell, 1958) showed that the more organized a list of words was the better it was recalled. Several later studies, however, reported results inconsistent with this conclusion. We report one such study in Box 5.1.

A second study by Puff (1970) also found results inconsistent with this conclusion. He divided his subjects into groups on the basis of whether they showed a significant amount of clustering in a free recall study. He found no differences in total recall between the group of subjects who showed a significant amount of clustering and the group who did not.

While the results of Cofer, Bruce, and Reicher (1966) and of Puff call into question the relationship between organization and our ability to remember, we should be cautious in rejecting such a relationship. It is possible that the clustering measures used in the studies of material-induced organization do not accurately measure how well organized a list of words is. In particular, it is entirely possible that a subject may recall a list perfectly and show no clustering. For example, in studies of category clustering a subject may decide to recall one word out of each category and repeat this operation many times. Such a recall pattern would show no clustering whatsoever even though recall could be perfect. In sum, there may be a very direct causative link between the amount of organization and the amount of recall, but the measures used for assessing organization in material-induced organizational studies may just not be tapping the organization.

In conclusion, studies of material-induced organization find extensive evidence that subjects cluster to-be-remembered words. This process appears to result from an effort on the subject's part to make information to be remembered more meaningful by relating it to the structures of semantic memory. This would then make the information more easily remembered. While the evidence for that conclusion is equivocal for the word list studies considered thus far, we will find strong evidence for this conclusion when we consider the retention of prose materials in Chapter 7.

SUBJECT-IMPOSED ORGANIZATION. When we study the material-induced structure in word lists, we may not get an accurate view of the subject's ability to organize. The principal reason for this is that we give credit for organization only if the subject organizes the words in the same way the experimenter does. Thus if the experimenter constructs a list with categories of animals and furniture and the subject tries to remember the list by alphabetizing the words or by making a story of them, the experimenter's clustering measures will indicate that the subject has done little organizing. This may be a very misleading conclusion. A better way to assess organization is to give subjects credit for any type of organizing they use. This sounds fine in principle, but has been hard to measure.

Tulving (1962) developed a technique that inspired a whole new look at the process of organization. He presented his subjects with a list of 16 unrelated words and then asked for free recall of the words. He then presented the list of 16 words a second time in a different order. Again he asked for free recall. He continued presenting the words for a total of 16 trials, each time in a new order and each time the subjects

> **Box 5.1 CLUSTERING: A SUFFICIENT CONDITION FOR RECALL?**
>
> A number of empirical studies in the late 1950s and early 1960s had established the existence of a relationship between clustering and recall. On the basis of these results some researchers argued that if subjects could be led to cluster a list of words more highly, their recall would necessarily improve. In effect, they argued that clustering is a sufficient condition for good recall.
>
> Cofer, Bruce, and Reicher (1966) tested this viewpoint by presenting subjects with word lists composed of 40 words, 10 words from each of four categories. Some of the lists were composed of the 10 highest frequency associates of the category name, and some were composed of 10 low-frequency associates of the category name. Subjects were presented the word lists in either a random or blocked format. In the random format the 40 words were presented to the subjects in a completely scrambled fashion. In the blocked format all words from one category were presented before any words in another category were presented.
>
> It was expected that the blocked presentation condition would lead to higher clustering scores and better recall than the random presentation condition. This was expected to hold regardless of the frequency of association of the words to the category name. Cofer et al. found that blocked presentation did aid clustering in both high and low frequency conditions, but it aided recall only in the high frequency condition. This pattern of results provides difficulty for the view that clustering is a sufficient condition for recall. Apparently subjects can improve their ability to cluster without necessarily influencing their ability to recall.
>
> While this study provided some difficulty for those who viewed organization as being tightly linked to recall, it does not conclusively prove that organization and recall are unrelated. It is of course possible that the clustering score is just too limited a measure of organization to accurately reflect the relationship between organization and recall. We explore this possibility further in the text.

were asked for free recall of the words. Tulving assessed the consistency of the recall order. To do so he developed a measure called *subjective organization,* which measured whether words that were recalled together during one recall trial were also recalled together on succeeding trials. He reasoned that since the words were never presented in the same order, any consistency in recall order must reflect an organizational structure that the subject was imposing on the words. Thus Tulving had a measure of organization which did not depend on the subject's using the same organizational structure as the experimenter.

As can be seen in Figure 5.4, Tulving's subjective organization measure was consistently related to recall. As the number of trials with the word list went up, the amount of subjective organization increased and the number of words the subjects recalled increased. As we saw with the clustering measures in studies of material-induced organization, recall was related to the extent of organization the subjects imposed on the word list.

It is tempting to conclude that organization caused the subject to be better able to recall the words. Unfortunately, a series of studies testing the relationship between subjective organization and recall found very mixed results. In some cases researchers even failed to find a systematic relationship between subjective organization and recall (Postman, 1970). The problem again appears to be in the measure of organization (Wood, 1972). Subjective organization reflects the extent to which subjects use a single organizational structure. Consequently, when an experimenter constantly changes the order of input of items, the subject may be hindered in developing a particular organizational plan. This may result in an underestimation of the amount of organization carried out by the subject and may depress the relationship between organization and recall.

At this point it may be worthwhile to summarize and draw some conclusions from the work on material-induced and subjective organization. The primary thrust of much of this work was to establish the fact that subjects do not just rote memorize words from lists they are given. Rather, they seem to search for a structure that provides some coherence to the word list, thus

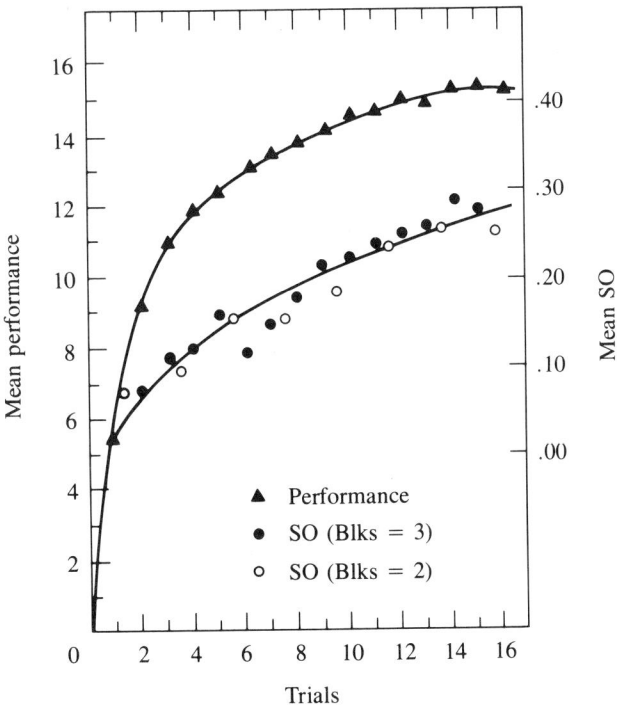

Figure 5.4 Mean recall performance (upper curve) and subjective organization (SO) as a function of trials. The subjective organization scores were calculated over blocks (Blks) of two or three trials. (From Tulving, 1962.)

making it easier to recall. However, research using word lists has not produced strong evidence for this process. (For a good overview and summary of the organizational work, we suggest the excellent book by Crowder, 1976).

It may be that the evidence is weak because subjects do not generate such structures. It is quite possible, however, that the weak evidence reflects the difficulty of getting a good measurement procedure to assess the structures that the subjects used.

It is possible that the difficulty that researchers have had in determining the importance of organization in memory has arisen from the stimulus materials they have used. In everyday situations most of us rarely memorize lists of words. Thus we have had relatively little practice with this type of task and when we are faced with it in a laboratory setting, we have no common approach to call upon. Therefore we probably generate any number of different plans or structures, making it difficult for researchers to measure what type of plan we have used. The consequence of this is the somewhat mixed set of results which has been reported.

Two major types of work, however, suggest that we not throw away our belief in the importance of organization in memory. One of these we will take up in Chapter 7 when we consider how people comprehend and remember prose materials, materials for which most of us have well-defined plans or schemata to help us remember. The other type of work we take up next as we consider the nature of mnemonics. In this section we will show that when subjects are given well-defined organizations, they can vastly improve their ability to remember even lists of unrelated words or numbers.

Mnemonics. Each of us has probably known someone who could perform some remarkable feat of memory. It may have been the woman who is a mnemonist recalling the name of every person seated in an auditorium. Or it may have been the parts man in a machinery store who when asked if he has a support rod for the husking bed for a 1962 John Deere pull-type corn picker says "Yes" and yells back to a boy to "Get part SP–1742."

Such feats of memory often seem to involve some type of trick that a person uses to aid his or her memory. The term *trick,* however, carries a connotation of stage magic or sleaziness. Yet this is not the case. The memory techniques (we prefer this expression to tricks) used by mnemonists are not essentially different from the processes used in the various organizational studies mentioned above. In all cases a person is attempting to generate a systematic plan that will effectively reduce the amount of information there is to remember. In the types of organization we have considered earlier, the plan usually involved finding an underlying structure that allowed the subject to remember fewer chunks of information. For example, when a subject finds that a list is composed of words from four different categories, he has reduced the amount of information to be remembered.

The mnemonic techniques we will describe operate in a similar fashion. They serve as a concise memory plan, which allows us to relate new information quickly and effectively to stored information so that the amount of information handling can be reduced. In some mnemonics we must learn some extra material to achieve this end. Some of the techniques described below, for example, require learning an elaborate rhyme or set of translation rules before they can be used in remembering other information.

It may seem at first blush that we must learn more new information when we use mnemonics than if we just rote memorized what had to be learned. While this is true on the surface, what we are learning are techniques that can be used in a variety of settings and that can provide a plan or schema for organizing information that has no inherent structure to it. This will become more clear as we consider some specific mnemonic techniques and how they are used.

"ONE IS A BUN, TWO IS A SHOE . . ." In 1960, Miller, Galanter, and Pribram published a book that was to have great influence on our understanding of human cognitive functioning. In that book they discussed a mnemonic technique that has proved to be a powerful procedure for remembering short lists of things, such as lists of names or grocery lists. The basis of this mnemonic is the use of imagery and the following simple rhyme:

one is a bun
two is a shoe
three is a tree
four is a door
five is a hive
six are sticks
seven is heaven
eight is a gate
nine is a line
ten is a hen (Miller et al., p. 135)

To use the technique, take the first word on the to-be-remembered list and create a mental image that interacts with the word *bun*. For example, if the first word is *newspaper,* you might visualize a large bun filled with a copy of the *New York Times* Sunday paper. Then take the second word and create an image with the word *shoe*. If the word is *street,* you might imagine a street created from old shoes. Continue in this fashion until the tenth word has been reached.

Now at the time of recall, you have a plan for recalling the words. Simply recite the rhyme and when the word *bun* is reached, the image created at the time of input will be available and the word *newspaper* will be recalled. The same holds for other words on the list. This mnemonic has additional advantages in that you can ask for the seventh word or ask what number a particular word was (*street*—second word). It has been shown that this technique can work well if subjects are given sufficient time to form the necessary visual images (Bugelski, Kidd, & Segmen, 1968). Surprisingly, the mnemonic can be used over and over again with little loss in its effectiveness. Researchers are not clear why subjects do not experience extensive interference with prior lists but such does not appear to be the case.

METHOD OF LOCI. One of the oldest and best-known mnemonics was used by the ancient Greek orators to aid them in giving their speeches. According to Yates (1966) the mnemonic received its name in a most unusual fashion. The Greek poet Simonides was attending a banquet when he was called from the banquet hall. During his absence from the hall the roof collapsed killing all who had remained inside. The bodies of the individuals were so mangled that their loved ones were unable to identify the remains. Simonides was able to recall each person by the place at which he sat at the banquet table. Hence the name *method of loci*.

In the method of loci the person is asked to place in memory a number of locations in his house or on his street. The locations are to be extensively practiced so that one can mentally walk through the house and "see" the objects in the same order each time. Thus we might start in the kitchen of our house and look first at the sink, then the range, the refrigerator, the table, and a picture on the wall. Moving to the living room, we might then look at the sofa, a lamp, and so on.

Once this list is firmly entered in memory, we are ready to employ the mnemonic. Let's say we wish to use it to remember a list of groceries. If the first item on the list is potato chips, we form an image of the potato chips interacting with the first location. Since our first location was the sink, we might image the sink outlet as a large mouth devouring potato chips (see Figure 5.5); then we go on to the second item and second location. If the second item is ketchup, we might image our range drinking from a ketchup bottle (see Figure 5.6), and so on. We continue to walk through the house mentally, imaging each grocery item at a different location.

Figure 5.5   A sink eating potato chips.

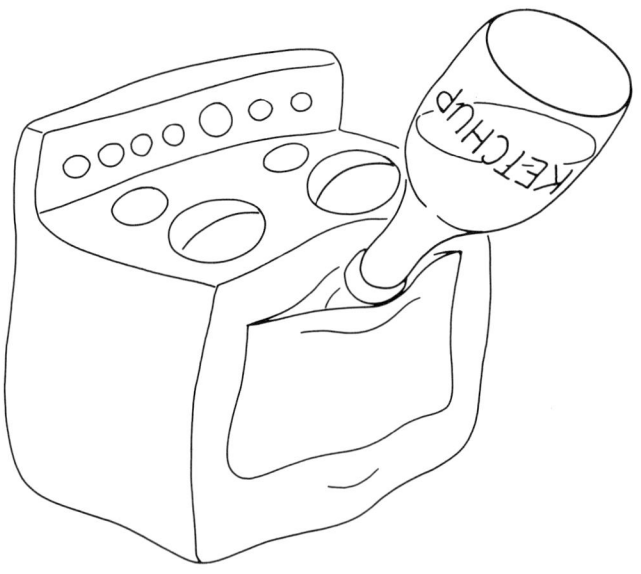

Figure 5.6   A range drinking ketchup.

At the time of recall we mentally go through our house reading off the items as we go. Looking at the sink we see the potato chips, at the range the ketchup bottle, and so on. (See Figure 5.7.)

Again, this mnemonic can be used over and over with little interference from previous lists. It can be effective for a variety of purposes in which one needs to remember materials in a particular serial order.

SUBSTITUTION. Perhaps one of the most difficult types of information to remember is numerical information. Phone numbers, social security numbers, library book call numbers, and birth dates have probably given all of us trouble at one time or another. The difficulty in learning numbers, of course, is that they have little meaning; they are abstract entities. Consequently, it is hard to integrate them into our semantic memory so that we can remember them well.

Figure 5.7 Mentally walking through the locations.

The techniques that mnemonists use to remember numbers make use of substitutions. Letters or sounds are substituted for numbers so that meaning can be created for the numbers. Once meaning has been assigned, other mnemonic devices are used to improve recall even further.

Probably the most widely used number mnemonic substitutes consonant sounds for the numbers 0 through 9. The origin of this technique is unclear. Some credit it to a German named Winckelmann in about 1648; others to a French mathematician named Herigon in 1634. (See Norman, 1976, for an interesting discussion of the method.) The method translates each number from 0 to 9 into particular consonant sounds as shown in Table 5.1. For example, each 0 in a

Table 5.1 A Number Mnemonic System Based on the Sounds of Letters

1	2	3	4	5	6	7	8	9	0
t	n	m	r	l	j	k	f	p	s
d					ch	ck	v	b	z
					sh	hard g	ph		soft c
					soft g	hard c			
					dg	q			
					tch	ng (hard)			

0. Zoo	25. NaiL	50. LaCe	75. eaGLe
1. haT	26. NiCHe	51. waLleT	76. CouCH
2. heN	27. NaG	52. LioN	77. CaKe
3. haM	28. kNiFe	53. LaMb	78. CoFfee
4. oaR	29. kNoB	54. LuRe	79. CaB
5. whaLe	30. MeSsiah	55. LiLy	80. oFfiCe
6. SHoe	31. MeaT	56. LeaSH	81. FooT
7. Key	32. MoNey	57. LaKe	82. VaN
8. wiFe	33. MoM	58. LoaF	83. FuMe
9. Pie	34. MaRe	59. LoBby	84. FiRe
10. ToyS	35. MaiL	60. CHeeSe	85. FiLe
11. ToT	36. MaTCH	61. SHaDow	86. FuDGe
12. TwiNe	37. MiKe	62. JohN	87. FoG
13. ThuMb	38. MuFf	63. JaM	88. FiFe
14. TiRe	39. MaP	64. JaR	89. ViP
15. TiLl	40. RoSe	65. JeweL	90. BuS
16. DiSH	41. heaRT	66. CHoo-CHoo	91. BoaT
17. DucK	42. hoRN	67. JoCKey	92. PeNny
18. DoVe	43. RaM	68. CHeF	93. BuM
19. TuB	44. waRrioR	69. CHiP	94. BeeR
20. NooSe	45. ReeL	70. KiSs	95. BaLl
21. kNighT	46. RaJah	71. KiTe	96. BeaCH
22. NooN	47. RaKe	72. GuN	97. BiKe
23. NaoMi	48. whaRF	73. CoMb	98. BeeF
24. NeRo	49. RoPe	74. CaR	99. PiPe
			100. DoZeS

Source: From Hersey (1963).

number is replaced by the *s, z,* or soft *c* sound. Each 1 is replaced by the *t,* or *d* sound. Each 2 is replaced by the *n* sound and so on. After all the appropriate substitutions have been made, vowel sounds are added to the consonants to produce words. The vowel sounds have no numerical meaning; the consonants *w* and *y* also have no meaning.

Let's look at some examples in order to see how the system operates. The number 1 can be represented by the word *toy* or *dew* (remember the consonants *w* and *y* carry no meaning in the system), the number 11 can be translated into *dot,* and the number 127 can be represented by the word *tank.* If we want to represent larger numbers we simply coin short phrases in a similar manner. Thus to remember the year in which Columbus discovered America (1492), we could substitute *deer pen, tar bin,* or *dear Ben.* To remember the telephone number 594-2158, we can simply recall *labor and love.*

Once we have translated the number into a word or phrase, we can use a variety of techniques to make the word or phrase more memorable. These might include imagery or other mnemonic techniques such as the method of loci. It is clear that it would take extensive practice with the number substitution technique before we could use it easily and effectively. However, learning to use this technique is similar to learning any other technical skill. Once mastered, it can be a powerful tool for remembering vast amounts of numerical information.

STORIES. A mnemonic technique that has proved useful in remembering serial lists of words involves weaving a story from the words. In particular, subjects may be told to "take the first word on a list and put it in a setting suitable for other words. Add each successive word to the developing story in a way that is meaningful to you." At the time of recall each subject is asked to remember the theme of his or her story in order to reconstruct the words composing the story. We describe evidence for the power of this technique in Box 5.2.

As our discussion in the past few pages suggests, the concept of organization has played an important role in psychologists' theorizing about human memory. One of the principal reasons for this is that the work on organization offers a reasonable and intuitive interpretation of what needs to happen for memory to occur. In particular, it suggests that good memory will necessarily follow if a person can determine a structure for incoming information that is compatible with semantic memory.

There is an interesting and important implication that arises from interpreting memory in this fashion. This concerns the concept of intentionality.

Intentionality and Memory. How important is it that we want to remember something? This question has become of increasing interest as researchers have tried to gain a better understanding of the role of organizational processes in memory. Even a cursory view of the situations in which we employ memory shows that in the great majority of cases in which we remember, there was no intent on our part at the time an event occurred to try to remember that event. It is unlikely that the fact that you can remember what you had for lunch yesterday or what you first did after rising this morning depends on an intention on your part to try to remember those events. But such analyses only show that intention is not necessary for recall. Is it possible that an intent to remember would make recall more efficient?

Mandler (1967), making use of a subject-imposed organization task, provided perhaps the clearest evidence on this point. He presented four groups of subjects with a list of 52 words. Two of the groups were told to sort the words into two to seven categories of their choice. The other two groups were simply required to list the words and were not required to categorize them. These two sets of two groups were further divided by instructions to recall. One group in each set was told to remember the words; the other group was told nothing about having to remember the words.

Box 5.2 THE STORY MNEMONIC

In order to test the effectiveness of the story mnemonic, Bower and Clark (1969) gave two groups of subjects 12 serial lists of words; each list was composed of 10 concrete nouns. One group was told to generate a story around the 10 words within each list, and they were allowed to work at their own speed. When they finished with the story, they gave the list back to the experimenter and were then asked to recall the 10 words. Here are two sample stories created by subjects in this condition.

1. A VEGETABLE can be a useful INSTRUMENT for a COLLEGE student. A carrot can be a NAIL for your FENCE or BASIN. But a MERCHANT of the QUEEN would SCALE that fence and feed the carrot to a GOAT.

2. One night at DINNER I had the NERVE to bring my TEACHER. There had been a FLOOD that day, and the rain BARREL was sure to RATTLE. There was, however, a VESSEL in the HARBOR carrying this ARTIST to my CASTLE.

The second group was given the same word lists, but they were simply told to study and learn the lists. Each subject in this group was yoked to a subject in the other group and allowed to study the list as long as the subject in the other group. Immediately after the study period for each list was over, these subjects were also asked to recall the words.

Bower and Clark found no differences in recall between the groups when they recalled immediately after studying the lists. Both groups recalled above 99 percent of the words. However, after the subjects completed the immediate recalls, Bower and Clark requested the subjects to recall all 12 of the previous lists, 1 at a time. As a cue to the list, Bower and Clark gave the subjects the first word in the list. The differences in recall between the two groups were now dramatic (see Figure 5.8). Subjects in the story groups recalled 93 percent of the words; subjects in the control group recalled only 13 percent. Creating a story around the words apparently provided an extremely effective mnemonic that served as a recall plan for the words on the lists.

This impressive study indicates that mnemonics can have a dramatic impact on our ability to remember information. They can provide us a means for remembering information that has little inherent structure and is consequently difficult to remember. Unfortunately, we have not had space to consider the numerous everyday applications to which mnemonics can be put to use, such as the retention of names, faces, activities to be done, and textual information. For those who would like to consider other uses of mnemonics, we recommend Cermak, 1975; Hersey, 1963; Lorayne and Lucas, 1974; and Norman, 1976.

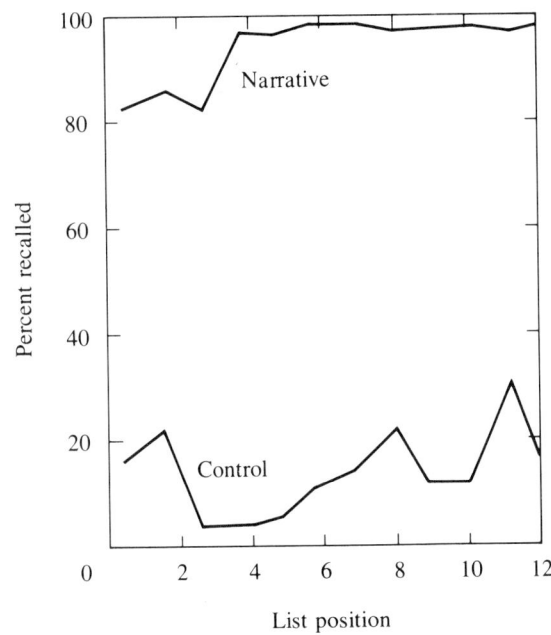

Figure 5.8 Median recall percentages for mnemonic and nonmnemonic subjects. (From Bower & Clark, 1969.)

The results are shown in Table 5.2. All the groups recalled equally well except for the group that simply listed the words and was not told to remember them. Subjects instructed to sort the words but given no intention to remember recalled as well as subjects who had been told to remember the words. Apparently instructions to remember the words meant the same thing as instructions to organize them.

Thus **intentionality,** or the desire to remember something, is important to memory only insofar as it leads to carrying out the processes of organizing incoming information so that it relates more efficiently to semantic memory. The actual desire to remember seems of little importance.

Table 5.2 Performance as a Function of Intentionality and Categorization Instructions

Categorizing Instructions	RECALL INSTRUCTIONS	
	Present	Absent
Present (sort)	31.4	32.9
Absent (list)	32.8	23.5

Source: From Mandler, (1967).

A number of later studies have reported similar findings and conclusions (Arkes, Schumacher, & Gardner, 1976; Hyde & Jenkins,

1969; Walsh & Jenkins, 1973). Although these studies suggest some subtle refinements to the above conclusions (see Arkes et al.), the basic conclusions remain unchanged.

The research on intentionality thus provides additional support for our interpretation that memory is intimately related to our ability to generate a structure for to-be-remembered material that is compatible with the structures found in semantic memory.

This brings to a close our discussion of storage processes in permanent episodic memory. We have discussed the range such processes can take from the quite automatic encoding processes to the more consciously controlled organization processes. In the latter part of this section we have suggested that memory may well involve finding or generating knowledge structures that provide a coherent interpretation of the to-be-remembered material. This concept has become firmly entrenched in our understanding of human memory processes. Although it arose from our discussion of memory for word lists, the concept has become the foundation of recent views of the procedures we use for learning from prose materials, a topic we take up in Chapter 7.

In the next section we shall see that the concept of organization and structuring of materials is an important one not only for the storage of new information but also for the retrieval of that which has been stored.

RETRIEVAL OF INFORMATION FROM PERMANENT MEMORY

We have all experienced the frustration of being unable to recall what we are certain we know. Surely the embarassment that comes with being unable to recall a friend's name is not an uncommon experience (we hope). Or who among us has not walked into a room to get something and then forgotten what it was we were to get? Such examples show that in order to understand memory we must be concerned not only with how we store information in memory, but also with how we retrieve it later. We will consider two major topics related to this issue: the relationship between storage and retrieval and the techniques for retrieval. The first of these topics is concerned with what has come to be called *encoding specificity*.

Encoding Specificity

We indicated in the section on organization that the ability to structure to-be-remembered materials plays an extremely powerful role in our ability to remember and recall information. A question that has puzzled psychologists for some time is the locus of this influence. Is the organization important at the time of input, at the time of retrieval, or both?

In an attempt to answer this question, Tulving and Osler (1968) presented subjects with word lists composed of 24 items. Some of their subjects saw these words alone, while others saw each word paired with a weak associate of the word. At retrieval these groups of subjects were divided again. Some of each of the presentation groups were given the list of low associates at the time of retrieval and some were not. Thus Tulving and Osler produced conditions under which specific organizational information (namely, low associate cue words) was available at both input and retrieval, input alone, retrieval alone, or at neither input nor retrieval.

The results from this study showed that performance improved only when cue words had been available at *both* storage and retrieval. Having the cues available at storage or at retrieval alone did not improve performance over having no cues available at all. Tulving and Osler concluded that organization plays a fundamental role in memory both at storage and at retrieval.

The findings of this study have been replicated in many settings and conditions and have become the foundation of a key principle in memory, **encoding specificity.** Generally this principle states that retrieval cues provide access to information about events in memory if and only if the cues have been stored as a part of the particular memory traces for the events (Tulving & Thomson, 1973). In other words, the context in which we are asked to recall has to be related to the context at the time of storage if we are to be able to recall information. We saw an example of this in our opening prison escape story. James had a flood of memories when he returned to the location of the initial events.

Some striking examples of the principle of encoding specificity have been reported in the memory literature. Tulving and Thomson (1973), for example, showed that in some cases subjects are able to recall words more easily than they can recognize these same words. They first showed subjects a series of word pairs such as *LADY–QUEEN* and told them that they had to remember the word *QUEEN* and that the first word might be a good cue for that word. In a second phase of the study the subjects were asked to free associate to words highly related to the to-be-remembered word, for example, *KING*. The subjects frequently gave as responses words that were on the initial list of words to be learned.

Tulving and Thomson then asked the subjects to circle any words generated in the free association task that were also on the to-be-remembered list. The subjects were correct only 24 percent of the time. In contrast, when the subjects were asked to recall the words with the help of the initial recall cue, the subjects were right 63 percent of the time. These results provide striking support for the principle of encoding specificity. When the context at the time of retrieval was much like it was at input *(LADY–QUEEN)* performance was good; however, when a word was presented in a different context *(KING–QUEEN)*, the subject was unable to remember it as being an item from the to-be-remembered list.

Anderson and Ortony (1975) provided evidence that this principle holds for the retention of sentence materials. They presented subjects sentences such as

1. The accountant pounded the stake

or

2. The accountant pounded the desk

They then gave cues such as *hammer* or *fist* to determine how effectively they aided memory. It was found that *fist* was a much better prompt for Sentence 2 and *hammer* was a much better prompt for Sentence 1. The effective cues were more closely related to the context that the original sentence established, and so they were more effective in aiding the subject to retrieve.

The concept of encoding specificity has come to play an important role in our understanding of human memory. It helps to explain some everyday occurrences that many of us have experienced. For example, in returning to your old neighborhood you may experience a flood of memories—the time you drove the tractor through the fence or the first time you kissed your date. These memories are more likely to occur at such times because we are reestablishing the context in which they were entered into memory.

Encoding specificity also suggests an important principle in preparing for examinations or for a lecture to be delivered. To the extent that we can establish at the time of storage the conditions that will hold at the time of retrieval, performance will be improved. Such techniques as testing oneself or studying in the room in which the test is to be taken should result in improved performance.

Finally, encoding specificity reminds us again of the importance of context. In setting up task situations to study human cognitive functioning, we must constantly keep in mind the context in which the task is set and, for that matter, the character of the task itself. If we forget the setting, we may be fooled in understanding the individual's performance. If we continue to choose unusual tasks (remembering word lists or nonsense syllables), we may fail to understand memory in the context in which it usually occurs (Neisser, 1976).

Processes of Memory Retrieval

A request to remember information may come with extensive information to help remembering or with relatively little information. At the first extreme we may be given a particular word, picture, or sentence and asked if that was the item we had been given before. This procedure is called a *recognition* procedure. In other situations we may simply be asked to remember who our first-grade teacher was, what words were on a given list, or what occurred on a particular day three years ago. Procedures such as these, which necessitate that we either *recall* or even *reconstruct* past events, provide much less information; they allow us to assess how people go about retrieving information with less information available to them.

Recall and Recognition. Numerous investigations using recall and recognition procedures have been carried out to determine how these processes work. A stable pattern of results is emerging which indicates that when subjects know they will have extensive information available at retrieval, including the item itself, they try to discriminate each item from the others so they can separate them from the distractor items (Kintsch, 1977). Distractor items are the items on a recognition test which were not part of the originally presented material. Preparation for recognition tests should be considerably different from the search for organizational structure which goes on in preparing for recall.

Certainly evidence has shown that people prepare themselves differently for recall and recognition tasks. Carey and Lockhart (1973), for example, found that subjects preparing themselves to recall a word list performed much more poorly on an actual recognition test than subjects who were preparing themselves for the recognition test.

Other investigators have found that organizational manipulations generally have little impact on recognition test performance. Kintsch (1968), for example, compared recall and recognition performance on 40-word lists composed of four categories of 10 words each. One such list was composed of frequent words in each category, while the other list was composed of infrequent words. For example, in the category of furniture, *chair* is a frequent response and *divan* an infrequent one. Kintsch found that subjects recalled much better the words from the list constructed of frequent members compared to the infrequent member list. Subjects, however, did not differ in their ability to recognize the words from these different lists. Apparently the organizational information that plays such a key role in aiding recall is of little importance in recognizing material.

We should not be misled, however, to conclude that organizational information is never important in recognizing what we have experienced before. When subjects cannot make a confident recognition decision based on the familiarity of an item, it appears that they may carry out a *recall check*. This involves an attempt to retrieve the item from memory as one would do in a recall task. To the extent that subjects carry out this strategy, we might expect organizational manipulations to play a larger role in performance. Mandler and Boeck (1974) have found this very result. They gave their subjects a 100-word list and determined how good an organizer each of their subjects was. Good organizers were defined as those using an optimal number of categories—six or seven—to organize a list of unrelated words. Poor organizers used only three or four categories.

Mandler and Boeck then gave their subjects a recognition test and determined whether the subjects made a fast or slow recognition decision. They assumed that fast responses indicated quick, confident decisions, while slow responses indicated difficult decisions. If this is so, then recall checks should be more likely in the latter case and hence organizational factors should play a more important role in slow decisions. This turned out to be the case. Mandler and Boeck found no difference between good and poor organizers on fast responses. On slow responses, however, the good organizers performed significantly better than the poor organizers.

It appears then that when subjects have extensive information available to them at the time of retrieval, they use a strategy of attempting to discriminate the presented items and do not attempt to establish recall plans using organizational information. In difficult situations, however, they may fall back on such procedures to try to improve their performance.

People who face situations in which they are given little information at the time of retrieval are forced to employ retrieval schemes that allow them to search memory systematically. The efficiency with which such memory searches are carried out is closely related to the types of organizational information available to them (see pages 109–118). Thus in recall tasks, subjects may look for categories in which the words can be placed *(I need to buy vegetables, fruit, and milk,* or *I had things to do at the hardware store, grocery store, and bank).* They may also look for mnemonics that allow them to systematically relate each item to be remembered to other items. As the section on encoding specificity notes, however, it is crucial that the type of encoding or organizational format employed at storage of information be available at the time of retrieval or performance will be very poor.

At the present time there is considerable debate over the issue of the similarity of recognition and recall procedures; this has been a topic of major interest for memory researchers during the mid-1970s. Two major positions are currently active. One, typified by the views of Flexser and Tulving (1978), suggests that recognition and recall are essentially independent procedures. The second, typified by Rabinowitz, Mandler, and Patterson (1977), suggests a degree of overlap between the procedures.

Craik (1979) strikes a balanced posture, suggesting that similar processes may well be operative in recognition and recall but that different information must be retrieved in the two situations. In recognition, the item is presented and its context needs to be retrieved; in recall, part of the context is presented and the item must be retrieved.

Reconstruction. The above discussion implies that at the time of retrieval, information is searched for and located in memory and simply read off. Thus all we need do is find where we stored the appropriate grocery list and read off its contents. This, as it turns out, is a misleading conception of memory. It assumes that the content of any single event is stored in its entirety and need simply be located and read off. If memory were structured in such a fashion, each of us would have to walk around in a small warehouse in which to keep all these episodic events.

If memory is not simply a reading off, however, what is it? A broad array of both old and new research suggests that it involves a process of *reconstruction*. That is, certain key events or characteristics of an event are stored in memory. We reconstruct our memory for a past event by retrieving these key events and putting them together with general knowledge from semantic memory about how events are related to one another.

Thus, for example, if we attend a baseball game and a friend later asks us how all the runs were scored, we probably remember certain key events and construct the rest. In this case we may remember how a particular runner got on base and who got the hit that scored him. However, we may have forgotten that he got to second base by a sacrifice fly and report instead that he was bunted over to second base. Errors such as this one should be expected to occur with some regularity if memory is reconstructive in character.

In general then, it should be clear that while a reconstructive memory retrieval system necessitates far less storage space, it also should be subject to a greater number of systematic errors. That is, we should expect recall to be fragmented occasionally or to show systematic distortions that reflect an improper reconstruction of an actual event. In fact, it is just these types of retrieval errors which led to the postulation of reconstructive memory.

In the early 1930s two important and often-cited studies were carried out that were to play a large role in the interpretation of memory as a reconstructive process. In 1932, F. C. Bartlett (1932/1967), an English psychologist, published a now famous book entitled *Remembering*. In this book he reported a number of interesting studies which launched the concept of reconstructive memory.

In one particularly well-known study, Bartlett presented subjects with a somewhat strange prose passage entitled "War of the Ghosts." He then had his subjects recall the passage after varying intervals. He noted that their recall for the passage was quite poor even at short intervals, but more importantly he noted that they often seemed to recall only a general conception or theme of the story. From this theme they constructed a plausible story that seemed to make sense of the information they had retained and that gave the story coherence. These reconstructed stories frequently included systematic distortions and errors. In effect, the subjects appeared to be reconstructing their memory of the story from relatively little information and making it fit into their own conception of a meaningful story.

At about the same time that Bartlett wrote his book, another group of researchers headed by Leonard Carmichael also found evidence for reconstructive memory in the retention of line drawings (Carmichael, Hogan, & Walter, 1932). These researchers presented three groups of subjects with line drawings such as those in Figure 5.9. One group of subjects was given the labels on the left of the drawings. A second group was

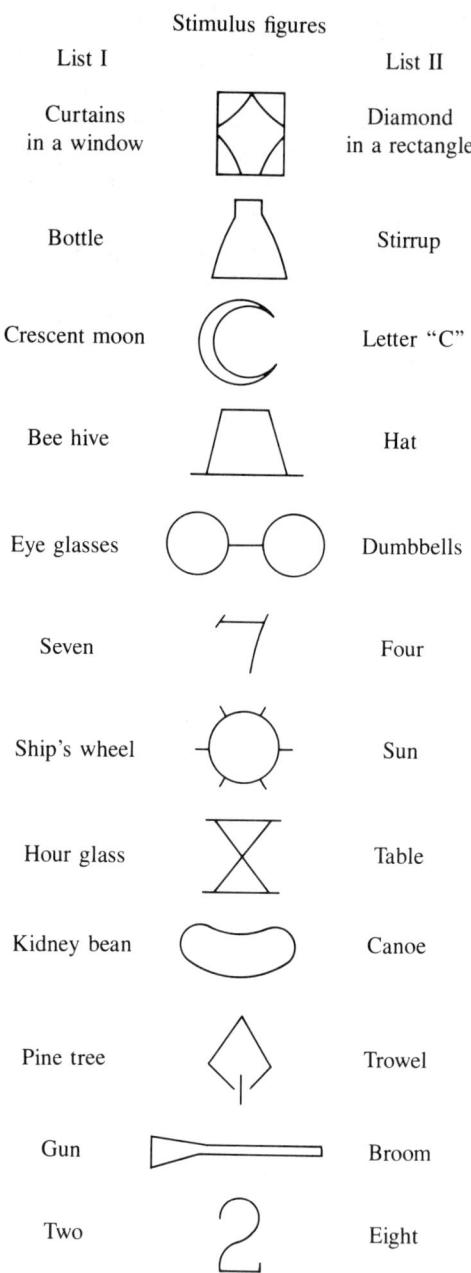

Figure 5.9 Line drawings used as stimulus figures by Carmichael, Hogan, and Walter (1932).

given the labels on the right. The third group (control group) was given the pictures with no labels. All three groups were then asked to recall all the pictures and to draw them.

The subjects in the first two groups tended to draw the pictures in a manner related to the presented word. For example, the drawing associated with eyeglasses tended to resemble eyeglasses more than did the drawings produced by the control group. It seems that the subjects' retrieval of the line drawings involved a reconstructive process that was biased by the labels for the drawings.

These studies provide evidence consistent with our description of reconstructive memory. There is thus suggestive evidence that memory involves more than just a simple reading off of the contents of memory. It appears that once information appropriate to a particular question is retrieved, a reconstructive process goes on in the production of a response.

Unfortunately, the researchers we have discussed above have been quite vague about how such reconstructive processes might be guided and when reconstructive errors are most likely to occur. This has led to frequent criticism of the concept of reconstructive memory (Cofer, 1973; Zangwill, 1972), and for several years little work was carried out on the topic. Since the mid-1970s, however, there has been a revival of interest in the topic, especially as it relates to the concept of schema. This has led to a clearer interpretation of how reconstructive memory occurs and when we are most likely to see reconstructive errors. We will consider this work in Chapter 7 after we have developed the concept of schema more fully.

CONCLUSION

We have reached the end of our tale of permanent memory. It has been a long and sometimes complex story. Perhaps we can sum up this story by once again returning to Peter in the midst of his late night studying. Our model depicting what Peter is doing is presented in Figure 5.10. When we last saw Peter, auditory and visual information had activated the Echo and Icon, been analyzed by the pattern recognition processes, and activated particular schemata in permanent memory. The information was being temporarily held in working memory and on the end of the episodic trace.

In the last two chapters, we have further expanded our discussion of what is involved in the permanent memory structure of our model. We reiterated our distinction between semantic and episodic memory and discussed in detail several views of the structure of semantic memory. These included network theories, set theory, feature comparison, and dual storage.

In Figure 5.10 we have not attempted to depict any particular one of these models but instead have tried to indicate that however we conceptualize semantic memory, there are clusters of information in it. We call these clusters schemata or concepts; these schemata are related closely to some other schemata and are unrelated to still others. These relationships are essential in explaining a variety of phenomena, from reaction time findings to clustering and subjective organization of new information. These relationships also represent the structure of our knowledge of the world.

A large segment of the present chapter was concerned with how Peter comes to put new information into his permanent memory. We noted that some processes for remembering information are carried out almost automatically. These are the encoding processes that relate incoming information to semantic information already stored in permanent memory. As these relationships are activated, a new trace is formed which becomes part of the episodic memory of the individual. We also noted that more effective permanent memory traces may result from taking into account the context in which a particular item is presented. This is the process of organization and it appears in many forms including mediation, clustering, subjective organization, and mnemonics.

In Figure 5.10 we have depicted Peter using a combination of imagery and mnemonic procedures to help him put new information in permanent memory so that he can perform better on his test. Peter is attempting to remember that purple flowers grow only in acid soil. He has called into working memory an image-forming schema to relate purple flowers to acid soil. By mentally putting a purple flower in a chemistry flask filled with acid, Peter images a happy flower. With this image placed in episodic memory, Peter now has a good link between purple flowers and acid soil. With repeated use, the tie between purple flowers and acid soil will become a part of Peter's semantic memory.

In choosing this particular image, Peter was also aware that the test will be given in the botany

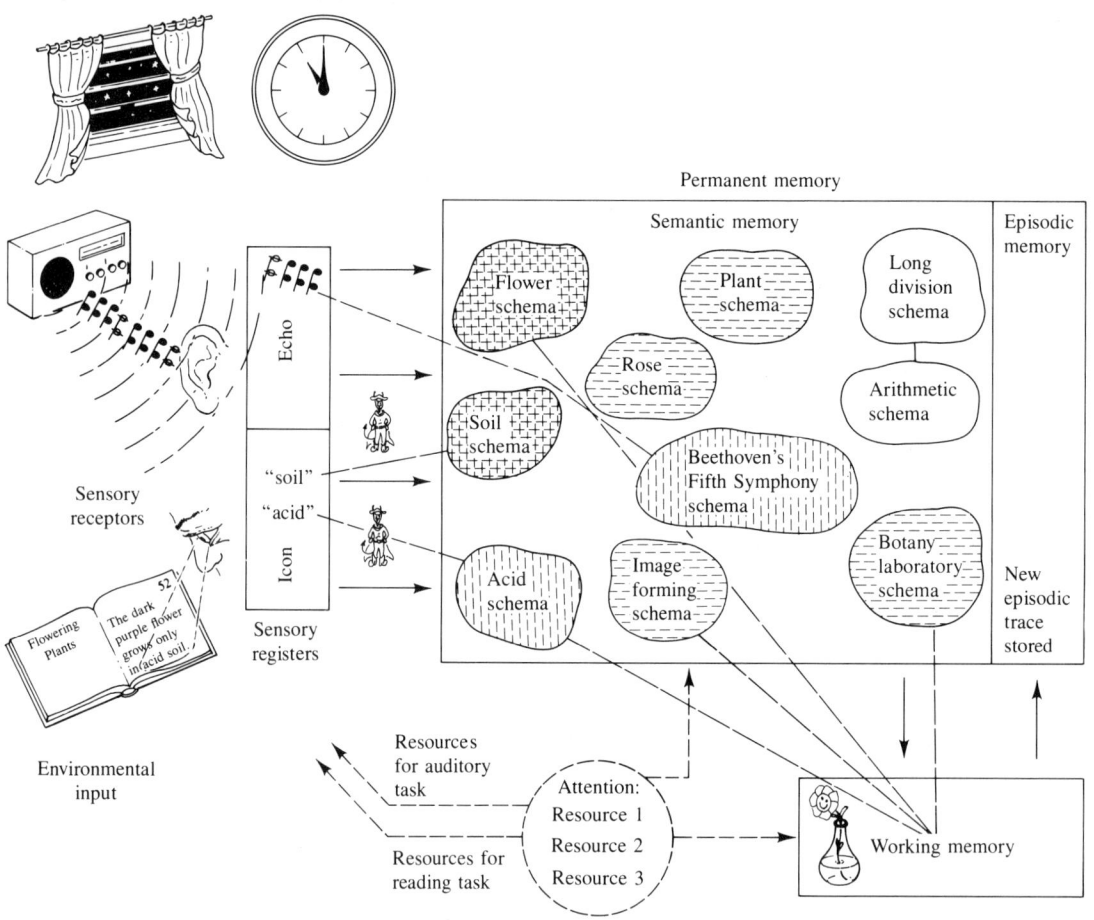

Figure 5.10 Expanded model of the components of the information-processing system.

laboratory, which is stocked with flasks. Peter has thus followed the crucial concept we have called encoding specificity, taking into account retrieval conditions at the time of storage.

The last section of this chapter dealt with what Peter will face when he walks in to take his test tomorrow. He will have to retrieve the information he has stored. Some of his retrieval will take the form of recognition, some will be recall, and some will be reconstruction. In the last case Peter may find himself filling in his answers with material he does not specifically remember but which he has assembled from what he knows.

6 Language

Properties of Language
    Creativity
    Rules
The Structure of Language
    Sentences
        Surface Structures and Underlying Representations
            The Syntactic Approach
            The Semantic Approach
        Surface Structure Clauses
    Words
        Content and Function Words
        Morphemes
    Sounds
Functions of Language
    Speech Acts
    Propositional Content
    Thematic Structure

Competence and Performance
Language Production
    Thought and Language
    Selecting a Meaning
    Creating Syntactic Structure
    Creating Phonemic Structure
    Evidence for the Order of Processing
    Motor Processes
Language Comprehension
    Speech Perception
        The Invariance Hypothesis
        Analysis by Synthesis
        The Auditory Processing Model
        Perception of Continuous Speech
    Lexical Analysis
        The Dictionary and the Encyclopedia
        Componential Analysis
        Procedural Semantics
    Syntactic Analysis
        Clause Analysis
        Surface Structure Analysis
    Memory for Meaning
A Computer Model of Language Processing
Conclusion

Language is our primary means of communicating with others. Through language we express our thoughts and feelings, our perceptions and our knowledge; and through language we receive the same kinds of information from others. You can appreciate the vast use we make of language simply by taking a vow of silence for one day.

The psychological study of language is often called *psycholinguistics,* and combines the study of language structure with the study of psychological processes that use that structure. In this chapter we shall see that language is a highly structured system, one that can be described by a set of rules. In the first part of the chapter we shall develop this system by examining some of the properties of language, the structure of language, and the functions of language.

In the second part of the chapter we shall look at how we use language, specifically in the processes of talking and understanding. There we shall try to show how the use of language involves such psychological processes as perception, memory, motor skills, and problem solving. In each case there is a major question we face: How does this process interact with our knowledge of language? Since it is generally assumed that one must have a clear understanding of the structure of language before one can understand the use of language, we will discuss language structure before talking about language use.

PROPERTIES OF LANGUAGE

There are about 2800 languages spoken in the world today (Pei, 1956), and each of them exhibits two rather interesting properties: They are *creative* and they are *rule governed.*

Creativity

The noted American linguist Noam Chomsky (1957) states that every natural language has a potentially infinite number of sentences. Though the number of sounds and words in a language is finite, the number of ways they can be combined into sentences is infinite. This potential is the *creativity* of language. No one of us, of course, ever uses all the sentences in our language (we should live so long), but the sentences we do use are all drawn from the infinite set for our language.

A simple demonstration of this aspect of creativity can be seen in the list of sentences *John loves one girl, John loves two girls, John loves three girls. . . .* This list could be continued (well beyond John's capacity) to infinity, yet it would constitute only a tiny fraction of the sentences in English.

A more significant way of creating new sentences is to expand a sentence by adding words, phrases, and clauses. *Automobile prices are up this year* can be expanded to *Retail automobile prices are up again this year for most American models.* A popular nursery rhyme begins with the simple sentence *This is the house that Jack built,* then adds two clauses to create *This is the malt that lay in the house that Jack built.* The tale continues to unfold by the addition of clauses until it reaches the impressive sentence,

> This is the farmer sowing his corn, that kept the cock that crowed in the morn, that waked the priest shaven and shorn, that married the man all tattered and torn, that kissed the maiden all forlorn, that milked the cow with the crumpled horn, that tossed the dog, that worried the cat, that killed the rat, that ate the malt that lay in the house that Jack built. (Opie & Opie, 1951, pp. 229–231.)

There is no grammatical reason for stopping the story with a sentence of this length. There is no upper limit on the length of a sentence, and there are sentences on record which are thousands of words in length. Every sentence, however, must be finite in length to qualify as a sentence, although there is no grammatical rule that limits how long the sentence may be.

A second aspect of creativity is novelty. Nearly every sentence we use is one we have not used before. In a sense, the sentence is the ultimate throwaway. Read through a newspaper or magazine article and you will typically find that no sentence occurs twice in the article. Although we repeat some of our sentences, such as *Thank you* and *How are you,* the vast majority are unique. Indeed, people who repeat their sentences, like people who repeat their jokes, will probably lose their audience.

The psychological implications of linguistic creativity are intriguing. Where do we get sentences? How do we decide which sentence to say at a given moment? Why is it so easy to understand most sentences even though we have never heard them before? These are questions we will take up in the sections on language use.

Rules

The second property of natural languages is that they are *rule governed*. Sentences are not created by randomly combining words. The sentence *The moon shone brightly* has four words that can be reordered in 4 factorial possible ways, where 4 factorial = $4 \times 3 \times 2 \times 1 = 24$. Most of these 24 orders (e.g., *Brightly moon shone the*) are not sentences. English has a set of rules that limit the ways words may be combined and thus determine what counts as a sentence. The rules are quite stringent, since they reject most word strings. In a ten-word sentence, nearly all the 3,628,800 possible orders of the ten words are rejected by these rules. The proportion of possible word strings that qualify as sentences is thus small; even so, it is an infinite set.

The rules for a language are descriptive, not prescriptive. Just as the laws of planetary motion are rules for describing the patterns of motion for the planets, so the rules of a language describe the patterns that speakers of that language follow. For most of us, the use of these rules is automatic and unconscious, just like the rules for how to walk.

In brief then, language structure strikes a balance between the freedom of creativity and the constraint of its rules. We want to know how the user of language operates within these limits.

THE STRUCTURE OF LANGUAGE

The task of formulating the rules of language falls to the linguist. In this section we shall examine the structure of language at the level of sentences, words, and sounds. We shall see first that sentences have both a surface structure and an underlying structure. We shall then look at word structure; and finally, we shall look at the set of sounds that combine to represent the spoken form of words and sentences.

Sentences

The sentence is the normal unit of conversation, and much of linguistic analysis focuses on the structure of the sentence. Words and sounds are integral parts of a sentence, but it is the relations among them that carry much of the information in a sentence. *Three blind mice* does not mean the same thing as *blind three mice* even though the words are the same. How shall we describe these relations? What rules will capture everything that a speaker knows about these relations?

Below we describe two levels of structure for a sentence, and we then discuss two linguistic theories of these structures. The discussion of the two theories is followed by an analysis of clauses and the way they combine in sentences. Our intent is to show that sentences are highly structured and that any theory of how people use language must take account of the structure of sentences.

Surface Structures and Underlying Representations. Most linguists agree that a sentence contains information at two levels, which we shall call the **surface structure** and the **underlying representation.** The surface structure of the sentence is the organization of the words in the sentence in its spoken form. The underlying representation is the way the meanings of the words are related to represent the meaning of the sentence.

Since most sentences have only one surface structure and one underlying representation, the distinction between these may be hard to see at first. The difference between the two is more evident in ambiguous sentences, which have a single surface structure and more than one underlying representation. Consider the ambiguous sentence *The shooting of the hunters was terrible*. It has a single surface structure, shown in the choice and order of the words in the sentence. However, there are two underlying representations for this sentence: one in which the hunters are doing the shooting, and the other in which the hunters are the hapless objects of the shooting. The meanings of the words in this sentence are related in two different ways, giving it two different underlying representations.

Ambiguous sentences occur more often than you might think. Reviewing the examples in Box 6.1 may sharpen the distinction between surface structure and underlying representation for you.

There are two schools of thought among linguists about how to represent the structure of a sentence. One takes syntax (grammatical rela-

---

Box 6.1 AMBIGUOUS SENTENCES

Many sentences that we hear and read are ambiguous, though the context in which they occur usually makes the intended meaning clear. The distinction between surface structure and underlying representation may be clearer if we examine some ambiguous sentences in isolation and try to determine how many meanings they have.

The simplest kind of ambiguity is lexical ambiguity. This occurs when one word in a sentence yields two or more meanings and hence two or more underlying representations. For example,

1. California is a great state to live in despite its faults.
2. There is a fork in the road ahead.

The two meanings of *faults* and *fork* lead to two different interpretations of these sentences. If you keep your mind limber, you will find similar examples almost daily. Consider these:

3. To a waiter: "Do you have frog legs?"
4. Newspaper name: *The Chattanooga News-Free Press*
5. One of the more gruesome examples, "He shot off his mouth," is so grisly you can hardly bear it.

The pun is a popular form of lexical ambiguity, though the surface structure for the pun often differs slightly for the two meanings, as shown in these examples by Bennett Cerf (1968):

6. And then there was the fellow who inherited 392 clocks and is now winding up the estate.
7. A Texan down on the range is suing for a divorce. He found his dear and an interloper playing.
8. Then there was the seashore eccentric who spent all his time throwing rocks at gulls. He left no tern unstoned.

A second level of ambiguity embraces units larger than the word and permits two or more entirely different interpretations of the same surface structure. For example.

9. The car was stopped by the tree.

can mean *The tree blocked the movement of the car* or *The car was parked alongside the tree.* Similarly, there are two very different underlying representations for

10. The magician made the prince a frog.

Students of ours have found at least eight meanings for

11. Jane reports that her neighbor had her second car stolen.

Two of these are

a. Jane's neighbor was the victim of car theft for a second time.

b. Jane's neighbor arranged the theft of Jane's old family jalopy.

How many meanings do you find for the following sentences?

12. The police were ordered to stop drinking at midnight.
13. She missed the boat.
14. Norman Rockwell painted me on his front porch.

tions) as its starting point, and the other takes semantics, which is the study of meaning.

THE SYNTACTIC APPROACH. The major linguist in the syntactic school is Chomsky (1965), who has concentrated on the development of transformational grammars to describe sentence structure. A *transformational grammar* is a set of rules that serves two purposes. First, it identifies which strings of words are sentences and which are not. Second, for those that are sentences it describes the grammatical relations in each sentence, such as which words serve as subject, verb, or object. A transformational grammar is generative. The rules of the grammar generate a sentence by analyzing the category *S* (sentence) into particular sentences. Different sentences require different rules to generate them, and the structure of each sentence is shown in the way the rules analyze *S* into the sentence.

Generating a sentence is something like using the rules of plane geometry to deduce a theorem from an axiom. Different rules must be used to prove different theorems, and only the expressions that can be derived by the rules count as theorems of plane geometry. So it is with sentences; only the word strings that can be generated by the rules of the grammar count as sentences.

A transformational grammar contains two major types of rules, *phrase structure rules* and *transformation rules*. Phrase structure rules generate the underlying structure of a sentence, and transformation rules generate its surface structure. A simple set of phrase structure rules is shown in Figure 6.1. The first rule is read "*S* (a sentence) may be rewritten as a noun phrase plus a verb phrase." This rule states that every sentence has both a noun phrase and a verb phrase. The second rule states that a noun phrase is composed of a determiner (e.g., *a, the, some*) plus an adjective plus a noun. The parentheses indicate that the determiner and the adjective are optional. The verb phrase in turn is composed of a verb and an optional noun phrase.

To generate a particular sentence, such as *George played the new organ*, these rules are applied to produce a tree structure, as shown in Figure 6.2. The part of the tree above the sentence is called the *phrase structure* of the sentence. We arrive at the sentence we are trying to generate by inserting words in the lowest level of categories in the phrase structure.

The second type of rule is the transformational rule. Chomsky (1965) argues that sentences such as *George played the new organ* (active), *The new organ was played by George* (passive), and *Did George play the new organ?* (question) are basically alike and can be represented by the same phrase structure. The differences in surface structure are produced by differ-

S ⟶ Noun phrase + Verb phrase

NP ⟶ (Determiner) + (Adjective) + Noun

VP ⟶ Verb + (Noun phrase)

Figure 6.1 Phrase structure rules for a simple grammar.

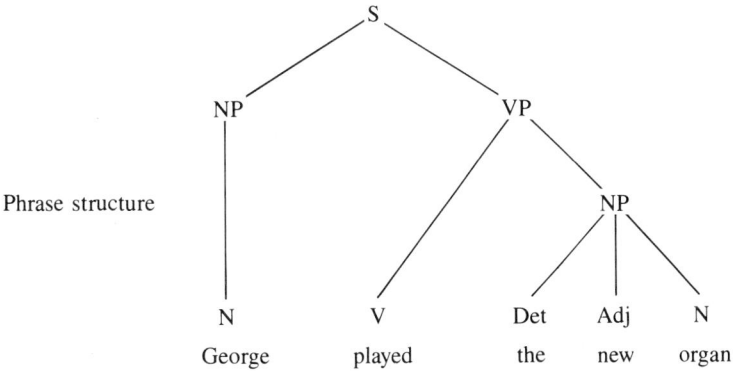

Figure 6.2 Tree structure for a sentence.

ent transformation rules that can be applied to the phrase structure.

An illustration of the passive transformation rule is shown in Figure 6.3. The string of categories on the left has been generated by phrase structure rules. The passive transformation rule converts it into the string on the right, which represents the surface structure of the passive sentence *The new organ was played by George*. Related sentences are thus shown to be related by having the same or similar phrase structures, while the differences among them are produced by different transformation rules.

In a transformational grammar the surface structure of a sentence is the form of the sentence after a transformation rule has been applied. The underlying representation of the sentence is based on the phrase structure of the sentence. A separate set of semantic rules interprets the phrase structure to generate the meaning of the sentence. Thus the syntactic relations of the sentence, as represented in the phrase structure of the sentence, are the basis for arriving at the meaning of the sentence.

THE SEMANTIC APPROACH. The semantic school is much like the syntactic school in its description of surface structure. It differs, however, in its description of underlying representations. Our description of this approach follows that of Clark and Clark (1977). The semantic school describes the underlying representation of a sentence by the use of **propositions,** a notion we discussed earlier in relation to memory (pages 84–85). A sentence of any complexity can be restated as a set of simple sentences, each of which expresses an underlying proposition.

For example, *A quizzical look crossed Patricia's face* can be restated as (a) *A look crossed the face,* (b) *The look was quizzical,* and (c) *The face was Patricia's*. A simple sentence is not the same thing as a proposition; it merely expresses one. A proposition is defined as a unitary idea consisting of a verbal unit plus one or more nouns. In (a), for instance, the verbal unit *crossed* joins the two nouns *look* and *face*.

The underlying representation of a sentence is its meaning, and it is shown by the way the propositions for that sentence combine. The main proposition in this sentence is expressed by *A look crossed the face,* which is qualified by the other two propositions. If the main proposition were expressed by *The look was quizzical,* and the other two qualified it, then the surface structure of the sentence would change to *The look that crossed Patricia's face was quizzical*. In this paraphrase only the relation of the propositions has changed.

The internal structure of propositions is based on the way verbs relate to nouns, and in particular on the various roles nouns can play. Fillmore (1968, 1971) has analyzed the roles nouns may play into the following six *case relations:*

1. *Agentive case (A)*. A noun that is the instigator or agent for the action in the verb.
    a. *Mike* hiked the Buckeye Trail.
    b. The tent was carried by *Dave*.
2. *Instrumental case (I)*. An instrumental noun is an inanimate force or object that is involved in the verb action.
    a. The *wind* blew the clouds across the darkening sky.

$NP_1 + V + NP_2 \Longrightarrow NP_2 + was + V + by + NP_1$

George played the new organ   The new organ was played by George

Figure 6.3 Rule for transforming a phrase structure into the passive.

b. *Leaves* drifted down from the trees.

3. *Experiencer case (E)*. An experiencer noun is being influenced by the action or psychological state named in the verb.
   a. *Mike* felt the rain begin to fall.
   b. *Chuck* was still damp from the last rain.

4. *Goal case (G)*. A goal noun refers to an object or state resulting from the verb action.
   a. Dave made a *shelter* out of the ground cloth.
   b. The wind whipped the rain into a *storm*.

5. *Locative case (L)*. A noun in the locative case refers to the location or orientation of the verb action.
   a. Chipmunks had nibbled holes in the *ground cloth*.
   b. The trees diverted the water *there*.

6. *Objective case (O)*. This is a somewhat general case for nouns whose role in the verb action or state depends on the meaning of the verb.
   a. The cascading water drenched *Chuck* again.
   b. Mike gave *Chuck* his handkerchief.

A proposition has a verb plus one or more nouns in these case relations. Here are some examples of propositions with varying numbers of nouns in them.

1. Chuck grinned. $(V + A)$
2. He sponged up the water with the handkerchief. $(V + A + O + I)$
3. He wrung out the handkerchief down Mike's back. $(V + A + O + L)$

Each case relation can appear only once in the proposition—for instance, there cannot be two *agentive* cases in a proposition. Sentences, of course, often contain more than one noun in a case relation, but that is because such sentences are complex surface structures that have more than one underlying proposition.

Propositions have been used in some models of semantic memory (see Chapter 4), as well as in models for processing prose material. The notion of a proposition is still being developed, but even now it provides a convenient way of analyzing the underlying structure of sentences.

The semantic approach thus chooses meaning, as expressed in propositions, as the basis for the underlying representation of a sentence. Few people dispute the relevance of both syntactic and semantic relations in describing the structure of a sentence. The debate between these two schools lies instead over which is the more fundamental for describing that structure.

Surface Structure Clauses. Most of the sentences we use are complex; that is, they are composed of two or more clauses. A clause can usually be stated as a simple sentence, but its syntactic structure is often altered when it appears in a complex sentence. Clauses commonly appear in the surface structure in one of three forms: *coordination, relativization,* and *complementation.* Coordination joins two clauses on an equal basis by a conjunction such as *and* or *but.* For example, *and* pairs the two clauses in *Dick is gregarious, and he has lots of friends* as does *but* in *The paper forecasts rain, but the skies are clear.*

In relativization and complementation one clause qualifies another. Relativization is expressed in relative clauses, as in *The club that Dale belongs to is fairly exclusive. That Dale belongs to* is a relative clause restricting the meaning of *club.*

Complementation permits a clause to take the role of a noun. The incomplete sentence *(noun) was a real accomplishment* can be completed by introducing a complement in place of the noun. English provides three forms for complements. The first is introduced by *that*—for example, *That Hal skied Devil's Run was a real accomplishment.* The second contains *for . . . to*—for example, *For Hal to ski Devil's Run was a real accomplishment.* The third contains the possessive plus *-ing* and *of*—for example, *Hal's skiing of Devil's Run was a real accomplishment.* These three forms each have specific surface structure markers for the complement, and we shall see in the comprehension section that listeners use these markers to recover the underlying representation.

The significance of coordination, relativization, and complementation is that they permit the creation of complex sentences. The rules for creating these three surface structures may be applied repeatedly, producing a still more complex sentence with each application. For example, the series of sentences in "This is the House that Jack Built" is an example of the repeated use of the relativization rule.

Rules that can be applied again and again are called *recursive* rules, and they are a major source of the creativity of language. The child who recounts an adventure with ". . . and then . . . and then . . . and then . . ." is using coordination recursively, just as the tale of Jack's house uses relativization recursively. In addition, these forms may appear together in sentences. Complementation and relativization both appear in *For Mary to visit Russia was an adventure that she would never forget.* To this we may readily add coordination, as in *For Mary to visit Russia was an adventure that she would never forget, and she thought about it often.*

In summary, we see that sentences have both a surface and an underlying representation. Linguists disagree over whether the underlying representation should be based on the syntactic relations among the words or should be based on semantic relations as expressed in propositions. At the level of surface structure, we find that clauses may be combined in several ways to produce complex sentences. The recursive application of rules for combining clauses is one important source of the creativity of language.

Let us turn now to an analysis of words.

Words

Words have internal structure just as sentences do, and the function of a word in a sentence influences the form it takes.

Content and Function Words. Words may be divided into two classes, *content words* and *function words*. Content words are nouns, verbs, adjectives, and adverbs. Examples of these are shown in Table 6.1. Most of the words in a language are content words, since these describe the infinite variety of objects, acts, and properties in the world. The growth of our vocabulary is devoted largely to learning new content words.

Function words are the prepositions, conjunctions, pronouns, and other forms that show the relationships among content words in a sentence. Examples of these are also shown in Table 6.1. There are only a few hundred function words and most of them are learned relatively early. Function words are used frequently, however, since their number is small and they are needed to construct almost any sentence. The word *the* is the most frequently used word in English, and most of the other frequently used words are also function words. You can check this for yourself just by tallying the frequency of each word that occurs in a conversation you are listening to.

Morphemes. Words are composed of one or more morphemes; a **morpheme** is the smallest unit of meaning in language. *Wallpaper* is composed of *wall* + *paper,* each of which contributes to the meaning of *wallpaper,* as is the case for *houseclean* and *finespun.* In these examples each syllable is a morpheme, but not all syllables are morphemes. *Vac-u-um* is a single morpheme word, as are *spir-it* and *rhy-thm,* though they have more than one syllable.

Inflections are a special type of morpheme which can be applied to many of the words of a particular class. Prefixes and suffixes are the

Table 6.1 The Major Word Classes in English

Content words
  Nouns: dog, apple, matriarchy, elation, etc.
  Verbs: go, receive, believe, trip, etc.
  Adjectives: happy, naughty, pusillanimous, etc.
  Adverbs: sadly, understandably, aptly, etc.

Function words
  Pronouns: I, you, she, . . . he.
  Determiners: a, an, the, this, . . . some.
  Quantifiers: much, a few, more, . . . three.
  Prepositions: in, on, beside, to, . . . of.
  Intensifiers: very, too, a little, . . . quite.
  Coordinate conjunctions: and, but, . . . or.
  Adverbial conjunctions: although, if, because, . . . before.
  Conjunctive adverbs: besides, nevertheless, . . . hence.
  Relative pronouns: who, which, whose, . . . that.
  Auxiliary verbs: can, may, have, . . . must.
  Linking verb: be.

Source: After Bolinger (1975).

most common types of inflection. For example, *-ed* can be added to most verbs to form the past tense. Since adding *-ed* changes the meaning of the verb, it is a morpheme. Other examples of inflections are shown in Table 6.2. Many languages make much greater use of inflections than does English, as anyone who has tackled German verb conjugations knows.

Table 6.2 Examples of Inflections Used in English

INFLECTION	FUNCTION	EXAMPLE
-ed	create past tense of verb	*worked, filled*
-s	create plural of noun	*birds, apples*
	create third person singular of verb	*sleeps, builds*
-ing	create progressive of verb	*running, singing*
-ness	make a noun of an adjective	*roughness, sadness*
-ate	make a verb of a noun	*chlorinate, captivate*
un-	negate meaning	*unhappy, unfinished*
re-	repeat action	*replay, refinish*

Since a word often has many inflected forms—for example, *cooks, cooking, cooker, cooked, recook, uncooked*—we should like to know whether each inflected form is stored in memory or whether stems and inflections are stored separately and combined at the moment of use. We shall take up this question when we discuss the use of language.

Sounds

Our last level of analysis is that of sounds. The spoken form of a word is composed of a sequence of sounds. The particular sounds used in a language as well as the order of the sounds in words are described by the rules for that language. Since speaking is a matter of converting meaning into sound and since understanding is a matter of recovering meaning from sound, these rules are of interest.

The sounds of a language are usually analyzed at two levels, the phonemic level and the phonetic level. At the phonemic level, the phoneme is the unit of analysis. The **phoneme** is the smallest unit of sound in which differences in sound can produce differences in meaning. The initial sounds in *pad* and *bad* are not only physically different but are also the source of the difference in the two word meanings. Hence *p* and *b* are different phonemes in English. There are approximately 40 phonemes in English, though different languages have different numbers of phonemes.

Phonemes are similar to letters of the alphabet, but they are usually shown with slashes (e.g., /p/) to distinguish them from letters of the alphabet. Most of the consonants in the alphabet are separate phonemes (e.g., /p/, /b/, /t/, /k/, /s/), though some are not. For example, the letter *c* always has the sound of /k/ *(cat)* or /s/ *(celery)* and is not a separate phoneme. The vowels of the alphabet each stand for more than one phoneme. For example, *a* has a different sound in *pa, pat,* and *pate*, and each of these sounds is a distinct phoneme. Linguists have developed a symbol for each phoneme, and we shall give a more detailed account of these in a later section.

The rules for a language describe, among other things, which sounds are permissable as phonemes in that language and the order in which phonemes may occur in that language. Many languages have phonemes not found in English, such as the trilled *r* in French or the umlaut vowels of German *(ö, ü)*. Similarly, the /ð/ phoneme in English, which is the *th* sound in *the* and *then,* does not occur in German and presents a problem for German speakers who are learning English.

The second level of analysis for sounds is the phonetic level. The phoneme is an abstract category, the individual instances of which are phones. A *phone* is the sound as it is actually pronounced, and phonetic analysis describes the physical features of these sounds. Linguists represent phones in brackets (e.g., [p]) to distinguish them from phonemes. Some phonemes are realized by more than one phone, though we are not always aware of the difference in pronounciation in these phones.

For example, there are two different phones for the phoneme /p/, as illustrated in the words *pin* and *nip*. The *p* in *pin* is accompanied by a small puff of air, called *aspiration,* and is represented as [p^h]. The *p* in *nip* is unaspirated and is represented as [p]. You can feel the difference between these two phones by holding the back of your hand near your lips as you say the two words. Though we are often not aware of it, there are contexts in which we systematically use [p^h] and others in which we use [p]. When a phoneme is realized by more than one phone, the phones are said to be *allophones* of the phoneme. Thus [p^h] and [p] are allophones of /p/.

In English, aspiration is a phonetic feature but not a phonemic one; that is, the difference between an aspirated phone and an unaspirated one does not produce a difference in meaning. In Thai it is a different matter. The word [paa] means *forest* while the word [p^{h}aa] means *to split,* though these words differ only in the aspiration of the *p*. Thus a feature of pronounciation which is phonetic in one language can be phonemic in another.

The rules governing the order of phones restrict the possible sequences of phones in a language. English does not permit sequences such as *tbkl* nor *npsh*, nor does it permit *ng* at the beginning of a word, though it does permit *ng* at the end of a word *(ring, sing)*. We shall see below that these rules bear on the way people perceive and produce speech sounds and especially on the kinds of errors they make in doing so.

FUNCTIONS OF LANGUAGE

The functions of language are more psychological in nature than is its structure, though function uses structure to achieve its goals. In this section we shall ask: What effects do speakers intend to have on their listeners, and how do they achieve them? How do they choose the content of what they say? What role does the listener play in this process?

Language provides a set of standard forms that a speaker may use to accomplish his or her purpose, such as uttering a question in order to gain information. The content of these standard forms varies with the speaker's purpose and can be analyzed separately from the forms. A speaker also keeps track of what the listener already knows, and selects utterances in a way that will meet the needs of the listener. We follow the analysis of Clark and Clark (1977) in describing these functions of language.

Speech Acts

A sentence can serve one of several functions. It can request information, command someone to do something, describe something, commit the speaker to something, and so on. Each of these functions is a *speech act,* and the speaker attempts to achieve the goal of the speech act by uttering a sentence. For example, the speaker utters a question in order to get information and utters a command in order to have someone do something. The intent, or goal, of the speech act is met if these things occur.

Speakers use the structure of their language to show which speech act they are performing. The general form for a speech act is *I (verb) to you (sentence complement)*. The particular form of speech act is shown by the choice of verb and sentence complement. Three of the most common forms of speech acts are assertions, questions, and commands. Assertions are illustrated by *I* **tell** *you that the train has already left* and *I* **say** *to you that the price of coffee is just too high.* The fact that these are assertions is signaled by the choice of the verb, in this case *tell* and *say.*

Questions are signaled by other verbs, as in *I* **ask** *you to tell me where we should meet* and *I* **request** *to know what time it is.* Similarly, commands are identified by the choice of verb, as in *I* **order** *you to be quiet* and *I* **command** *you to hand me that pencil.*

These sentences sound awkward to us and for good reason. Since assertions, questions, and commands are so common in English, speakers usually leave out much of the surface structure of these forms and utter only abbreviated structures, such as *The price of coffee is just too high, What time is it?* and *Hand me that pencil.* Listeners, of course, must be able to fill in the unspoken part if they are to respond appropriately to the speech act.

Thus the question of what effects a speaker intends to have on a listener is answered by a description of speech acts and the form of sentence chosen to carry out a speech act, and it is the content of these forms we turn to now.

Propositional Content

The information contained in a speech act varies with the speaker's purpose and is called the *propositional content* of the speech act. The propositional content is the expression of the underlying propositions that the speaker intends to convey by the speech act. Vendler (1967) states that propositions have three functions: (1) to denote events or states, (2) to denote facts about events or states, and (3) to qualify other propositions.

For example, in the assertion *I tell you that a robin built a nest on my porch,* the propositional content of *a robin built a nest on my porch* denotes an event, the building of a nest. If we expand the assertion to *I tell you that I was pleased to see that a robin built a nest on my porch,* the added propositional content denotes a fact about the event. *I was pleased to see* expresses the speaker's reaction to the event and constitutes a fact about that event.

Expanding the assertion once more will illustrate the remaining function of qualifying a proposition. *I tell you that I was pleased to see that a robin built a nest on my porch while I was away* contains the added phrase *while I was away.* The proposition expressed in this phrase qualifies the expression of the event by telling when the event occurred.

The spoken form of this assertion would probably be *I was pleased to see that a robin built a nest on my porch while I was away.* It is a complex sentence since it contains a relative clause *(that . . .).* As English sentences go, it is not very long, and it could easily be expanded. However, the added propositional content would serve one or more of the three functions of denoting an event, denoting a fact about an event, or qualifying an event.

Thematic Structure

The final aspect of language function involves the role of the listener. To communicate effectively, the speaker must keep track of several things about the particular listener. What does the listener already know? What new things will be of interest? The speaker's judgments about these questions are reflected in the *thematic structure* of his or her speech. We shall be interested in two aspects of thematic structure: the use of given and new information, and the use of subject and predicate.

Given information is the information in a sentence which the speaker assumes the listener already knows. *New information* is that information the speaker assumes the listener does not know. The speaker who says, "It was Bruce who taught in Bangkok," assumes his listener already knows someone taught in Bangkok, but does not know who. He puts the new information up front in the sentence and ties it to what she already knows with a relative clause. If the speaker thought his listener already knew Bruce had taught, but did not know where, he might say, "It was in Bangkok that Bruce taught."

New information is usually signaled by the *focal stress* of a sentence—that is, the word or phrase having the greatest emphasis in the sentence. In the following examples, focal stress is shown by capital letters: *Rudy finally won his BLACK BELT. Linda bought a new CAR.* The speaker assumes the listener knows Rudy and Linda but does not know what they did. Thus he signals the new information by the focal stress in the sentence.

The use of subject and predicate is related to the use of given and new information. The subject of a sentence identifies what the speaker wants to talk about, and the predicate describes what he wants to say about it. *Bill* is featured as the subject in *Bill took the emcee's part,* and the predicate says something about Bill. If the speaker wished to talk about the emcee's part, however, he might say, *The emcee's part was taken by Bill.* Thus the choice of subject signals what the speaker wishes to talk about.

In English the subject is often the given information, and the predicate is the new information. This aspect of sentence structure thus aids one of the functions of the sentence, which is to help the listener relate new information to given information.

In summary, the functions of language are manifested in speech acts, propositional content, and thematic structure. The speaker's choice of speech act signals his intent, whether he wishes to tell something, ask something, command something, or so on. The propositional content expressed in the speech act is the particular information he wishes to tell, ask, or command. This is given thematic structure by stressing new information and relating it to given information, often through the choice of subject and predicate. Each of these functions takes advantage of the structure of language to achieve its end.

COMPETENCE AND PERFORMANCE

Up to this point we have concentrated on the characteristics of language. The remainder of this chapter focuses on how people use language. Before taking up that topic, we wish to reiterate a distinction we made earlier between what people *know* about their language and how they *use* that knowledge. Chomsky (1965) labels these *competence* and *performance*. The section above on the structure of language partly describes the speaker or listener's competence — that is, what each knows about the language.

In general, the study of competence is the province of linguistics. Competence is an abstract system, a set of rules which a speaker and listener share and implicitly abide by in communicating. Competence is not a process, however, and the question of how people use their knowledge is a question of performance. In general, the study of performance is the province of psychology. The rules of chess describe the permissible moves for the game, but they do not tell us when to make these moves. Good chess players know something more; they know how to use these rules to play the game well. Similarly, having described the structure of language, that is, the rules, we shall examine some of the processes that use that structure.

Performance processes fall under two major topics, language production and language comprehension. In the language production section, we shall describe some of the present thinking about how people use their competence in creating speech. We shall ask: How do we choose what to say? How is that meaning translated into sound? In the language comprehension section, we shall analyze how people understand speech. There we shall ask: How do we translate sound into meaning? What psychological processes do we use in this task?

LANGUAGE PRODUCTION

The act of talking is at once natural and mysterious. There are few things we spend more time at; yet it is one of the least understood cognitive processes. Our knowledge of our language enables us to utter an infinity of sentences. How do we choose which sentence to say at any one moment? How do we use our knowledge of language to create that sentence? Karl Lashley (1951) broached this issue in a classic article entitled, "The Problem of Serial Order in Behavior." Lashley was one of the first to suggest that a schema orders speech elements and that the schema is independent of both thought and motor processes.

We shall examine a recent version of this notion, one that describes how thoughts are given syntactic and phonemic form. We shall then discuss how phonemic forms are converted into motor commands for speaking. As we go, we shall see that language production has many processes in common with problem solving, memory, and motor skills. The selection of the thought to be expressed has many of the goal-oriented characteristics of problem solving. Words are stored in semantic memory and must be retrieved as we speak. Finally, speaking itself is one of the most commonly used motor skills.

Thought and Language

We shall take the position that thought and language are separate symbolic systems, and that talking requires conceiving a message in the thought system and then translating it into linguistic form. It is often assumed that thinking is internal speech, as suggested by the fact that we sometimes carry on private conversations with ourselves. Fodor and his colleagues (Fodor, 1975; Fodor, Bever, & Garrett, 1974), however, offer several reasons for believing thought to be a separate system from language. First, if thinking is speaking internally, then those without language should not be able to think. Thus children who have not yet learned language should not be able to think; yet they regularly display rational behavior.

Second, many thoughts are very difficult to articulate. Our efforts to describe an odor, to express certain feelings, or to convey a complex idea do not always succeed fully; yet any thought should be easy to express if thought is conducted in language. Finally, such diverse processes as seeing, tasting, and using motor skills do not seem to be linguistically coded even though they interact with thinking. Fodor argues that, instead of assuming thinking to be internal speech, it is more plausible to assume a separate central processing system that coordinates information received through the sensory systems and that is expressed through language, gestures, facial expressions, or other motor behavior.

Fodor offers an analogy between thinking and computer processing. We may input information into a computer in several ways, such as punched cards, magnetic tape, or electric typewriter. In each case the computer converts the information into a central processing language called *machine language* and carries out its operations in this system. The results are then translated for output into numbers, English, or some other system for human use. Thus machine language serves as a central system that carries out computational functions and is common to all the input and output systems.

By analogy, humans may receive information in several perceptual systems, such as the visual code, the auditory code, or the olfactory code. Information in these codes is then translated into a central processing system, which we call thinking, for further processing. The results of this processing may be translated into language or other motor codes for expression. Thought thus serves as a central system for processing all the information received by the perceptual systems or produced in the expressive systems. It seems clear that the system for thought must be at least as complex as any perceptual or expressive system. In particular, thought must be at least as complex as language, if every sentence begins as a thought.

Although this interpretation is only an analogy, it does give us a framework for interpreting language production. A schematic of the processes that seem to be involved in language production is shown in Figure 6.4, which is adapted from analyses by Fromkin (1973) and MacNeilage and MacNeilage (1973). The seven stages for creating a sentence can be grouped into four basic processes: selecting a meaning, creating syntactic structure, creating phonemic structure, and motor processes. We will describe each of these processes and examine some of the evidence for them.

Selecting a Meaning

Stage 1 in producing a sentence requires selecting a meaning to be expressed. Like most of the processes involved in talking, this one is unconscious. Few of us are conscious of our sentences before we speak them. Speaking seems instead to be a matter of engaging the tongue to an efficient but well-hidden engine that delivers the sentence fully prepared to the tongue. Since selecting a meaning cannot be observed, we can only speculate about what goes on, but it appears to bear many similarities to problem solving.

The issues here revolve around the functions of language (see pages 147–149). The major question is, "What is the speaker's goal? Does he want to comment, persuade, ask, describe, or offend? Each of these goals leads to a different meaning, even though each goal may occur at the same point in the conversation as the others. The

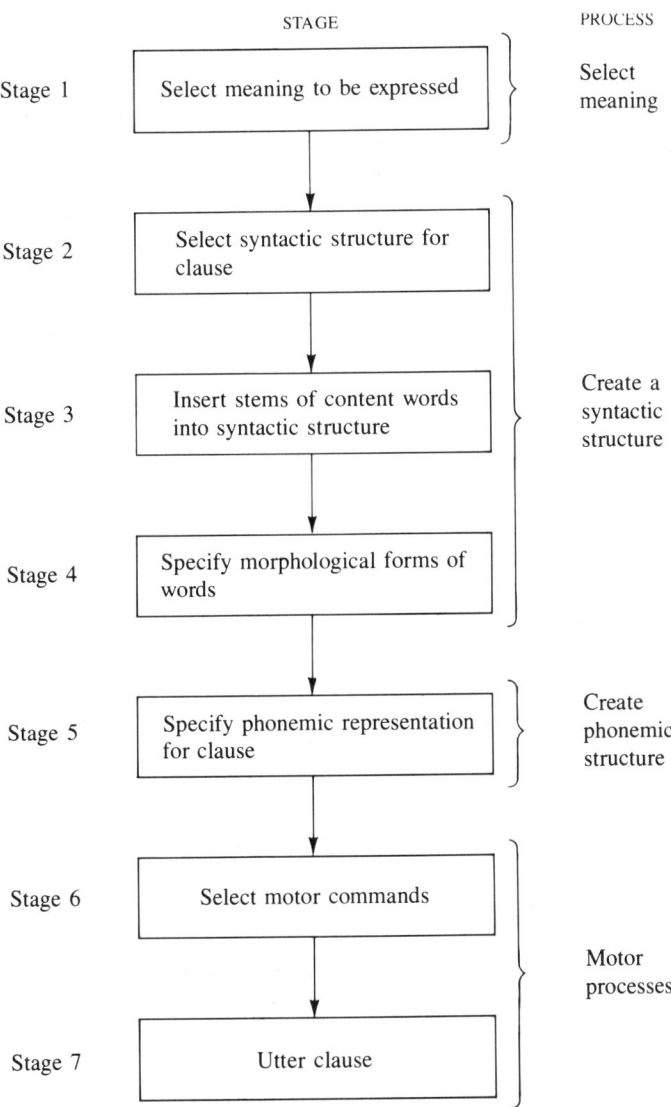

Figure 6.4 Schematic view of speech production.

follow-up question for the speaker is, "How do I get to the goal? The speaker's strategy in this problem will be based on his personal knowledge, the context of the conversation, and what he knows about his listener.

In describing, for example, he attempts to say something that the listener does not know and will be interested in hearing. He draws his information from semantic and episodic memory and fits it to the context of the conversation. In doing so, he focuses on information he thinks will be new for his listener. The importance of not telling your listener something she already knows is easily shown by telling a friend about the time you snuck into the movies and got caught. Bring the conversation around to the same story three times within the same hour. For the best effect (or worst effect), tell it with a straight face each time.

Creating Syntactic Structure

The meaning to be expressed is assigned a syntactic structure in Stage 2. The syntactic structure for the sentence to be produced will take the form of one or more surface structure clauses of the kind we described on pages 143–144. For example, the sentence *Larry chopped the logs that we had gathered in the woods* contains two surface structure clauses—*Larry chopped the logs* and *that we had gathered in the woods*. Each of these expresses a simple proposition in the underlying representation of the sentence.

At the end of Stage 2 in the development of this sentence, these two underlying representations will have been assigned syntactic structures of the form *noun phrase + verb + noun phrase,* and the form *noun phrase + verb + noun phrase + prepositional phrase,* respectively. In addition, the syntactic structure will specify the grammatical relations among the terms as well as the stress pattern of each clause. The grammatical relations for the first clause are *subject + verb + object* and its stress pattern is 1-3-2, where smaller numbers indicate greater stress.

In Stage 3 the stems for the content words (nouns, verbs, etc.) are selected, plus symbols indicating the morphological form the word is to take. For the first clause these would be *Larry chop+PAST log+PLURAL.*

In Stage 4 appropriate function words (prepositions, determiners, etc.) are selected, and the morphemic changes are made. In this example, *chop+PAST* is changed to *chopped* and *log+PLURAL* is changed to *logs.* The syntactic form of the clause is now *Larry chopped the logs.*

Creating Phonemic Structure

In Stage 5 the clause is given its phonemic representation. Each word is assigned the string of phonemes which represents how the word is to be pronounced. Table 6.3 shows the phonemes of

Table 6.3 English Phonemes and Their Pronounciation

SYMBOL	EXAMPLES	SYMBOL	EXAMPLES	SYMBOL	EXAMPLES
p	*p*at, ta*p*, hiccou*gh*	ð	*the*, mo*ther*, wrea*the*	e	b*a*te, b*ai*t, *eigh*t
b	*b*at, ta*b*, am*b*le	š	*sh*oe, mu*sh*, deduc*t*ion	ε	b*e*t, s*ai*d, d*ea*d
m	*m*at, da*m*, co*mb*	ž	a*z*ure, vi*s*ion, deci*s*ion	æ	p*a*n, *a*ct, l*au*gh
t	*t*ap, pa*t*, kiss*ed*	č	*ch*oke, ma*tch*, fea*t*ure	u	b*oo*t, tw*o*, thr*ough*
d	*d*ip, ca*d*, love*d*	j	*j*udge, *G*eorge, resi*d*ual	U	p*u*t, f*oo*t, c*ou*ld
n	*n*ap, ca*n*, sig*n*	l	*l*eaf, fee*l*, pa*l*ace	Λ	b*u*t, t*ou*gh, *o*ven
k	*k*it, *c*riti*c*, *c*ritique	r	*r*eef, fea*r*, ca*r*p	o	b*oa*t, g*o*, th*ough*
g	*g*uard, bur*g*, o*g*re	y	*y*ou, ba*y*, feu*d*	ɔ	b*ough*t, *aw*e, *au*thor
ŋ	si*ng*, lo*ng*, fi*ng*er	w	*w*itch, mo*w*ing, *qu*een	a	p*o*t, f*a*ther, mel*o*dic
f	*f*at, cou*gh*, *ph*ilosophy	ʍ	*wh*ich, *wh*ere, *wh*ale	ə	s*o*fa, *a*lone, telegr*a*ph
v	*v*at, do*v*e, ri*v*al	h	*h*at, *wh*o, re*h*ash	ay	b*i*te, s*igh*t, *i*sland
s	*s*ap, pa*ss*, pea*c*e	ʔ	bo*tt*le, glo*tt*al	æω	*a*bout, d*ou*bt, c*ow*ard
z	*z*ip, pa*ds*, *x*ylophone	i	b*ee*t, b*ea*t, bel*ie*ve	oy	b*oy*, d*oi*ly
θ	*th*igh, wra*th*, ari*th*metic	I	b*i*t, *i*njury, cons*i*st		

Source: Adapted from Fromkin and Rodman (1974).

English and how they are pronounced. As you can see from the table, the phonemic representation of *Larry chopped the logs* would be /læri čapt ðə lagz/. You might try writing the second clause yourself. At this point in the development of the sentence, the surface structure has been completed.

We will return to a discussion of the last two stages of the production process, but first let us examine some evidence for the ordering of the preceding five stages.

Evidence for the Order of Processing

We have assumed here that the creation of syntactic structure in the development of the sentence precedes the creation of phonemic structure. These two creative processes are unobservable, but we may infer something about them from the types of errors that occur in speaking. Speech errors commonly arise from adding, omitting, or misordering speech units and may occur at several stages in the production of a sentence.

One of the best known speech errors is the *spoonerism,* so called in deference to an English clergyman, Reverend William Spooner. The good reverend is credited with the following lines in upbraiding a student:

You've hissed all my mystery lectures (You've missed all my history lectures).

I saw you fight a liar in the back quad (light a fire).

In fact, you've tasted the whole worm (wasted the whole term).

Errors of this kind occur even among professional speakers (see Box 6.2, page 154). Fromkin (1973) has discussed additional types of speech errors, including the following examples.

1. A 50-pound dog of bag food (a 50-pound bag of dog food): Word misorder
2. laternoon classes (late afternoon classes): Omission of morpheme
3. Seven innings in one run (seven runs in one inning): Suffix relocated and word stems reversed
4. Shmut his mouth (shut his mouth): Phoneme addition
5. face spood (space food): Phoneme misorder

Analyses of the several types of speech errors suggest that the syntactic structure of a clause is created before the phonemic structure, since some errors involve misplacing whole syntactic units such as words and phrases. If phonemic structure were assigned before syntactic structure, however, one would expect such errors to arbitrarily interrupt word and phrase units.

Boomer and Laver (1968) collected a sample of 100 speech errors from recordings of conversations and broadcasts. The errors they reported were sequence errors—that is, misorderings of phonemes. A later analysis of these errors by Garrett and Shattuck (1974) showed that only two of the errors crossed clause boundaries. This suggests that the syntactic structure that governed the selection of the phonemes was already in place and that an error had occurred merely in locating the phonemes in their proper place within that structure. One would expect sound exchanges to cross clause boundaries if the syntactic structures for two or more clauses were simultaneously available and the selection of phonemes for all these clauses were being made at the same time. Present evidence, however, suggests that clauses are developed one at a time and in the order in which they are to be spoken.

Further evidence for this hypothesis comes from the fact that errors that do cross clause boundaries are primarily word exchanges rather than phoneme exchanges. Fromkin (1973) cited the example, *If you'll meet him, you'll stick around (If you'll stick around, you'll meet him).* In this example whole words have been exchanged across clause boundaries, but the phonemic structure of the exchanged words is correct. Apparently the syntactic structures for the words were selected, though in the wrong

Box 6.2 BLOOPERS

Speech errors are often called "bloopers" in the radio and TV world. They are the bane of every performer, and the stress of live performance seems to invite them. The following examples are adapted from Kermit Schafer's *Your Slip Is Showing*. See if you can identify the type of speech error in each one. Note that some display more than one type of error.

1. On "Exploring the Unknown," a science program, Andre Baruch, reading a commercial for a large corporation, called it "the largest producers in the United States of magnoosium, alleminum, and stool."
2. Introduction: "Ladies and gentlemen, the President of the United States, Hoobert Heever."
3. Announcer: "We now bring you, 'Mister Keene, loser of traced persons.'"
4. Introducing the "Friendly Homemaker Program," the announcer said, "And now we present our homely friendmaker."
5. Commentator: "All the world was thrilled with the marriage of the Duck and Doochess of Windsor."
6. On "Young Doctor Malone": "The doctor just fainted—he was lechering the nurse, and passed out."
7. On "Crime Photographer," Casey said to the T-man, "If you're not afraid to get some fingernails under your paint. . . ."
8. "The jockey got his foot caught in the syrup."
9. Commentator, covering the visit of England's King and Queen: "When they arrive, you will hear a twenty-one son galute."
10. Announcer: "Don't forget to visit your A and Poo Feed Store."
11. Broadcaster, introducing a woman who was about to broadcast a news show from Spain: "NBC now brings you the only woman correspondent in pain. . . ."
12. When a network was doing a series of classic romances, one of radio's most dependable announcers said, "And so ends another virgin of a famous love story."
13. Madison Square Garden announcer: "It's a hot night at the Garden, folks, and at ringside I see several ladies in gownless evening straps."
14. Commercial: "And Dad will love Wonder Bread's delicious flavor too. Remember it's Wonder Bread for the breast in bed."

order, before the phonemic structure of the words was assigned. Similarly, words may be exchanged within clauses and remain phonemically intact — for example, *I wouldn't buy kids for the macadamia nuts (I wouldn't buy macadamia nuts for the kids)* (Fromkin, 1973), and *Does your close store at six? (Does your store close at six?)* (Garrett & Shattuck, 1974).

Words are uttered as whole units, but we have assumed that the stem of a word is selected first (Stage 3) and then morphemic changes are made to the stem (Stage 4). The independence of these stages is evidenced by exchanges of affixes (prefixes and suffixes)—for example, *singing sewer machine (Singer sewing machine)* (Fromkin, 1973), and *He made a lot of money intelephoning stalls (He made a lot of money installing telephones)* (Garrett & Shattuck, 1974).

MacKay (1978) offers additional evidence that word stems are selected first, followed by morphemic changes. His subjects were given a verb and asked to produce a related noun as fast as possible using one of the suffixes *-ment, -ence,* or *-ion*. For example, given *equip* they were to produce *equipment* and given *decide* to produce *decision*. MacKay hypothesized that such words are stored as a stem plus rules for applying the suffix, rather than being stored independently as whole words. For some nouns, he observed, the stem must undergo several changes when the suffix is added. For example, in *decide/decision* the vowel changes from /ay/ to /I/, and /d/ goes to

---

Box 6.3   BLENDS

Some speech errors are a phonemic blend of two words having similar meanings, like *stray* for *straw* and *hay*. The speaker is apparently undecided about which word better expresses his meaning, and his indecision is carried through the phonemic structuring of the word. Fromkin (1973) lists a number of examples of such blends:

striving/trying → strying
public/popular → poplic
insufficient/inferior → insufferior
edited/annotated → editated
slick/slippery → slickery
spank/paddle → spaddle
person/people → perple
grizzly/ghastly → grastly
draft/breeze → dreeze
tummy/stomach → stummy
near/close → clear
dealer/salesman → dealsman
terrible/horrible → herrible
transposed/transcribed → transpised

Though most blends are not a true word, they do follow English rules of pronunciation. *Spank/paddle* does not result in *spakdnl* or a similarly unpronounceable string, but in *spaddle*, a perfectly pronounceable nonword.

/ž/ when *-ion* is added. However, in *equip/ equipment* no change occurs in the stem when *-ment* is added. MacKay reasoned that the amount of time required to produce the noun form should increase with the number of stem changes, and his reaction time data confirmed this hypothesis.

The assignment of phonemes to a word seems to be related to the syllable structure of the word. When phonemes are exchanged, they tend to come from the same place in the syllable; some examples from Fromkin are *canpakes (pancakes), relevation (revelation), serp is souved (soup is served),* and *with this wing I thee red (with this ring I thee wed).* Although some errors result in actual words (as in the last example), most do not.

The general pattern that emerges from these data is one in which the syntactic structure of the clause is created first, followed by the assignment of word stems, affixes, and phonemes, in that order. The existence of speech errors at each of these levels suggests that the levels are independent stages in the development of the clause. The fact that errors involving affixes and phonemes rarely cross clause boundaries suggests that the assignment of these elements occurs relatively late in the development of the clause. In general, errors occur in the stressed syllables of the words of a clause, but the stress pattern of the clause remains unchanged, indicating that it is fixed relatively early in the development of the syntactic structure of the clause.

Motor Processes

Let us return now to Stages 6 and 7, which involve the motor commands for uttering the clause. The final product of Stage 5 is a phonemic representation of the clause /læri čapt ðə lagz/. In Stage 6 the phonemic representation is coded into a set of motor commands for uttering the clause. The motor commands specify the movements of the lips, tongue, jaw, vocal folds, and other components of the vocal tract involved in uttering the clause. A critical question at this stage is, What is the code?

A plausible hypothesis, which is known as the *motor command hypothesis,* assumes that each phonemic representation of a clause is encoded from left to right. The commands for one phoneme are issued simultaneously, followed by the commands for the next phoneme, and so on. This assumption accounts for the ordering of sounds in speaking.

The motor command hypothesis has encountered some serious difficulties, however. First, the transmission speed of motor commands to the different articulators varies. For example, the speed of transmission of a command to the lips is faster than that to the jaw. If all the motor commands for a phoneme were initiated at the same time, they would reach the articulators at different times and so would not be properly coordinated for uttering that phoneme.

Second, the muscle contractions associated with speaking a particular phoneme vary significantly with the context in which the phoneme appears. MacNeilage and DeClerk (1969), for example, measured contractions in the muscles of the mouth and jaw for subjects who pronounced 27 syllables such as /bæd/(*bad*), /big/(*beeg*), /dub/(*doob*), and /dɔb/(*daub*). The results of these measures showed that in nearly every case the muscle contractions for a phoneme differed according to the phoneme that preceded or followed it. For example, the contractions for /d/ differed according to whether it occurred in /bæd/(*bad*), /bid/(*beed*), /gud/(*gude*), /dɔg/(*dog*), and /dæb/(*dab*).

Differences in the pronunciation of a phoneme, produced by differences in the context in which the phoneme occurs, are called *coarticulation effects,* and are common in normal speech. An example of coarticulation is the pronunciation of /t/ in *too* and *tea*. The vowel in *too* is pronounced with rounded lips, while the vowel in *tea* is pronounced with spread lips. However, the rounding/spreading is anticipated in the pronouncing of /t/, so that the /t/ in *too* is pronounced

Box 6.4 THE TIP-OF-THE-TONGUE PHENOMENON

Many of us have had the mildly frustrating experience of being very close to recalling a word, yet not quite being able to. Brown and McNeill (1966) found they could induce this state experimentally by reading subjects definitions of uncommon words and asking the subjects to give the word. See if you can give the correct word for the following definitions. Answers are given below.

1. A small boat used in the rivers of China and Japan, rowed from the stern, and often having a sail.

2. The practice of appointing relatives to positions of influence without regard to their qualifications.

3. The study or collection of coins and medals.

Brown and McNeill found many subjects were unable to give an answer; others knew the correct word immediately. In a small number of cases, however, subjects reported having the tip-of-the-tongue feeling. These subjects were asked if they could tell (1) what the first letter of the word was, (2) how many syllables the word had, and (3) what some similar sounding words were.

In a surprising number of cases their answers were correct, even though they could not say what the correct word was. The first letter was correctly reported 62 percent of the time, though chance success was a mere 8 percent. The number of syllables was reported correctly 57 percent of the time, though chance performance was only twenty percent. In giving similar sounding words, subjects often gave words having the same initial letter and same number of syllables. Thus for *sextant*, subjects reported such words as *secant*, *sextet*, and *sexton*. Though subjects could not report the correct word, they could reject incorrect candidates. At some level the word was available, though it was not immediately accessible.

Brown and McNeill concluded that the various aspects of the phonemic structure of words are stored separately. In normal speaking, we retrieve all the phonemic aspects of a word, but once in a while only some of these aspects are accessible.

This interpretation of the tip-of-the-tongue phenomenon is consistent with the notion that, in speaking, meaning is developed before the selection of the phonemic structure of a word.

Answers: sampan, nepotism, numismatics.

with rounded lips while the /t/ in *tea* is pronounced with spread lips.

The effect of preceding context is illustrated in the pronunciation of /k/ in *hawk* and *beak*. The back vowel in *hawk* produces a point of closure for /k/ which is relatively far back in the mouth, while the front vowel in *beak* produces a point of closure for /k/ which is relatively farther forward in the mouth. In general, coarticulation occurs when some of the articulatory gestures for one phoneme overlap with those of another phoneme. Thus there is no clear boundary between the two. The implication of this effect is that several phonemes must be readied in advance of what is being spoken so that the effects of context can be introduced. Our discussion of slips of the tongue also indicated that phonemes are planned ahead.

A second hypothesis about how the phonemic representation is coded into motor commands is the *articulatory target hypothesis*. MacNeilage (1970) argues that a speaker has an internal representation of the ideal vocal tract configuration for each of the 40 phonemes. Motor commands are thus governed by an internal spatial target. This hypothesis accounts for coarticulation effects by adjusting the motor commands for achieving a target phoneme to the context in which the phoneme occurs.

MacNeilage offers the analogy of a tennis player whose goal is always to return the ball. As the ball comes across the net on each play, the player finds herself in a different position relative to where the ball is headed, and so she must produce a new set of movements each time to reach her goal of returning the ball. Similarly in articulating a particular phoneme, the target shape for the vocal tract is always the same, but the shape of the vocal tract just prior to uttering that phoneme varies greatly. Thus the motor commands for achieving the target must be adjusted to the starting position of the vocal tract and vary greatly according to linguistic context.

An important issue in the articulatory target hypothesis is the role of feedback in influencing motor commands for a phoneme. We shall see in the motor skills chapter that feedback provides a major source of control for some motor acts. In speaking, feedback comes in the form of hearing the sound and feeling the movements of the articulators. Given the rapidity of speech (10 to 20 phonemes per sec), it is unlikely that feedback mechanisms operate quickly enough to control motor commands. MacNeilage suggests that the motor commands for phonemes may be under open loop control; that is, the adjustments for each target are specified in advance. Since the sequence of phonemes to be uttered is probably programmed well in advance of articulation, the opportunity exists to make these adjustments to motor commands prior to their issuance.

In Stage 7 the motor commands that have been created in Stage 6 are carried out. The movement of the articulators modifies the flow of air through the vocal tract to produce speech. It has taken us many pages to describe the processing of a clause from thought to speech, incomplete as our description is. Yet the whole act takes but a moment and is certainly one of the marvels of cognitive processing.

In summary, the act of talking begins with the development of a thought to be expressed. Since thinking is a nonlinguistic system, the thought must be translated into linguistic form to be expressed. The translation begins with the creation of a syntactic structure for the thought, the clause being the unit of syntactic structure. The translation then progresses through the selection of content words to fill in the syntactic structure, the assignment of the proper morphological forms for the words, and the assignment of phonemic forms to the words.

Evidence from slips of the tongue suggests that each of these stages is separate and that errors can occur in each stage. The order of the stages is indicated by the fact that errors in the latter stages rarely cross clause boundaries.

The phonemic representation is coded into a set of motor commands for each phoneme. These commands are governed by an articulatory target for each phoneme. The motor commands for each target are adjusted to the context in which the target occurs, probably in advance, and the commands are then carried out to produce speech.

LANGUAGE COMPREHENSION

On an average day most of us hear and understand thousands of sentences. Most of them are ones we have never heard before; yet we rarely have difficulty in understanding them. In this section we shall explore the processes that underlie this awesome capacity. We shall ask: What are the decoding operations for relating sound to meaning? How is the lexicon represented? How is knowledge of the world related to comprehension? Our answers to these questions suggest that comprehension is not a passive process, but an active one in which listeners construct meaning. In doing so, they use the sound pattern of the sentence they hear as well as their knowledge of language and of the world.

Our analysis of this constructive process will take us into the areas of speech perception, syntactic analysis, and meaning. Speech perception is the process of analyzing the sound pattern of a sentence. Syntactic analysis takes clues from the surface structure of the sentence to determine its meaning. As for meaning, we shall examine how meaning is represented and how it is processed in memory.

To aid our discussion of these processes, we shall use the schematic shown in Figure 6.5. In this schematic the acoustic signal is analyzed by the speech perception system into a string of perceived speech sounds. This perceptual string is then syntactically analyzed; the lexical search identifies the meaning of each word, and the syntactic processes identify the relations among the word meanings. The output of syntactic processing is the meaning of the sentence or clause, and the meaning is stored in memory.

Speech Perception

Only sounds reach the listener's ear. Their meaning is supplied by the listener. As a first step the

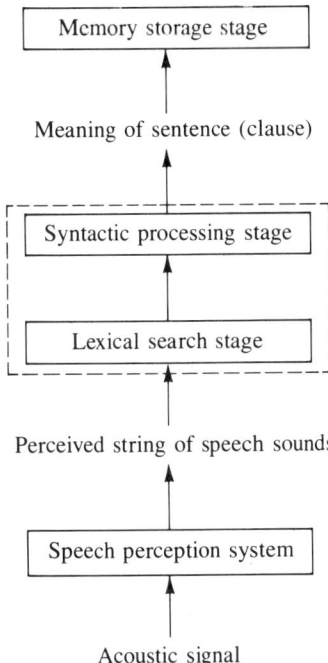

Figure 6.5 Major processes in comprehending a clause or sentence. (From Cairns & Cairns, 1976.)

acoustic vibrations reaching the ear are transformed into the string of perceived sounds. These are the speech sounds as they occur in consciousness, and they are represented by a phonemic transcription of the sentence. The transformation from acoustic to perceptual form seems to be complex, though it has not always been thought so.

The Invariance Hypothesis. An early hypothesis assumed that each phoneme has an invariant acoustic pattern, and that hearing is thus simply a matter of associating that acoustic pattern with perceiving the phoneme. This hypothesis led to the prospect of a "voice typewriter," an electronic device that would detect each acoustic pattern and link it to the appropriate typewriter key.

You would then be able to dictate to the typewriter and have your speech typed out. Unhappily for those of us who are poor typists, this hypothesis proved to be flawed. Let us see why.

The acoustic pattern of a sentence can be analyzed by a speech spectrograph, a device that records the intensity, pitch, and duration of an acoustic pattern on paper. Figure 6.6 shows a spectrogram of the sentence *I can see you.* Pitch is shown on the ordinate in cycles per sec. Intensity is shown by the darkness of the shading on the spectrogram. Above the spectrogram is a phonemic transcription of the sentence.

Early research showed that each phoneme displays a distinct set of formants in the spectrogram. A *formant* is a dark area in the spectrogram indicating greater sound intensity, as shown in Figure 6.7. It represents a concentration of energy which occurs at various pitches and for varying lengths of time. When simplified copies of formants are printed on tape and fed into a pattern playback, a device that converts the printed copies into an electronic signal and amplifies it through a speaker, the sounds you hear are quite recognizable speech. Thus the formants for each phoneme seemed to be the key to the invariant acoustic pattern for the phoneme.

Subsequent research, however, has revealed a number of problems with the invariance hypothesis (Liberman, Cooper, Shankweiler, & Studdert-Kennedy, 1967). For example, when /d/ is paired with different vowels, you would expect the formants for /d/ to remain the same if each phoneme has an invariant pattern of formants.

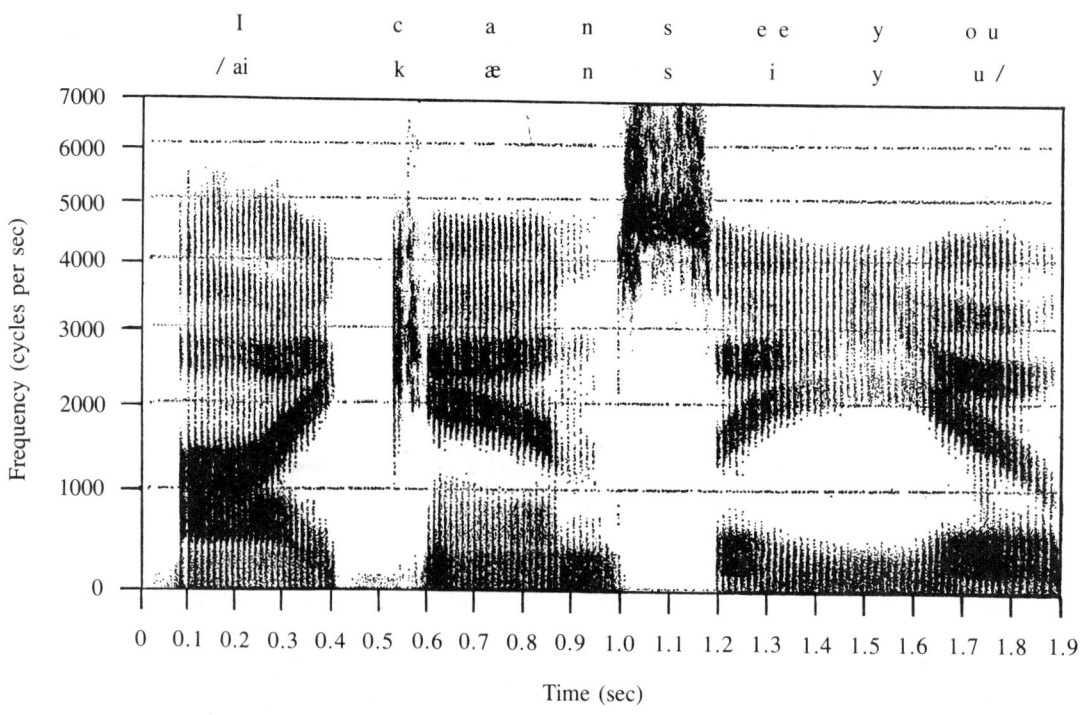

Figure 6.6 Speech spectrogram of *I can see you.* (From Denes & Pinson, 1963.)

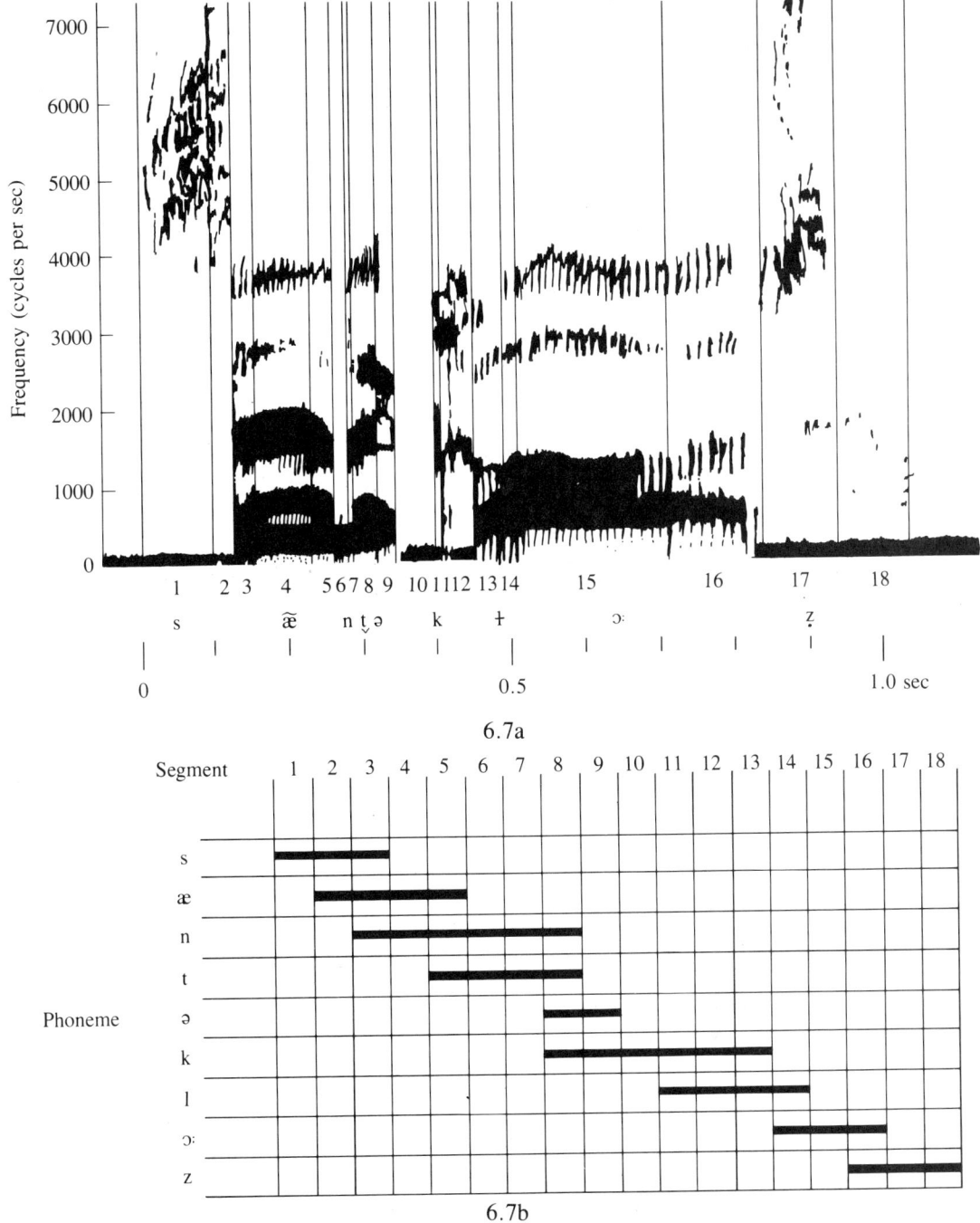

Figure 6.7 Perceptually, speech sounds seem to follow one another like a train of independent speech segments. Acoustically, however, there is considerable overlap. Speech spectrogram of the words Santa Claus (6.7a), where vertical lines mark acoustically different segments, and the assignment of phonemes to those segments (6.7b). (After Cutting & Pisoni, 1976.)

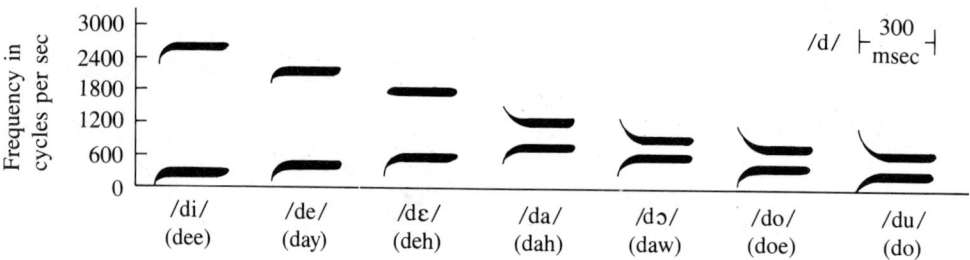

Figure 6.8 Spectrograms for the first two formants of /d/ followed by different vowels. (From Liberman, Cooper, Shankweiler, & Studdert-Kennedy, 1967.)

Liberman et al. found this not to be so. Figure 6.8 shows the formants for the syllables given at the bottom of the figure. In each pair of formants, the left side of the formant should carry the information for perceiving /d/, while the right side should carry the information for perceiving the vowel.

Note that the left side of the formants for /di/ shows a rising pitch for both formants, but the pattern changes as one moves toward /du/, which has a rising pitch for the lower formant but a falling pitch for the upper formant. Yet all these patterns are heard as /d/ when they occur in the context of the vowel shown. Similar effects have been found for the phonemes /b, g, p, t, k/. Thus different acoustic cues are perceived as the same phoneme, which contradicts the invariance hypothesis.

Efforts to isolate the acoustic pattern for /d/ have also been unrewarding. Liberman et al. took a recording of the formant pattern for /di/ and progressively erased the right end of the formants, hoping to remove the cues for /i/, leaving only the cues for /d/. When all the acoustic cues for /i/ had been removed, however, the remaining acoustic cues produced only a chirp that sounded nothing at all like /d/. Thus it appeared that /d/ not only had no invariant pattern of acoustic cues, but it had no isolable pattern of acoustic cues at all. This disconfirmed a second part of the invariance hypothesis—namely, that there is a distinct acoustic pattern for each phoneme.

From this and related work, Liberman et al. concluded that the acoustic cues for the phonemes in a syllable are not ordered serially but are transmitted *in parallel*. Information about the consonant and the vowel is intermixed and is being transmitted simultaneously to the ear (see Figure 6.9). Perceptually, however, the consonants and vowels occur serially, each lined up after the other like donkeys in a pack train. Thus the order of acoustic cues does not match the order in which they are perceived. Decoding

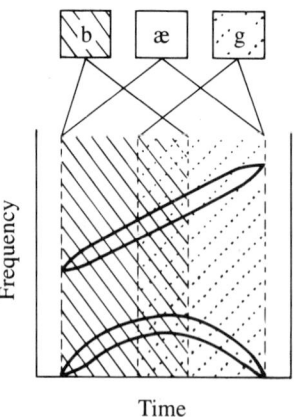

Figure 6.9 Parallel transmission: Information in the speech signal for each phone overlaps rather than being independent. (From Liberman, 1970.)

acoustic cues into perceptual events seems to be a complex process.

The complexity of the relation between acoustic patterns and *percepts* (that which we perceive) may be less surprising if we recall the discussion of coarticulation effects from the section on motor processes in language production (pages 156–159). There we saw that the lips are rounded in pronouncing the /t/ in *too* while they are spread in pronouncing the /t/ in *tea*. One of the articulatory gestures for the vowel is thus anticipated in the preceding consonant. Similarly, we saw that articulatory gestures for a phoneme frequently carry over to influence the pronunciation of a following phoneme. Thus the phonemes are not articulated in a linear order and so they do not occur in a linear order in the acoustic waveform that strikes the ear.

Analysis by Synthesis. Several theories have been offered to explain how the acoustic signal is transformed into a perceived string of phonemes. Although none of these seems fully adequate, let us examine two fairly different ones.

The first of these is the analysis-by-synthesis model proposed by Halle and Stevens (1964). This model assumes that the perceptual system generates strings of percepts which are hypotheses about the incoming acoustic signal. The strings of percepts are converted into internal representations of waveforms, much as would happen overtly if the strings of percepts were uttered as speech. The waveforms for the hypothesized strings of percepts are then matched against the waveform for the incoming acoustic signal. The best match indicates which string of percepts is to be heard.

This model is called *analysis by synthesis* because it analyzes the incoming acoustic signal by synthesizing (generating) perceptual strings that are to be tested against the incoming acoustic signal. The perceptual strings are synthesized from the listener's knowledge of the rules for phonemes and how they may be ordered. The fact that the strings are synthesized accounts for the linear order of the percepts. This model clearly assumes that the decoding operation is a very active, constructive one, since it involves the continuous creation of perceptual hypotheses about the incoming acoustic signal.

A second important assumption in this model is that speech perception is closely related to speech production. The hypothesized perceptual strings are converted into internal representations of how they would sound if they were uttered. This is matched with the incoming speech signal. As a result, speech perception and speech production have in common the operations that convert a phonemic representation into articulatory gestures. Although listening and speaking are obviously different at the peripheral level, they converge at the more central level of phonemic representation.

The Auditory Processing Model. The second theory of speech perception has been presented by Massaro (1975) and Paap (1975) and is distinguished from the first theory by the fact that it does not assume that production processes are involved in perception. The *auditory processing theory* instead assumes that the incoming acoustic signal is analyzed into sets of acoustic features, such as pitch, intensity, and duration. These sets of acoustic features are stored briefly while permanent memory is searched for a matching set of acoustic features that will lead to the proper percept. The sets of acoustic features stored in permanent memory are called *signs,* and it is at this level that phonemic knowledge is stored. Each sign represents a V (vowel), CV (consonant-vowel) or VC (vowel-consonant). Note that the auditory processing theory differs from the analysis-by-synthesis theory by storing phonemes in combination rather than individually.

Once the search process has identified a matching sign, the sign initiates commands for synthesizing the perceptual unit for that sign, that is, a V, CV, or VC. These perceptual units are what we hear as speech. In this manner this theory, too, accounts for the linear order of percepts.

Both these theories account for the linear order of percepts as well as for coarticulation effects. The analysis-by-synthesis theory accounts for coarticulation effects by introducing a portion of the production process into the perception process; and it is the production process, of course, that creates the coarticulation effects. The auditory processing theory accounts for coarticulation effects by using CVs and VCs as the unit of recognition for acoustic patterns. Whether one of these theories or still another theory will provide us a complete account of speech perception remains to be seen.

One message that is common to these and other current theories, however, is that speech perception is a constructive process. Such an assumption seems necessary to account for the complex relation between acoustic patterns and percepts, as well as to explain perceptual illusions—that is, perceptions that do not have the usual acoustic basis.

One example is the *slit-split* phenomenon (Liberman et al., 1967). A tape recording of *slit* can be made to sound like *split* simply by inserting a piece of blank tape of about 75 msec duration between the /s/ and the /l/. Perceptually, the effect is very compelling; the word sounds exactly like *split*. The perceptual system has taken an interval of silence somewhat similar to the acoustic cue for /p/ and produced a perfectly natural-sounding /p/. It is noteworthy that the perceptual system does not synthesize /t/ or /k/ or some other stop consonant that has partial silence in its acoustic signal. The reason seems to lie in the rules for ordering sounds in English. Only /p/ is permissible in this location; the perceptual system is constrained by these rules and /skIIt/ and /stIIt/ violate these rules.

Warren and Warren (1970) offer a similar example in the after-dinner-speaker effect. They recorded a sentence containing the word *legislature* and then removed the /s/ and replaced it with a cough. Subjects who heard the recording of the sentence failed to notice the missing /s/ and indeed were unable to tell which sound was missing even when told that one was absent.

A related effect was reported by Cole (1973) who had subjects listen to a passage that contained frequent mispronunciations. For example, *confusion* might have been pronounced *gunfusion, bunfusion,* or *sunfusion.* Subjects frequently failed to notice the mispronunciations even though they were easily able to identify the mispronounced syllables (e.g., *gun, bun, sun*) when they heard them in isolation. These results suggest that the subjects' perceptions were constructed not only from the acoustic signal but also from context information based on the structure of words and of the sentence.

Perception of Continuous Speech. The support provided by context is even more apparent in the perception of continuous speech. In normal conversation we hear the speaker's words as separate perceptual units. At the acoustic level, however, there is often no physical separation between words. The sound stream is more or less continuous as you can see in the spectrogram in Figure 6.6. There only the first two words show an appreciable separation, and this separation is due to the initial phoneme in *can;* /k/ is a stop consonant that requires a complete momentary blockage of the airstream when it is uttered.

If words often have no acoustic break between them, why do they sound distinct perceptually? The answer seems to lie once again in the constructive nature of the perceptual process. Listeners synthesize words on the basis of the speech signal, but the synthesis is constrained by the semantic and syntactic structure that is developing for the sentence. Thus the structure of the sentence, and indeed of the whole conversation, gives the listener a set of expectations about what is to come next.

These expectations can be violated, of course. Tell someone the sentence *The matadors fish on Friday,* and then ask her the meaning of *The cat on the mat adores fish on Friday.* Having been primed with *matadors* in the first sentence, she will probably fail to segment *mat* and *adores* in the second sentence and so will not be able to understand it.

Miller, Heise, and Lichten (1951) gave evidence of the influence of context in word identification by having people try to identify words against a background of white noise. Some subjects heard the words in sentences, while others heard them in isolation. Regardless of the noise level, those who heard the words in sentences identified more words correctly. A similar effect was reported by Pollack and Pickett (1964), who tape-recorded conversations and then played back isolated words snipped from the tape to a different group of subjects. The subjects were able to identify only 47 percent of these isolated words, though the words were presumably fully intelligible in the context of the conversation.

Pollack and Pickett found the proportion of identifiable words increased when they gave their subjects longer and longer segments of the conversations. Interestingly, the subjects' subjective experience in identifying the words was not one of "being close" to recognizing a word, but rather one of either recognizing it clearly or not at all. It was as if they were unconsciously offering hypotheses about what the word might be. When the hypothesis was wrong, the acoustic pattern was unintelligible; but when the hypothesis was correct, the word suddenly became perfectly clear.

Misperceptions provide a clue to such hypothesizing. Garnes and Bond (1977) have collected hundreds of such "slips of the ear" from everyday conversations. Here are some examples:

Intended: There's some ice tea made.
Perceived: There's a nice team mate.

Intended: You swallowed a watermelon.
Perceived: You smiled at a watermelon.

Intended: He worked in an herb and spice shop.
Perceived: He worked in an urban spice shop.

Intended: Speech science.
Perceived: Speech sinus.

Most of these errors show a conformity to the syntactic constraints of the sentence; that is, nouns replace nouns, verbs replace verbs, and so on. These results suggest that listeners are creating hypotheses about what they are hearing and sometimes accept wrong hypotheses. The hypotheses, which are synthesized perceptions of what the listener is hearing, reflect the contextual constraints of the sentence structure as well as being based on the acoustic signal.

Reddy and Newell (1974) have written a computer program that models the speech perception process for the restricted world of playing chess. The program contains syntactic, semantic, and phonemic information about the things people say in chess games and uses this information to interpret acoustic signals that represent utterances in a chess game. The semantic information represents knowledge such as how to play the game and the current state of the conversation. The syntactic information contains a vocabulary of 31 words related to chess and rules for combining them. The phonemic information defines the available phonemes and gives rules for detecting junctures between phonemes, predicting missing phonemes in mumbled speech, and so forth.

The program accepts a speech spectrogram of a sentence and attempts to analyze it into a sentence. As we have seen, the acoustic information (in the spectrogram) is insufficient to permit an accurate analysis by itself. Working from left to right, the program advances hypotheses about what each phoneme might be. As the phonemic string develops, it is matched against hypotheses that are being advanced at the syntactic and semantic levels. The final interpretation of the sentence is the one most satisfactory at all three levels of analysis. The advantage of such a computer model is that it provides a working model of the assumption that levels of analysis interact in speech perception. Of course, this model applies to the very limited world of chess conversation, but it may be possible to expand upon it.

The conclusion that emerges from these studies is that the perception of continuous speech is a constructive process that recruits information at all levels of the sentence structure to synthesize the perceived sentence. The developing syntactic and semantic structures of the sentence operate in a top-down fashion (see Chapter 2) to limit the possible perceptions, while the acoustic string operates in a bottom-up manner to further limit hypotheses. Collectively these interacting levels of analysis provide the context for determining the most acceptable perception of the acoustic signal.

In summary, a critical question in speech perception is how the acoustic signal is coded into the perceived string of phonemes. The invariance hypothesis suggested that each phoneme has a unique acoustic pattern that leads to the perception of that phoneme. Spectrographic analyses, however, showed that different acoustic patterns were perceived as the same phoneme, and that no acoustic pattern could be isolated for some phonemes. Thus the speech code seems to be complex, and the complexity probably derives from coarticulation in speaking. Analysis by synthesis interprets perception as being mediated by production processes, while the auditory processing theory assumes complex acoustic patterns are stored as signs. Both theories assume that perception is constructive in that perceptions are synthesized.

Now we turn to the level of lexical analysis to see how the meanings of words are recovered once their phonemic form has been perceived.

Lexical Analysis

At this stage the phonemic representation of a word is paired with its meaning. A college graduate knows 25,000 to 50,000 words, and the meanings of these are stored in memory. In this section we shall ask (1) how are meanings coded in the mental lexicon, (2) how are meanings retrieved from the lexicon during comprehension, and (3) how much information is available at the moment of retrieval? Our attempts to answer these questions will necessarily lead us to reconsider some issues we first raised in Chapter 4 on the structure of permanent memory and should help us formulate a more complete view of memory.

The question of how meanings of words are coded is part of the problem of semantics, one of the thorniest problems in linguistics. There are two attractively simple theories that we shall describe, but only to show that they must be discarded. These are the *reference theory* and the *image theory*.

The reference theory states that the meaning of a word is simply the object the word refers to. For example, the meaning of *giraffe* is simply the delightful beast we are all familiar with. Of the several problems with this theory, a major one is that many words have no object to which they refer. What, for instance, is the object denoted by *however, if, and, above,* or *in?* Second, words that refer to the same object often do not mean the same thing. In the sentence *Emily is a speech therapist and a marvelously funny woman,* the words *Emily, therapist,* and *woman* all refer to the same person; yet we can hardly claim that they have the same meaning. Meaning is more than just reference.

The image theory states that the meaning of a word is the image the word evokes. The problems with this theory are similar to those with the reference theory. Many words appear to have no image—for example, such abstract words as *mercy, proof, or, however,* and *during.* Moreover, images are particular, while words are often general. Does the word *flower* evoke the image of a tulip, a begonia, or a rose? Clearly these are only particular instances of flowers, and we do not have an image that has all the characteristics of all flowers. Although many words evoke images, it seems that we cannot equate these images with the meanings of the words.

The Dictionary and the Encyclopedia. An absorbing question about the mental lexicon is whether it is organized more like a dictionary or more like an encyclopedia. If it is like a dictionary, then each lexical entry holds phonemic information about the entry, its syntactic category, and its meaning. For example, *stool* would be represented as "/stul/; noun; a single seat without a back or arms, supported on three or four legs." If it is like an encyclopedia, however, the meaning of the entry would contain all our knowledge about stools—that is, what they are made of, how they are used, what they look like, and all the experiences we have had with them.

The encyclopedia metaphor suggests that each of us should have a different meaning for *stool* since we each have had different experiences with stools, and that furthermore the meaning should change with each new experience. Both of these metaphors are useful. The dictionary metaphor seems appropriate, since it suggests that all speakers share a common meaning for the term. However, it seems reasonable to suppose that the meaning of a term should give us access to all our knowledge about that term; that is, the dictionary should somehow be linked to the encyclopedia.

Two contemporary theories of meaning offer insight into this issue, though we shall see that they raise new questions as well. The first of these was developed by linguists and was primarily intended to be a formalism for representing the semantic structure of words. The second was developed by psycholinguists and incorporated some of the work of the first. It attempts to represent the psychological operations used in processing lexical information and shows some parallel to the semantic memory models we described in Chapter 4.

Componential Analysis. Many words can be analyzed into a set of component features. *Girl*, for example, can be analyzed into *human, female, nonadult;* while the word *boy* has the features *human, male, nonadult*. In like manner, *woman* has the features *human, female, adult;* while *man* is composed of *human, male, adult*. The similarities and differences among these four words can be shown more clearly if they are expressed as:

girl: *+human, −male, −adult*
boy: *+human, +male, −adult*
woman: *+human, −male, +adult*
man: *+human, +male, +adult*

Several efforts have been made (e.g., Katz & Fodor, 1963) to show that each word in the lexicon can be described by a set of semantic features of this kind. The total number of features is assumed to be relatively small, providing an economical way of representing meaning. If two words are similar in meaning, they are assumed to have similar feature patterns. For example, the patterns for *girl* and *boy* differ in only one feature. Words having quite different meanings, such as *girl* and *plow,* are represented by quite different feature patterns. Further, many words have more than one meaning. Among the meanings for *board,* for example, are "a plank," "a governing committee," and "a meal plan." In systems of this kind each of the meanings is shown by a unique feature pattern, though they have the common phonemic representation /bord/.

Componential analysis has been used effectively for several kinds of terms—kinship terms, for instance, such as *father, mother, aunt,* and *uncle* (Romney & d'Andrade, 1964). This approach is not without problems, however. The words *girl, boy, woman,* and *man* can be analyzed into a set of binary features (± *human,* ± *male,* ± *adult*), but many terms cannot be described by binary features. For example, the class of metals (iron, zinc, gold, copper, and so on) does not seem to yield to this type of analysis.

A second problem lies in what may be called "fuzzy categories." Wittgenstein (1953, 1958) argues that the category *games* has no properties that are common to all its members, such as chess, checkers, softball, basketball, hopscotch, or canasta. Although different subsets of games may have common properties, there appear to be no properties that are shared by all games, which means that *game* and other fuzzy terms cannot be handled by componential analysis.

Although there are difficulties in applying componential analysis, it has an important advantage that invites its continued investigation. The semantic features defining a word can be translated directly into propositions (Clark & Clark, 1977). As we saw on pages 142–143, propositions are one way of describing the underlying representation of a sentence. The meaning of a sentence is based in part on the meanings of its individual words and in part on how these meanings are related. As Miller (1965) notes, a *venetian blind* is different from a *blind Venetian*. The fact that semantic features can be translated into propositions thus gives an attractive coherence to this semantic system.

Our second semantic theory parallels componential analysis in many respects but has the important advantage that it ties this type of analysis more directly to psychological processes.

Procedural Semantics. One of the functions of language for a speaker is to get his listener to attend to certain parts of the listener's knowledge. The speaker who uses *man* in a sentence is directing his listener's attention to the listener's concept of *man* which is stored in her lexicon. We shall discuss concepts more fully in Chapter 8, but a brief description here will aid our understanding of procedural semantics.

A **concept** is a name for a category of objects. The category is defined by a rule that states what objects are members of the category and what objects are not. There are several kinds of rules. A *conjunctive rule* states that an object must have all the properties listed in the rule to be a member of the category. The category of *insects,* for example, is defined by a rule that states that every member of the category is invertebrate *and* has six legs *and* has a head, thorax, and abdomen. Any object that does not meet all these criteria is not a member of the category, such as a spider, for instance, which has eight legs.

A second kind of rule is the *disjunctive rule,* which states that an object must have one or more of the listed properties to be a member. For example, the concept of *strike* in baseball is defined as any pitched ball that the batter swings at and misses *or* that goes between the batter's shoulders and knees without his swinging *or* that is hit beyond the foul line. A pitched ball that meets any one of these conditions is defined as a strike.

There are still other rules, of course, which we shall describe later; the important notion here is that a concept is defined by a rule. In procedural semantics the rule is treated as a mental operation for determining whether a word applies to an object. Table 6.4 illustrates the procedures for determining whether *man* should be applied to an object. Note that the procedures are essentially those of a computer program, which means that procedural semantics can be modeled and tested by computer simulation.

As you have probably realized, the concept of *man* in procedural semantics is defined in the same way that it is defined in componential analysis, that is, by the presence of the properties *human, male,* and *adult*. In general, a concept is also defined by the presence of certain properties, as the examples above show, which means that all the applications of componential analysis can be extended to procedural semantics. Fur-

Table 6.4 Semantic Procedure for Determining Whether *Man* Applies to x

Step 1. Is x human?
  If so, continue to 2
  If not, go to 5
Step 2. Is x adult?
  If so, continue to 3
  If not, go to 5
Step 3. Is x male?
  If so, continue to 4
  If not, go to 5
Step 4. The procedure succeeds: x is a man
Step 5. The procedure fails: x is not a man

Source: From Clark and Clark (1977).

thermore, procedural semantics rises above some of the limitations of componential analysis. Componential analysis uses only the conjunctive rule. Procedural semantics, however, uses several kinds of rules and so gains greater flexibility in defining terms.

We noted above that procedural semantics ties semantic representations more closely to psychological processes than does componential analysis. How is this done? The procedures used to determine when a word is appropriate are assumed to be mental operations based in such processes as perceiving, attending, and deciding. Miller and Johnson-Laird (1976), for example, have analyzed many words in terms of the perceptual operations linked to these words. Procedural semantics thus merges the dictionary into the encyclopedia, since the procedures for defining a word are linked to the very cognitive processes we use in coding and storing our experience of the world and in operating on that stored knowledge.

An example of how perceptual and decision-making processes are involved in semantic procedures may be helpful. Johnson-Laird (1977) has analyzed verbs of motion in terms of these processes. An illustration of his analysis is shown in the decision table in Table 6.5. K and Q are two billiard balls; K is moving toward Q. What verb should we use to describe this motion? Johnson-Laird argued that this depends on the action of Q. The four steps at the top of the table are procedural tests the observer makes, where t_0 and t_1 are two different times in this event. The answers to these tests may be either *Yes* or *No*, and the possible outcomes for these answers are shown under Test Outcomes.

The lower part of the table shows which verb is most appropriate for each test outcome. The *x* under the column of answers for Test Outcome 1 indicates that *meet* is the most appropriate verb for that event. Test Outcome 2, which has a different pattern of answers, identifies *converge* as the proper word, since it does not

Table 6.5 A Decision Table for Six Motion Verbs

		TEST OUTCOMES					
PROCEDURE STEPS		1	2	3	4	5	6
Step 1: Is K moving toward Q at t_0?		yes	yes	yes	yes	yes	yes
Step 2: Is Q moving at t_0?		yes	yes	yes	yes	no	no
Step 3: Is Q moving toward K at t_0?		yes	yes	no	no	no	no
Step 4: Do K and Q touch at t_1?		yes	no	yes	no	yes	no
VERBAL DESCRIPTIONS FOR THE SIX TEST OUTCOMES							
K and Q *meet*		x					
K and Q *converge*		(x)	x				
K *catches up with* Q				x			
K *gains on* Q				(x)	x		
K *joins* Q		(x)		(x)		x	
K *moves toward* Q		(x)	(x)	(x)	(x)	(x)	x

Source: Based on Johnson-Laird (1977).

satisfy the same conditions that *meet* does. An *x* in parentheses (*x*) indicates that the verb is acceptable, though it is not the most appropriate one.

The procedure steps are essentially the same ones we saw in componential analysis and the fact that the same steps can be used for defining several different words shows the semantic relationships among the words. Note, however, that these procedure steps are also basic perceptual processes that the observer carries out, and the decisions about these are also inherently cognitive processes. Grounding its semantic operations in basic psychological processes is one of the most significant contributions of procedural semantics.

Because of its recent emergence, it is not yet clear how procedural semantics will fare as a theory of semantic processes. Although it offers serious promise, it also faces several problems, among them the fact that many concepts have fuzzy boundaries. When, for example, is a stool wide enough to be a bench, or a bud open enough to be a blossom? We will encounter this particular problem again in the chapters on concepts and prose retention. Given the increasing interrelation among areas of cognitive research, we may find that developments in one area offer solutions to another.

In summary, the question of how words are stored in the mental lexicon seems to lead either to a mental dictionary or a mental encyclopedia. Componential analysis opts for a dictionary and defines terms by the presence or absence of a limited set of semantic features. This analysis has the advantage of capturing the uniformity of word meanings as well as showing how meanings are related and how they may be integrated into the propositions underlying sentences. Procedural semantics incorporates the techniques of componential analysis and links them to the encyclopedia. It also allies semantic operations more fully with psychological processes.

Syntactic Analysis

In the section on speech perception we saw that there is not a simple relation between the acoustic signal and the perceptual string. At the syntactic level we find a similar lack of invariance between the perceptual string and the underlying meaning of the sentence. Hearing the word *ring* alone does not tell us whether to think about weddings, telephones, or the leftovers in the bathtub. At a broader level, very similar strings of words may have quite different meanings. The sentences *Wrestling bears are exciting* and *Wrestling bears is exciting* are worded very similarly; yet the speaker is an observer in one and a participant in the other.

In this section we shall see how syntax mediates the relation between the perceptual level and meaning. We shall want to know how a listener recovers the underlying meaning from the surface structure of a sentence. What strategies does he or she use to do so?

Once again we shall find that comprehension is a constructive process in which listeners use their knowledge of syntactic structure, their lexical knowledge, their knowledge of the world, and their assumptions about how the speaker has coded his intentions into thematic structure. We shall also see that in this process of constructing meaning, the clause is the syntactic unit of processing. Listeners gather incoming words in working memory until a clause is complete, whereupon they analyze the meaning of the clause and store it in permanent memory.

Given that the function of speaking is to communicate a meaning, listeners typically assume that a speaker intends to make sense, and they try to construct a plausible meaning from what the speaker says. The degree to which listeners abide by this implicit contract is illustrated in a series of studies by Fillenbaum (1971; 1974a,b). His subjects were asked to paraphrase a series of "perverse" sentences, such as *John dressed and had a bath* and *Don't print that or I won't sue you.* We would normally expect John to have a bath and *then* dress, or to sue someone *for* printing something. Fillenbaum's subjects apparently thought so too, since more than 60 percent of them paraphrased the sentences in a way that changed the meaning to a more plausible one (e.g., *If you print that, I'll sue you*).

Even when Fillenbaum asked his subjects to check very closely to see whether there was any difference in meaning between the original sentence and their paraphrase of it, more than half the subjects saw no difference. Clearly, they expected the sentence to make sense and had not accepted the meaning required by the syntactic structure of the sentence. Even the subjects who saw that their paraphrases were incorrect defended their misinterpretations by saying they knew what the speaker had actually intended and had given a paraphrase of that. Thus the listener's assumptions about the speaker's intentions influence comprehension.

Clause Analysis. In the section on language structure we noted that the surface structure of a sentence is composed of one or more clauses. Several kinds of evidence suggest that listeners process the meaning of a sentence in clause units. As the words arrive, listeners store them in working memory. They assign each word a meaning and construct the meaning of the clause on the basis of the internal structure of the clause, their lexical knowledge, their knowledge of the world, and what they think the speaker intends.

Garrett, Bever, and Fodor (1966) offered perceptual evidence that the clause is a unit. They used pairs of sentences in which the end of a clause occurred on opposite sides of a word in the two sentences. For example,

1. In her hope of marrying / Anna was surely impractical.
2. Your hope of marrying Anna / was surely impractical.

The slash (/) marks the break between clauses. Note that in (1) the clause break comes before *Anna*, whereas in (2) it comes after *Anna*. Six pairs of such sentences were recorded and played to subjects through headphones. In one ear the subjects heard the sentence, and in the other they heard a sharp click ($\sqrt{}$) at some point in the sentence. Their task was to write down the sentence and show where the click had occurred.

Objectively, the click was located in the middle of one of the two words shown in (1) and (2). Subjects' reports of the location of the click, however, were often in error. For sentences like (1), the most frequently reported location of the click was just before *Anna*, which is in the clause break; whereas for sentences like (2), the most frequently reported location was in the clause break after *Anna*. Garrett et al. concluded that the clause is a perceptual unit that resists interruption by nonlinguistic sounds. The fact that the clicks tended to be misperceived as occurring at the boundary of the clause rather than within it supports this interpretation.

Critics of earlier studies of this type had argued that the mislocation of the clicks was not due to the perceptual unity of the clauses, but was due instead to pauses that often occur at the boundary of clauses. Experimental evidence has shown that such pauses tend to attract clicks (Garrett, 1965). To rule out this interpretation, Garrett, Bever, and Fodor (1966) prepared their sentence pairs so that the parts of the sentence being compared for click location were acoustically identical.

In (1) and (2), for example, the sentences have the same words except for the initial word or two. The tape recordings of the two sentences were made by making a single recording of the identical part and then splicing the two different beginnings on to copies of this part. Thus no difference in pauses at clause breaks could exist to influence the perceived location of the click. Garrett et al. concluded that the mislocation of the clicks was due to the fact that subjects organize the clause as a perceptual unit, and that such units resist interference.

If the clause is the perceptual unit of processing, then comprehension should be easier when material is presented in clause units rather than in some arbitrary unit. To test this hypothesis, Graf and Torrey (1966) gave readers a prose passage and then tested how well they understood the passage. The passage was shown one line at a time. For half the readers each line was a phrase or clause, as shown in Form A below, while for the other readers each line contained the end of one such unit and the beginning of another, as shown in Form B. If the clause is the normal unit of processing, then Form A should have been easier to comprehend than Form B; and Graf and Torrey indeed found comprehension scores for Form A to be better than those for Form B.

Form A

During World II,
even fantastic schemes
received consideration
if they gave promise
of shortening the conflict.

Form B

During World War
II, even fantastic
schemes received
consideration if they gave
promise of shortening the
conflict.

Once a clause is complete in working memory, its meaning is analyzed and dispatched to permanent memory. It has generally been observed that the meaning of a sentence is retained much longer than are its phonemic and syntactic structure. Phonemic and syntactic structure appear to be vehicles for conveying the meaning of a sentence, but are themselves often lost soon after that meaning has been determined. You can test this notion for yourself by asking someone to repeat a sentence you spoke one or two minutes earlier in a conversation. Your listener will usually have little trouble paraphrasing the meaning of that sentence, but will have more trouble in repeating the sentence verbatim.

A more systematic test of this hypothesis appears in a study by Sachs (1967). She read her subjects a series of passages of normal, descriptive material. Each passage contained a test sentence, such as (1).

1. He sent a letter about it to Galileo, the great Italian scientist.

The subjects did not know which sentence in the passage was the test sentence. Shortly after hearing each passage, the subjects were shown either the test sentence or an alternate form of the test sentence, and were asked to tell whether that sentence was one that had occurred in the passage. The alternate forms of the sentence consisted either of a formal change, which reordered the words in the sentence, such as (2), a syntactic change such as (3), or a semantic change such as (4).

2. He sent Galileo, the great Italian scientist, a letter about it.

3. A letter about it was sent to Galileo, the great Italian scientist.

4. Galileo, the great Italian scientist, sent him a letter about it.

Sachs found subjects were not able to detect the formal and syntactic changes after a delay of only 27 sec between hearing the test sentence in the passage and being presented the recognition sentence. However, they were able to detect the semantic change (4) even after a delay of about 46 sec.

Apparently subjects retained the form of the sentence only long enough to recover its meaning. Interestingly, however, if the test sentence occurred at the end of the passage and just before the recognition sentence was presented, subjects were able to detect each type of change. This indicates that syntactic information was still available in working memory, though it was not retained for very long.

Two additional studies support the hypothesis that the clause is the unit of processing in working memory. Stewart and Gough (1967) used a probe technique in which subjects heard a sentence and then were given two words. Their task was to say whether both words had occurred in the sentence. Stewart and Gough compared reaction times for this decision in two conditions. In the first, the two words came from the same clause in the sentence; but in the second, the two words straddled a clause break in the sentence. For example, the two words *large corporations* occur in the same clause in the sentence *The presidents of large corporations / pay millions of dollars in taxes each year*. The same two words occur in separate clauses, however, in *When profits are large / corporations pay millions of dollars in taxes each year*.

Stewart and Gough hypothesized that the two probe words should be easier to recover if they occurred within the same clause than if they occurred in different clauses. Their results showed that reaction times were significantly faster for word pairs within a clause than for those that crossed clauses, indicating that the two clauses were at different stages of processing.

Caplan (1972) also used the probe technique in testing a related hypothesis. His subjects heard a sentence and then 100 msec later were given a single probe word. If they recognized the probe word as having occurred in the sentence, they were to press a lever that recorded their reaction time. In a series of studies, Caplan found that reaction time was significantly faster if the probe word came from the last clause of a sentence than if it came from the next-to-last clause. For example, the probe word *rain* occurs in the next-to-last clause in *When the sun warms the earth after the rain / clouds soon disappear,* but it occurs in the last clause in *When a high-pressure front approaches / rain clouds soon disappear*. The reaction time to *rain* was faster in the latter sentence.

Note that the two sentences are alike following the probe word, and therefore the differences in reaction time cannot be explained by differences in this information. The results instead support the hypothesis that the first clause in the sentence has already been processed for meaning, and information about specific words is less available than it is in the last clause of the sentence. The last clause is presumably still in working memory when the probe word is given, so that lexical items are more available.

Additional support for this interpretation appears in work by Jarvella (1971), who read subjects short stories. Jarvella interrupted the story from time to time to ask the subjects to recall the preceding material as accurately as possible. He found words from the clause immediately preceding interruption were best recalled, and word recall was much poorer for clauses that preceded this one. Jarvella not only found that clause boundaries produced this effect, but that sentence boundaries did too. Consider the following examples:

1. The tone of the document was threatening //
   Having failed to disprove the charges /
   Taylor was later fired by the President.

2. The document had also blamed him /
   for having failed to disprove the charges //
   Taylor was later fired by the President.

The single slash (/) marks a clause boundary within the sentence, while a double slash (//) marks a clause boundary that is also the end of a sentence. Note that the middle clause in (1) is part of the last sentence, while in (2) it is part of the next-to-last sentence. Jarvella found subjects recalled the middle clause better if it was part of the last sentence than they did if it was part of the next-to-last sentence. In either case, of course, the last clause was recalled best. Sentence boundaries thus show the same effect that is produced by clause boundaries.

Interestingly, Jarvella found that words within a clause were equally well recalled regardless of where they occurred in the clause. For example, words at the end of the clause were not better recalled than those at the beginning. This supports our hypothesis that the clause is processed as a unit.

In a second part of these studies, Jarvella explored his subjects' recall of the meaning of the stories by asking them questions about the content of the stories they had heard. Unlike the word recall task, the meaning recall task showed almost no influence from the number of clauses occurring between the information to be recalled and the point of interruption. Jarvella concluded that the clauses initially held in working memory were being transferred into a semantic form for storage in permanent memory.

Surface Structure Analysis. To recover the underlying meaning of a sentence, the listener must identify the clauses in the sentence, the relations among them, and the internal structure of each clause. The surface structure of the sentence contains much information to aid in this task, and Kimball (1973) has proposed a series of strategies by which a listener might use this information. For example, to identify how a clause is related to the rest of the sentence, Kimball suggests that subjects may employ the strategy,

> Use the first word (or major constituent) of a clause to identify the function of that clause in the current sentence.

In the section on surface structure clauses in the structure of language, we saw that relative clauses and complementizers are two common types of clauses. Kimball's strategy suggests that relative clauses can be identified by the fact that they begin with a relative pronoun (*who, which, that*, etc.), and this indicates that the clause modifies a noun in the sentence. For example, the *who* clause in *The man who is the clown likes kids* qualifies *man*.

In contrast, complementizers function as a noun in the sentence and are identified by *for . . . to, possessive + -ing,* or *that*. Thus, *For Jim to find a job* is the subject noun in *For Jim to find a job was good news for everyone.* As with any strategy, these do not work every time. For example, *that* can begin either a relative clause or a complementizer. However, the strategy reduces the number of possible interpretations enormously and so makes comprehension more efficient.

If people do use such strategies, then we might suspect that removing the surface structure cue would make a sentence harder to comprehend. In English it is often permissible to use a relative clause without the relative pronoun. For example, *The music that Johnny composed was delightful* can also be stated *The music Johnny composed was delightful.* Fodor and Garrett (1967) tested comprehension for sentences without the relative pronoun against those that had the relative pronoun. They measured comprehension by scoring the accuracy of their subjects' paraphrasing of the sentences.

The sentences they chose contained embedded relative clauses and were sufficiently complex that the subjects could not paraphrase them perfectly each time. Sample sentences with and without the relative pronouns are shown in (1) and (2), and a paraphrase of these is shown in (3).

1. The pen which the author whom the editor liked used was new.
2. The pen the author the editor liked used was new.
3. The editor liked the author, who used the pen, which was new.

Fodor and Garrett found that paraphrases of sentences having the relative pronouns were much better than paraphrases of sentences not having the relative pronouns. This supports the hypothesis that people use the relative pronoun as a cue to the existence of a relative clause.

Hakes and Cairns (1970) tested the same hypothesis in a different kind of task. They used the same sentences Fodor and Garrett had used, but asked their subjects merely to listen to the sentence and press a key when they heard a certain phoneme. In sentences (1) and (2), the phoneme was the *u* in *used*. Hakes and Cairns hypothesized that subjects would have more difficulty in comprehending sentences that did not have the relative pronouns, and so would give less attention to monitoring the phoneme.

This hypothesis relates to the work we described in Chapter 3 on temporary memory, which showed that working memory has a limited capacity and is easily overtaxed. The reasoning of Hakes and Cairns was supported by the results of this task, since the reaction times to the phoneme were significantly faster for sentences having the relative pronouns than for those not having them.

Hakes (1972) reported a similar effect using the phoneme-monitoring task with simpler sentences. His sentences contained a complementizer introduced by *that,* such as *Everyone who was at the party saw (that) Ann's date had made a complete fool of himself.* The complementizer in this sentence is the noun clause serving as the object of *saw.* Hakes presented his sentences with and without the word *that* at the beginning of a complementizer and selected a phoneme occurring shortly after the location for *that.* In the above sentence it was the *d* in *date.* Hakes assumed that at this point the listener would still be having difficulty in determining whether a complementizer were present and so would be less attentive to the monitoring task. His results bore out this assumption, since reaction times to the phoneme were significantly longer in the sentences not having the word *that*.

Collectively these studies suggest that Kimball's strategy is correct. Listeners seem to use surface structure clues for a clause, and they falter when these clues are removed. This does not mean that listeners cannot understand the sentence without the clause clue, but only that understanding is easier when it is there.

Thus far we have discussed a strategy for identifying clauses and relating them to the rest of the sentence. Now we should ask, Are there strategies for identifying the internal structure of a clause? Clearly, the way words are related within a clause is important to our understanding of it, and a listener must identify these relations in order to construct an underlying representation of the clause.

Fodor, Bever, and Garrett (1974) suggest one such strategy, which we shall call the SVO strategy. They argue that people look for certain patterns of noun phrases and verb phrases in sentences to aid their comprehension of these sentences. In particular, Fodor et al. observe that many sentences begin with a noun phrase that is followed immediately by a verb phrase and that may be followed immediately by another noun phrase—for example, *The old man dug a well.* They state that the underlying representation for most such sentences is one of subject-verb-object (SVO), where the first noun phrase is the subject and the second noun phrase, if there is one, is the verb object. Fodor et al. suggest that people expect this type of sentence construction and process sentences accordingly.

An occasional sentence having this surface structure will not have the same simple underlying representation, and such sentences are often more difficult to comprehend. For example, *The horse raced past the barn fell* has a surface structure that begins with a noun phrase, verb phrase, and noun phrase. However, these are not related as subject-verb-object. Instead, the subject and verb *(fell)* are separated by a relative clause, *(that was) raced past the barn.* The difficulty of comprehending sentences where this strategy does not apply suggests its common use when it does apply.

Further strategies for identifying internal structure are given by Kimball (1973). Let us close this section by looking at brief examples of two of them. Kimball notes that the presence of an article *(a, an, the)* or a quantifier *(one, all, many, three,* etc.) is usually the clue for a noun phrase. On hearing one of these, one should listen for a noun that completes the noun phrase, such as *the tired waitress* or *some black swans.*

This strategy, of course, contributes to the SVO strategy described above.

A second example of Kimball's strategies draws the listener's attention to affixes. Most affixes are attached to words of only one syntactic category. For example, *-ing* and *-ed* signal a verb, while *-ly* signals an adverb, and *-ness* and *-ion* signal a noun. Of course, *-s* may signal either a noun *(birds)* or a verb *(sleeps),* but at least the options are few.

Kimball (1973) gives a number of other strategies, but perhaps these illustrations will convey the general notion of how a listener may use the surface structure of a sentence to construct its underlying representation. Constructing an underlying representation involves, in part, identifying the meaning of each word in the sentence, as we saw in the section on lexical analysis (see pages 166–170). But the meaning of a sentence is not a simple sum of the meanings of its words. The relations among the word meanings are also a necessary part of the sentence meaning, and the surface structure of the sentence is a ready source of this information.

In this section on comprehension we have assumed that listeners believe that a speaker intends to make sense. Their comprehension is thus guided by their expectations of what they think the speaker is saying. On the other hand, their comprehension is constrained by the surface structure of the sentence they hear. They must identify the meaning of each word and the relations among them to recover the underlying meaning of the sentence.

Schank (1973) has characterized these two components of comprehension as "top-down" and "bottom-up" approaches to comprehension. We first identified these terms in Chapter 2 in discussing perception; they refer to analogous processes here. The top-down approach to comprehension is guided by the conceptual base—that is, what we expect or are listening for. The bottom-up approach is guided by what we hear—that is, the surface structure of the sentence. Used alone, either of these is inefficient.

Schank suggests that it is more plausible to think that the two methods combine for efficient comprehension.

Schank's analysis suggests that the process of comprehending language is very similar to the process of perceiving any type of environmental event. In the same manner that our expectations influence our ability to perceive the world around us, our expectations influence how we comprehend the language we hear.

In summary, the processing of the surface structure of a sentence leads to the recovery of the meaning of the sentence. Several kinds of evidence suggest that a listener processes the sentence in clause units. Words are gathered in working memory until the clause is complete; then the meaning of the clause is analyzed and sent to permanent memory. Syntactic and lexical information about the clauses may be lost from memory fairly quickly once the meaning of the clause has been analyzed.

The listener may use a number of strategies to analyze the surface structure of a clause as well as the way clauses are related in a sentence. These strategies use surface structure clues to signal the presence of such elements as noun phrases and relative clauses.

Memory for Meaning

What happens to the meaning of a sentence once it is stored in permanent memory? It is plausible to think that it stays there relatively unchanged until it is needed. There are several studies, however, which show that sentence meanings are not stored independently but are integrated into a holistic semantic form. Bransford and Franks (1971) first demonstrated this effect in a recognition memory task. They took a complex sentence and broke it into four simple sentences, each stating a simple idea in the complex sentence. For example, one of the complex sentences was *The ants in the kitchen ate the sweet jelly which was on the table.* This was broken into the four simple sentences:

1. The ants were in the kitchen.
2. The jelly was on the table.
3. The jelly was sweet.
4. The ants ate the jelly.

These can be combined, two at a time, into TWOS that express two ideas, such as

5. The ants in the kitchen ate the jelly.
6. The ants ate the sweet jelly.

They can be combined also, three at a time, into THREES that express three ideas, such as

7. The ants ate the sweet jelly which was on the table.
8. The ants in the kitchen ate the jelly which was on the table.

In the first part of their study, Bransford and Franks presented their subjects with sets of 24 sentences, which included two ONES, two TWOS, and two THREES from the same complex sentence. The complete complex sentence (a FOUR), however, was never presented.

In the second part of the study, the subjects heard a new list of sentences. For each sentence they were asked first, to decide whether they recognized the sentence and second, to rate how confident they were about this decision. The list of sentences they were given contained some of the ONES, TWOS, and THREES they had heard in the first part of the study, plus the FOUR (which they had not heard), plus some new ONES, TWOS, and THREES and some control sentences that were unrelated to the ideas in the original FOUR.

The results of the confidence ratings were quite striking. The highest confidence ratings were for the FOUR, the sentence they had never heard. Seemingly, the subjects had integrated the ideas in the ONES, TWOS, and THREES into a holistic representation, which they falsely recognized when the FOUR was presented in the test list. The surface structures of the sentences they had heard were lost as their meanings were processed into memory.

It is not surprising that subjects tended to forget the surface structure of the original sentences, since they heard a number of sentences that were highly similar. Small (1975) has shown that subjects are able to remember the surface structures when sentences have unrelated meanings. However, he found that subjects still integrate the meaning into a holistic semantic representation. The important effect then is that memory is constructive; that is, meanings are integrated into semantic wholes. Surface structures are retained in some conditions but lost in others.

A second constructive process in memory is related to inferences. Not only do people integrate meaning into semantic wholes, but they also tend to incorporate reasonable inferences into these semantic wholes. Bransford, Barclay, and Franks (1972) demonstrated this by having subjects listen to sentences such as

1. Three turtles rested <u>on</u> the floating log and a fish swam beneath them.
2. Three turtles rested <u>beside</u> the floating log and a fish swam beneath them.

Note that these two differ only in the underlined prepositions. Three minutes later the subjects heard sentences like (3) and (4) in a recognition test:

3. Three turtles rested on the floating log and a fish swam beneath it.
4. Three turtles rested beside the floating log and a fish swam beneath it.

Notice that these two sentences differ from the first two only in the last word of the sentence. In the recognition task, subjects were quite confident they had heard (3), though in fact they had not. Bransford et al. suggested that (3) is a reasonable inference from (1), and this inference was incorporated into the semantic representation of the sentence. If the fish swam beneath the turtles, then it must have swum beneath the log, since the turtles were on the log. This inference is not reasonable for (4), however, since the turtles were merely beside the log, and subjects correctly rejected (4) in the recognition task.

The inference that got incorporated into the semantic representation was based on spatial relationships, not on syntactic relationships. *On* and *beside* refer to the relation of two objects in space, in this case where the turtles were relative to the log. Listeners had to use their knowledge of the world to infer that the fish swam beneath the log, and so we have in this study an illustration of the way a listener's conceptual structure enters into the comprehension process.

Thus memory for meaning also appears to be a constructive process in which simple meanings are integrated into a holistic form. Inferences from these meanings may also be integrated into this holistic form.

A COMPUTER MODEL OF LANGUAGE PROCESSING

Now that you have had a look at the various processes used in language production and comprehension, it may help to try to put them all together. One of the ways to do this is to model them in a computer program. No program today can match the way humans use language, but efforts to write programs are instructive, since they force us to be explicit in our assumptions and they point the way to new problems for research.

One of the best of these computer programs was created by Winograd (1972). The world of the program is somewhat limited; it consists of a set of toy blocks and a box, all of which are set on a table. This scene is shown on a cathode-ray tube screen. You can give commands to the program *(Put the red block in the box)* on an electric typewriter and see them carried out by an imaginary robot arm on the screen. You can also give it new information and ask it questions and receive intelligent answers. An example of a dialog with the program is shown in Box 6.5.

Winograd's program contains three subprograms: one for syntax, one for semantics, and one for a conceptual world of toy blocks. The syntax program, called PROGRAMMAR, analyzes the syntactic structure of inputs and generates replies. It uses comprehension strategies similar to those suggested by Kimball (1973). For example, in line 1 *(Pick up a big red block)*, it analyzes the sentence into a verb group and a noun group, and further analyzes the noun group into an article *(a)*, two adjectives *(big, red)* and a noun *(block)*.

The semantic program is a bridge from the syntactic program to the conceptual world. It identifies the meaning of each word and relates it to the conceptual world using procedural semantics. Each object in the conceptual world is represented by a set of semantic features (e.g., BLOCK: BIG, RED) in a way that is sufficient to distinguish it from every other object.

The third program, called PLANNER, represents the conceptual world and can make inferences about that world in order to answer questions appropriately. For example, if all three pyramids were on the table and two blocks were in the box, it could infer that no block in the box supported a pyramid. PLANNER is a problem-solving program. We shall see other examples of such programs in Chapter 9, but this one has the special merit of being integrated with a language-using program.

PROGRAMMAR has several interesting linguistic features. For example, it stores words in stem form (e.g., *grasp*), and then applies a subroutine to recognize or produce the various inflected forms of the word (e.g., *grasps, grasped, grasping*). It thus simulates human processes, as we saw in the production and comprehension sections above. PROGRAMMAR also keeps track of words and phrases in the dialog and can identify the reference for pronouns such as *it* and *that*. When it encounters one of these, it searches the most recent part of the dialog for a word or phrase that fits semantically. This is an example of using context, a topic we shall explore more fully in the next chapter.

Box 6.5 EXAMPLE OF A COMPUTER DIALOGUE

The following dialog (Winograd, 1972, pp. 8–10) typifies the type of conversation which can occur between man and computer. In this case, the input to the computer is shown in boldface and its replies are shown in capitals. The brief descriptions following each exchange describe what has occurred, and Figures 6.10 and 6.11 show the "world" setting at different points in the conversation.

1. **pick up a big red block.**
   OK.

   The system answers "OK" when it carries out a command. In order to pick up the red block, it had to clear it off by finding a space for the green one and moving the green one away.

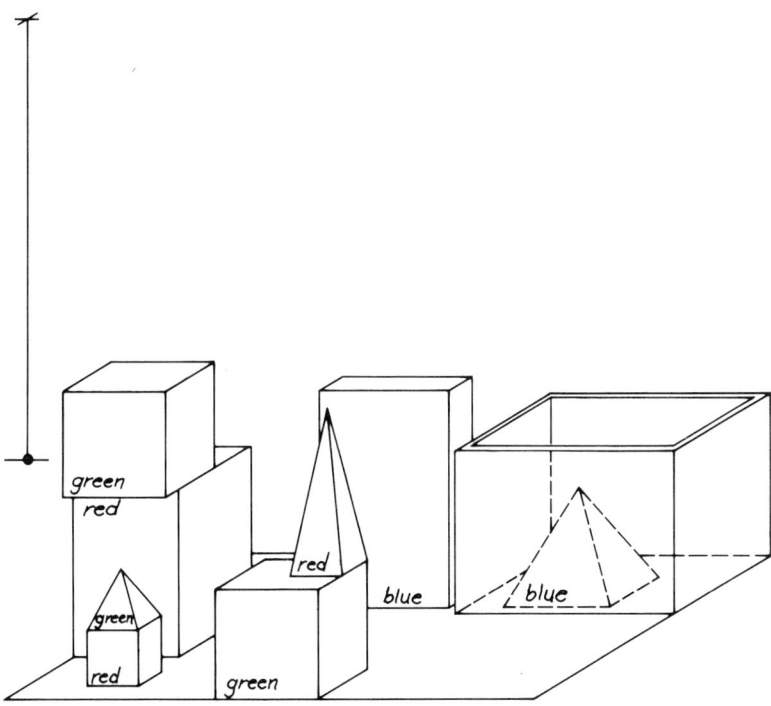

Figure 6.10 The setting that exists when the computer is asked to "Pick up a big red block." (From Winograd, 1972.)

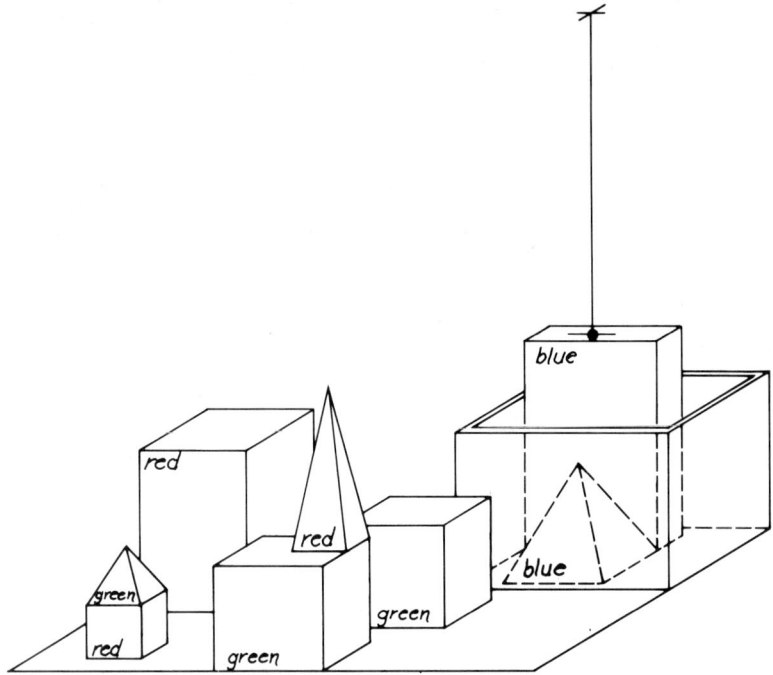

Figure 6.11 The setting that exists when the computer has completed responding to the question "Find a block which is bigger than the one you are holding and put it into the box." (From Winograd, 1972.)

2. **grasp the pyramid.**

   I DON'T UNDERSTAND WHICH PYRAMID YOU MEAN.

   There are three pyramids in the scene, so the program does nothing.

3. **find a block which is taller than the one you are holding and put it into the box.**

   The system has to figure out what is meant for "one" and "it," as well as using deduction to decide which block it is holding.

   BY "IT," I ASSUME YOU MEAN THE BLOCK WHICH IS TALLER THAN THE ONE I AM HOLDING.

   Printed out to keep us informed.

   OK.

   The hand has to set down the red block to pick up the taller blue one. Figure 6.11 shows the result of the system's manipulations so far.

4. **what does the box contain?**

   THE BLUE PYRAMID AND THE BLUE BLOCK.

5. **what is the pyramid supported by?**

Earlier the system responded to "the pyramid" by saying "I don't understand which pyramid you mean." Now, it assumes that we mean the one just mentioned.

THE BOX.

6. **how many blocks are not in the box?**

Negatives such as "not" and "no'" are handled whether they appear in clauses or noun groups (such as "no boxes").

FOUR OF THEM.

7. **is at least one of them narrower than the one which I told you to pick up?**

The phrase "at least one of them" must be analyzed to refer back to the previous question, and "the one which . . ." must also refer to blocks. Noun groups can have complicated numbers such as "at least one," "more than three," "exactly seven," etc. The memory of past events is used to deduce which block is "the one which I told you to pick up." Notice the complicated syntactic structure in which "the one" is actually the object of a clause embedded two levels deeper.

YES, THE RED CUBE.

8. **is it supported?**

Passives can be used without a "by . . ." phrase.

YES, BY THE TABLE.

9. **can the table pick up blocks?**

NO.

The semantic rules make this a nonsensical question which therefore must be false.

10. **can a pyramid be supported by a block?**

YES.

The deductive system finds an actual example, so it knows this is possible.

For all its impressive accomplishments, Winograd's model is still limited in many ways. For example, its conceptual world is restricted to a set of toy blocks, and it is not clear whether the processes embodied in this program can be generalized to represent the enormous body of knowledge which a human has. However, the model does capture some important aspects of language use and points the way to new developments.

CONCLUSION

Let us conclude this chapter by recalling a few of the highlights about language and its use. We have seen that language is both creative and rule governed. The rules describe its structure at the level of sounds, words, and even sentences. The structure of a sentence can be divided into its surface structure and its underlying representation. Our knowledge of the structure of a sentence, which is our competence, interacts with other psychological processes in talking and understanding.

Talking involves the translation of a thought into a sentence through the progressive selection of syntactic structure, lexical items, and then phonemic forms. Understanding operates somewhat in reverse, analyzing the phonemic and syntactic structure of the sentence to recover its meaning. These processes are not passive but constructive. Moreover, they are integrative. They pull together our knowledge of our language with our knowledge of the world and our understanding of our partner in the communication process.

7 Comprehension and Retention of Prose Materials

Context and Language Comprehension
    Context and the Meaning of Words
    Context and the Meaning of Sentences
    Context, Passages, and Importance
        Pictorial Settings
        Themes
        Instructions
        Reader Background
Schemata
The Role of Schemata in Processing Prose Materials
    Comprehension
    Comprehension and Memory
Inference Processes in Comprehension and Retention
    Inference Processes at Comprehension
    Inference Processes at Retrieval
Schemata and Semantic Memory
Conclusion

We begin this chapter by relating a simple account of an event with which we are all familiar:

> The procedure is actually quite simple. First you arrange things into different groups. Of course, one pile may be sufficient depending on how much there is to do. If you have to go somewhere else due to lack of facilities that is the next step, otherwise you are pretty well set. It is important not to overdo things. That is, it is better to do too few things at once than too many. In the short run this may not seem important but complications can easily arise. A mistake can be expensive as well. At first the whole procedure will seem complicated. Soon, however, it will become just another facet of life. It is difficult to foresee any end to the necessity for this task in the immediate future, but then one never can tell. After the procedure is completed one arranges the materials into different groups again. Then they can be put into their appropriate places. Eventually they will be used once more and the whole cycle will have to be repeated. However, this is part of life. (Bransford & Johnson, 1973, p. 400)

Your reaction is probably one of puzzlement. You thought you were going to hear a simple account of a familiar event, but this passage makes no sense. How can a simple passage be so difficult to understand?

How, in fact, do we understand and remember any type of prose materials? Are the same perceptual and memory processes involved in working with prose passages as in working with geometric patterns or word lists? These are some of the questions we address in this chapter on the comprehension and retention of prose materials.

Several major issues will concern us as we move through this chapter. We first consider how dramatic an impact the context in which a word or paragraph is located has on our ability to understand and remember information. This fact makes it clear why the study of prose materials has become so popular in recent years. Prose processing not only provides a means to study context, but also more accurately reflects the type of processing we are asked to carry out in our daily lives.

Second, we consider the powerful role that schemata play in our ability to comprehend and remember prose materials. This will lead us to a consideration of the types of inference processes we go through in comprehending and retrieving information contained in prose passages. Finally, we consider how our more complete understanding of schemata and their role in prose processing help us to generate a model of semantic memory different from those discussed in Chapter 4.

With this chapter overview in mind let us return to the question regarding the simple passage we presented at the beginning of this chapter. How can such a simple passage be so difficult to understand? The answer is really quite simple; the passage is out of *context*. Try rereading it with the commonplace event of "washing clothes" in mind. You will find that it makes a substantial difference in the ease with which you understand the passage.

CONTEXT AND LANGUAGE COMPREHENSION

At the close of Chapter 6 we reported that people employ a number of strategies in their attempts to understand sentences. These strategies use such cues as word order, relative pronouns, and inflections to gain an understanding of sentence meaning. Viewing sentence comprehension as strategy based was an important advance in our understanding of how we comprehend sentences. However, recent evidence suggests that if we are to fully understand the comprehension of sentences and textual materials, we must better understand the role of context.

We first introduced context in Chapter 2 as we considered the process of perception. At that point we illustrated how what people perceive is influenced not only by what information they get from the environment but also by the expectations they have about that information. These expectations are thought to arise from the context in which the to-be-perceived information is coming. Thus we noted that the features of a face, such as eyes, ears, or nose, are more easily perceived in the context of the outline of a face than if they are isolated from the facial context (see figures 2.21 and 2.22).

In a similar manner we find that how we understand language is a function of the context in which it is found. This is the case whether we are concerned with the understanding of a word in a sentence, a sentence in a paragraph, or passages as a whole. Let us briefly consider each of these levels.

Context and the Meaning of Words

We are all probably confident that we know what such terms as *mess, person, inside,* or *cleaned* mean. They are quite common terms that we employ on an everyday basis. We could easily produce synonyms that could be used in place of these terms. A study by Strange and Jenkins (Jenkins, 1977) suggests an important restriction on this conclusion, however. Strange and Jenkins created two stories using the four words mentioned above in the first few sentences. The stories began as follows:

> Raggedy Ann was in trouble. The spray from the painting fell on her and her face was a *mess*. A kind *person* picked her up and carried her *inside*. She *cleaned* Raggedy Ann's face carefully with turpentine.
>
> The team was in trouble. It had been a tough half playing in the rain and their uniforms were a *mess*. The *person* in charge followed them *inside* in anger. He *cleaned* off a space on the bench and stood on it.

A careful consideration of the four italicized terms in these two stories suggests that they take on different meanings in the two stories. A *mess* in the first story means paint spattered; in the second story it means muddy. A *person* in the first story is probably a lady; in the second story it must be the coach. *Inside* in the first story is probably in a house; in the second story it is probably in a locker room. *Cleaned* in the first story probably means washed; in the second story it probably means cleared.

It appears that the meaning of a term depends on the situation into which the term is projected. A mess in a yard suggests a much different situation than a mess on a desk or a mess in which one finds himself.

Strange and Jenkins provided support for this interpretation in a recognition memory study using the stories sketched above. Subjects were presented either the Raggedy Ann or the football story. After having heard the story, the subjects were tested for word recognition. They were presented words that were actually in the passage they read, words that were synonyms of these words, or words that were synonyms of these words when they were presented in the other form of the passage.

Strange and Jenkins found that the subjects recognized the words actually presented in the stories in about 80 percent of the cases. The interesting results from the study occurred when the subjects were given the synonyms of the story words in the recognition test. Performance differed dramatically depending on whether the synonyms had been selected from the same or different story perspective. When the subjects were given synonyms selected from the perspective from which they'd read the story, they incorrectly identified 50 percent of the words as ones they had seen before. That is, subjects who read the Raggedy Ann story incorrectly recognized synonyms of the words obtained from the Raggedy Ann perspective about half the time. However, when the subjects were given synonyms selected from the other perspective, they incorrectly identified the words only about 20 percent of the time. Apparently the identical words in these two stories were interpreted quite differently depending on the story version which was read.

Anderson and Ortony (1975), in an article aptly titled "On Putting Apples into Bottles—a Problem of Polysemy," came to a similar conclusion. They found that the word *bottle* would be a good memory prompt for the sentence *The container held the cola*, but that it would not be a good prompt for the sentence *The container held the apples*. Studies such as these provide convincing evidence that the meaning of words within sentences is highly dependent upon the context in which those words are set.

Context and the Meanings of Sentences

The sentence *The cupboard was a large one* seems simple and straightforward. Surely we can all agree what the meaning of this sentence is. Unfortunately, some evidence presented by Smith (Jenkins, 1977) suggests otherwise. She presented this sentence at different places within the same story and found that the meaning the subjects gave the sentence varied. If the sentence was placed in the context of attempts at putting something on top of a kitchen cupboard, it was interpreted to mean *the cupboard was tall*. This was shown by the fact that subjects' estimates of the dimensions of the cupboard emphasized the cupboard's height.

If the sentence was placed later in the story in the context of a boy trying to hide something in the cupboard by pushing it to the back of the cupboard, the sentence was interpreted to mean *the cupboard was deep*. In this case estimates of the dimensions of the cabinet stressed its depth. Apparently even sentences take on differential meanings depending on the context in which they are embedded.

Certainly ambiguous sentences such as *They are eating apples* and *The police were ordered to stop drinking* are rarely ambiguous in context. When the first of these sentences is produced as the speaker stands admiring a bowlful of bright red Delicious apples, the meaning he is conveying is likely to be quite clear. Indeed, Gottfried (Jenkins, 1977) found that subjects interpreted ambiguous sentences in an unambiguous fashion when they were embedded in a plausible story context.

Context, Passages, and Importance

We have already demonstrated in our opening passage about washing clothes that the context in which we read a passage influences our ability to understand the meaning of the passage. We now consider the types of contextual situations which influence the interpretation and retention of passages. By analyzing these various situations, we hope to suggest an explanation for how context influences prose comprehension and retention.

Pictorial Settings. In a now classic study, Bransford and Johnson (1973) showed that pictorial information can dramatically influence our ability to comprehend and retain prose passages. They presented subjects the following passage:

> If the balloons popped the sound wouldn't be able to carry since everything would be too far away from the correct floor. A closed window would also prevent the sound from carrying, since most buildings tend to be well insulated. Since the whole operation depends on a steady flow of electricity, a break in the middle of the wire would also cause problems. Of course, the fellow could shout, but the human voice is not strong enough to carry that far. An additional problem is that a string could break on the instrument. Then there could be no accompaniment to the message. It is clear that the best situation would involve less distance. Then there would be fewer potential problems. With face to face contact, the least number of things could go wrong. (pp. 392–393)

Some subjects were shown the picture in Figure 7.1 before reading the passage; the other subjects read the passage with no accompanying information. Those who had seen the picture found the passage completely comprehensible; those who had not found it incomprehensible. These differences were dramatically reflected in the subjects' recall of the contents of the passage. Those subjects who had seen the picture recalled twice as much as those who had not seen the picture.

Themes. With some passages a simple word or two that reminds the reader of a familiar theme can serve to make a passage more understandable. Dooling and Lachman (1971) explored the impact of such contextual themes with stories such as the following one:

> With hocked gems financing him, our hero bravely defied all scornful laughter that tried to prevent his scheme. "Your eyes deceive," he had said, "an egg not a table correctly typifies this unexplored planet." Now three sturdy sisters sought proof, forging along sometimes through calm vastness, yet more often over turbulent peaks and valleys. Days become weeks as many doubters spread fearful rumors about the edge. At last from nowhere welcome winged creatures appeared signifying momentous success. (p. 217)

Using a methodology similar to that employed by Bransford and Johnson, Dooling and Lachman gave some of their subjects the title for the passage—"Christopher Columbus Discovering America"—while others were not told the title. Again the results were clear. Those who were given the title recalled 18 percent more words than those who were not given the title.

In a follow-up study by Dooling and Mullet (1973), subjects given the title of similar vague passages prior to reading the passages recalled almost twice as many words and sentences as subjects given no title or subjects given the title after having read the passage (see Table 7.1). In addition, subjects given the title before reading the passage made twice as many intrusion errors as other subjects. (Intrusion errors are recalled words that are consistent with the theme of the passage but were not actually presented in the passage.)

Instructions. Many of the passages we have described have been vague and metaphorical. You might argue that context is only important when people have to deal with such materials. Some recent research on the role of instructions suggests that this is not at all the case. Probably the most striking example is seen in a study by Pichert and Anderson (1977). These authors presented three groups of subjects the story in Box 7.1 about two boys playing hooky from school. One group was told to read the story from the perspective of a potential home buyer, one from the perspective of a burglar, and one was given no special perspective.

Table 7.1 Recall of Passages as a Function of Title Placement

	TITLE OF PASSAGE		
Dependent measure	*Before*	*After*	*None*
Number of correct words recalled	18.6	11.8	12.2
Number of correct sentences recalled	3.0	1.4	1.2
Number of intrusion errors	8.5	4.0	5.1

Source: From Dooling and Mullet (1973).

easily eliminated because it was unimportant to the theme of the passage. Pichert and Anderson calculated a rank order correlation coefficient. This coefficient indicates whether the subjects from the various perspectives thought the same idea units were important. A correlation approaching 1 would suggest that the same idea units were important from each perspective. A correlation of 0 would suggest that different idea units were thought to be important.

The mean correlation was .11, suggesting that the subjects using the two perspectives thought that different idea units were important. A close analysis of the story suggests why this is the case. A burglar is likely to be interested in the color TV set but unconcerned about a leaky roof. A home buyer is likely to reverse these preferences.

This difference in importance is reflected in the subjects' ability to recall idea units. On an immediate test, subjects recalled 48 percent of the idea units rated as important from their perspective but only 25 percent of those idea units rated as being of little importance. Apparently the instructional set we bring to a clear, straightforward story influences not only what we find important in the story but what we are able to recall at a later point.

Reader Background. Each of us has special areas of interest, competence, or experience. Some of us are fascinated by politics or automobiles; others by gourmet cooking, gardening, or sports. Such interests result in specialized knowledge about these areas, knowledge that may make us more likely to interpret environmental events in certain ways. Thus we may use a sports analogy to describe a political situation ("The ball is in their court," "It's a whole new ball game," "She's got two strikes against her as she starts"), or we make use of our knowledge of automobiles to understand how a space vehicle works ("Putting on the reverse rockets is like hitting the brakes").

That such background knowledge can influence our comprehension of prose passages was

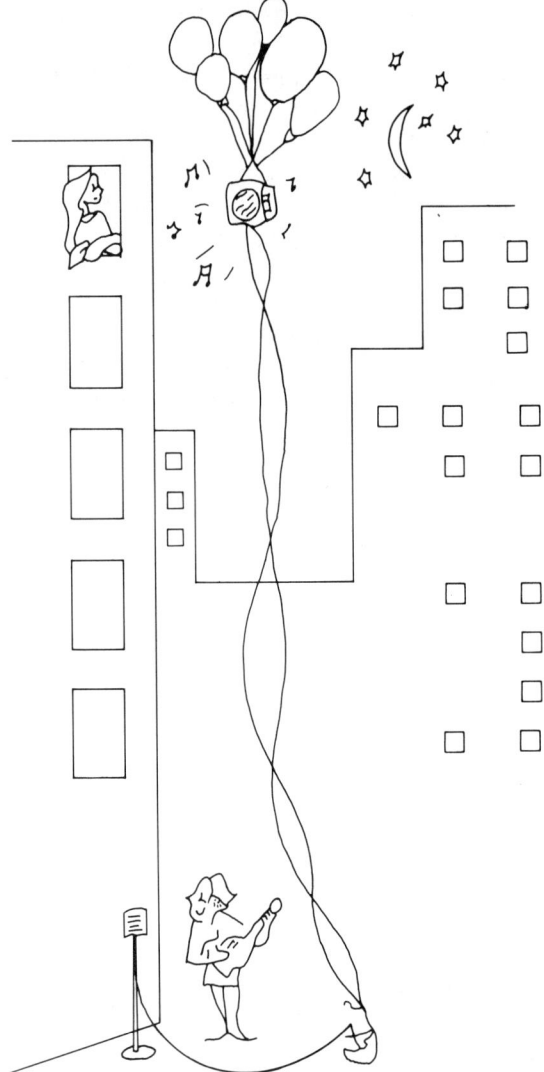

Figure 7.1 Contextual drawing for the balloon passage of Bransford and Johnson (1973).

The subjects were then asked to rate 72 idea units in this passage on a 5-point scale in which 5 meant the idea unit was essential to the meaning of the passage, and 1 meant the idea unit could be

> **Box 7.1   PLAYING HOOKY FROM SCHOOL**
>
> The two boys ran until they came to the driveway. "See, I told you today was good for skipping school," said Mark. "Mom is never home on Thursday," he added. Tall hedges hid the house from the road so the pair strolled across the finely landscaped yard. "I never knew your place was so big," said Pete. "Yeah, but it's nicer now than it used to be since Dad had the new stone siding put on and added the fireplace."
>
> There were front and back doors and a side door which led to the garage which was empty except for three parked 10-speed bikes. They went to the side door, Mark explaining that it was always open in case his younger sisters got home earlier than their mother.
>
> Pete wanted to see the house so Mark started with the living room. It, like the rest of the downstairs, was newly painted. Mark turned on the stereo, the noise of which worried Pete. "Don't worry, the nearest house is a quarter of a mile away," Mark shouted. Pete felt more comfortable observing that no houses could be seen in any direction beyond the huge yard.
>
> The dining room, with all the china, silver and cut glass, was no place to play so the boys moved into the kitchen where they made sandwiches. Mark said they wouldn't go to the basement because it had been damp and musty ever since the new plumbing had been installed.
>
> "This is where my Dad keeps his famous paintings and his coin collection," Mark said as they peered into the den. Mark bragged that he could get spending money whenever he needed it since he'd discovered that his Dad kept a lot in the desk drawer.
>
> There were three upstairs bedrooms. Mark showed Pete his mother's closet which was filled with furs and the locked box which held her jewels. His sisters' room was uninteresting except for the color TV which Mark carried to his room. Mark bragged that the bathroom in the hall was his since one had been added to his sisters' room for their use. The big highlight in his room, though, was a leak in the ceiling where the old roof had finally rotted. (Pichert & Anderson, 1977, p. 310)

demonstrated by Anderson, Reynolds, Schallert, and Goetz (1977). These authors gave the following passage to two groups of students, one composed of students from weight-lifting classes and the other from an educational psychology course:

Rocky slowly got up from the mat, planning his escape. He hesitated a moment and thought. Things were not going well. What bothered him most was being held, especially since the charge against him had been weak. He considered his present situation. The lock that held him was strong but he thought he could break it. He knew, however, that his timing would have to be perfect. Rocky was aware that it was because of his early roughness that he had been penalized so severely—much too severely from his point of view. The situation was becoming frustrating; the pressure had been grinding on him far too long. He was being ridden unmercifully. Rocky was getting angry now. He felt he was ready to make his move. He knew that his success or failure would depend on what he did in the next few seconds.(p. 372)

In prior testing this passage had typically been thought to be about a convict planning his escape from prison, although it could also be interpreted to be about a wrestler breaking a hold. The subjects were given test items such as the following one:

How had Rocky been punished for his aggressiveness?

A. He had been demoted to the "B" team.
B. His opponent had been given points.
C. He lost his privileges for the weekend.
D. He had been arrested and imprisoned.

Each such item had two correct answers, one for each story perspective.

Test performance was scored from the nondominant, or wrestling, point of view. Students from the weight-lifting classes, probably more familiar with wrestling than those from the educational psychology course, got 64 percent of the answers correct. Students from the educational psychology course got only 28 percent correct. Just as striking was the fact that only about 25 percent of the subjects were aware during reading of the passage that an interpretation different from the one they took was possible. Thus our experience apparently does prepare us to see the world in a select fashion.

It is clear from our discussion that context dramatically influences the manner in which we process prose materials. It influences our interpretation of words, sentences, and even whole passages, whether these be ambiguous or straightforward.

What type of cognitive process or mechanism can handle such a diversity of findings? To answer that question we need to analyze carefully the different types of contextual factors influencing prose comprehension. What is common to pictorial information, themes, instructions, and reader background?

Although these factors appear different, they do accomplish one common outcome. They provide a structure that brings the passage being read under a single, coherent interpretation. Consider each of the contextual situations. The pictorial information used by Bransford and his colleagues provides a single framework in which to fit all the pieces about the flow of electricity, the balloons popping, and the human voice. The statement of a theme such as Columbus discovering America activates a coherent piece of knowledge that most of us have about an important historical event. This knowledge provides us with a means to understand eggs and planets, turbulent peaks and valleys, and edges and winged creatures. Instructions serve a similar end in activating collections of knowledge we may have stored, such as what burglars or home owners do. The extensive background readers may have in sports (or gardening or politics) prepares them with well-organized knowledge that can be imposed upon new information to make it meaningful.

The key then to our question of the cognitive mechanism underlying the contextual findings seems to lie in a structure or process that produces a coherent ordering of an individual's knowledge. The mechanism most frequently proposed to meet these characteristics is the cognitive structure that we have labeled the schema.

SCHEMATA

Before you continue reading we would like you to pause and sketch out a response to the following question: What is involved in the physical process of constructing a house?
Finished?

Your reply probably contains several of the features sketched out in Figure 7.2. The type of knowledge it represents is yet another example of what we earlier called a schema—in this case, a schema of the events involved in constructing a house. When we first introduced the concept of **schema** in Chapter 2, we tentatively described it as generalized knowledge about events, situations, or objects. We maintain that basic description here. Consequently, we say that people have schemata for how to do long division, what happens at a restaurant (Schank & Abelson, 1977), how to hit a tennis backhand, or how to build a house.

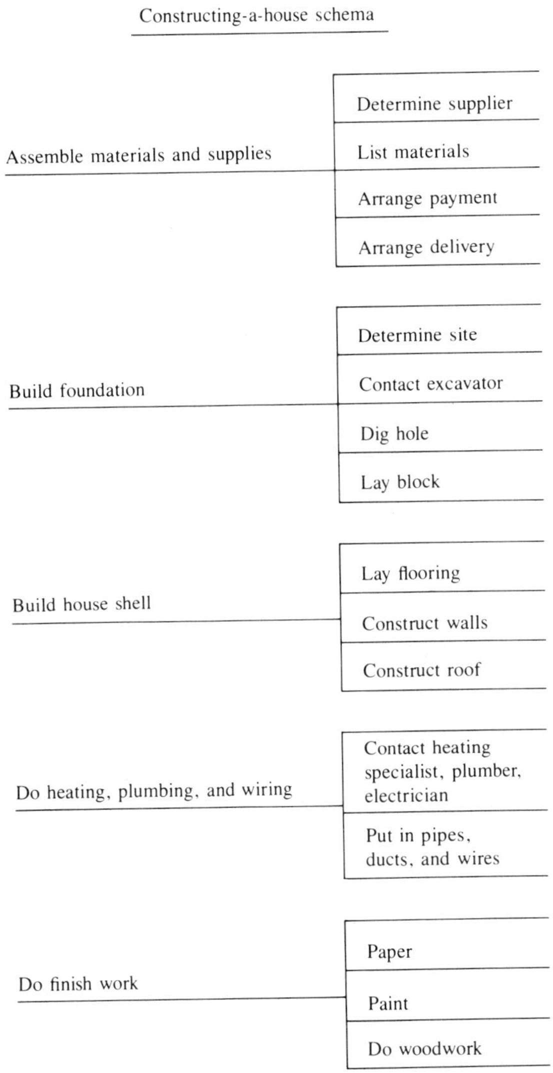

Constructing-a-house schema

Assemble materials and supplies	Determine supplier
	List materials
	Arrange payment
	Arrange delivery
Build foundation	Determine site
	Contact excavator
	Dig hole
	Lay block
Build house shell	Lay flooring
	Construct walls
	Construct roof
Do heating, plumbing, and wiring	Contact heating specialist, plumber, electrician
	Put in pipes, ducts, and wires
Do finish work	Paper
	Paint
	Do woodwork

Figure 7.2 Sketch of a house-building schema.

We need, however, to elaborate upon our earlier description in order to see how schemata play an important role in how people process prose materials. In particular, we need to describe four key characteristics of schemata which help us better understand the role of schemata in cognition. These characteristics are that (1) schemata have slots or variables; (2) schemata can be embedded within other schemata; (3) schemata vary in their level of abstractness; and (4) schemata represent general knowledge of the world rather than definitions of objects or events (Rumelhart & Ortony, 1977). We briefly describe each of these before we consider the role of schemata in processing prose materials.

Schemata involve generalized knowledge about events, situations, or objects; they do not include specific information about specific settings. Thus we might have a schema about giving, which contains general knowledge about the fact that there must be a giver, a gift, and a recipient of the gift. These three categories are called *slots* or *variables,* and can be filled in a variety of ways. For example, if John gives Bill the ball, or the government gives food stamps to miners, then John and the government are the givers, the ball and food stamps are gifts, and Bill and the miners are the recipients. Similarly, in our house-constructing schema there are variables or slots for who assembles the supplies, what kind of house shell is constructed, or where the foundation will be placed.

The fact that schemata are general entities means that they can apply to many different situations. In each of these situations the slots are filled with different specific values. The process of filling these slots is called the *instantiation* of the schema. It is a process that plays a fundamental role in comprehending prose materials as we will see below.

Generally the slots in a schema are filled with environmental information. For example, people watching a house being constructed can determine from what they see where the house foundation is located or what type of house shell is being constructed. In some situations, however, the environment may provide no information as to how to fill some of the slots. For example, when we approach a house site, the building materials may have already been delivered. Thus we may have no information about who delivered the materials. In such cases a slot may be filled by *default* or by *inference*. That is, we may know from past experience that lumber companies have delivery trucks, that there is only one lumber company in town, and that the nearest town is 75 miles away. Under these conditions the slot for who delivered the materials may be filled by inference: Don's Lumber Company delivered the materials. This process of default assignment plays a large role in text comprehension.

The second major characteristic of schemata is that they can embed within one another. By this we mean that the components of a schema may themselves be schemata. For example, in Chapter 2 we discussed a face schema described by Palmer (1975). In this schema there are slots for information about eyes, nose, ears, and mouth and how these relate to each other. However, we also have a schema for the eye, which includes slots for information concerning the pupil, retina, iris, and eyelid. In a similar manner the face schema itself may be a subschema for a larger, more inclusive, person schema.

Thus we see that our knowledge of the world is hierarchically organized, allowing for both the interrelationships between certain "important" aspects of a situation or event (eyes, ears, nose, and mouth for face) and access to information of lesser importance but still related (eyelids, iris, nostril).

This leads us directly to the third characteristic of schemata: They vary in their level of abstractness. The knowledge that we have about our environment varies dramatically in abstractness. We have very specific knowledge, for instance, about the number and types of line segments which make up the letter *A* (see Chapter 2), and more general knowledge about the relationships among words, such as the fact that canaries are birds and peaches are fruit (see Chapter 4).

More recently some insightful work by Rumelhart (1975) and Kintsch and van Dijk (cited in Kintsch, 1977) suggests that humans have even more abstract collections of knowledge. For example, Kintsch and van Dijk showed that people from western cultures have a schema for the structure of narrative prose passages. Individuals from these cultures know that such prose passages involve the establishment of a setting for a story *(exposition),* which includes a variable number of episodes about a central figure (the hero or heroine). Within each episode there is a *complication* followed by a *resolution*.

When subjects read narratives, they attempt to fill in these slots for exposition, complication, and resolution in order to gain an understanding of the story. When subjects are presented stories that do not have this form, they find the stories difficult to understand. Other such abstract schemata are involved in comprehending scientific technical reports or scholarly articles. Clearly, the range of knowledge we possess varies from the very specific to the highly abstract.

The fourth and final characteristic of schemata is that schemata are representations of the general knowledge that people have of their world. In this sense, schemata are not definitions of concepts, which specify some particular relationship that must always hold. For example, a definition of the term *student* might indicate that a student is a person who is officially enrolled at an institution of learning. Such definitions are useful, but they do not characterize the type of knowledge humans have of their environment.

Our knowledge seems much more probabilistic; that is, it is much better described as that which normally or typically occurs. Thus our schema of student is likely to involve individuals formally enrolled in a school, those who attend class but are not enrolled, and those who have dropped out for a short period. Rumelhart and Ortony (1977) made the point about the probabilistic character of schemata succinctly when they said,

> Schemata attempt to represent knowledge in the kind of flexible way which reflects human tolerance for vagueness, imprecision, and quasi inconsistencies. (p. 111)

Our elaborated characterization of schemata suggests that they play an important role in the processing of information about the world around us. To see how this is the case in the processing of prose materials, we consider now the role of schemata in comprehending and retaining prose passages.

THE ROLE OF SCHEMATA IN PROCESSING PROSE MATERIALS

We must face a number of knotty issues if we are to understand how people process prose materials. First, we must come to an understanding of what is involved in the initial comprehension of a passage by the reader. This involves establishing a clear interpretation of the meaning of the passage. Second, we need to consider how our comprehension of a passage is related to our ability to remember that passage. Third, readers of prose passages commonly go beyond the information given them in a passage and reach conclusions about the text that are not explicitly stated in the text. We need to understand how and when this is done. These three issues will be the focal points in our discussion of the role of schemata in prose processing.

Comprehension

There is a strong tradition in psychology and education that prose passages, text books, and other printed materials have specific meanings inherent in them. From this viewpoint, the process of comprehending a passage is the extraction of the meaning it contains. This general approach has led a number of researchers to develop elaborate procedures for analyzing and diagraming the structure and interrelationships among the words and propositions contained in prose passages—all in an attempt to better understand how passages convey their meaning. Some researchers who have used this approach are Crothers (1972), Chafe (1972), and Meyer (1975).

Meyer, for example, used an elaborate analysis to construct hierarchically arranged tree structures that specify the structure of a passage. The nodes in these tree structures are content words, and the lines connecting the nodes indicate how the content is organized. A portion of such a tree structure is shown in Figure 7.3. Meyer (1977) finds that tree structures are useful in predicting subjects' recall of prose passages. In particular, she finds that subjects are more likely to recall information that is from the top levels of the hierarchy—for example, the information from the leftmost part of the hierarchy in Figure 7.3—than that which is lower in the hierarchy.

Recently the view that meaning is inherent in the passage has come under increasing attack. The criticism has arisen principally from those psychologists who have considered the impact of context on the comprehension of prose materials. As we saw from the work on context, the same passage, the same sentence, and even the same word may be comprehended differently depending on the context in which they are set. For example, the story about the two boys playing hooky was interpreted much differently if one viewed it from the perspective of a home buyer rather than a burglar. Similarly, the passage about the wrestler/prisoner had a much different meaning depending on the point of view from which we approached the passage.

Since the physical structure of these passages does not change when the reader changes perspective, how are we to account for the different meanings that the reader attains? The answer lies in our giving up the belief that meaning is to be found in the passage and that comprehension involves extracting that meaning. Instead, we need to view comprehension as an interactive process involving both the text and what the reader brings to the text in the way of background knowledge.

In essence, comprehension of textual materials involves the discovery of a formulation that coherently explains the content of a passage (Anderson, 1978). Using the language of schemata, comprehension consists of selecting schemata whose slots are reasonably filled by information from the passage and thus "account for" the material to be comprehended (Rumelhart & Ortony, 1977). This view of comprehension was keenly expressed by Anderson (1977): "Text is gobbledygook unless the reader possesses an interpretive framework to breathe meaning into it" (p. 423).

In order to make this interpretation of comprehension more clear, it is instructive to reconsider some of the contextual research that we discussed at the beginning of this chapter. First, consider the washing clothes passage from Bransford and Johnson with which we opened the chapter. A schema about washing clothes probably includes slots for information about where it is carried out (laundromat, at home), how one sorts the clothing for washing, whether one folds the clothes once they have been washed, the type of water one uses (hot, warm, cold), and whether one uses detergents or bleaches.

When we read the washing clothes passage with such a schema in mind, the various statements in the passage become interpretable. The statement about going somewhere because of a lack of facilities suggests that under some conditions we will have to go to a laundromat. The statement that it is difficult to foresee any end to the task can be interpreted as due to the cyclic nature of clothes getting dirty, being washed, and getting dirty again. The statement about the mistake being expensive can be seen to fit with the variable of the type and amount of detergents or bleaches which should be used. Thus we see that the schema accounts for the various words and sentences in the passage, and we feel that we have comprehended what was written.

Parakeet Paragraph

The wide variety in color of parakeets that are available on the market today resulted from careful breeding of the color mutant offspring of green-bodied and yellow-faced parakeets. The light green body and yellow face color combination is the color of parakeets in their natural habitat, Australia. The first living parakeets were brought to Europe from Australia by John Gould, a naturalist, in 1840. The first color mutation appeared in 1872 in Belgium; these birds were completely yellow. The most popular color of parakeets in the United States is sky-blue. These birds have sky-blue bodies and white faces; this color mutation occurred in 1878 in Europe. There are over 66 different colors of parakeets listed by the Color and Technical Committee of the Budgerigar Society. In addition to the original green-bodied and yellow-faced birds, colors of parakeets include varying shades of violets, blues, grays, greens, yellows and whites.

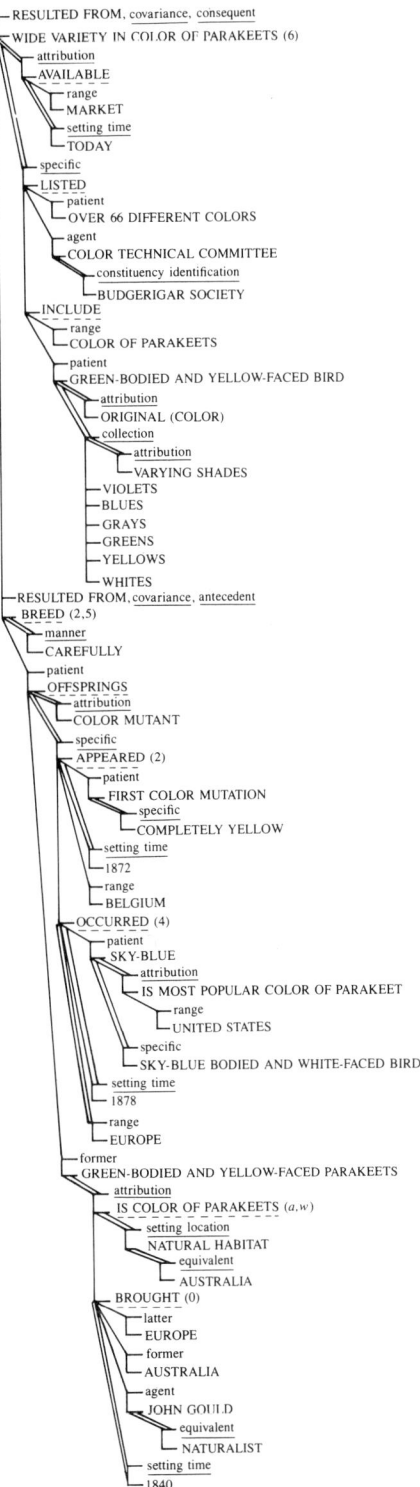

Figure 7.3 Example of a passage and tree structure as described by Meyer (1975).

Similar arguments can be made about the passages used by Dooling and Lachman (Columbus discovering America) and Anderson et al. (wrestler/prisoner). Schemata with slots for ocean travel, how Columbus's voyage was financed, and the types of ships he used, make the first passage easily interpretable. Schemata with slots for methods of prison escape or methods of scoring points in wrestling lead to particular interpretations in the second case.

It seems clear that the process of comprehension involves the schemata that the reader brings to the reading task as well as the information that is presented in the passage itself.

This description of the comprehension process speaks primarily to a final state of the comprehension process, a state in which the reader has located the appropriate schema and has filled its slots acceptably. It is likely, of course, that comprehension involves a series of intermediate steps as the person is finding and checking the appropriate schemata. Evidence for this hypothesis has been provided by Collins, Brown, and Larkin (in press). These psychologists presented subjects with five short, difficult passages and then recorded in-depth protocols for how each subject processed the passages. The subjects were asked to describe any intermediate hypotheses they had about the meaning of the passage and whether these hypotheses were satisfactory or not.

Collins et al. found that subjects proceeded through intermediate stages before reaching a final decision about the appropriate meaning for the passages. Furthermore, their subjects employed several problem-solving strategies as they attempted to develop their conceptualization of the meaning of the passages. This is an interesting observation and suggests that the process of comprehending a prose passage may not be dramatically different from the process of problem solving, a topic we will take up in greater detail in Chapter 9.

An astute reader has probably noted a major problem with the view of comprehension which we have outlined above. Since we have argued that comprehension involves the selection of a schema that accounts for the passage, is it not the case that we have to have an unlimited number of schemata for comprehension to occur? For example, if we are given the following sentences (from Rumelhart & Ortony, 1977):

> Mary heard the ice-cream man coming
> She remembered her pocket money
> She rushed into the house

do we need a special schema about hearing ice-cream men in order to comprehend the sentences? Indeed, do we need a special schema for any situation with a novel twist to it? If so, we would be unable to comprehend even simple variations of common settings unless we had access to warehouses of schemata.

Rumelhart and Ortony suggest that this is not the case because of two of the characteristics of schemata which we described above: Schemata can be at various levels of abstractness, and schemata can embed one within another. Thus in our example above, a very specific schema about hearing ice-cream men is unnecessary. Rather, more general problem-solving schemata combined with a schema of ice-cream men may be sufficient. For an in-depth discussion of the character of these problem-solving schemata see Rumelhart (1977c). The ice-cream-man schema probably has subschemata dealing with selling and ice cream, and the ice-cream subschema has further subschemata dealing with liking and buying. By filling slots in these various subschemata and noting overlaps, a reader is able to develop a coherent formulation for this relatively unique situation.

Similar arguments allow for a schema-based view of comprehension to explain a wide variety of novel situations that may face an individual. We do not mean to imply, of course, that all novel situations may be comprehended. Surely there are situations for which we do not have even highly abstract schemata that provide a reasonable interpretation. The mathematics novice certainly has no appropriate schemata to interpret the problem

$$\int_{-\pi}^{-\delta} + \int_{\delta}^{\pi} f(x-t)\,Dn(t)\,dt$$

and attempts to comprehend it must consequently result in a state of little meaning.

Comprehension and Memory

Do you remember those frustrating moments when you have just finished reading a complicated section in a text and you close the book and try to remember what the author said? And all that you can recall are a few isolated phrases or words; you cannot even state the major point of the section. This situation aptly illustrates the extremely close relationship between comprehension and memory.

Memories are side effects of the comprehension process. As we explained above, the process of comprehension involves the selection and instantiation of a schema that can account for the information found in a passage. Part or all of this instantiated schema is subsequently stored in memory and forms the basis for all attempts to remember the passage. As time goes by, of course, some aspects of the initially instantiated schema may become unavailable, leaving only fragments of the instantiated schema.

If we wish to remember the event at some later time, these fragments must serve as the foundation from which our reconstruction of the event is produced. As Rumelhart and Ortony (1977) note, however, this reconstruction is not an unguided process. In order to provide a meaningful interpretation of the fragments, we again search for schemata that can systematically account for the remaining fragments. These schemata provide a framework for guiding our reconstruction of the event.

Thus we see that schemata play a crucial role not only at the time when we encode information into memory, but also at the time when we attempt to retrieve that which we have stored. Interestingly, this suggests that comprehension and retrieval are very similar processes in that both employ schemata. In one case the principal information used in filling the schema slots is environmental information; in the other case it is memorial information (Rumelhart & Ortony, 1977).

Several studies by Anderson and Pichert (Anderson & Pichert, 1978; Pichert & Anderson, 1977) provide evidence that schemata influence our ability to remember passages both at the time of initial comprehension (and encoding) and at the time of retrieval. In these studies Anderson and Pichert made use of the playing hooky passage with which we are now familiar. In order to determine if the schemata the reader used in interpreting the passage had any influence at the point of retrieval, Anderson and Pichert (1978) had half of their subjects read the hooky passage from the perspective of the home buyer and half from the perspective of the burglar. Each subject then recalled the passage from the perspective with which he or she had read the passage. All the subjects were then asked to recall the passage a second time from the opposite perspective.

Subjects were now able to recall a significant amount of new information relevant to the new perspective that they were unable to recall the first time. The particular recall patterns of the subjects are shown in Table 7.2. In this table the first two columns of numbers refer to the proportion of burglar information recalled from the passage. The last two columns refer to the proportion of home-buyer information recalled.

The recall pattern noted above can be seen in the increase from the first to second recall in row one for burglar information when the subjects' second recall was from the burglar perspective (.51 to .61); a similar pattern is seen for the other recall order in the bottom row of the home-buyer information (.40 to .50). It is not possible

Table 7.2 Proportion of Information Recalled as a Function of Recall Perspective and Type of Information

	INFORMATION CLUSTER			
	Burglar		Homebuyer	
First/Second perspective	1st Recall	2nd Recall	1st Recall	2nd Recall
Homebuyer/Burglar	.51	.61	.59	.48
Burglar/Homebuyer	.68	.36	.40	.50

Source: From Anderson and Pichert (1978).

to interpret this increased recall in terms of encoding mechanisms, since the shift in perspective occurred after the passage had been read and recalled. Apparently schemata can function at the time of retrieval to aid our recall of prose materials.

Schemata do not influence memory just at the point of retrieval, as was shown in another study by these same investigators (cited in Anderson, 1978). In this study subjects were asked to recall a story only once, either from the perspective from which they had read the story or from a different one. They found that

> both the perspective from which the story was read and the perspective from which it was recalled . . . had a substantial effect on performance. Thus, both encoding and retrieval influences were demonstrated. (Anderson, 1978, p. 21)

These studies suggest that schemata play a role in our ability to remember what we have read. We can understand better now why the context effects we described in the opening pages of this chapter not only have an effect on our ability to comprehend what is being read, but also influence our ability to remember it at a later time. Comprehension and retention seem to be cut from the same cloth.

This view of the relationship between comprehension and memory also suggests an interesting interpretation of the concept of encoding specificity, which we first introduced in Chapter 5. If you recall, encoding specificity refers to the fact that a retrieval cue will only be effective in aiding recall if that cue is related to the material at the time of encoding. In our discussion of the role of schemata in memory, we have noted that the context in which a passage is initially set will determine the type of schemata used to comprehend the passage. If the same passage or part of it is presented as a retrieval cue in a different context, subjects may employ different schemata to interpret it and fail to recognize the material as being the same that they initially saw. Thus the concept of encoding specificity is clearly interpretable from a schema-theoretical view of memory.

From our discussion to this point, it is apparent that schemata are involved in the comprehension of and memory for prose materials. However, there is an important characteristic of the processing of prose materials which has not been discussed. Frequently our interpretation of a passage goes beyond that which is explicitly stated in the passage. That is, we appear to infer information that logically follows from a passage but is not explicitly stated. In order to complete our understanding of the processing of prose materials, we must consider the role of such inferential processes in how we comprehend and remember prose materials.

INFERENCE PROCESSES IN COMPREHENSION AND RETENTION

There is an interesting and important consequence of viewing comprehension and retention of prose materials as involving the selection and instantiation of schemata. Whenever a schema is selected to aid our comprehension of new information or to guide our retrieval of an event, there will probably be a large number of slots in the schema for which there is no information available.

For example, when the passage about the boys playing hooky is viewed from the perspective of a home buyer, the appropriate schema probably contains slots for information about the quality of the heating system and type of exterior materials (wood siding, brick, stone). However, no information was presented in the passage that was appropriate to these slots. Similarly, at the time of retrieval the information about the leaking roof may have been forgotten, if it was ever encoded in the first place. Consequently, if the subject were using a home-buyer schema to aid reconstruction, there would be no memorial information available for a schema slot dealing with the quality of the roof. In cases such as these, we find that subjects frequently go beyond the information available and fill in the missing information by inference. This inference process appears to occur both at encoding and at retrieval.

Inference Processes at Comprehension

We have all chuckled over (or been embarrassed by) sentences such as the following:

> Did you walk into the door *again* last night?
> My wife, Kathy, gave me a glass of vinegar last night and told me it was wine. When my lips get unpuckered, I'm going to have a word with her.

A special feature of these sentences is that they permit inferences about events that have occurred earlier (I walk into doors often; I drank the vinegar). In many cases these inferences are of greater importance than the direct meaning of the sentence.

There is considerable empirical evidence that subjects make such inferences while comprehending prose materials. In Chapter 6, for example, we reported that subjects drew inferences from sentences such as

> Three turtles rested on a floating log, and a fish swam beneath them.

In this case subjects were found to falsely recognize a sentence stating that the fish swam under the log as one they had seen before (Bransford, Barclay, & Franks, 1972). They did not make such inferential errors when the initial sentence was

> Three turtles rested beside a floating log, and a fish swam beneath them.

Apparently certain spatial relations are integrated into the subjects' schemata at the point of comprehension. Later, when they are tested for their retention of sentence information, subjects are unable to differentiate information actually presented in the passage from that which could be logically inferred from the information presented.

Such inference processes occur not only when subjects are processing sentences but also when they process complete prose passages. Frederiksen (1975), for example, presented subjects 500-word essays and then scored the subjects' recall for both veridical recall and for various constructions or inferential errors. He found that about 40 percent of the subjects' recall consisted of three types of inferential errors. These were overgeneralizations (e.g., recalling *best proven administrators* as *administrators*), pseudodiscriminations (e.g., recalling *administrators* as *successful administrators*) and inferences (e.g., recalling *wealthy ranchers* when they were given *senators are ranchers* and *senators are rich*).

It is important to question whether these inferential errors occurred at the time of comprehension or at retrieval. Frederiksen suggested that they occurred at comprehension; he argued in this fashion: Veridical recall increased over a series of four recall trials and the number of inferences correlated positively with the number of veridical responses. If the constructions were due to processes at the time of retrieval, there should be a negative correlation. That is, as the subjects recalled more information accurately, there should have been less need for inference. Therefore it appears the constructions were due to processes occurring at the time of comprehension. We conclude then that drawing inferences as we are comprehending prose materials is a practice that may influence our recall at later times.

While the study by Frederiksen suggests that events at the time of comprehension may influence our memory, we should also consider whether events at the time of recall influence how accurately we remember.

Inference Processes at Retrieval

We have described the process of retrieval as one in which the individual uses schemata to guide the reconstruction of past events. In this process the slots in the schemata are filled with the fragments of the initially encoded information which are still available at the time of recall. This view suggests that a number of inferences will be made at the time of retrieval when there is insufficient information for the various slots in the schemata guiding retrieval. Is there evidence that such inferences occur?

Certainly in our everyday functioning something like this seems to occur. When we try to recall events from long ago, it is easy to remember events that might have happened but actually did not. For example, remembering what we did on Christmas day two years ago might lead us to recall that we had lunch and then opened the traditional gifts. This is the normal series of events that has happened on Christmas day for many of us. However, on this particular Christmas we may have needed to see a sick friend after lunch, so the gift-opening ceremony occurred before lunch. The schema we have for the series of Christmas day events has thus led us to reconstruct the day's happenings inaccurately.

Examples such as these suggest that we make inferences at the point of retrieval; however, more controlled evidence is necessary. The most famous empirical study of inferential processes was carried out by Bartlett (1932/1967). He presented subjects the somewhat complex story entitled "War of the Ghosts." (See pages 129–131 on memory retrieval processes.) Many of Bartlett's subjects appeared to recall only a general theme for the story; from this theme they constructed a plausible interpretation of the story. Other subjects seemed to recall only a few events, sometimes only one isolated detail. These subjects would then weave this detail into a plausible story, making use of general schematic knowledge to generate or infer information for vacant slots in the story. As a result, the stories the subjects recalled often differed greatly in detail from the original and frequently had a stereotyped style. Bartlett's work thus suggested that inferential processes do play a significant role at the time of retrieval.

A number of later studies (Cofer, 1973; Zangwill, 1972) were unable to replicate Bartlett's findings, and the notion of reconstructive recall came under attack. Zangwill (1972), a student of Bartlett's, even went so far as to say that the theory, "in my view never very plausible, is perhaps best forgotten" (p. 127). However, some insightful work by Spiro (1977) differs with this pessimistic view and reports some compelling support for the notion of reconstructive processes.

Many of the critics of the reconstructive notion argued that recall is usually quite accurate and does not show all the inferential errors that Bartlett reported. They contended that if the concept of reconstruction is correct, inferential errors should be far more common. Spiro (1977) strongly disagreed with this notion, arguing that the number of errors is not a good index of whether memory is reconstructive. He cogently argued that such errors should only occur under two major conditions.

First, the number of reconstructive errors should increase the more an individual attempts to integrate the to-be-remembered material into his or her overall knowledge base. The more a person does this, the more the particular identity of the story is lost and the more recall will depend on inferences made from existing cognitive structures. Since most of the research studies of reconstructive memory have been carried out in laboratory situations where the subjects are highly unlikely to attempt to integrate presented stories into their permanent knowledge base, inferential errors should be at a minimum. In effect, Spiro argued, we have rarely tested reconstructive memory.

The second major condition leading to inferential errors, according to Spiro, occurs when the schema by which a story is comprehended is modified by later information. This may lead to a situation in which the schema guiding retrieval is different from the one used to encode the material.

Spiro's own research has paid particular attention to these two conditions. By manipulating the schemata through which a person encoded a story and the amount of interaction with existing cognitive structures, he found compelling evidence for inferential processes at the point of retrieval as Bartlett had originally suggested. Spiro had subjects read one of two different stories dealing with an engaged couple, Bob and Margie. In one story Bob indicates a strong desire not to have children and after some delay informs Margie. Margie it turns out has similar beliefs and they are both relieved. The second story is identical to the first except that Margie is horrified by Bob's revelation and there is a bitter discussion as the story ends.

Some subjects were given these stories in a setting that indicated the story was concerned with memory. The other subjects were told that the experiment concerned interpersonal relations and that the stories were true. It was thought this latter condition would lead to greater cognitive interaction and attempts to integrate the material more with the subjects' own cognitive structures.

After the subjects read the stories, they filled out some forms for a few minutes. During this period the experimenter either (1) casually mentioned that Bob and Margie got married and are living happily together, or (2) casually mentioned that they never did get married and broke off the engagement, or (3) did not mention them at all. Some of this information would result in a modification of the expectations engendered by the stories, while other information was consistent with the story expectations. Subjects returned after either 2 days, 3 weeks, or 6 weeks and were asked to recall the story as well as they could.

It was predicted that there would be more inferential errors among those subjects who thought they were in a study of interpersonal relations. It was also predicted that there would be more errors when the expectations were changed by the subsequent information. Subjects in these conditions would be attempting to remember using a more recent schema inconsistent with the manner in which the information was encoded. Finally, it was predicted that there would be more inferential errors the longer the delay period, which would indicate that the errors were occurring at retrieval and not at comprehension.

Spiro found that all his predictions were conclusively demonstrated. Some examples of errors that subjects showed when told that Bob and Margie were happily married after disagreeing violently were:

> They separated but realized after discussing the matter that their love mattered more.

They underwent counseling to correct the major discrepancy.

They discussed it and decided they could agree on a compromise: adoption.

She was only a little upset at the disagreement. (Spiro, 1977, p. 150)

These results in combination with the evidence in the prior section indicate that inferential processes play an important role in the processing of prose materials both at comprehension and at retrieval. It seems clear that what we remember from what we have read depends both on what we

---

Box 7.2 INFERENTIAL PROCESSES IN AN EVERYDAY SETTING: AUTOMOBILE ACCIDENTS

Is there such a thing as a leading question? Can the manner in which we are asked about an event that we have witnessed influence how we recall that event? A study by Loftus and Palmer (1974) provides convincing evidence that it can. These authors had 150 students view a film depicting a multiple-car accident. The film lasted less than a minute and the accident scene lasted about 4 sec.

After the film was over, the subjects were asked to answer a series of questions about the accident. One question was critical: It asked about the speed at which the cars were going. To 50 of the subjects the question was asked in this fashion, "About how fast were the cars going when they *smashed* into each other?" Another group of 50 was asked, "About how fast were the cars going when they *hit* each other?" A final group of 50 subjects was not questioned about the speed of the car.

A week later the subjects returned and without reviewing the film answered a set of questions. Again, one question was critical: "Did you see any broken glass?" It is important to realize that there had been no broken glass in the film. However, since broken glass would be a likely piece of information for a slot in a schema dealing with cars smashing (but not so likely with hitting), it was expected that subjects who heard the "smash" question would answer *Yes* more often.

This was in fact what occurred, as we can see by looking at the distribution of *Yes* and *No* responses. For those subjects who heard the question with the verb *smash*, 32 percent said they had seen glass, while only 14 percent of the subjects who had the verb *hit* and 12 percent of the control subjects reported that they had seen glass. The simple procedure of changing the initial verb describing the automobile accident had led to more than twice as many subjects reporting that they had seen glass.

Is it possible that even *recognition* of visual scenes can be biased by misleading information? Loftus, Miller, and Burns (1978) found that it could. They showed subjects a series of 30 slides including one in which a red Datsun stops at an intersection having either a stop or yield sign (see Figure 7.4). At varying intervals (up to 1 week) after viewing the slides, the subjects were given a set of questions including one that asked, "Did another car pass the red Datsun while it was stopped at the stop (yield) sign?"

For some subjects this question was consistent with the slide they had seen, and for some it was misleading. Later, the subjects were given a forced choice recognition test involving several pairs of slides. The critical pair included the red Datsun at either the stop or yield sign. Subjects were to pick which slide they had seen before. Loftus et al. found that subjects given consistent information picked the correct slide 75 percent of the time, while those given misleading information were correct only 41 percent of the time. They also found that the misleading information had a more powerful impact if it were given just prior to the time of testing. Apparently even recognition of previously seen information can be biased by misleading information.

Evidence such as this makes it clear why the legal concept of leading questions has been developed and why there are rules indicating when such questions can be used. Unfortunately, there are many other settings in which regulations on the use of leading statements have not been set up. Listen carefully to commercial advertisements and the claims they make. For example, what is actually claimed in, and what do people infer from, the following statement,

"No one does it better than *brand X*"?

Most of us would infer that brand X is better than all the other products. However, this statement is also true if there are no significant differences among any of the brands. Apparently the manner in which we process information makes us susceptible to (sometimes) unwarranted conclusions.

Figure 7.4 Critical slides used in study by Loftus, Miller, and Burns (1978). Note that the slides differ only in the nature of the traffic signs.

have been presented in the passage and what our knowledge background leads us to infer.

Inferential processes such as the ones described here play important roles in our everyday functioning. This fact was shown in some recent studies by Loftus (Loftus, Miller, & Burns, 1978; Loftus & Palmer, 1974). They are described in detail in Box 7.2 and illustrate the importance to lawyers and judges of the concept of leading questions. In addition, these studies suggest that we should be generally aware that inference making is a common phenomenon in human information processing.

We began this chapter by considering the role of context in prose processing. It is appropriate and instructive to return briefly to this topic to show how the concept of schema helps us interpret that work. We indicated that the meaning of words in sentences, sentences in passages, and even passages in text, may be altered by context. In light of our discussion of schemata, it appears likely that the psychological mechanism that accounts for these findings is the schema.

The context in which a word is set plays a significant role in what schema a subject employs in comprehending each word in a sentence. Thus the context in which the word *mess* is set—a paint-smeared dress or muddy uniform—determines which schema and hence which slots are filled. Similarly, sentences and passages must be filtered through the schemata that have been activated by the context in which they are set.

In addition, we can now more clearly see the relationship between the varieties of contextual situations that influence comprehension. Pictorial settings, themes, instructions, and our own background are all factors that influence the schemata through which we approach prose materials. The first three of these are all variables that suggest to us which particular schemata we should use in reading a particular passage. The fourth of these factors is slightly different. It suggests that our general set of background experiences influences the types of schemata we will have at hand to interpret our world.

In the same manner that Anderson, Reynolds, Schallert, and Goetz's (1977) weightlifters brought a general knowledge of wrestling and sports, each of us brings sets of schemata generated by our idiosyncratic set of experiences. The individual raised in a poverty-striken ghetto where the actions of someone approaching her on a street suggest danger may interpret quick movements in other settings through a similar schema. The senator who has been through numerous political skirmishes may be set to interpret statements and decisions by others as more devious than a layman inexperienced in politics would. Context, it seems, suggests the type of background knowledge we should bring to bear upon the situation before us.

Before we conclude this chapter we need to consider one additional topic. At the end of Chapter 4 we indicated that we would need to consider the impact of the concept of schema on our view of permanent memory structure, and now that we have elaborated the concept of schema we are ready to carry out that task.

SCHEMATA AND SEMANTIC MEMORY

In our earlier discussion of the structure of permanent memory we described several different theories of semantic memory. These included network models, dual-storage models, feature comparison models, and set theory models. We found that these models could explain a wide variety of evidence such as the category size effect, typicality effect, and various priming effects. In addition, they explain a number of everyday phenomena, such as how one word leads us to think of others or how we judge similarities and differences among words. Thus these theories provide an explanation for how we store and use information we have about our environment.

However, psychologists who are interested in topics such as perception and prose retention—topics that necessitate discussion of the nature of stored knowledge—have not made extensive use of the semantic memory theories in their work. Instead, they have increasingly called on the concept of schema, as we have seen earlier in this chapter and in Chapter 2. The question we must ask is whether these two views of our world knowledge are the same or whether they are fundamentally different in character. In order to do this, we need to compare these views.

A careful analysis of schema theory (as defined by Neisser, 1976; Rumelhart & Ortony, 1977) and the semantic memory theories we discussed in Chapter 4 indicates at least three major ways that these views are alike. First, both schema theory and semantic memory theory contend that our knowledge system must represent not only a particular concept or idea but also the vast network of relationships which are thought to exist among concepts. In fact, schema theory and several of the semantic memory models seem to argue for some type of hierarchical structure to knowledge, whether it be the embedding of subschemata in schemata or the elaborate structures of the Collins and Loftus network model.

Second, there are examples of each theoretical approach which claim that our representational system represents our knowledge of the world rather than just a record of concept meanings. In other words, they claim that our memory is not like a list of definitions but rather is an indication of what associations or relationships exist among concepts.

Finally, both views claim to represent generalized knowledge that we have of objects, situations, or events, and not just highly specific, time-tagged knowledge of a specific situation or event. That is, they do not claim a vast taperecorder system which has faithfully represented all the fine detail of a given situation.

But schema theory and the semantic memory theories do appear to differ on two major characteristics. First, while both semantic memory theories and schema theory agree that our representational systems represent our knowledge of the world, they sometimes differ on the role that this world knowledge is thought to play in our ability to understand language. Schema theory places heavy emphasis on the fact that how we understand a passage or a sentence depends on the particular background knowledge a person has of the situation. Such knowledge is not necessarily given an important role in language understanding by semantic memory theories.

The second way in which schema theory and semantic memory theories differ is in the emphasis they place on semantic flexibility. Schema theory views schemata as information-accepting systems that can take on a tremendous diversity of meanings. In contrast, the semantic memory theories portray our knowledge system as a large collection of links between conceptual nodes in the system. According to this latter view, our performance on a priming task or typicality task depends upon presence or absence of a particular link. But the manner in which this link is influenced by the particular situation at hand has not been well detailed.

In marked contrast, schema theory suggests that a new or different interpretation may be given to an event depending on the context in which it is embedded. We reviewed a large number of perceptual and prose-processing studies that spoke to this point. For example, we saw in the beginning of this chapter how the word *mess* can take on a large number of meanings depending on the context in which the word is set. This is the case even though the nominal meaning of the term is the same. Thus we seem to have different meanings for a mess on a table, a mess in the yard, and a mess in a house (Jenkins, 1977). It is difficult to conceptualize a static system of links between conceptual nodes which could be complete enough to have an established link to represent every possible context in which a mess can occur.

On the other hand, the slot or variable notion proposed by schema theory allows for the formation of an infinite number of different interpretations to a setting. In effect, the slots in a schema will be differentially filled depending on the context, thus allowing for the great diversity of meanings which perceptual and prose-processing situations seem to call for.

In sum, the evidence from two major areas of cognitive functioning—perception and prose processing—seems to call for people to have a highly flexible means to represent the world around them. This is a new demand we have placed on our models of the structure of permanent memory. While it is not impossible for semantic memory theories to handle this semantic flexibility, this notion seems most adequately filled by the concept of schema.

CONCLUSION

As we conclude this chapter on the processing of prose materials, we would like to comment briefly on the important role we have assigned the concept of schema in our view of prose processing in particular and cognition in general. The concept of schema is not new (see Bartlett, 1932/1967; Kant, 1781/1915; Piaget, 1962), but its resurrection in the past few years has presented a new way to view prose retention, perception, and memory. The concept is not without its problems (see Brown, 1978); in particular, the lack of a rigorous definition makes it difficult to test. However, the concept integrates topics as diverse as perception, motor skills, and prose retention; it allows us to speak to a great number of everyday situations; and further, it allows us to account for the role of context in cognitive functioning.

These benefits are likely to keep the concept of schema an active one in the field of cognitive psychology for years to come.

8. Concepts

Concept Structure
Learning Concepts
    Discovering the Attributes
    Discovering the Rule
    Hypothesis Testing
    Strategies
Concepts, Memory, and Language
    The Internal Structure of Concepts
        Perceptual Categories
        Semantic Categories
    Concepts and Semantic Memory
    Concepts and Language
Conclusion

Human beings have an awesome ability for telling things apart. In the color spectrum alone we are able to distinguish some seven million different values. A consequence of this refined ability is that almost every experience we have is unique. As many times as you have been with some friend—Harry, let's say—you find that each experience is distinctive and can be separated from every other experience. From week to week or moment to moment friend Harry is detectably different in hair style (combed, partly combed, windblown, slept on), choice of clothes, posture, facial expression, or angle from which you see him. Your auditory experience of him changes momentarily with the sounds of his moving, speaking, or the growling of his stomach, as do your experiences of his feel and smell. Like a series of snapshots, each slice of time in this continuing experience is noticeably different from the others.

This raises a bit of a philosophical puzzle. If each momentary experience of friend Harry is unique, how do you know each time that it's friend Harry? If each experience is different, why treat them as being of the same person? Experience of Shirley and Alex are different too, but you do not treat them as being of the same person.

The solution to this puzzle is that we ignore the differences and instead group our experiences on the basis of some common features. Even though our many experiences of friend Harry are detectably different, they also have many characteristics in common which lead us to categorize them as being of the same person. Similarly, we group all our experiences of boats into the category BOAT, and all our experiences of tomatoes into the category TOMATO, and so on for thousands of objects and events.

The mental structure with which we represent a category is called a **concept**. A concept is abstract; it represents a class of things, not any particular member of the class. The concept of HORSE cannot be represented by a particular horse, such as Man O' War, nor by any image of a horse we may create. Each of these is particular and leaves out much of the information about horses in general.

In many cases a concept is equivalent to the mathematical notion of *set*. It is defined by a list of properties; any entity that has those properties is a member of the set. Many concepts will have finite sets, such as that of PLANETS IN THE SOLAR SYSTEM. Others will have indefinitely large sets, as the concept of HUMAN BEING or of WALNUT TREE. Still others will have empty sets, such as the concept of LIVING DINOSAURS or of GOLD PENNIES. Concepts having empty sets are especially revealing of the inventive nature of concept formation. We do not have to have experience with instances of a concept to conceive it, as is illustrated in the literature of fairy tales and myths or the hypothetical entities of science.

What would life be like without concepts? We would be unable to eat, since we would have no concept for what things are edible. Nor drink. Just imagine. With no way of grouping past experiences, we would as likely make love to telephone poles as to people. We could not count (numbers are concepts), nor tell time. Our cars would go unrecognized, since their sameness from one experience to the next would be lost. With no conceptual structure, science would not be possible.

In fact, each of us already has learned a large number of concepts with which we solve the problem of overwhelming novelty. To recognize something is to identify it as a member of a known concept and thus to permit us to respond appropriately to unique objects and events. Moreover, we can relate concepts in such a way that identifying x as a frog suggests what may happen if we capture it, hold it, kiss it, and so on. Representing the world to ourselves this way is enormously economical, since the finite number of concepts we have lets us react adaptively to an indefinitely large number of unique experiences. We have seen this process in perception, memory, and language, and we will see it again in problem solving and motor skills.

In the balance of this chapter we will address two major topics on concepts. The first deals with the way researchers in this area have defined concepts and how they have explored the phenomena involved in the learning of concepts. The second topic focuses on the relationship of concepts to some of the cognitive processes we have discussed in earlier chapters, including memory structure and language.

CONCEPT STRUCTURE

A concept is defined by one or more **attributes** related by a **rule.** An attribute is any feature of an object or event which may change noticeably from one instance to another. For example, seagulls are noticeably different in height, weight, coloring, wingspan, and so on. An attribute has two or more *values,* which are degrees of difference in the attribute. Some attributes have discrete values, such as *male, female* for the attribute of sex, or *single, married, widowed,* and so on for the attribute of marital status. Other attributes have continuous values, as in the case of the dimensions of time, weight, and temperature, though we often break these into arbitrary units. A concept having continuous dimensions will usually have a range of acceptable values for each dimension. The concept of VOTER, for instance, is defined by a range of acceptable ages, of which 18 is usually the lower limit.

One of our major tasks in learning a concept is to separate *relevant* and *irrelevant* attributes. Relevant attributes define the concept. Instances of the concept, however, will have other attributes that are unrelated to the concept. The concept of VOTER is defined by such relevant attributes as age and citizenship, but matters of sex, education, and employment are irrelevant to whether a person may be a voter in this country today.

Most objects have a large number of attributes, only some of which are relevant to the concept to which we assign that object. The relevant attributes change according to the concept we use. For example, Charlie Brown's dog Snoopy can be categorized variously as a PET, DOG, ANIMAL, MAMMAL, FICTIONAL CREATURE, and so on, each category having a different set of relevant attributes. Assigning Snoopy to any one of these is a coding process of determining that Snoopy has the relevant attributes for the concept.

Coding is quite selective, since the attributes for one concept may be irrelevant for another and so are ignored. Regardless of the concept into which an object is coded, the coding is selective and many of the attributes of the object will not be attended to.

In addition to its relevant attributes, a concept is defined by a **rule** that combines these attributes in a particular way. For example, a concept may require the joint presence of two attributes (e.g., tall *and* dark), the presence of one or the other attributes (tall *or* dark), and so on. The attributes and the rule defining a concept are separate components of the concept. The same attributes may be combined by different rules to produce different concepts.

LEARNING CONCEPTS

To learn a concept we must discover its relevant attributes and the rule relating them. To acquire the concept of POISON IVY, for example, we must learn that it is a vine that has three-leaf clusters. Each leaf is pointed and has toothed edges. The stems for the three leaves are red at the base. These are the relevant attributes, and we may ignore such irrelevant attributes as the length of the vine and the number of three-leaf clusters on the vine. The rule for this concept is the *conjunction* rule; that is, all of the relevant attributes must be present in a plant for it to be an instance of the concept.

Once we have learned the relevant attributes and the rule, we have the concept POISON IVY and can distinguish examples of it from plants that have some but not all of the relevant attributes. The Virginia Creeper vine looks something like poison ivy, but it has five leaves to a cluster instead of three. Seedlings of the box elder tree look even more like poison ivy, since they have a three-leaf cluster whose stems are red at the base. But the box elder is a tree and even its seedlings have a central stem that is straight rather than vinelike.

Learning the concept of POISON IVY, of course, requires practice in discriminating true instances from look-alikes. Such practice sets the concept firmly in permanent memory and makes it available for the pattern recognition process of identifying new instances. We study this learning process by observing how people discover the relevant attributes for a concept and the rule relating them. It appears that people often use an hypothesis-testing approach in learning concepts, and we will explore this approach below. A good understanding of the requirements for learning a concept will give us better control over our own learning as well as helping those whose work involves teaching concepts.

We will consider four processes that are involved in learning a concept: (1) discovering the relevant attributes, (2) discovering the rule that relates the attributes, (3) testing hypotheses, a notion that underlies many theories of concept learning, and (4) using strategies, which are systematic procedures that may be used for learning a concept.

An example of a standard experimental procedure for studying concept learning may help in understanding this section. Figure 8.1 shows an array of cards put before a subject in a typical concept-learning situation. They vary in shape of figure (square, circle, or triangle), size of figure (large or small), and position of figure (left, middle, or right). The experimenter has a concept in mind, such as LARGE CIRCLES, which the subject must discover. The subject is shown a positive instance of the concept (e.g., card 3) and asked to choose other cards one at a time until she can say what the concept is. After each card choice she is told whether the card is a positive or negative instance of the concept. For example, if she chooses card 18, she is told that it is a negative instance of the concept, since it is not a large circle.

Table 8.1 shows the card choices made by a sophisticated subject, as well as the feedback given by the experimenter for each card and the inference the subject draws. This hypothetical experiment illustrates the two aspects of a concept-learning task. The subject had to learn the relevant attributes of the concept, which in this example are size (large) and shape (circle).

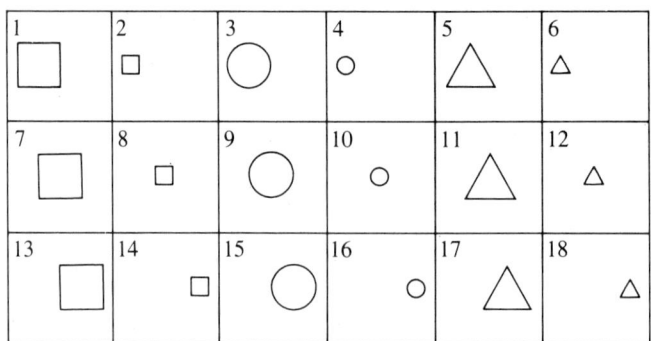

Figure 8.1 Array of cards presented to a subject in an hypothetical concept-learning experiment.

Table 8.1 Sequence of Card Choices, Feedback, and Inferences Drawn in an Hypothetical Experiment

Card choice	Feedback given	Inference drawn
Experimenter presents card 3 (circle, large, left)	Positive instance	"Since this is positive, shape, size, and position could all be part of the concept."
Subject chooses card 1 (square, large, left)	Not an instance	"Only shape is different from the first card, so *circle* must be part of the concept."
Subject chooses card 9 (circle, large, middle)	Positive instance	"Only position is different from the first card, but this card is still positive, so position must not be part of the concept."
Subject chooses card 4 (circle, small, left)	Not an instance	"Only size is different from the first card, so *large* must be part of the concept."
		Conclusion: "The concept is LARGE CIRCLES."

She also had to learn the rule for combining the attributes, which in this example is the rule of conjunction. Let us look at the aspects of concept learning in more detail.

Discovering the Attributes

In the first stages of learning a concept, a person faces a profusion of attributes. We saw in Chapter 2 on attention that the environment holds far more information than we take in at a given moment. Inevitably, we select. Our task here is to attend to the relevant attributes and ignore the irrelevant ones. A geology instructor may develop the concept of SEDIMENTARY ROCKS by pointing out the layering in several sample rocks. Her students may observe that the layers vary in thickness and color and so will not code these irrelevant attributes into their concept.

One factor influencing attention to attributes is the *salience* of the attributes. This term describes the fact that some features are noticed quickly in a concept-learning task while others are only noticed later if at all. To identify airplanes, aircraft enthusiasts commonly attend to such distinctive attributes as wing and fuselage shape, but rely less on tail shape and length of fuselage. Similarly, in a standard laboratory task we may notice immediately that the figures differ in shape and color, but we may fail to see that they have different positions on the card.

When the salient attributes are relevant, learning the concept is easy; but it is understandably more difficult when irrelevant attributes are salient. During wartime, for example, enemy aircraft spotters have more difficulty identifying enemy aircraft when salient attributes such as wing shape are similar for both friendly and enemy aircraft. When friendly and enemy aircraft differ in these salient attributes, the spotter's job is made much easier.

Although people differ in which attributes are most salient for them, external conditions can be manipulated to change the salience of attributes. Archer (1962) increased salience by increasing the difference between the values of the attribute. Taking size as an example, he found that a large difference between big and small figures gave greater salience than did a slight difference. If size were relevant, the increased salience aided discovery of the concept; if size were irrelevant, the increased salience slowed discovery. Increasing the difference between values of an attribute is thus one way of increasing its salience.

Discovering the relevant attributes is often depicted as a process of testing hypotheses. Assuming the relevant attributes are within the set of attributes a person has attended to, the person selectively tests them until the irrelevant ones have been discarded and the relevant ones remain. Before we examine hypothesis testing more fully, let us look at the discovery of the rule that relates the relevant attributes.

Discovering the Rule

Since concepts are defined both by their relevant attributes and a rule of combination, learning the concept requires discovering both attributes and rule. Concepts having more complex rules should, of course, be more difficult to learn.

Neisser and Weene (1962) have identified ten rules that may relate the attributes of a concept having two attributes, each with two values. Table 8.2 describes six of these rules, and Figure 8.2 shows the positive instances under each rule. The simplest rules are the *affirmation* and *negation* rules, which apply only to concepts having a single relevant attribute. The affirmation rule states that any instance having the proper value of the attribute is a positive instance. If the concept were LARGE OBJECTS, as defined by the single attribute of size (large, small) and the value *large*, then any object that was large would be a positive instance under this rule. For the same attribute, the negation rule states that any object not large would be a positive instance.

Most concepts have more than one relevant attribute and so involve more complex rules. One of the most common is the *conjunction* rule, which states that the proper values of *all* relevant attributes must be present for an instance to be positive. Consider the attributes of size (large, small) and shape (circle, square), with *large* and *circle* being the proper values. By the conjunction rule any object that is both large and a circle is a positive instance. The *disjunction* rule states that any object with the proper value for one or more of the relevant attributes is a positive instance. Thus in our example any object that is large or a circle or both is a positive instance under this rule.

Table 8.2 Rules for Relating Attributes in a Concept

Rule	Symbolic description	Verbal description
Affirmation	L	Any large object
Negation	L̄	Any object not large
Conjunction	L ∩ C	Any object both large and a circle
Disjunction	L ∪ C	Any object either large or a circle or both
Conditional	L ⇒ C	Any large object if it is a circle
Biconditional	L ⇔ C	Any large object if and only if it is a circle

Source: After Haygood and Bourne (1965).

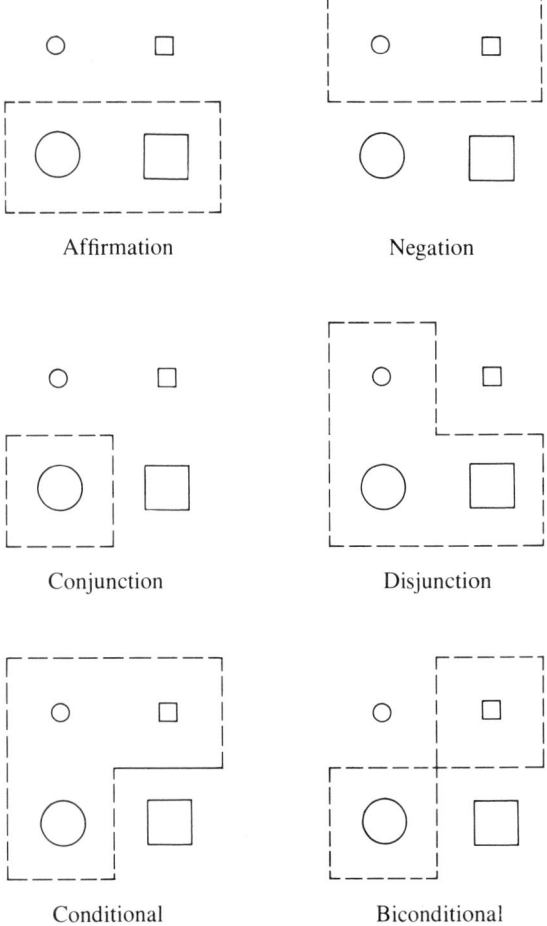

Figure 8.2 Positive instances according to six different rules. Positive instances for each rule are enclosed by dashed lines.

Two additional rules are the *conditional* (if ... then) and *biconditional* (if and only if) rules familiar to those who have studied logic. The conditional rule states that all objects are positive instances with certain exceptions. The exception comes in the condition that *if* an instance has the antecedent relevant attribute (the one stated in the *if* clause), *then* it must have the consequent relevant attribute (the one stated in the *then* clause) to be a positive instance; otherwise it is a negative instance. If the concept is defined as IF LARGE THEN CIRCLE, large figures would have to be circles in order to be positive instances. Large figures that were not circles would be negative instances, but any other objects that were not large would be positive. Intuitively this rule is not as obvious as the simpler ones.

The *biconditional* rule is logically related to the conditional rule and requires the joint presence of both relevant attributes or neither attribute in order to have a positive instance. For the biconditional concept LARGE IF AND ONLY IF CIRCLE, any object that was both large and a circle would be a positive instance as would be any object that was neither large nor a circle. Any object that was large but not a circle, or a circle but not large, would be a negative instance. There are still other rules, which we will not pursue here, but you will find a discussion of them in Kintsch (1977).

Throughout the examples above we have kept the same two attribute values for the concept, those of *large* and *circle*. Note that with each new rule we got a different partition of figures differing in size and shape into positive and negative instances. The subsets of positive and negative instances are not the same for any two rules. This illustrates the independence of attributes and rules in defining a concept and also indicates the way concepts are allied to set theory.

Neisser and Weene (1962) grouped rules into three levels of complexity. For the six rules described above, they were: Group I, affirmation and negation; Group II, conjunction and disjunction; Group III, conditional and biconditional. When they asked subjects to learn concepts based on each of the rules, they found the difficulty of learning the concepts was ordered as they had expected, with those from Group I being the easiest, those from Group II harder, and those from Group III hardest.

There are two problems that must be noted with this conclusion. First, it is possible that some rules such as the conjunction rule are more familiar, and concepts based on them are easier to learn because of the amount of previous experience subjects have had with them rather than because the rule is intrinsically easier. For example, in a study of conjunctive and disjunctive concepts, Wells (1963) found subjects initially showed a strong preference for conjunctive concepts, but became more adept at solving disjunctive concepts after learning four concepts based on the disjunction rule. Thus differences in rule difficulty may be reduced by practice.

The second problem, pointed out by Haygood and Bourne (1965), is that the discovery of rules is often confounded with the discovery of attributes in concept learning, and one cannot be sure how much of the difficulty comes from rule discovery alone. To get a purer measure of differences due to rule difficulty, these authors devised three separate tasks: attribute learning, rule learning, and concept learning.

In the attribute-learning task, the nature of the rule was explained to the subjects and they merely had to discover the relevant attributes. In the rule-learning task, the relevant attributes were given to the subjects and they had only to discover the rule. In concept learning, neither the attributes nor the rule were given and the subjects had to learn both. Subjects learned five successive concepts based on one of four rules: conjunction, disjunction, joint denial, and conditional. *Joint denial* has as its positive instances all instances having neither of the relevant attributes (e.g., figures that are neither large nor circles). The results of this study are shown in Figure 8.3.

Attribute learning and rule learning were both significantly easier than concept learning, showing that these two processes contribute separately to concept learning. In rule learning there were marked differences in the ease of learning the rules at the outset. The conjunction rule was the easiest. The other rules showed improvement with successive problems, however; and by the third problem, disjunction and joint denial were no more difficult than conjunction. The conditional rule remained more difficult, but in a later experiment Bourne (1967) showed that even the conditional and biconditional rules could be learned, with sufficient practice, to the efficiency seen in the use of these other rules. In general then, it seems that the ease with which rules are learned may differ, but these differences can be overcome with practice.

Some of the differences in rule difficulty may be related to the cognitive processes required to use the rules. Trabasso, Rollins, and Shaughnessy (1971) argued that the more complex

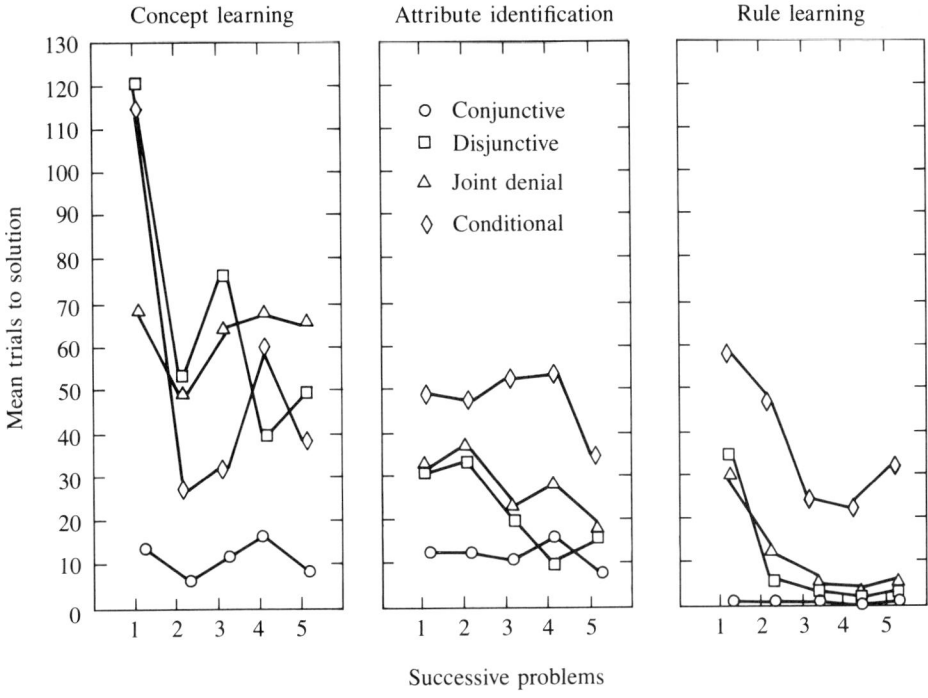

Figure 8.3 Mean trials to learning of concepts based on four different rules. (From Bourne, 1967.)

rules are difficult to use because more mental operations are required in applying complex rules than are required in simpler rules. Each mental operation takes time. The larger the number of operations, the greater the time.

To test their hypothesis, these researchers measured reaction time in a verification task. They first gave their subjects a concept and then showed them a slide depicting a possible instance of the concept. The subjects were to decide as quickly as possible whether the slide depicted a positive or negative instance of the concept.

Trabasso et al. used a decision tree to represent the mental operations a subject was hypothesized to use in making this decision. Figure 8.4 shows the decision trees for three of their rules: conjunction (A_1 and A_2), disjunction (A_1 or A_2 or both), and exclusive disjunction (A_1 or A_2, but not both), where A_1 and A_2 are the two relevant attributes. As you can see, the number of mental operations for the conjunction and disjunction rules is the same; but for exclusive disjunction, the number is larger and therefore a decision should take longer.

The instances in this task were somewhat different from those we have described earlier. Instead of representing all attributes in a single figure, this task used a different figure for each of the two relevant attributes. The two figures were shown on a slide. In each case the slide showed a triangle on the left and a circle on the right. The two relevant attributes were size (large or small) and color (orange or green).

Before the slide was shown, the experimenter gave the subject a rule—for example, the disjunction rule—and then the values of the two

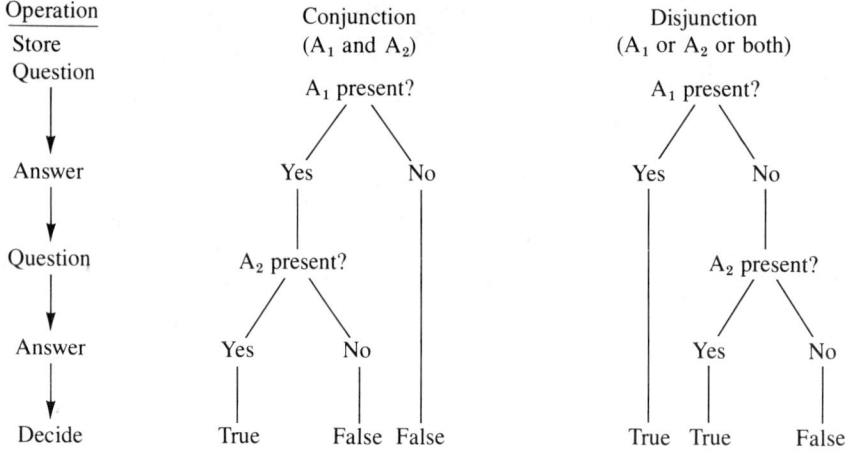
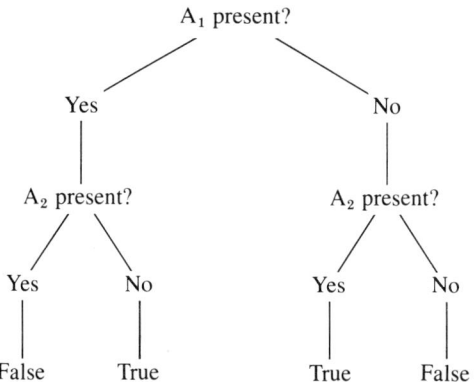

Figure 8.4 Decision trees for three rules. (From Trabasso, Rollins, & Shaughnessy, 1971.)

relevant attributes, for example, *large, green*. The first value referred to the triangle and the second value to the circle. When the slide was shown, the subject checked the triangle to see if it was large and then the circle to see if it was green. If the rule was disjunction and the first test true, the subject could respond immediately that the instance was positive. If the rule was conjunction, however, the subject would then have to make the second test.

The mean verification times for the three rules were: conjunction, 895 msec; disjunction, 758 msec; and exclusive disjunction, 1330 msec. As predicted by the decision tree analysis, the times for conjunction and disjunction were not significantly different, but the time for exclusive disjunction was significantly longer. These results were stable over many hours of practice. Such results suggest that rules that involve more mental operations take longer to carry out.

Note that the difference in difficulty for conjunction and disjunction rules which we reported as occurring at the beginning of learning tasks did not appear in this verification task. Posner (1973) suggests that the reason lies in the difference between the two tasks. In the verification task the two attributes appear in two different figures (the triangle and the circle), while in the typical learning task the two attributes appear in the same figure. In the verification task the two attributes are probably tested separately, but in the learning task they can be tested simultaneously. This suggests that the step-by-step processing of attributes described by a decision tree analysis does not necessarily occur for all uses of concepts.

Hypothesis Testing

A common assumption in theories about concept learning is that the subject forms hypotheses about the relevant attributes and their correct values and then tests them. Consider, for example, a farmer named Fitzgerald who was coming down with a cold. To cure the cold, he decided to (1) take an aspirin, (2) drink a beer, and (3) go to bed early. Upon rising the next morning he discovered his cold was cured. "My problem now," he said, "is I don't know which one cured the cold." Mr. Fitzgerald will not be able to resolve his dilemma because he failed to test his hypotheses systematically. Such a testing procedure would require that he test his hypotheses one at a time.

Of course, we do not always have to experience such travail in order to test hypotheses. A subject in a standard laboratory task may test her hypotheses against a set of instances presented to her by an experimenter. Each hypothesis is tested against instances that fit the hypothesis; if the subject is told an instance is positive, she continues to test the hypothesis on other instances. If she is told it is negative, she rejects the hypothesis and tries a new one. Ultimately she should come to the hypothesis that is the concept the experimenter has in mind.

Three things are notable about the assumption that hypothesis testing is a fundamental part of learning concepts. First, it portrays concept learning as a constructive process, one in which the subject generates candidate hypotheses. The constructive nature of the cognitive processes is a theme that appears throughout the literature on cognition. Second, it stresses the role of feedback in learning a concept; without feedback, in fact, one cannot learn a concept. The necessity of feedback in cognitive processes is also widespread, as we shall see in the study of problem solving and motor skills. Finally, hypothesis testing is selective; it focuses on certain attributes to the neglect of others. This reduces the strain on resources in working memory, but does so at the risk that the correct hypothesis may not be among those being tested.

The act of generating hypotheses is a private mental act. Since this act is unobservable, how can we know whether or not a subject is testing hypotheses or using some other strategy for learning a concept? In traditional methodology subjects are asked to verbalize their hypotheses as they work through a task. This methodology has several uncertainties, however, which researchers would like to avoid. We discuss some of these uncertainties in Box 8.1. In order to avoid some of these problems, Levine (1966) devised a novel technique for determining whether subjects use hypotheses and whether they use them systematically.

Levine's procedure began with a regular feedback trial, which was followed by four nonfeedback trials in which he determined the hypothesis the subject had used in the feedback trial. In the feedback trial the subject was presented a card that contained two figures differing in four attributes: position (left or right), size (large or small), shape (x or T), and color (black

Box 8.1 VERBALIZING HYPOTHESES

Hypothesis-testing theories face a serious methodological problem. By its very nature, the hypothesis a subject is testing is private, hidden in the recesses of the mind and barred from direct inspection. How then can an experimenter know whether a subject is testing hypotheses and, if so, which ones?

A common methodology for dealing with this problem is to have subjects verbalize their hypotheses. On each trial a subject tells the experimenter what he or she thinks the concept might be, thereby enabling the experimenter to assess the way the subject is discovering the concept.

There are several problems with this methodology. First, a subject may not be aware of having an hypothesis. Hull (1920) observed this in a classic experiment in which he asked subjects to sort letters from the Chinese alphabet. Those letters that exhibited a particular element were positive instances of the concept, while those that did not were negative. The subjects were not told the basis for defining the concept but were given feedback as they sorted each letter into the positive or negative pile.

Hull observed that some subjects learned to sort the letters correctly but were unable to verbalize the basis for their sorting. Hull introduced the phrase "functional concept" to describe the behavior of subjects who can perform correctly but cannot tell why. This notion is the basis of Levine's (1966) procedure (see text).

Second, verbalizing an hypothesis may bias the subjects' behavior by committing them to their stated hypothesis. Hislop and Brooks (1968) had subjects sort cards showing pictures of animals. The cards differed in several attributes, but the concept was defined as all those showing two animals of the same species. In one condition subjects were asked to state their basis for sorting the cards before classifying them. In a second condition they classified the cards before stating their basis for doing so.

The subjects who classified first made significantly more correct classifications than those who verbalized first. Hislop and Brooks concluded that the subjects who verbalized first tended to be guided by their stated hypotheses, while those who classified first relied more on nonverbal information they had coded from the cards. Posner (1973) describes the use of nonverbal information more fully in a discussion of "spectator behavior."

One of the questions which underlies this methodological problem is, What is the role of consciousness in dealing with concepts? (See Chapter 2 for a discussion of the role of consciousness in cognition.) Is the processing of a concept fully conscious? If not, which processes are unconscious or to what degree are they unconscious? These questions are as old as psychology, and we make no pretense of answering them here. However, they pose a continuing barrier to the resolution of our methodological problem. We have some evidence that verbalizing hypotheses is an invalid procedure, but to what degree is not clear. How shall we resolve this problem?

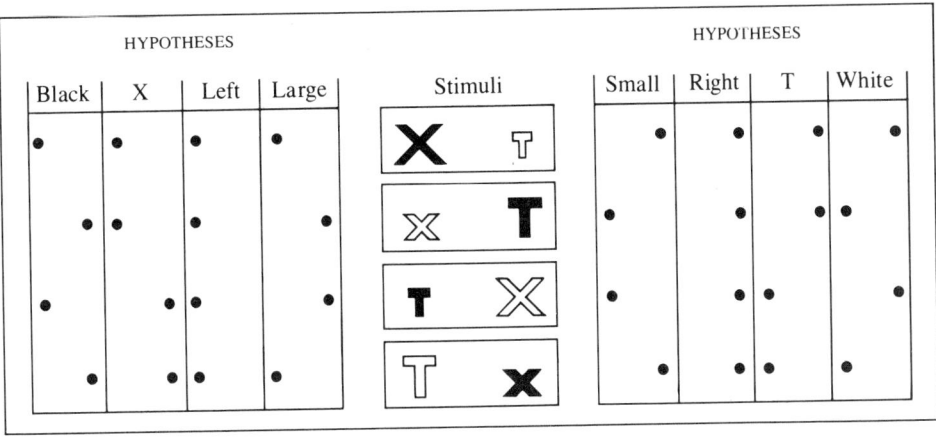

Figure 8.5 The pattern of choices for each of eight hypotheses when the four stimulus pairs are presented without feedback. (From Levine, 1966.)

or white). The subject had to guess which figure was correct and was told whether or not the guess was correct. In the four following trials the subject was presented the four cards shown in the middle column of Figure 8.5. For each card the subject was asked to say which figure was correct according to the decision he or she had made on the first card.

There are eight possible hypotheses in this task, and these are also shown in Figure 8.5. The pattern of dots below each hypothesis indicates the pattern of choices the subject would make on the four cards when using that hypothesis. There are numerous patterns of choices, of course, which do not correspond to any of these hypotheses. Since each pattern is different, the hypothesis the subject is using can be uniquely determined in the four nonfeedback trials, assuming the subject is using an hypothesis-testing procedure.

Levine found that in about 92 percent of the tests his subjects (college students) followed a pattern consistent with one of the hypotheses. Moreover, he found that a subject who had been told a choice was correct on the first feedback trial would stick with that hypothesis about 95 percent of the time on the second feedback trial, the trial following the four nonfeedback trials. If the subject had been told a choice was incorrect, however, he or she would change the hypothesis on the next feedback trial about 98 percent of the time. This tactic is often called a "win stay, lose shift" strategy. Levine's evidence thus strongly suggests that subjects not only use hypothesis testing in learning a concept but also that they use it in a systematic fashion.

Another question frequently asked in hypothesis-testing theories is, How much do subjects rely on memory when testing hypotheses? Do they test only one hypothesis at a time, thereby reducing strain on working memory; or do they test several hypotheses at the same time for greater efficiency? Levine was able to explore this question also.

On the first trial, if the subject had chosen the large black T on the left and was told it was correct, the subject could infer that the concept was one of the four hypotheses LARGE, BLACK, T, or LEFT. He or she could also reject the hypotheses of SMALL, WHITE, X, and RIGHT. Ideally a subject could eliminate half the possible hypotheses on each feedback trial, discovering the correct hypothesis in only three feedback trials (try it). But this requires keeping in memory all the hypotheses that are still possible while simultaneously inferring which ones can be rejected after each feedback trial and dropping those from memory. The combined memory and inferential strain is heavy, but Levine found his subjects operated much more efficiently than one would predict had they merely been testing one hypothesis at a time.

Levine's results are shown in Figure 8.6. The top line in that figure depicts the performance of an hypothetical subject who tests only one hypothesis at a time and has no memory for the hypotheses he has already tested. The bottom line depicts the performance of an hypothetical subject who uses memory fully, following the idealized strategy above. As you can see, Levine's subjects came close to this ideal use of memory.

There are a number of pitfalls involved in testing hypotheses. These are of special interest in view of the close parallel between hypothesis testing in concept learning and hypothesis testing in developing scientific theories. Wason (1960) has demonstrated some of these pitfalls in a study investigating how subjects decide whether an hypothesis is correct.

Wason's subjects were given a series of numbers, such as 2, 4, 6, and asked to discover the simple rule for the series by generating other

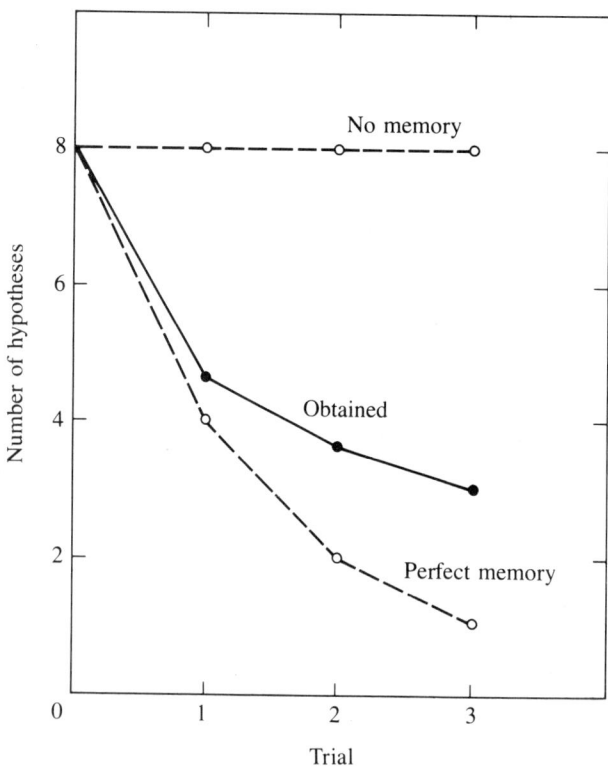

Figure 8.6 The size of the set of hypotheses from which the subject is sampling immediately following a *wrong* on trials 1, 2, and 3. (From Levine, 1966.)

series to test their hypotheses. For each series the subject generated, the experimenter told him whether it conformed to the rule. When a subject felt he had the correct rule, he was to announce it. The experiment is a standard concept identification task except that the subject generates instances rather than using ones supplied by the experimenter.

The correct rule was *numbers increasing in magnitude,* but there are a great many specific cases of this rule which will always lead to positive instances of this rule, such as *numbers increasing by 2, increasing even numbers, ascending numbers separated by regular intervals,* and so forth. Wason (1968) noted that the purpose of the experiment was not to see whether a subject could discover the correct rule, but to see how he behaved when a series he generated supported his hypothesis.

In the 1960 study, Wason reported that subjects tended to generate only series that were positive instances of the hypothesis they had in mind, but did not generate negative instances that would test the possible falsity of the hypothesis. For example, a subject who developed the hypothesis *numbers increasing by 2* tested the series 8, 10, 12; 7, 9, 11; and 1, 3, 5; but he did not test a series such as 2, 5, 8, which would have been positive and would have shown that he had the wrong hypothesis. Since the subject could generate an indefinite number of series that would confirm his hypothesis, he would never discover his hypothesis was false by this method. Only by generating a series that was negative according to his hypothesis could he discover his hypothesis was wrong.

In later experiments, Wason (1968) reported that subjects were often unable to use the procedure of negative proof, that it appeared to be a "totally alien concept." This difficulty is not limited to laboratory studies; even good scientists may find it difficult to reject an hypothesis (see Box 8.2).

These studies have a strong bearing on the testing of scientific hypotheses. Popper (1935/1959) noted that it is not usually possible to prove an hypothesis true. This requires testing all possible events predicted by the hypothesis and showing that they all confirm the hypothesis. Since there are an infinite number of events (instances) to be tested for most hypotheses, an hypothesis usually cannot be proved. Thus one must search for instances that would disconfirm an hypothesis. Finding these will let us discredit a false hypothesis, but true hypotheses will have no such disconfirming instances. In the Wason experiments the false hypothesis of *numbers increasing by 2* would have been disconfirmed by the test series 2, 5, 8, but the true hypothesis of *numbers increasing in magnitude* would not.

Strategies

In a seminal early work on concept learning, Bruner, Goodnow, and Austin (1956) observed that some of their subjects were not only able to learn concepts but also sometimes used a strategy for discovering the concept. A **strategy** is a systematic procedure for discovering a concept. Strategies are typically more efficient than a trial-and-error procedure and often reduce the strain on working memory.

One of the more efficient strategies that Bruner et al. observed was the conservative-focusing strategy. It requires subjects to take the first positive instance they find and use it as a focus card. On each trial thereafter the subjects choose a card that differs from the focus card in only one attribute. If they are told the card is negative, they know the attribute they changed is relevant. If they are told the card is positive, they know the attribute is irrelevant. Thus they can discover the concept in as many trials as there are attributes.

The use of this strategy is illustrated in Table 8.1 and Figure 8.1 (at the beginning of the chapter) for the concept LARGE CIRCLES. On the first trial the experimenter gives the subject card 3, which is a positive instance of the concept. Using this card as a focus card, the subject then chooses

Box 8.2 ON REJECTING FALSE HYPOTHESES IN SCIENCE

The growth of science relies on the ability of scientists to develop hypotheses that explain their observations. For any particular set of observations, however, there are many separate hypotheses that explain the observations equally well, as we saw in the Wason (1960) study. The task of the scientist is to discover which hypotheses are false and reject them, while retaining the true hypothesis.

Testing an hypothesis requires an experimental situation in which one outcome of the experiment would support the hypothesis, while a different outcome would show the hypothesis to be false and permit us to reject it. Wason's subjects generally did not generate number strings which would be false according to their hypotheses, and so they did not discover that their hypotheses were false. Their reluctance to test their hypotheses in a way that could show them to be false is comparable to the scientist's reluctance to test a scientific hypothesis in a way that could show it to be false. Consider an example from the history of medical science, reported by Eisenberg (1977).

Benjamin Rush was one of the foremost physicians of the eighteenth century. He received his medical training at the University of Edinburgh and was a professor at the College of Pennsylvania, soon to become the first medical school in America. In 1793 an epidemic of yellow fever struck Philadelphia causing thousands to flee the city and ultimately taking more than 4000 lives. Rush was one of three physicians who remained in the city to care for the sick. Eisenberg writes:

> Rush was an adherent of the Brunonian system of medicine, according to which febrile illnesses [illnesses induced by fever] resulted from an excess of stimulation and a corresponding excitement of the blood. In keeping with this theory, he ministered to his patients by vigorous bleeding and purging, the latter to "divert the force of the fever to [the bowels] and thereby save the liver and brains from a fatal and dangerous congestion." Rush went from patient to patient, letting blood copiously and purging with vigor. His desperate remedies, contemporary critics contended, were more dangerous than the disease, a criticism history has borne out.
>
> His beliefs were not something he reserved for others. He himself was taken with a violent fever. He instructed his assistant to bleed him "plentifully" and give him "a dose of the mecurial medicine." From illness and treatment combined, he almost died; his convalescence was prolonged. That he did recover persuaded him that his methods were correct. Thus, when the epidemic subsided, he wrote: "Never before did I experience such sublime joy as I now felt on contemplating the success of my remedies. . . . The conquest of a formidable disease was through the triumph of a principle in

> medicine." ... Neither dedication so great that he risked his life to minister to others, nor willingness to treat himself as he treated others, nor yet the best education to be had in his day was sufficient to prevent Rush from committing grievous harm in the name of doing good. Convinced of the correctness of his theory of medicine and lacking a means for the systematic study of treatment outcome, he attributed each new instance of improvement to the efficacy of his treatment and each new death that occurred despite it to the severity of the disease. (Eisenberg, 1977, p. 1106)

card 1, which differs from card 3 only in shape. He is told that it is negative, so he infers that shape is relevant to the concept and *circle* must be the correct value. He then chooses card 9, which differs from the focus card only in position. He is told that it is positive, so he infers that position is not relevant in the concept. Finally, he chooses card 4, which differs in the size of figure. He is told this card is negative and so infers that size is relevant. He has now tested all three attributes and knows that LARGE CIRCLES is the concept. As you can readily see, the only information subjects have to carry in working memory is a list of the attributes plus the outcomes of the tests they have conducted.

The conservative-focusing strategy is appropriate only for conjunctive concepts, and of course not all subjects use it even for these concepts. Its use, however, is one of the interesting phenomena of concept learning. Bruner et al. (1956) described a number of other strategies that subjects sometimes use. These fall into two categories—hypothesis-testing strategies and focusing strategies such as the conservative-focusing strategy described above. Bruner's initial evidence for the use of strategies has been supplemented by more exhaustive investigations by Laughlin (1973) and Johnson (1978).

We close this section with an example of an application of concept learning—namely, the discovery of a mathematical function from a set of examples. Huesmann and Cheng (1973) observe that mathematical functions are a qualitatively different kind of concept from the kind we have described thus far, and yet subjects still use hypothesis testing and a type of strategy in discovering these concepts.

The concepts in their study were the functions addition, subtraction, multiplication, division, and exponentiation, or some combination of these. In the learning task, they gave subjects six instances of the form $a \$ b = c$ and asked them to say what function described the relation among the numbers for all six instances. For example, the instances $2 \$ 2 = 4$, $1 \$ 5 = 6$, and $-3 \$ 2 = -1$ are described by the function of addition. Which of their functions do you think describes the instances $3 \$ 2 = 9$, $2 \$ 4 = 16$, $6 \$ 1 = 6$?*

To determine whether the subjects were testing hypotheses or using strategies, Huesmann and Cheng asked them to verbalize their thoughts as they worked on each concept. The authors also measured the amount of time required for a subject to discover each concept. The results showed that solution times were significantly shorter for simple functions than for complex ones—that is, for functions having more operations in them.

More interestingly, an analysis of the protocols (the reports of the subjects' verbalizations) showed that subjects made extensive use of hypothesis testing. A sample protocol might read something like: "Let's try $a + b$. It works on number 1. It works on number 2, but it doesn't work on number 3. OK, let's try another one. Ah,

*Answer: exponentiation: $3^2 = 9$, $2^4 = 16$, $6^1 = 6$.

how about $a \times b$? It works on number 1 but it won't work on number 2. Well, let's see, maybe we should try $a - b$." Clearly the subject is drawing from the set of possible functions and trying to see which one fits the instances.

Huesmann and Cheng also observed that subjects used a general strategy for discovering the function, though the strategy was not as formal as the conservative-focusing strategy. This strategy arranged the hypotheses in order of complexity. Hypotheses about simple functions were tested first, and only if these failed did the subject try hypotheses about functions having a larger number of operations. In brief, Huesmann and Cheng found that subjects who are trying to discover a mathematical function from a set of instances use much the same approach as has been reported for other types of concept learning. This does not mean, however, that this approach is used for all types of concept learning, as we shall see in the next section.

We shall return to the topic of strategies in the chapter on problem solving. Strategies are used frequently in problem solving, and so the topic of concept learning has often been treated as a special form of problem solving.

In summary, there are two aspects of learning a concept: the discovery of the relevant attributes and the discovery of the rule that combines them. Rules partition a set of objects in different ways, and some rules are more difficult to learn than others. The difficulty in learning a rule has been attributed to experience with the rule as well as to the complexity of decision making in the use of the rule.

Many theories of concept learning assume that a subject forms and tests hypotheses about the concept. The work of Levine (1966) supports this assumption and further indicates that subjects are able to remember which hypotheses have been rejected and which are still viable. Many subjects develop a strategy for learning a concept, which typically reduces memory strain and renders the task more efficient.

CONCEPTS, MEMORY, AND LANGUAGE

In recent years the study of concepts has merged increasingly with the study of other cognitive processes. One of the most prominent areas of this convergence has been the relation of concepts to semantic memory and the kindred area of language. This more recent work emphasizes the internal structure of concepts, a viewpoint that is consonant with the work on the structure of semantic memory which we discussed in Chapter 4. In this section we explore first the nature of that internal structure and then sketch some of the ways it relates to processing concepts in semantic memory. Finally, we explore the relation of concepts to language. Here the focus is on the conceptual basis of lexical information and the way it is tied to experience through perceptual operations.

The Internal Structure of Concepts

Some of the colors we call red seem "redder" than others; some of the animals we call dogs seem "doggier" than others. In a series of studies, Rosch (1973, 1975) has given evidence that many categories have a *prototype,* a clear case that is a good example of the category. Other members of the category show varying degrees of similarity to the prototype such that some are good examples of the category while others are poor examples. Categories thus have internal structure and ill-defined boundaries.

Rosch's interpretation of a concept (she prefers the term *category*) differs from the interpretation used in the earlier part of this chapter. That work assumed that a concept has well-defined boundaries and that all instances of the concept are equivalent members. Rosch has challenged this interpretation in a number of studies of both perceptual and semantic categories.

Perceptual Categories. The color spectrum is a physically continuous dimension, but languages sort and label that dimension in different ways. For example, the language of the Zuni people has a single term for approximately the same segment of the spectrum which English divides into orange and yellow. Many psychologists, linguists, and anthropologists have taken such observations as evidence that languages sort and code the world in arbitrarily different ways (e.g., Whorf, 1956).

Berlin and Kay (1969), however, have argued that there are a limited number of basic colors which are organized around *focal points*. The English names for these focal points are black, white, red, green, yellow, blue, pink, orange, brown, and purple. Languages differ in where they put the boundaries for these colors, but the focal points are the same for all human beings regardless of their language. Focal points are thus universal and may be physiologically based.

If focal points are universal, then they should serve as prototypes for learning color names for people who have very few color names in their language. Rosch (1973) tested this hypothesis among the Dani, a stone-age people of New Guinea whose language has only the color terms *mili* and *mola,* which mean roughly "dark" and "light." We report two of Rosch's tests.

In the first, she selected eight sets of three colors. In each set of three, one color was a focal color and the other two were slightly above and below it on the color spectrum (e.g., the focal green with a slightly yellowish green and a slightly bluish green). She asked her Dani subjects to learn a name for all the colors. The name was the same for the three colors in a set and different for each set. Learning trials continued until a subject named all colors correctly in a single trial.

The second test differed from the first only in choice of colors for a set. These sets also contained a focal color and two nonfocal colors, but the nonfocal colors were one and two steps to the same side of the focal color rather than being one step on each side of it.

The results of these two name-learning tasks revealed that the names were learned faster for focal colors than for nonfocal colors, even when focal colors were not at the center of the set. Second, it was easier for Dani to learn names for a category of colors when the focal color was at the center of the category than when it was peripheral to the category. Rosch (1973) interpreted these results to mean that a focal color is the prototype for a color category, and a color category is most easily learned when it is organized around a prototype.

Semantic Categories. Since color categories may have a physiological basis, which would account for their internal structure, it is possible that other kinds of categories do not have internal structure. Rosch (1975) explored this question for certain kinds of semantic categories—specifically, categories of concrete objects such as furniture, fruit, and clothing. She selected ten such categories and then for each category chose 50 to 60 objects that are examples of that category (e.g., *furniture: table, chair, bed, . . .*). Subjects then rated each object in each category on a 7-point scale measuring how good an example the object was of the category. A subject who judged *table* to be a very good example of *furniture* would rate it 1, while a poor example such as a *telephone* might be rated 6.

The results showed very high agreement among the subjects in their ratings. For example, in nine of the ten categories, 95 percent of the subjects agreed on a rating of 1 for the object that overall was rated the best example of the category. These results reflect an internal structure for categories of concrete objects comparable to that which Rosch has found for color categories.

Rosch (1975) further explored the internal structure of these categories in a series of priming tasks. The general design for these tasks calls for subjects to be either in a primed or unprimed condition. In the primed condition, they are given the name of a category (e.g., *furniture*) and

2 sec later are shown two objects. In the unprimed condition, they are given the word *blank* and then 2 sec later are shown the two objects. In both conditions, if the objects are members of the same category (e.g., *chair, table*), the subjects are to respond *same;* if not (e.g., *chair, apple*), they are to respond *different.* Their reaction time in responding *same* or *different* is recorded. The category prime lets the subjects activate a mental representation for the category in anticipation of the objects they are to react to.

Using this methodology Rosch reported two major conclusions. First, priming of a category with the category name led to faster reaction times in making the judgments of *same* and *different* than did priming with the word *blank.*

Second, and more importantly, priming with the category name produced faster reaction times for good examples of a category than for poor ones. For example, Rosch found that subjects responded *same* more quickly to the words *chair, dresser,* which are good examples of the category *furniture,* than to *rug, stove,* which are poor examples. This finding suggests that the mental representation of the category takes the form of a prototype or best example of the category. This effect provides further evidence for the internal structure of categories.

How is the mental representation for a category represented? Is it a word, an image, a list of properties? What is the form that makes it an effective prime? In a further part of this study, Rosch (1975) compared reaction times to words and to pictures to see if priming aided one more than the other. If it did, one might have a clue about the form of the mental structure for a category.

The design for this task was the same as that described above, except that on half the trials the subjects saw a pair of words and on the other half they saw a pair of simple line drawings of the objects. The pattern of results was also the same as in the two tasks described above. Most importantly, reaction times to pictures did not differ from those to words, suggesting that the mental structure aroused by the prime was neither a particular word nor a particular visual image, but a more abstract representation that prepared the subject equally well for words and pictures.

In summary, Rosch suggests that concepts of color and of some concrete objects have internal structure, a notion not found in the literature on the learning of concepts. In her view the typical attributes of a concept are represented in a prototype, and examples of the concept share these attributes in varying degrees. The boundaries of the concept are consequently ill-defined and membership in the concept becomes difficult to judge at the boundaries. The notion that concepts have internal structure is consistent with the work on the structure of permanent memory (see Chapter 4), and in the next section we see how this notion integrates with one of the models of the structure of permanent memory.

Concepts and Semantic Memory

Technically speaking, a chicken is a bird. Such statements seem to imply that some birds are better birds than others. Lakoff (1972) identifies qualifications such as *technically speaking* as hedges. Hedges vary in the degree to which they qualify a statement. For example, *Loosely speaking, a bat is a bird* qualifies its proposition considerably, while *A robin is a true bird* does not. Lakoff's linguistic analysis of hedges served as one of the bases of the feature comparison model of semantic memory (Smith, Shoben, & Rips, 1974) which we discussed in Chapter 4.

The linguistic idea of hedges also bears a close resemblance to Rosch's interpretation of the internal structure of concepts, for both views suggest that some exemplars of a category are better than are others. The feature comparison model, in fact, takes this notion as the foundation for its structure of concepts in semantic memory.

You will remember that the feature comparison model identified concepts by lists of features. These features are separated into *defining* and *characteristic* features. Defining features are essential to the concept, while characteristic features are often present in examples of the concept but are not essential. When both defining and characteristic features are present in an example, one kind of hedge is used *(A cardinal is a true bird),* but when only defining features are present, one uses a different kind of hedge *(Technically speaking, a penguin is a bird).* When only characteristic features are present, still another kind of hedge is used *(A decoy is a fake bird).*

Rosch's work on the internal structure of concepts thus seems to converge with recent work in the structure of semantic memory. This point of convergence, which hinges on the notion that some exemplars of a concept are better than others, allows for a richer representation of the world, which in turn allows for degrees of membership in categories.

Zadeh (1965) has formalized this kind of representation in what he calls "fuzzy logic." In brief, fuzzy logic is a mathematical analysis of entities that have multiple values. Propositions in this logic can be assigned a "degree of truth" ranging between 0 and 1 rather than being simply true or false. For example, *A robin is a bird* might be assigned a value of .9, while *A robin is a car* might be assigned a value of .1. Fuzzy logic promises to be a useful way of representing psychological concepts in a more rigorous fashion.

Concepts and Language

Thus far we have suggested that at least some concepts have internal structure and that such internal structure is reflected in semantic memory. Now we would like to broaden the notion of concepts once more to include functions; by doing this we are better able to relate concepts to language.

Most discussions of concepts define them by perceptual attributes, such as size, shape, and color. Such treatments neglect one form of knowledge which we commonly have about an object—namely, its *function*. We not only know what a spoon *looks* like but also how we may *use* it. Developmental studies (e.g., Nelson, 1973) suggest that children's early concepts include information about how an object may be used and what actions may be performed on it. Does it roll? Does it bounce? Can it be thrown? If so, it must be a ball.

How can this knowledge be represented? The problem is a thorny one, but Miller (1977) offers a solution. Consider the couple who stop for a picnic lunch in the woods. The wife says, "This stump will make a good table." Now a stump fits the perceptual attributes of *table* rather poorly. How then can one say it is a *good* table and still make sense?

Miller suggests that an item in the mental lexicon such as *table* is a concept defined by both perceptual and functional criteria. An object that fits both sets of criteria is literally a table, but an object that fits only the perceptual criteria (such as a picture of a table) or only the functional criteria (such as a stump) may still be called a table. By either set of criteria, some objects are better examples than others; that is, concepts have internal structure. A stump is a *good* table because it fits the functional criteria well: It is a flat surface on which one can serve a meal.

Functional criteria are part of the definition of an item in the mental lexicon. The method of testing whether an object fits these functional criteria, however, is not part of the definition but provides a link from lexical knowledge to practical knowledge—that is, to what we know about the world.

We can say x is a table if it is possible to show that x fits the functional criteria for *table*. To establish this possibility draws upon practical knowledge to show (1) the means are readily at hand to make x serve as a table, or (2) a search of our practical knowledge reveals no reason why x cannot serve as a table. Either of these is sufficient to establish that it is possible for x to serve as a table, though in the latter case we must still search for the means to carry it out.

This notion of a concept is developed more fully by Miller and Johnson-Laird (1976). Figure 8.7 shows the components of an entry in one's lexicon. The label (e.g., *table*) is the word we use for the concept (TABLE), and the syntactic information includes its syntactic category (noun) and the syntactic rules for the use of the word. The schemata are procedures for testing whether an object meets the perceptual and functional criteria for the concept. The concept is also linked to other concepts (e.g., *furniture*).

The perceptual schema has a set of identification procedures for testing whether an object meets the perceptual criteria for that concept. Consider an imaginary world that has only three kinds of objects: tables, chairs, and beds. These objects can be sorted by two identification procedures:

1. Does it have a seat? If so, call it a chair. If not, go to 2.
2. Does it have a work top? If so, call it a table. If not, call it a bed.

These identification procedures can be represented in a flowchart as is shown in Figure 8.8. A flowchart is the format a computer programmer uses for laying out the sequence of operations in a computer program. It has the advantage of being precise about the exact operations and their order. In the case of a perceptual schema, however, it has the disadvantage of committing us to a particular order of the identification procedures. We could have begun the flowchart with *Does it have a work top?* and then moved to *Does it have a seat?* and we might have had no good reason for preferring one of these flowcharts over the other. The arbitrariness of this decision becomes more apparent as we increase the number of tests in the flowchart.

A more flexible way of representing a set of identification procedures is by the use of a *decision table*. Table 8.3 is a decision table for the identification procedures in our imaginary world. The three columns can be thought of as three rules for the outcomes of the identification procedures. In column 1, for example, Y (yes) indicates the condition for (1) has been met and the *x* indicates the action to take, call it a *chair*.

Each rule indicates the conditions that are to be met to sort objects into tables, chairs, and beds. You do not have to start the testing with condition (1), but may enter the table at any con-

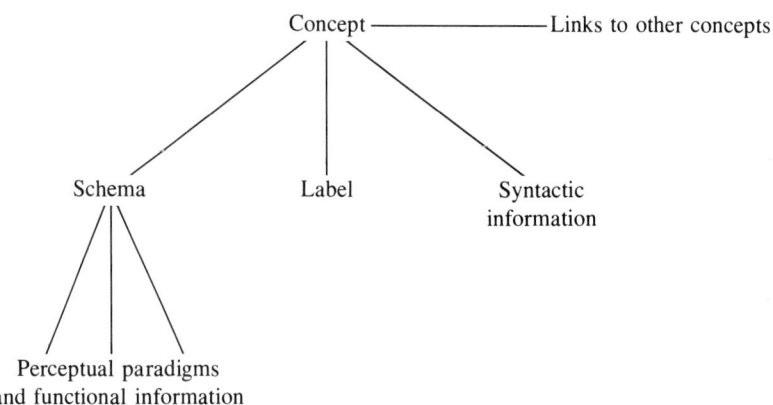

Figure 8.7 Representation of a lexical concept. (From Miller & Johnson-Laird, 1976.)

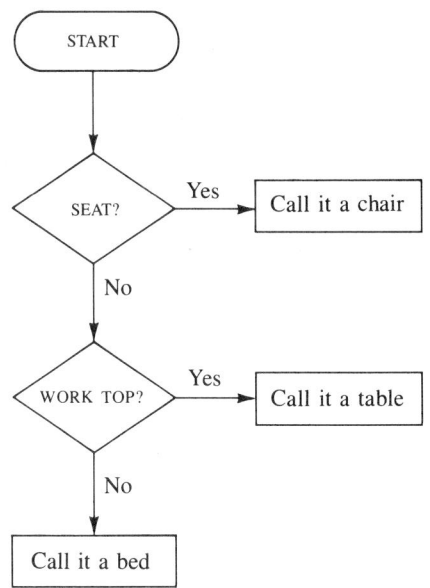

Figure 8.8 Flowchart for an identification procedure. (From Miller & Johnson-Laird, 1976.)

dition. This option yields flexibility to our testing, especially in a decision table having many conditions for identifying many different objects. Thus decision tables offer a better formalism than do flowcharts for representing identification procedures.

Table 8.3 Decision Table

	1	2	3
Conditions			
(1) It has a SEAT?	Y	N	N
(2) It has a WORK TOP?		Y	N
Actions			
"chair"	x		
"table"		x	
"bed"			x

Source: From Miller and Johnson-Laird (1976).

We introduced decision tables in Chapter 6 on language in the context of procedural semantics (see pages 168–170). Our purpose there was to show how a semantic feature analysis for words can be integrated with perceptual operations to decide upon the use of the right word. Here we have expanded upon that description to suggest that items in the mental lexicon contain concepts. In this analysis, concepts do not reside in splendid isolation from the other cognitive processes, but are linked to perception by the use of identification procedures and to other concepts in semantic memory. The significance of this analysis is thus that it integrates concepts with certain other cognitive processes in a way that may shed light on each of them.

CONCLUSION

We began this chapter with a discussion of how concepts help us respond to the awesome uniqueness of the world. By conceptualizing the recurring similarities of our experience, we can adapt to continuing novelty in appropriate ways. The learning of a concept is an active, often systematic, process of constructing a mental structure of the attributes of objects and the way they are related. For many subjects, learning a concept appears to involve developing and testing hypotheses about the concept.

As the study of concepts has begun to make contact with research in other cognitive processes, a new interpretation of the structure of a concept has emerged. Research in the context of semantic memory and language portrays a concept as a set of features that identify some objects as better examples of the concept than others.

In general, the study of concepts has been limited to categories of concrete objects. This may be the easiest part of the problem. What can we say about abstract objects, actions, or properties? What about, for example, laws, ideals, or thinking? Are they concepts? If so, how can they be represented? How do we show *relations* among features? A table has a working surface and legs, but the legs *support* the working surface. How can we represent such relations in a concept? And how do concepts relate to other cognitive processes?

The chapters on permanent memory and language have touched on these issues, but the questions continue to outnumber the answers. Miller and Johnson-Laird offer a well-integrated interpretation of many of these topics, though we have described only a small segment of their work here. Other recent work (e.g., Bobrow and Winograd's knowledge representation language, 1977; Hayes-Roth, 1977; Hayes-Roth & Hayes-Roth's property set model, 1977) also offers expanded interpretations for conceptual phenomena, and it appears likely that the study of concepts will show increasing integration with the other cognitive processes in coming years.

9. Problem Solving

Gestalt Theory
    Restructuring
    Set and Functional Fixity
        Set
        Functional Fixity
    Stages of Problem Solving
        Preparation
        Incubation
Information-processing Theory
    The Problem Space
    The Computer as a Model
        Computer Simulation
        Algorithms and Heuristics
            Working Backward
            Means-Ends Analysis
    Executive Control

> Simulation Programs
> > Problem-solving Programs
> > > GPS
> > > Checkers
> > > Chess
> > Programs Involving Memory
> > > Retrieving from Permanent Memory
> > > Working Memory
> > Programs for Comprehension
> > Programs for Rule Induction
> > > Concept Identification and Problem Solving
> > > Series Completion
> > > GRI
> > Ill-defined Problems
> Conclusion

Miss Benson's body had been taken away, but her desk was otherwise untouched. Detective Lieutenant MacDonald stood in the doorway to her office, the spot from which the killer had fired. In the hallway were the only four people who had been in that end of the library at the time. Since that part of the building was a cul-de-sac, one of them had to be the murderer, though why anyone would want to kill the aging head of a branch library was a mystery. Miss Stella Swift, a junior librarian, had discovered the body, followed shortly by Mrs. Cora Jarvis, the kittenish children's librarian. Mr. James Stickney, a youngish man with no tie and wild hair was a library patron, as was Mr. Norbert Utter, a high-school teacher.

"Does anyone know what this means?" MacDonald pulled the page from the typewriter where Miss Benson had been at work and handed it around to the four.

Davies: MISSION TO MOSCOW (2 cop)
Kernan: DEFENSE WILL NOT WIN THE WAR
 FIC
MacInnes: ABOVE SUSP
QL 696 .C9

"It looks like a list of needed replacements," said Mrs. Jarvis, "except that last line doesn't make any sense. Do you suppose she was trying to tell us something?"

"We were always teasing her about working for the FBI," said Miss Swift, "because she was always sending off stuff to them about suspicious people—you know, somebody who checked out too many books on high explosives and how to make bombs and who might be going to blow up factories and such. She took it all very seriously."

"Yes," said Mrs. Jarvis, "her love of her country was matched only by her love of cataloging, She knew every system down to a gnat's eye, and nothing distressed her more than finding an entry with the wrong category or. . . ."

"And birds," Miss Swift interrupted. "She loved birds too. She got a set of field glasses when she was a girl and she could identify just about anything."

Back at the office, detective Lieutenant MacDonald was reading through the FBI report on Miss Benson's information-gathering activities. Apparently she was involved in more than a game, since the report noted that in recent months several FBI suspects had been observed visiting the library for no apparent reason. His attention was interrupted by a call from Mrs. Jarvis.

"I think I have a clue," she said. "It's about the QL 696 .C9. You see . . ." A dull thud came over the line, and MacDonald heard her moan only "Elsie . . ." before the receiver clicked. Shortly after, the police found her lying on the floor with a severe concussion.

In one of the great traditions of mystery stories, the puzzled lieutenant takes the mystery to a friend with a known talent for solving mysteries, in this case one Nick Noble, a man of insight and sure logic, whose reasoning is not blurred by his penchant for sherry. The lieutenant relates his problem and takes a small measure of pride in noting that Noble is equally perplexed until MacDonald mentions "Elsie," at which point Noble's eyes brighten, and he promises the lieutenant a solution within 24 hours. The next morning a book is delivered to the lieutenant which unravels the meaning of QL 696 .C9 and gives the identity of the killer.

Now this is a rather abbreviated version of Mr. Anthony Boucher's original fine story (1947), and it would be unfair to its creator to deliver a swift solution without first noting that it falls within the ranks of many masterful stories by giving the reader a proper set of clues for solving the puzzle. Indeed, our Noble hero got on the right track without leaving his sherry.

Pause for a moment. What clues do you think led him to the solution?

Noble reasoned that "Elsie" was not a woman's name but the letters *L.C.*, for Library of Congress, a cataloging system with which Miss Benson would have been intimately familiar but the murderer would not. The book delivered to MacDonald, *U.S. Library of Congress Classification Q: Science,* also revealed her knowledge of ornithology, as MacDonald discovered in thumbing through the pages. "QL: Zoology. QL 600, Vertebrates. QL 696 Birds, QL 696.C9 Cypseli, (Swifts)."

Without going into detail, we will close by adding that Miss Swift had been relaying messages for a foreign power, using books in the stacks as a pickup for the enemy agents who drifted into the library. She suffered the fate of most villains—having to stand in silence while the hero modestly takes the spotlight to explain the reasoning that solved the mystery.

Nick Noble's problem was much like those that abound in our own lives, whether we are trying to find a lost umbrella, write a paper, or get into our car when we have locked the keys safely inside. Such problems have three parts: (1) a *given state,* which is the state one is in, (2) a *goal state,* which is the state one wants to reach, and (3) a *path* from the given state to the goal state.

The path from the given state to the goal state is not immediately known but must be discovered in order to solve the problem. The given state for Nick Noble was the fact of the murder and MacDonald's report of its circumstances. Less obvious, but just as important, was the knowledge he could draw upon—for example, the minor fact that L.C. is an abbreviation for the Library of Congress cataloging system. His goal state was the name of the murderer. In most problems the goal state is described by a set of general requirements. The solution is a particular state that meets these requirements; in Nick Noble's case it is a particular name.

As stated, the path to the goal is not immediately known and must be discovered; in fact if the path is immediately known, there is no problem. Initially, Nick Noble was as puzzled as detective Lieutenant MacDonald, though not for so long. Had he not been, only MacDonald would have had a problem. The discovery of the path to the solution is the primary activity in problem solving. What was going on in Nick Noble's head that was not going on in MacDonald's?

In the remainder of this chapter we will describe two major interpretations of what goes on in the process of solving problems. The first of these, *gestalt theory,* is responsible for defining many of the basic phenomena of problem solving. Its major contribution has been to develop the role of the structure of problems in the problem-solving process.

The second of these, *information-processing theory,* has offered a more rigorous interpretation of some of the phenomena identified in gestalt theory. It has been especially concerned with detailing the specific cognitive processes involved in problem solving. Much of this work has been accomplished through the use of computer simulation techniques.

GESTALT THEORY

One of the classic debates in problem solving developed between Edward L. Thorndike, an early American behaviorist, and Wolfgang Köhler, one of the founders of the German school of gestalt psychology. Thorndike (1898) conducted a series of studies on animal intelligence, one of them requiring a cat to escape from a wooden cage by pulling a string. The string released the latch to the cage and freed the cat to get to a bowl of fish. When the cat was first put in the cage, it tried to squeeze between the bars, bit the bars, and clawed at random until it chanced to claw at the loop in the end of the string and released the latch. In succeeding trials Thorndike observed that the cat showed less and less of the random biting and clawing and that the time lapse before it pulled the string also decreased. In the final trials the cat pulled the string and escaped in about 10 sec.

Thorndike called the random behavior preceding the correct response *trial-and-error* behavior and noted that its gradual replacement by the correct response was characteristic of learning. This interpretation relied heavily on the role of chance in producing the correct response and minimized any assumptions about reasoning in solving the problem. It became one of the foundations of behaviorism, in which Thorndike was to be a central figure.

Köhler challenged this interpretation, arguing that the test situation was artificial for the cat. The mechanism by which the string released the latch was hidden from view and precluded any intelligent behavior. Along with other gestalt psychologists, Köhler held that a problem situation is perceived as a total structure—a **gestalt** —whose parts must be reorganized to meet the requirements of the solution. Such *restructuring* uses the relationships among the component parts and reformulates them to provide a new gestalt, which is the solution to the problem.

During World War I, Köhler was trapped on the island of Tenerife by a British blockade. He took the opportunity to develop his theory of problem solving, using the apes and chimpanzees on the island. This work was later published under the title of *The Mentality of Apes* (1925).

In a typical study, Köhler hung a basket of fruit well out of reach at the top of the cage of Sultan, an ape, and waited to see how Sultan would get the fruit. Several sticks and two crates were scattered around the cage. Sultan first tried to knock the fruit down with the sticks, but they were too short. Throwing the sticks aside, he slumped into a heap. After a moment his gaze fell on the crates. Suddenly he leaped up, dragged one under the fruit, and clambered to his prize.

Sultan had reorganized the problem situation into a new structure, which was the solution state. Köhler observed that a number of his subjects seemed to experience a flash of insight just prior to solving the problem, and he concluded that such sudden insightful restructuring of the problem situation is characteristic of problem solving.

Gestalt psychologists distinguish between two kinds of thinking: *productive* and *reproductive*. Productive thinking requires putting the parts of a problem situation together in a novel way to create a solution, as Sultan did. Reproductive thinking involves applying familiar habits or past solutions to a problem. Thorndike's cats, once they had learned to pull the string to release the latch, were engaging in reproductive thinking.

The Problem
Given matchsticks which form five squares, move three sticks to form four squares.

Group Mem
The complete solution steps are presented to the subject in order, moving one stick at a time, and repeating six times. For the above problem, the required moves shown are:

Group Help
The second method involves giving a series of hints to the subject accompanied by the comment, "Try to understand what I am doing."

Results
Typical proportion correct on retention and transfer tests were as follows:

Group	Test after 1 week		Test after 3 weeks	
	Practice tasks	New tasks	Practice tasks	New tasks
Mem	.67	.25	.53	.14
Help	.58	.55	.52	.55
Con	.12	.12	.12	.12

Figure 9.1 Katona's matchstick problem (After Katona, 1940.)

Katona (1940) compared several conditions for solving a matchstick problem, two of which illustrate productive and reproductive thinking. The matchsticks were arranged to form five squares, as shown in Figure 9.1, and the subject was to move three matchsticks to form four squares.

A memory group (reproductive thinking) was shown the exact steps to the solution seven times and asked to memorize them. A help group (productive thinking) was given a series of hints to help them solve the problem by understanding it. For example, the experimenter shaded the squares that appeared in the solution and pointed out the matchsticks that had to be moved. These hints encouraged the subjects to discover the principle of the solution, which was that the closed figure had to be broken up in order to solve the problem. A control group was given no instruction at all in how to solve the problem.

All of the subjects were given a pretest to be sure they did not know how to do this kind of problem; they then practiced on two more tasks of this kind. After 1 week some of the subjects were transferred to a new task of this kind, and 3 weeks later the remaining subjects were transferred to the same new task.

The results are shown in Figure 9.1 as the proportion of subjects who solved the problems. The memory group was better in retaining the practiced tasks than the help group after 1 week. However, the help group was much better in solving the new tasks after both 1 and 3 weeks. Katona concluded that they had learned the principle for solving the problems, which helped them in solving new problems of a similar type.

Restructuring

A basic thesis of gestalt psychology is that perception and thinking occur in organized wholes. When you look at Figure 9.2, you see several things shaped like bowls. The shape is a property of the whole, not of its parts. The relationship among the parts provides a gestalt, a structure worthy of study in its own right.

It is in this sense that gestalt psychologists claimed that the whole is more than the sum of its parts. When you look at the Big Dipper on a clear night, it ceases to be the Big Dipper if you look at the stars individually through a telescope. Similarly, a melody loses its form quality when the notes are widely spaced. Try playing "Oh, Susanna" ("Oh, I come from Alabama . . .") on the piano with the notes spaced ten seconds apart. The form quality returns if you play it at normal speed and is still there if you change the key you play it in.

In the same way, a person perceives a problem situation as a whole. To solve the problem is to understand the relations among the parts of the situation and then to restructure them into a new gestalt that satisfies the requirements of the goal state. The restructuring often occurs suddenly and is experienced as an *insight*, the "Aha!" or "Eureka!" experience. Nick Noble's eyes brightened when MacDonald mentioned "Elsie," and he promised a solution within 24 hours. He had apparently perceived the relation *Elsie = L.C. = Library of Congress,* plus the possibility that *QL 696 .C9* was a category in that system. Since Miss Swift had the name of a bird and Miss Benson was a knowledgeable bird-watcher as well as cataloger, the pieces fitted together in a new relationship that led to the solution of the mystery.

Gestalt psychologists also describe a problem as having *direction*. The restructuring process is not a random process, but is guided by the structure of the problem. They use a metaphor of

Figure 9.2 Examples of whole properties.

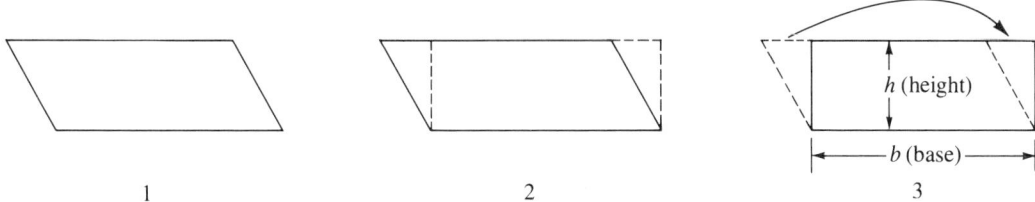

Figure 9.3 Steps involved in finding the area of a parallelogram. (After Wertheimer, 1959.)

"forces" inherent in the relations among the parts of the problem which aid in restructuring the problem situation. In an absorbing account of problem solving, Wertheimer (1959) describes an example of a child finding the area of a parallelogram.

The child knows that the area of a rectangle is equal to base times height. However, the shape of the parallelogram is different from that of a rectangle, so he cannot use this knowledge. Then the child notices that the "extra" triangle on one end of the parallelogram can be fitted into the gap at the other end to produce a rectangle, whose area he can solve for (see Figure 9.3). The discrepancy between the two shapes is the force that provides the direction for restructuring the problem situation into the goal state.

Past experience plays a role in restructuring many problems. In the example above, the child knew how to find the area of a rectangle, though the relevance of that knowledge was not immediately clear. Since our knowledge base is very large, however, the relevance of some of that knowledge is not always clear. Duncker (1945) gives an example in the "13" problem. Why can you divide 13 evenly into all numbers of the form *abc, abc,* such as 134,134; 721,721; and 806,806?

Duncker found most subjects could not solve this problem immediately, and he explored the use of hints to direct their thinking toward relevant knowledge. General hints that gave the principle for solving the problem were of no help (e.g., "If a divisor of a number is divisible by p, then the number itself is divisible by p"). The only hints that helped were specific ones that drew the subject's attention to the number 1001, either through the hint "The numbers are divisible by 1001" or the hint "1001 is divisible by 13." With these hints subjects often realized that the numbers could be factored into *abc* times 1001 and that 1001 is divisible by 13.

Duncker found that the relevance of this knowledge became apparent even without hints if he selected numbers such as 274,274, 275,275, 276,276, and so on, in which the common factor of 1001 was more evident. In this case, the likelihood that subjects would find the solution leaped from .08 to .75.

Set and Functional Fixity

Prior experience may inhibit problem solving just as it may help it. Here we face the larger question of why problem solving fails. If we can get an idea of how it can go wrong, perhaps we will have a clearer idea of how it works when it succeeds. Gestalt psychologists identified several types of difficulty people have in solving problems, among them being *set* and *functional fixity.*

Set. The tendency to approach a problem the same way each time—that is, to use a reproductive style of problem solving—is known as **set.** It is based on familiar or habitual types of solution. Luchins (1942) illustrated this effect in a water jar problem. He asked his subjects to measure out a given amount of water using three pitchers of specified size. Table 9.1 lists the sizes of the pitchers and the amount desired for 11 problems. In problem 1, pitcher A holds 29 quarts and pitcher B holds 3 quarts. The goal is to measure out 20 quarts. An unlimited supply of water is at hand. See if you can solve all the problems before reading further.

Problem 1 is a practice problem that Luchins gave to all his subjects. He then gave problems 2 through 11 one at a time to all members of an experimental group. Subjects in a control group were given the practice problem and then problems 7 through 11. Most subjects in the experimental group discovered that problems 2 through 6 could be solved in the same way—that is, Goal $= B - A - 2C$. Luchins used these problems to induce a set, a habitual way of approaching new problems. Problems 7, 8, 10, and 11 can be solved in this way too, but can also be solved in a simpler way, either $A + C$ or $A - C$. How did you fare? Problem 9 can be solved by $A - C$, but cannot be solved by the $B - A - 2C$ formula.

Table 9.1 Luchins's Water Jar Problem

PROBLEM	GIVEN JARS OF THE FOLLOWING SIZES			OBTAIN THE AMOUNT
	A	B	C	
1.	29	3		20
2. E1	21	127	3	100
3. E2	14	163	25	99
4. E3	18	43	10	5
5. E4	9	42	6	21
6. E5	20	59	4	31
7. C1	23	49	3	20
8. C2	15	39	3	18
9.	28	76	3	25
10. C3	18	48	4	22
11. C4	14	36	8	6

E = Experimental group
C = Control group

Source: From Luchins (1942).

Luchins inserted this problem into the series to try to break the set induced by problems 2 through 6.

Luchins gave this task to more than 900 people. He found the control group almost always found the short solution, but experimental subjects frequently used the long method even on problems 10 and 11. Luchins concluded that set, or "mechanization" as he called it, was a grave source of difficulty in problem solving, one that blinded people to fresh ways of exploring problems.

This conclusion was strengthened by Gardner and Runquist (1958), who found that the more problems subjects could solve by the same method, the less likely they were to see a simpler method for problems having two solutions. They also found that problems that could not be solved by the first method at all but required a different method were more difficult to solve. The set induced by the familiar method led the subjects to try this method (inappropriately) on these problems.

Functional Fixity. When the solution to a problem calls for the novel use of a familiar object, it may be hard to discover the solution. The phenomenon, called **functional fixity,** describes the difficulty of using an object in a new way rather than for a familiar function. For example, the normal function of a dime is to buy things, but in an emergency we may use it as a screwdriver.

Duncker (1945) showed how easily one may fixate on the normal function of an object in a task that required subjects to mount a candle on a wall. Figure 9.4 illustrates the materials given to the subjects: a candle, some matches, and a box of tacks. The goal is to mount the candle on the wall in such a way that it will burn without dripping wax on the table or floor. See if you can figure out how to do it without reading further.

The solution is shown in Figure 9.5. It calls for the subject to empty the box of tacks, tack the box to the wall, and mount the candle on the horizontal surface of the box. Duncker found that

Figure 9.4 The candle problem. The figure contains a candle, matches, and a box full of tacks. Your task is to think of a way of getting the candle on the wall so that it would burn properly, using only the objects illustrated in the figure. (After Dunker, 1945.)

most of his subjects were unable to discover this solution. He argued that they perceived the box in its familiar function—to hold the tacks—and could not restructure that perception to permit a novel use of the box as a ledge to support the candle. As evidence for this interpretation, he cited the performance of a control group which was given the box and the tacks separately (see Figure 9.6). This presentation tended to reduce their perception of the box as a container for the tacks and led more of them to discover the solution.

Duncker's conclusion was somewhat questionable, since he had only 14 subjects in his experiment and he performed no statistical analysis of his data. Adamson (1952) repeated this and other Duncker experiments with an improved methodology. His results were similar to Duncker's; for example, 86 percent of those who were given an empty box solved the problem within 20 min, while only 41 percent of those who were given a box containing tacks succeeded within that time. Adamson's results thus support Duncker's original hypothesis.

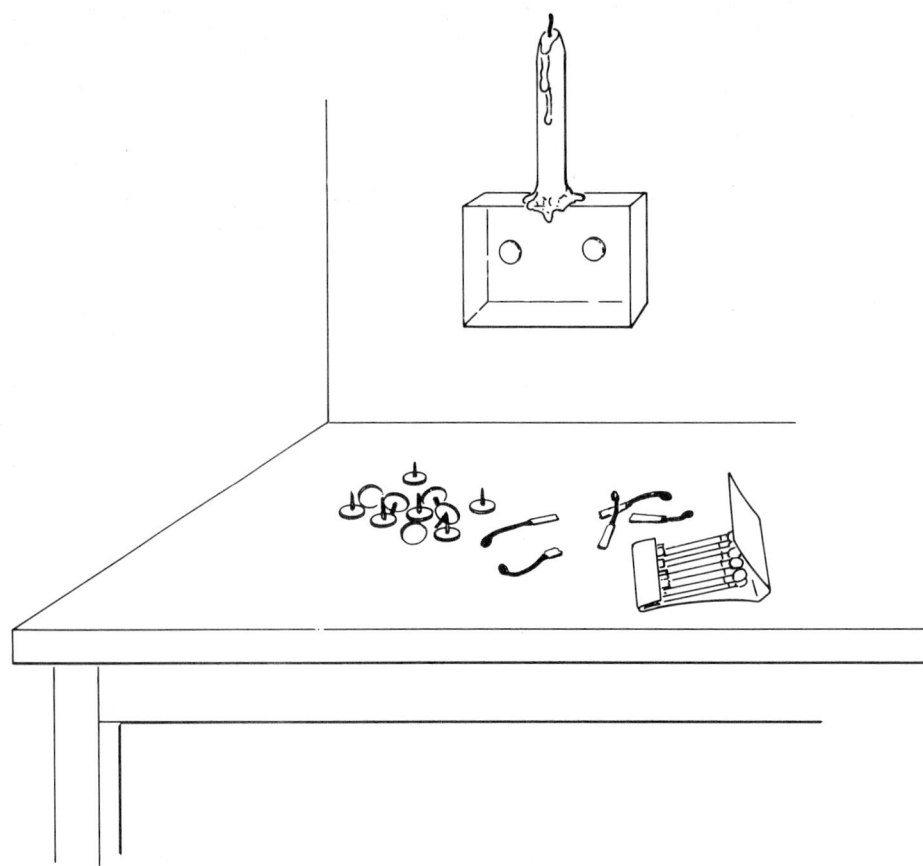

Figure 9.5 Solution to Duncker's candle problem. (After Duncker, 1945.)

A further refinement in methodology was added by Birch and Rabinowitz (1951). It is not clear in the Duncker and Adamson experiments how much previous experience the subjects had with the objects in the experiment and what role this experience plays in functional fixity. Birch and Rabinowitz used a transfer design in which they first established a function for two objects and then tested how the objects were used in a second task.

In the first task subjects were asked to complete an electrical circuit. Some were given a switch to complete the circuit with, others were given a relay. All subjects were then introduced to the two-string problem (Maier, 1930, 1931). For this problem the subjects were brought one at a time into a room having two strings attached to the ceiling at some distance apart (see Figure 9.7). The subjects were to tie the ends of the strings together, but they discovered quickly that the strings were too far apart to hold one and reach the other. Two heavy objects, the switch and relay, were available to aid in solving this problem. Before reading further, see whether you can figure out what they should do.

The solution lies in making a pendulum out of one of the strings by tying the switch or the relay to it, setting it swinging, grabbing the other

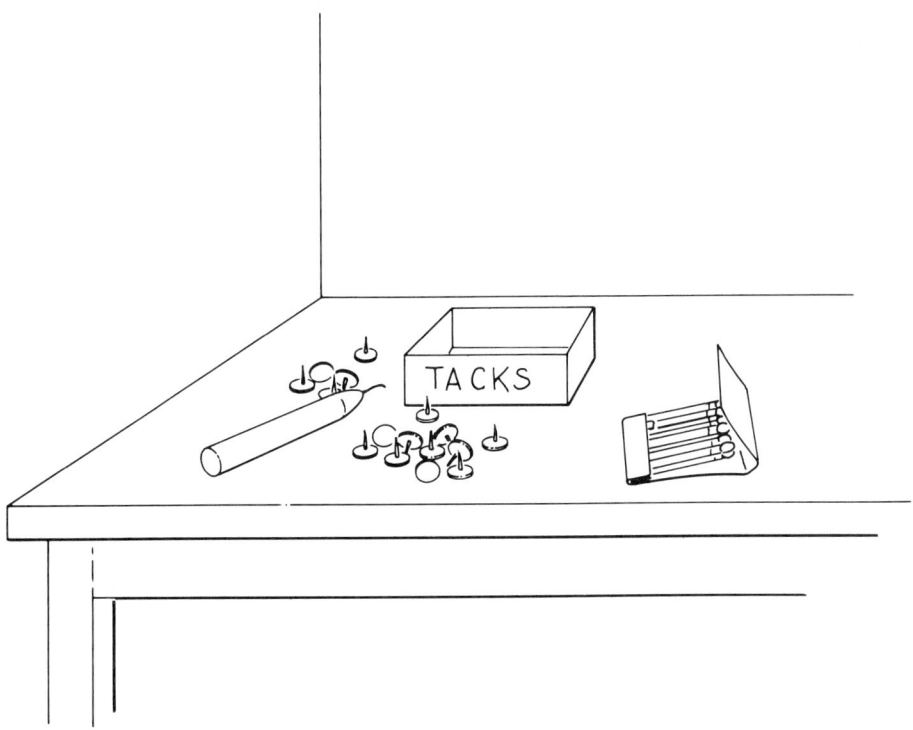

Figure 9.6 An alternative presentation of the candle problem that leads to an easier solution. (After Duncker, 1945.)

string, and then catching the first on the return swing. For those subjects who did not discover the solution initially, one of the experimenters gave a hint by "accidentally" bumping into one of the strings and setting it swinging. All subjects eventually discovered the solution and the results are shown in Figure 9.8.

All the subjects who had used the relay to solve the circuit problem used the switch to solve the pendulum problem, while nearly all those who had used the switch to solve the circuit problem used the relay to solve the pendulum problem. Control subjects who had not solved the circuit problem, and hence had not established a particular function for the switch or relay, were evenly divided in their use of these to solve the pendulum problem. The pretraining in the circuit problem had established a particular function for the switch and relay, which made it hard for subjects to use them in a novel way, namely, as a pendulum weight. Control subjects, on the other hand, had had no previous experience with the switch and relay, and so the function of these was not fixed for them.

There are many unanswered questions about functional fixity. Does the effect hold for all the functions of an object or only the most familiar one? How can the fixation be broken? How long does it last? Adamson and Taylor (1954) indicated that fixity may decrease with time. Their subjects first solved the electrical circuit problem using either the switch or relay, and then they were transferred to the two-string problem. The time period between the pretraining and transfer

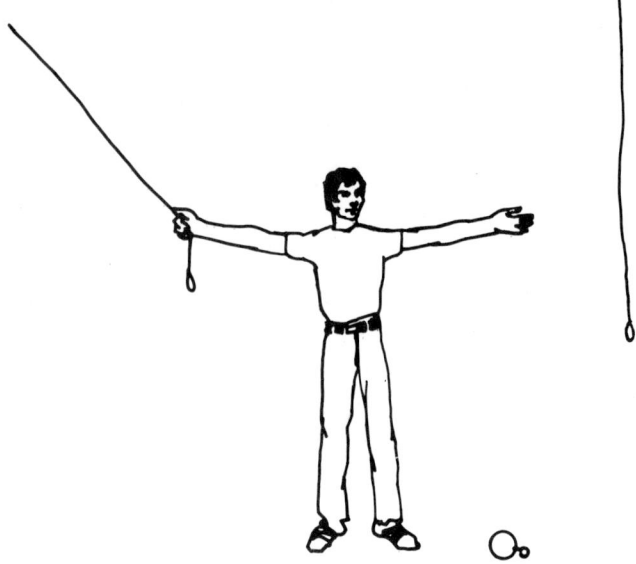

Figure 9.7 Given two strings hanging from the ceiling and heavy objects around the room, tie the strings together. (After Maier, 1930.)

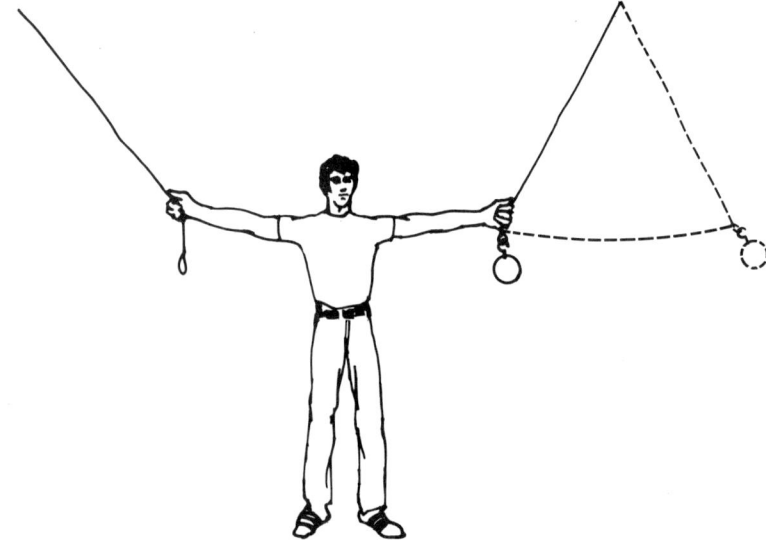

Group	N	Number using relay	Number using switch
Preutilization with relay	10	0	10
Preutilization with switch	9	7	2
No preutilization	6	3	3

Figure 9.8 Frequency of choice of objects in problem solving. (After Birch & Rabinowitz, 1951.)

problems was either 1 minute, 30 minutes, 1 hour, 1 day, or 1 week. Adamson and Taylor observed less functional fixity as the delay increased.

The knowledge we bring to a problem may help or hinder our solving the problem, depending on whether we can access relevant knowledge. In Chapter 8 on concepts, we noted that the entry in the mental lexicon for an object may contain the function for that object. If only familiar functions are given in the entry, it is understandable why they should be accessed first and lead to functional fixity. In that account we saw that novel functions *(This stump will make a good table)* require a search of the knowledge base to determine whether it is possible for the object to serve this novel function.

Retrieving a novel function is also made more difficult by the fact that the search of the knowledge base is backward. In the candle problem, for example, we do not ask, *Will this box made a good ledge?* but instead ask, *What will support the candle?* We must work backward to the more specific question, *Can we make a ledge for the candle?* Only then are we likely to consider the possibility that the box may serve the novel function of a ledge.

In brief, set and functional fixity, which are based in previous experience with methods or objects, can be hindrances to problem solving. Using previous experience is adaptive for most kinds of problems; but in problems of the type described above, it may blind one to other ways of approaching the problem.

Stages of Problem Solving

Problem solving is a process, a movement from the given state to the goal state, however erratic the movement may be. On the basis of introspection, Wallas (1926) divided this process into four stages and tried to analyze what goes on in each stage. These were:

Preparation. Gathering information and making the first attempts at a solution.

Incubation. Putting the problem aside for a while.
Illumination. Experiencing an insight into how to solve the problem.
Verification. Checking the solution to be sure that it is correct.

The first two stages are the more creative parts of problem solving, and we discuss them more fully below. Although they are the more interesting stages psychologically, the evidence for them is largely introspective and hard to evaluate. They thus offer a case study of the methodological difficulties involved in investigating problem solving.

Preparation. The first stage involves gathering information about the problem and structuring it. At this stage we may also draw upon such relevant experience as we can think of. The role of such knowledge is significant. Louis Pasteur was wont to say "In experimental science chance favors only the prepared mind" (Dubos, 1960, p. 34). The observer who brings a rich knowledge base to the task will be able to use information that would be useless to a more naive observer. "Accidental" scientific discoveries are more likely to be made by a knowledgeable scientist than by a naive observer. Nick Noble was able to relate "Elsie" to the library context of his problem; detective Lieutenant MacDonald was not.

The way we first structure a problem may affect the ease of solving it. Posner (1973) offers the following example:

Two train stations are fifty miles apart. At 2 P.M. one Saturday afternoon two trains start toward each other, one from each station. Just as the trains pull out of the stations, a bird springs into the air in front of the first train and flies ahead to the front of the second train. When the bird reaches the second train it turns back and flies toward the first train. The bird continues to do this until the trains meet.

If both trains travel at the rate of twenty-five miles per hour and the bird flies at a hundred miles per hour, how many miles will the bird have flown before the trains meet? (pp. 150–151)

If the problem is represented as the distance the bird travels, then calculating the length of all these trips is difficult. However, if the problem solver focuses on the time the bird is in the air, the problem becomes easy. At 25 miles per hour each, the two trains are approaching one another at 50 miles per hour and will cover the 50-mile distance in 1 hour. The bird flies at 100 miles per hour and so will cover 100 miles in that time. Representing the problem as a time problem rather than a distance problem makes it much easier to solve.

Adding relevant knowledge to what we know about the problem situation will sometimes let us represent the problem in a much easier form. Consider the geometry example in Figure 9.9 from Köhler (1969). See if you can figure out the length of line L, given that the radius of the circle is 5 inches.

The solution is shown in Figure 9.10. The first representation focuses on line L as the hypotenuse of a right triangle. Representing it

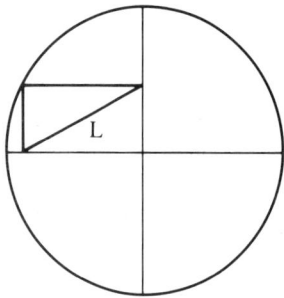

Figure 9.9 The problem is to determine the length of line L if you know the radius of the circle is 5 inches. The difficult structure shows line L as a side in a right triangle. (After Köhler, 1969.)

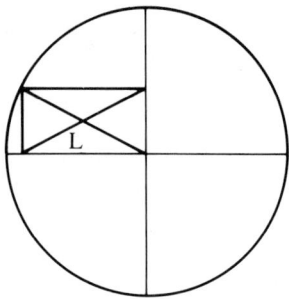

Figure 9.10 The easier structure. Line L is one of two diagonals in a rectangle. (After Köhler, 1969.)

as a diagonal of a rectangle, however, quickly suggests that the other diagonal is the radius of the circle and the answer thus is 5 inches. A relatively small addition to the given from what we know transforms the representation into a much more solvable problem.

Sometimes it is hard to break up the structure in the given state of a problem. This effect has been the most clearly demonstrated with anagrams. An anagram is a string of letters that can be rearranged to form a word (e.g., *kbolc* = *block*). Beilin and Horn (1962) gave subjects anagrams that were either in the usual nonsense form (*obave* for *above*) or were words (*froth* for *forth*, *leash* for *shale*). The latter took significantly longer to solve. In gestalt terms, anagrams that are themselves words are already well structured and resist reorganization.

Thus the preparation of a problem involves the way we first structure it and the knowledge we bring to bear on it. These have an important influence on how easy the problem is to solve; and if success eludes us, we may turn to the second stage of problem solving.

Incubation. Artists, mathematicians, and scientists have reported experiencing a sudden insight into a problem after a period of neglecting the problem (e.g., Ghiselin, 1952; Hadamard, 1945; Koestler, 1964). The period of neglect is called *incubation* by Wallas, a term that suggests that work on the problem continues unconsciously. Preparation for the problem has been intense but unsuccessful, and the thinker deliberately puts the problem aside to attend to other matters. After an indeterminate time, a key to the solution suddenly appears *(illumination)* and the thinker checks the solution *(validation)*, thus completing the final two stages of the process Wallas described. The French mathematician Poincaré (1913) reports a vivid example of this process. He had spent 15 days working on the properties of Fuchsian functions.

> Just at this time I left Caen, where I was then living, to go on a geologic excursion under the auspices of the school of mines. The changes of travel made me forget my mathematical work. Having reached Coutances, we entered an omnibus to go some place or other. At the moment when I put my foot on the step the idea came to me, without anything in my former thoughts seeming to have paved the way for it, that the transformations I had used to define the Fuchsian functions were identical with those of non-Euclidean geometry. I did not verify the idea; I should not have had time, as, upon taking my seat in the omnibus, I went on with a conversation already commenced, but I felt a perfect certainty. On my return to Caen, for conscience' sake I verified the result at my leisure. (pp. 387–388)

The first part of Poincaré's account describes his intense, conscious attack on the problem. The geological excursion interrupts his work and he seemingly devotes no attention to the problem until a key to an unresolved part of the problem suddenly leaps into consciousness as he boards the bus. This and similar accounts suggest that the plan set in motion during preparation may have continued unconsciously.

The hypothesis of unconscious processing is difficult to test, though the advance that has been made in a given problem at the moment of insight is a compelling indication. Posner (1973) describes several ways the advance might occur, including the possibility that the thinker forgets an inappropriate set during the rest period or that he continues to work on the problem periodically but forgets that he has done so. These speculations require evidence, however, before they can be accepted.

Posner reports an empirical study on incubation by Silveira (1971). The problem Silveira presented to her subjects was as follows:

> A man had 4 chains, each 3 links long. He wanted to join the 4 chains into a single closed chain. Having a link opened cost 2¢ and having a link closed cost 3¢. The man had his chains joined into a closed chain for 15¢. How did he do it?

The subjects soon discovered that they could not simply link the four chains end to end. Instead, they had to disassemble one of the chains and use the links to join the other three chains.

A control group of subjects, who worked continuously for about half an hour, achieved only about 50 percent success on this task. Four experimental groups varied in the amount of time given to incubation and in the amount of time given to preparation. Two groups spent a relatively brief time in preparation; one then took a ½-hour break before returning to the problem, while the other took a 4-hour break. Two other groups spent a relatively long time in preparation before entering the ½-hour or 4-hour incubation period. During the incubation period the subjects were involved in activities unrelated to the problem.

None of the subjects experienced an insightful solution to the problem during the incubation period. However, when the groups with long preparation resumed the problem, their success rate on the problem was much greater than that of the control group. The group taking a ½-hour break showed 64 percent success and the group taking the 4-hour break showed 85 percent success. Silveira had her subjects talk aloud as they worked on the problem. She found that when they returned to the problem following the break, they seemed to have made no notable progress on the problem but simply picked up where they had left off.

Silveira's task is thus somewhat different from Wallas's stages in that incubation did not

---

Box 9.1 TIPS ON SOLVING PROBLEMS

What is the best way to attack a problem? As you can see from the description above, gestalt psychology offers no ultimate answers, although searching for new ways to conceptualize the problem seems to be important. We often think of creativity as being an element of good problem solving, and we look to creative thinkers for clues about how to be creative. Ghiselin (1952) and Vernon (1970) have described the thinking of a number of creative people, and their descriptions may shed some light on this process. The notion of creativity, however, is difficult to define and there is not much consensus at present on what it is or how it occurs. Practical aids to solving problems have been offered by Polya (1957, 1965) and Wickelgren (1974). From these and similar sources, we offer some tips you may find helpful on how to attack a problem.

1. *Broaden your knowledge.* The prepared mind brings greater resources to the problem. The more diverse your knowledge is, the better the chance that some of that knowledge will be relevant to the problem at hand. Gordon (1961) recommends that professional problem-solving groups be composed of people from different disciplines in order to expand the source of ideas.

2. *Look for new relations.* Try representing the problem in different ways, as in the bird and train problem. Look for new relations in what is given or draw analogies from previous problems you have solved. Polya (1957) suggests working backward from the goal state toward the given state as a way of getting fresh ideas. Wickelgren (1974) gives many techniques and useful examples.

3. *Explain the problem to someone.* Talking about the problem may bring out hidden assumptions or errors in your thinking.

4. *Put the problem aside.* Incubation seems to work for some of the people some of the time. You may also find during the waiting period that a seemingly unrelated experience offers a new conceptualization of the problem.

end with illumination. However, it is noteworthy that the interruption did produce a higher success rate for those who had done intensive preparation, and the longer interruption produced the higher success rate.

In summary, the work on Wallas's (1926) four stages of preparation, incubation, illumination, and verification stresses the importance of intense work during preparation and a search for relevant information and the right structure for the problem. If these efforts fail, incubation may lead to an insight into the problem which can later be verified. It is not clear, however, whether these processes occur in all problem solving, and objective evidence for them is hard to secure.

In conclusion, gestalt psychology has offered some challenging ideas about whole properties, restructuring, sources of fixation in problem solving, and stages in problem solving. Many of these ideas are especially compelling because they are part of our everyday experience. Research on these ideas has added to our understanding of problem solving; yet critics of gestalt psychology argue that many of their notions are vague and difficult to test. The subjective character of such concepts as structure, direction, insight, and set makes it hard to develop explicit hypotheses about them or to know whether an experimental test truly represents the concept in question. Information-processing theorists have sought to conceptualize these notions in a more explicit and testable form, as we shall see in the following section.

INFORMATION-PROCESSING THEORY

Information-processing theory is primarily concerned with the mechanisms, structures, and processes people employ in operating upon environmental stimuli. Its application to the area of problem solving has developed since World War II; it has been especially stimulated by the advent of digital computers, and of cybernetics (Weiner, 1948)—the comparative study of complex calculating machines and the human nervous system. Its success has been encouraged largely by technological advances in these areas as well as in applied mathematics. Information-processing theory accepts many of the goals and assumptions of gestalt theory but seeks a more objective and analytic form for them. We introduce some of its concepts with a particular example.

Try to solve the following problem. Say aloud everything that comes to mind as you go, especially things you notice about the problem and steps you take in trying to solve it. Write down anything you want to.

$$\begin{array}{r} DONALD \\ +GERALD \\ \hline ROBERT \end{array} \quad D = 5$$

This is a problem in cryptarithmetic. There are ten different letters; each stands for a different number for the numbers 0 to 9, with $D = 5$. Find the right number for the other nine letters. Once you get the code, you will find that the sum is arithmetically correct. Work on the problem for at least 5 minutes before reading further.

In an information-processing (IP) analysis it is important to find out what the problem solver is thinking. This helps us better understand all the activities that occur in problem solving. Since thinking is covert, the experimenter asks the subject to say aloud everything that comes to mind. The written record of this report is called a *protocol*. The following selection is the first part of a protocol from a single subject working on the DONALD + GERALD problem. The protocol and its analysis (here paraphrased) come from Newell (see Newell & Simon, 1972, pp. 230–231. Also Lindsay & Norman, 1977).

Each letter has one and only one numerical value—

(This is a question to the experimenter, who responds, "One numerical value.")

There are ten different letters and each of them has one numerical value.

Therefore, I can, looking at the 2 D's—each D is 5; therefore, T is zero. So I think I'll start by writing that problem here. I'll write 5, 5 is zero.

Now, do I have any other T's? No, but I have another D. That means I have a 5 over the other side.

Now I have 2 A's and 2 L's that are each—somewhere—and this R—3 R's. Two L's equal an R. Of course, I'm carrying a 1 which will mean that R has to be an odd number because the 2 L's—any two numbers added together has to be an even number and 1 will be an odd number. So R can be 1, 3, not 5, 7, or 9.

(At this point there is a long pause; so the experimenter asks, "What are you thinking now?")

Now G—since R is going to be an odd number and D is 5, G has to be an even number.

I'm looking at the left side of this problem here where it says D + G. Oh, plus possibly another number, if I have to carry 1 from the E + O. I think I'll forget about that for a minute. Possibly the best way to get this problem is to try different possible solutions. I'm not sure whether that would be the easiest way or not.

What is going on in this protocol? The subject quickly notes that T = ∅ (we use ∅ for zero to avoid confusion with the letter O). He also notes that D appears on the left of the problem. Having recorded this much, he turns to another area of the problem.

Now I have 2 A's and 2 L's that are each—somewhere—and this R—3 R's. Two L's equal an R. Of course, I'm carrying a 1, which will mean that R has to be an odd number because the 2 L's—any two numbers added together has to be an even number and 1 will be an odd number. So R can be 1, 3, not 5, 7, or 9.

Now he brings in his knowledge that the sum of any two numbers is an even number. He uses this to conclude that R has to be odd and records this. He seems unable to find a way to reduce the possibilities for R at the moment, so he turns to another area.

Now G—since R is going to be an odd number and D is 5, G has to be an even number.

Here he introduces his knowledge that the sum of two odd numbers is an even number. Since R and D are both odd, G has to be even. Though he does not yet know G, he has reduced the options.

This is but a fragment of the 20-minute protocol that Newell recorded. The analysis of it is somewhat informal, but it reflects the steps the problem solver goes through, the operations he performs, and the information he gains at each step. These processes are assumed to be general to all kinds of problem solving, including mathematics, games, puzzles, and designing a house. The goal of IP theory is to explicate these processes fully and objectively.

To improve the objectivity of protocol analysis, Newell developed the *problem behavior graph*, a visual display of the steps in solving a problem. The protocol is analyzed into a series of *knowledge states*, each one showing what the subject knows at that point in the process (see Figure 9.11). For example, in the first state, the subject knows only that D = 5; in the next state, he has discovered that T = ∅. The knowledge states reflect the information he has accumulated as he works through the problem. The *operation* he performs on a knowledge state is shown as an arrow. The operation creates new knowledge, which is shown in the next knowledge state. The problem behavior graph thus represents the pro-

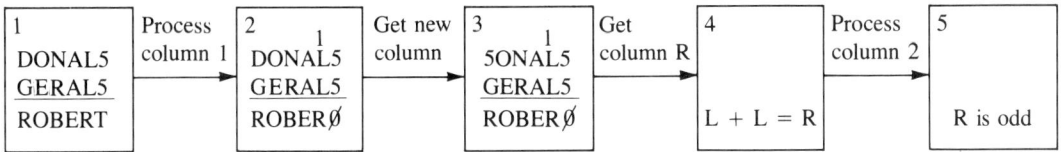

Figure 9.11 Representation of states in a problem behavior graph. (From Lindsay & Norman, 1977.)

tocol as a path from one knowledge state to the next.

The first five knowledge states for this protocol are shown in Figure 9.11. State 1 shows that the subject knows D = 5. He then operates on column 1 to produce 5 + 5 = ∅. The columns are numbered from right to left, 1–6. The operation produces new knowledge shown in State 2. The next move is to find a new column having T or D in it and to substitute there. He does not find another T, but he does find a D in column 6 and substitutes 5, producing State 3. Now the subject explores first column 3 and then column 2.

Now I have 2 A's and 2 L's that are each—somewhere—and this R—3 R's.

He does nothing in column 3 but decides to process column 2. Thus we add State 4. The processing leads to his conclusion that R is odd, shown in State 5.

At this state the subject backs up. At State 5 he says,

Two L's equal an R. Of course, I'm carrying a 1, which will mean that R has to be an odd number. . . .

Then he decides to generate the possible numbers. To do so, he backs up to State 4, concludes again that R must be odd, and then generates the possible numbers.

. . . because the 2 L's—any two numbers added together has to be an even number and 1 will be an odd number. So R can be 1, 3, not 5, 7, or 9.

Backing up is common in protocols and is shown in the graph by dropping an arrow from the backup state down to the next state, which is a duplicate of the backup state (see Figure 9.12). Processing from that state then moves horizontally until a new backup occurs. Here State 7 shows the subject has again concluded that R is odd, and State 8 shows the numbers he has generated for R. Note that it shows that he explicitly considered the possibility that R = 5 and rejected it.

The complete graph for this protocol is shown in Figure 9.13 and contains 238 states. Each dot represents one state, such as those shown in Figures 9.11 and 9.12. To read the graph, start in the upper left-hand corner (which represents the five states shown in Figure 9.11) and read horizontally to the end, then back up until you reach the first vertical line, drop to the next row, read to the end, back up until you reach the first vertical line, drop to the next row, and so on. Do not go through any state twice.

A problem behavior graph can be applied to many different kinds of problems. The knowledge states and operations change among problems, though interestingly the subject in this protocol used only four different operations throughout the protocol. The general pattern in this and other graphs seems to be one in which a subject breaks the overall problem into subproblems and attacks these one at a time. The knowledge states show the information he or she has

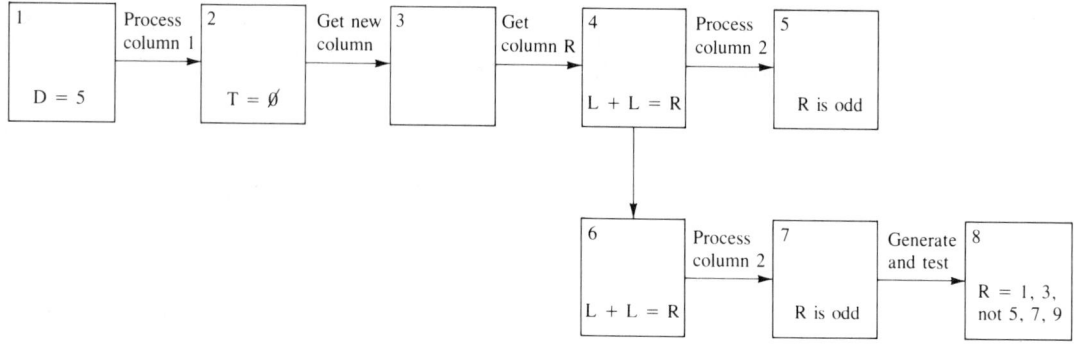

Figure 9.12 Sequence of states in a problem behavior graph. (From Lindsay & Norman, 1977.)

gathered up to that point. Movement across states is somewhat erratic as a subject explores first one subproblem and then another, often backing up. In the next section we describe a more formal way for representing the structure of a problem and the way it unfolds as a subject works on it.

The Problem Space

At the beginning of this chapter we noted that a problem is defined by a given state, which sets the initial conditions for the problem, a goal state, which is the desired state, and a path from the given state to the goal state. IP theory treats problem solving as a search for a path through a *problem space* (Newell & Simon, 1972). A problem space is composed of all the possible knowledge states that can be generated by applying the available operations to knowledge states. The problem space for a given problem may vary from individual to individual; this is particularly the case for ill-defined problems, which we discuss later in this chapter. For certain well-defined problems, however, the problem space is probably similar from individual to individual.

The problem behavior graph we described above represents some, but not all, of the states for the problem space for the DONALD + GERALD problem. The subject might have generated other states by tackling the problem in different ways, as you probably did when you tried the problem. The number of possible knowledge states for most problems is quite large, and a typical problem solver will generate only a small portion of these as he or she works on the problem.

A problem space can be shown graphically by a *tree*. Consider a very simple problem: to discover the combination of a lock that has only two dials, each with the letters A, B, and C. It is now set at AA. A tree of the possible states is shown in Figure 9.14. To find the combination one starts the search at AA, which is Node 1. There are two possible operations at this node. We may move Dial 1 one place, yielding BA, the state shown at Node 2, or we may move Dial 2 one place, yielding AB, the state shown in Node 3. Similarly, for nodes 2 and 3 there are two possible actions each, resulting in the states shown in nodes 4 through 7.

Thus a tree represents the set of possible

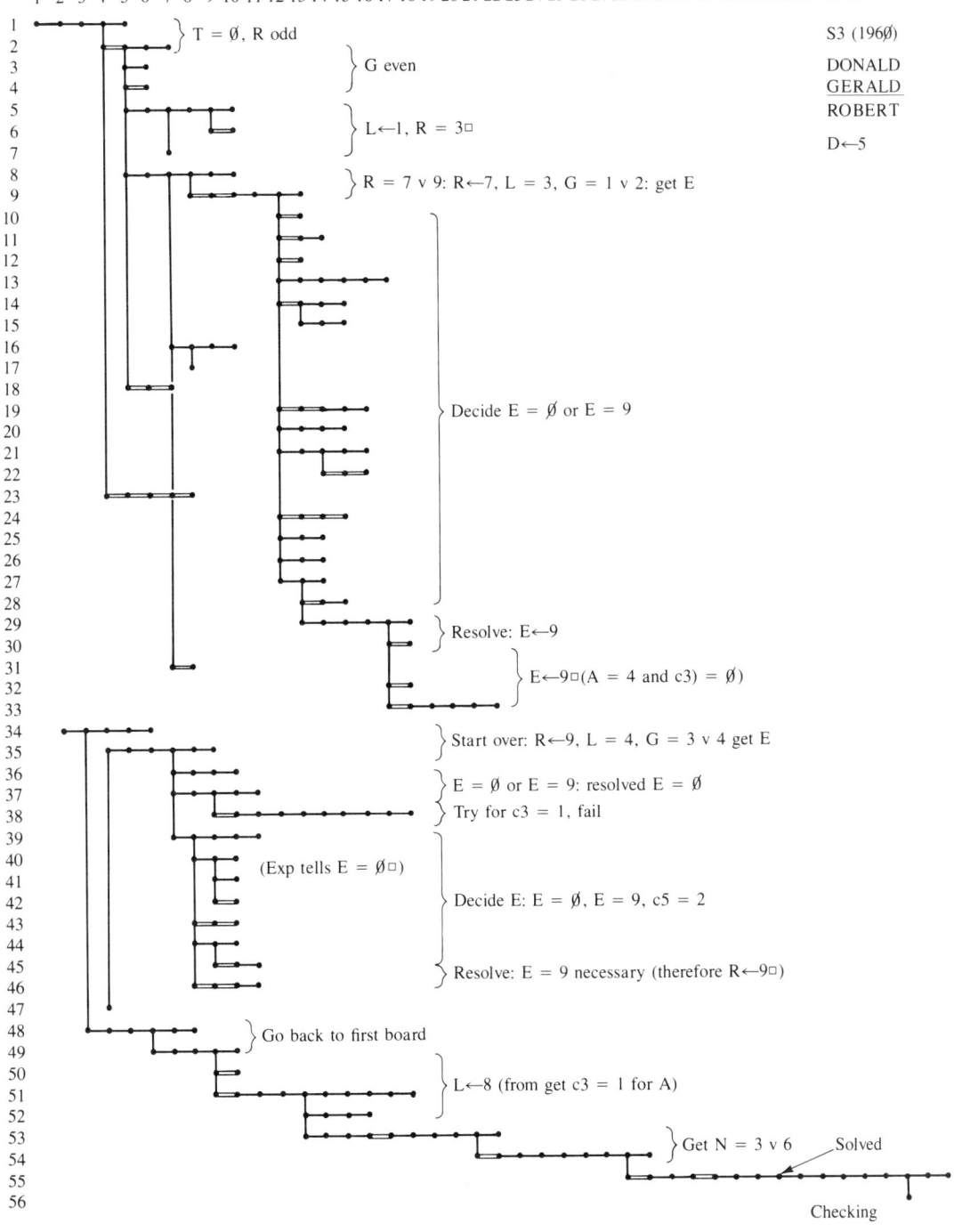

Figure 9.13 Problem behavior graph for single subject solving DONALD + GERALD problem. The symbols to the right of the dots are the experimenters' notations for what the subject is doing at that stage of the problem. (From Newell & Simon, 1972.)

> **Box 9.2 SOLUTION TO DONALD + GERALD**
>
> Many protocols have been collected for the DONALD + GERALD problem, each of them unique in its attack on the problem. Most reveal a somewhat fumbling, torturous path through the problem space like the one that begins on page 247. One of the most efficient is shown below (Lindsay & Norman, 1977, pp. 559–560).
>
> ```
>      (Column 6 5 4 3 2 1)
>             DONALD   D = 5.
>           + GERALD
>           ─────────
>             ROBERT
> ```
>
> 1. $D = 5$, so T must be 0 (with a carry to column 2).
> 2. Look at column 5: $O + E = O$. This can happen only if 0 or 10 is being added to O. Therefore, E must be 9 (plus a carry) or 0. But T is already 0, so E must be 9 (with a carry from column 4).
> 3. If E is 9, then in column 3 A must be 4 or 9 (with a carry in either case). E is already 9, so A must be 4.
> 4. In column 2, $L + L$ plus a carry $= R$ plus a carry to column 3. R must be odd. The only odd numbers left are 1, 3, and 7. But from column 6, $5 + G = R$, so R must be greater than 5. So R must be 7, which makes $L = 8$ and $G = 1$.
> 5. In column 4, $N + 7 = B +$ carry. Therefore, N is greater than or equal to 3. The only numbers left are 2, 3, and 6, so N is 3 or 6. But if N were 3, B would be 0, so N must be 6. That makes $B = 3$.
> 6. That only leaves the letter O and the number 2: $O = 2$.
>
> ```
>      5 2 6 4 8 5
>    + 1 9 7 4 8 5
>    ─────────────
>      7 2 3 9 7 0
> ```

operations at each juncture in the problem and the states these operations lead to. To solve the problem is to find a path through the tree to the correct state—that is, the combination of letters that will open the lock. If *BC* were the solution, it might be reached by the path 1-3-7-13. Note that a particular state may occur several times when the problem space is shown in this form and may be reached by different paths. For most problems the solution to the problem may be reached by more than one path.

A problem space gives a more objective representation of a problem than is commonly found in gestalt discussions of problem solving. Each

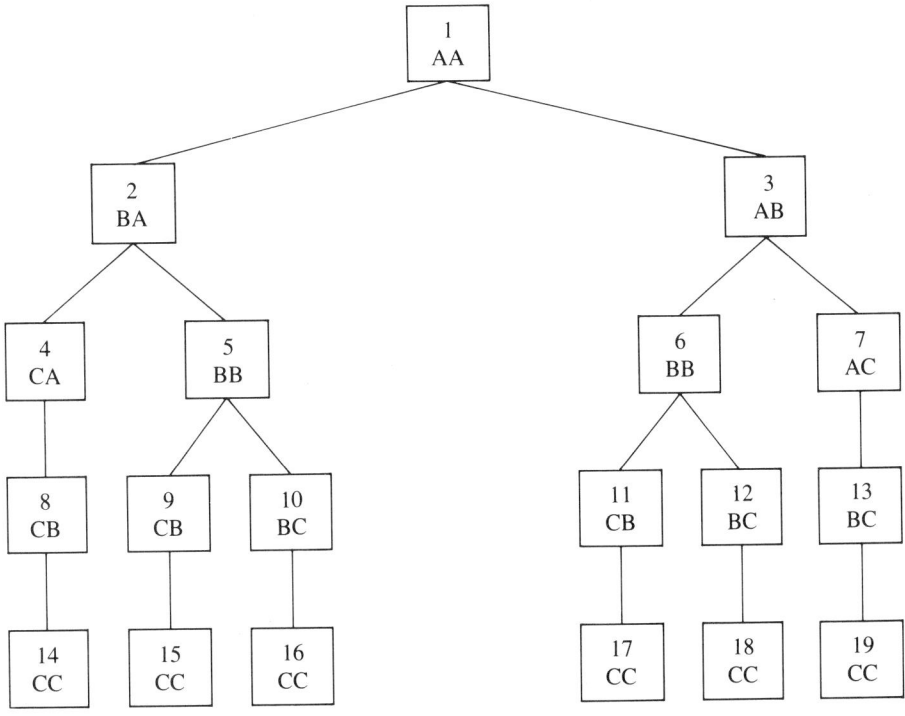

Figure 9.14 Tree of action states for a combination lock of two dials having three letters each. The left letter in each two-letter combination is the setting for Dial 1; the right letter is the setting for Dial 2.

knowledge state is a discrete state. It can be produced by an operation on some other state. Of course, a good problem space can be produced only when the researcher can determine what the possible operations are. In the example of the combination lock, these are limited to the movements of the dials.

A common technique for determining the operations subjects use in solving a problem is the "thinking-aloud" process we saw in the crypt-arithmetic example. The experimenter asks the subjects to report everything they are thinking as they work on the problem. The experimenter then abstracts the operation from the protocols.

Reports of this kind provide much information, but they must be used with some caution. A subject may not tell all that he or she is thinking and sometimes must be prompted. Also, for a given subject the processes may not all be conscious. In insight problems, for example, the solution may come so quickly that the subject can tell us little about how it developed. In other tasks the reasons given for moves may be of little help —"It seemed right," for example, or "Only possible move."

Finally, it is not clear what effects thinking aloud has on the problem-solving process itself. Dansereau and Gregg (1966), for instance, reported no differences in the times for doing mental arithmetic problems in silent and thinking-aloud conditions. Nonetheless, although a number of questions remain unanswered about this technique, it has proved useful as a first step in analyzing many problem tasks. Newell and

Simon (1972), for example, reported that the several protocols they examined for the cryptarithmetic problem revealed only a small number of operations, which in turn produced very similar problem spaces for these subjects.

In short, a problem space is the set of all possible knowledge states for a particular problem. A path through this space can be shown by a problem behavior graph, though we cannot be sure the graph completely captures the problem solver's thought processes. Nonetheless, this kind of analysis is more objective and, as we shall see below, is especially well suited to computer modeling of problem solving.

The Computer as a Model

The digital computer has had a tremendous influence on IP theories of problem solving. The parallel between computer functions and human cognitive processes is close enough to suggest the computer as a model for problem-solving processes. Like humans, computers have

1. input and output devices for receiving information (card readers, tapes) and displaying stored or processed information (printers, cathode-ray tubes)
2. a memory for storing information
3. a processing unit for operating on information that is input or is in memory
4. a control unit for ordering the processes

The parallel is far from perfect, but it has excited a great many efforts to write computer programs that solve human kinds of problems—for example, geometry problems (Gelernter, 1959), algebra problems—a program named STUDENT (Bobrow, 1968), and analogies—a program named ARGUS (Reitman, 1965).

The first general purpose digital computer was the Mark I, which began operating in 1944. It was an electromechanical machine, which is to say that it had moving parts. The first purely electronic computer was the ENIAC, which was developed at the University of Pennsylvania in 1946 and had no moving parts. A major advance occurred in 1949 with the development of EDVAC, a computer that used stored programs. Storing a program of instructions for the computer, rather than reading them in from cards or tape, permits much faster and more flexible operations. In the intervening years computer technology has greatly reduced the size of computer components and increased their speed. Present day computers can carry out basic operations in nanoseconds (billionths of a second), which is a million times faster than the earliest computers.

Digital computers are general-purpose machines. They can be programmed to carry out many different functions. The program is input to the computer along with a set of data to be processed, and both are stored in memory until the control unit begins work. A program thus converts a computer from being a general-purpose machine to being a special-purpose machine. Since a great many programs can be written for a computer, it can serve many different special purposes, such as doing a statistical analysis, solving analogies, computing a payroll, and projecting the trajectory of a rocket.

The notion of a machine as a model for human processes is very old (Apter, 1970), and the computer is only the latest such machine model. The question in such machine modeling is, How well does the operation of the machine help us understand human processes? Newell and Simon (1972) used a program entitled the GENERAL PROBLEM SOLVER (GPS) to solve cryptarithmetic problems. How does it work? What can we learn from such programs? Let us look first at some of the basic concepts of these programs, and then we shall return to GPS and similar programs.

Computer Simulation. Efforts to program computers to carry out human kinds of activities have taken two directions. In *artificial intelligence* one tries to write a program that will carry out some human activity in the best possible way. In *computer simulation* one tries to write a program that will carry out some human activity exactly the way humans do it. As Feigenbaum and Feldman (1963) explain,

> An artificial intelligence researcher interested in programming a computer to play chess would be happy only if his program played good chess, preferably better chess than the best human player. However, the researcher interested in simulating the chess-playing behavior of a given individual would be unhappy if his program played chess better (or worse) than that individual, for this researcher wants his program to make the same moves as the human player, regardless of whether these moves are good, bad, or indifferent. (p. 269)

Good simulation is the aim of those who take the computer as a model of human problem solving. The program is the researcher's theory of the cognitive processes underlying the problem solving. Simon and Newell (1971) state that *"an explanation of an observed behavior of the organism is provided by a program of primitive information processes that generates this behavior"* (p. 147). The program is usually tested by having it solve problems (such as cryptarithmetic problems) and then matching the steps it went through against problem behavior graphs of humans who solved the same problems. Where discrepancies occur, the program must be revised to improve the fit. Simon and Newell (1971) give a very clear account of this approach in a short history of their own work.

The computer itself is only a convenient tool. It carries out the instructions in the program, but it is the program that serves as a theory of the cognitive processes, not the computer. In principle, one could dispense with the computer and sit down with paper and pencil to trace out the activities called for by the program instructions in solving the problem. In practice, of course, this would probably be a monumental job—one that the computer could do much more efficiently.

A successful program is a theory in the usual sense that it is an organized set of statements for predicting and explaining a set of phenomena. Many theories are written in plain language (e.g., gestalt theories); others are written in mathematical form. A program is written in computer language. A theorist is at liberty to choose the symbolic system he or she prefers, so long as the theory predicts and explains the phenomena satisfactorily.

The advantages of using a program as theory are that a program is objective and explicit. Theories in plain language are sometimes vague about just what processes are going on or how they occur, a problem we saw in gestalt theory. A computer program, on the other hand, must be very explicit. In fact, computers have been called dumb machines in the sense that they only do what they are told to do (some people may quarrel with this statement; see Box 9.3). A single missing or vague instruction will usually bring the computer to a halt. And yet, because a program must be explicit about every stage of processing, it is an objective statement about the cognitive processes it simulates.

Algorithms and Heuristics. We have characterized problem solving as a search through a problem space. For a combination lock, the problem space is the set of all possible combinations of the dials. The intriguing thing about combination locks is that any thief who will take the time to try all possible combinations is guaranteed admission. An exhaustive search of the problem space is thus one way of assuring a solution to the problem. Any method that guarantees a solution to a problem is an **algorithm.** It is a series of actions that have a sure path from the given state to the solution state. An algorithm does not have to be an exhaustive search. For example, the rules we apply in multiplying or dividing two numbers

Box 9.3 CAN COMPUTERS THINK?

As computers have become more sophisticated, a popular question has arisen about whether computers can think. Behind this question sometimes lurks the fear that computers may some day "take over" as HAL tried to do in the movie *2001*. Armer (1963) summarizes several of the early arguments against the possibility that machines can think. The first of these assumes that computers can only process numbers. This was indeed true of the earliest computers, but present-day computers process letters and other kinds of symbols as well.

A second type of argument states that computers cannot think because the hardware for computers (circuits, relays, etc.) is different from that of brains (neurons, synapses, etc.). A related argument calls for computers to do things exactly the way humans do (e.g., in chess to recognize each of the pieces the way humans do). This is a little like saying planes can't fly because they don't flap their wings and roost in trees the way birds do. At what level are we seeking similarity?

Here we should ask, What do we mean by *thinking*? Is thinking a matter of carrying on such cognitive processes as perceiving, remembering, solving problems, and playing games? If so, we may have to admit that computers can think, at least when they are running under the right programs. Simulation programs are available for many of the cognitive processes now, and it is likely that other (and better) ones will be written in the future.

The logic of simulation, of course, requires only that the *behavior* of the program be the same as that of a human (e.g., that a program for playing checkers play by the rules of the game and that it have a goal to win). If the behavior is the same, can we infer that the processes that led to the behavior are the same for computer and human? We have no guarantee of that, but neither do we have a guarantee that they are not. This leads us back to the question, What is thinking? Should any set of processes that produces human-like behavior be called thinking? If not, what other characteristic should these processes have in order to be called thinking?

One candidate is consciousness. We think of thinking as a conscious activity. Yet some of the cognitive processes are not conscious—for example, retrieving familiar items from memory, talking and other highly practiced motor skills, and perhaps some problem-solving activities such as incubation. Are these processes not to be called thinking, or shall we say that consciousness is not necessary for thinking? If we decide that thinking must be conscious, then we may ask, Can computers have consciousness? Apter (1970) gives a delightful review of the issues underlying machine consciousness, and we will not tip his hand except to say that his discussion is quite provocative.

In brief then, the answer to the question *Can computers think?* awaits a clearer definition of what we mean by thinking. Definitional problems of this kind are not uncommon in scientific practice when we are called upon to give scientific meaning to popular terms.

guarantee a correct answer without an exhaustive search.

In most problems the only available algorithm is exhaustive search, and when the problem space is large, that may be too costly. In the game of checkers, for instance, an exhaustive search would require that you consider all the possible moves you could make at the beginning of the game, then examine all the replies your opponent could make, all the counterreplies you could make, and so on, to all the possible outcomes of the game. Many of the combinations of moves would lead to your winning, and you could simply chose one of these paths. Samuel (1959) has calculated that such an approach to checkers would involve about 10^{40} possible moves, "which at 3 choices per millimicrosecond would still take 10^{21} centuries to consider" (p. 212). For chess he estimates the number of possible moves to be about 10^{120}.

Clearly, exhaustive search is not the way to win these games. It is a brute force technique that is too demanding for humans or even modern computers. An alternative is the **heuristic,** a selective search of certain paths through the problem space, a search that offers a good chance of finding a solution, but does not guarantee success. Heuristics thus reduce the cost of search at the risk of not solving the problem.

Research on human problem solving has concentrated on the use of heuristics rather than algorithms, since the use of a heuristic is both more common and more creative than the routine application of an algorithm. There are many heuristics; two examples we will consider are *working backward* and *means-ends analysis*.

WORKING BACKWARD. In plane geometry one proves a theorem by showing how the theorem can be derived from the axioms of plane geometry. A useful approach is to start with the theorem and work backward to the axioms. The number of paths leading from the theorem back to the axioms is relatively small, while the number of paths leading away from the axioms is relatively large (hundreds of theorems can be proved from the axioms). Thus it is relatively easier to work backward from the information given in the theorem to the axioms.

Working backward is a commonly used heuristic in mathematics and other formal systems (Polya, 1957). Consider the *Logic Theorist,* a program developed by Newell, Shaw, and Simon (1958b) to prove theorems in symbolic logic. The system is an axiomatic system with strict rules of inference for proving theorems, just as is the case in plane geometry. Newell et al. observed that human subjects working on such proofs typically worked backwards from the theorem to the axioms, and so they designed the *Logic Theorist* to work in this fashion.

To test the program, they gave it 52 of the theorems from Whitehead and Russell's monumental *Principia Mathematica* (1935). It succeeded with 38 (73 percent) of these, was unable to prove 1 more, and failed for lack of memory space on the rest. Like the human problem solvers it simulates, it does not solve all problems. Moreover, for difficult problems it takes more time and more operations to prove the theorem.

The efficiency of the working backward heuristic is illustrated by the British Museum algorithm: If three monkeys sat down to three typewriters and typed at random for eternity, they would eventually produce all the books in the British Museum. Most of what they produced, of course, would be nonsense, and it would probably be eons before even a single book appeared by chance.

Newell et al. programmed the *Logic Theorist* in something of this manner to work forward from the axioms to derive theorems. Figure 9.15 shows the number of proofs derived and the number of steps required for each proof. The program derived 246 theorems with proofs that took no more than 8 steps. Of the 246 proofs only 5 are among the 52 theorems in *Principia*. Newell et al. estimate that this procedure would require "eons and eons" to prove the remaining theorems in *Principia*. Thus the working back-

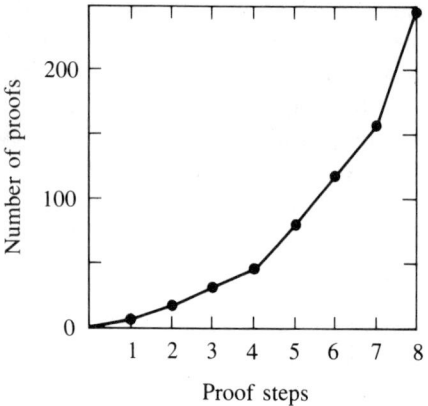

Figure 9.15 Number of proofs generated by first few steps of British Museum algorithm. (From Newell & Simon, 1972.)

ward heuristic used in the *Logic Theorist* is a highly efficient heuristic for proving theorems.

MEANS-ENDS ANALYSIS. This heuristic breaks a given problem into a set of subproblems; solving these may lead to the solution of the main problem. Newell and Simon (1972) cite a homely example:

> I want to take my son to nursery school. What's the difference between what I have and what I want? One of distance. What changes distance? My automobile. My automobile won't work. What is needed to make it work? A new battery. What has new batteries? An auto repair shop. I want the repair shop to put in a new battery; but the shop doesn't know I need one. What is the difficulty? One of communication. What allows communication? A telephone . . . and so on. (p. 416)

Means-ends analysis notes the difference between the given state and the goal and tries to reduce that difference by setting up subproblems. Applying an operator to the goal creates a subproblem, which may be more solvable. In this example, the automobile will solve the parent's problem of getting to the nursery school, but first she must make it work. This is a subproblem whose solution (a battery) leads to a lower subproblem. The heuristic continues to reduce differences and produce subproblems until it reaches a subproblem it can solve. It then works back up the sequence, solving each subproblem, until it reaches the goal state.

Note that the means-ends heuristic can place significant demands on working memory. Each subproblem must be held in memory until the ones below it are solved. One way of representing the sequence of subproblems in memory is the *push-down stack,* as shown in Figure 9.16, which is similar to the devices used in some cafeterias for holding plates. The topmost goal goes in first and is pushed down as subgoals are added. When a subgoal is solved, the stack pops up to the next subgoal.

Heuristics are a very selective search of the problem space; yet they can be effective. We describe the use of heuristics in more detail below, but first we should take up the question of how to control the flow of processes in a program.

Executive Control. The gestalt psychologists spoke of "direction" in problem solving. Human problem solving is rarely a random search through the problem space, but rather is organized around the requirements of the problem. In computer simulation, such organization is often represented by an *executive routine,* which controls the order of operations. In many programs certain sequences of operations are often repeated (e.g., the operations for multiplying two numbers). For efficiency these sequences are stored as *subroutines* and are called upon by the executive routine as needed. The *Logic Theorist* has a small number of subroutines for attacking a theorem in symbolic logic. Its executive routine determines which of these subroutines are to be used, the order for trying them, and when to quit trying.

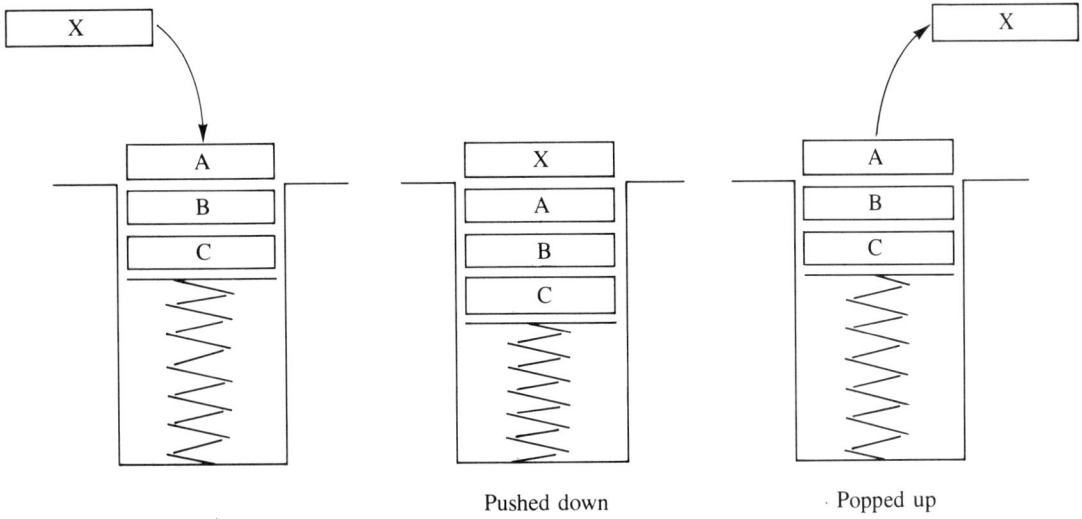

Figure 9.16 A push-down stack of subproblems, in which subproblem X is first added and then popped up. (After Hayes, 1978.)

The purposiveness of human behavior is thus achieved in a program by an executive routine. The list of instructions for this routine determines which operations of subroutines are to be used in any given situation. At each stage of processing, the executive conducts certain tests to determine which operations are to be applied next. The flexibility of the executive lies in the choice of tests. Each test may have two or more outcomes, and for each outcome there is a particular operation to be applied.

As the managerial metaphor suggests, the executive routine "decides" which operation to apply on the basis of the feedback from the tests it conducts. The direction of the search is determined by the outcomes of the series of tests that are made. In this manner the search is limited to a relatively small part of the problem space, but one that is likely to yield a solution if the executive routine is well conceived.

The operation of the executive routine is sometimes compared to consciousness or working memory. Demanding tasks, such as deciding what steps to take next in a problem, appear in consciousness. In contrast, routine tasks place little demand on working memory and are comparable to subroutines. Highly practiced subroutines become automatic and may require no conscious control at all, as we shall see in Chapter 11 on motor skills.

A programmer will often use a *flowchart* to outline the sequence of tests and operations in an executive routine. Since most simulation programs are quite complex, the flowchart guides the programmer in writing the instructions for the program. Such a "road map" as the flowchart is also a convenient way of describing what the program does for people who do not know the program language.

Consider a flowchart for the game of nim. Two players, A and B, spread seven matches between them. Each player in turn may take away either one or two matches. The objective is to leave the opponent with the last match to take away. Figure 9.17 is a tree for the game of nim. Player A makes the first move at *Begin* by taking

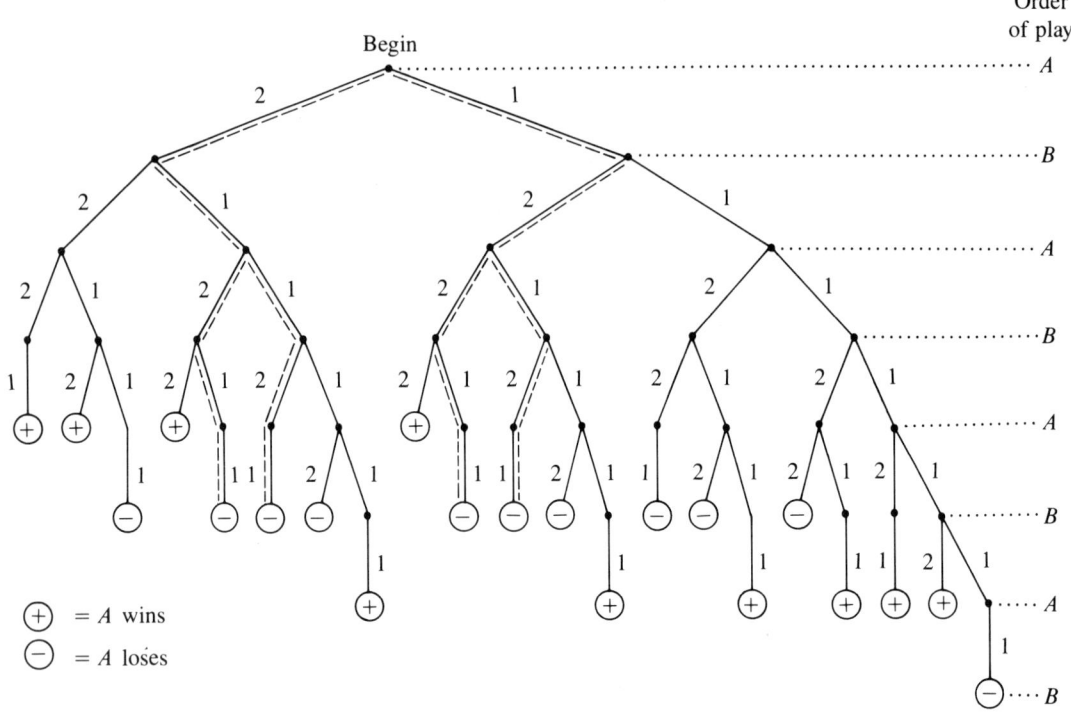

Figure 9.17 Tree diagram for nim for seven matches and two players, A and B. (After Trakhentenbrot, 1963.)

either one match (the right branch) or two matches (the left branch). At each node thereafter the player indicated in the right-hand column must also choose one or two matches. The tree represents all possible combinations of moves in the game.

There is a strategy for playing nim that guarantees that B will always win if A goes first. It has two rules: (1) if A takes two matches, B should take one; (2) if A takes one match, B should take two. The dashed-line paths show all the possible game sequences under this strategy which end in a win for B. Note that this strategy prunes the tree substantially, even trimming some branches that lead to a win for B. However, the strategy guarantees a win for B. Nim may also be played under other conditions—for example, with nine matches and each player taking either one, two, or three matches in a turn. You might try figuring out the strategy for this variation of the game.

Since the strategy for winning at nim is well defined, we could write a program that would play nim using this strategy. A flowchart for such a program is shown in Figure 9.18, and it contains two kinds of entries: tests (shown in circles) for determining what state the game is in, and operations (shown in rectangles). Since each outcome of a test has an operation tied to it, the feedback from a test determines the next operation. All the paths permitted by the strategy (the dashed-line paths in Figure 9.17) are captured in this flowchart.

In short, the control processes in a problem are contained in an executive routine, a series of tests and consequent operations, which directs

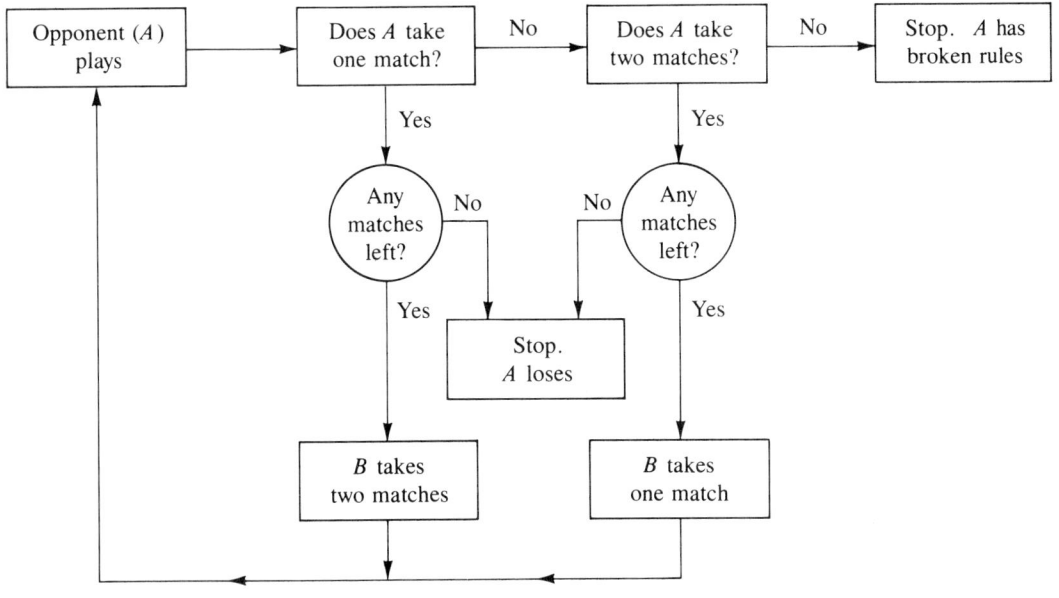

Figure 9.18 Flowchart of strategy for winning at nim.

the search through the problem space. A flowchart of an executive routine shows the overall plan of the executive routine in an easily understood form.

Simulation Programs

The general principles of simulation described above have been applied in a rapidly growing body of programs simulating human problem solving. For a good overview of these programs, see Winston (1977). Though the early efforts focused on basic processes in problem solving, more recent efforts have begun to show the involvement of related cognitive processes. In the following section we describe examples of four kinds of simulation programs: (1) programs limited to basic problem-solving processes, (2) programs that represent the use of memory in solving problems, (3) programs that relate linguistic comprehension to setting up a problem space, and (4) programs for inducing rules.

Problem-solving Programs. There are several types of basic problem-solving programs. These include general programs that can be adapted to a variety of problems and more specialized programs dealing with topics such as checkers and chess.

GPS. One of the best known programs is the GENERAL PROBLEM SOLVER (GPS) (Newell & Simon, 1961; Simon & Newell, 1962). This is a general-purpose program that can be tailored to many different kinds of problems. GPS begins by setting up an internal representation of the given state and the goal state. Its task environment consists of a set of *objects* and *operators* that vary with the kind of problem to be solved. Problem solving proceeds by means-ends analysis, the heuristic we described earlier.

In general, the heuristic discovers differences between a current state and a desired state and tries to reduce the differences by applying one or more operators. There may be several differences between a current state and a desired state, and reducing each one may become a subgoal. An operator may not reduce a difference completely; a new subgoal is then set up to reduce the difference further. In this manner the heuristic recursively generates a hierarchy of subgoals until it reaches a subgoal it can solve. The solution to this one may permit solving the subgoal next above, which in turn may help solve the subgoal above it, and so on.

For each kind of problem that GPS attempts (proving theorems, playing chess, etc.), one must specify the kinds of operators which can be used. An operator is also called a *production,* as discussed in our description of ACT in Chapter 4. A production has two parts, a *condition* and an *action,* written as

$$C \to A$$

The condition (C) is a test to be made on some knowledge state (e.g., in chess, "Test if it is black's move"). If the test is satisfied, the action (A) is executed; if not, control passes to another production. An action may be a motor act, an act of retrieving information from permanent memory, or an act of changing something stored in temporary memory.

Productions operate serially—only one at a time, a practice that Newell and Simon have found is common to human problem solving. A set of productions may be organized into a *production system* whose function is to work on a particular type of problem or part of a problem.

An executive routine governs GPS operations by determining which differences to pursue, which productions to apply and in what order, and how long to pursue the deepening of a subgoal hierarchy. For example, if the subgoals are becoming more distant from the goal state, then the executive abandons that hierarchy and sets up a new subgoal. Similarly, the executive will halt the deepening of subgoals once the list exceeds a certain length, an effect somewhat similar to overtaxing working memory.

GPS can solve a variety of problems, including the hobbits and orcs problem, water jar problems (see page 238), and calculus problems. An example will make its operation clearer.

In the hobbits and orcs problem (also called the missionaries and cannibals problem), three hobbits and three orcs come to a river, which they want to cross. A boat is available, but it will hold no more than two creatures at a time. How shall they get across? The problem is further complicated by the disposition of the orcs. If at any time there are more orcs than hobbits on one side of the river, the orcs will fall upon the hobbits and devour them. You might see if you can solve the problem before reading on.

This was one of the first problems GPS solved (Ernst & Newell, 1969). To simplify the description of its solution, we will use a reduced version of the problem adapted from Rumelhart (1977a) in which there are only two hobbits and two orcs. GPS is a general purpose program, so we must specify several things for it before it can start:

The given state: Two hobbits, two orcs, and the boat, all on the left side of the river.

The goal state: Two hobbits, two orcs, and the boat, all on the right side of the river.

Operators: MOVE is the only operator. It transports either one or two creatures at a time across the river in the boat; it cannot cross the river empty. MOVE can be applied only if the boat is on the side of the river from which creatures are to be transported and if the orcs do not outnumber the hobbits on either side of the river.

States: A state is a description of the number of hobbits and orcs on each side of the river and where the boat is at any stage of the problem. Applying MOVE to any state, including the given state, produces a new state.

Figure 9.19 shows the states GPS goes through in solving this problem. The given state

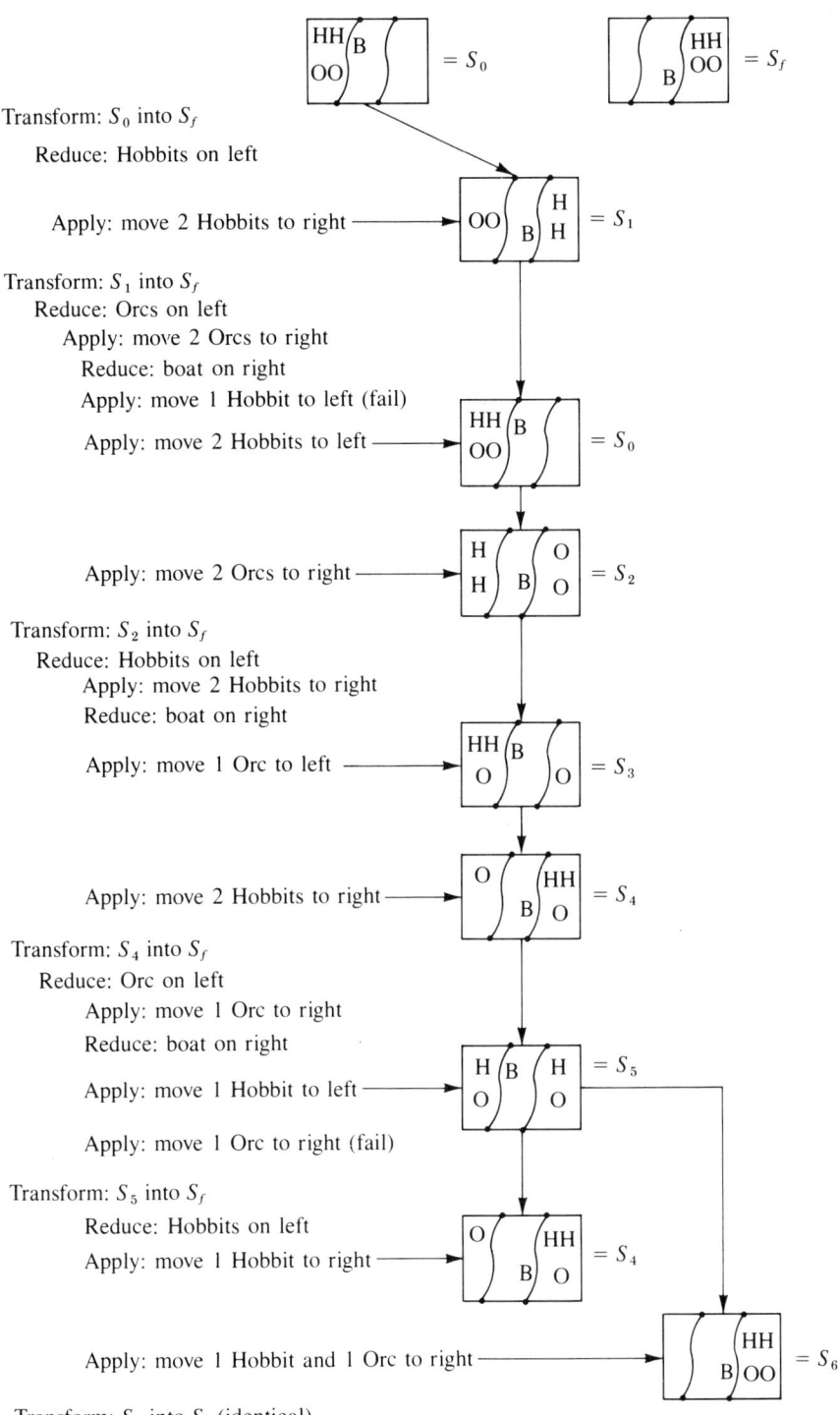

Figure 9.19 Sequence of subgoals involved in the solution of the hobbits and orcs problem. H stands for hobbits, O for orcs, and B for boat. (From Rumelhart, 1977a.)

is labeled S_0 and the goal state is labeled S_f. GPS begins by trying to transform S_0 into S_f, a method of first detecting a difference between the two and then trying to reduce the difference. This is the method for setting up subproblems, and it is used repeatedly in solving the main problem.

The first time GPS uses this method, it decides there are too many hobbits on the left bank. It tries to reduce this difference by applying MOVE to carry two hobbits to the right bank. This produces State S_1. Next it decides there are too many orcs on the left bank and tries to reduce this number. But MOVE cannot be used since the boat is still on the right bank. It attempts to solve this subproblem by moving one hobbit in the boat back to the left bank. This attempt fails, since that would leave two orcs and only one hobbit on the left bank. Thus it moves two hobbits in the boat back to the left bank.

Unhappily, GPS is now back where it started, in S_0. It now moves two orcs to the right bank, producing S_2. Detecting too many hobbits on the left, it tries to move them to the right but first must retrieve the boat, which it does with one orc aboard. GPS continues in this fashion until it gets to S_5, where it makes a false move that leads it back to S_4. It remembers that it has been in this state before and so backs up to S_5, where it makes the move that carries it to S_f, the goal state. GPS takes 27 steps to solve this version of the problem. In the original version of the problem (three hobbits and three orcs) it took 54 steps, exactly twice as many as in this reduced version.

Research on human solutions to the hobbits and orcs problem has been reported by Thomas (1974) and Greeno (1974). These authors suggest that subjects divide the problem into three subproblems. Thomas, for example, measured the mean times subjects took to make each move and the number of errors at each state. These peaked at two different states in the problem, and Thomas inferred that these states marked the beginning of work on new subgoals. The times and error rates tended to drop off as the subjects reached each of these subgoals. These results are evident in the two graphs in Figure 9.20.

Greeno (1974) reached a similar conclusion by giving subjects part of the problem to solve and then transferring them to the whole problem. The significance of these studies is that they suggest that subjects tend to look ahead and break the problem into subgoals as a means-ends analysis would do.

Jeffries, Polson, Razran, and Atwood (1977) give a different interpretation of this problem in a program that solves both river-crossing problems and water jar problems. Their program incorporates a means-ends heuristic as well as a memory component that keeps track of the states a subject has visited. Together these components determine the next state a subject will enter at any stage of solving the problem. Jeffries et al. argued that memory limitations preclude the multistate look ahead used by other programs (which have no memory component) and limit the subject to looking ahead to only one state. By showing the influence of memory on problem solving, they thus constrain hypotheses about how problem solving occurs.

CHECKERS. One of the exciting early programs was Samuel's (1959) program for playing checkers. The most interesting aspect of this program is that it learns from its game-playing experience. The problem space for checkers is so immense that it is not possible to search it exhaustively for a winning game path. Samuel uses a set of heuristics that focus on such subgoals as preserving more pieces than your opponent, advancing your men (especially to kings), and maintaining mobility for pieces.

At each move the program looks ahead at possible moves for each piece and possible countermoves by its opponent, generating a tree of possible moves which is several moves deep. An evaluator determines the relative gain for each move, based on weights assigned to each subgoal. The move with the greatest relative gain is then made.

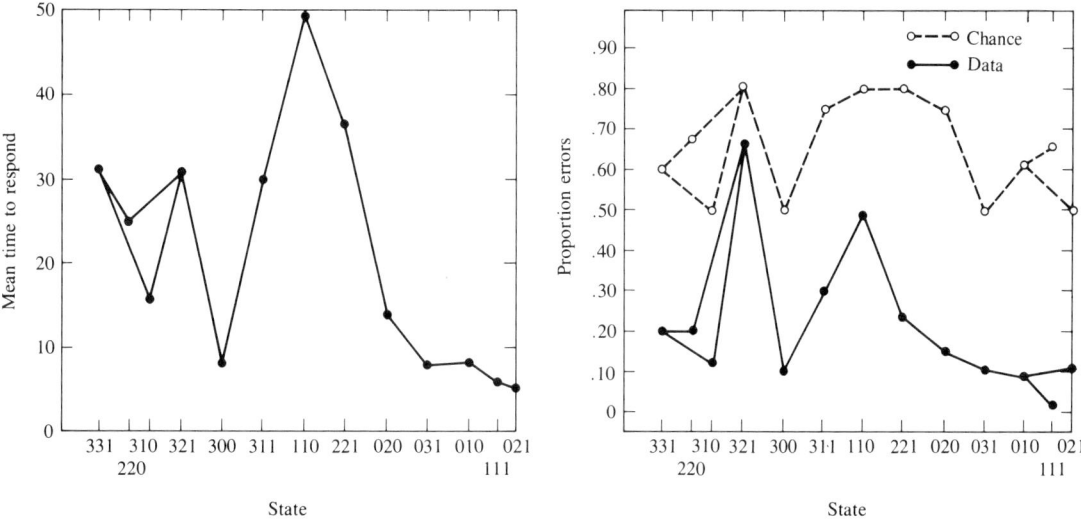

Figure 9.20 Steps in solving the hobbits and orcs problem. The numbers on the abscissa refer to different states in the problem solution. (From Thomas, 1974.)

The learning component is somewhat complex. Basically, it is a way of evaluating a set of possible tactics for the game. Winning a game increases the weights for the tactics used in that game, while losing a game decreases the weights for that game's tactics. Thus effective tactics come to dominance with experience. In 1962 the program beat a checkers champion of national rank, who later commented, "The machine . . . played a perfect ending without one misstep. In the matter of the end game, I have not had such competition from any human being since 1954, when I lost my last game" (Samuel, 1963, p. 104).

CHESS. Chess is a complex game, which never seems to lose its interest. Professional players typically take 10 years or more to master its intricacies. Simulating chess is accordingly difficult, and early efforts concentrated on programs that generated acceptable moves rather than on ones that played complete games (e.g., Bernstein, 1958; Newell, Shaw, & Simon, 1958a). These programs show a common structure. They use forward search, unlike the backward search of theorem-proving programs. The search is conducted by a move generator that creates a tree of possible moves. The tree becomes large very quickly; but the program, like humans, tends to explore one move in depth rather than exploring the branches of the tree. Such a strategy reflects the limitations of working memory.

The selection of a move from the tree is based on a principle of *minimaxing*—that is, minimizing the chances of loss by a move and maximizing the chances of a gain. This principle assumes that the opponent will usually make the best possible move, and so one must select a move that gives the opponent the least chance for advantage. The evaluation of possible moves is based on a set of goals, such as controlling the center of the board, preserving material balance, and developing pieces. An analysis procedure assigns values to each potential move, and these are evaluated against the goals to select a move.

These programs show interesting similarities to human protocols as well as to games reported in chess books. They tend to consider only a limited number of moves, usually ones supported by chess analysts. They also follow a course of progressive deepening—a process of going up the same branch several times, extending the search deeper and exploring side branches on each trip. After each exploration, the player returns to the base position rather than backing up part way to explore branches of the tree. This practice is assumed to reduce the burden on working memory.

The construction of these programs was derived from studies of the psychological processes that are involved in good chess playing. There have been a number of such attempts to understand what makes a chess player good. These have focused on both memory and perceptual processes. The results of the memory work, which we reviewed in Chapter 3, suggest that a key to the good chess player's performance is linked to his ability to store large amounts of chess information in permanent memory. This information is organized into chunks that represent clusters of chess pieces. This chunking process not only provides a better organization of the player's chess knowledge, but also enables him to use his information more effectively in working memory.

In addition, this chunking process seems to play an important role in the perception of a chess board. For example, Chase and Simon (1973a, b; Simon & Chase, 1973) asked chess players to reconstruct the positions of an unfinished chess game. The game was placed before them and they were asked to place pieces in the same positions on an empty board alongside it. Chase and Simon found that a glance of about 2 sec was used to perceive a chunk and store it in working memory. These pieces were then placed on the empty board without glancing back at the game board. The members of a chunk were "local clusters of pieces in arrangements that recur with high frequency in actual chess positions" (1973a, p. 400). Glances of more than 2 sec tended to code pieces that were not chunks for the player, but instead had been distributed in more or less random arrangements.

The chunking process observed in the perceptual and memory tasks is the foundation of a program simulating how chess players reconstruct the pattern of pieces on a chess board (Simon & Gilmartin, 1973). This program is called MAPP and incorporates two other programs, PERCEIVER and EPAM. EPAM learns what the familiar patterns of pieces are and stores them in a permanent memory network. In the reconstruction task, PERCEIVER scans an unfinished game for major pieces, such as queen or castle, and then checks the memory network to see which of these pieces belong to stored patterns. If a pattern is found, PERCEIVER checks whether the other pieces in the stored patterns match what is on the board. If so, this pattern is stored in working memory, and the search continues.

Reconstruction involves retrieving the patterns stored in working memory. MAPP's success approximates that of an excellent chess player. Thus the Chase and Simon (1973) and Simon and Gilmartin (1973) studies both suggest that the nature of the patterns (chunks) stored in permanent memory plays an important role in the quality of a chess player's game.

Programs Involving Memory. Early problem-solving programs focused on problems that required little use of memory, such as cryptarithmetic and theorem-proving in logic. More recent efforts have tried to capture the interplay between memory and problem solving to show how memory is a resource for problem solving as well as a limitation on it. Heuristics, for example, may draw upon permanent memory in constructing subgoals for a problem. This was demonstrated in a study by Bhaskar and Simon (1977);

> **Box 9.4 TURING'S TEST**
>
> In writing computer programs to simulate human behavior such as playing chess, one is faced with the question of when the simulation is good enough for the program to be an adequate theory of that behavior. This is often called the "goodness of fit" question. Turing (1950) proposed a now famous solution, which is usually called Turing's Test. Put two teletypewriters in a room with a person to act as a judge. One teletypewriter is hooked to a computer having a simulation program. The other goes to a second room where a man sits, typing out his answers. The judge must decide which teletypewriter goes to the man and which to the computer. She types questions to both until she gets enough answers to decide. Turing reasoned that the computer simulation would be effective if the judge (or a set of judges) could not tell which teletypewriter led to the computer.
>
> While Turing's Test is thoroughly behavioral and intuitively plausible, it still has been criticized as a test of the adequacy of simulation programs. Feldman (1962), for example, claims that the procedure lacks rigor; while Colby and Hilf (1974) argue that the test is too global and fails to show specifically where a simulation may be weak. Thus the question of what will serve as a definitive test of goodness of fit is a continuing one for psychologists interested in the computer simulation of behavior.

they studied a chemical engineering student who was solving problems in thermodynamics.

Using an extensive protocol analysis, these authors found that the student used a means-ends heuristic to reduce the problems to equations having one unknown and then to solve for the unknown. It was evident from the protocols that the equations and the knowledge of how to apply them were in permanent memory. Bhaskar and Simon thus showed that a problem-solving program must incorporate not only heuristics for solving a problem but also a representation of the knowledge base relevant for solving that problem.

It is evident that memory plays a key role in our attempts to simulate human problem-solving behavior. There are several facets of memory which simulation programs must deal with; two important ones are the retrieval of information from permanent memory and dealing with the limitations of working memory.

RETRIEVING FROM PERMANENT MEMORY. The knowledge we have in permanent memory can be represented as a set of propositions (see pages 91–95) that are stored in semantic memory as a set of nodes and links that represent relations among the nodes. Greeno (1976) discussed the use of such knowledge in solving problems in plane geometry. Consider the problem shown in Figure 9.21. Given that $P = 30°$, find Q. One subject solved the problem in the way shown in Figure 9.22. "Angle A and angle P are congruent, because they are corresponding angles, so $A = 30°$. Angles A and B are congruent for the same reason, so $B = 30°$. Angles B and Q are

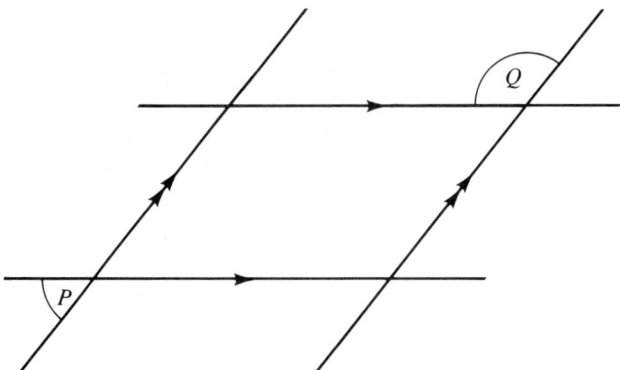

Figure 9.21 Diagram for a problem in angles and parallel lines. (From Greeno, 1976.)

supplementary because together they form a straight angle; thus, angle Q is shown to have measure $Q = 180° - 30° = 150°$" (p. 136). Knowledge about congruent angles, corresponding angles, supplementary angles, and so forth, is stored as a set of propositions. How is this knowledge to be used in solving the problem?

Greeno uses a production system to search among the propositions in semantic memory for information that will help solve the problem. The condition for a production is defined by a set of features that can be matched against concepts in the propositions. Since propositions in semantic memory are related, a match to a concept permits inferences to related propositions that may help solve the problem (e.g., that $A = 30°$). Testing a related proposition becomes a subgoal, and a separate production system searches within the available information to see whether that subgoal can be met. If so, it is added to the available

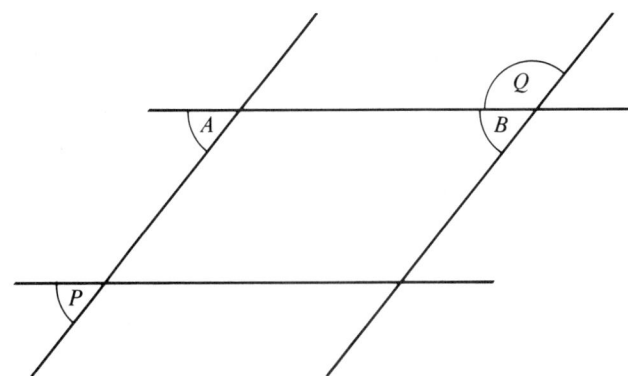

Figure 9.22 Solving for Q by finding the values of A and B. (From Greeno, 1976.)

information and may contribute to the solving of the main problem. If not, other related propositions may become subgoals.

The key to the system proposed by Greeno lies in the features for defining the productions. Since they are the same features used to define concepts in the semantic network, they provide the link between permanent memory and other production systems for working on the problem. Hunt and Poltrock (1974) offer a similar (and very readable) analysis, treating permanent memory as a system of propositions to be operated upon by production systems to solve problems.

Studies such as these demonstrate how retrieving from permanent memory can be incorporated into simulation models of problem solving. Similar efforts are under way in attempting to incorporate the concept of working memory into simulations of problem solving.

WORKING MEMORY. The small capacity of working memory imposes a heavy constraint on

---

Box 9.5 RECONSTRUCTIVE MEMORY

We can sometimes gain insight into a phenomenon by viewing it from a different perspective. This seems to be the case for the concept of reconstructive memory, which we discussed in Chapters 5 and 7. As we noted there, retrieving information from permanent memory is sometimes difficult, neither automatic nor guaranteed of success. In such cases it can be thought of as a form of problem solving, a search for the right information. Lindsay and Norman (1977, p. 372) give an example:

What were you doing on Monday afternoon in the third week of September two years ago?

(Try answering this before you read on.)
A typical answer, constructed from various people's answers to this question, might go like this:

1. **Come on. How should I know? (Experimenter: Just try it, anyhow.)**
2. **OK. Let's see: Two years ago....**
3. **I would be in high school in Pittsburgh....**
4. **That would be my senior year.**
5. **Third week in September—that's just after summer—that would be the fall term....**
6. **Let me see. I think I had chemistry lab on Mondays.**
7. **I don't know. I was probably in the chemistry lab....**
8. **Wait a minute—that would be the second week of school. I remember he started off with the atomic table—a big, fancy**

> chart. I thought he was crazy, trying to make us memorize that thing.
> 9. You know, I think I can remember sitting. . . .
>
> The subject's initial resistance makes it clear that he cannot retrieve the answer the way he would toss off the name of a good friend. Instead, he begins a process of reconstruction, breaking the retrieval problem into a set of subgoals and working on these in turn. In line 2 he starts with the problem of what he was doing two years ago. Having answered that, he moves to a more specific subproblem (line 5) which he works on in lines 6 and 7. He reaches a momentary dead end in line 7, when some unreported search seems to open up new routes and sends him on his way.
>
> Reconstructive memory is a constructive search. When the exact answer cannot be retrieved, we set up subproblems, whose solution (if they can be solved) may lead us closer to the answer. The solution to some subproblems leads to new subproblems; for example, *solution:* "I think I had a chemistry lab on Mondays"; new *subproblem:* "What would I have been doing there?"; *solution:* "Working on the periodic table of elements." The cycle continues to solution. The final answer, however, is not a simple recall but a mixture of construction and remembered experiences.

problem solving. Working memory must contain what the current plan of attack is (the heuristic), where one is in the problem space, and what has been learned in exploring the space. This burden usually limits the exercise of a heuristic, even though in principle the heuristic may be very powerful. Players of checkers and chess limit their search to a small part of the problem space and even then will often retrace some of the paths several times. Such rehearsal preserves the paths and the newly generated knowledge in working memory.

The interplay between working and permanent memory (as well as perception and attention) is displayed in a game study and simulation by Eisenstadt and Kareev (1975). The ancient games of go and gomoku are both played with black and white stones on a 19 × 19 grid, but the games follow different rules. Players of the games seem to learn patterns of pieces that lead to capture or defense, though the patterns are different for the two games.

Evidence of such specific learning was shown by presenting players with various unfinished games and telling them that these were either from go or from gomoku. When the players later reconstructed the board positions, the reconstructions differed significantly according to whether the player thought the game was go or gomoku. The players' knowledge of patterns for each game had structured their perceptual organization and subsequent reconstruction of the pieces on the board.

Memory for these patterns was also the basis for two strategies (heuristics) that Eisenstadt and Kareev discovered were used in both games. In the *top-down* strategy a player would search the board for patterns that matched those in memory, especially those leading to a win. The search is a matter of directing attention to various squares in the grid to discover what pieces might be in them. Eisenstadt and Kareev were able to observe what pattern was guiding the search by an ingenious method that permitted the player to attend to only one square at a time. A player's choice of squares indicated the pattern he or she was searching for. The authors call this strategy an "Are you there?" strategy, since a pattern in memory directs the search of the board.

The *bottom-up* strategy is guided by the presence of various pieces on the board. The presence of various subpatterns suggests the possibility of full patterns stored in memory, which are then searched for by the top-down strategy. These two strategies thus combine efficiently to limit the search through the problem space.

Eisenstadt and Kareev constructed a program to simulate the psychological processes they observed in players of go and gomoku. This program has an executive that organizes the use of these two strategies, a permanent memory for storing familiar patterns, and (of particular interest here) a working memory that stores information from the scanning activities as well as information about which patterns are to be searched next. The limited storage capacity of working memory is simulated by the decay of information in working memory. Attention is simulated by limiting the number of spaces that can be searched at any time, so that the choice of spaces is guided by a strategy. Thus the model shows how strategies are used within the constraints of attention, perception, and memory.

Eisenstadt and Kareev's simulation program was successful in reproducing many of the performance patterns found in players of go and gomoku. Of particular interest was how the program simulated the relationship between working memory and the use of strategies. In the course of a game, both players and the simulation program look to see what the next move should be. The look ahead generally follows a progressive deepening, a retracing of a potential path that shows only limited branching or backup. This effect was earlier noted by de Groot (1965) and Newell and Simon (1972) in chess. It is produced by working memory, which can store only a small number of possible moves and is overtaxed by exploring multiple branches or backing up.

In summary, memory is intimately related to problem solving. Semantic memory contains knowledge that may help solve the problem, as we saw in the gestalt notion of preparation. IP theory formalizes access to semantic memory through production systems, which retrieve propositions from semantic memory. In addition, any retrieved information must compete for the limited space in working memory with other information that is being used to work on the problem.

Programs for Comprehension. The first step in solving a problem is to understand what the problem is. This means constructing a problem space and often involves getting instructions on what is given and what the solution must look like. Several programs have been written that attempt to integrate this comprehension stage with the problem-solving stage, such as Bobrow's STUDENT (1968) and Moore and Newell's MERLIN (1974).

Simon and Hayes (Hayes & Simon, 1974; Simon & Hayes, 1976a, b) have developed a program called UNDERSTAND, which comprehends instructions and sets up a problem space to be used by GPS. Human subjects tend to start work on a problem as soon as they have constructed enough of the problem space to do anything. When they hit a snag, they return to the instructions for further clarification. The alternation between comprehension and solving is shown in Figure 9.23, which is a flowchart for UNDERSTAND and its relation to GPS.

UNDERSTAND has two parts, a language part for interpreting the plain language instructions, and a construction part for creating the problem space. The language part first analyzes the syntax of the instructions, breaking them down into such units as noun phrases, verb phrases, and prepositional phrases, and then further into nouns, verbs, adjectives, and so on. The analysis extracts the deep structure of a sentence and represents this in a case grammar. Semantic analysis then identifies important relations among the objects in the problem.

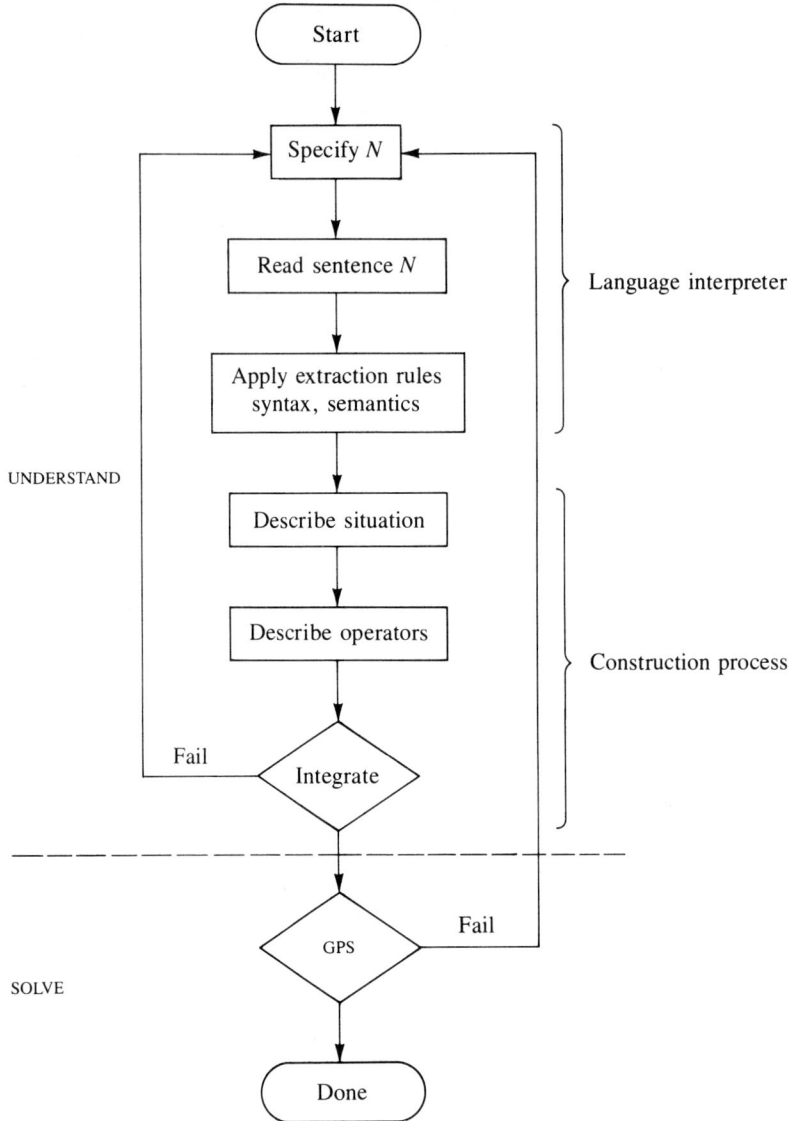

Figure 9.23 Flowchart for UNDERSTAND and its relation to GPS. (From Hayes & Simon, 1974.)

The output of the language part is the input for the construction part, which builds the problem space. The problem space contains a situation and a set of operators, which must be in a form usable by GPS. The situation is composed of the objects in the problem (e.g., missionaries, cannibals, a river, and a boat—and the relations among them, such as the threat from the cannibals and the capacity of the boat). The set of operators is a production system for making various changes in the states of the situation, such as moving two missionaries across the river in the boat. Once the problem space is built, it is turned over to GPS, which then attempts the problem.

The significance of UNDERSTAND and like programs is that they link comprehension to problem solving in a holistic manner and reflect the influence of one upon the other. Although these attempts are still in a developmental stage, they have implications for education (Klahr, 1976) as well as for a better understanding of the cognitive processes.

Programs for Rule Induction. You have perhaps guessed by now that concept identification, as described in Chapter 8, is a problem-solving task. This observation applies more broadly to a class of tasks called *rule-induction tasks*. These can be covered in a common theoretical framework that interprets them as problem-solving tasks.

CONCEPT IDENTIFICATION AND PROBLEM SOLVING. The given state in a concept-identification task is a set of instances having differing attributes and values. The goal state is a concept defined by a rule joining the relevant attributes. As Miller, Galanter, and Pribram (1960) have observed, the attainment of the concept is a search through the problem space of possible concepts. Different rules can join attributes in many different ways to produce many possible concepts (see pages 212–217). Since a concept is composed of a set of attributes and a rule joining them, both attributes and rules are the objects of the search through the problem space. This interpretation is straightforward when concepts are defined as a set of attributes joined by a rule, though it is unclear whether it applies when concepts are defined as having internal structure (see pages 224–226).

A concept can often be discovered by the use of a strategy (see pages 221–224), such as the conservative-focusing strategy for conjunctive concepts. Such strategies are essentially heuristics for solving the problem of finding the concept. A relatively simple one is the generate-and-test heuristic, which generates hypotheses about the concept at random and tests them on appropriate instances. When a test is negative, the hypothesis is discarded and a new hypothesis generated.

A more efficient approach is the conservative-focusing strategy, which requires only as many tests as there are attributes. The latter is an example of an algorithm, which guarantees a solution, and is generally of less interest in research on problem solving, since it can be applied routinely and without the more constructive search that usually characterizes problem solving. In most cases of concept identification, however, the subject either has no strategy or is discovering one, so his thinking is a form of problem solving.

SERIES COMPLETION. An additional type of rule-induction task will perhaps bring home the parallel between rule learning and problem solving. This is the *series-completion task*. In IQ tests one is often given a series of letters and asked to discover the pattern and continue the string—for example, *atbataatbat___*. Such a string is a sequential concept; the letters serve as attributes and are related by a rule. Simon and Newell (1974) observe that the search for the relevant attributes and rule is a problem-solving task. Discovering the concept permits you to extend the string correctly and indefinitely, just as you can identify new positive instances of a concept you have learned.

Simon and Kotovsky (1963) have written a program simulating the discovery of such rules. It assumes one knows the alphabet forward and backward, has the two relations *equal* and *next*, and has the concept *cycle*. For the string *atbataatbat___* the rule is represented as [a, t, (b, a)], which specifies that the series is composed of a cycle of three letters, the initial one being a, the second one t, and (a, b) alternating in the third position. The program discovers the relevant letters, what the cycle is, and what relations *(equal, next)* to apply to which letters. The program then translates this rule into a set of instructions for continuing the sequence.

Kotovsky and Simon (1973) report that the program accords well with human efforts at discovering such rules, especially in terms of the difficulty of the rules. A string such as *wxaxybyzczadab___* puts special strain on working memory, since the alphabet is advancing in two separate places in the cycle.

A second program for solving series completions has been written by Hunt and Poltrock (1974). It employs an executive routine that controls subroutines for discovering the cycle and the relations among letters. The subroutines are production systems—that is, sets of operators which are applied to the letters to test various hypotheses about the length of the cycle and the relations among the letters.

Hunt and Poltrock report that their program compares favorably with the performance of human subjects in that it takes longer for more difficult series and it fails to solve some of the same ones humans fail to solve. This program is of special interest because of its use of production systems, which Hunt and Poltrock argue are general enough to model almost any cognitive process.

GRI. The similarities between concept learning and series-completion tasks have been noted by Egan and Greeno (1974), who classify them both as rule-induction tasks. In both tasks a person must discover a rule that relates certain objects (attributes or letters), and the discovery proceeds by induction—that is, by observing one or more examples in which the rule is used.

Simon and Lea (1974) have written a program, the GENERAL RULE INDUCER (GRI), which simulates both concept-learning and series-completion tasks. GRI has two basic processes, one for generating rules and one for generating the test instances. In concept learning, the process for generating and testing instances simulates the subject's selection of instances and the feedback the subject gets about whether or not they are instances of the concept.

In some concept tasks the experimenter selects the order of instances, so that the experimenter rather than the subject becomes the instance generator. This is also the case in series completion. The experimenter gives the instances (the letters) which the subject is to extrapolate (e.g., *abmcdmefm___*). However, the subject may select which instances are to be tested. For example, the subject may note that *m* is the third letter in the string and test the hypothesis that it is always the third letter in a cycle of three letters.

The test results for instances are fed to the rule generator to guide the type of rule to be generated and tested. The rules for concept learning are hypotheses about what the concept is. For series completion they are relations *(same, next)* among the letters.

GRI is distinct from problem solving in that it has two problem spaces, one for rules and one for instances. The search through these spaces proceeds in much the same manner as in problem solving, though the results from one search may feed back to the other search to make it more selective.

GRI is like GPS in many respects. Not only does it construct a problem space and conduct a search through it, but it also must be tailored to the particular kind of problem being solved. This includes a description of the objects (instances of the concepts or letters in the series) and the ways they may be operated upon in the search process. The significance of GRI lies in its ability to solve both series-completion tasks and a wide range of concept-learning tasks by the same procedures. It thus compares to GPS in its generality for interpreting rule induction.

In summary, our review of computer simulation activities indicates the major role that simulation currently plays in scientific efforts to understand problem solving. These efforts extend over a wide range of problem tasks, including games, mathematics, puzzles, and rules. Recent programs have attempted to incorporate related cognitive processes such as permanent memory, working memory, and comprehension.

Ill-defined Problems

Most of the problems we have considered thus far are said to be well-defined; that is, they have a clear structure that guides the attack on the problem. Problems in logic and plane geometry state exactly what is to be proved and provide explicit rules for going about it. Checkers and chess have simple rules for moving the pieces and a simple way of telling when the game is over.

In contrast, ill-defined problems seem to have vague specifications that give little direction to the problem. Hayes (1978) gives an example of an architect who is asked to design a shop. He is told where the shop is to be, that it will sell contemporary furniture, the limits on cost, and a few other details. The design of the shop, however, is left largely to the architect, who faces many decisions about space, function, facade, materials, and so forth. Hayes gives an excellent account of how a particular architect went about solving this problem.

Ill-defined problems are our daily fare, whether we are looking for a job, shopping for a car, or trying to patch up a relationship with a friend. Consider the case of writing a term paper. The given state is a topic, a generally large body of literature on that topic, and our own as yet undigested ideas about it. The solution state merely requires that the paper have a beginning, a middle, and an end, that it be of some length and depth, and that it be an "intelligent" treatment of the topic. How can problem-solving principles be generalized to such ill-defined tasks?

Reitman (1965) suggests that solving ill-defined problems involves closing the open definition of the problem by generating additional structures that bring the problem closer to being a well-defined one. He reports the experience of a composer writing a fugue, a task with few constraints. As the composer worked, he rejected certain possible forms for the fugue and explored others, thus limiting the definition of the final form.

Similarly, to write a term paper we first select a topic, say ecology. This closes the definition of the problem considerably. Our reading on ecology then discloses several subtopics on ecology which are important to the topic, such as

1. Interdependence of humans and environment
2. Sources of human pollution
   a. Air pollution
   b. Water pollution
   c. Solid waste pollution
3. Influence of pollution on environment

Subtopics further define the problem, and each of these can be broken down still more. What we have done is to *construct* the problem so that it is now amenable to our usual problem-solving procedures.

The subtopics for the paper are a set of subproblems that we solve one at a time. Solving subproblems may require setting up a hierarchy of additional subproblems. For water pollution we may list pollution of lakes, rivers, and oceans, and under these set goals for describing the forms and extent of pollution. Solving each subproblem adds to the solution of the subproblem above it, and so we are led to the solution of our original goal of writing a term paper.

Simon (1973) argues that this approach is used for both well-defined and ill-defined problems, and that the difference between the two is more apparent than real. In chess, for example, there are hundreds of paths that lead to winning. The player decomposes the goal into a set of manageable subproblems that limit his search, such as protecting his king and gaining control of the center of the board. An ill-defined problem thus becomes a well-defined problem by such structuring.

Well-defined problems then are simply ill-defined problems that have been formalized by analyzing them into a hierarchy of clearly stated subproblems that are easier to attack. This kind of information-processing analysis has been applied to problems as various as designing a shop (Hayes, 1978), writing a fugue (Reitman, 1965), and building a warship (Simon, 1973). IP methods for solving problems are still being developed, but the extension of these methods to such vague problems as these encourages us to think that they may be general to all kinds of human problems.

CONCLUSION

Gestalt psychologists had a remarkable flair for capturing the intuitive aspects of problem solving and, in particular, for showing how we use the pieces of a problem to structure a solution for it. One of the aims of IP theory has been to formalize the sometimes vague gestalt ideas so that they are more testable. IP theory thus depicts problem solving as a search through a problem space, a selective search directed by a set of heuristics. Simulating this search with a computer program is one way of theorizing about how humans solve problems—one that lets us analyze processes of a rather challenging complexity. Although these programs are incomplete in many ways, the attempts to write them may clarify our thinking about the processes we use for solving problems.

10 Deductive Reasoning

Linear Series Problems
    Image Theory
    Linguistic Theories
    An Integrated Model
    Related Models
Propositional Reasoning
    Formal and Natural Reasoning
        Formal Reasoning
        Natural Reasoning
    Models of Reasoning
        Formal Logic
        A Natural Logic
Reasoning with Syllogisms
    The Logic of Syllogisms
    The Psychology of Syllogisms
        The Set Analysis Theory
        The Analogical Theory
Conclusion

Pam is older than Jill
Jill is older than Kate
Is Pam older than Kate?

Max is not as young as Gene
Mark is not as young as Max
Is Mark older than Gene?

These are linear series problems (the answer is *Yes* in both cases). You probably found the first one easier than the second one. Now try these two problems:

1. All A are B
   All B are C
   Therefore:
   a. All A are C
   b. All A are not C
   c. Some A are C
   d. Some A are not C
   e. None of these conclusions is valid
2. All B are A
   No C are B
   Therefore:
   a. All A are C
   b. All A are not C
   c. Some A are C
   d. Some A are not C
   e. None of these conclusions is valid

These problems are syllogisms, familiar fare in any introductory logic course. Once again you probably found the first one (answer: a) easier than the second one (answer: d). Why is this? In this chapter we shall explore the cognitive processes involved in *deductive reasoning*—the act of deducing a conclusion from a given set of premises. This is the process that underlies proving theorems in mathematics as well as the more familiar verbal inferences described above.

Deductive reasoning stands in contrast to two other forms of reasoning—abduction and induction. *Abduction* is the process of generating an hypothesis to explain some observation (Peirce, 1901/1957). *Induction* is the testing of an hypothesis by making new observations that are suggested by the hypothesis. Both abduction and induction are illustrated at length in Chapters 8 and 9; we introduce them here only to clarify the nature of deductive reasoning.

In deductive reasoning a set of premises and rules is given, and the reasoner uses this information to derive a conclusion that can be proved correct. In abduction, however, one proceeds from one or more specific observations to a general hypothesis that would account for these and many other observations. It is a process of generalizing and, as such, it does not lead to a provable conclusion—that is, there are no rules that assure a correct hypothesis. Similarly, an inductive conclusion is not provable. It is always possible that further observations would alter that conclusion. Thus only deductive reasoning permits a provable conclusion since only deductive reasoning involves rules for testing whether the conclusion follows from what is given.

A key issue in the study of deductive reasoning is whether systems of deductive logic, as postulated by logicians and philosophers, can serve as models of deductive reasoning. Does the formal system for representing premises and testing conclusions accurately portray the cognitive processes involved in deductive reasoning? The nineteenth century Irish mathematician George Boole considered his system of logic to do just that. His treatise *The Laws of Thought* was designed "to investigate the fundamental laws of those operations of the mind by which reasoning is performed" (1854, p. 1).

Was Boole correct? Can formal logic systems serve as models of the cognitive operations that occur in reasoning? More recent investigators think not. They note that formal logic systems do not tell what conclusion to draw from a set of premises but only whether some particular conclusion was correctly drawn. That is, they do not say how to get from the premises to a conclusion, but only whether it was properly done. Since logic systems do not describe how conclusions are reached in reasoning tasks, it becomes apparent that reasoning is very similar to the process of problem solving. The reasoner has a given state (the premises), a goal state (some valid conclusion), and does not at the moment know the route from the given to the goal.

In fact, we have already described a computer program—the *Logic Theorist*—that treats deductive reasoning in a problem-solving format (see pages 257–258). The *Logic Theorist* is a program for proving theorems in propositional logic, and it uses a set of heuristics for discovering a proof. The heuristics are not part of the propositional logic itself, but are a separate set of cognitive operations for finding a logical link between the axioms (the premises) and a theorem. The heuristics do not guarantee a solution to the problem. Like human reasoners they sometimes find a proof and other times fail. Moreover, the errors they make are often like the errors human reasoners make.

It may be helpful in understanding the link between logic systems and reasoning to draw an analogy to the distinction between linguistic competence and linguistic performance (see page 149). There we saw that competence represents grammatical knowledge (the rules of the language), while performance is the set of processes involved in the speaker/listener's use of that knowledge. Is a formal system of logic a model of logical competence or a model of logical performance? Boole opted for the latter, arguing that the processes for reaching conclusions are the same as the rules of logic. The *Logic Theorist*, however, treats the logic system as competence and provides a separate performance system, a set of heuristics for manipulating knowledge about the logic system in proving a theorem.

In conclusion, mortals that we are, we human beings often make errors in deductive reasoning. The source of such errors, as well as an understanding of how successful reasoning occurs, becomes clearer if we distinguish between *logic*—a formal system for deriving valid conclusions—and *reasoning*—the cognitive processes involved in using logic.

In this chapter we will examine three kinds of deductive reasoning, each of which deals with problems found in a system of formal logic. *Linear series problems* are based on relational terms within assertions as illustrated in the *Pam is older than Jill* example at the beginning of the chapter. *Propositional reasoning* is based upon connections between propositions, for example, the *if . . . then* connection in *If it is raining, then I will get wet.* Such reasoning has been formalized in the propositional logic. *Syllogisms* are also a form of propositional reasoning, but one in which the propositions contain quantifiers such as *all, some,* or *none.* Syllogisms are illustrated in the *All A are B* example at the beginning of the chapter and are the most familiar type of quantificational logic.

We will discuss only a few topics and problems related to each of these types of reasoning. However, these topics are the ones that have been most thoroughly studied in psychology. The underlying question throughout this chapter will be, How do people reason within these different types of logic systems?

LINEAR SERIES PROBLEMS

> John is taller than Mary
> Mary is taller than David
> Is John taller than David?

This is a linear series problem. It sets up relations among terms in sentences—in this case, among *John, Mary,* and *David.* The first two sentences in these problems are called *premises.* To solve such problems we must create some kind of representation that orders the terms in the premises in a linear sequence. What kind of cognitive operations are involved in representing and solving such problems? In the following sections we will consider several answers that have been offered to this question.

Image Theory

De Soto, London, and Handel (1965) suggested that people solve series problems by combining the premises into a unified visual image. The image for some terms is a vertical array and for other terms is a horizontal one. In vertical arrays, people show a preference for ordering terms from top down. For example, the premises *Alice is better than Jean, Jean is better than Susan* would be ordered

>Alice
>Jean
>Susan

In horizontal arrays, the preference is to order terms from left to right. Jones (1970) has shown that the choice of a vertical or horizontal ordering may be more a matter of convenience than a true indication of the internal spatial representation. The important point, however, is that people show a preferred ordering for terms in a unified array.

The second assumption of the image theory is the *end-anchor* principle. A new premise is easier to incorporate into the array if its first term will become the end anchor in the array, that is, the first or last term in the array. For example, in the problem above, it would be easier to incorporate the new premise *Helen is better than Alice* than it would be to incorporate *Susan is better than Nancy*.

The evidence collected by De Soto et al. to test their hypotheses is shown in Table 10.1 and clearly supports these two assumptions. Problems 1 through 4 illustrate the first assumption of a preferred order. Performance was best when the order of the terms in the premises was from better to worse (Problem 1). A mixed order of better to worse and worse to better was more difficult (Problems 2 and 3), and the poorest performance occurred when terms were given in reverse order of worse to better (Problem 4).

The end-anchor assumption is illustrated in Problems 5 through 8. The first term in the premises for Problems 5 and 6 is an end term in the array. This lets the subjects construct the array from the ends, which is easier than constructing it from the middle, as shown in Problems 7 and 8. In these problems, the first term of the premises is the middle term in the array, which required the array to be built from the middle to ends and was more difficult.

Linguistic Theories

The premises for linear series problems are usually presented as sentences. Two theories suggest that comprehension of these sentences plays a major role in solving the problem.

In the first of these linguistic theories, Huttenlocher (1968) assumed that one takes the two terms from the first premise and starts building the array. The third term for the array is given in the second premise, and it must be inserted in the array next. She proposed that the insertion is easiest when the third term is the logical subject of the premise. The logical subject of a sentence is the person or thing carrying out the action.

Unfortunately it has proved somewhat difficult to provide a definitive test of this hypothesis since certain types of sentences do not have logical subjects in the usual sense. Relational sentences, for example, merely state the relative positions of two items on some dimension. A good example of such a sentence is *Tom is taller than John*. On the basis of prior research, Huttenlocher argued that in relational sentences people treat the grammatical subject as the logical subject. Thus, for example, in the problem

>Tom is taller than John
>Sam is taller than Tom

the third term, *Sam,* is the grammatical subject of the sentence and, according to Huttenlocher, is also treated as the logical subject. Huttenlocher found error rates for *Who is taller?* to be lower when she gave the second premise in this form

Table 10.1 Proportion of Correct Responses for Eight Deduction Problems

Premises	Proportion correct response	FORM OF PREMISES	
		Within premises	Between premises
1. A is better than B B is better than C	.61	better-to-worse	better-to-worse
2. B is better than C A is better than B	.53	better-to-worse	worse-to-better
3. B is worse than A C is worse than B	.50	worse-to-better	better-to-worse
4. C is worse than B B is worse than A	.43	worse-to-better	worse-to-better
5. A is better than B C is worse than B	.62	ends-to-middle	better-to-worse
6. C is worse than B A is better than B	.57	ends-to-middle	worse-to-better
7. B is worse than A B is better than C	.41	middle-to-ends	better-to-worse
8. B is better than C B is worse than A	.38	middle-to-ends	worse-to-better

The question for the subjects was stated in each of four ways:

Is A better than C? Is C better than A? Is A worse than C?
Is C worse than A?

Source: From De Soto, London, and Handel (1965).

than when she gave it as *John is taller than Sam.* In the latter case *Sam* is the logical object rather than the logical subject of the sentence.

As indicated above, however, examples of this kind require the assumption that subjects treat the grammatical subject as a logical subject. It would be preferable to have a direct test of the importance of the role of the logical subject in such reasoning tasks. Huttenlocher carried out such a test in a second experiment that used the relation *is leading.* For example, *Pam is leading Linda* can be taken as a premise about a footrace. This premise sets up a relation along the dimension of who is ahead, and it also contains a logi-

cal subject in the usual sense—that is, Pam is performing the action of leading.

Huttenlocher put the second premise in both the active and passive voices, so that the third term was sometimes the grammatical subject and other times the grammatical object. In either case error rates were lower so long as the third term was the logical subject. If the third term was made the logical object of the premise, however, error rates increased, regardless of whether it was the grammatical subject or the grammatical object. Thus, for example, subjects answered the question *Who is first?* more accurately for problems of form A than form B.

Form A

Pam is leading Linda
Nikki is leading Pam
   (third term is logical subject
   and grammatical subject)

Pam is leading Linda
Pam is led by Nikki
   (third term is logical subject
   but grammatical object)

Form B

Pam is leading Linda
Nikki is led by Linda
   (third term is logical object
   but grammatical subject)

Pam is leading Linda
Linda is leading Nikki
   (third term is logical object
   and grammatical object)

Huttenlocher's results then suggest that it is easiest to solve a linear problem when the third term is the logical subject of the second premise.

Note that Huttenlocher's proposal is essentially a reformulation of the end-anchoring principle. She too makes the assumption that people image a linear array, but argues that the ease of constructing the array is based on the deep structure of the second premise.

The second linguistic theory is that of Clark (1969). It is based on purely linguistic assumptions, unlike Huttenlocher's, which contains a mixture of linguistic and spatial imagery assumptions. Clark proposed three principles to account for performance on linear series problems. These he calls:

1. *The primacy of functional relations.* According to this principle, one interprets the premises into their linguistic deep structures and stores them. For example, *A is led by B* will be stored as *B leads A*. Similarly, *Tom is worse than Jerry* will be stored as *(Tom is bad) more than (Jerry is bad)*. The simple relations in parentheses are easier to retrieve than the relation between the two clauses.

2. *The principle of lexical marking.* Unmarked adjectives, such as *long* and *good*, are neutral and are used to refer to a whole scale, such as length and goodness. Questions such as *How long is X?* make no assumptions about where X falls on the scale of length. In contrast, marked adjectives, such as *short* and *bad*, refer to the scale and also imply a position on the scale. Questions such as *How short is X?* imply that X lies on the lower end of the scale of length.

   In their comparative form, unmarked adjectives *(longer, better)* simply refer to the relative positions of two items on the scale. Marked forms *(shorter, worse)* assume in addition that the two items are toward the lower end of the scale. Clark claims that unmarked adjectives are stored and retrieved more easily than marked adjectives, since marked adjectives make an extra assumption. Thus *A is better than B* should be easier to process than *B is worse than A*.

3. *The principle of congruence.* The question that is asked (e.g., *Who is better?*) is compared with the deep structure of the premises that are stored in memory. If the form of the question is congruent with the deep structures, it will be answered faster than if it is not. For the premises *A is better than B, B is better than C,* the question *Who is best?* matches the deep structure form of the premises and should be answered quickly. The question *Who is worst,* however, is incongruent and must be translated into the form *Who is least best,* and thus response time should be longer.

The results of a test of Clark's principles are shown in Table 10.2. Note that the affirmative premises in the first 8 problems take less time

Table 10.2 Mean Solution Time (sec) for Linear Series Problems

Premises	Who is best?	Who is worst?	Mean
1. A better than B; B better than C	5.4	6.1	5.8
2. B better than C; A better than B	5.0	5.5	5.2
3. C worse than B; B worse than A	6.3	6.5	6.4
4. B worse than A; C worse than B	5.9	5.0	5.5
5. A better than B; C worse than B	5.4	5.3	5.3
6. C worse than B; A better than B	4.8	5.8	5.3
7. B worse than A; B better than C	5.0	6.0	5.5
8. B better than C; B worse than A	6.1	5.4	5.8
9. A not as bad as B; B not as bad as C	6.8	6.0	6.3
10. B not as bad as C; A not as bad as B	7.2	6.6	6.8
11. C not as good as B; B not as good as A	5.6	6.6	6.1
12. B not as good as A; C not as good as B	6.1	6.6	6.4
13. A not as bad as B; C not as good as B	6.3	6.7	6.5
14. C not as good as B; A not as bad as B	6.7	6.3	6.5
15. B not as good as A; B not as bad as C	6.1	6.2	6.1
16. B not as bad as C; B not as good as A	5.5	7.1	6.2

Source: After Clark (1969).

than the negative premises in problems 9 through 16 as suggested by the principle of functional relations. An extra step is required in encoding the negative premises to remove the negation. Similarly, the principle of lexical marking predicts that problems with *bad* or *worse* (3, 4, 9, and 10) should take longer than those with *good* or *better* (1, 2, 11, and 12). Finally, the principle of congruence predicts that *Who is worst?* will be answered faster when the premises are given in terms of *worse than* than it will when they are given in terms of *better than*. Similarly, *Who is best?* is congruent with *better than* premises and should be answered faster than for *worse than* premises.

These predictions are generally supported in the data. Note that the response times for the first eight problems are in accord with predictions made by De Soto et al. and by Huttenlocher. Times were faster when each of the comparisons within a premise went from better to worse (1 and 2) rather than worse to better (3 and 4). Also, times were faster when the third term was the logical subject of the second premise (2, 4, 5, and 6) rather than the logical object (1, 3, 7, and 8).

Thus most of Clark's predictions match those of De Soto et al. and Huttenlocher, although Clark makes different assumptions about how these effects arise. We shall see presently that all three of these theories are incomplete in some respects.

An Integrated Model

Potts (1972, 1974) has presented linear series problems in a story format that contains four and sometimes six terms. A sample story is,

In art class, Sally showed her nature painting to the teacher. Her teacher felt that certain parts of the picture were drawn better than others. The teacher said her tree was better than her grass, her sky was better than her bird, and her bird was better than her tree. Upon hearing this, Sally decided to drop art and major in psychology. (Potts, 1974, p. 433)

The terms in this story can be arranged in the series *sky > bird > tree > grass* or $A > B > C > D$. The terms that occur together in the story are *adjacent pairs*, namely, $A > B, B > C, C > D$. The terms that do not occur together are *remote pairs* $(A > C, B > D, A > D)$. After subjects heard the story, Potts asked them questions of the form *Was X better than Y*, for example, *Was the tree better than the sky?*

The results showed a "distance effect"; that is, answers to remote pairs were more accurate and faster than answers to the adjacent pairs, even though subjects had to deduce their answers about remote pairs from their knowledge of adjacent pairs. Potts concluded that subjects were integrating the pairs in the story into a unified list, which they then drew upon to answer the questions.

Potts also observed a strong end-anchoring effect; that is, questions containing the *A* term, such as *Is $A > C$?*, produced the fastest RT (reaction time). Questions containing a *D* term had slower RTs, and questions containing only *B* and *C* terms yielded the slowest RTs. To explain these results, Potts developed the model shown in Figure 10.1. The model assumes that one has represented the terms in an integrated series, and it represents the cognitive processes used to answer the questions.

Note that the first test in the model is whether an *A* term is the first term in the question. If it is, an immediate response *True* is given. If not, the model tests for a *D* term as the second term of the question. If it is there, the immediate answer is *False*. These two tests account for the end-anchoring effect. Failing these two tests, the model must probe more deeply and so takes longer to answer the question. This model makes the assumption of an integrated representation, as do the theories of De Soto et al. and Huttenlocher; but Potts's model gives a more explicit account of the end-anchoring effect.

In 1975, Potts and Scholz attempted a more thorough test of the Clark (1969) and Huttenlocher (1968) theories. The usual method of testing linear series problems is to present both premises and the test question at the same time. However, this method makes it difficult to determine whether the subject is spending more time encoding the premises or in comparing the question to the encoded form of the premises. Potts and Scholz timed these processes separately. The premises were first shown on a screen. When a subject felt she understood the premises, she pressed a button that recorded her time for encoding the premises and flashed the test question on the screen. When she pressed a second button to answer the question, her reaction time for answering the question was also recorded. The premises contained both unmarked adjectives (e.g., *better*) and marked adjectives (e.g., *worse*).

The results showed that Clark's congruence effect disappeared when subjects were given ample time to study the premises. Reaction times to the question *Who is best?* were faster than to *Who is worst?* regardless of the form of the adjective used in the premises. These results suggest that subjects stored marked and unmarked adjectives in the same form, probably in an unmarked form since RTs were faster to the unmarked form of the question. In measuring the reading times for the premises, however, the authors did note some evidence that marked adjectives led to longer encoding times. Similar effects have been reported by Carpenter (1974) and Higgins (1976).

Potts and Scholz's data also provided only partial support for Huttenlocher's theory. Her theory predicts that it is easiest to construct a unified form of the linear series when the third term of the series is the logical subject of the second premise. The reading times for premises showed this was true for many but not all of the premises. Potts and Scholz noted, however, that other parts of their data supported Huttenlocher's

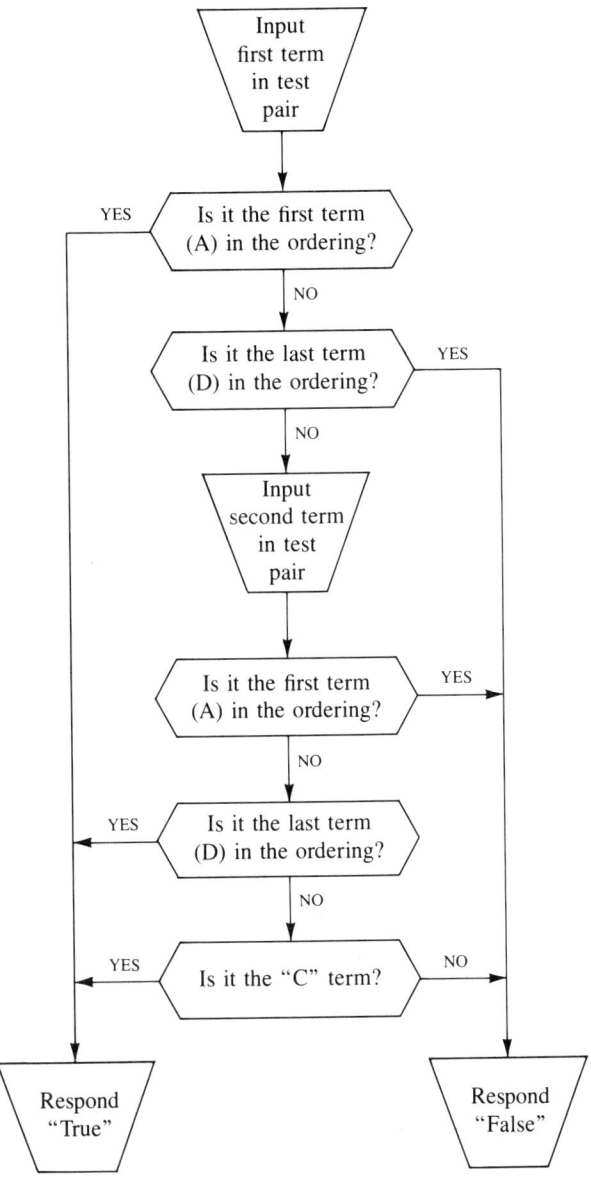

Figure 10.1 A flowchart showing a possible strategy for answering test questions. (From Potts, 1972.)

assumption that premise terms are integrated into a unified representation. Thus both theories were partly supported though neither was shown to be completely accurate.

Related Models

Our discussion of linear series problems has concentrated on studies in which subjects are given two premises stated as sentences and a question that they must answer *True/False* or *Yes/No*. These studies illustrate some of the major effects that occur in solving series problems. Other studies, however, have used a different methodology that produces somewhat different effects. For example, Trabasso and Riley (1975) used colored sticks of different lengths to establish the array. They found distance and end-anchor effects that were qualitatively different from those reported by Potts (1972, 1974).

Such differences have also been noted by Polich and Potts (1977) and Mayer (1978). Mayer suggested that these qualitative differences are produced by differences in the meaningfulness of the materials. Linguistic materials, such as the stories Potts used, invite one kind of strategy for coding and solving series problems, while nonlinguistic materials invite a different strategy. A series of experimental tests by Mayer (1978) supported this hypothesis.

In conclusion, the cognitive processes people use to solve linear series problems seem to divide into encoding and comparison processes. Encoding the premises involves constructing a unified representation of the terms and is affected by the order of the terms in the premises as well as the marking of the adjectives in the premises. The comparison process yields both end-anchor and distance effects. In the end-anchor effect, RTs are fastest to questions that contain one of the end terms in the array. For terms in between the anchor terms, the distance effect reflects the fact that RTs are faster as the distance between terms increases.

These effects vary somewhat with the methodology used, but it is significant that they can be produced by models that contain only a few basic cognitive activities such as coding and matching. Some questions remain unanswered, but it is encouraging to note that solving linear series problems seems to be based on some of the same fundamental cognitive processes that we have seen in previous chapters.

PROPOSITIONAL REASONING

The most common kind of reasoning in everyday affairs is *propositional reasoning*. It is based upon the relations among propositions. For example, we may say,

> If the car won't start, I will miss the party
> The car won't start
> Therefore, I will miss the party

The propositions in such reasoning are the simple assertions described in Chapter 6 on language. The relations are the connectives *and, or,* and *if . . . then*.

The psychological study of how people reason with propositions is not very advanced. There is, for example, no model of the cognitive processes that are used in propositional reasoning. Language is clearly a major part of propositional reasoning, and our difficulty in understanding how language is used has probably contributed to the slow development in this area.

One approach to studying propositional reasoning is to determine if propositional logic can be a model for such reasoning. Propositional logic has been formalized in the propositional calculus, a familiar topic in many logic courses. In this section we will briefly examine the propositional calculus, focusing on the *if . . . then* relation—the most difficult and the most studied one in the propositional calculus. We will then consider the propositional calculus as a model of everyday reasoning. To anticipate, it appears that it is not a very good model. Thus we will turn to a natural logic, which seems to conform more fully to everyday reasoning.

Formal and Natural Reasoning

The *propositional calculus* is an axiomatic system for organizing the inferences among propositions. In this system propositions are symbolized by p, q, r . . . , and the relations *and, or,* and *if . . . then* by &, V, and $\supset$. For example, we may use p for *The sun is shining* and q for *I will get tan* to produce the expressions p & q, *The sun is shining and I will get tan,* and $p \supset q$, *If the sun is shining, then I will get tan.*

One of the rules of inference in this system is *modus ponens,* which takes the form

If the sun is shining, then I will get tan	$p \supset q$
The sun is shining	p
Therefore, I will get tan	$\therefore q$

Given the two premises $p \supset q$ and p, the conclusion q is valid.

The function of the propositional calculus is to derive valid conclusions from premises. The content of the propositions plays no role in this process; only the relations among propositions are important. Once the propositions have been reduced to their symbolic form, it is a relatively easy matter to apply the rules of inference to arrive at valid conclusions.

Within this system propositions have only two values; they are either true or false. For example, p asserts that a proposition such as *The sun is shining* is true. *Not-p,* which is symbolized $\bar{p}$, asserts that the proposition is false, *The sun is not shining.* When propositions are combined into expressions, the truth value of the whole expression depends on the connective. For example, p & q is true when both p and q are true. If either one or both were false, the whole expression would be false.

Interpretations in this truth-value system sometimes do not fit very well with everyday reasoning. For instance,

He rented a car and went to Chicago

does not seem to be the same as

He went to Chicago and rented a car

yet they are the same within the truth-value system.

A similar problem arises with the $\supset$ connective, which comes closest to *if . . . then* in ordinary English. The expression $p \supset q$ is true in the propositional calculus, since both p and q are true. This fits ordinary English usage of *if . . . then: If the sun is shining, then I will get tan.* However, the expression is also true if p is false and q is true—that is, $\bar{p} \supset q$. The ordinary English equivalent *If the sun is not shining, I will get tan* does not seem to square with this interpretation. A closer look at formal and natural reasoning will give us a clearer idea of just where the problems lie.

Formal Reasoning. The major rule of inference in the propositional calculus as mentioned above is *modus ponens,* which contains two premises and a conclusion. The first premise is a conditional expression of the form $p \supset q$. In this expression p is the *antecedent* and q is the *consequent.* Both the antecedent and the consequent may be either true or false, which permits four arguments. Two of these are valid and two are invalid, as shown in Box 10.1.

Box 10.1 MODUS PONENS ARGUMENTS

1. $p \supset q$	If Sam is neurotic, then he is anxious		Conditional expression
p	Sam is neurotic		Antecedent is true
$\therefore q$	Therefore, Sam is anxious		Valid argument

2. $p \supset q$	If Sam is neurotic, he is anxious	Conditional expression
$\bar{q}$	Sam is not anxious	Consequent is false
$\therefore \bar{p}$	Therefore, Sam is not neurotic	Valid argument
3. $p \supset q$	If Sam is neurotic, he is anxious	Conditional expression
q	Sam is anxious	Consequent is true
$\therefore p$	Therefore, Sam is neurotic	Invalid argument, affirming the consequent
4. $p \supset q$	If Sam is neurotic, he is anxious	Conditional expression
$\bar{p}$	Sam is not neurotic	Antecedent is false
$\therefore \bar{q}$	Therefore, Sam is not anxious	Invalid argument, denying the antecedent

The two fallacies demonstrated in (3) and (4) above are common logical errors (e.g., see Wason & Johnson-Laird, 1972). They are the fallacies of *affirming the consequent* and *denying the antecedent,* respectively. Scientific reasoning is as vulnerable to these as are homier kinds of reasoning. Argument (3), for example, is sometimes mistakenly used to "prove" that an hypothesis is true. It rests on the assumption that an hypothesis (the antecedent) predicts an observation (the consequent) and therefore must be true. Since most hypotheses are plausible, the argument is easy to accept. The incorrectness of the argument is easier to see in a foolish example:

If the moon is made of cheese, then it will be yellow
The moon is yellow
Therefore, the moon is made of cheese

There are, of course, any number of hypotheses that predict that the moon is yellow, and the observation that it is indeed yellow supports them all but does not prove any of them.

Natural Reasoning. The inferences that occur in natural reasoning are somewhat different from those that are permitted in formal reasoning. For example, in addition to logical relations, temporal and causal relations may exist in an expression. The *and* in *He rented a car and went to Chicago* expresses a temporal relation between the two propositions, not a logical one. Similarly, a causal relation exists in *If Jon gets a job, then Jeanette will marry him.* In formal reasoning, this expression is true even if it is false that Jon gets a job. In natural reasoning, however, this would probably not be acceptable, at least in Jeanette's mind.

A second disparity lies in the "communal assumptions" that often underlie natural reasoning. Johnson-Laird (1975) suggested that a speaker may leave many things unsaid, assuming a listener will infer them from general knowledge. Upon hearing *Michael went to three drugstores,* the listener may infer that the first two drugstores did not have what Michael wanted. The inference is based on a communal base of knowledge that includes such assumptions as

> Drugstores are shops that have certain sorts of goods.
>
> People visit shops in order to buy goods.
>
> If one shop does not have an item that it normally stocks, then another shop of the same sort may have it. (Johnson-Laird, 1975, p. 51)

Inferences based on communal assumptions are not necessarily valid, though they are usually plausible. Thus they depart from the strict inference rules of the propositional calculus.

Observations such as the ones we have described in this section have led to more thorough investigations of the kind of logic that underlies natural reasoning.

Models of Reasoning

A model of reasoning may be either a competence model, a performance model, or both (Osherson, 1975). A *competence model* would generate all the expressions that a reasoner believes to be valid on purely logical grounds. A *performance model* would display the actual cognitive processes a reasoner goes through in reaching his or her conclusions. Braine (1978) noted that a performance model would contain the competence model and would also specify comprehension processes, heuristics for selecting inference rules, and the kinds of limits that working memory would impose. These are the components commonly found in the problem-solving models in the last chapter.

A natural question is, Is the propositional calculus a model of either logical compctence or performance?

Formal Logic. Several theorists have argued that the axiomatic system of the propositional calculus is not an appropriate model of human reasoning (Braine, 1978; Johnson-Laird, 1975). People do not reach conclusions by deriving them from axioms, they say. Osherson (1974, 1975) conducted an experimental test of this hypothesis by comparing the proof procedures for solving propositional logic problems with the difficulty subjects had in solving them. More difficult problems should take longer and produce more errors if people use the standard proof procedures of the propositional calculus.

Osherson gave his subjects problems that contained several connectives and that varied in difficulty. He then correlated the number of errors made and the solution times with the number of steps in the formal proof procedure. These correlations were generally nonsignificant, and Osherson concluded that the propositional calculus does not correspond to either the competence or the performance processes of human subjects.

A Natural Logic. The poor fit between natural reasoning processes and those required in the propositional calculus has led Braine (1978) to propose a natural logic that represents natural reasoning processes more accurately. The model defines the deductive steps available to a reasoner in any deductive task. These steps use the connectives *and, or,* and *if . . . then* according to the meanings they have in ordinary English rather than the special meanings they have in the propositional calculus.

The deductive steps that Braine uses are called inference rules. He defines an *inference rule* as one in which "a certain proposition can immediately be concluded when certain other propositions have been established" (1978, p. 3). For example,

Either Ford won or Carter won	Ford did not win

Carter won

When the propositions above the line have been

established, the one below the line can be concluded immediately.

Each inference rule is a particular instance of an *inference rule schema,* which is a formula that defines the form for inference rules. The schema for the inference rule above is

$$\frac{p \text{ or } q \quad \text{not } p}{q}$$

Many different inference rules can be created from this schema, since many different propositions can be substituted for p and q.

Braine (1978) proposed 18 inference rule schemata, which he believes to be the forms for all inferences that occur in natural reasoning. Each schema describes the form for a unique, elementary inference. For example, another of the schemata takes the form

$$\frac{p_1, p_2, \ldots p_n}{p_1 \text{ AND } p_2 \text{ AND } \ldots \text{ AND } p_n}$$

Given that a set of individual propositions have been established, one may conclude their conjunction. Logically speaking, this is a simple step, but all the schemata are for such elementary steps. They may be combined to produce an argument of any complexity.

The schemata contain the connectives *and* and *or* plus negation. They do not contain the $\supset$ connective of propositional logic, since it fits the ordinary English usage of *if . . . then* poorly. The *if . . . then* relation is expressed by the form of a schema: If the material above the line has been established, then one may conclude what lies below the line. This gives a ready explanation of the ease of handling *modus ponens* when it takes the form

$$\frac{\text{If } p \text{ then } q}{\therefore q}$$

The first premise takes the form

$$\frac{p}{q}$$

and since p is established in the second premise, then q follows immediately. If something other than p is established (i.e., $\bar{p}$, q, or $\bar{q}$), then the reasoner must go through additional inference rules to reach a conclusion.

These rules may lead to a conclusion that is valid in the propositional logic or to one of the fallacies in the propositional logic: denying the antecedent or affirming the consequent. In either event subjects should handle the first case of *modus ponens* correctly and quickly, while the other cases should take longer and lead to more errors within the framework of the propositional calculus. Research on reasoning in the propositional calculus confirms this prediction.

Braine's natural logic resolves a number of problems for a theory of propositional reasoning. It defines the place of logic in the reasoning process. A reasoner codes information into the forms described by the inference rule schemata and uses these to reach some conclusion. The logic does not say how the coding is done nor which schemata a reasoner will use in a particular case. In this respect the logic is a competence model rather than a performance model. It describes the schemata that are available but does not describe how they are used. Braine (1978) suggested, however, that the logic might be incorporated into a performance model, such as GPS, to account for the performance aspects of the reasoning process.

In addition, this natural logic defines connectives in a way that corresponds more closely to the way conjunctions are used in ordinary English and thus gives an insight into natural reasoning. Finally, it provides an account of the difficulties of using propositional logic by showing how the schemata of natural logic are applied to problems in the propositional calculus.

Research on Braine's proposal is still limited, but the problems it resolves suggest that it is

Box 10.2 ANALYTICAL ABILITY

Reasoning with propositional information is part of our daily activities, and skill at such reasoning is important for many tasks. The Graduate Record Examination, a test used nationwide for evaluating applicants to graduate school, has a special subtest for assessing skill at propositional reasoning. One type of item on the test measures ability to determine the relation of a statement to a previously described situation. Identifying the correct relation draws upon the reader's ability to analyze the situation and fit the statement to it appropriately. Here is a sample item from the test. It begins with a set of directions, followed by the situation and the set of statements to be evaluated. Try to respond to the statements before reading the answers.

Analysis of Explanations

Directions: For each set of questions, a fact situation and a result are presented. Several numbered statements follow the result. Each statement is to be evaluated in relation to the fact situation and result. Consider each statement separately from the other statements. For each one, examine the following sequence of decisions, in the order A, B, C, D, E. Each decision results in selecting or eliminating a choice. *The first choice that cannot be eliminated is the correct answer.*

- A. Is the statement *inconsistent* with, or contradictory to, something in the fact situation, the result, or both together? If so, choose A.
  If not,
- B. Does the statement present a *possible adequate explanation* of the result?
  If so, choose B.
  If not,
- C. Does the statement have to be true if the fact situation and result are as stated?
  If so, the statement is *deducible* from something in the fact situation, the result, or both together; choose C.
  If not,
- D. Does the statement either support or weaken a possible explanation of the result?
  If so, the statement is *relevant* to an explanation; choose D.
- E. If not, the statement is *irrelevant* to an explanation of the result; choose E.

Problem

Situation: In an attempt to end the theft of books from Parkman University Library, Elnora Johnson, the chief librarian, initiated a stringent inspection program at the beginning of the fall term. At the library entrance, Johnson posted inspectors to check that each library book leaving the building had a checkout slip bearing the call number of the book, its due date, and the borrower's identification number. The library retained a carbon copy of this slip as its only record that the book had been checked out. Johnson ordered the inspectors to search for concealed library books in attaché cases, bookbags, and all other containers large enough to hold a book. Since no new personnel could be hired, all library personnel took turns serving as inspectors, though many complained of their embarrassment in conducting the searches.

Result: During that term Margaret Zimmer stole twenty-five library books.

Statement:
1. Zimmer stole the books before the inspection system began.
2. Zimmer dropped the books out of a second-story window into a clump of bushes and retrieved them after she left the building.
3. The library had at one time kept two carbon copies of each checkout slip.

Answers

The correct answers to statements 1 through 3 and the rationale for them are as follows:

1. The answer to this question of average difficulty is A, because the statement is inconsistent with the information given in the result, which states that Zimmer stole the books during the term in which the inspection was initiated.
2. Since the statement could be true given the information in the situation and the result, this statement is consistent with the information given, so the correct answer is not A. The next option to be considered is B. The statement is a possible explanation of the result, since Zimmer could have avoided the inspection system in this way. The question is an easy one.
3. This statement is not inconsistent with the information given, is not a possible explanation of the result, cannot be deduced from the information given, and does not support or weaken a possible explanation of the result. Information about the system used in the past is not relevant to any explanation of the result, so the correct answer is E.

a promising alternative to the propositional calculus as a model of propositional reasoning.

In summary, propositional reasoning is a system for arriving at conclusions, stated in the form of propositions, on the basis of their relations to other propositions. The propositional calculus is an axiomatic system for arriving at valid conclusions; however, its definitions for some of the connectives, especially ⊃, do not conform very well to the ordinary use of these connectives in English. Osherson's work (1974, 1975) suggested that the propositional calculus is not a plausible model of competence in natural reasoning; and Braine (1978) has offered an alternative, a natural logic, which appears to conform more closely to the steps that are used in natural reasoning with propositions.

REASONING WITH SYLLOGISMS

Propositions often use terms referring to quantity (*all, some, none,* etc.), as in the syllogism

> All whales are mammals
> Moby Dick is a whale
> Therefore, Moby Dick is a mammal

The *logic of quantification* is based on deductions that use quantifiers; it contains the propositional calculus but is more powerful because it also relates quantities. The syllogism is the most familiar form of quantificational logic, and much of the logic of syllogisms stems from the work of Aristotle.

In this section we will concentrate on the psychological processes that underlie reasoning with syllogisms. First, we will have a look at the logic of syllogisms, and then we will examine two psychological theories for reasoning with syllogisms. The two major questions that seem to underlie these theories are (1) How do people encode propositions that contain terms for quantity? and (2) How do people reason from the coded forms to a conclusion? Our analysis is similar to the analysis of linear series problems, which is not surprising since linear series problems are often treated as a form of quantificational logic.

The Logic of Syllogisms

A **syllogism** is a set of logical statements that contains two premises and a conclusion in the form

All A are B	All moviegoers are property owners
All B are C	All property owners are taxpayers
∴ All A are C	Therefore, all moviegoers are taxpayers

A and C are the subject and predicate noun of the conclusion, while B is the middle term that mediates between A and C. The terms in the premises can be arranged in four different ways to produce four standard figures, and these are shown in Table 10.3.

Table 10.3 The Four Standard Figures for Syllogisms

I	II	III	IV
B–C	C–B	B–C	C–B
A–B	A–B	B–A	B–A
A–C	A–C	A–C	A–C

The premises and conclusion in a syllogism can each take one of four forms called *moods*. These are:

| Universal affirmative: | All A are B | All moths are insects |
| Universal negative: | No A are B | No children are senators |

Particular affirmative:	Some A are B	Some carpenters are Republicans
Particular negative:	Some A are not B	Some pianists are not parents

The relation between A and B in these propositions is that of inclusion—for example, in the universal affirmative all members of set A are included in set B, while in the particular affirmative some and possibly all members of set A are included in set B. In the universal negative no members of set A are included in set B, and in the particular negative some and possibly all of the members of set A are not included in set B.

The major concern in the logic of syllogisms lies with the validity of the conclusion; that is, does the conclusion follow logically from the premises. Validity is based on the form of the syllogism, not on the truth of the premises. The truth of a conclusion is a separate matter from its validity, and a false conclusion may nonetheless be a valid one. If the premises are both true, however, then a valid conclusion is necessarily

---

Box 10.3 FORM AND CONTENT IN CHILDREN'S THINKING

Jean Piaget, the famous Swiss developmental psychologist, states that children progress through stages in which their reasoning increasingly approximates adult reasoning (Phillips, 1975). Attaining what Piaget terms the formal operations stage is necessary in order for children to be able to reason with syllogisms, since only at this stage is it possible to separate the logical form of an argument from its content.

Take the syllogism

> All children like spinach
> Boys are children
> Therefore, boys like spinach

The child who has not reached formal operations will respond to the content of the syllogism with such statements as "Spinach is terrible" and "I don't like spinach." The child at formal operations, however, can appreciate the form of the argument and recognize that the syllogism is valid, even though the child knows that the first premise is false, so that the conclusion may be false too.

The distinction between the truth and the validity of an argument is critical for the use of syllogisms. The truth of the premises is established inductively—that is, by gathering evidence that the statement is accurate. The validity of a syllogism, however, is established from the logical form of the syllogism. Children are sensitive to the truth of a statement at an early age, but they do not develop an appreciation for the logical form of a syllogism until the advent of the formal operations stage at about age 11.

true. The relation between truth and validity may be more easily seen by considering some developmental changes in the ability of children to reason. We take up this issue in Box 10.3.

The Psychology of Syllogisms

Reasoning with syllogisms is difficult. Even the simplest syllogisms are usually more difficult than a linear series problem. The psychological question in this task is, What mental operations do people use? Even when people reach an invalid conclusion, it is important to determine what cognitive process led to that conclusion.

One of the earliest explanations of logical errors in syllogistic reasoning was the *atmosphere effect* proposed by Woodworth and Sells (1935). It stated that two premises in the same mood (see page 293) create an atmosphere that invites the reasoner to draw a conclusion stated in the same mood. For example,

All A are B	All neurotic people are anxious
All C are B	All my close friends are anxious
∴ All A are C	Therefore, all neurotic people are my close friends

The reasoner's friends may indeed be neurotic, but the logic here does not establish that. Logically, this error is the fallacy of the *undistributed middle*. The middle term *(B)* is not related to the other two in a way that permits a valid conclusion.

Woodworth and Sells suggested, however, that reasoners do not follow the logic of the argument but merely accept the *all* in the two premises as justification for the *all* in the conclusion. In general, they argued that two universal premises lead to a universal conclusion, and two particular premises lead to a particular conclusion. Similarly, affirmative premises lead to affirmative conclusions and negative premises lead to negative conclusions. The effect is akin to that of set in problem solving.

A second explanation of errors in syllogistic reasoning suggests that they arise from *invalid conversion* of premises (Chapman & Chapman, 1959). *All A are B* may lead one to convert the premise to *All B are A,* a tempting but not necessarily valid inference. The problem is easy to see in a concrete example: *All dimes are coins* is not the same as *All coins are dimes*. In some cases, however, the conversion is valid. For example, *No A are B* means the same as *No B are A*. Whether the conversion is valid or not, it will sometimes lead to true conclusions in everyday reasoning, which may explain the use of conversions.

Since the research for these two explanations is based primarily on logical errors, the hypotheses say little about how people reach valid conclusions. In addition, these explanations portray the reasoning process as fairly superficial. More recent interpretations have sought a more general account of reasoning which encompasses both valid and invalid conclusions. In general, these interpretations suggest that syllogistic reasoning is a rational process, but that errors may arise either from the manner in which premises are encoded or from the deductions made from the coded form of the premises.

The Set Analysis Theory. Several investigators have observed that premises are open to more than one interpretation of the relation between the two terms. For example, *All A are B* can mean either that *A* is a subset of *B* or that *A* and *B* are identical sets. Understanding how a reasoner encodes the premises should give at least a partial account of his or her conclusions, regardless of whether they are valid.

Erickson (1974, 1978) has developed this assumption in the set analysis theory of syllogistic reasoning. The terms in a premise are viewed as sets, and the relations between them are described by Venn diagrams. Table 10.4 shows the possible set relations for premises in each of the four moods. *All A are B* can have either the subset or identity relations, while *No A are B* has only an exclusion relation. Note that *Some A are B* has four possible relations. In logic *some* means "at least one and possibly all"; so its relations include the relations for *All A are B*. We will return to Erickson's theory shortly, but first let us look at some of the evidence that people encode premises in different ways.

Ceraso and Provitera (1971) sought to reduce the ambiguity of premises by writing them in a modified form that made clear exactly which relation was being described. For example, instead of stating *All A are B,* a modified premise might state *All A are B, but there are some B that are not A,* thus identifying the subset relation. They then gave subjects syllogisms using the modified forms and compared their conclusions with those of a control group of subjects using the traditional forms. The group using the modified forms produced only about half as many errors as the traditional group, suggesting that the ambiguity of traditional forms is a major source of error.

Evidence of a different kind was produced by Neimark and Chapman (1975). They gave subjects a series of premises in the traditional form and a set of Venn diagrams for each premise. The Venn diagrams were the five relations shown in Table 10.4 plus a sixth choice of "incompatible," which meant that the relation could not exist. For each premise the subjects were asked to circle all the diagrams that might apply for that premise. The subjects were college students plus high school students in the 7th to 12th grades. The results are shown in Figure 10.2.

A correct response is one in which the subject circled all the possible relations permitted by the premise, as shown in Table 10.4. Universal premises were interpreted correctly at a high level, though older students did better than younger ones. The negative form, which has only one relation, was significantly better than the affirmative form, which has two possible relations. Premises using *some* showed poor agreement with the logically acceptable relations at all ages. In general *some* was interpreted too narrowly. Many subjects chose only the overlap relation; subjects who recognized inclusive relationships added the subset relation and occasionally the identity relation.

Table 10.4 Possible Set Relations Implied by Syllogistic Sentences

	Subset	Superset	Identity	Overlap	Exclusion
All A are B	X		X		
No A are B					X
Some A are B	X	X	X	X	
Some A are not B		X		X	X

Source: From Erickson (1974).

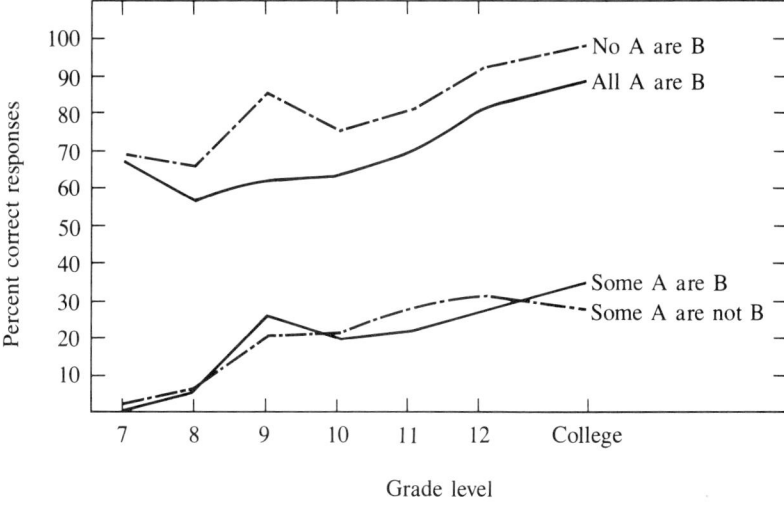

Figure 10.2 Group mean percent correct responses on simple propositions as a function of grade level. (From Neimark & Chapman, 1975.)

These results are very much in accord with those of Ceraso and Provitera, and support the hypothesis that people interpret premises in a more restricted fashion than logical convention permits. Let us return now to Erickson's set analysis theory, which embodies this hypothesis.

The set analysis theory (Erickson, 1974) assumes that reasoning with syllogisms occurs in three stages. Stage I assumes people interpret premises in something like Venn diagrams. In Stage II, encoded premises are combined, again in the form of Venn diagrams. In Stage III, a conclusion is selected from the combined form. At each stage the analysis may be incomplete, and this is the source of errors in reasoning. A sample problem within this framework is illustrated in Table 10.5. A subject is given two premises and asked to draw a conclusion. The possible interpretations of the premises are shown at Stage I and the possible combinations of these at Stage II.

In line with evidence described above, the theory assumes people do not consider all possible interpretations of the premises, nor do they consider all possible combinations of the premises. Stage III shows the relations between A and C which are permitted by the possible combinations in Stage II. Reasoners tend to select the relation common to *all* the combinations they are considering, in this case *Some A are C*, which is the correct conclusion. Clearly the degree to which reasoners consider all possible interpretations of the premises and all possible combinations of them influences their success in solving the syllogism.

Erickson (1978) has reported several tests of the set analysis theory. First, he established the relative frequency with which subjects would choose interpretations in Stages I and II. This enabled him to predict the conclusion they would draw for a syllogism. The predictions correlated about .85 to .95 with data from valid syllogisms and .80 to .85 with data from invalid syllogisms. The theory also accounts for the results of the

Table 10.5 Analysis of Problem of Drawing a Conclusion from Premises in a Syllogism

Task: Draw a conclusion from premises (or state that no conclusion is logical)

All A are B	Major premise
All B are C	Minor premise
? ? ?	Conclusion

Stage I: Interpretation of premises

Possible interpretations

All A are B

    1   2

(A B) or (AB)

All B are C

    3   4

(B C) or (BC)

Stage II: Combination of interpreted premises

Possible combinations

1 and 3	1 and 4	2 and 3	2 and 4
((A) B) C	(A) BC	(AB) C	ABC

Stage III: Labeling of set relation of C to A

Possible labels

1 and 3
Some C are A
or
Some C are not A

1 and 4
Some C are A
or
Some C are not A

2 and 3
Some C are A
or
Some C are not A

2 and 4
All C are A
or
Some C are A

Logical conclusion: Some C are A

Source: From Erickson (1974).

Ceraso and Provitera (1971) study simply by changing the way traditional and modified premises are interpreted in Stage I.

The results for this theory are promising. It accords well with earlier research on interpretation of premises and can be applied to both valid and invalid syllogisms. Thus it has an attractive degree of generality. The results reported above, however, are based on abstract materials *(All A are B)* rather than real-life materials *(All cows are mammals),* and it is well known that the concreteness of the material has an important influence on syllogistic reasoning (e.g., Wilkins, 1928). Our next theory applies to concrete materials.

The Analogical Theory. Ordinary reasoning with syllogisms does not use abstract materials but concrete materials of the kind

> All senators are elected officials
> Mr. Harper is a senator
> Therefore, Mr. Harper is an elected official

Concrete syllogisms are generally easier to solve than abstract ones; and since they are more common to our experience, a theory about them is of special interest. Johnson-Laird and Steedman (1978) have proposed such a theory in the analogical theory of reasoning with quantifiers. The theory accounts for the conclusions drawn in both valid and invalid syllogisms and takes special note of the effects of the figure of the syllogism (see Table 10.3).

As a first step in developing the theory, the authors asked 20 subjects to draw a conclusion, or state that no valid conclusion was possible, for a syllogism in each of the valid and invalid forms. As we have described, each of the premises in a syllogism can take one of four moods, and the two terms in each premise can be in one of two orders. Thus there were $4 \times 4 \times 2 \times 2 = 64$ syllogisms that the subjects solved. The syllogisms were of neutral content about occupations and interests, such as

> All of the gourmets are storekeepers
> All of the storekeepers are bowlers
> Therefore, ?

The results showed a strong effect for the figure of the syllogism. When premises were of the form $A-B/B-C,$ subjects showed a strong preference for drawing a conclusion of the $A-C$ form. For the $B-A/C-B$ figure, however, there was a strong preference for drawing a conclusion of the $C-A$ form.

When a figure had only one valid conclusion, subjects tended to draw this conclusion when it was compatible with the figure but not when it was incompatible with the figure. For example, in the $A-B/B-C$ figure, 85 percent of the valid conclusions drawn were of the compatible $A-C$ form, and in the $B-A/C-B$ figure 77.5 percent of the conclusions drawn were in the compatible $C-A$ form. When a valid deduction was incompatible with the figure, however, it occurred only 20 percent of the time.

Similar preferences for a compatible conclusion occurred when two valid conclusions were possible and even when no valid conclusion was possible. The effect of figure on the choice of conclusion was largely limited to the $A-B/B-C$ and $B-A/C-B$ figures; the other two figures showed little effect.

The proportion of correct solutions varied greatly among the syllogisms (30 percent–85 percent). The figure of the syllogism influenced correctness but in a way that depended heavily on the mood of the premises in the syllogism.

Johnson-Laird and Steedman (1978) proposed the *analogical theory* to account for these results as well as those of other experiments on syllogistic reasoning. The theory assumes there are four stages in reasoning which a person goes through in reasoning with syllogisms, as follows:

1. an interpretation of the premises
2. a heuristic for combining interpretations of the two premises
3. the formation of a conclusion that fits the combined interpretations

4. a logical test that may lead to modifying or abandoning the conclusion

In the first stage, the four moods for premises are interpreted into the following forms:

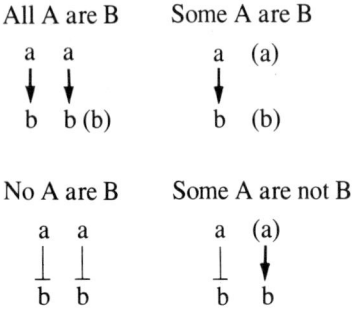

The arrows stand for class membership. For example, in *All A are B,* all the *a*'s are linked to *b*'s with the option that there may be *b*'s for which there are no *a*'s. In *Some A are B,* the *(a)* and *(b)* indicate that there may be *a*'s for which there are not *b*'s, and *b*'s for which there are not *a*'a. The ⊥ sign indicates a negative link—that is, a relation that is blocked between *a* and *b*. Note that the relations shown for these four premises match closely those described by Erickson (see Table 10.4).

In the second stage, the interpretations of the two premises are combined. The heuristic for combining them seeks links wherever possible between *a* and *c* terms by way of *b* terms. A combined interpretation takes the form

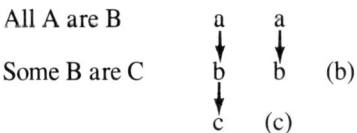

The heuristic has dutifully created an *a* → *b* → *c* link that, in this case, leads to the invalid conclusion *Some A are C.*

In the third stage, a conclusion is formed which reflects the kind of paths between *a* and *c* terms. When all paths are positive, it takes the form *All A are C.* When all paths are negative, it takes the form *No A are C.* When there is at least one positive path, it is *Some A are C;* and when there is at least one negative path, it is *Some A are not C.* Where there are only indeterminate paths, no valid conclusion can be drawn. For example,

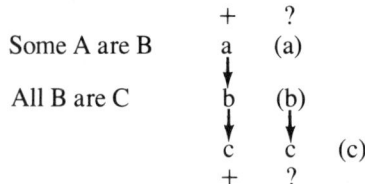

The + indicates a positive path, one which links *a* to *c*. The ? indicates an indeterminate path, one in which links from *a* to *c* cannot be established with certainty.

Since there is at least one positive path, *Some A are C* is a valid conclusion, and it was selected by 16 of the 20 subjects in the study described above. *Some C are A* is equally valid, but it is incompatible with the figure and was selected by only 3 subjects. The explanation for the figure effect lies in the direction of the *a* → *b* → *c* path. It is much easier to go with the arrows than against them. This assumption provides an account of all the figure effects described above.

In the fourth stage, a logic test attempts to break the paths between *a* and *c* items without violating the meanings of the premises. It seeks the most limited relation permissible between these terms. If the heuristic has created the combined representation

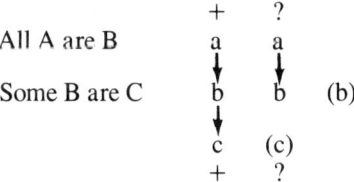

this would be modified by the logical test to

The modification preserves the meaning of the premises, but in a more limited form. Since only indeterminate paths remain, no valid conclusion can be drawn.

The first three stages of this theory are heuristic in the sense that they constitute a plausible search for a conclusion. The fourth stage, however, is purely logical and assures a correct conclusion if the logical test is carried out properly. Johnson-Laird and Steedman note that "the essence of the theory is that subjects are very good at drawing conclusions on heuristic grounds but generally less efficient at submitting them to logical tests" (1978, p. 82).

The analogical theory predicted 95 percent of the subjects' responses in the experiment reported above. For example, it predicted that syllogisms that require no modifications by logical testing should be easier than those that do. The proportions correct in these two cases were 80 percent and 46 percent respectively. The theory also predicted the effect for figures. For example, it predicted the easiest problems to be those where the correct conclusion follows the arrows and the hardest ones to be where the conclusion goes against the arrows. The proportion correct in these cases was 73 percent and 20 percent respectively.

Johnson-Laird and Steedman noted that the analogical theory predicts the atmosphere effect (Woodworth & Sells, 1935) but is more general in that it also accounts for figure effects and for responses of "No valid conclusion." They noted further that Erickson's set analysis theory, while plausible in many respects, fails to include any directional component that would predict the substantial figure effect that they have observed.

The analogical theory then is especially interesting because of its generality. It applies to ordinary reasoning with concrete materials in both valid and invalid syllogisms. The data on which the theory is based have revealed a strong effect for figure, not observed in less exhaustive studies, an effect that the theory explains. Its accuracy in explaining these data is encouraging and invites additional research on this theory.

In summary, the logic of syllogisms is an ancient and mature discipline. It tells us when the conclusion to a syllogism is valid; but, interestingly for the psychologist, it does not tell us how to reach a conclusion from two premises. Drawing a conclusion thus becomes something of a problem-solving task, and errors are common for the novice.

Early psychological interpretations of syllogistic reasoning, such as invalid conversion and the atmosphere effect, depicted this process as somewhat irrational. The more recent theories of Erickson (1974, 1978) and Johnson-Laird and Steedman (1978) offer a more generous view. Erickson's set analysis theory suggests that the initial interpretation of premises may be incomplete, but the reasoning from the interpreted forms is fairly rigorous. In contrast, the analogical theory assumes that people are quite good at interpreting premises but relatively inefficient at reasoning from them.

In both theories, interpreted premises are represented as relations between sets of objects, though the analogical theory contains a directional component not found in the set analysis theory. Both theories apply to both valid and invalid syllogisms, though Erickson's was developed on abstract materials while Johnson-Laird and Steedman used concrete materials. It remains to be seen whether either of these theories can be extended, but their current success gives hope for a truly comprehensive theory of syllogistic reasoning.

CONCLUSION

Deductive logic is a method for determining whether a valid conclusion has been derived from given information. Systems of logic, however, do not provide a method for deriving a conclusion; that is, they lack a method of discovery. Deductive reasoning is thus a form of problem solving in which the reasoner conducts a heuristic search for an acceptable conclusion.

Systems of logic do not seem to provide good models of the psychological processes people use in deductive reasoning. The psychological interpretations for reasoning with linear series, propositional reasoning, and syllogistic reasoning all embody cognitive processes that are outside the realm of logic. A common theme among these interpretations is that the initial stage of encoding relations is difficult. In propositional and syllogistic reasoning especially, people do not seem to interpret the relations in the way the formal logic requires.

A second common theme lies in the use of cognitive operations to manipulate the encoded representations. These operations are elementary cognitive processes such as matching or combining; and, like the encoding process, they are subject to error. Each of the theories and models we have described assumes an opportunity for errors in reasoning, but they nonetheless concur in treating human reasoning as a rational process.

There is at present no unified theory of deductive reasoning. Moreover, current theories make only limited assumptions about the relation of reasoning to memory, language, and problem solving. The field has grown rapidly in the last two decades, however, and in the future we may hope for a unified theory that fully integrates reasoning with the other cognitive processes.

11 Motor Skills

Properties of Motor Skills
Learning a Motor Skill
    Early Phase
    Intermediate Phase
    Late Phase
Feedback
Processing Information
    Discrete Skills
    Continuous Skills
Practice
    Compatibility
    Distributed versus Massed Practice
    Whole-Part Learning
    Limits of Skill
Central Processes

A Theory of Continuous Skills
   Inner-loop Control
   Higher-order Control
   Voluntary Control
A Theory of Discrete Skills
   The Recall Schema
   The Recognition Schema
   Integrating Motor Schemata
Conclusion

When Roger Bannister broke the 4-minute mile in 1954, he managed the supreme feat of the track world. We often think of skill as being just one of these moments of peak performance, but psychologists use the term for any instance of using the muscles in a coordinated manner: walking, running, playing golf, tennis, or basketball; singing, playing the guitar, piano, or other musical instrument; typing, driving, or manipulating other machines.

We use motor skills in almost every waking activity, and we can perhaps appreciate their value to us by putting ourselves in the place of someone who does not have them—namely, the newborn infant, who can neither drive a car, sew a button, talk, walk, or even hold its head upright, not to mention playing the piccolo. The learning and use of motor skills are thus pervasive psychological processes, and we shall explore them in this chapter.

The unity of motor skills with the other cognitive processes is suggested by Bartlett in *Thinking* (1958):

All skilled behaviour is set into a form of significant sequence within which it must be studied if understanding is to be reached. . . . it submits to a control which lies outside itself and is appreciated, at the bodily level, by the receptor system; . . . proper timing, the ways in which transition is made from one direction of move to another, "point of no return," and the character of direction and how it is appreciated are all critical features of skilled behaviour. From time to time, and in relation to all the kinds of thinking which I have discussed, I have returned particularly to those properties of skill, and it has seemed not only that thinking of all kinds possesses them, but also that their study does throw some real light upon the thinking processes themselves.

. . . thinking is an advanced form of skilled behaviour; . . . it has grown out of earlier established forms of flexible adaptation to the environment; . . . the characteristics which it possesses and the conditions to which it submits can best be studied as they relate to those of its own earlier forms. (pp. 198–199)

In this chapter we shall expand on some of Bartlett's observations by showing how motor skills share processes with other cognitive skills. We shall discuss the learning of a motor skill and the role of feedback, information, and practice in carrying out a skill. Finally, we shall consider two schema models, one for controlling discrete skills and one for continuous skills. In all these topics we shall see that the movement of the body is only the visible part of a complex cognitive process. Motor skills are like language in that they are a particularly vivid expression of cognitive activities. Thus their relation to the other cognitive processes is of special interest.

In one of the earliest studies of motor skill learning, Bryan and Harter (1897, 1899) observed some of the significant features of skills in telegraph operators who were learning Morse code. The operators tended to learn the simple letters first and then the more complex ones. With practice they began to group the letters for familiar words, such as *the, of* and *on,* and with further practice even to group words into phrases. This resulted in an hierarchical structure for the code.

Practice also brought increased speed and fewer errors, though the rate of learning with continued practice dropped off, as is shown in Figure 11.1. Although Bryan and Harter give the data for only one subject in Figure 11.1, the form of the curve is common to many skill-learning tasks. Continual practice leads to continual improvement, but the rate of learning diminishes.

Fitts (1964) defined a **motor skill** response as "one in which receptor-effector-feedback processes are highly organized, both spatially and temporally," adding that "the central problem for the study of skill learning is how such organization or patterning comes about" (p. 244). The

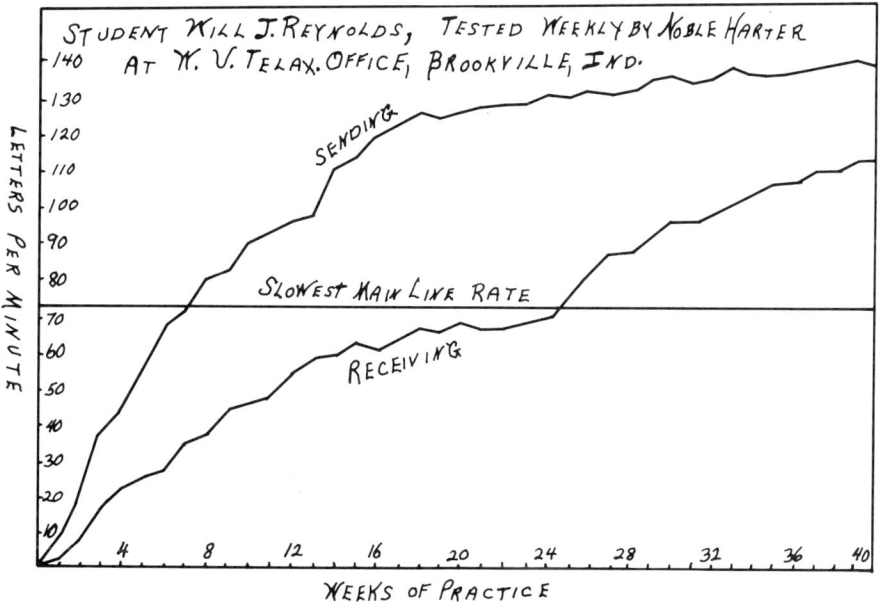

Figure 11.1 Rates for sending and receiving Morse code across weeks of practice for one student. (From Bryan & Harter, 1897.)

spatial pattern is the path the body traces through space as the skill is carried out. Instant playbacks on TV allow us to see this path more clearly and also reveal the temporal pattern—that is, the precise timing of each movement, as when a diver does a flip in midair and then slips into the water. The movements of many skills are coordinated to within millimeters and fractions of a second, and even the casual observer may be aware of when that coordination is poor.

Fitts noted that the psychological question is, Where does the organization come from? Given that a person is able to make a great many different movements, and that he or she could combine these into a still larger number of orders, why does the person choose these particular movements in this particular order? It is the same problem we have seen in other cognitive processes: the sequencing of instances in identifying a concept, the choice of actions in solving a problem, the choice of words in creating a sentence.

In each of these cases the process is hierarchically organized, and so it is with motor skills. Bryan and Harter (1897, 1899) observed that telegraph operators organize Morse code letters into words and words into phrases. Although each of the letters could be produced independently, they were structured hierarchically to meet the goal of sending a particular message. Similarly, in playing the guitar, we make chords with the left hand by choosing selected positions for each finger from among the many possible positions each finger might assume. Moreover, the progression of the chords is ordered, yielding an hierarchical structure for the positioning of the fingers in space and time. You might try analyzing some of the other motor skills you are familiar with in this same way.

In the following sections we will interpret the use of motor skills as a form of information processing. The process can be modeled by a program composed of an executive routine and any number of subroutines. The latter are relatively independent, repeatable acts that can be integrated into many different skills as dictated by the executive. The executive controls the order and timing of the subroutines and relies heavily on feedback in this control. Learning a motor skill is the process of choosing the appropriate subroutines and integrating them with increasing precision through practice.

PROPERTIES OF MOTOR SKILLS

There are several properties of skilled behavior which are especially revealing of its nature. These properties provide a convenient taxonomy of skills—that is, a set of categories for describing different skills. In addition, they are important characteristics that a proper theory of motor skills should explain. We shall describe them in this section and in later sections try to show how they arise from the way the motor skill processes are organized.

Fitts (1964) has described three properties of skilled behavior. *Continuity* is the evenness of the movement in space and time. The act of pulling the drawstring on a set of curtains requires little change in either the direction of the movement or its timing. In playing the piano, however, the fingers must change the direction of their movement frequently and at irregular intervals.

Coherence is the patterning of the movement in space and time. Swimming the backstroke is highly coherent, since the order and timing of the movements are quite patterned and predictable; but playing Ping-Pong has lower coherence since each return of the ball is made from a unique height, angle, speed, and so on.

Complexity is the number of stimuli and responses involved in the skill, or in information-processing terms, the amount of information which must be taken in, processed, and then output. Playing the organ is more complex, for instance, than playing the piano because there are usually three lines of music to read instead of two and there are many more controls to operate for both the hands and the feet. These properties provide a descriptive framework for motor skills, and a skill may be described by the measure it has on each of these properties.

To these three properties we may add two more, the first of which is *appropriateness*. Most skills are suited to the situation at hand and are not produced randomly, except perhaps in convulsive states. They thus display the goal-directed character that is found in so many of the other cognitive processes.

Second, virtually every motor act is *novel;* that is, it can be distinguished from other examples of the same act in some manner. Although you have written your signature thousands of times, it is unlikely that any two instances of it are indentical.

LEARNING A MOTOR SKILL

In learning a new skill, one brings many already well-developed skills to the task. The overall plan for a new skill may be compared to an executive routine that maps out the basic requirements of the skill and then draws upon relevant subroutines from known skills. At first these are coordinated clumsily, but with practice they may be integrated smoothly and the skill carried out unconsciously.

Fitts (1964) has described three phases for learning a skill. They are not discrete phases but shade gradually into one another as the skill becomes hierarchically organized. In the *early phase* we determine the basic requirements of the skill through instructions or watching someone else perform the skill. We also make some preliminary efforts at putting together the component movements of the skill and try to discover how they are patterned.

The *intermediate phase* involves practice at integrating the components, discovering how the borrowed subroutines should be modified, discovering more precisely what the timing requirements are for the movements and integrating them accordingly into a well-coordinated act. The new skill must also be integrated with ongoing skills; for example, in learning a new dance step, the skills for posture and locomotion must be maintained.

The *late phase* involves the continual polishing of the acquired skill. At present it appears that a skill will continue to improve so long as one practices it, although the rate of improvement will diminish. With this overview, let us look at these three phases in more detail.

Early Phase

In learning a new skill, one must first get a "Plan" for the skill, to use Miller, Galanter, and Pribram's (1960) term. Someone tells us how to carry out the act and perhaps demonstrates it so that we can code a schematic of the various movements and their order. Getting the pattern right at this conceptual level is important preparation for integrating the movements. In driving a car with a standard shift we must learn to depress the clutch before moving the gear shift. A tennis instructor may demonstrate how to return a ball by going through the act in slow motion and pointing out the important movements as she goes. By observing these we can code what is required for the act.

Integrating movements at this stage is largely a conscious process and the strain on working memory is substantial. In learning to return a tennis shot we must simultaneously remember to go to where the ball is going to be, keep our knees bent, elbow straight, racquet drawn back, and eye on the ball. The action will be erratic until some of these become automatic and take the load off of working memory. In conscious control, we also rely on forms of feedback which will drop away as the skill becomes automatic, as when we watch our fingers in learning to type or our feet in learning a dance step.

Intermediate Phase

The skill becomes more efficient through practice. The plan for the skill becomes more sharply defined as one adjusts the intensity and timing of each movement to a more smoothly executed flow. The strain on working memory is still heavy, since it must call up each movement at the right time as well as store feedback from each completed movement. The strain is steadily reduced, however, as corrective feedback refines the program instructions for each movement and the movements are integrated into larger units. Miller et al. cite an excellent example of these processes in a study by Book (1908) on learning to touch-type.

> People first memorized the positions of the different letters on the keyboard. Then they would go through several discrete steps: look at the next letter in the material that was to be copied, locate this letter in their image of the keyboard, feel around on the actual keyboard for the key corresponding to the remembered position, strike the key, and look to see if it was correct. After a few hours of practice these components of the Plan began to fit together into skilled movements, and the learner had acquired dependable "letter habits." Further speed resulted when they began to anticipate the next letter and build up small subroutines to deal with familiar sequences like *-ing* and *the*. By then dependable "word habits" were developing. (Miller, Galanter, & Pribram, 1960, p. 86)

This selection describes both the early and intermediate phases of learning to touch-type. The intermediate phase appeared after the first few hours of practice as the typists began to increase speed and to integrate their movements into larger units.

Typing is fairly low in continuity. Kay (1969) has described the development of a skill that is higher in continuity: catching a ball. In studying films of children aged 2, 5, and 15, he observed that the 2-year-olds tended not to close their fingers immediately after the ball hit their hands. Their hands moved slowly, tending to cradle the ball against the body, and the ball often rolled away. These children watched their hands or the thrower instead of the ball. The 5-year-olds moved their hands to meet the ball and watched the ball as well as their hands. The 15-year-olds kept their eye on the ball even while moving their hands to meet the ball and closed their fingers immediately. The separate movements were integrated into a smooth sequence attuned to the action of the ball.

Late Phase

Once established, a skill continues to improve both in speed and proficiency so long as it is practiced. Although there are few studies of long-range learning, an extensive review by Crossman (1959) indicates no leveling off of performance so long as practice continues. In a study of workers in a Cuban cigar-manufacturing company, for example, he found that even workers who had rolled as many as ten million cigars continued to increase their speed of rolling cigars (see Figure 11.2). As with most skills, however, the rate of improvement decreased. The only limit to improvement appears to arise not from the learning process but from a drop in motivation for practice or from physiological changes such as aging. Reports from athletes and musicians also indicate that further practice continues to produce improvement in a skill even after years of intensive practice.

With practice, a skill also becomes increasingly autonomous. It is a simple matter to walk and talk at the same time because both of these skills are highly practiced. The experienced pianist can carry on a conversation as he plays. Autonomy is reflected in a minimum of interference to a skill when two or more skills are carried on simultaneously. It is also reflected in a minimum of conscious control, which frees the performer to concentrate on larger features of the skill, as a violinist when she is interpreting the mood of a concerto.

In brief, the learning of a motor skill progresses from a conscious representation of the re-

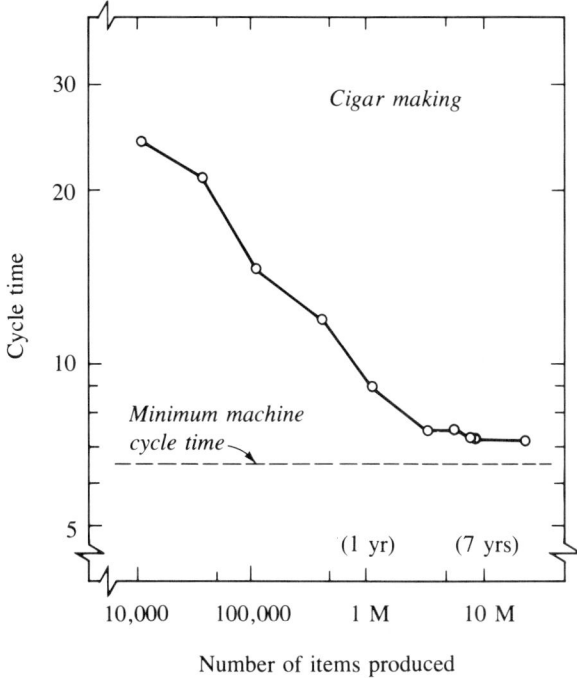

Figure 11.2 Gradual improvement in the performance of an industrial task over several years of work. (From Crossman, 1959.)

quirements of the skill through a phase of increasing hierarchical organization and coordination to a level of smooth, autonomous mastery. Such learning occurs only with continual practice. In addition, feedback is critical to learning, and it is to this topic that we turn next.

FEEDBACK

Motor skills have often been referred to as "perceptual motor skills" to emphasize the importance of sensory feedback in controlling the motor act. In Chapter 1 we stated that **feedback** is a form of information that stems from the consequences of an act and provides guidance about whether the act is achieving its intended goal.

In Figure 11.3 we have diagrammed a TOTE unit that illustrates the use of feedback. (TOTE is an acronym for Test-Operate-Test-Exit.) After each operation with the hammer a visual test determines whether the nail head is flush with the board. The results of the test are feedback; if the nail head is not flush, hammering continues; but if it is, then hammering stops. A thermostat is an example of a familiar device that uses feedback. The thermostat controls when the furnace turns on and off, and the output of the furnace is input to the thermostat. Control devices that use feedback are called *servomechanisms* and are applications of cybernetic theory.

In a human motor skill, feedback may be either intrinsic or extrinsic. *Intrinsic feedback* is sensory information that is a natural consequence of the act. In reaching for a doorknob, you may see that your hand has reached the knob as well as feel the touch of it. Similarly, you know that you

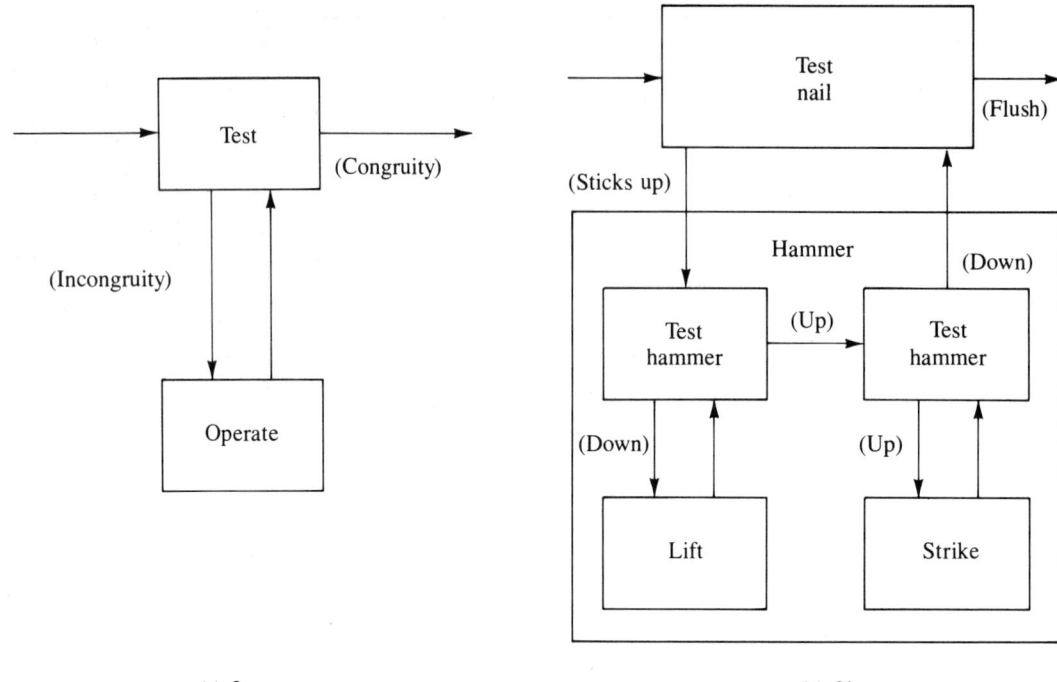

Figure 11.3 The TOTE unit as conceptualized by Miller, Galanter, and Pribram (11.3a) and an example of a TOTE unit involved in hammering a nail (11.3b). (From Miller, Galanter, & Pribram, 1960.)

have lit your pipe when you hear the crackle of the tobacco and perhaps see it flame, as well as taste the smoke, smell the aroma, and feel the heat. Intrinsic feedback may flow through any of the senses—sight, audition, taste, smell, touch, balance, and proprioception.

Proprioceptive feedback is signaled by receptors in the joints and tells us where the limbs are located in space (Adams, 1977). Try closing your eyes, holding your hands straight out from your sides, and then bringing your arms around until your forefingers touch. The control for this surprisingly successful movement lies in proprioceptive feedback. This sense is one we often do not think about but it is one of the most significant sources of feedback for motor skills.

Extrinsic feedback comes from external sources such as an observer or a machine signal. When you execute a dive, a poolside observer may tell you whether your legs were still straight as you entered the water; similarly, the bell on a typewriter tells you when you have reached the margin. Extrinsic feedback may come from several sources at the same time, just as intrinsic feedback may, and it usually supplements intrinsic feedback.

Learning a motor skill does not occur without feedback. You may instruct your muscles to perform, but if the accuracy of the action is unknown no improvement is possible. Although it is very difficult to remove all feedback, especially proprioceptive feedback, Laszlo and Bairstow

(1971) attempted to do so in a task requiring subjects to draw letters with their index fingers. Visual and auditory feedback were removed by closing the eyes and stopping the ears, and proprioceptive feedback was removed by a tight cuff around the wrist. Subjects reported they could not feel the movements of their hands while the cuff was on.

Under these conditions of no feedback, extended practice in drawing letters produced no improvement. Other evidence suggests that the success of learning depends on the clarity of sensory feedback (Adams & Goetz, 1973; Newall, 1974) and is reduced when the feedback is distorted or equivocal (Hunt, 1964; Shelly, 1961).

Since learning involves matching an actual movement to an intended movement, feedback about the discrepancy between the two is especially helpful for learning. Leonard (1959) asked subjects to turn a wheel at a certain rate. Between trials some subjects held the wheel while a machine turned it at the desired rate, thus telling them what the target rate was. Other subjects held the wheel while the machine turned it at a rate that matched the difference between the target rate and how fast they had actually turned it, giving them feedback about how far off target they were. The latter group learned to turn the wheel at the target rate significantly faster.

Studies in which feedback is reduced (e.g., Gould, 1965) usually indicate that learning is impaired in proportion to the degree that feedback is reduced. Smith and Sussman (1969) have reported a series of studies in which television monitors and other electronic links were used to delay intrinsic feedback for varying intervals. They concluded that "observed effects of feedback delays indicate that little or no learning actually occurs in most response systems with feedback delays longer than 0.4 second, or if limited learning occurs, it is likely to be unstable" (p. 126).

Reducing or delaying feedback will also inhibit the carrying out of an already learned skill (see Annett, 1969, for a review). Speaking, for example, relies heavily on auditory feedback. If a person's speech is tape recorded and played back through earphones at a delay of about 200 msec, the individual will begin to hesitate, falter, and slow down. Normal feedback is partly preserved through bone conduction, but the delay in the feedback that comes through the ears creates a severe disturbance. Similarly, although you can write in the dark, the extra visual feedback from light usually makes the result more legible.

When feedback is delayed, reduced, or distorted in some manner, you can often adapt to these circumstances with practice, though the adaptation is not usually complete. Stratton (1896, 1897) developed a special pair of glasses which inverted the visual image so that the wearer saw everything upside down and reversed from right to left. Stratton found coordination was a bit difficult at first for such simple acts as reaching for a doorknob (he tended to reach to the wrong side of the door) or even walking across the room without bumping into things. After wearing the lenses for a number of days, however, Stratton found his coordination in these and other tasks began to improve. Kohler (1964) reported similar effects for lenses that only inverted the visual image, as well as for lenses that merely reversed the image from left to right.

The disorientation induced by such lenses arises from conflict among the sources of feedback. In normal circumstances, intrinsic feedback comes through several sensory systems and these are all in agreement. If you let the wheel of your car stray off the edge of the road, visual feedback signals the same thing as the shiver of the steering wheel and the crunch of gravel. With distorting lenses, however, vision signals that an object you wish to pick up is in one place while proprioception and other sensory systems indicate that it is in another; as the wearer of the lenses you are thus in understandable confusion about what movement would be required to pick up the object.

Adapting to such conflict appears to be a matter of bringing the sensory systems back into accommodation (Harris, 1965; Kornheiser, 1976). In analyzing the effects of distorting lenses, Harris (1965) describes proprioceptive information as a sense of *felt position,* which also includes the effects of the pull of gravity in determining when one is upright. From the work of Stratton (1896, 1897), Kohler (1964), and many others in this field, Harris concluded that the visual system is largely inflexible and that it is the position sense that changes with experience to restore the accord between these sources of feedback.

For example, when a wearer of inverting lenses was permitted to use only one of his arms within his field of vision, the position sense for that arm adapted to the new visual field. Lenses that invert the visual field, of course, also reverse the visual field; thus the wearer had to move his arm to the right to reach something that appeared to be on the left in the reoriented visual field.

After wearing the lenses for a while, the position sense for this arm adapted to the reversed movement. The position sense for the unseen arm, however, was unaffected. When the subject was then blindfolded and asked to point in a certain direction with first one arm and then the other, the two arms did not agree. The pointing was guided solely by the position sense, and the position sense for one arm had been reoriented by its adaptation to the reversed visual field.

In summary, feedback is perceptual information from the consequences of a motor act which signals how well the act is being carried out. Feedback may be either intrinsic or extrinsic and can be received through any of the perceptual systems. Learning does not occur without feedback and is retarded if feedback is reduced, distorted, or delayed. Also, the performance of a familiar skill is impaired when feedback is reduced, distorted, or delayed, although some adaptation to these conditions occurs with practice. An interesting real-life setting where feedback plays an important role is described in Box 11.1.

PROCESSING INFORMATION

As with the other cognitive processes, carrying out a motor skill can be viewed as an information-processing activity. Shannon and Weaver (1949) developed a method for quantifying information which is often used in research on motor skills. The term *information* is defined in a somewhat special sense. It assumes that information is a measure of uncertainty in a situation; that is, it is a measure of the number of possible events that may occur.

If someone gives you a number, for instance, the number conveys more information if it is drawn from the set of 1–100 than if it is only drawn from the set of 1–10. Your uncertainty about which number you will get is much greater with the 100 than with the 10. Thus the amount of information conveyed increases with the uncertainty of what the event will be. If there were only one possible event, you would gain no information when it occurred, since the single possibility was perfectly predictable.

The significance of defining information in this way is that it permits a quantitative measure of information. The ability to quantify terms lends greater precision and testability to an hypothesis or theory and is usually greeted with approval. Quantifying the term *information* led to new ways of thinking about some of the cognitive processes (e.g., see Attneave, 1959; Pierce, 1961), though we should warn you that information-processing theorists do not always use the term in this specialized sense.

The basic unit of information is the *bit,* an abbreviation of the words *binary digit.* A bit is the amount of information gained from knowing which of two equally likely events will occur. Flipping a coin has two equally likely outcomes, heads or tails; knowing which outcome will occur for a particular flip gives one bit of infor-

> **Box 11.1 FEEDBACK IN SINGING**
>
> Professional opera singing is a truly demanding skill. Behind the splendor of the vocal line lies a controlled outpouring of energy that can cost a singer five pounds in a single night's performance. Following a highly acclaimed production of *Norma*, opera singers Joan Sutherland and Marilyn Horne gave an inside report on some of the vocal techniques that brought them to the top of their profession (Meryman, 1970). Sutherland is a statuesque Australian soprano who specializes in coloratura roles. The music for these roles is filled with vocal runs, trills, and leaps of such daring as to make a nightingale blanch. Dramatic arias, saving the hardest work until last, sometimes end on a pitch so high that it is beyond the range of most singers. Horne, in contrast, sings in the lower register, delivering a rich, velvet tone with a power that commands and captivates her listeners.
>
> Both singers concentrate intensely on tone quality. Wobble, flattening, and squeezing are all to be avoided. They strive for a big, roomy tone—one that is round and bright and capable of filling a large auditorium. Surprisingly, singers rely heavily on proprioceptive feedback in the control of tone quality rather than on auditory feedback. Sensations of vibration as the tone resonates in the chest and head are the sought-after cues that the proper tone is reaching the listener. These sensations are often difficult to identify, and Sutherland reports that singers vary greatly in how they describe them.
>
> Given the difficulty of labeling these sensations, the art of teaching good vocal technique taxes a coach's ingenuity. Horne reports that singers often spend years in searching for the proprioceptive sensations that produce the desired tone. Vocal coaches work with them to give them feedback (extrinsic) about what the tone sounds like. Over the years a coach and a singer may develop a common set of labels—words for identifying the proprioceptive sensations the singer experiences and the tone quality the coach experiences. For example, Horne reports that it was several years before she and her coach came to a common understanding for the use of the term *forward*. She discovered that he was using *forward* for the sounds that she produced by singing deeper in the throat while resonating in the mask (that is, the nose, cheekbones, mouth, and sinuses).

mation. If there are eight equally likely outcomes for an action, you gain three bits of information from knowing which one will occur.

For example, if someone holds eight playing cards and asks you which one is the ace of spades, you may ask whether it is in cards 1–4 or 5–8, and the answer will give you one bit of information (see Figure 11.4). If it is in 5–8, you then ask whether it is in cards 5, 6 or 7, 8; and the answer gives you one more bit of information. If

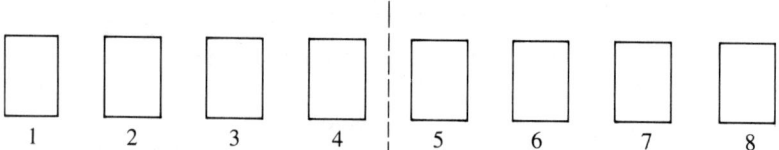

Q: Is the ace in the left set or right set of cards?
A: Right set (produces one bit of information)

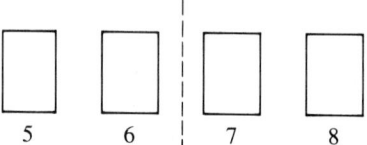

Q: Is the ace in the left set or right set of cards?
A: Left set (produces a second bit of information)

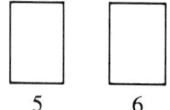

Q: Is the ace the left or right card?
A: Left card (produces a third bit of information)

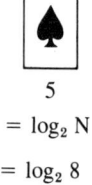

$H = \log_2 N$

$3 = \log_2 8$

Figure 11.4 Finding the ace of spades in a set of eight playing cards produces three bits of information.

you are told it is in 5, 6, you then ask which and the answer—say, 5—gives the third bit of information.

This method of successive halving of possible outcomes provides the measure of information for any set of equally likely outcomes. In general the formula for calculating information is

$$H = \log_2 N \qquad (1)$$

where H is the number of bits of information and N is the number of equally likely outcomes. H is simply the number of times 2 must be multiplied by itself to yield N.

Quite commonly the possible outcomes of

an event are not equally likely. In a horse race some mounts are more likely to win than others. The more likely an outcome is, the less information it conveys when it actually occurs. The perfectly predictable outcome—for example, that a light goes out when you turn off the power—conveys no information at all; while an unlikely outcome is highly informative, as when a long shot wins the horse race. When the possible outcomes are not equally likely, the formula for calculating information for an outcome is

$$H = \log_2 1/p \qquad (2)$$

where p is the probability of that outcome. Note that this formula is identical to formula (1) when the outcomes are equally likely.

People carrying out a motor skill are transmitting information in the sense that each response they make is one of many possible responses that they might make. Different tasks call for different amounts of information to be transmitted, and the comparison between discrete and continuous tasks is of special interest.

Discrete Skills

In an RT (reaction time) task a subject is asked to respond as quickly as possible to a signal. Varying the number of signals changes the information being transmitted in the task. Hyman (1953) showed that increasing the information in the signals increases the RT to them in a linear manner. Using lights as signals, he asked his subjects to give a different verbal response to each light. When he varied the number of lights from one to eight, he found this relation held even when some lights occurred more frequently than others or when certain lights regularly followed others. In all cases the RT increased as the information value of the signals increased (see Figure 11.5). Other studies have shown the same effect (e.g., Brainard, Irby, Fitts, & Alluisi, 1962; Hick, 1952).

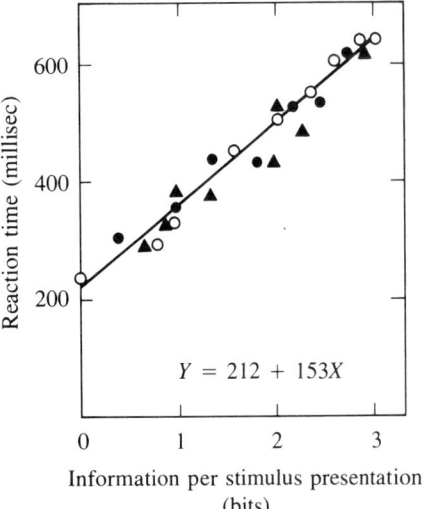

Figure 11.5 RT as a function of the average information in sets of stimuli with equal probabilities (circles), unequal probabilities (filled circles), and sequential dependencies (triangles). Data are for one subject. (From Hyman, 1953.)

This relation also holds when speed is traded for accuracy. Speeding up the task increases the number of errors subjects make, but only correct responses can be counted in calculating the amount of information transmitted. A subject making many errors in responding to signals having four bits of information might be transmitting no more information than a subject who makes no errors in responding to signals having two bits of information. Hick (1952) varied the speed of an RT task, thereby increasing errors in the more speeded conditions, and found that the linear relation between amount of information transmitted and RT still appeared.

Thus RT appears to be governed not by the number of different signals and responses in the task, but by the amount of information being transmitted. Together, the Hyman (1953) and Hick (1952) experiments, plus other supporting studies, have established a broad range of conditions in which RT increases in constant proportion to the amount of information being transmitted in the skill task.

Although RT increases as the amount of information being transmitted increases, the rate of increase in RT varies with the task. The rate of increase is shown by the slope of the line relating the two, as in Figure 11.5; the steeper the slope, the greater the rate of increase in RT.

One factor that has an important effect on the rate of increase is the *compatibility* of the task. This is an index of how directly related a response is to its signal. Crossman (cited in Welford, 1976) established a high compatibility task by arranging lights in a horizontal row and putting the correct key for each light immediately beneath the light. A low compatibility condition was created by randomly ordering the keys under the lights. Some subjects had only two lights to react to, while others had eight lights. As was to be expected, those having eight lights (greater information) showed longer RTs to the lights. Moreover, the increase in RT was greater in the low compatibility task than in the high compatibility one.

Other studies that have investigated the effects of compatibility without varying the number of choices also show that high compatibility produces faster RTs. Moreover, intermediate levels of compatibility, as when the lights and keys are ordered in opposite directions, still produce faster RTs than do random orderings of the keys (Fitts & Deininger, 1954; Morin & Grant, 1955; Smith, 1977).

The notion of compatibility carries over to the relation between equipment controls and their effects. When you turn the tuning knob of a radio clockwise, you expect the station marker to move to the right, not to the left. This relation and similar ones shown in Figure 11.6 are matters of convention in designing equipment controls. Such conventions lead to an easy control of the equipment. Unconventional relations can be overcome with practice but still may lead to confusion in moments of stress (Taylor & Garvey, 1959).

Continuous Skills

Continuous skills are those that involve a series of movements, such as typing or playing the piano. The amount of information transmitted in these tasks is based on the number of keys being used (e.g., about 45 on a typewriter or 88 on a piano keyboard), as well as the rate of striking them.

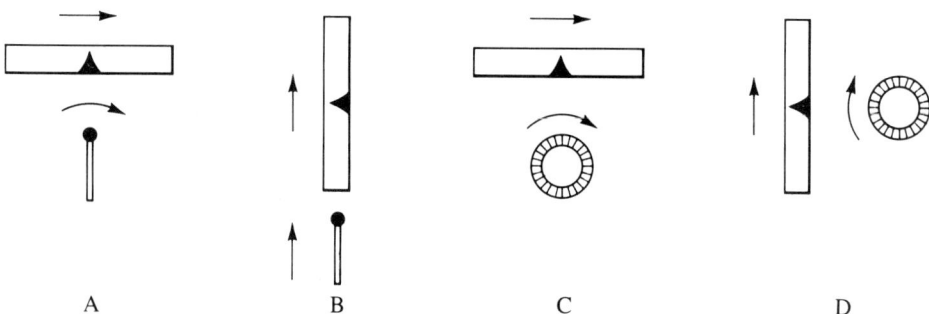

Figure 11.6 Expected relationships between the movements of controls and displays. Movements of the levers and knobs are expected to produce corresponding movements of the pointers in the directions indicated by the arrows. (From Welford, 1976.)

Each response contains so many bits of information, and we can calculate the rate of transmission by the number of bits per sec.

Most typewriters have about 45 keys, which are for letters, numbers, and punctuation. Striking one of these keys conveys 5.49 bits of information by formula (1). If a typist averages two keys per sec, then there are $2 \times 5.49 = 10.98$ bits per sec being transmitted. Quastler and Wulff (1955) have calculated the amount of information being transmitted by a skilled typist to be about 15 bits per sec and for a skilled pianist about 22 bits per sec. These rates are stable even when the task is speeded up, since errors increase with speed and must be discounted in calculating amount of information.

The upper limit for the rate of transmitting information has been estimated to be 25 to 35 bits per sec for highly practiced tasks such as typing, piano playing, reading, and speaking (Newman, 1959; Pierce & Karlin, 1957). These limits, however, may vary with the efficiency of the coding strategy being used for processing incoming information. The skilled pianist reads ahead, coding and storing music in working memory so that she is ready to turn the page while her fingers still lag several bars behind. Similarly, an analysis of typing reveals that the typist looks ahead in the copy, coding groups of letters or words even as his fingers are typing out groups already coded (Shaffer, 1976).

These strategies illustrate the chunking process we observed in the discussion of temporary memory in Chapter 3. It is a very efficient way of encoding information, and it occurs most commonly in highly practiced skills. However, it represents a qualitatively different way of processing information, since the elements of a chunk are not independent but are processed as a whole. This is the major reason for the high rates of transmitting information in well-practiced skills.

At the beginning of this chapter we stated that motor skills differ in terms of their complexity. Complexity can now be understood in part as the amount of information being transmitted. Flying a plane is more complex than driving a car because there are more gauges to attend to and more controls to operate, which results in more information being transmitted.

PRACTICE

Practice is an indispensable requirement for learning a motor skill. Countless experiments attest to this as does the personal experience of anyone who has ever undertaken a new skill. Practice means the repetition of a motor act with feedback. Both repetition and feedback are necessary for learning a motor act; repetition without feedback leads only to fatigue. The major effect of practice is to improve the speed, timing, and precision of a motor skill—that is, its spatial and temporal coordination. The mechanism of improvement is the organization of the individual movements of the skill into larger units that constitute subroutines in the program guiding the skill.

Timing is a key element in the program. Skilled movements are hierarchically structured in time; they are not just a succession of movements but are rhythmically patterned (Michon, 1974). Moreover, the rhythm has a minimum tempo, and if the pace of the movements drops below this minimum, the rhythm cannot be recognized.

Kalsbeek (1964) illustrated the development of a rhythm in two tasks that were to be performed concurrently. His subjects were to react to tones of two different pitches by pressing pedals with their feet while simultaneously sorting rods of different lengths with their hands. The subjects were free to regulate the order and timing of their movements for both hands and feet. Kalsbeek reported that with practice the subjects combined the tasks into a single, complex rhythm that reduced errors in both tasks.

Practice also changes the speed and timing in the execution of a skill. Times between individual movements seem to diminish, although the time devoted to the movements themselves changes less. For example, in a simple task such as grasping an object, moving it over to a box and dropping it into the box, the time required for moving the object diminishes faster with practice than the times devoted to grasping and dropping (Seymour, 1959; von Treba & Smith, 1952; Wehrkamp & Smith, 1952). The central decision process is presumably being modified with practice more than the execution times for individual movements.

The improvement that comes with practice seems in part to come from an increasing reliance on proprioceptive feedback. West (1967), for example, noted that typists do better in early training sessions if allowed to see what they have just typed. Visual feedback, however, later gives way to a reliance on proprioceptive feedback (see Box 11.2). If the trainee becomes dependent upon these external sources of feedback instead of shifting to proprioceptive feedback, then performance drops when the trainee transfers to the actual job (Annett, 1959; Goldstein & Rittenhouse, 1954; Thorsheim, Houston, & Badger, 1974).

Long-term studies of practice under controlled conditions are relatively few. One of the better examples was conducted by Snoddy (1926), who had subjects trace a pattern while they watched their actions in a mirror. Visual feedback was thus reversed, which led to initially awkward tracing. The subjects were asked to trace a pattern with a pencil once a day for 60 days. Snoddy scored the tracings for speed and number of errors, with the results shown in Figure 11.7. When the scales for trials (days) and performance are both converted to log scales, the relationship between practice and performance can be graphed as a simple straight line. Note that the tracing skill continued to improve throughout the 60 days.

Extensive practice of a skill, well beyond the level of mastery of it, makes it easier to recover after a long period of disuse. The experienced typist who returns to the keyboard after a year away will recover reasonable proficiency after only a few minutes of renewed practice. The ease of remembering a motor skill for a long time is in surprising contrast to the substantial forgetting that occurs for verbal materials within the same time period.

Fleishman and Parker (1962) investigated this effect in a study that simulated an airborne

---

Box 11.2 PROPRIOCEPTIVE FEEDBACK: HOW A DRUMMER KEEPS HIS BEAT

One night I stopped in at a local tavern to hear some friends who had formed a country music band. The drummer, who was about 20, sat in a nest of five drums and five cymbals. He almost never looked at his instruments but stared intently into space as he played. During a break, I asked him why he didn't watch what he was doing (even though he was doing very well without watching), and he said it would break his timing if he did. He had once played in a nightclub lighted only by a swirling stroboscopic beam. The timing of the strobe light conflicted with the rhythm of the music and he had had to learn to play with his eyes closed to keep his rhythm. He always set up his drums and cymbals in the same places so that he would know (proprioceptive knowing) where they were and could play them without looking at them.

—Danny Moates

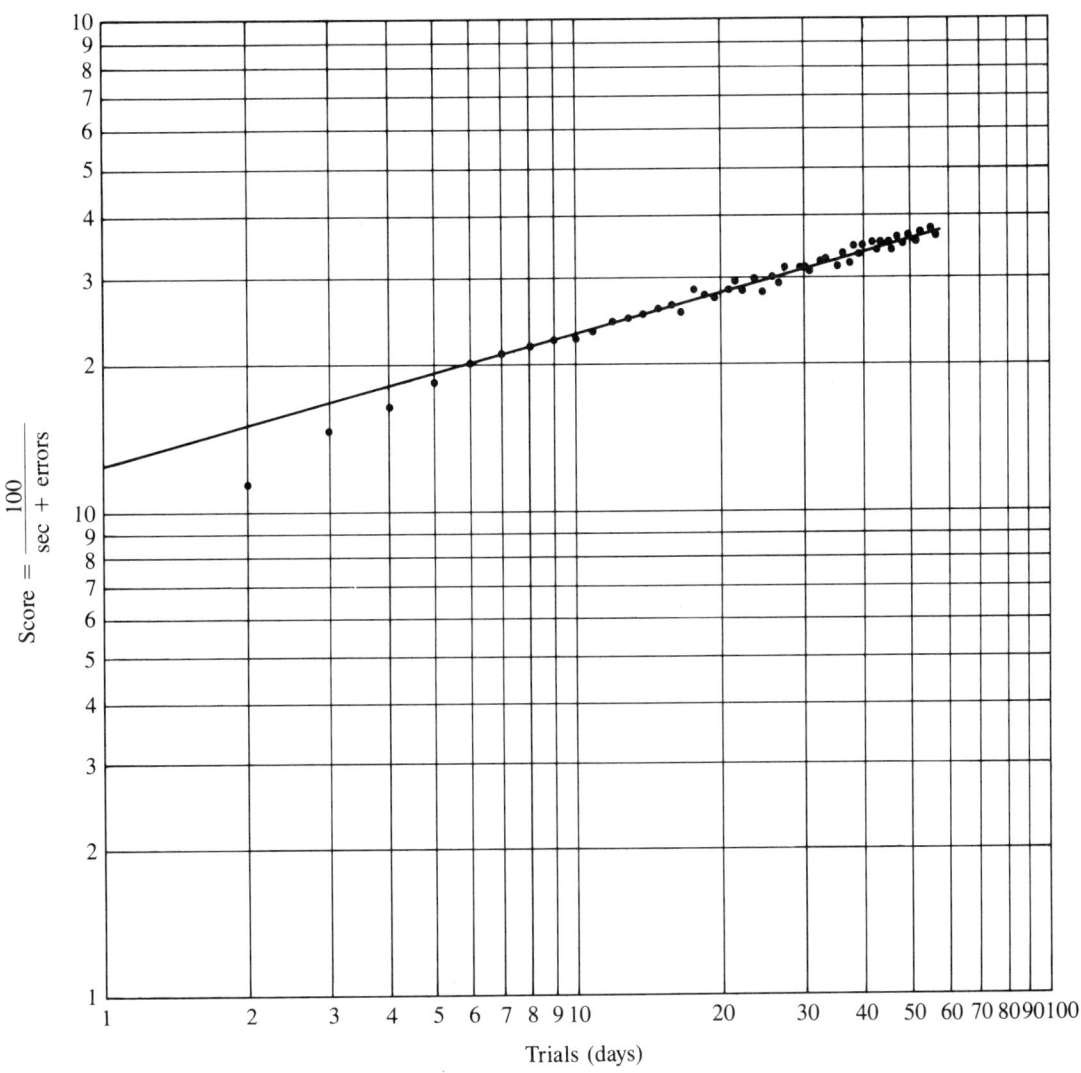

Figure 11.7 Improvement with practice, one trial per day. (From Snoddy, 1926.)

radar intercept mission. The equipment consisted of a cathode-ray tube that displayed a target dot; the dot was programmed to move off center continually in both horizontal and vertical directions. Beneath the cathode-ray tube was a voltmeter whose needle was also programmed to move off center continually.

The subjects were asked to keep the dot centered with a control stick that could be moved in two dimensions, and to keep the needle centered by foot control of a rudder bar. All subjects had 17 daily sessions for the initial training. They were then divided into three groups, which returned for retraining after intervals of

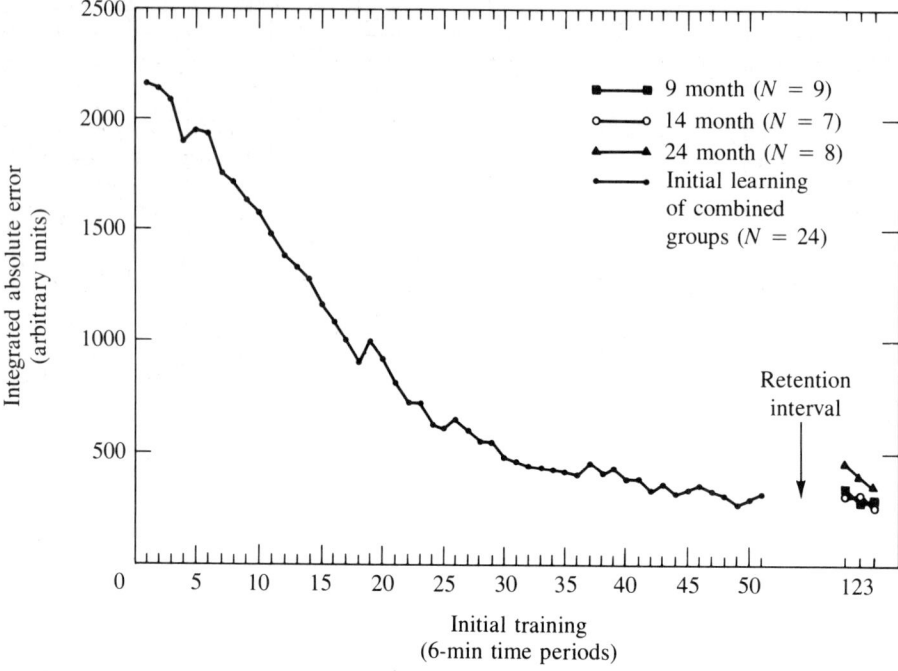

Figure 11.8 Performance during initial training and following varying periods without practice. (From Fleishman & Parker, 1962.)

either 9, 14, or 24 months. Figure 11.8 shows their error rate in both the initial and retraining sessions.

The initial training shows a large reduction in errors, and performance has nearly leveled off by the end of training. To the right of the figure are error rates for the three groups at retraining. These show almost no loss in proficiency even after months without practice. Even the 24-month group showed only a slight increase in errors, and they recovered their original proficiency within 20 minutes of retraining. Fleishman and Parker came to the ready conclusion that retention of this complex skill was extremely good for these long intervals and that even the small losses could be recovered easily.

Compatibility

We saw in an earlier section that reaction times are linearly related to the amount of information being transmitted in a task. In highly compatible tasks the reaction times are generally quite fast, and increasing the amount of information being transmitted does not increase the reaction time very much (Brainard, Irby, Fitts, & Alluisi, 1962; Hellyer, 1963; Leonard, 1959).

Practice also reduces reaction times, especially in a several-choice task (high-information load) as Teichner and Krebs (1974) have illustrated. Mowbray and Rhoades (1959) found that the reaction time to a four-choice task was reduced to that of a two-choice task after 42,000 heroic trials. With practice subjects can thus process increased information loads with minimum increases in reaction time. Even in an incompatible task practice reduces reaction time though not as much as in a compatible one.

Distributed versus Massed Practice

The schedule for practicing a skill plays an important role in acquiring it, especially in the early stages of learning. Periodic pauses for rest *(distributed practice)* generally produce better learning than does uninterrupted rehearsal *(massed practice)*. In a pursuit rotor task, Bourne and Archer (1956) asked subjects to try to keep a pointer fixed on a spot on a revolving disc. They found that the longer the rest periods between trials, up to 60 sec, the better the performance. Bourne and Archer also gave all their subjects a rest interval of 5 min between trials 21 and 22. This interval produced an especially marked improvement for all subjects (see Figure 11.9). Massed practice may result in fatigue and thus induce errors. If an error is repeated, then the error rather than the correct movement, may be learned. Errors thus should be a signal for a brief rest.

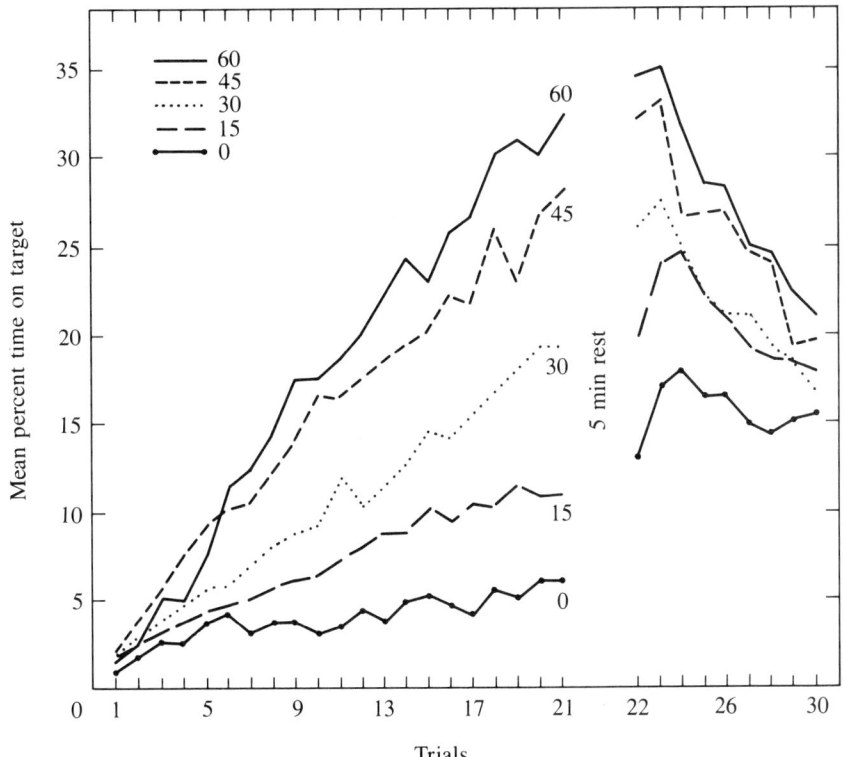

Figure 11.9 Time on target as a function of distribution of practice. Subjects had intervals of 0 to 60 sec between trials. (From Bourne & Archer, 1956.)

Whole-Part Learning

A skill is often more easily mastered if it can be broken into several parts that are practiced separately (part learning) rather than all practiced together (whole learning) (e.g., Bahrick, 1957). The critical question is how independent the components of the skill are. Seymour (1954, 1955, 1956) noted that the operation of a capstan-lathe (a type of industrial equipment) could be divided into four fairly distinct operations. He had subjects practice these four independently at first, then in pairs, then triplets, and finally all together, resulting in faster learning than occurred in a control group that learned the task as a whole.

When a task is not easily divided, however, such as flying an aircraft, it is better to learn it as a whole. Much of the learning then lies in the coordination of the individual movements and dividing the task destroys coordination and outweighs the advantage of mastering different portions of the task (Knapp, 1963; Naylor & Briggs, 1963).

Limits of Skill

There is no known limit to the number of skills a person can learn, and there is no clear limit to how well a person can learn a particular skill. In the section on practice we saw that workers in a cigar-making plant continued to improve even after rolling ten million cigars (Crossman, 1959). We often read news accounts of an athlete or musical artist who has reached some new limit in mastering a skill. The 4-minute mile was not broken until 1954; yet since that time several seconds have been knocked off the record. Reports from those who have devoted their lives to a particular skill indicate that continual practice is necessary for the skill to go on improving. Physical decline with age puts a ceiling on improvement; but prior to that, the major limit is a person's willingness to practice.

One of the final marks of a well-mastered skill is *automaticity*, the ability to carry out a skill without conscious control (see Chapter 2). Mature pianists can often carry on a conversation while playing your favorite rag. They let their hands do the playing while they devote conscious processing to the conversation. When a skill becomes automatic, feedback operates at a higher level in controlling the skill. The finger strokes of a musician may reach 16 per sec in some passages, and the succession of these movements is simply too quick for even visual feedback to provide any control over the movements (Lashley, 1951).

Keele and Posner (1968) established that it takes about 190–260 msec for visual feedback to be useful in correcting a movement. The fact that several individual movements can be produced within this time period suggests that the movements are not being controlled by feedback but may be controlled by a central program that directs the order and intensity of individual movements.

Feedback to this program is assumed to apply to some larger unit of action than the individual movement (Glencross, 1977). Central monitoring of feedback from the skill is more periodic, and the limited capacity of working memory is now more free for other activities. The conscious control required in the early stages of learning a motor program has now been discarded, replaced by the largely automatic functioning of a highly refined and well-rehearsed motor program. We turn now to a discussion of motor programs and their role in controlling a motor skill.

CENTRAL PROCESSES

Only in recent years have theorists begun to treat a motor skill as an information-processing activity that is centrally controlled and draws upon other central processes such as attention, perception, and memory (e.g., Adams, 1971). Earlier explanations had stressed the role of sensory feedback as a stimulus for a subsequent response —for example, the feedback from striking a particular typewriter key as a stimulus for striking the next key. Thus the serial nature of a motor skill was interpreted as a chain of stimulus-response events.

The "chaining" interpretation, however, faces several problems. First, a person can start, carry out, and stop a movement in 100 msec; yet the time required to make use of sensory feedback seems to be about 190–260 msec for vision (Keele & Posner, 1968) and 120–125 msec for the more rapid proprioceptive feedback (Chernikoff & Taylor, 1952). Clearly these times are too long to permit such sensory feedback to control motor movements. Similarly, in a complex skill such as playing the piano, the individual movements occur far too rapidly to be influenced by the relatively sluggish flow of sensory feedback (Lashley, 1951; Pew, 1966).

A second problem is that most motor acts are novel. The choice and sequence of movements in each act is unique; thus there has been no opportunity to learn a stimulus-response chain, since the act has not occurred before.

These difficulties have led to the hypothesis of a **motor program,** a stored set of commands that is structured before the act and permits the act to be carried out without feedback. Although theories about motor programs have only recently appeared, the notion of a motor program appeared as early as Lashley (1917). Lashley described a patient who had a gunshot wound in his back and had lost all sensory feedback below the knees, though he had not lost the efferent pathways for controlling these limbs. Despite the loss of sensory feedback, the patient showed a surprising ability to control movement in his legs and feet, leading Lashley to suggest the movement was controlled centrally rather than by sensory feedback.

A motor program is essentially a schema, as we have used the term in earlier chapters (see particularly Chapters 2 and 7), following Bartlett (1932/1967) and more recently Neisser (1976). As such, it is a general plan for a class of acts, such as throwing something, returning a serve, or diving. Each time an act from that class is performed, the schema or program must be tailored to the specific situation. Throwing a tennis ball is different from throwing a Ping-Pong ball.

Each use of the program not only provides control for the present act but also adds new information to the program for carrying out future acts. Continuing use of the program thus provides for its continuing refinement. The new information is in the form of feedback from the act. Most theories about motor programs not only provide for central control of an act by a motor program but also postulate varying degrees of peripheral influence from sensory feedback (e.g., Glencross, 1977; Pew, 1974; Schmidt, 1976).

Defining a motor schema as a general plan rather than a set of specific muscle movements resolves problems related to novelty and storage. Virtually every motor act is unique, varying with the starting position of the body and the state of the environment. As many times as we may shake hands, each time the act will be detectably different from all others of the same class. Hypothesizing a specific schema for each unique act would entail the storage of an enormous number of schemata and would still leave unanswered the question of how we acquired the schemata in the first place.

Current theories about motor schemata thus define a schema as a general plan for carrying out a class of acts and provide a mechanism for tailoring the schema to the individual requirements of the situation each time the schema is called up. This approach not only accounts for novelty but reduces the storage problem to more reasonable limits.

The following discussion of two current theories about motor programs is broken into a description of first, a theory of continuous motor skills and second, a theory of discrete motor skills, though the two theories have much in common.

A Theory of Continuous Skills

A *continuous skill* is one that may be carried out in an unbroken fashion for an indefinite period of time, such as speaking, singing, typing, or walking. These skills are carried out linearly in time; yet they have an hierarchic structure that can be captured readily in a motor program. Pew (1974) has developed a theory that describes the organization and control of such skills at three levels: (1) inner-loop control, (2) higher-order control, and (3) voluntary movement.

Inner-loop Control. The lowest level of control is *inner-loop control* (often called *closed-loop control* by other investigators). In such control all corrections in a behavior are in response to external stimulation. This level of control applies to simple acts, such as pressing on a control stick with a force equal to the force with which the control stick is pressing back. If the force from the control stick is varied randomly, then the subjects must adjust their pressure accordingly. Pew noted that RT for making adjustments in such tasks was about 200 msec. This is a tracking task in which the subjects try to follow the changes in pressure. A model of this tracking process requires only that subjects be able to determine the pressure from the stick, to detect any discrepancy between their pressure and that of the stick, and to reduce the discrepancy to zero.

These processes constitute a closed-loop control system, the simplest feedback control system, and are the same ones used by a thermostat: identify, match, reduce discrepancy to zero. Closed-loop control systems require a minimum of intelligence and operate in a great variety of simple tracking tasks.

Higher-order Control. The second level of control applies to tasks in which the signal to be tracked is not random but organized and therefore predictable, as in tracing a circle or keeping a car on the road. As subjects gain experience with the signal or have a chance to look ahead at what they must track, they detect the pattern in the signal they are tracking and create a motor program to represent it. The motor program then generates commands that will reproduce the pattern. Initially the pattern developed in the motor program will contain inaccuracies, but the subjects continue to match the pattern generated against the pattern in the incoming signal and use this feedback to modify the pattern in the motor program. The role of practice is thus to refine the pattern in the motor program.

A well-practiced subject should then be able to track a signal without feedback about how he or she is doing. Such an act is then under what is called *open-loop control;* that is, the act is directed solely by the motor program and without benefit of feedback. Open-loop control is in contrast to *closed-loop control* (described in the previous section), in which the direction of the movements is controlled by feedback.

Pew suggested that motor programs normally operate under closed-loop control, so long as feedback is available. Subjects continue to test the pattern they are generating against the pattern in the signal, modifying the pattern in the motor program if necessary. The time span in such testing, however, is longer than the 200 msec used by closed-loop control systems and may span a period of several seconds.

The motor program and closed-loop control systems are thus separate control systems operating in concert to produce the tracking behavior. Each operates in closed-loop fashion, using feedback to correct movements, but the motor program operates at a higher level by correcting the pattern generator that issues movement commands.

A final component of higher-order control involves the effector system of the machine being operated. Driving a car with manual steering requires more force than driving a car with power steering; similarly, the precision in the two systems is likely to differ. The commands issued by the motor program must be adjusted to take account of the effector system, in this case the steering system. Steering a truck is different from driving a car, though the object is the same: to keep the vehicle on the road. In general, the speed, power, and precision of the effector system must be represented in the motor program to bring the motor commands to the desired goal.

Voluntary Control. The third level of control differs from the preceding two in that in voluntary movement (1) the path of movement is less important than the goal, (2) the pattern of movement is generated internally from experience with similar goals, and (3) the conduct of the movement is paced by internal control rather than by external conditions.

Voluntary control arises from a motor schema that has been developed from previous experience with similar goals and is stored in memory. Invoking such a schema is a voluntary act that can be applied to a class of acts, such as signing your name. As we have pointed out, the thousands of signatures you have produced are similar and distinctively yours despite differences in their size (signing a check versus signing your name on a blackboard) and the speed with which they are carried out.

This raises a question of what is coded in the motor schema. Clearly it does not specify either particular muscle movements or timing, since these change each time you sign your name. What is more likely is that the motor schema contains some features that are fixed, such as the spatial pattern to be produced; while other features, such as size and timing of the movements, are left open, to be specified by the requirements of the particular situation.

Henderson (1977) has offered evidence for this assumption in a study of dart throwing. In one of the conditions of her study, subjects threw darts at a well-lighted target for 100 trials. In the following 20 trials the room was dark and the subjects threw darts at a luminescent target. Thus they received no visual feedback about the accuracy of their throws. Henderson found that the accuracy of throws in the dark condition deteriorated, but the consistency of throws did not. Consistency was measured by the distance between the point of impact for successive throws.

Henderson interpreted these results to mean that consistency is controlled by factors intrinsic to the schema for the voluntary act of dart throwing. These central control factors are unaffected by the loss of visual feedback. Accuracy, however, requires specifying motor commands at each throw to adjust for the position of the thrower and his relation to the target. Thus accuracy is affected by visual feedback.

Figure 11.10 diagrams the process of generating a voluntary act. The motor schema for an act is contained in schema memory. When the conditions are such that the individual desires to carry out a movement, a specific instance of the schema is selected. This selection depends on the state of the organism and the environment. In the next stage of the production of the response, the specific program is converted into a sequence of motor commands. Finally, the muscles are activated to carry out the motor command. As indicated in the figure a number of feedback loops serve to modify the selection procedure and the schema itself.

We may see this process in the act of returning a tennis shot. Although each shot (forehand, backhand, volley) has a fairly standard form, a particular instance of a shot must be selected for a particular situation. This will depend on the speed and angle of the incoming ball as well as whether the player is near the net or the baseline, is moving, or is still. Thus the momentary state of the player and the environment will influence which specific instance is selected. Once the instance is selected a string of motor commands is generated and finally the muscles will be activated to carry out the shot.

Feedback in such voluntary movements serves two roles. First, visual, auditory, and proprioceptive feedback indicate whether the act achieved its goal (e.g., whether the tennis shot was returned successfully). Feedback thus tells whether the motor schema and the specific instance of it selected for this act were correct or should be modified for future acts.

Second, feedback—especially proprioceptive feedback—tells whether the act is being carried out properly. Pew suggests that the motor schema not only generates a set of muscle commands, but that it also retains a copy of these and further that it generates a set of expected sensory consequences of the muscle acts. Actual sensory

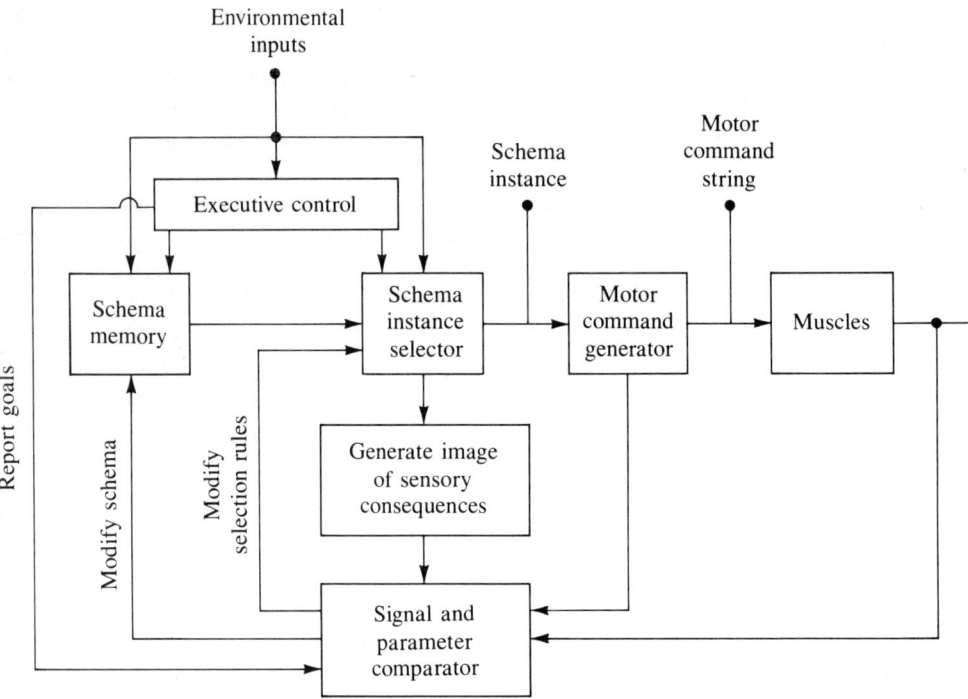

Figure 11.10 Flowchart for a model of the performance of voluntary movements. (From Pew, 1974.)

feedback is compared with expected sensory consequences as the act is carried out; where a mismatch occurs, a correction may be made if time permits. A good tennis player, for instance, may know that his serve is incorrect even before his arm completes the arc of the serve. The actual sensory feedback from an act provides information about whether the act was carried out properly in yet another way. The sensory feedback is compared with the copy of the motor commands to determine whether these were the right commands for carrying out the act or should be modified in future selections of a specific instance.

In summary, Pew's analysis of continuous skills indicates that control of these skills may operate at several levels, the lowest being inner-loop control, followed by higher-order mechanisms and voluntary control. Although this model is probably not complete, it nonetheless supports the hierarchical interpretation of skill organization that we have seen in Bryan and Harter (1897, 1899) and in Miller, Galanter, and Pribram (1960).

Pew does not assume that a motor program exists only for one level of a continuous skill, but that the skill is organized at all three levels and the control of the skill may move among the levels as circumstances require. In the early stages of learning a skill, control focuses at the lowest level; with practice, it moves to higher levels as the motor program for the skill is refined. Automaticity thus appears only with efficient control at the higher levels.

A Theory of Discrete Skills

A *discrete skill* is one that has a recognizable beginning and end and that is carried out in a relatively brief time (e.g., fewer than 5 sec). These skills include such acts as throwing something (a dart), reaching for something (a doorknob), or moving an object to a particular spot (a chess piece). In particular, they include ballistic tasks—that is, rapid movements that occur in a time span of fewer than 200 msec.

Schmidt (1975a, 1975b, 1976) has developed a schema theory of discrete motor acts which has a number of features in common with Pew's (1974) theory of continuous motor acts. Both assume a general schema for each class of acts which must be tailored to the specific situation each time it is called up, and which is refined with practice. Both also assume that with practice the need for sensory feedback is reduced so that a skill may progress from closed-loop control to increasingly open-loop control.

Schmidt suggests that a motor schema for a discrete act develops from four sources of information that are stored each time an act of that type is produced: (1) the initial conditions, (2) the response specifications for the act, (3) the sensory consequences of the movements produced, and (4) the outcome of the act.

Initial conditions refer to the position of the body and the state of the environment at the moment the act is to be produced. Response specifications are the particular choices of speed, force, and so on, necessary to carry out the act. Since most acts are novel, response specifications will differ for nearly every act.

Sensory consequences are the feedback from the act from such sources as proprioception, vision, and audition. The outcome of the act is the success of the act relative to what was intended. This information serves as knowledge of results and may come from an experimenter ("Your dart landed three cm to the left of the target") or from other sources such as seeing or hearing.

Information from these four sources is stored after each act; and after a number of similar acts have been performed, the subject begins to abstract a schema from this information. The schema is in two parts, a recall schema and a recognition schema (see Figure 11.11). These are stored in memory and operate together to control motor acts of a similar form.

The Recall Schema. The recall schema is built up from past experience and is abstracted from the relationship among initial conditions, response specifications, and the actual outcome. Each time the subjects carry out the act, they determine the relation among the initial conditions, the response specifications, and the actual outcome. With practice these relations are abstracted to form the recall schema, which continues to be updated with continuing practice.

After the schema is established, the subjects can produce a novel act—that is, an act never before produced in its exact form—by entering the recall schema with the initial conditions and the intended outcome. The schema then produces the response specifications for the novel act. The response specifications determine the particular speed, force, and so forth, of muscle commands for carrying out the act. Once these conditions have been determined, muscle commands are issued and the act is carried out.

The Recognition Schema. The recognition schema operates in a similar way. Each time the act is carried out, the subjects determine the relation among the initial conditions, the sensory consequences, and the actual outcome. With practice these relations are abstracted to form the recognition schema, which is also updated with continued experience. In preparing an act, the intended outcome and initial conditions are entered into the recognition schema and it generates the expected sensory consequences. After the act, the expected sensory consequences are compared with the actual sensory consequences,

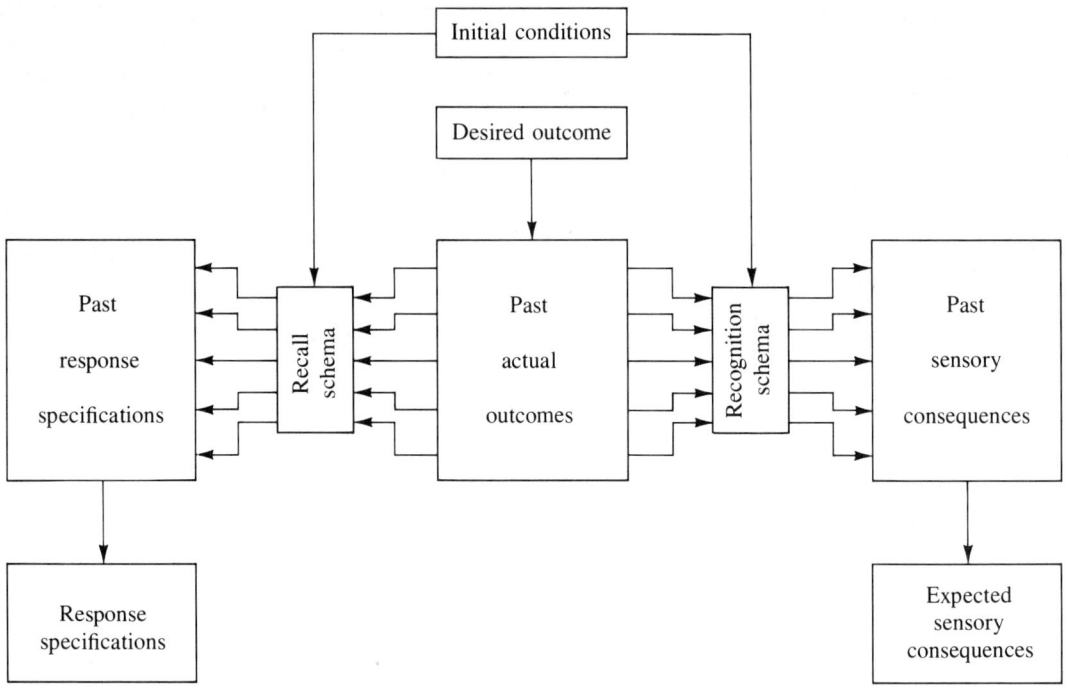

Figure 11.11 The recall schema and recognition schema and their sources of information. (From Schmidt, 1975a.)

including the actual outcome of the act, to determine whether an error occurred. An error indicates that the initial conditions selected for the intended act were not correct and must be modified.

The general function of the recognition schema is thus to determine whether the intended act was carried out. When this fails, the recall schema must be modified, since it generates the response specifications for the act. Since most acts are novel, the response specifications for a new act must be interpolated from previous experience and these will often be incorrect, especially in the early development of the recall schema.

Schmidt (1976) suggests that both the recall and recognition schemata improve with practice and further that they improve more rapidly with more varied experience. The greater the variety of prior acts, the broader will be the range of information from which the recall and recognition schemata are abstracted, thereby improving their precision.

Evidence for Schmidt's schema theory of discrete skills is still incomplete, but the theory accounts for a broad range of presently available evidence. Moreover, the theory offers a promising interpretation of the interplay between central control through motor schemata and sensory feedback.

Integrating Motor Schemata

As we saw in Chapter 2 on perception and attention, there is a fairly widely held assumption that working memory is limited and can be easily overtaxed. In the area of motor skills, this assumption has been used to explain why people may have difficulty in carrying on two skills at once, such as typing and talking. All of us have had the experience of trying to do two things at once and ending up doing both badly. Yet we all know people who are capable of performing two complex skills well simultaneously, and we ourselves usually have little difficulty in talking while driving. Why are simultaneous activities possible in some cases and not in others?

A resolution to this issue seems to lie in how well one has learned the schemata for the two activities. Neisser (1976) suggested that the assumption of a fixed, central capacity for processing information is misguided. Instead, he suggested that people have an indefinitely large capacity for acquiring skills and the limits on the use of these skills are tied only to people's proficiency at them. He cited a study by Allport, Antonitis, and Reynolds (1972) in which college students majoring in piano were asked to sight-read new music while simultaneously shadowing (repeating aloud) passages on Norse history played to them over earphones.

The students handled these two skills almost as well simultaneously as they did individually, even though the shadowing task is one normally assumed to demand full attentional capacity. In this case, however, the students were quite proficient at both tasks and so were able to deploy the two schemata simultaneously. A more extensive study of simultaneous tasks is given in Shaffer (1975). You may also find it instructive to review our discussion of resource-limited processes in Chapter 2. A highly practiced task necessitates fewer resources and hence can more likely be carried out with some additional task.

How do we develop such proficiency? In the section on learning a skill we saw that a person starts by constructing a general plan for the choice of movements and their order. Initially the use of this plan is conscious and somewhat awkward, but with practice the precision and timing of it are refined. Norman (1976) interpreted this process as the particularization of a schema. He suggested that we have very general schemata that can be used in all kinds of acts—for example, a schema for throwing something. A virtue of the generality is that the schema can be applied to all kinds of situations. A drawback to that same generality, however, is that tailoring the schema to a specific act requires a reasonable amount of computation and may strain working memory.

Alternatively, a person may develop a set of particular schemata, each limited to a narrow range of acts but also much easier to carry out. Thus from the general schema for throwing an object, we might develop particular schemata for throwing a baseball, throwing a Frisbee, skipping stones, and so on. Each of these, of course, would require special practice, but with practice comes the automaticity that relieves working memory. Particularizing schemata requires expanded storage, but long-term memory for schemata seems to be indefinitely expandable.

It is apparent that carrying on two skills at once will put the greatest strain on working memory when general schemata must be used. If the two skills are well practiced, however, particular schemata will control them, and their performance will be much more proficient.

In summary, most current theories about motor skills assume that a skill is controlled by a central schema or motor program. A motor schema is a general plan for structuring motor commands in advance of an act, and it permits the act to be carried out without feedback. Since a schema is general to a class of acts, the muscle commands for an individual act must be tailored to the unique position of the body, the state of the environment, and the intended outcome of the act. Such tailoring explains how a person can produce a novel act, since the muscle commands for a novel act are interpolated from experience with previous, similar acts as represented in the motor schema.

The generality of the schema also minimizes the problem of storage, since a single schema is sufficient for controlling each of the indefinitely large number of individual acts in a class, such as shooting a basketball. Finally, the motor schema explains how one can carry out an act that is too rapid to be controlled by the relatively slow sensory feedback from the motor movements.

The role of feedback in motor schema theories is to provide corrective information for acts that are relatively extended in time. In both continuous and discrete skills, an act that exceeds approximately 200 msec can be adjusted if sensory feedback indicates that the muscle commands are not meeting the intended goal. Moreover, sensory feedback leads to changes in the motor schema when the feedback reveals that motor commands generated by the motor schema are consistently in error. Learning a motor schema thus proceeds through practice and the continual adjustment of the schema through feedback.

In the early stages of learning, or when the requirements of the act are unpredictable, control of the skill relies heavily on feedback and thus is under closed-loop control. When the motor schema is well learned, however, feedback exerts much less influence; and in the extreme case, when feedback is not available or the act is very brief, control is lodged solely in the motor schema and constitutes open-loop control.

CONCLUSION

Fitts (1964) has defined a motor skill act as "one in which receptor-effector-feedback processes are highly organized, both spatially and temporally" (p. 244). The structure of the act is hierarchical, and the carrying out of the act is an information-processing activity of the same kind as memory, attention, speaking, and so on.

We have shown that feedback and practice are two important factors influencing how we learn such motor skills. These factors are influential in our ability to develop increasingly larger units of the skill so that the skill can be carried out more smoothly and quickly. Establishing larger units in learning a motor skill is analogous to the chunking process we described in our discussion of temporary memory in Chapter 3. A highly polished skill also exhibits the automaticity we described in our discussion of attention in Chapter 2.

Current theories of motor skills have placed heavy emphasis on the role of the schema in understanding motor skill performance. This fact shows the very substantial overlap between motor skill performance and general human cognitive functioning. As with the other cognitive processes, motor skills are an integral part of continuing cognitive functioning that suffuses every activity of our daily lives.

References

ADAMS, J. A. A closed-loop theory of motor learning. *Journal of Motor Behavior,* 1971, *3,* 111–149.

ADAMS, J. A. Feedback theory of how joint receptors regulate the timing and positioning of a limb. *Psychological Review,* 1977, *84,* 504–523.

ADAMS, J. A., & GOETZ, E. T. Feedback and practice as variables in error detection and correction. *Journal of Motor Behavior,* 1973, *5,* 217–224.

ADAMSON, R. E. Functional fixedness as related to problem solving: A repetition of three experiments. *Journal of Experimental Psychology,* 1952, *44,* 288–291.

ADAMSON, R. E., & TAYLOR, D. W. Functional fixedness as related to elapsed time and to set. *Journal of Experimental Psychology,* 1954, *47,* 122–126.

ALLPORT, D. A., ANTONITIS, B., & REYNOLDS, P. On the division of attention: A disproof of the single channel hypothesis. *Quarterly Journal of Experimental Psychology,* 1972, *24,* 225–235.

ANDERSON, J. R. *Language, memory, and thought.* Hillsdale, N.J.: Lawrence Erlbaum Associates, 1976.

ANDERSON, J. R. Arguments concerning representations for mental imagery. *Psychological Review,* 1978, *85,* 249–277.

ANDERSON, J. R., KLINE, P. J., & LEWIS, C. H. A production system model of language processing. In M. A. Just & P. A. Carpenter (Eds.), *Cognitive processes in comprehension.* Hillsdale, N.J.: Lawrence Erlbaum Associates, 1977.

ANDERSON, R. C. The notion of schemata and the educational enterprise: General discussion of the conference. In R. C. Anderson, R. J. Spiro, & W. E. Montague (Eds.), *Schooling and the acquisition of knowledge.* Hillsdale, N.J.: Lawrence Erlbaum Associates, 1977.

ANDERSON, R. C. Schema-directed processes in language comprehension. In A. M. Lesgold, J. W. Pellegrino, S. D. Fokkema, & R. Glaser (Eds.), *Cognitive psychology and instruction.* New York: Plenum Press, 1978.

ANDERSON, R. C., & ORTONY, A. On putting apples into bottles—a problem of polysemy. *Cognitive Psychology,* 1975, *7,* 167–180.

ANDERSON, R. C. & PICHERT, J. W. Recall of previously unrecallable information following a shift in perspective. *Journal of Verbal Learning and Verbal Behavior,* 1978, *17,* 1–12.

ANDERSON, R. C., REYNOLDS, R. E., SCHALLERT, D. L., & GOETZ, E. T. Frameworks for comprehending discourse. *American Educational Research Journal,* 1977, *14,* 367–381.

ANNETT, J. Learning a pressure under conditions of immediate and delayed knowledge of results. *Quarterly Journal of Experimental Psychology,* 1959, *11,* 3–15.

ANNETT, J. *Feedback and human behaviour.* Harmondsworth, England: Penguin Books, 1969.

APTER, M. J. *The computer simulation of behaviour.* London: Hutchinson, 1970.

ARCHER, E. J. Concept identification as a function of obviousness of relevant and irrelevant information. *Journal of Experimental Psychology,* 1962, *63,* 616–620.

ARKES, H. R., SCHUMACHER, G. M., & GARDNER, E. T. Effects of orienting tasks on the retention of prose material. *Journal of Educational Psychology,* 1976, *68,* 536–545.

ARMER, P. Attitudes toward intelligent machines. In E. A. Feigenbaum & J. Feldman (Eds.), *Computers and thought.* New York: McGraw-Hill, 1963. (Reprinted from *Symposium on bionics,* 1960, Wadd Technical Report 60 600.)

ATKINSON, R. C. Mnemotechnics in second-language learning. *American Psychologist,* 1975, *30,* 821–828.

ATKINSON, R. C., & SHIFFRIN, R. M. Human memory: A proposed system and its control processes. In K. W. Spence & J. T. Spence (Eds.), *The psychology of learning and motivation* (Vol. 2). New York: Academic Press, 1968.

ATTNEAVE, F. *Applications of information theory to psychology.* New York: Holt, Rinehart & Winston, 1959.

AVERBACH, E., & CORIELL, A. S. Short-term memory in vision. *Bell System Technical Journal,* 1961, *40,* 309–328.

BACHRACH, A. J. Diving behavior. In *Human performance and SCUBA diving: Proceedings of the symposium on underwater physiology.* Chicago: The Athletic Institute, 1970.

BADDELEY, A. D. The trouble with levels: A reexamination of Craik and Lockhart's framework for memory research. *Psychological Review,* 1978, *85,* 139–152.

BADDELEY, A. D., GRANT, S., WIGHT, E., & THOMPSON, N. Imagery and visual working memory. In P. M. A. Rabbitt & S. Dornic (Eds.), *Attention and performance V.* London: Academic Press, 1975.

BAHRICK, H. P. An analysis of stimulus variables influencing the proprioceptive control of movement. *Psychological Review,* 1957, *64,* 324–328.

BANKS, W. P. & BARBER, G. Color information in iconic memory. *Psychological Review,* 1977, *84,* 536–546.

BARTLETT, F. C. *Thinking: An experimental and social study.* London: Allen & Unwin, 1958.

BARTLETT, F. C. *Remembering: A study in experimental and social psychology.* Cambridge: Cambridge University Press, 1967. (Originally published, 1932.)

BEILIN, H., & HORN, R. Transition probability effects in anagram problem solving. *Journal of Experimental Psychology,* 1962, *63,* 514–518.

BELLEZZA, F. S., CHEESMAN, F. L., & REDDY, B. G. Organization and semantic elaboration in free recall. *Journal of Experimental Psychology: Human Learning and Memory,* 1977, *3,* 539–550.

BERLIN, B., & KAY, P. *Basic color terms: Their universality and evolution.* Berkeley: University of California Press, 1969.

BERNSTEIN, A. A chess-playing program for the IBM-704. *Chess Review*, July 1958, 208–209.

BHASKAR, R., & SIMON, H. A. Problem solving in semantically rich domains. *Cognitive Science,* 1977, *1,* 193–215.

BIRCH, H. G., & RABINOWITZ, H. S. The negative effect of previous experience on productive thinking. *Journal of Experimental Psychology,* 1951, *41,* 121–125.

BJORK, R. A. Short-term storage: The ordered output of a central processor. In F. Restle, R. M. Shiffrin, N. J. Castellan, H. R. Lindman, & D. B. Pisoni (Eds.), *Cognitive theory* (Vol. 1). Hillsdale, N.J.: Lawrence Erlbaum Associates, 1975.

BOBROW, D. G. Natural language input for a computer problem-solving system. In M. Minsky (Ed.), *Semantic information processing.* Cambridge, Mass.: M. I. T. Press, 1968.

BOBROW, D. G., & WINOGRAD, T. An overview of KRL, a knowledge representation language. *Cognitive Science,* 1977, *1,* 3–46.

BOLINGER, D. *Aspects of language* (2nd ed.). New York: Harcourt Brace Jovanovich, 1975.

BOOK, W. F. *The psychology of skill.* Missoula: Montana Press, 1908.

BOOLE, G. *An investigation of the laws of thought.* London: Walton & Maberley, 1854.

BOOMER, D. S., & LAVER, J. D. M. Slips of the tongue. *British Journal of Disorders of Communication*, 1968, *3*, 1–12.

BOUCHER, A. QL 696 .C9. In R. T. Bond (Ed.), *Famous stories of code and cipher*. New York: Rinehart, 1947.

BOURNE, L. E., JR. Learning and utilization of conceptual rules. In B. Kleinmuntz (Ed.), *Concepts and the structure of memory*. New York: Wiley, 1967.

BOURNE, L. E., JR., & ARCHER, E. J. Time continuously on target as a function of distribution of practice. *Journal of Experimental Psychology*, 1956, *51*, 25–33.

BOUSFIELD, W. A. The occurrence of clustering in the recall of randomly arranged associates. *Journal of General Psychology*, 1953, *49*, 229–240.

BOUSFIELD, W. A., COHEN, B. H., & WHITMARSH, G. A. Associative clustering in the recall of words of different taxonomic frequencies of occurrence. *Psychological Reports*, 1958, *4*, 39–44.

BOWER, G. H. Mental imagery and associative learning. In L. W. Gregg (Ed.), *Cognition in learning and memory*. New York: Wiley, 1972. (a)

BOWER, G. H. A selective review of organizational factors in memory. In E. Tulving & W. Donaldson (Eds.), *Organization of memory*. New York: Academic Press, 1972. (b)

BOWER, G. H., & CLARK, M. C. Narrative stories as mediators for serial learning. *Psychonomic Science*, 1969, *14*, 181–182.

BOWER, G. H., & SPRINGSTON, F. Pauses as recoding points in letter series. *Journal of Experimental Psychology*, 1970, *83*, 421–430.

BRAINARD, R. W., IRBY, T. S., FITTS, P. M. & ALLUISI, E. A. Some variables influencing the rate of gain of information. *Journal of Experimental Psychology*, 1962, *63*, 105–110.

BRAINE, M. D. S. On the relation between the natural logic of reasoning and standard logic. *Psychological Review*, 1978, *85*, 1–21.

BRANSFORD, J. D., BARCLAY, J. R., & FRANKS, J. J. Sentence memory: A constructive versus interpretive approach. *Cognitive Psychology*, 1972, *3*, 193–209.

BRANSFORD, J. D., & FRANKS, J. J. The abstraction of linguistic ideas. *Cognitive Psychology*, 1971, *2*, 331–350.

BRANSFORD, J. D., & JOHNSON, M. K. Considerations of some problems of comprehension. In W. G. Chase (Ed.), *Visual information processing*. New York: Academic Press, 1973.

BROADBENT, D. E. *Perception and communication*. London: Pergamon Press, 1958.

BROADBENT, D. E. The magical number seven after fifteen years. In A. Kennedy & A. Wilkes (Eds.), *Studies in long term memory*. London: Wiley, 1975.

BROOKS, L. R. Spatial and verbal components of the act of recall. *Canadian Journal of Psychology*, 1968, *22*, 349–368.

BROWN, A. Theories of memory and the problems of development: Activity, growth, and knowledge. In F. I. M. Craik & L. Cermak (Eds.), *Levels of processing and memory*. Hillsdale, N.J.: Lawrence Erlbaum Associates, 1978.

BROWN, R., & MCNEILL, D. The "tip of the tongue" phenomenon. *Journal of Verbal Learning and Verbal Behavior*, 1966, *5*, 325–337.

BRUNER, J. S., GOODNOW, J. J., & AUSTIN, G. A. *A study of thinking*. New York: Wiley, 1956.

BRUNER, J. S., & POTTER, M. C. Interference in visual recognition. *Science*, 1964, *144*, 424–425.

BRYAN, W. L., & HARTER, N. Studies in the physiology and psychology of the telegraphic language. *Psychological Review*, 1897, *4*, 27–53.

BRYAN, W. L., & HARTER, N. Studies on the telegraphic language. The acquisition of a hierarchy of habits. *Psychological Review*, 1899, *6*, 345–375.

BUGELSKI, B. R., & ALAMPAY, D. A. The role of frequency in developing perceptual sets. *Canadian Journal of Psychology*, 1961, *15*, 205–211.

BUGELSKI, B. R., KIDD, E., & SEGMEN, J. Image as a mediator in one-trial paired-associate learning. *Journal of Experimental Psychology*, 1968, *76*, 69–73.

CAIRNS, H. S., & CAIRNS, C. E. *Psycholinguistics: A cognitive view of language*. New York: Holt, Rinehart & Winston, 1976.

CANTOR, N., & MISCHEL, W. Traits as prototypes: Effects on recognition memory. *Journal of Per-

sonality and Social Psychology, 1977, *35,* 38–48.

CAPLAN, D. Clause boundaries and recognition latencies for words in sentences. *Perception and Psychophysics,* 1972, *12,* 73–76.

CAREY, S. T., & LOCKHART, R. S. Encoding differences in recognition and recall. *Memory and Cognition,* 1973, *1,* 297–300.

CARMICHAEL, L., HOGAN, H. P., & WALTER, A. A. An experimental study of the effect of language on the reproduction of visually perceived form. *Journal of Experimental Psychology,* 1932, *15,* 73–86.

CARPENTER, P. A. On the comprehension, storage, and retrieval of comparative sentences. *Journal of Verbal Learning and Verbal Behavior,* 1974, *13,* 401–411.

CERASO, J., & PROVITERA, A. Sources of error in syllogistic reasoning. *Cognitive Psychology,* 1971, *2,* 400–410.

CERF, B. *Bennett Cerf's treasury of atrocious puns.* New York: Dell, 1968.

CERMAK, L. S. *Improving your memory.* New York: McGraw-Hill, 1975.

CHAFE, W. L. Discourse structure and human knowledge. In J. B. Carroll & R. O. Freedle (Eds.), *Language comprehension and the acquisition of knowledge.* Washington, D.C.: Winston, 1972.

CHAPMAN, L. J., & CHAPMAN, J. P. Atmosphere effect reexamined. *Journal of Experimental Psychology,* 1959, *58,* 220–226.

CHARNESS, N. Memory for chess positions: Resistance to interference. *Journal of Experimental Psychology: Human Learning and Memory,* 1976, *2,* 641–653.

CHASE, W. G., & SIMON, H. A. The mind's eye in chess. In W. G. Chase (Ed.), *Visual information processing.* New York: Academic Press, 1973. (a)

CHASE, W. G., & SIMON, H. A. Perception in chess. *Cognitive Psychology,* 1973, *4,* 55–81. (b)

CHERNIKOFF, R., & TAYLOR, F. V. Reaction time to kinesthetic stimulation resulting from sudden arm displacement. *Journal of Experimental Psychology,* 1952, *43,* 1–8.

CHOMSKY, N. *Syntactic structures.* The Hague: Mouton, 1957.

CHOMSKY, N. *Aspects of the theory of syntax.* Cambridge, Mass.: M. I. T. Press, 1965.

CLARK, H. H. Linguistic processes in deductive reasoning. *Psychological Review,* 1969, *76,* 387–404.

CLARK, H. H., & CLARK, E. V. *Psychology and language.* New York: Harcourt Brace Jovanovich, 1977.

COFER, C. N. Constructive processes in memory. *American Scientist,* 1973, *61,* 537–543.

COFER, C. N., BRUCE, D. R., & REICHER, G. M. Clustering in free recall as a function of certain methodological variations. *Journal of Experimental Psychology,* 1966, *71,* 858–866.

COLBY, K. M., & HILF, F. D. Multidimensional evaluation of a simulation of paranoid thought processes. In L. W. Gregg (Ed.), *Knowledge and cognition.* Potomac, Md.: Lawrence Erlbaum, 1974.

COLE, R. A. Listening for mispronunciations: A measure of what we hear during speech. *Perception and Psychophysics,* 1973, *13,* 153–156.

COLLINS, A., BROWN, J. S., & LARKIN, K. M. Inference in text understanding. In R. J. Spiro, B. C. Bruce, & W. F. Brewer (Eds.), *Theoretical issues in reading comprehension.* Hillsdale, N.J.: Lawrence Erlbaum Associates, in press.

COLLINS, A., & LOFTUS, E. F. A spreading activation theory of semantic processing. *Psychological Review,* 1975, *82,* 407–428.

COLLINS, A., & QUILLIAN, M. R. Retrieval time from semantic memory. *Journal of Verbal Learning and Verbal Behavior,* 1969, *8,* 240–247.

COLLYER, S. C., JONIDES, J., & BEVAN, W. Images as memory aids: Is bizarreness helpful? *American Journal of Psychology,* 1972, *85,* 31–38.

CONRAD, C. Cognitive economy in semantic memory. *Journal of Experimental Psychology,* 1972, *92,* 149–154.

CONRAD, R. Acoustic confusion in immediate memory. *British Journal of Psychology,* 1964, *55,* 75–84.

CONRAD, R., & HULL, A. J. Information, acoustic confusion, and memory span. *British Journal of Psychology,* 1964, *55,* 429–432.

CONRAD, R., & HULL, A. J. Input modality and the serial position curve in short-term memory.

Psychonomic Science, 1968, *10,* 135–136.

CRAIK, F. I. M. Human memory. *Annual Review of Psychology,* 1979, *30,* 63–102.

CRAIK, F. I. M., & JACOBY, L. L. A process view of short-term retention. In F. Restle, R. M. Shiffrin, N. J. Castellan, H. R. Lindman, & D. B. Pisoni (Eds.), *Cognitive theory* (Vol. 1). Hillsdale, N.J.: Lawrence Erlbaum Associates, 1975.

CRAIK, F. I. M., & LOCKHART, R. S. Levels of processing: A framework for memory research. *Journal of Verbal Learning and Verbal Behavior,* 1972, *11,* 671–684.

CRAIK, F. I. M., & TULVING, E. Depth of processing and the retention of words in episodic memory. *Journal of Experimental Psychology: General,* 1975, *104,* 268–294.

CRAIK, F. I. M., & WATKINS, M. J. The role of rehearsal in short-term memory. *Journal of Verbal Learning and Verbal Behavior,* 1973, *12,* 599–607.

CROSSMAN, E. R. F. W. A theory of the acquisition of speed-skill. *Ergonomics,* 1959, *2,* 153–166.

CROTHERS, E. J. Memory structure and the recall of discourse. In J. B. Carroll & R. O. Freedle (Eds.), *Language comprehension and the acquisition of knowledge.* Washington, D.C.: Winston, 1972.

CROWDER, R. G. The sound of vowels and consonants in immediate memory. *Journal of Verbal Learning and Verbal Behavior,* 1971, *10,* 587–596.

CROWDER, R. G. Inferential problems in echoic memory. In P. M. A. Rabbitt & S. Dornic (Eds.), *Attention and performance V.* London: Academic Press, 1975.

CROWDER, R. G. *Principles of learning and memory.* Hillsdale, N.J.: Lawrence Erlbaum Associates, 1976.

CROWDER, R. G., & MORTON, J. Precategorical acoustic storage (PAS). *Perception and Psychophysics,* 1969, *5,* 365–373.

CUTTING, J. A., & PISONI, D. B. An information-processing approach to speech perception. In *Status report on speech research* (Document SR-48). New Haven, Conn.: Haskins Laboratories, 1976.

DANSEREAU, D., & GREGG, L. W. An information processing analysis of mental multiplication. *Psychonomic Science,* 1966, *6,* 71–72.

DARWIN, G. J., & BADDELEY, A. D. Acoustic memory and the perception of speech. *Cognitive Psychology,* 1974, *6,* 41–60.

DARWIN, G. J., TURVEY, M. T., & CROWDER, R. G. An auditory analogue of the Sperling partial report procedure: Evidence for brief auditory storage. *Cognitive Psychology,* 1972, *3,* 255–267.

DE GROOT, A. D. *Thought and choice in chess.* The Hague: Mouton, 1965.

DENES, P. B., & PINSON, E. N. *The speech chain: The physics and biology of spoken language.* Garden City, N.Y.: Anchor Books, 1973.

DE SOTO, C., LONDON, M., & HANDEL, S. Social reasoning and spatial paralogic. *Journal of Personality and Social Psychology,* 1965, *2,* 513–521.

DOOLING, D. J., & LACHMAN, R. Effects of comprehension on retention of prose. *Journal of Experimental Psychology,* 1971, *88,* 216–222.

DOOLING, D. J., & MULLET, R. L. Locus of thematic effects in retention of prose. *Journal of Experimental Psychology,* 1973, *97,* 404–406.

DUBOS, R. *Pasteur and modern science.* Garden City, N.Y.: Doubleday, 1960.

DUNCKER, K. [On problem-solving.] *Psychological Monographs,* 1945, *58,* (Whole No. 270).

EGAN, D. E., & GREENO, J. G. Theory of rule induction: Knowledge acquired in concept learning, serial pattern learning, and problem solving. In L. W. Gregg (Ed.), *Knowledge and cognition.* Potomac, Md.: Lawrence Erlbaum, 1974.

EISENBERG, L. The social imperatives of medical research. *Science,* 1977, *198,* 1105–1110.

EISENSTADT, M., & KAREEV, Y. Aspects of human problem solving: The use of internal representations. In D. A. Norman & D. E. Rumelhart (Eds.), *Explorations in cognition.* San Francisco: W. H. Freeman, 1975.

ELMES, D. G., & BJORK, R. A. The interaction of encoding and rehearsal processes in the recall of repeated and nonrepeated items. *Journal of Verbal Learning and Verbal Behavior,* 1975, *14,* 30–42.

ERICKSON, J. R. A set analysis theory of behavior in formal syllogistic reasoning tasks. In R. L. Solso (Ed.), *Theories in cognitive psychology: The*

Loyola symposium. Potomac, Md.: Lawrence Erlbaum, 1974.

ERICKSON, J. R. Research on syllogistic reasoning. In R. Revlin & R. E. Mayer (Eds.), *Human reasoning.* Washington, D.C.: Winston, 1978.

ERNST, G. W., & NEWELL, A. *GPS: A case study in generality and problem solving.* New York: Academic Press, 1969.

FEIGENBAUM, E. A., & FELDMAN, J. (Eds.), *Computers and thought.* New York: McGraw-Hill, 1963.

FELDMAN, J. Computer simulation of cognitive processes. In H. Borko (Ed.), *Computer applications in the behavioral sciences.* Englewood Cliffs, N.J.: Prentice-Hall, 1962.

FILLENBAUM, S. On coping with ordered and unordered conjunctive sentences. *Journal of Experimental Psychology,* 1971, *87,* 93–98.

FILLENBAUM, S. Or: Some uses. *Journal of Experimental Psychology,* 1974, *103,* 913–921. (a)

FILLENBAUM, S. Pragmatic normalization: Further results for some conjunctive and disjunctive sentences. *Journal of Experimental Psychology,* 1974, *102,* 574–578. (b)

FILLMORE, C. J. The case for case. In E. Bach & R. T. Harms (Eds.), *Universals of linguistic theory.* New York: Holt, Rinehart & Winston, 1968.

FILLMORE, C. J. Some problems for case grammar. In R. J. O'Brien (Ed.), Linguistics: Developments of the sixties—Viewpoints for the seventies. *Monograph Series on Languages and Linguistics,* 1971, *24,* 35–56.

FITTS, P. M. Perceptual-motor skill learning. In A. W. Melton (Ed.), *Categories of human learning.* New York: Academic Press, 1964.

FITTS, P. M., & DEININGER, R. L. S-R compatibility: Correspondence among paired elements within stimulus and response codes. *Journal of Experimental Psychology,* 1954, *48,* 483–492.

FLEISHMAN, E. A., & PARKER, J. F., JR. Factors in the retention and relearning of perceptual-motor skill. *Journal of Experimental Psychology,* 1962, *64,* 215–226.

FLEXSER, A. J., & TULVING, E. Retrieval independence in recognition and recall. *Psychological Review,* 1978, *85,* 153–171.

FODOR, J. A. *The language of thought.* New York: Crowell, 1975.

FODOR, J. A., BEVER, T. G., & GARRETT, M. F. *The psychology of language.* New York: McGraw-Hill, 1974.

FODOR, J. A., & GARRETT, M. F. Some syntactic determinants of sentential complexity. *Perception and Psychophysics,* 1967, *2,* 289–296.

FREDERIKSEN, C. H. Acquisition of semantic information from discourse: Effects of repeated exposures. *Journal of Verbal Learning and Verbal Behavior,* 1975, *14,* 158–169.

FREEDMAN, J. L., & LOFTUS, E. F. Retrieval of words from long-term memory. *Journal of Verbal Learning and Verbal Behavior,* 1971, *10,* 107–115.

FROMKIN, V. A. The non-anomalous nature of anomalous utterances. In V. A. Fromkin (Ed.), *Speech errors as linguistic evidence.* The Hague: Mouton, 1973.

FROMKIN, V. A., & RODMAN, R. *An introduction to language.* New York: Holt, Rinehart & Winston, 1974.

FROST, N. Encoding and retrieval in visual memory tasks. *Journal of Experimental Psychology,* 1972, *95,* 317–326.

GARDNER, R. A., & RUNQUIST, W. N. Acquisition and extinction of problem-solving set. *Journal of Experimental Psychology,* 1958, *55,* 274–277.

GARNES, S., & BOND, Z. S. *A slip of the ear: A snip of the ear? A slip of the year?* Paper presented at the meeting of the 12th International Congress of Linguists, Vienna, September 1977.

GARRETT, M. F. *Syntactic structures and judgments of auditory events.* Unpublished doctoral dissertation, University of Illinois, 1965.

GARRETT, M. F., BEVER, T. G., & FODOR, J. A. The active use of grammar in speech perception. *Perception and Psychophysics,* 1966, *1,* 30–32.

GARRETT, M. F., & SHATTUCK, S. R. *An analysis of speech errors.* (Quarterly Progress Report No. 113). Research Laboratory of Electronics, M.I.T., 1974.

GELERNTER, H. Realization of a geometry-theorem proving machine. In E. A. Feigenbaum & J. Feldman (Eds.), *Computers and thought.* New York: McGraw-Hill, 1963. (Reprinted from *Proceedings of an International Conference on Information Processing.* Paris: UNESCO House, 1959.)

GHISELIN, B. (Ed.), *The creative process*. Berkeley: University of California Press, 1952.

GIBSON, E. *Principles of perceptual learning and development*. New York: Appleton-Century-Crofts, 1969.

GLANZER, M., & RAZEL, M. The size of the unit in short-term storage. *Journal of Verbal Learning and Verbal Behavior,* 1974, *13,* 114–131.

GLENBERG, A., SMITH, S. M., & GREEN, C. Type I rehearsal: Maintenance and more. *Journal of Verbal Learning and Verbal Behavior,* 1977, *16,* 339–352.

GLENCROSS, D. J. Control of skilled movements. *Psychological Bulletin,* 1977, *84,* 14–29.

GOLDSTEIN, M., & RITTENHOUSE, C. H. Knowledge of results in the acquisition and transfer of a gunnery skill. *Journal of Experimental Psychology,* 1954, *48,* 187–196.

GORDON, W. J. *Synectics*. New York: Harper & Row, 1961.

GOULD, J. D. Differential visual feedback of component motions. *Journal of Experimental Psychology,* 1965, *69,* 263–268.

GRAF, R., & TORREY, J. W. Perception of phrase structure in written language. *Proceedings of the 74th Annual Convention of the American Psychological Association,* 1966, *1,* 83–84.

GREENO, J. G. Hobbits and orcs: Acquisition of a sequential concept. *Cognitive Psychology,* 1974, *6,* 270–292.

GREENO, J. G. Cognitive objectives of instruction: Theory of knowledge for solving problems and answering questions. In D. Klahr (Ed.), *Cognition and instruction*. Hillsdale, N.J.: Lawrence Erlbaum Associates, 1976.

HADAMARD, J. *The psychology of invention in the mathematical field*. New York: Dover, 1945.

HAKES, D. T. Effects of reducing complement constructions on sentence comprehension. *Journal of Verbal Learning and Verbal Behavior,* 1972, *11,* 278–286.

HAKES, D. T., & CAIRNS, H. S. Sentence comprehension and relative pronouns. *Perception and Psychophysics,* 1970, *8,* 5–8.

HALLE, M., & STEVENS, K. N. Speech recognition: A model and a program for research. In J. A. Fodor & J. J. Katz (Eds.), *The structure of language: Readings in the philosophy of language*. Englewood Cliffs, N.J.: Prentice-Hall, 1964.

HARRIS, C. S. Perceptual adaptation to inverted, reversed, and displaced vision. *Psychological Review,* 1965, *72,* 419–444.

HAYES, J. R. *Cognitive psychology*. Homewood, Ill.: Dorsey, 1978.

HAYES, J. R., & SIMON, H. A. Understanding written problem instructions. In L. W. Gregg (Ed.), *Knowledge and cognition*. Potomac, Md.: Lawrence Erlbaum, 1974.

HAYES-ROTH, B. Evolution of cognitive structures and processes. *Psychological Review,* 1977, *84,* 260–278.

HAYES-ROTH, B., & HAYES-ROTH, F. Concept learning and the recognition and classification of exemplars. *Journal of Verbal Learning and Verbal Behavior,* 1977, *16,* 321–338.

HAYGOOD, R. C., & BOURNE, L. E., JR. Attribute and rule learning aspects of conceptual behavior. *Psychological Review,* 1965, *72,* 175–195.

HELLYER, S. Stimulus-response coding and amount of information as determinants of reaction time. *Journal of Experimental Psychology,* 1963, *65,* 521–522.

HENDERSON, S. E. Role of feedback in the development and maintenance of a complex skill. *Journal of Experimental Psychology: Human Perception and Performance,* 1977, *3,* 224–233.

HERSEY, W. D. *How to cash in on your hidden memory power*. New York: Award Books, 1963.

HICK, W. E. On the rate of gain of information. *Quarterly Journal of Experimental Psychology,* 1952, *4,* 11–26.

HIGGINS, E. T. Effects of presupposition on deductive reasoning. *Journal of Verbal Learning and Verbal Behavior,* 1976, *15,* 419–430.

HISLOP, M. W., & BROOKS, L. R. *Suppression of concept learning by verbal rules* (Technical Report No. 28). Hamilton, Ontario, Canada: McMaster University, Department of Psychology, December 1968.

HOWE, M. J. A. Consolidation in short-term memory as a function of rehearsal. *Psychonomic Science,* 1967, *7,* 355–356.

HUBEL, D. H., & WIESEL, T. N. Receptive fields, binocular interaction and functional architecture in the cat's visual cortex. *Journal of Physiology,* 1962, *160,* 106–154.

HUBEL, D. H., & WIESEL, T. N. Shape and arrangement of columns in cat's striate cortex. *Journal of Physiology,* 1963, *165,* 559–568.

HUBEL, D. H., & WIESEL, T. N. Receptive fields and function architecture in two nonstriate visual areas (18 and 19) of the cat. *Journal of Neurophysiology,* 1965, *28,* 229–289.

HUBEL, D. H., & WIESEL, T. N. Receptive fields and functional architecture of monkey striate cortex. *Journal of Physiology,* 1968, *195,* 215–243.

HUESMANN, L. R., & CHENG, C. A theory for the induction of mathematical functions. *Psychological Review,* 1973, *80,* 126–138.

HULL, C. L. Quantitative aspects of the evolution of concepts. *Psychological Monographs,* 1920, *28* (Whole No. 123).

HUNT, D. P. Effects of nonlinear and discrete transformations of feedback information on human tracking performance. *Journal of Experimental Psychology,* 1964, *67,* 486–494.

HUNT, E. B., & POLTROCK, S. E. The mechanics of thought. In B. H. Kantowitz (Ed.), *Human information processing: Tutorials in performance and cognition.* Hillsdale, N.J.: Lawrence Erlbaum Associates, 1974.

HUTTENLOCHER, J. Constructing spatial images: A strategy in reasoning. *Psychological Review,* 1968, *75,* 550–560.

HYDE, T. S., & JENKINS, J. J. Differential effects of incidental tasks on the organization of recall of a list of highly associated words. *Journal of Experimental Psychology,* 1969, *82,* 472–481.

HYDE, T. S., & JENKINS, J. J. Recall for words as a function of semantic, graphic, and syntactic orienting tasks. *Journal of Verbal Learning and Verbal Behavior,* 1973, *12,* 471–480.

HYMAN, R. Stimulus information as a determinant of reaction time. *Journal of Experimental Psychology,* 1953, *45,* 188–196.

JACOBY, L. L. Encoding processes, rehearsal, and recall requirements. *Journal of Verbal Learning and Verbal Behavior,* 1973, *12,* 302–310.

JAMES, W. *The principles of psychology* (Vol. 1). New York: Holt, 1904. (Originally published, 1890.)

JARVELLA, R. J. Syntactic processing of connected speech. *Journal of Verbal Learning and Verbal Behavior,* 1971, *10,* 409–416.

JAYNES, J. *The origin of consciousness in the breakdown of the bicameral mind.* Boston: Houghton Mifflin, 1976.

JEFFRIES, R., POLSON, P. G., RAZRAN, L., & ATWOOD, M. E. A process model for Missionaries-Cannibals and other river-crossing problems. *Cognitive Psychology,* 1977, *9,* 412–440.

JENKINS, J. J. *Context conditions meaning.* Paper presented at the meeting of the Midwestern Psychological Association, Chicago, May 1977.

JENKINS, J. J., MINK, W. D., & RUSSELL, W. A. Associative clustering as a function of verbal association strength. *Psychological Reports,* 1958, *4,* 127–136.

JENKINS, J. J., & RUSSELL, W. A. Associative clustering during recall. *Journal of Abnormal and Social Psychology,* 1952, *47,* 818–821.

JOHNSON, E. S. Validation of concept-learning strategies. *Journal of Experimental Psychology: General,* 1978, *107,* 237–266.

JOHNSON-LAIRD, P. N. Models of deduction. In R. J. Falmagne (Ed.), *Reasoning: Representation and process in children and adults.* Hillsdale, N.J.: Lawrence Erlbaum Associates, 1975.

JOHNSON-LAIRD, P. N. Psycholinguistics without linguistics. In N. S. Sutherland (Ed.), *Tutorial essays in psychology* (Vol. 2). Hillsdale, N.J.: Lawrence Erlbaum Associates, 1977.

JOHNSON-LAIRD, P. N., & STEEDMAN, M. The psychology of syllogisms. *Cognitive Psychology,* 1978, *10,* 64–99.

JONES, S. Visual and verbal processes in problem-solving. *Cognitive Psychology,* 1970, *1,* 201–214.

JONIDES, J., KAHN, R., & ROZIN, P. Imagery instructions improve memory in blind subjects. *The Bulletin of the Psychonomic Society,* 1975, *5,* 424–426.

KALSBEEK, J. W. H. On the measurement of deterioration in performance caused by distraction stress. *Ergonomics,* 1964, *7,* 187–195.

KANT, I. [Critique of pure reason] (F. M. Muller, trans.). New York: Macmillan, 1915. (Originally published, 1781.)

KATONA, G. *Organizing and memorizing.* New York: Columbia University Press, 1940.

KATZ, J. J., & FODOR, J. A. The structure of a semantic theory. *Language,* 1963, *39,* 170–210.

KAY, H. The development of motor skills from birth to adolescence. In E. Bilodeau (Ed.), *Principles of skill acquisition.* New York: Academic Press, 1969.

KEELE, S. W., & POSNER, M. I. Processing of feedback in movements. *Journal of Experimental Psychology,* 1968, *77,* 353–363.

KIMBALL, J. P. Seven principles of surface structure parsing in natural language. *Cognition,* 1973, *2,* 15–47.

KINNEY, G. C., MARSETTA, M., & SHOWMAN, D. J. *Studies in display symbol legibility, part XII. The legibility of alphanumeric symbols for digitalized television* (ESD-TR-66-117). Bedford, Mass.: The Mitre Corporation, November 1966.

KINTSCH, W. Recognition and free recall of organized lists. *Journal of Experimental Psychology,* 1968, *78,* 481–487.

KINTSCH, W. *Memory and cognition* (2nd ed.). New York: Wiley, 1977.

KINTSCH, W., & BUSCHKE, H. Homophones and synonyms in short-term memory. *Journal of Experimental Psychology,* 1969, *80,* 403–407.

KLAHR, D. (Ed.), *Cognition and instruction.* Hillsdale, N.J.: Lawrence Erlbaum Associates, 1976.

KLATZKY, R. L. *Human memory: Structures and processes.* San Francisco: W. H. Freeman, 1975.

KNAPP, B. *Skill in sport: The attainment of proficiency.* London: Routledge and Kegan Paul, 1963.

KOESTLER, A. *The act of creation.* New York: Macmillan, 1964.

KOHLER, I. [The formation and transformation of the perceptual world] *Psychological Issues,* 1964, *3*(4).

KÖHLER, W. *The mentality of apes.* New York: Harcourt, 1925.

KÖHLER, W. *The task of Gestalt psychology.* Princeton, N.J.: Princeton University Press, 1969.

KORNHEISER, A. S. Adaptation to laterally displaced vision: A review. *Psychological Bulletin,* 1976, *83,* 783–816.

KOSSLYN, S. M., BALL, T. M., & REISER, B. J. Visual images preserve metric spatial information: Evidence from studies of visual scanning. *Journal of Experimental Psychology: Human Perception and Performance,* 1978, *4,* 47–60.

KOTOVSKY, K., & SIMON, H. A. Empirical tests of a theory of human acquisition of concepts for sequential patterns. *Cognitive Psychology,* 1973, *4,* 399–424.

KROLL, N. E. A. Visual short-term memory. In D. Deutsch & J. A. Deutsch (Eds.), *Short-term memory.* New York: Academic Press, 1975.

LAKOFF, G. Hedges: A study in meaning criteria and the logic of fuzzy concepts. *Papers from the eighth regional meeting, Chicago Linguistics Society.* Chicago: University of Chicago Linguistics Department, 1972.

LASHLEY, K. S. The accuracy of movement in the absence of excitation from the moving organ. *American Journal of Physiology,* 1917, *43,* 169–194.

LASHLEY, K. S. The problem of serial order in behavior. In L. A. Jefress (Ed.), *Cerebral mechanisms in behavior.* New York: Wiley, 1951.

LASZLO, J. I., & BAIRSTOW, P. J. The compression block technique: A note on procedure. *Journal of Motor Behavior,* 1971, *3,* 313–317.

LAUGHLIN, P. Selection strategies in concept attainment. In R. L. Solso (Ed.), *Contemporary issues in cognitive psychology: The Loyola symposium.* Washington, D.C.: Winston, 1973.

LEONARD, J. A. Tactual choice reactions. *Quarterly Journal of Experimental Psychology,* 1959, *11,* 76–83.

LEVINE, M. Hypothesis behavior by humans during discrimination learning. *Journal of Experimental Psychology,* 1966, *71,* 331–336.

LIBERMAN, A. M. The grammars of speech and language. *Cognitive Psychology,* 1970, *1,* 301–323.

LIBERMAN, A., COOPER, F. S., SHANKWEILER, D. P., & STUDDERT-KENNEDY, M. Perception of the speech code. *Psychological Review,* 1967, *74,* 431–461.

LINDSAY, P. H., & NORMAN, D. A. *Human information processing: An introduction to psychology* (2nd ed.). New York: Academic Press, 1977.

LOCKHART, R. S., CRAIK, F. I. M., & JACOBY, L. Depth of processing, recognition and recall. In J. Brown (Ed.), *Recall and recognition.* London: Wiley, 1976.

LOFTUS, E. F., MILLER, D. G., & BURNS, H. J. Semantic integration of verbal information into a visual memory. *Journal of Experimental Psychology: Human Learning and Memory,* 1978, *4,* 19–31.

LOFTUS, E. F., & PALMER, J. C. Reconstruction of automobile destruction: An example of the interaction between language and memory. *Journal of Verbal Learning and Verbal Behavior,* 1974, *13,* 535–589.

LOFTUS, G. R., & LOFTUS, E. F. *Human memory: The processing of information.* Hillsdale, N.J.: Lawrence Erlbaum Associates, 1976.

LORAYNE, H., & LUCAS, J. *The memory book.* New York: Ballantine, 1974.

LUCHINS, A. S. Mechanization in problem-solving: The effect of *Einstellung*. *Psychological Monographs*, 1942, *54* (6, Whole No. 248).

MACKAY, D. G. Derivational rules and the internal lexicon. *Journal of Verbal Learning and Verbal Behavior,* 1978, *17,* 61–71.

MACNEILAGE, P. F. Motor control of serial ordering of speech. *Psychological Review,* 1970, *77,* 182–196.

MACNEILAGE, P. F., & DECLERK, J. L. On the motor control of coarticulation in CVC monosyllables. *Journal of the Acoustical Society of America,* 1969, *45,* 1217–1233.

MACNEILAGE, P. F., & MACNEILAGE, L. A. Central processes controlling speech production during sleep and waking. In F. J. McGuigan (Ed.), *The psychophysiology of thinking.* New York: Academic Press, 1973.

MAIER, N. R. F. Reasoning in humans I: On direction. *Journal of Comparative Psychology,* 1930, *10,* 115–143.

MAIER, N. R. F. Reasoning in humans II: The solution of a problem and its appearance in consciousness. *Journal of Comparative Psychology,* 1931, *12,* 181–194.

MANDLER, G. Organization and memory. In K. W. Spence & J. T. Spence (Eds.), *The psychology of learning and motivation: Advances in research and theory* (Vol. 1). New York: Academic Press, 1967.

MANDLER, G. *Mind and emotion.* New York: Wiley, 1975.

MANDLER, G., & BOECK, W. J. Retrieval processes in recognition. *Memory and Cognition,* 1974, *2,* 613–615.

MASSARO, D. W. Preperceptual images, processing time, and perceptual units in auditory perception. *Psychological Review,* 1972, *79,* 124–145.

MASSARO, D. W. Preperceptual images, processing time and perceptual units in speech perception. In D. W. Massaro (Ed.), *Understanding language: An information-processing analysis of speech perception, reading, and psycholinguistics.* New York: Academic Press, 1975.

MAYER, R. E. *Thinking and problem solving: An introduction to human cognition and learning.* Glenview, Ill.: Scott, Foresman, 1977.

MAYER, R. E. Qualitatively different storage and processing strategies used for linear reasoning tasks due to meaningfulness of premises. *Journal of Experimental Psychology: Human Learning and Memory,* 1978, *4,* 5–18.

MCLEAN, R. S., & GREGG, L. W. Effects of induced chunking on temporal aspects of serial recitation. *Journal of Experimental Psychology,* 1967, *74,* 455–459.

MELTON, A. W. Implications of short-term memory for a general theory of memory. *Journal of Verbal Learning and Verbal Behavior,* 1963, *2,* 1–21.

MERYMAN, R. A tour of two great throats. *Life,* June 26, 1970, *68,* 63–71.

MEYER, B. J. F. Identification of the structure of prose and its implications for the study of reading and memory. *Journal of Reading Behavior,* 1975, *7,* 7–47.

MEYER, B. J. F. The structure of prose: Effects on learning and memory and implications for educational practice. In R. Anderson, R. Spiro, & W. Montague (Eds.), *Schooling and the acquisition of knowledge.* Hillsdale, N.J.: Lawrence Erlbaum Associates, 1977.

MEYER, D. E. On the representation and retrieval of stored semantic information. *Cognitive Psychology,* 1970, *1,* 242–300.

MEYER, D. E. & SCHVANEVELDT, R. W. Meaning, memory structure, and mental processes. In C. Cofer (Ed.), *The structure of human memory.* San Francisco: W. H. Freeman, 1976.

MEYER, D. E., SCHVANEVELDT, R. W., & RUDDY, M. G. Loci of contextual effects on visual word recognition. In P. M. A. Rabbitt & S. Dornic (Eds.), *Attention and performance V*. London: Academic Press, 1975.

MICHON, J. A. Programs and "programs" for sequential patterns in motor behavior. *Brain Research*, 1974, *71*, 413–424.

MILLER, G. A. The magical number seven, plus or minus two: Some limits on our capacity for processing information. *Psychological Review*, 1956, *63*, 81–97.

MILLER, G. A. Decision units in the perception of speech. *IRE Transactions on Information Theory*, 1962, *IT-8*, 81–83.

MILLER, G. A. Some preliminaries to psycholinguistics. *American Psychologist*, 1965, *20*, 15–20.

MILLER, G. A. Practical and lexical knowledge. In P. N. Johnson-Laird & P. C. Wason (Eds.), *Thinking: Readings in cognitive science*. New York: Cambridge University Press, 1977.

MILLER, G. A., GALANTER, E., & PRIBRAM, K. H. *Plans and the structure of behavior*. New York: Holt, Rinehart & Winston, 1960.

MILLER, G. A., HEISE, G., & LICHTEN, W. The intelligibility of speech as a function of the context of the test materials. *Journal of Experimental Psychology*, 1951, *41*, 329–335.

MILLER, G. A., & JOHNSON-LAIRD, P. N. *Language and perception*. Cambridge, Mass.: Harvard University Press, 1976.

MINSKY, M. A framework for representing knowledge. In P. H. Winston (Ed.), *The psychology of computer vision*. New York: McGraw-Hill, 1975.

MONTAGUE, W. E., ADAMS, J. A., & KIESS, H. D. Forgetting and natural language mediation. *Journal of Experimental Psychology*, 1966, *72*, 829–833.

MOORE, J., & NEWELL, A. How can MERLIN understand? In L. W. Gregg (Ed.), *Knowledge and cognition*. Potomac, Md.: Lawrence Erlbaum, 1974.

MORAY, N. *Attention: Selective processes in vision and hearing*. New York: Academic Press, 1970.

MORIN, R. E., & GRANT, D. A. Learning and performance on a key-pressing task as function of the degree of spatial stimulus-response correspondence. *Journal of Experimental Psychology*, 1955, *49*, 39–47.

MOWBRAY, G. H., & RHOADES, M. V. On the reduction of choice-reaction times with practice. *Quarterly Journal of Experimental Psychology*, 1959, *11*, 16–23.

MURDOCK, B. B., JR. The retention of individual items. *Journal of Experimental Psychology*, 1961, *62*, 618–625.

MURPHY, G., & KOVACH, J. K. *Historical introduction to modern psychology*. New York: Harcourt Brace Jovanovich, 1972.

NAYLOR, J. C., & BRIGGS, G. E. Effects of task complexity and task organization on the relative efficiency of part and whole training methods. *Journal of Experimental Psychology*, 1963, *64*, 217–224.

NEIMARK, E. D., & CHAPMAN, R. H. Development of the comprehension of logical quantifiers. In R. J. Falmagne (Ed.), *Reasoning: Representation and process in children and adults*. Hillsdale, N.J.: Lawrence Erlbaum Associates, 1975.

NEISSER, U. Visual search. *Scientific American*, 1964, *210*, 94–102.

NEISSER, U. *Cognitive psychology*. New York: Appleton-Century-Crofts, 1967.

NEISSER, U. *Cognition and reality*. San Francisco: W. H. Freeman, 1976.

NEISSER, U., & KERR, N. Spatial and mnemonic properties of visual images. *Cognitive Psychology*, 1973, *5*, 138–150.

NEISSER, U., & WEENE, P. Hierarchies in concept attainment. *Journal of Experimental Psychology*, 1962, *64*, 640–645.

NELSON, K. Some evidence for the cognitive primacy of categorization and its functional basis. *Merrill-Palmer Quarterly of Behavior and Development*, 1973, *19*, 21–39.

NEWALL, K. M. Knowledge of results and motor learning. *Journal of Motor Behavior*, 1974, *6*, 235–244.

NEWELL, A., SHAW, J. C., & SIMON, H. A. Chess-playing programs and the problem of complexity. *IBM Journal of Research and Development*, 1958, *2*, 320–335. (a)

NEWELL, A., SHAW, J. C., & SIMON, H. A. Elements of a theory of human problem-solving. *Psychological Review*, 1958, *65*, 151–166. (b)

NEWELL, A., & SIMON, H. A. GPS, a program that simulates human thought. In E. A. Feigenbaum & J. Feldman (Eds.), *Computers and thought.* New York: McGraw-Hill, 1963. (Reprinted from *Lernende Automaten.* Munich: R. Oldenbourg KG, 1961.)

NEWELL, A., & SIMON, H. A. *Human problem solving.* Englewood Cliffs, N.J.: Prentice-Hall, 1972.

NEWMAN, E. F. Men and information: A psychologist's view. *N.2 del Supplemento del Neuovo Cimento,* 1959, *13,* 539–559.

NORMAN, D. A. *Memory and attention* (2nd ed.). New York: Wiley, 1976.

NORMAN, D. A., & BOBROW, D. G. On data-limited and resource-limited processes. *Cognitive Psychology,* 1975, *7,* 44–64.

NORMAN, D. A., & BOBROW, D. G. On the role of active memory processes in perception and cognition. In C. N. Cofer (Ed.), *The structure of human memory.* San Francisco: W. H. Freeman, 1976.

OPIE, I., & OPIE, P. (Eds.), *The Oxford dictionary of nursery rhymes.* London: Oxford University Press, 1951.

OSHERSON, D. N. *Logical abilities in children* (Vol. 2), *Logical inference: Underlying operations.* Hillsdale, N.J.: Lawrence Erlbaum Associates, 1974.

OSHERSON, D. N. Logic and models of logical thinking. In R. J. Falmagne (Ed.), *Reasoning: Representation and process in children and adults.* Hillsdale, N.J.: Lawrence Erlbaum Associates, 1975.

PAAP, K. R. Theories of speech perception. In D. W. Massaro (Ed.), *Understanding language: An information-processing analysis of speech perception, reading, and psycholinguistics.* New York: Academic Press, 1975.

PAIVIO, A. *Imagery and verbal processes.* New York: Holt, Rinehart & Winston, 1971.

PAIVIO, A. Language and knowledge of the world. *Educational Researcher,* 1974, *3,* 5–12.

PAIVIO, A. Imagery and long-term memory. In A. Kennedy & A. Wilkes (Eds.), *Studies in long-term memory.* London: Wiley, 1975.

PALMER, S. E. Visual perception and world knowledge: Notes on a model of sensory-cognitive interaction. In D. A. Norman, D. E. Rumelhart, & the LNR Research Group (Eds.), *Explorations in cognition.* San Francisco: W. H. Freeman, 1975.

PARKS, T. E., KROLL, N. E. A., SALZBERG, P. M., & PARKINSON, S. R. Persistence of visual memory as indicated by decision time in a matching task. *Journal of Experimental Psychology,* 1972, *92,* 437–438.

PEI, M. *Language for everybody.* New York: Devin-Adair, 1956.

PEIRCE, C. S. *Essays in the philosophy of science* (V. Tomas, Ed.). New York: Liberal Arts Press, 1957. (Originally published as *Collected Papers of Charles Sanders Peirce.* Cambridge, Mass.: Harvard University Press, 1931–1935.)

PENFIELD, W. The interpretive cortex. *Science,* 1959, *129,* 1719–1725.

PETERSON, L. R., & PETERSON, M. J. Short-term retention of individual verbal items. *Journal of Experimental Psychology,* 1959, *58,* 193–198.

PEW, R. W. Acquisition of hierarchical control over the temporal organization of a skill. *Journal of Experimental Psychology,* 1966, *71,* 764–771.

PEW, R. W. Human perceptual-motor performance. In B. H. Kantowitz (Ed.), *Human information processing: Tutorials in performance and cognition.* New York: Wiley, 1974.

PHILLIPS, J. L., JR. *The origins of intellect: Piaget's theory* (2nd ed.). San Francisco: W. H. Freeman, 1975.

PIAGET, J. *Play, dreams and imitation in childhood.* New York: Norton, 1962.

PIAGET, J. Piaget's Theory. In P. Mussen (Ed.), *Carmichael's Manual of Child Psychology* (Vol. 1, 3rd ed.). New York: Wiley, 1970.

PICHERT, J. W., & ANDERSON, R. C. Taking different perspectives on a story. *Journal of Educational Psychology,* 1977, *69,* 309–315.

PIERCE, J. R. *Symbols, signals and noise: The nature and process of communication.* New York: Harper & Row, 1961.

PIERCE, J. R., & KARLIN, J. E. Reading rates and the information rate of a human channel. *Bell System Technical Journal,* 1957, *36,* 497–516.

POINCARÉ, H. Mathematical creation. In *The founda-*

tions of science (G. H. Halstead, trans.). New York: Science Press, 1913.

POLICH, J. M., & POTTS, G. R. Retrieval strategies for linearly ordered information. *Journal of Experimental Psychology: Human Learning and Memory,* 1977, *3,* 10–17.

POLLACK, I., & PICKETT, J. M. Intelligibility of excerpts from fluent speech: Auditory vs. structural context. *Journal of Verbal Learning and Verbal Behavior,* 1964, *3,* 79–84.

POLYA, G. *How to solve it.* Garden City, N.Y.: Doubleday Anchor, 1957.

POLYA, G. *Mathematical discovery: On understanding, learning and teaching problem solving* (Vol. II). New York: Wiley, 1965.

POPPER, K. R. [The logic of scientific discovery] (K. R. Popper, trans.). Basic Books, 1959. (Originally published, 1935).

POSNER, M. I. Abstraction and the process of recognition. In G. H. Bower & J. T. Spence (Eds.), *The psychology of learning and motivation* (Vol. 3). New York: Academic Press, 1969.

POSNER, M. I. *Cognition: An introduction.* Glenview, Ill.: Scott, Foresman, 1973.

POSNER, M. I., & BOIES, S. J. Components of attention. *Psychological Review,* 1971, *78,* 391–408.

POSNER, M. I., BOIES, S. J., EICHELMAN, W. H., & TAYLOR, R. L. Retention of visual and name codes of single letters. *Journal of Experimental Psychology Monograph,* 1969, *79* (1, Pt. 2).

POSNER, M. I., GOLDSMITH, R., & WELTON, K. E., JR. Perceived distance and the classification of distorted patterns. *Journal of Experimental Psychology,* 1967, *73,* 28–38.

POSNER, M. I., & KEELE, S. W. On the genesis of abstract ideas. *Journal of Experimental Psychology,* 1968, *77,* 353–363.

POSNER, M. I., & KEELE, S. W. Retention of abstract ideas. *Journal of Experimental Psychology,* 1970, *83,* 304–308.

POSNER, M. I., & MITCHELL, R. F. Chronometric analysis of classification. *Psychological Review,* 1967, *74,* 392–409.

POSTMAN, L. Effects of word frequency on acquisition and retention under conditions of free-recall learning. *Quarterly Journal of Experimental Psychology,* 1970, *22,* 185–195.

POSTMAN, L. Verbal learning and memory. *Annual Review of Psychology,* 1975, *26,* 291–335.

POTTS, G. R. Information processing strategies used in the encoding of linear orderings. *Journal of Verbal Learning and Verbal Behavior,* 1972, *11,* 727–740.

POTTS, G. R. Storing and retrieving information about ordered relationships. *Journal of Experimental Psychology,* 1974, *103,* 431–439.

POTTS, G. R., & SCHOLZ, K. W. The internal representation of a three-term series problem. *Journal of Verbal Learning and Verbal Behavior,* 1975, *14,* 439–452.

PUFF, C. R. Role of clustering in free recall. *Journal of Experimental Psychology,* 1970, *86,* 384–386.

PYLYSHYN, F. W. What the mind's eye tells the mind's brain: A critique of mental imagery. *Psychological Bulletin,* 1973, *80,* 1–24.

QUASTLER, H., & WULFF, V. J. *Human performance in information transmission* (Control Systems Laboratory Report No. 62). Urbana: University of Illinois, 1955.

QUILLIAN, M. R. Semantic memory. In M. Minsky (Ed.), *Semantic information processing.* Cambridge, Mass.: M. I. T. Press, 1968.

RABINOWITZ, J. C., MANDLER, G., & PATTERSON, K. E. Determinants of recognition and recall: Accessibility and generation. *Journal of Experimental Psychology: General,* 1977, *106,* 302–329.

REDDY, R., & NEWELL, A. Knowledge and its representation in a speech understanding system. In L. Gregg (Ed.), *Knowledge and cognition.* Potomac, Md.: Lawrence Erlbaum, 1974.

REED, S. K. Pattern recognition and categorization. *Cognitive Psychology,* 1972, *3,* 382–407.

REITMAN, J. S. Mechanisms of forgetting in short-term memory. *Cognitive Psychology,* 1971, *2,* 185–195.

REITMAN, J. S. Without surreptitious rehearsal, information in short term memory decays. *Journal of Verbal Learning and Verbal Behavior,* 1974, *13,* 365–377.

REITMAN, W. R. *Cognition and thought.* New York: Wiley, 1965.

ROGERS, T. B., KUIPER, N. A., & KIRKER, W. S. Self-reference and the encoding of personal information. *Journal of Personality and Social Psychology,* 1977, *35,* 677–688.

ROMNEY, A. K., & D'ANDRADE, R. G. Cognitive aspects of English kin terms. In A. K. Romney & R. G. d'Andrade (Eds.), Transcultural studies in cognition. *American Anthropologist*, 1964, *66* (3, Pt. 2), 146–170.

ROSCH, E. H. On the internal structure of perceptual and semantic categories. In T. E. Moore (Ed.), *Cognitive development and the acquisition of language*. New York: Academic Press, 1973.

ROSCH, E. H. Cognitive representations of semantic categories. *Journal of Experimental Psychology: General*, 1975, *104*, 192–233.

ROSENHAN, D. L. On being sane in insane places. *Science*, 1973, *179*, 250–258.

ROTHKOPF, E. F. Structural text features and the control of processes in learning from written materials. In J. B. Carroll & R. O. Freedle (Eds.), *Language comprehension and the acquisition of knowledge*. Washington, D.C.: Winston, 1972.

RUMELHART, D. E. Notes on a schema for stories. In D. G. Bobrow & A. M. Collins (Eds.), *Representation and understanding: Studies in cognitive science*. New York: Academic Press, 1975.

RUMELHART, D. E. *Human information processing*. New York: Wiley, 1977. (a)

RUMELHART, D. E. Toward an interactive model of reading. In S. Dornic (Ed.), *Attention and performance VI*. Hillsdale, N.J.: Lawrence Erlbaum Associates, 1977. (b)

RUMELHART, D. E. Understanding and summarizing brief stories. In D. LaBerge & S. J. Samuels (Eds.), *Basic processes in reading: Perception and comprehension*. Hillsdale, N.J.: Lawrence Erlbaum Associates, 1977. (c)

RUMELHART, D. E. & ORTONY, A. The representation of knowledge in memory. In R. C. Anderson, R. J. Spiro, & W. E. Montague (Eds.), *Schooling and the acquisition of knowledge*. Hillsdale, N.J.: Lawrence Erlbaum Associates, 1977.

SACHS, J. S. Recognition memory for syntactic and semantic aspects of connected discourse. *Perception and Psychophysics*, 1967, *2*, 437–442.

SAKITT, B. Iconic memory. *Psychological Review*, 1976, *83*, 257–276.

SAMUEL, A. L. Some studies in machine learning using the game of checkers. In E. A. Feigenbaum & J. Feldman (Eds.), *Computers and thought*. New York: McGraw-Hill, 1963.

SCHAFER, K. *Your slip is showing*. New York: Grayson, 1953.

SCHANK, R. C. Identification of conceptualizations underlying natural language. In R. C. Schank & K. M. Colby (Eds.), *Computer models of thought and language*. San Francisco: W. H. Freeman, 1973.

SCHANK, R. C., & ABELSON, R. P. *Scripts, plans, goals and understanding*. Hillsdale, N.J.: Lawrence Erlbaum Associates, 1977.

SCHMIDT, R. A. A schema theory of discrete motor skill learning. *Psychological Review*, 1975, *82*, 225–260. (a)

SCHMIDT, R. A. *Motor skills*. New York: Harper & Row, 1975. (b)

SCHMIDT, R. A. The schema as a solution to some persistent problems in motor learning theory. In G. E. Stelmach (Ed.), *Motor control: Issues and trends*. New York: Academic Press, 1976.

SCHNEIDER, W., & SHIFFRIN, R. M. Controlled and automatic human information processing: I. Detection, search, and attention. *Psychological Review*, 1977, *84*, 1–66.

SELFRIDGE, O. G. Pandemonium: A paradigm for learning. In *Symposium on the Mechanization of Thought Processes* (Vol. 1). London: HM Stationery Office, 1959.

SEYMOUR, W. D. Experiments on the acquisition of industrial skills. *Occupational Psychology*, 1954, *28*, 77–89.

SEYMOUR, W. D. Experiments on the acquisition of industrial skills. Part 2. *Occupational Psychology*, 1955, *29*, 82–98.

SEYMOUR, W. D. Experiments on the acquisition of industrial skills. Part 3. *Occupational Psychology*, 1956, *30*, 94–104.

SEYMOUR, W. D. Experiments on the acquisition of industrial skills. Part 4. Assembly tasks. *Occupational Psychology*, 1959, *33*, 18–35.

SHAFFER, L. H. Multiple attention in continuous verbal tasks. In P. M. A. Rabbitt & S. Dornic (Eds.), *Attention and performance V*. London: Academic Press, 1975.

SHAFFER, L. H. Intention and performance. *Psychological Review*, 1976, *83*, 375–393.

SHALLICE, T. On the contents of primary memory. In P. M. A. Rabbitt & S. Dornic (Eds.), *Attention and performance V.* London: Academic Press, 1975.

SHANNON, C. E., & WEAVER, W. *The mathematical theory of communication.* Urbana: University of Illinois Press, 1949.

SHELLY, M. W. Learning with reduced feedback information. *Journal of Experimental Psychology,* 1961, *62,* 209-222.

SHEPARD, R. N., & METZLER, J. Mental rotation of three-dimensional objects. *Science,* 1971, *171,* 701-703.

SHIFFRIN, R. M. Short-term store: The basis for a memory system. In F. Restle, R. M. Shiffrin, N. J. Castellan, H. R. Lindman, & D. B. Pisoni (Eds.), *Cognitive theory* (Vol. 1). Hillsdale, N.J.: Lawrence Erlbaum Associates, 1975.

SHIFFRIN, R. M., & GARDNER, G. T. Visual processing capacity and attentional control. *Journal of Experimental Psychology,* 1972, *93,* 72-82.

SHIFFRIN, R. M., & GEISLER, W. S. Visual recognition in a theory of information processing. In R. Solso (Ed.), *The Loyola Symposium: Contemporary issues in cognitive psychology.* Washington, D.C.: Winston, 1973.

SHIFFRIN, R. M., PISONI, D. B., & CASTANEDA-MENDEZ, K. Is attention shared between the ears? *Cognitive Psychology,* 1974, *6,* 190-215.

SHULMAN, H. G. Encoding and retention of semantic and phonemic information in short term memory. *Journal of Verbal Learning and Verbal Behavior,* 1970, *9,* 499-508.

SHULMAN, H. G. Semantic confusion errors in short-term memory. *Journal of Verbal Learning and Verbal Behavior,* 1972, *11,* 221-227.

SILVEIRA, J. *Incubation: The effect of interruption timing and length on problem solution and quality of problem processing.* Unpublished doctoral dissertation, University of Oregon, 1971.

SIMON, H. A. The structure of ill structured problems. *Artificial Intelligence,* 1973, *4,* 181-201.

SIMON, H. A. How big is a chunk? *Science,* 1974, *183,* 482-488.

SIMON, H. A., & CHASE, W. G. Skill in chess. *American Scientist,* 1973, *61,* 394-403.

SIMON, H. A., & GILMARTIN, K. A simulation of memory for chess positions. *Cognitive Psychology,* 1973, *5,* 29-46.

SIMON, H. A., & HAYES, J. R. Understanding complex task instructions. In D. Klahr (Ed.), *Cognition and instruction.* Hillsdale, N.J.: Lawrence Erlbaum Associates, 1976. (a)

SIMON, H. A., & HAYES, J. R. The understanding process: Problem isomorphs. *Cognitive Psychology,* 1976, *8,* 165-190. (b)

SIMON, H. A., & KOTOVSKY, K. Human acquisition of concepts for sequential patterns. *Psychological Review,* 1963, *70,* 534-546.

SIMON, H. A., & LEA, G. Problem solving and rule induction: A unified view. In L. W. Gregg (Ed.), *Knowledge and cognition.* Potomac, Md.: Lawrence Erlbaum, 1974.

SIMON, H. A., & NEWELL, A. Simulation of human thinking. In M. Greenberger (Ed.), *Computers and the world of the future.* Cambridge, Mass.: M. I. T. Press, 1962.

SIMON, H. A., & NEWELL, A. Human problem solving: The state of the theory in 1970. *American Psychologist,* 1971, *26,* 145-159.

SIMON, H. A., & NEWELL, A. Thinking processes. In D. H. Krantz, R. C. Atkinson, R. D. Luce, & P. Suppes (Eds.), *Contemporary developments in mathematical psychology* (Vol. 1). San Francisco: W. H. Freeman, 1974.

SMALL, D. W. The abstraction of arbitrary categories. *Memory and Cognition,* 1975, *3,* 581-585.

SMITH, E. E., SHOBEN, E. J., & RIPS, L. J. Structure and process in semantic memory: A featural model for semantic decisions. *Psychological Review,* 1974, *81,* 214-241.

SMITH, G. A. Studies in compatibility and a new model of choice reaction time. In S. Dornic (Ed.), *Attention and performance VI.* Hillsdale, N.J.: Lawrence Erlbaum Associates, 1977.

SMITH, K. U., & SUSSMAN, H. Cybernetic theory and analysis of motor learning and memory. In E. A. Bilodeau & I. McD. Bilodeau (Eds.), *Principles of skill acquisition.* New York: Academic Press, 1969.

SNODDY, G. S. Learning and stability. *Journal of Applied Psychology,* 1926, *10,* 1-36.

SORKIN, R. D., & POHLMANN, L. D. Some models of observer behavior in two channel auditory signal detection. *Perception and Psychophysics,* 1973, *14,* 101–109.

SPERLING, G. The information available in brief visual presentations. *Psychological Monographs,* 1960, *74* (Whole No. 498).

SPERLING, G. A model for visual memory tasks. *Human Factors,* 1963, *5,* 19–36.

SPIRO, R. J. Remembering information from text: The "state of schema" approach. In R. C. Anderson, R. J. Spiro, & W. E. Montague (Eds.), *Schooling and the acquisition of knowledge.* Hillsdale, N.J.: Lawrence Erlbaum Associates, 1977.

STEWART, C., & GOUGH, P. Constituent search in immediate memory for sentences. *Proceedings of the Midwestern Psychology Association,* 1967.

STRATTON, G. M. Some preliminary experiments on vision without inversion of the retinal image. *Psychological Review,* 1896, *3,* 611–617.

STRATTON, G. M. Vision without inversion of the retinal image. *Psychological Review,* 1897, *4,* 341–360, 463–481.

TAYLOR, F. V., & GARVEY, W. D. The limitation of a "Procrustean" approach to the optimization of man-machine systems. *Ergonomics,* 1959, *2,* 187–194.

TEICHNER, W. H., & KREBS, M. J. Laws of visual choice reaction time. *Psychological Review,* 1974, *81,* 75–98.

THOMAS, J. C., JR. An analysis of behavior in the Hobbit-Orcs problem. *Cognitive Psychology,* 1974, *6,* 257–269.

THORNDIKE, E. L. Animal intelligence. *Psychological Monographs,* 1898, II, No. 4 (Whole No. 8).

THORSHEIM, H. I., HOUSTON, L., & BADGER, C. Visual and kinesthetic components of pursuit-tracking performance. *Journal of Motor Behavior,* 1974, *6,* 199–203.

TILL, R. E., & JENKINS, J. J. The effects of cued orienting tasks on the free recall of words. *Journal of Verbal Learning and Verbal Behavior,* 1973, *12,* 489–498.

TRABASSO, T., & RILEY, C. A. On the construction and use of representations involving linear order. In R. L. Solso (Ed.), *Information processing and cognition: The Loyola symposium.* Hillsdale, N.J.: Lawrence Erlbaum Associates, 1975.

TRABASSO, T., ROLLINS, H., & SHAUGHNESSY, E. Storage and verification stages in processing concepts. *Cognitive Psychology,* 1971, *2,* 239–289.

TRAKHTENBROT, B. A. [*Algorithms and automatic computing machines*] (J. Kristian, J. D. McCawley & S. A. Schmitt, trans.). Lexington, Mass.: Heath, 1963.

TREISMAN, A. M. Contextual cues in selective listening. *Quarterly Journal of Experimental Psychology,* 1960, *12,* 242–248.

TREISMAN, A. M., & GEFFEN, G. Selective attention: Perception or response? *Quarterly Journal of Experimental Psychology,* 1967, *19,* 1–17.

TULVING, E. Subjective organization in free recall of "unrelated" words. *Psychological Review,* 1962, *69,* 344–354.

TULVING, E. Episodic and semantic memory. In E. Tulving & W. Donaldson (Eds.), *Organization of memory.* New York: Academic Press, 1972.

TULVING, E., & OSLER, S. Effectiveness of retrieval cues in memory for words. *Journal of Experimental Psychology,* 1968, *77,* 593–601.

TULVING, E., & THOMSON, D. M. Encoding specificity and retrieval processes in episodic memory. *Psychological Review,* 1973, *80,* 352–373.

TURING, A. M. Computing machinery and intelligence. *Mind,* 1950, *59,* 433–460.

TURVEY, M. T. On peripheral and central processes in vision: Inferences from an information-processing analysis of masking with patterned stimuli. *Psychological Review,* 1973, *80,* 1–52.

VENDLER, Z. *Linguistics in philosophy.* Ithaca, N.Y.: Cornell University Press, 1967.

VERNON, P. E. (Ed.), *Creativity.* Harmondsworth, England: Penguin Books, 1970.

VON TREBA, P., & SMITH, K. U. The dimensional analysis of motion: 4. Transfer effects and direction of movement. *Journal of Applied Psychology,* 1952, *36,* 348–353.

VON WRIGHT, J. M. On the problem of selection in iconic memory. *Scandinavian Journal of Psychology,* 1972, *13,* 159–171.

WALLAS, G. *The art of thought.* New York: Harcourt, 1926.

WALSH, D. A., & JENKINS, J. J. Effects of orienting tasks on free recall in incidental learning: "Difficulty," "effort," and "process" explanations. *Journal of Verbal Learning and Verbal Behavior,* 1973, *12,* 481–488.

WARREN, M., & WARREN, P. Auditory illusions and confusions. *Scientific American,* 1970, *223,* 30–43.

WASON, P. C. On the failure to eliminate hypotheses in a conceptual task. *Quarterly Journal of Experimental Psychology,* 1960, *12,* 129–140.

WASON, P. C. Reasoning about a rule. *Quarterly Journal of Experimental Psychology,* 1968, *20,* 273–281.

WASON, P. C., & JOHNSON-LAIRD, P. N. *Psychology of reasoning.* Cambridge, Mass.: Harvard University Press, 1972.

WATKINS, M. J., WATKINS, O. C., CRAIK, F. I. M., & MAZURYK, G. Effect of nonverbal distraction on short-term storage. *Journal of Experimental Psychology,* 1973, *101,* 296–300.

WAUGH, N. C., & NORMAN, D. A. Primary memory. *Psychological Review,* 1965, *72,* 89–104.

WEHRKAMP, R., & SMITH, K. U. Dimensional analysis of motion: 2. Travel-distance effects. *Journal of Applied Psychology,* 1952, *36,* 201–206.

WEINER, N. *Cybernetics.* New York: Wiley, 1948.

WELFORD, A. T. *Skilled performance: Perceptual and motor skills.* Glenview, Ill.: Scott, Foresman, 1976.

WELLS, H. Effects of transfer and problem structure in disjunctive concept formation. *Journal of Experimental Psychology,* 1963, *65,* 63–69.

WERTHEIMER, M. *Productive thinking.* New York: Harper & Row, 1959.

WEST, L. J. Vision and kinesthesis in the acquisition of typewriting skill. *Journal of Applied Psychology,* 1967, *51,* 161–166.

WHITEHEAD, A. N., & RUSSELL, B. *Principia mathematica* (Vol. 1, 2 ed.). Cambridge: At the University Press, 1935.

WHORF, B. L. *Language, thought, and reality: Selected writings of Benjamin Lee Whorf.* (J. B. Carroll, Ed.). New York: Wiley, 1956.

WICKELGREN, W. A. Acoustic similarity and retroactive interference in short-term memory. *Journal of Verbal Learning and Verbal Behavior,* 1965, *4, 53–61.*

WICKELGREN, W. A. *How to solve problems.* San Francisco: W. H. Freeman, 1974.

WILKINS, M. C. The effect of changed material on ability to do formal syllogistic reasoning. *Archives of Psychology,* 1928, *16* (Whole No. 102).

WINOGRAD, T. *Understanding natural language.* New York: Academic Press, 1972.

WINSTON, P. H. *Artificial intelligence.* Reading, Mass.: Addison-Wesley, 1977.

WITTGENSTEIN, L. *Philosophical investigations.* New York: Macmillan, 1953.

WITTGENSTEIN, L. *The blue and brown books.* New York: Harper & Row, 1958.

WOLLEN, K. A., WEBER, A., & LOWRY, D. H. Bizarreness versus interaction of mental images as determinants of learning. *Cognitive Psychology,* 1972, *3,* 518–523.

WOOD, G. Organizational processes and free recall. In E. Tulving & W. Donaldson (Eds.), *Organization of memory.* New York: Academic Press, 1972.

WOODWARD, A. E., JR., BJORK, R. A., & JONGEWARD, R. H., JR. Recall and recognition as a function of primary rehearsal. *Journal of Verbal Learning and Verbal Behavior,* 1973, *12,* 608–617.

WOODWORTH, R. S., & SELLS, S. B. An atmosphere effect in formal syllogistic reasoning. *Journal of Experimental Psychology,* 1935, *18,* 451–460.

YATES, F. A. *The art of memory.* Chicago: University of Chicago Press, 1966.

YERKES, R. M., & DODSON, J. D. The relation of strength of stimulus to rapidity of habit-formation. *Journal of Comparative Neurology and Psychology,* 1908, *13,* 459–482.

ZADEH, L. Fuzzy sets. *Information and Control,* 1965, *8,* 338–353.

ZANGWILL, O. L. Remembering revisited. *Quarterly Journal of Experimental Psychology,* 1972, *24,* 123–138.

Acknowledgments and Copyrights

(Continued from page iv)

Figure 2.17, p. 27. From Hubel & Wiesel, 1965, p. 251. Copyright 1965 by the American Physiological Society. Reprinted by permission.

Table 2.1, p. 31. From *Principles of perceptual learning and development* by Eleanor J. Gibson, © 1969, p. 88. Reprinted by permission of Prentice-Hall, Englewood Cliffs, N.J.

Table 2.2, p. 32. From Kinney, Marsetta, & Showman, 1966. Copyright 1966 by The Mitre Corporation. Reprinted by permission.

Figure 2.19, p. 33. From "Visual Search" by Ulric Neisser, p. 97. Copyright © 1964 by Scientific American, Inc. All rights reserved. Reprinted by permission.

Figure 2.20, p. 34. From Bugelski & Alampay, 1961, p. 206. Copyright 1961 by the Canadian Psychological Association. Reprinted by permission.

Figure 2.21, p. 37. From *Explorations in cognition,* edited by Donald A. Norman, David E. Rumelhart, and the LNR Research Group, p. 296. W. H. Freeman and Company. Copyright © 1975. Reprinted by permission.

Figure 2.22, p. 37. From *Explorations in cognition,* edited by Donald A. Norman, David E. Rumelhart, and the LNR Research Group, p. 296. W. H. Freeman and Company. Copyright © 1975. Reprinted by permission.

Figure 2.24, p. 40. Photo by Edgar J. Cheatham, Jr., and Patricia Cheatham.

Figure 2.27, p. 43. From Kintsch, 1977, p. 130. Copyright 1977 by John Wiley & Sons. Reprinted by permission.

Figure 3.1, p. 56. From Murdock, 1961, p. 619. Copyright 1961 by the American Psychological Association. Reprinted by permission.

Figure 3.2, p. 62. Lyrics copyright © 1959 by Richard Rodgers & Oscar Hammerstein II; Williamson Music, Inc., owner of publication and allied rights throughout the Western Hemisphere and Japan. International copyright secured. All rights reserved. Used by permission.

Table 3.1, p. 64. From Conrad, 1964, p. 78. Copyright 1964 by the British Psychological Society. Reprinted by permission.

Table 3.2, p. 64. From Conrad, 1964, p. 78. Copyright 1964 by the British Psychological Society. Reprinted by permission.

Figure 3.4, p. 68. From Peterson & Peterson, 1959, p. 275. Copyright 1959 by the American Psychological Association. Reprinted by permission.

Figure 3.5, p. 74. From Atkinson & Shiffrin, 1968, p. 93. Copyright 1968 by Academic Press, Inc. Reprinted by permission.

Figure 3.6, p. 76. From Shiffrin, 1975. Copyright 1975 by Lawrence Erlbaum Associates, Inc., Publishers. Reprinted by permission of the author and the publisher.

Figure 4.3, p. 89. From Collins & Quillian, 1969, p. 241. Copyright 1969 by Academic Press, Inc. Reprinted by permission.

Figure 4.7, p. 97. From Smith, Shoben, & Rips, 1974, p. 222. Copyright 1974 by the American Psychological Association. Reprinted by permission.

Figure 4.8, p. 100. From Brooks, 1968, p. 350. Copyright 1968 by the Canadian Psychological Association. Reprinted by permission.

Figure 4.9, p. 102. From Kosslyn, Ball, & Reiser, 1978, p. 51. Copyright 1978 by the American Psychological Association. Reprinted by permission.

Figure 4.10, p. 102. From Kosslyn, Ball, & Reiser, 1978, p. 52. Copyright 1978 by the American Psychological Association. Reprinted by permission.

Figure 5.1, p. 112. From Wollen, Weber, & Lowry, 1972, p. 520. Copyright 1972 by Academic Press, Inc. Reprinted by permission.

Figure 5.2, p. 113. From Wollen, Weber, & Lowry, 1972, p. 520. Copyright 1972 by Academic Press, Inc. Reprinted by permission.

Figure 5.3, p. 114. From Atkinson, 1975, p. 822. Copyright 1975 by the American Psychological Association. Reprinted by permission.

Figure 5.4, p. 117. From Tulving, 1962, p. 349. Copyright 1962 by the American Psychological Association. Reprinted by permission.

Quotation, p. 119. From *Plans and the structure of behavior* by George A. Miller, Eugene Galanter, and Karl H. Pribram, p. 135. Copyright © 1960 by Holt, Rinehart and Winston, Inc. Reprinted by permission of Holt, Rinehart, and Winston.

Table 5.1, p. 122. From Hersey, 1963, p. 47. Copyright 1963 by Award Books. Reprinted by permission of Robert J. Abramson & Assoc., Inc., as agent for Award Books.

Figure 5.8, p. 125. From Bower & Clark, 1969, p. 182. Copyright 1969 by the Psychonomic Society, Inc. Reprinted by permission.

Table 5.2, p. 125. From Mandler, 1967, p. 356. Copyright 1967 by Academic Press, Inc. Reprinted by permission.

Figure 5.9, p. 130. From Carmichael, Hogan, & Walter, 1932.

Table 6.1, p. 145. After Bolinger, 1975. From *Psychology and language: an introduction to psycholinguistics* by Herbert H. Clark and Eve V. Clark, p. 22. © 1977 by Harcourt Brace Jovanovich, Inc. Reprinted by permission of the publishers.

Table 6.3, p. 153. Adapted from *An introduction to language* by Victoria Fromkin and Robert Rodman, pp. 37–39. Copyright © 1974 by Holt, Rinehart and Winston, Inc. Reprinted by permission of Holt, Rinehart and Winston.

Box 6.2, pp. 153–154. From *Your slip is showing: broadcasting's classic bloopers* collected by Kermit Schafer. Reprinted by permission of Kermit Schafer.

Quotations, pp. 154–156. From "The non-anomalous nature of anomalous utterances" by V. A. Fromkin. In V. A. Fromkin (Ed.), *Speech errors as linguistic evidence*. Copyright 1973 by Mouton Publishers. Reprinted by permission of the publishers.

Figure 6.5, p. 159. From *Psycholinguistics: a cognitive view of language* by S. Cairns and C.E. Cairns, p. 158. Copyright © 1976 by Holt, Rinehart and Winston. Reprinted by permission of Holt, Rinehart and Winston.

Figure 6.6, p. 160. Excerpted from *The speech chain* by P. B. Denes and E. N. Pinson, p. 160. Copyright © 1963 by Bell Telephone Laboratories, Inc. Reprinted by permission of Doubleday & Company, Inc.

Figure 6.7, p. 161. After Cutting & Pisoni, 1976, p. 311.

Figure 6.8, p. 162. From Liberman, Cooper, Shankweiler, & Studdert-Kennedy, 1967. Copyright 1967 by the American Psychological Association. Reprinted by permission.

Figure 6.9, p. 162. From Liberman, 1970, p. 309. Copyright 1970 by Academic Press, Inc. Reprinted by permission.

Table 6.4, p. 168. From *Psychology and language: an introduction to psycholinguistics* by Herbert H. Clark and Eve V. Clark, p. 440. © 1977 by Harcourt Brace Jovanovich, Inc. Reprinted by permission of the publishers.

Table 6.5, p. 169. Based on Johnson-Laird (1977). From *Psychology and language: an introduction to psycholinguistics* by Herbert H. Clark and Eve V. Clark, p. 441. © 1977 by Harcourt Brace Jovanovich, Inc. Reprinted by permission of the publishers.

Figure 6.10, p. 179. From Winograd, 1972, p. 8. Copyright 1972 by Academic Press, Inc. Reprinted by permission.

Figure 6.11, p. 180. From Winograd, 1972, p. 9. Copyright 1972 by Academic Press, Inc. Reprinted by permission.

Quotations, pp. 184, 186. From Bransford & Johnson, 1973, pp. 392–393, 400. Copyright 1973 by Academic Press, Inc. Reprinted by permission.

Figure 7.1, p. 187. From Bransford & Johnson, 1973, p. 393. Copyright 1973 by Academic Press, Inc. Reprinted by permission.

Table 7.1, p. 188. From Dooling & Mullet, 1973, p. 405. Copyright 1973 by the American Psychological Association. Reprinted by permission.

Figure 7.3, p. 195. From Meyer, 1975, pp. 31–32, 40. Copyright 1975 by the National Reading Conference, Inc. Reprinted with permission of the National Reading Conference and B. J. F. Meyer.

Table 7.2, p. 198. From Anderson & Pichert, 1978, p. 8. Copyright 1978 by Academic Press, Inc. Reprinted by permission.

Figure 7.4, p. 203. Photos from Loftus, Miller, & Burns, 1978, p. 20. Copyright 1978 by the American Psychological Association. Reprinted by permission.

Table 8.2, p. 212. After Haygood & Bourne, 1965. Copyright 1965 by the American Psychological Association. Reprinted by permission.

Figure 8.3, p. 215. From Bourne, 1967. Copyright 1967 by John Wiley & Sons, Inc. Reprinted by permission.

Figure 8.4, p. 216. From Trabasso, Rollins, & Shaughnessy, 1971. Copyright 1971 by Academic Press, Inc. Reprinted by permission.

Figure 8.5, p. 219. From Levine, 1966. Copyright 1966 by the American Psychological Association. Reprinted by permission.

Figure 8.6, p. 220. From Levine, 1966. Copyright 1966 by the American Psychological Association. Reprinted by permission.

Quotation, pp. 222–223. From "The social imperatives of medical research" by L. Eisenberg. *Science,* 1977, *198,* 1105–1110. Copyright 1977 by the American Association for the Advancement of Science. Reprinted by permission.

Figure 8.7, p. 228. From Miller & Johnson-Laird, 1976, p. 279. Copyright 1976 by the Belknap Press of the Harvard University Press. Reprinted by permission of the publishers.

Figure 8.8, p. 229. From Miller & Johnson-Laird, 1976, p. 284. Copyright 1976 by the Belknap Press of the Harvard University Press. Reprinted by permission of the publishers.

Table 8.3, p. 229. From Miller and Johnson-Laird, 1976, p. 284. Copyright 1976 by the Belknap Press of the Harvard University Press. Reprinted by permission of the publishers.

Story, pp. 232–233. Condensed from "QL 696.C9" by Anthony Boucher. Reprinted by permission of Curtis Brown Ltd. Copyright © 1943 by Anthony Boucher. Copyright renewed 1975 by Davis Publications.

Figure 9.1, p. 236. Presentation and diagrams of problem from Katona, 1940. Copyright 1940 by Columbia University Press. Reprinted by permission. Other text from *Thinking and problem solving: an introduction to human cognition and learning* by Richard E. Mayer, p. 63. Copyright © 1977 by Scott, Foresman and Company. Reprinted by permission.

Figure 9.3, p. 237. After Wertheimer, 1959.

Table 9.1, p. 238. From Luchins, 1942.

Figure 9.4, p. 239. From Rumelhart, 1977a, p. 261; after Duncker, 1945. Copyright 1977 by John Wiley & Sons, Inc. Reprinted by permission.

Figure 9.5, p. 240. From B.F. Anderson, 1975; after Duncker, 1945. Copyright 1975 by Academic Press, Inc. Reprinted by permission.

Figure 9.6, p. 241. From Rumelhart, 1977a, p. 263; after Duncker, 1945. Copyright 1977 by John Wiley & Sons, Inc. Reprinted by permission.

Figure 9.7, p. 242. After Maier, 1930, from *Thinking and problem solving: an introduction to human cognition and learning* by Richard E. Mayer, p. 80. Copyright © 1977 by Scott, Foresman and Company. Reprinted by permission.

Figure 9.8, p. 242. After Birch & Rabinowitz, 1951. From *Thinking and problem solving: an introduction to human cognition and learning* by Richard E. Mayer, p. 99. Copyright © 1977 by Scott, Foresman and Company. Reprinted by permission.

Figure 9.9, p. 244. From *The task of gestalt psychology* by Wolfgang Köhler, with an introduction by Carroll C. Pratt; p. 146. Copyright © 1969 by Princeton University Press; Princeton Paperback, 1972. Reprinted by permission of Princeton University Press.

Figure 9.10, p. 244. After Köhler, 1969. From *Thinking and problem solving: an introduction to human cognition and learning* by Richard E. Mayer. Copyright © 1977 by Scott, Foresman and Company. Reprinted by permission.

Excerpts, pp. 247–249. From *Human problem solving* by Allen Newell and Herbert A. Simon, Appendix 6.1, pp. 230–231. Copyright © 1972 by Prentice-Hall, Inc. Reprinted by permission.

Figure 9.11, p. 249. From Lindsay & Norman, 1977. Copyright 1977 by Academic Press, Inc. Reprinted by permission.

Figure 9.12, p. 250. From Lindsay & Norman, 1977. Copyright 1977 by Academic Press, Inc. Reprinted by permission.

Figure 9.13, p. 251. From Allen Newell and Herbert A. Simon, *Human problem solving*, © 1972, p. 181. Reprinted by permission of Prentice-Hall, Inc., Englewood Cliffs, New Jersey.

Box 9.2, p. 252. From Lindsay & Norman, pp. 559–560. Copyright 1977 by Academic Press, Inc. Reprinted by permission.

Figure 9.15, p. 258. From Newell & Simon, 1972, p. 109. Copyright 1972 by Prentice-Hall, Inc. Reprinted by permission.

Figure 9.16, p. 259. From J. R. Hayes, *Cognitive psychology* (Homewood, Ill.: The Dorsey Press, 1978), p. 189. © 1978 by The Dorsey Press. Reprinted by permission.

Figure 9.17, p. 260. After Trakhentenbrot, 1963.

Figure 9.19, p. 263. From Rumelhart, 1977a, p. 258. Copyright 1977 by John Wiley & Sons, Inc. Reprinted by permission.

Figure 9.20, p. 265. From Thomas, 1974. Copyright 1974 by Academic Press, Inc. Reprinted by permission.

Figure 9.21, p. 268. From Greeno, 1976a. In D. Klahr (Ed.), *Cognition and instruction,* p. 136. Copyright 1976 by Lawrence Erlbaum Associates, Inc. Reprinted by permission of the editor and Lawrence Erlbaum Associates, Inc., Publishers.

Figure 9.22, p. 268. From Greeno, 1976a. In D. Klahr (Ed.), *Cognition and instruction,* p. 137. Copyright 1976 by Lawrence Erlbaum Associates, Inc. Reprinted with the permission of the editor and Lawrence Erlbaum Associates, Inc., Publishers.

Box 9.5, pp. 269–270. From Lindsay & Norman, 1977, p. 372. Copyright 1977 by Academic Press, Inc. Reprinted by permission.

Figure 9.23, p. 272. From Hayes & Simon, 1974. Reprinted with the permission of the authors and Lawrence Erlbaum Associates, Inc., Publishers.

Table 10.1, p. 281. From DeSoto, London & Handel, 1965, p. 156. Copyright 1965 by the American Psychological Association. Reprinted by permission.

Figure 10.1, p. 285. From Potts, 1972, p. 738. Copyright 1972 by Academic Press, Inc. Reprinted by permission.

Box 10.2, pp. 291–292. Excerpt of sample question from *1977–78 information bulletin, graduate record examinations,* pp. 18–19. Reproduced by permission of Educational Testing Service, the copyright owner.

Table 10.2, p. 283. From Clark, 1969. Copyright 1969 by the American Psychological Association. Reprinted by permission.

Table 10.4, p. 296. From Erickson (1974). In R. L. Solso (Ed.), *Theories in cognitive psychology: the Loyola symposium,* p. 309. Copyright 1974 by Lawrence Erlbaum Associates, Inc. Reprinted with the permission of the editor and Lawrence Erlbaum Associates, Inc., Publishers.

Figure 10.2, p. 297. Neimark & Chapman, 1975. In R. J. Falmagne (Ed.), *Reasoning: representation and process in children and adults.* Copyright 1975 by Lawrence Erlbaum Associates, Inc. Reprinted with the permission of the editor and Lawrence Erlbaum Associates, Inc., Publishers.

Table 10.5, p. 298. From Erickson (1974). In R. L. Solso (Ed.), *Theories in cognitive psychology: the Loyola symposium,* p. 310. Copyright 1974 by Lawrence Erlbaum Associates, Inc. Reprinted with the permission of the editor and Lawrence Erlbaum Associates, Inc., Publishers.

Quotation, pp. 304–305. From *Thinking: an experimental and social study* by F. C. Bartlett, pp. 198–199. Copyright 1967 by George Allen & Unwin Ltd. Reprinted by permission.

Quotation, p. 308. From *Plans and the structure of behavior* by George A. Miller, Eugene Galanter, and Karl H. Pribram, p. 86. Copyright © 1960 by Holt, Rinehart and Winston, Inc. Reprinted by permission of Holt, Rinehart and Winston.

Figure 11.2, p. 309. From Crossman, 1959. Copyright 1959 by Taylor & Francis, Ltd. Reprinted by permission.

Figure 11.3, p. 310. From *Plans and the structure of behavior* by George A. Miller, Eugene Galanter, and Karl H. Pribram, pp. 26, 36. Copyright © 1960 by Holt, Rinehart and Winston, Inc. Reprinted by permission of Holt, Rinehart and Winston.

Figure 11.5, p. 315. From Hyman, 1953, p. 192. Copyright 1953 by the American Psychological Association. Reprinted by permission.

Figure 11.6, p. 316. From *Skilled performance: perceptual and motor skills* by A. T. Welford, p. 74. Copyright © 1976 by Scott, Foresman and Company. Reprinted by permission.

Figure 11.8, p. 320. From E. A. Fleishman & J. F. Parker, "Factors in the retention and relearning of perceptual-motor skill." *Journal of experimental psychology,* 1962, *64,* 218. Copyright 1962 by the American Psychological Association. Reprinted by permission.

Figure 11.9, p. 321. From Bourne & Archer, 1956, p. 27. Copyright 1956 by the American Psychological Association. Reprinted by permission.

Figure 11.10, p. 326. From Pew, 1974, p. 31. Reprinted with the permission of Lawrence Erlbaum Associates, Inc., Publishers.

Figure 11.11, p. 328. From Schmidt, 1975a, p. 236. Copyright 1975 by the American Psychological Association. Reprinted by permission.

Name Index

Abelson, R.P., 191
Adams, J.A., 110, 310, 311, 322
Adamson, R.E., 239–243
Alampay, D.A., 36
Allport, D.A., 329
Alluisi, E.A., 315, 320
Anderson, J.R., 54, 75, 85, 92, 94–95, 103–104
Anderson, R.C., 107, 127, 186, 187, 189–190, 194, 196, 197–198, 204
Annett, J., 311, 318
Antonitis, B., 329
Apter, M.J., 254, 256
Archer, E.J., 212, 321
Aristotle, 293
Arkes, H.R., 72, 108, 125–126
Armer, P., 256
Atkinson, R.C., 53, 73, 74, 111, 114
Attneave, F., 312
Atwood, M.E., 264
Austin, G.A., 221
Averbach, E., 11

Bachrach, A.J., 47
Baddeley, A.D., 15, 54, 101
Badger, C., 318
Bahrick, H.P., 322
Bairstow, P.J., 310–311
Ball, T.M., 101–103
Banks, W.P., 13
Barber, G., 13
Barclay, J.R., 177–178, 199
Bartlett, F.C., 33, 130, 200–201, 206, 304–305, 323
Beilin, H., 244
Bellezza, F.S., 110
Berlin, B., 225
Bernstein, A., 265
Bevan, W., 111
Bever, T.G., 150, 171, 175
Bhaskar, R., 266-267
Birch, H.G., 240–241, 242
Bjork, R.A., 48, 61, 63
Bobrow, D.G., 35, 45, 230, 254, 271
Boeck, W.J., 128-129
Boies, S.J., 44, 65
Bolinger, D., 145
Bond, Z.S., 165
Book, W.F., 308
Boole, G., 278–279
Boomer, D.S., 153-154
Boucher, A., 233
Bourne, L.E., Jr., 212, 214, 215, 321

Bousfield, W.A., 114-115
Bower, G.H., 58, 110–111, 124, 125
Brainard, R.W., 315, 320
Braine, M.D.S., 289–290, 292–293
Bransford, J.D., 176–178, 184, 186–188, 190, 194, 199
Briggs, G.E., 322
Broadbent, D.E., 41, 42, 43, 44, 57, 72–73
Brooks, L.R., 99, 100–101, 103, 218
Brown, A., 206
Brown, J.S., 196
Brown, R., 157
Bruce, D.R., 115, 116
Bruner, J.S., 35, 221, 223
Bryan, W.L., 305, 306, 326
Bugelski, B.R., 36, 119
Buschke, H., 65
Burns, H.J., 202–203, 204

Cairns, C.E., 159
Cairns, H.S., 159, 174–175
Cantor, N., 22, 23
Caplan, D., 173
Carey, S.T., 128

Carmichael, L., 130-131
Carpenter, P.A., 284
Castaneda-Mendez, K., 44
Ceraso, J., 296–298
Cerf, B., 139
Cermak, L.S., 124
Chafe, W.L., 194
Chapman, J.P., 295
Chapman, L.J., 295
Chapman, R.H., 296, 297
Charness, N., 59
Chase, W.G., 46, 59, 60, 266
Cheatham, E., 40
Cheatham, P., 40
Cheesman, F.L., 110
Cheng, C., 223–224
Chernikoff, R., 323
Chomsky, N., 137, 140, 141–142, 149
Clark, E.V., 142, 147, 168
Clark, H.H., 142, 147, 168, 282–283, 284
Clark, M.C., 124, 125
Cofer, C.N., 115, 116, 131, 200
Cohen, B.H., 115
Colby, K.M., 267
Cole, R.A., 164
Collins, A., 85–91, 94, 98, 196, 205
Collyer, S.C., 111
Conrad, C., 90
Conrad, R., 15, 63–64, 65
Cooper, F.S., 160, 162
Coriell, A.S., 11
Craik, F.I.M., 53–54, 61, 69, 71, 72, 73–77, 107, 108, 129
Crossman, E.R.F.W., 308, 309, 316, 322
Crothers, E.J., 194
Crowder, R.G., 11, 13–15, 71, 118
Cutting, J.A., 161

d'Andrade, R.G., 167
Dansereau, D., 253
Darwin, G.J., 13–15
DeClerk, J.L., 156
de Groot, A.D., 58, 271

Deininger, R.L., 316
Denes, P.B., 160
De Soto, C., 280, 281, 283, 284
Dodson, J.D., 47
Dooling, D.J., 187, 188, 196
Dubos, R., 243
Duncker, K., 237, 238–240, 241

Egan, D.E., 274
Eichelman, W.H., 65
Eisenberg, L., 222–223
Eisenstadt, M., 270–271
Elmes, D.G., 61, 63
Erickson, J.R., 296–298, 300, 301
Ernst, G.W., 262

Feigenbaum, E.A., 255
Feldman, J., 255, 267
Fillenbaum, S., 170–171
Fillmore, C.J., 142–143
Fitts, P.M., 305–306, 307, 315, 316, 320, 330
Fleishman, E.A., 318–320
Flexser, A.J., 129
Fodor, J.A., 150, 167, 171, 174, 175
Franks, J.J., 176–178, 199
Frederiksen, C.H., 199–200
Freedman, J.L., 91
Freud, S., 48
Fromkin, V.A., 150, 152, 153–155, 156
Frost, N., 103

Galanter, E., 119, 273, 307, 308, 310, 326
Gardner, E.T., 72, 108, 125
Gardner, G.T., 44
Gardner, R.A., 238
Garnes, S., 165
Garrett, M.F., 150, 153, 155, 171, 174, 175
Garvey, W.D., 316
Geffen, G., 43–45

Geisler, W.S., 71
Gelernter, H., 254
Ghiselin, B., 245, 246
Gibson, E., 31
Gilmartin, K., 266
Glanzer, M., 57
Glenberg, A., 63
Glencross, D.J., 322, 323
Goetz, E.T., 189–190, 204, 311
Goldsmith, R., 21
Goldstein, M., 318
Goodnow, J.J., 221, 223
Gordon, W.J., 246
Gottfried, 186
Gough, P., 173
Gould, J.D., 311
Graf, R., 172
Grant, D.A., 316
Grant, S., 101
Green, C., 63
Greeno, J.G., 264, 267–269, 274
Gregg, L.W., 60, 253

Hadamard, J., 245
Hakes, D.T., 174-175
Halle, M., 163
Handel, S., 280, 281
Harris, C.S., 312
Harter, N., 305, 306, 326
Hayes, J.R., 259, 271, 272, 275, 276
Hayes-Roth, B., 230
Hayes-Roth, F., 230
Haygood, R.C., 212, 214
Heise, G., 165
Hellyer, S., 320
Henderson, S.E., 325
Herbart, F., 107
Herigon, P., 122
Hersey, W.D., 122, 124
Hick, W.E., 315–316
Higgins, E.T., 284
Hilf, F.D., 267
Hislop, M.W., 218
Hogan, H.P., 130–131

Horn, R., 244
Horne, M., 313
Houston, L., 318
Howe, M.J.A., 61
Hubel, D.H., 23, 27
Huesmann, L.R., 223–224
Hull, A.J., 15, 65
Hull, C.L., 218
Hunt, D.P., 311
Hunt, E.B., 269, 274
Huttenlocher, J., 280–283, 284–285
Hyde, T.S., 72, 108, 125
Hyman, R., 315–316

Irby, T.S., 315, 320

Jacoby, L.L., 54, 61, 72, 75–77
James, W., 39, 48
Jarvella, R.J., 173–174
Jaynes, J., 49
Jeffries, R., 264
Jenkins, J.J., 72, 108, 114, 115, 125, 126, 185–186, 205
Johnson, E.S., 223
Johnson, M.K., 184, 186–188, 194
Johnson-Laird, P.N., 169, 228, 229, 230, 288–289, 299–301
Jones, S., 280
Jongeward, R.H., Jr., 61, 63
Jonides, J., 100, 111

Kahn, R., 100
Kalsbeek, J.W.H., 317
Kant, I., 206
Kareev, Y., 270–271
Karlin, J.E., 317
Katona, G., 235, 236
Katz, J.J., 167
Kay, H., 308
Kay, P., 225
Keele, S.W., 21–23, 322, 323
Kerr, N., 99–100
Kidd, E., 119

Kiess, H.D., 110
Kimball, J.P., 174, 175–176, 178
Kinney, G.C., 30, 32
Kintsch, W., 9, 43, 54, 65, 128, 193, 214
Kirker, W.W., 108
Klahr, D., 273
Klatzky, R.L., 21, 60
Kline, P.J., 54, 92
Knapp, B., 322
Koestler, A., 245
Kohler, I., 311, 312
Köhler, W., 234–235, 244
Kornheiser, A.S., 312
Kosslyn, S.M., 101–103
Kotovsky, K., 273–274
Kovach, J.K., 107
Krebs, M.J., 320
Kroll, N.E., 66
Kuiper, N.A., 108

Lachman, R., 187, 196
Lakoff, G., 226
Larkin, K.M., 196
Lashley, K.S., 149, 322, 323
Laszlo, J.I., 310–311
Laughlin, P., 223
Laver, J.D.M., 153–154
Lea, G., 274
Leonard, J.A., 311, 320
Levine, M., 217–220, 224
Lewis, C.H., 54, 92
Liberman, A.M., 160, 162, 164
Lichten, W., 165
Lindsay, P.H., 23–28, 247–250, 252, 269–270
Lockhart, R.S., 53–54, 73–75, 107, 128
Loftus, E.F., 85–91, 94, 98, 202–204, 205
Loftus, G.R., 98
London, M., 280, 281
Lorayne, H., 124
Lowry, D.H., 111, 112, 113
Lucas, J., 124
Luchins, A.S., 237–238

MacKay, D.G., 155–156
MacNeilage, L.A., 150
MacNeilage, P.F., 150, 156, 158
Maier, N.R.F., 240, 242
Mandler, G., 48, 71, 72, 110, 123, 125, 128–129
Marsetta, M., 30, 32
Massaro, D.W., 71, 163
Mayer, R.E., 286
Mazuryk, G., 69
McLean, R.S., 60
McNeill, D., 157
Melton, A.W., 53
Meryman, R., 313
Metzler, J., 103
Meyer, B.J.F., 194, 195
Meyer, D.E., 36, 88, 95–96
Michon, J.A., 317
Miller, D.G., 202–204
Miller, G.A., 35, 55, 57, 119, 165, 168, 169, 227, 228, 229, 230, 273, 307, 308, 310, 326
Mink, W.D., 115
Minsky, M.A., 34
Mischel, W., 22, 23
Mitchell, R.F., 65
Moates, D., 318
Montague, W.E., 110
Moore, J., 271
Moray, N., 42
Morin, R.E., 316
Morton, J., 71
Mowbray, G.H., 320–321
Mullet, R.L., 187, 188
Murdock, B.B., Jr., 55, 56, 58
Murphy, G., 107

Naylor, J.C., 322
Neimark, E.D., 296, 297
Neisser, U., 30, 33, 34, 35, 39, 99–100, 111, 128, 205, 212, 214, 323, 329
Nelson, K., 227
Newall, K.M., 311

Newell, A., 165, 247, 248, 250, 251, 253–254, 255, 257–258, 261, 262, 265, 271, 273
Newman, E.F., 317
Norman, D.A., 23–28, 35, 45, 47, 48, 53, 57, 73, 122, 124, 247, 249, 250, 252, 269, 329

Opie, I., 137
Opie, P., 137
Ortony, A., 127, 186, 192, 193, 194, 196, 197, 205
Osherson, D.N., 289, 293
Osler, S., 126

Paap, K.R., 163
Palmer, J.C., 202, 204
Palmer, S.E., 36, 37, 192
Paivio, A., 85, 98–99, 101
Parker, J.F., Jr., 318–320
Parkinson, S.R., 66
Parks, T.E., 66
Pasteur, L., 243
Patterson, K.E., 129
Pei, M., 137
Peirce, C.S., 278
Penfield, W., 82
Peterson, L.R., 68, 69, 70
Peterson, M.J., 68, 69, 70
Pew, R.W., 323, 324–326, 327
Phillips, J.L., Jr., 294
Piaget, J., 33, 206, 294
Pichert, J.W., 187–189, 197–198
Pickett, J.M., 165
Pierce, J.R., 312, 317
Pinson, E.N., 160
Pisoni, D.B., 44, 161
Pohlmann, L.D., 44
Poincaré, H., 245
Polich, J.M., 286
Pollack, I., 165
Polson, P.J., 264
Poltrock, S.E., 269, 274

Polya, G., 246, 257
Popper, K.R., 221
Posner, M.I., 21–23, 44, 65–66, 217, 218, 243–244, 245, 322, 323
Postman, L., 57, 65, 117
Potter, M.C., 35
Potts, G.R., 283–286
Pribram, K.H., 119, 273, 307, 310, 326
Provitera, A., 296–298
Puff, C.R., 115
Pylyshyn, F.W., 99

Quastler, H., 317
Quillian, M.R., 85, 88, 89, 90

Rabinowitz, H.S., 240–241, 242
Rabinowitz, J.C., 129
Razel, M., 57
Razran, L., 264
Reddy, B.G., 110
Reddy, R., 165
Reed, S.K., 23
Reicher, G.M., 115, 116
Reiser, B.J., 101–103
Reitman, J.S., 69, 70
Reitman, W.R., 254, 275, 276
Reynolds, P., 329
Reynolds, R.E., 189–190, 204
Rhoades, M.V., 320–321
Riley, C.A., 286
Rips, L.J., 96, 97, 226
Rittenhouse, C.H., 318
Rodman, R., 152
Rogers, T.B., 108
Rollins, H., 214–216
Romney, A.K., 167
Rosch, E.H., 224–226, 227
Rosenhan, D.L., 23
Rothkopf, E.F., 108–109
Rozin, P., 100
Ruddy, M.G., 36
Rumelhart, D.E., 34, 192, 193, 194, 196, 197, 205, 262, 263

Runquist, W.N., 238
Rush, B., 222–223
Russell, B., 257
Russell, W.A., 114, 115

Sachs, J.S., 172–173
Sakitt, B., 13
Salzberg, P.M., 66
Samuel, A.L., 257, 264–265
Schafer, K., 154
Schallert, D.L., 189–190, 204
Schank, R.C., 176, 191
Schmidt, R.A., 323, 327–328
Schneider, W., 46
Scholz, K.W., 284–285
Schumacher, G.M., 72, 108, 125
Schvaneveldt, R.W., 36, 95–96
Segmen, J., 119
Selfridge, O.G., 28, 29
Sells, S.B., 295, 301
Seymour, W.D., 318, 322
Shaffer, L.H., 317, 329
Shallice, T., 65
Shankweiler, D.P., 160, 162
Shannon, C.E., 312
Shattuck, S.R., 153–155
Shaughnessy, E., 214–216
Shaw, J.C., 257, 265
Shelly, M.W., 311
Shepard, R.N., 103
Shiffrin, R.M., 44–45, 46, 53, 54, 71, 72, 73, 74, 75, 76
Shoben, E.J., 96, 97, 226
Showman, D.J., 30, 32
Shulman, H.G., 66
Silveira, J., 245–247
Simon, H.A., 46, 57, 59, 60, 247, 250, 251, 254, 255, 257–258, 261, 262, 265, 266, 267, 271, 272, 273–274, 275, 276
Simonides, 119
Skinner, B.F., 3
Small, D.W., 177
Smith, 186

Smith, E.E., 96–97, 226
Smith, G.A., 316
Smith, K.U., 311, 318
Smith, S.M., 63
Snoddy, G.S., 318, 319
Sorkin, R.D., 44
Sperling, G., 11–12, 13
Spiro, R.J., 200–202
Spooner, W., 153
Springston, F., 58
Steedman, M., 299–301
Stevens, K.N., 163
Stewart, C., 173
Strange, 185–186
Stratton, G.M., 311, 312
Studdert-Kennedy, M., 160, 162
Sussman, H., 311
Sutherland, J., 313

Taylor, D.W., 241, 243
Taylor, F.V., 316, 323
Taylor, R.L., 65
Teichner, W.H., 320
Thomas, J.C., Jr., 264, 265
Thomson, D.M., 101, 127
Thorndike, E.L., 3, 234–235
Thorsheim, H.I., 318
Till, R.E., 72, 108
Torrey, J.W., 172

Trabasso, T., 214–216, 286
Trakhentenbrot, B.A., 260
Treisman, A.M., 42, 43–45
Tulving, E., 54, 83, 107, 108, 115–117, 126–127, 129
Turing, A.M., 267
Turvey, M.T., 13–14, 71

van Dijk, 193
Vendler, Z., 147–148
Vernon, P.E., 246
von Treba, P., 318
von Wright, J.M., 12

Wallas, G., 243, 245, 246, 247
Walsh, D.A., 108, 126
Walter, A., 130–131
Warren, M., 164
Warren, P., 164
Wason, P.C., 220–221, 222, 288
Watkins, M.J., 61, 69
Watkins, O.C., 69
Watson, J.B., 3
Waugh, N.C., 48, 53, 57, 73
Weaver, W., 312
Weber, A., 111, 112, 113
Weene, P., 212, 214
Wehrkamp, R., 318

Weiner, N., 247
Welford, A.T., 316
Wells, H., 214
Welton, K.E., 21
Wertheimer, M., 237
West, L.J., 318
Whitehead, A.N., 257
Whitmarsh, G.A., 115
Whorf, B.L., 225
Wickelgren, W.A., 65, 68–69, 70, 246
Wiesel, T.N., 23, 27
Wight, E., 101
Wilkins, M.C., 299
Winckelmann, J.J., 122
Winograd, T., 178–181, 230
Winston, P.H., 261
Wittgenstein, L., 167
Wollen, K.A., 111, 112, 113
Wood, G., 117
Woodward, A.E., Jr., 61, 63
Woodworth, R.S., 295, 301
Wulff, V.J., 317

Yates, F.A., 119
Yerkes, R.M., 47

Zadeh, L., 227
Zangwill, O.L., 131, 200

Subject Index

Abduction, 278
Abstract schemata, 192–193
Acoustic features, 163
Acoustic information, memory for, 63–65, 73
Acoustic intrusions, 63
Acoustic pattern, 159–162
Actions in GPS computer program, 262
ACT model of human cognition, 54, 75, 85, 91–95, 262
Activation, 75, 87–88, 91, 94
  model of memory, 54–55
Active list (ALIST), 54, 94
Affirmation rule, 212
Affixes in sentence structure analysis, 176
After-dinner-speaker effect, 164
Agentive case, 142
Algorithms, 255, 257, 258
ALIST (Active List), 54, 94
Allophone, 146
Alphabet, English, distinctive features of, 30, 31
Ambiguity in syllogisms, 296–297
Ambiguous sentences, 139–140, 186
Anagrams and problem solving, 244
Analogical representation in memory, 84–85

Analogical theory of syllogistic reasoning, 299–301
Analysis-by-synthesis model of speech perception, 163, 164
Analytical ability, 291–292
Animal intelligence studies, 234–235
Antecedent, logical, 287
Apperceptive mass, 107
APPLY LIST in ACT model, 95
ARGUS computer program, 254
Arousal and automaticity, 47
Articles in sentence structure analysis, 175–176
Articulatory target hypothesis, 158
Artificial intelligence, 254–255
Aspiration (phoneme), 146
Assertions, 147–148
Associations in ACT model, 94
Assumptions, communal, in natural reasoning, 288–289
Atmosphere effect, 295, 301
Attention, 8, 9, 10, 39–46
  focal, 48
Attenuation model of attention, 43–45
Attributes and concepts, 209, 210–212, 214
Auditory processing model of speech perception, 163, 164

Auditory registers, 13–16
Automaticity, 46–47, 48, 58
  of skilled behavior, 308–309, 322, 326
Awareness and memory, 10, 82. *See also* Consciousness

Ballistic tasks, 327
Behaviorism, 2–3, 85, 234
Biconditional rule, 212, 213–214
Binary features in componential analysis, 167
Bit (measure of information), 312–314
Bizarre images and recall, 111, 113
Blends, speech, 155
Bloopers, 154
Bottom-up approach to cognition, 36, 176, 271
Brain activity in visual perception, 23–28
British Museum algorithm, 257, 258

Candle problem, 238–239, 240, 241
Capacity limitations in attention theories, 41–44
Case relations of nouns, 142–143
Categorization and memory, 123, 125

Category, 224–226. *See also* Concept
  clustering, 114–115
  size effect, 88–89, 96, 98
Central processor, 48
Chaining theory of motor skills, 322–323
Characteristic features, 96–97, 98, 226–227
Checkers, computer programs for, 264–265
Chess and computers, 165, 265–266
Chess memory, 58–60, 266
Children's thinking, 294
Chunking, 55–56, 58–60, 78, 266, 317
Clauses, 143–144, 170–174
Closed loop control of motor skills, 324
Clustering and recall, 114–115, 116
Coarticulation effects, 156, 158, 163, 164
Cognitive demons, 28, 29
Cognitive economy, 88, 89, 90
Cognitive overload, 55
Cognitive psychology, development of, 1–4
Congruence in reasoning, 282–284
Coherence of skilled behavior, 306
Color focal points, 225
Collins and Loftus model of permanent memory, 85–88, 94, 205
Commands, 147–148
Comparison in problem solving, 286
Compatability of tasks and reaction time, 316, 320–321
Competence, linguistic, 149
Competence, logical, 279, 289, 290
Complementation of clauses, 143–144
Complexity of skilled behavior, 306, 317
Componential analysis of words, 167–169
Comprehension
  computer models of, 271–273
  and expectations, 170–171
  and memory, 197–198
  of prose, 184–190
Computer(s), 3–4, 247, 254
  dialogue, 178–181
  and thinking, 256
Computer language, 255

Computer simulation, 168, 254–275
  involving memory, 266–271
  of checkers and chess, 264–266
  of cognitive function, 91–92
  of comprehension, 271–273
  of language processing, 178–181
  of problem solving, 261–264
  of rule induction, 273–275
  of speech perception, 165
Concept(s), 17, 168, 207–230. *See also* Category, Schemata
  abstract, 229–230
  in children, 227
  in comprehension, 177–178
  and consciousness, 218
  and function, 227–229
  identification problems, 273–274
  and language, 227–229
  learning of, 209–224, 274
  and memory, 83, 85, 86–87, 226–227
  relations in, 229–230
  structure of, 83, 85, 209, 224–226
Conceptual nodes, 205
Conceptually driven schemata, 36
Conditions, in GPS computer program, 262
Condition-action pair, 95
Conditional rule, 212, 213
Conditioning, 3
Confusion matrix, 30, 32, 63, 64
Conjunction rule, 168, 209, 212
Consciousness, 47–49. *See also* Attention; Awareness; Central processor; Memory, primary; Memory, working
  and computers, 256
  and concepts, 218
  and memory, 10, 54, 71, 99, 109
  and problem solving, 245
  in skill learning, 307–308
Consequent, logical, 287–288
Conservative-focusing strategy, 211, 221, 223, 273
Consistency of skills and motor schemata, 325
Consonants and modality effect, 15
Constructive processes in concept learning, 217. *See also* Memory, reconstructive
Content words, 144, 145

Context
  and language, 181, 184–190, 204
  and memory, 107, 126–127, 205–206
  in perception, 16, 35–38, 164–165
  and phoneme production, 156–158
  in schema theory, 205–206
Continuity of skilled behavior, 306, 308
Continuous speech perception, 164–166
Coordination of clauses, 143, 144
Creativity of language, 137–138
Creativity and problem solving, 246
Criteria, concept-defining, 227–228
Criteriality in theories of permanent memory, 87, 91
Cues in memory storage and retrieval, 126–127
Cues in sentence analysis, 174–175
Cybernetics, 247
Cyclic processes in perception, 17, 33

Dampening process in ACT model, 94
Dani (New Guinea people), 225
Data base in ACT model, 54
Data-driven schemata, 36
Data limitations and attention, 45–46
Decay theory of forgetting, 67–70
Decision demon, 28, 29
Decision table, 169–170, 228–229
Decision tree, 215–216
Declarative knowledge in ACT model, 92, 94
Deductive reasoning, 277–302
Default assignment in prose comprehension, 192
Defining features, 96–97, 98, 226–227
Demons, 28, 29
Dichotic listening task, 41
Dictionary analogy of mental lexicon, 166–167, 169
Dictionary in Collins and Loftus model, 87
Direction of problems in gestalt theory, 236–237
Disjunction rule, 168, 212
Distance effect, 284
Distinctive features, 19, 28–33

Distinctiveness in memory retrieval, 76
Distractor items, 128
Distractor task, 68–69
Distributed practice in motor skills, 321
DONALD + GERALD problem, 247–252
Dual-coding theories of memory, 85, 99

Early selection model of attention, 41–43
Echo, 14–16, 71
EDVAC computer, 254
Effector system, 324
Edge detector brain cells, 23–24
Encoding, 72, 78, 107
 in linear series problem solving, 284, 286
 in permanent memory, 107–109
 in reasoning, 293, 295, 296–297
 specificity, 126–128, 198
 in temporary memory, 63–67
Encyclopedia analogy of mental lexicon, 166–167, 169
End-anchor principle, 280, 281, 282, 284
English language
 inflections, 145
 phonemes, 153
 word classes, 145
ENIAC computer, 254
EPAM computer program, 266
Equipment controls and compatibility, 316
Errors in memory retrieval, 129–131. *See also* Logical errors, Misperceptions, Speech errors
Executive control, 258–261
Expectations and comprehension, 170–171, 176
Expectations and perception, 33–37
Experience and problem solving, 237–243
Experiencer case, 143
Expertise, automatic processes in, 46
Eyes and iconic memory, 13

Face, human, schematic drawing of, 17
Facial features, context in perception of, 36, 37, 185

Feature analysis, 23–33
Feature comparison model of semantic memory, 96–98, 226–227
Feature demons, 28, 29
Feedback, 309–310
 in concept learning, 217
 in hypothesis testing, 217, 219–220
 and motor skills, 307–312, 317, 322, 323, 324
 proprioceptive, 310, 312, 313, 318
 in speech processes, 158
 in voluntary acts, 325–326
Figure effect in syllogistic reasoning, 301
Flowchart, 259–261
 for identification procedure, 228–229
Focal attention and consciousness, 48
Focal stress of sentences, 148
Focusing strategies, 223
Foreign language learning, keyword method of, 111, 114
Forgetting from temporary memory, 67–70
Formants, 160, 162
Formats, computer, 34
Full-processing model of attention, 44–45
Functions and concepts, 227–229
Functions of language, 147–149
Function words, 144, 145
Functional concept, 218
Functional fixity, 237, 238–243
Functional relations in reasoning, 282–283
Fuzzy categories, 167
Fuzzy logic, 227

Galvanic skin response (GSR), 42
Game strategies and working memory, 270–271
GENERAL PROBLEM SOLVER (GPS) computer program, 254, 261–264, 271–273, 274, 290
GENERAL RULE INDUCER (GRI) computer program, 274–275
Generate-and-test heuristic, 273
Gestalt theory of problem solving, 234–247
Given state of problems, 233–234

Go and gomoku, computer simulation of, 270–271
Goals, orientation of cognitive functions toward, 5
Goal case, 143
Goal state of problems, 233–234
"Goodness of fit" question, 267
GPS (GENERAL PROBLEM SOLVER) computer program, 254, 261–264, 271–273, 274, 290
Graduate Record Examination, 291–292
Graphic tasks and recall, 108
GRI (GENERAL RULE INDUCER) computer program, 274–275
GSR (galvanic skin response), 42

HAM model, 92
Hedges, linguistic, 226–227
Heuristics, 255, 257–258
 in *Logic Theorist* program, 279
 memory in, 266–267
 and syllogistic reasoning, 299–301
Higher order control of continuous skills, 324
Hobbits and orcs problem, 262–264
Horizontal array in image theory, 280
Hypotheses and language, 165
Hypothesis testing, 210, 212, 217–224

Icon, 11–13, 71
Identification procedures for concepts, 228–229
Identity match task, 65, 66
Ill-defined problems, 250, 275–276
Illumination in problem solving, 243, 245, 246–247
Image(s), 98–104
 demon, 28, 29
 in deductive reasoning, 280
 interacting, 111, 112, 113
 memory storage of, 98–104
 and word meaning, 166
Imagery, 99–100, 110–111
 in mnemonics, 119–121, 123
 value, 111
Improvement of skills, rate of, 308–309
Incubation in problem solving, 243, 245–247

Induction, 278
Inference
  errors in, 199–201
  in comprehension and memory, 177–178, 199–204
  rules of, 286–290
Inflections, word, 144–146
Information
  measurement of, 312–315
  and sentence structure, 148
Information processing
  and attention, 41–46
  and motor skills, 312–317
  schemata in, 34, 35
  system, 8–10, 37–39, 49–50, 77–79, 131–133
  theory of problem solving, 234, 247–276
Information transmission rates, 316–317
Information value and reaction time, 315–316
Inner-loop control of continuous skills, 324
Insight in gestalt theory, 235–236
Instantiation of schemata, 192
Instructions and prose comprehension, 188, 190
Instrumental case, 142–143
Intentionality and memory, 123, 125–126
Interference theory of memory, 53, 67–70
Intersection search, 87–88
Interstimulus interval (ISI), 65–66
Intrusion errors, 187
Invalid conversions, 295, 301
Invariance hypothesis of phonemes, 159–163
ISI (interstimulus interval), 65–66

Joint denial rule, 214

Keyword method in foreign language learning, 111, 114
Knowledge in ACT model, 92–95
Knowledge base and chunking, 60
Knowledge representation language, 230
Knowledge states in problem solving, 248–252

Language, 135–182. *See also* Prose, Sentences
  comprehension, 159–178, 184–190
  and concepts, 227–229
  functions, 147–149, 150–152
  in network models of memory, 85
  processing, 15–16, 178–181
  production, 149–159
  properties, 137–138
  rules in, 138
  structure, 138–147
  and thought, 149–150
Laws of Thought, The, 278
Leading questions, 202–203
Learning
  in checkers computer program, 264–265
  of concepts, 209–224
  feedback in, 217, 307–311, 312
  of motor skills, 305–311, 312
Learning theory, 3
Levels of analysis in speech perception, 165
Levels-of-processing theory of memory, 53–54, 72, 73–77
Lexical ambiguity, 139–140
Lexical analysis in language comprehension, 166–170
Lexical concepts, 228
Lexical marking, 282–283, 284
Lexical network, 87
Lexicon, mental, 227
Line detector brain cells, 24, 26
Linear series problems, 278, 279–286, 293
Linguistics and cognitive theory, 3
Linguistic theories of reasoning, 280–283
Links, 86–87, 89, 91, 92, 93, 205
Listening confusion matrix, 63, 64
Literal copy view of images, 99–100
Locative case, 143
Loci, method of, 119–121
Logic, 278–297, 286–290, 292–295. *See also* Propositional calculus, Reasoning, Syllogisms
Logic Theorist computer program, 257–258, 279
Logical errors, 287–288, 295, 296–297
Logical subject, 280–282, 284–285
Long term memory store, 53, 73

Machine language, 150
MAPP computer program, 266
Mark I computer, 254
Matchstick problem, 235, 236
Material-induced organization, 114–115
Maintenance rehearsal, 61–63, 78
Massed practice in motor skills, 321
Mathematical functions, learning of, 223–224
Means-ends analysis, 258, 261
Meaning
  and language, 150–152, 155, 194
  and memory, 172–174, 176–178
  and perception, 9
  and problem solving, 286
Mechanization in problem solving, 238
Mediation and recall, 110
Memory, 8, 53–55, 82–84. *See also* Encoding, Recall, Retention, Retrieval, Storage
  and attention, 44
  in chess, 58–60, 266
  in clause analysis, 172–174
  and comprehension, 197–198
  in computer simulation, 264, 266–271
  episodic, 75–76, 82–83
  in hypothesis testing, 219–220
  intentionality and, 123, 125–126
  for meaning, 176–178
  for motor skills, 318–320
  permanent, 9, 81–104, 105–133
    for chess, 59
    and pattern recognition, 17–19
    processes, 105–133
    structure, 83–104
  primary, 48, 53, 73
  and problem solving, 266–271
  reconstructive, 76–77, 128, 129–131, 266, 269–270
    inference in, 177–178, 199–204
  schemata in, 197–198
  searches, 129
  secondary, 53
  semantic, 82–83, 85–104, 204–206, 226–227
  sensory, 11–16, 70–71
  short-term, 53, 56, 57–58, 75–76
  span, 55, 56
  temporary, 51–79
    in ACT model, 94
    capacity, 55–56, 57–58
    characteristics, 55–70

Memory, *(Continued)*
　practical implications, 78
　structures, 70–77
　traces, 71, 72–77
　working, 9, 10, 48, 71–72
　　in ACT model, 54, 94
　　in computer simulation studies, 269–271
　　and consciousness, 48
　　and motor skills, 307–308, 329
Mental lexicon, 166–170
Mental operations in rule learning, 214–217
Mental photograph view of imagery, 99, 100
Mentality of Apes, The, 234–235
MERLIN computer program, 271
Minimaxing, 265–266
Misperception, 35, 37, 165
Mnemonics, 118–123
Modality effect, 14–15
Modifier links, 86, 87
Modus ponens, 287–288, 290
Moods of syllogisms, 293–294
Morphemes, 144–146
Morse code, learning of, 305, 306
Motor command hypothesis, 156
Motor processes in language production, 156, 158–159
Motor programs, 322–330
Motor schemata, 323, 325, 327–330
Motor skill(s), 303–330
　continuous, 316–317, 323–326
　discrete, 315–316, 327–328
　learning of, 305–306, 307–309
　limits of, 322
　properties of, 306–307
　response, 305

Narratives, schemata for, 193
Negation rule, 212
Negative proof procedure, 221
Network models of semantic memory, 85–95
Nim, 259–261
Node, 86–87
Nouns, 142–143

Novelty, 5, 138, 196–197, 307, 323
Numerical information, mnemonic techniques for, 121–123

Objects in GPS computer program, 261
Objective case, 143
"One is a bun, two is a shoe . . ." mnemonic technique, 119
Open-loop control of continuous skills, 324, 330
Operations in problem solving, 248-254
Operators in GPS computer program, 261
Order of processing in language production, 150–156, 158
Ordering in deduction, 280, 281
Organization in permanent memory, 107, 109–126
Orienting tasks, 107–108

P system, 72–73
Paired-associate tasks, 111
Pandemonium model of feature detection, 28, 29, 30
Parallel transmission of acoustic cues, 162–163
Parallelogram area, steps in finding, 237
Partial report procedure, 11, 12
Particular affirmative, 294
Particular negative, 294
Particularization of schema, 329
Paths in problem solving, 233–234, 251–252, 257
Pattern recognition, 9–10, 17–33, 44
PERCEIVER computer program, 266
Perception, 7, 8, 9
　expectations and, 35–37
　processes of, 16–39
　of speech, 159–166
Perceptual analysis and memory, 73–75
Perceptual categories, 224–225
Perceptual criteria of concepts, 227–228
Perceptual illusions, 164
Performance, linguistic, 149
Performance, logical, 279, 289, 290

Personality traits as prototypes, 22, 23
Phone, 146–147
Phonemes, 146–147, 152, 156, 163
Phoneme-monitoring task, 175
Phonemic structure, 152–153, 172
Phrase structure rules, 141–142
Physiological bases of concepts, 225
Physiological mechanisms in feature analysis, 23–28
Piano playing, information transmission in, 316–317
Pictorial settings and prose comprehension, 186–187, 190
Pitch and the Echo, 15–16
PLANNER computer program, 181
Practice
　and chunking, 58–60
　and motor skills, 305, 307–309, 317–322, 323, 327
　in rule learning, 214
Predicate and thematic structure, 148–149
Premise, 279
Preparation in problem solving, 243–244, 246–247
Priming, 91, 93, 225–226
Principia Mathematica, 257
Probe technique, 66–68, 173
Problems, linear series, 278, 279–286, 293
Problem behavior graph, 248–251
"Problem of Serial Order in Behavior, The," 149
Problem solving, 231–276
　computer models of, 254–261
　computer programs for, 254–255, 261–275
　and concept identification, 273
　and simulation programs involving memory, 266–271
　and reasoning, 278–279
　schemata, 196
　tips, 246
Problem space, 250–254, 274
Procedural knowledge in ACT model, 94–95
Procedural semantics, 168–170, 181
Productions, 95, 262

Production system, 262, 268–269, 274
Productive thinking in gestalt theory, 235
Proficiency in motor skills, 329
PROGRAMMAR computer program, 178, 181
Pronunciation of phonemes, 153, 156, 158
Proof and reasoning, 278
Property set model, 230
Propositions in ACT model, 94
Propositions in linguistics, 142–143
Propositional calculus, 286–288, 289, 290, 292–293
Propositional content of language, 147–148
Propositional representation in memory, 84–85
Prose, 106–107, 108–109, 183–206. *See also* Language, Sentence
   comprehension, 184–190, 193–197, 199–200
   retention, 130, 197–198, 199, 200–204
   schemata, 190–198
Protocol in information-processing analysis, 247–250, 252
Prototypes, 21–23, 224, 225, 226
Psycholinguistics, 137
Puns, 139–140
Pursuit rotor task, 321
Push-down stack, 258, 259

Quantificational logic, 293
Questions, 147–148

Reaction time (RT) and information value, 315–316
Reaction time studies in semantic memory, 88–91
Reader background and prose comprehension, 188–189, 190
Reading, schemata in, 35
Reasoning, 277–302
   formal, 286–288
   models of, 280–286, 289–290, 292–293

   natural, 288–289
   propositional, 279, 286–293
   syllogistic, 293–301
Recall. *See also* Memory, Retention, Retrieval
   check, 128–129
   organization in free, 111–118
   perspective, importance of, 197–198
   procedures, 128–129
   reconstructive, 129–131, 200–203
   and retention interval in temporary memory, 68
   schema, 327, 328
Recency effect, 57
Recognition procedure, 128–129
Recognition schema, 327–328
Reconstruction. *See* Memory, reconstructive
Recursive rules, 144
Reference theory of word meaning, 166
Registration in memory, 72
Rehearsal, 60–63, 70, 78
Relation-argument associations, 94
Relativization of clauses, 143, 144
Relevance of attributes in concept learning, 209–212
Remembering, 130
Repetition in motor skill practice, 317
Representational formats in memory, 84–85
Reproductive thinking in gestalt theory, 235
Resources, 45–46, 56
Restructuring, 236–237
Retention of prose, 197–198, 199, 200–204. *See also* Memory
Retention systems, auditory, 13–16
Retrieval, 72, 106, 126–131, 200–204
   and computer simulation, 267–269
   and inference, 200–203
   schemata in, 197–198
Rhythm in motor skills, 317, 318
River-crossing problems, 262–264
RT. *See* Reaction time
Rules and concepts, 168, 209, 210–217
Rule induction, computer simulation of, 273–275

S system, 72–73
Salience of attributes, 211–212
Schemata, 5, 17–18, 190–193, 206. *See also* Concept
   activation of, 36
   inference rule, 290
   in memory, 104, 197–198, 204–206
   motor, 323–330
   in perception, 17–18, 33–35
   problem solving, 196
   properties of, 190–193
   in prose processing, 193–198, 204
   and speech, 149
Science, rejection of false hypotheses in, 221, 222–223
Selection
   in hypothesis testing, 217
   in information processing, 46
   studies, 12, 13, 14
   of task and attention, 39–46
Self-reference in encoding, 108
Semantic approach to language, 142–143
Semantic categories, 225–226
Semantic codes in temporary memory, 66–67
Semantic flexibility, 205–206
Semantic intrusions, 63
Semantic network, 87, 92
Semantic procedures, 168, 169–170
Semantic tasks and recall, 108
Sensory receptors, 9
Sensory registers, 9, 10–16, 28, 70–73
Sentence structure, 138–144
Sentence(s), 137–138
   ambiguous, 139–140
   comprehension and reasoning, 280–283
   and encoding specificity, 127
   meaning and context, 186
   and memory, 172–174
   organization of information in, 148
Serial learning tasks, 111
Serial position, 15
Series-completion task, 273–274
Servomechanisms, 309
Set in problem solving, 237–238
Sets, mathematical, and concepts, 208
Set analysis theory of reasoning, 295–299, 301
Set theory model of semantic memory, 95–96

Shadowing procedure, 42–44, 66
Signs in auditory processing model, 163
Signal detection task, 69, 70
Simultaneous activities, 329
Singing, feedback, in, 313
Skills. *See* Motor skills
"Slips of the ear," 165
Slit detector brain cells, 23, 24, 25
Slit-split phenomenon, 164
Slots in schemata, 192
Sounds and language structure, 138, 146–147
Spatial information, representation in memory, 100–101, 103–104
Spectator behavior, 218
Speech. *See* Language
Speech acts, 147
Speech errors, 153, 156
Speech perception, 159–166
Speech production, 151, 156, 158–159, 163
Speech spectrogram, 160, 161, 162
Spoonerism, 153
Stereotypes, 23
Storage in memory, 53, 72, 106, 107–126, 323
Stories as a mnemonic technique, 123, 124–125
Strategy(ies)
    in concept learning, 210, 221–224, 273
    conservative-focusing, 210, 211, 221, 223, 273
    in games, 270–271
Stress pattern in language production, 156
Structuring in problem solving, 243–244, 275
STUDENT computer program, 254, 271
Subject of sentence and thematic structure, 148
Subject predicate associations, 94
Subjective organization (SO), 115–117
Subroutines, 258, 259
Substitution as a mnemonic technique, 121–123
Superordinate links, 86–87, 89, 91

Surface structure of sentences, 138–140
    analysis, 174–176
    clauses in, 143–144
    memory for, 172–173, 177
    in semantic approach, 142
    in transformational grammar, 141–142
SVO (Subject-verb-object) strategy, 175–176
Switching capability, 41
Syllable structure and language production, 156
Syllogisms, 278, 279, 293–301
Syntactic analysis of language, 159, 170–176
Syntax
    and language production, 152, 153, 154
    and memory, 172–173
    and sentence structure, 139–142

Task types and rule difficulty, 217
Task type and semantic memory, 96
Template, 18–21
Test answering strategy flowchart, 285
Thematic structure of language, 148–149
Themes and prose comprehension, 187–188
Thinking, 304–305
Thinking and computers, 256
Thinking aloud in problem solving, 253–254
"13" problem, 237
Thought and language, 149–150
Time and perceptual analysis, 9, 10
Timing and motor skill practice, 305, 306, 307–308, 317–318
Tip-of-the-tongue phenomenon, 157
Top-down approach to comprehension, 176
Top-down perception, 36
Top-down strategy and game pattern memory, 270–271
TOTE (Test-Operate-Test-Exit) unit, 309, 310
Training and resource limits, 46–47
Transformational grammar, 140–142

Tree structures in prose analysis, 194, 195
Tree structures of sentences, 141
Trial-and-error behavior, 234
Truth in logic, 287, 294–295
Turing's Test, 267
Two-store theory of memory, 53, 58, 72–73, 75, 82
Two-string problem, 240-243
Typicality effect, 89–91, 98
Typing as a skill, 308, 316–317, 318

Unattended information, processing of, 41–44
Uncertainty as measure of information, 312
Unconscious processing and problem solving, 245
Underlying representation of sentences, 138–144, 176
UNDERSTAND computer program, 271–273
Undistributed middle, 295
Universal affirmative, 293–294
Universal negative, 293–294

Validation in problem solving, 243, 245
Validity in logic, 294–295
Values of attributes, 209
Verbs in semantic school of linguistics, 142–143
Verbal information, representation in memory, 85, 94, 100–104
Verification in problem solving, 243, 245
Verification process in set theory model of memory, 95–96
Verification task in study of rule-learning, 215–217
Vertical array in image theory of reasoning, 280
Visual images in memory, 85, 98–104
Visual registers, 10–13
Vocabulary size, 60, 166
Voluntary act, 325–326

Voluntary control of skills, 325–326
Vowels and modality effect, 15

"War of the Ghosts," 130, 200
Water jar problems, 237–238, 264
Whole-part learning, 322
Whole properties, 235, 236
Word(s), 144–146. *See also* Language, Speech
  classes in English, 145
  meaning, 166–170, 185–186
  storage in memory, 155–156, 157
  structure, 138, 144–146
Word-list studies, 106
Working backward in problem solving, 257–258

Yellow fever epidemic of 1793, Philadelphia, 222–223
Yerkes-Dodson law, 47
Your Slip Is Showing, 153

Zuni people, 225

LIBRARY OF DAVIDSON COLLEGE